MIHI CREDENTI

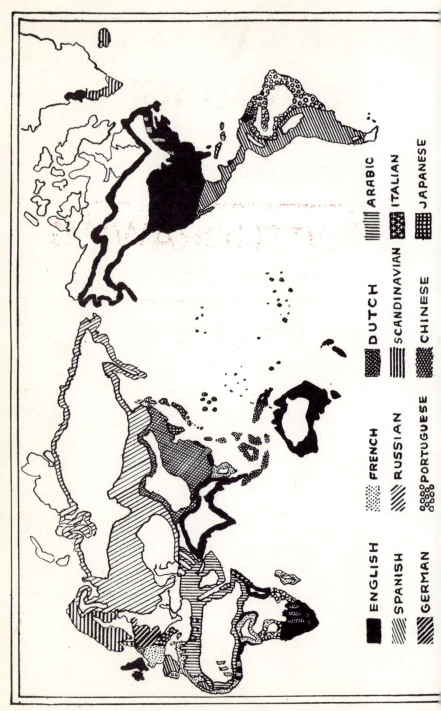

ENGLISH
SPANISH
GERMAN
FRENCH
RUSSIAN
PORTUGUESE
DUTCH
SCANDINAVIAN
CHINESE
ARABIC
ITALIAN
JAPANESE

THE WORLD'S CHIEF LANGUAGES

Formerly

LANGUAGES FOR WAR AND PEACE

WITHDRAWN

MARIO A. PEI, Ph, D.

Professor of Romance Languages
Columbia University

S. F. VANNI
Publishers and Booksellers
30 WEST 12TH STREET
NEW YORK 11, N. Y.

TABLE OF CONTENTS

LINGUISTIC MAPS

ALPHABETS AND ILLUSTRATIONS

FOREWORD

The man who speaks another language besides his own has "another string to his bow".

In the late war, if he knew the language of the enemy, he was able to avoid capture, or, if taken prisoner, to make his escape far more easily; he could question prisoners and obtain from them valuable information, or glean such information from their notebooks and letters; he could even derive it from a military sign-post in the enemy's language. He could communicate directly with the allies whose language he knew, make things infinitely more comfortable for himself and his unit when billeted in an allied or enemy country, give and receive directions, speak the language of friendship, of command, of common everyday needs. Striking examples of the way in which linguistic training could be put to military uses appeared in the early days of the war, when German parachutists came down in Holland equipped not only with Dutch uniforms, but also with a command of the Dutch tongue, and German motor-cyclists, disguised as French soldiers, swept across Belgium and northern France spreading disorder and panic in excellent French.

Now that peace is restored to a war-weary world, the benefits of linguistic training will be equally vast and far more enduring. American soldiers, scattered throughout the four corners of the globe in the post-war days while the preliminaries of a permanent peace are being worked out, need languages. Later, when world economy is put on a far more stable footing and commercial exchanges become far more intense than ever before, men and women with linguistic training will be at a premium. The demand for diplomatic and consular representatives, for government employes, for commercial travellers with a knowledge of foreign languages will exceed anything ever known. More foreigners will come to our shores, more Americans will travel abroad. Travelling for pleasure, in the post-war world, will no longer be restricted to a few tourists. The men who have been abroad, to a hundred different lands, on a military mission, will wish to revisit those lands, to continue and tighten the bonds of friendship and comradeship and interest formed there. American commercial and industrial enterprises in foreign countries, expanding because of the imperative needs of nations whose industries have been disrupted by war, will call for American-born, American-trained skilled workers who are conversant with the language of the country to which they are destined. Politically, as well as economically, present indications are that the world will become more closely welded together than it has been in the past. In any political arrangement in which races and nationalities are drawn closely together, the need for linguistic interchange will be more keenly felt than ever before. In the world of tomorrow, political, economic and military isolation will be things of the past. Linguistic isolationism and self-sufficiency, the sort of thing that some American educators have been preaching during the last two decades, will be regarded as something just as outmoded and ridiculous as political isolationism and economic autarchy have been proved to be.

So the study of foreign languages becomes imperative. Our immediate war need was of a military nature — to equip as many members of our fighting forces as possible with a quickly acquired, practical knowledge of a few important foreign tongues, to be used in their ordinary intercourse with allied or enemy troops and populations. Our present need is to create the world-minded attitude that will lead to the proper kind of international relations, commercial, economic, diplomatic and cultural, now that the war is over, making a recurrence of the recent conflict unlikely, and to endow a considerable segment of our population with the sort of linguistic training that will enable them, to their own personal advance-

ment and to the benefit of the Nation and the world at large, to take advantage of the innumerable opportunities that peace is bringing in its wake.

How shall we go about this? What languages are to be studied, and how? The traditional method has been one of high specialization. Most high-school and college students have normally been required to choose one of an extremely limited number of languages (French, Spanish, German, occasionally Italian), to study it for a two- or three- or four-year period, mastering every intricacy of grammar and syntax, then go on with it and imbue themselves with the literature, customs and habits of life of the particular nation speaking this particular language, more or less to the exclusion of the rest of the world. There is nothing wrong with this specializing method, save the fact that it is restrictive. Let it by all means be continued. But let us also have, for the people who do not wish to become specialists and literary and cultural experts in any one language, and for those who do, but who also want to know something about other languages, a method that will enable the individual of average linguistic ability to acquire the basic facts about the world's chief languages, where they are spoken and by whom, to identify them readily, and to handle more than just one of them in a comprehensible and acceptable fashion, even if without absolute grammatical correctness and literary style.

The purpose of the present work is to present the main facts about languages, not in the form of a philosophical or psychological or literary essay, not from the historical and scientific point of view, but as something of an immediate, practical value. The world's main languages and their geographical distribution, the linguistic families and the elementary relationships among their members, the identification of the written and possibly the spoken form of several important tongues, and lastly the description of the sounds and grammatical structure, together with a limited vocabulary, of seven of the world's most widely-spoken languages — all this will serve the purpose of giving the reader the elementary linguistic *consciousness that the soldier of yesterday needed in his military activities on foreign soil and that the man and woman of tomorrow will need in a world destined, by reason of the constant advances in our mechanical civilization and spiritual point of view, to become more and more a single political, economic and cultural unit.*

FOREWORD TO THE THIRD EDITION

At the time of this book's first appearance, in 1944, the world was in the throes of the Second Great War. While the outcome was no longer in doubt, the shape of things to come was as yet unclear. Once the smoke of battle lifted, would the earth settle down again to the sort of political set-up that had prevailed in the past, with some nations in possession of large colonial holdings, others, so to speak, disinherited? Would there emerge from the chaos of war a world government that would effectively take over the undeveloped regions of the earth, and hold them in trusteeship until such a time as they should be ready for admission to the ranks of full-fledged nations? Would there be a more or less gradual process of emergence from colonial or semi-colonial status for some more fortunate areas, coupled with a return to colonialism for others?

It is not our purpose to discuss the political set-up of the past, present or future, save insofar as it affects the world's language picture. The world of 1960 is in a kaleidoscopic process of change, with new nations rising out of the wreckage of the great colonial empires of the past. The last three decades have seen the emergence to fully independent status of such large national units as India, Indonesia, Pakistan, Ceylon, Malaya, North and South Vietnam, North and South Korea, Laos, Cambodia, Iraq, Jordan, Lebanon, Israel, the United Arab Republic (a merger of Egypt and Syria), Libya, Morocco, the Sudan, Tunisia, Ghana, to mention only some. Other areas are in a state of transition, with new nations about to arise out of what was once French West and Equatorial Africa, the Cameroons, Somaliland, the Belgian Congo, Nigeria. No one can at this point predict what lies in store for Algeria, Kenya, South Africa, or a dozen other major areas.

Under the circumstances, any complete revision of this work along political lines would be largely wasted, since

I

there is no crystallizing the course of present-day history. Maps and descriptions of political units based upon the fleeting present situation would probably be subject to new major revisions within a year or two. We have therefore decided to leave the political arrangement appearing in Chapter II unchanged, leaving it to the reader to make the necessary adjustments with the aid of an up-to-date world atlas.

Population figures for the various countries are subject to change almost as much as political boundaries. Since 1944, the world's population has grown enormously. For purposes of the present edition, we have presented, a little farther on in this Foreword, approximate population figures for 1960, together with a revised chart of languages and the number of people who speak them. Here we are in many instances faced with an element of conjecture. Certain areas of the earth have had a far greater proportional increase in population than others, partly by reason of higher birth and lower death rates, partly because of immigration. The question of bilingualism also looms large, and leads to overlapping. Are we justified in assigning to a country's predominant, official language all the inhabitants of that country? Should all of Mexico's 32 million inhabitants be credited to Spanish, despite the fact that at least two million of them still speak nothing but native Indian languages? What of countries like the USSR, where Russian is the "binding" tongue, learned and used for official purposes by practically all the inhabitants, but 145 minor languages, unhampered and even encouraged, live side by side with it? What of India, where Hindi is spreading, but somewhat slowly, or Indonesia, where an artificial Bahasa Indonesia encounters the resistance both of the local languages and of the widespread Malay?

We have endeavored, in our new chart of languages and speakers that follows, to present as accurate and reasonable a picture as possible, crediting each language not only with those who speak it as a mother-tongue, but also with those who may have satisfactorily acquired it, either as a language of common areal intercourse or as a cultural

II

tongue. The figures are sometimes precise, sometimes based on rough estimates, which may be quite at variance with other estimates. We have amplified each figure somewhat in accordance with current trends, to make allowance for population expansion in the course of the next three or four years.

Least subject to the ravages of time and the fluctuations of politics are the languages themselves and their distribution. Languages inevitably change, but the rate of change is slow. Even where new languages have been evolved, as in the case of Indonesian, the link with the older Malay is so strong as to make the speakers practically interchangeable, because the speech is mutually comprehensible. Vietnamese is still overwhelmingly the old Annamese, Thai the old Siamese. In addition, the old languages of colonization still thrive, even where nations have proclaimed their full independence. Morocco and Tunisia have severed their link with France, but French is still a widespread tongue in those countries. More people speak English today in India, Pakistan, Ceylon, Burma and Malaya than was the case when those newly independent countries formed part of the British Empire (in fact, most of them continue to form part of the British Commonwealth of Nations). African areas that have gained or are gaining their political independence continue to use, of their own free will, the language of the former colonial power, not so much for reasons of sentimental attachment, as because it gives them a tongue of common intercourse among peoples speaking a variety of different, often unrelated local tongues. Practical considerations often force this solution even upon countries that in principle rebel against it. India, Pakistan, Ceylon, the Philippines are glaring examples: Hindi, Urdu, Singhalese, Tagalog, though proclaimed official in the place of English, still fall far short of universal adoption by the speakers, and English supplies a highly convenient koiné, quite aside from the fact that it gives those populations contact with the western world. Even in Indonesia, Vietnam, Morocco and Tunisia, where the former Dutch and French rules are viewed with

III

some disfavor, it is idle to suppose that Dutch and French have disappeared from the linguistic scene.

For these reasons, the purely linguistic, as apart from the political picture, appearing in the earlier editions of this work, is in the main unchanged. Whatever may be the status of colonialism as such, the languages of colonization are still very much in existence, and it is unlikely that they will disappear during the balance of this century.

Other language changes are few and trifling, and hardly of such a nature as to warrant a complete recasting of our work. They apply for the most part to elements of slang and vulgarisms in the various tongues, which have a habit of falling into desuetude and being replaced by new terms of the same nature. A few minor spelling changes appear in Dutch, Portuguese and some of the Scandinavian tongues, but since most of the written materials available to the student are in the older spelling, and since new changes may be expected at any moment, it has been thought best to reserve them for a future edition which will also present, it is hoped, a more stable political picture. The same may be said of changes in the system of writing of languages like Chinese and Japanese, which are at the present time in the experimental stage.

For the convenience of the reader of the present edition, we append two extensive tables, one of countries, populations and predominant languages, the other of languages and speakers, with references to the pages in the text to which the new descriptions and figures apply.

The first of these tables applies specifically to Chapter II (pages 41-61), entitled "Geography and Languages." It has seemed desirable to leave the material of the original edition untouched, for comparative purposes, so that those wishing to study population and language growth in the course of the past two decades may have an opportunity to do so.

IV

TABLE I — GEOGRAPHY AND LANGUAGES
(See pp. 41-61 of text)

(All population figures are based on 1960 United Nations estimates, with a slight projection, based on existing trends, into the future).

1. NORTH AMERICA

Country	Approximate Population	Notes
Alaska	150,000	Now a State of the Union.
Bermudas	50,000	
Canada (including Labrador and Newfoundland)	17,000,000	French speakers, mostly bilingual, now estimated at about 5,000,000.
Greenland	50,000	
Mexico	32,000,000	
U.S.A.	180,000,000	This figure includes military personnel and civilians stationed abroad, as well as the populations of the new States of Alaska and Hawaii.

2. CENTRAL AMERICA AND WEST INDIES

Country	Approximate Population	Notes
Bahamas	100,000	
British Honduras	100,000	
Canal Zone	70,000	
Costa Rica	1,000,000	
Cuba	6,000,000	
Dominican Republic	3,000,000	
Guadeloupe and Martinique	600,000	
Guatemala	3,500,000	
Haiti	3,500,000	
Honduras	2,000,000	
Nicaragua	1,500,000	
Panama	1,000,000	

Puerto Rico	2,500,000	
Salvador	2,500,000	
Virgin Islands	30,000	
West Indian Federation	3,500,000	This new political unit includes Jamaica, Trinidad-Tobago, Barbados, and the Leeward and Windward Islands (Antigua, Monserrat, Saint Christopher-Nevis, Anguilla; Dominica, Grenada, St. Lucia, St. Vincent, etc.).

3. SOUTH AMERICA

Country	Approximate Population	Notes
Argentina	21,000,000	
Bolivia	3,500,000	
Brazil	65,000,000	
Chile	7,500,000	
Colombia	13,500,000	
Ecuador	4,000,000	
Guiana, British	500,000	
Guiana, Dutch	500,000	Including Surinam and Netherlands Antilles: Curaçao, etc.
Guiana, French	50,000	
Paraguay	2,000,000	
Peru	10,000,000	
Uruguay	3,000,000	
Venezuela	6,000,000	

*   *   *

South American speakers of Spanish are now roughly 70,000,000; South American speakers of Portuguese, about 65,000,000.

The Western Hemisphere shows in 1960 well over 200,000,000 speakers of English; over 125,000,000 speakers of Spanish; 65,000,000 speakers of Portuguese; perhaps 10,000,000 speakers of French; 50,000 speakers of Dutch; 50,000 speakers of Danish.

VI

4. EUROPE

Country	Approximate Population	Notes
Albania	1,500,000	
Austria	7,500,000	Previously included in total for Germany.
Belgium	9,500,000	
Bulgaria	8,000,000	
Czechoslovakia	14,000,000	Population loss as a result of World War Two.
Denmark	4,500,000	
Finland	4,500,000	
France	45,000,000	
Germany	75,000,000	About 55,000,000 in Federal Republic of Germany (West Germany); 20,000,000 in German Democratic Republic (East Germany).
Greece	8,500,000	
Hungary	10,000,000	
Iceland	200,000	
Ireland (Eire)	3,000,000	
Italy	50,000,000	
Luxembourg	500,000	
Netherlands	12,000,000	
Norway	4,000,000	
Poland	30,000,000	Population loss as a result of World War Two.
Portugal (including Azores)	9,000,000	
Rumania	18,000,000	Population loss as a result of World War Two.
Spain	30,000,000	
Sweden	8,000,000	
Switzerland	5,500,000	
U.S.S.R. (in Europe)	160,000,000	Including European portion of Russian S.F.S.R. (about 100,-000,000); Ukrainian S.S.R. (40,000,000); Byelorussian S. S. R. (10,000,000); Karelo-Finnish S.S.R. (1,000,000); Moldavian S.S.R. (3,000,000);

		Lithuanian S.S.R. (3,000,000) ; Latvian S.S.R. (2,000,000) ; Estonian S.S.R. (1,000,000).
United Kingdom	55,000,000	Including England (44,000,-000) ; Wales (3,000,000) ; Scotland (6,000,000) ; Northern Ireland (2,000,000).
Yugoslavia	18,500,000	

*   *   *

English, in 1960, has nearly 60,000,000 native European speakers, in the United Kingdom and Eire, and is spoken as an acquired language by an estimated 10 to 20 million Europeans in continental countries. German has nearly 90,000,000 native speakers in Germany, Austria and Switzerland, and is spoken and understood by at least 20,000,000 additional Europeans. French has over 55,000,000 native speakers in France, Belgium and Switzerland, and is the acquired tongue of between 10 and 20 million additional Europeans. Other languages are fairly well represented by the population figures of their respective nations. Note the absorption of Lithuania, Latvia and Estonia, as well as of various areas of pre-war Poland, Rumania, Czechoslovakia, Finland and German East Prussia, by the U.S.S.R., where Russian is almost universally spoken and understood, even by populations whose mother-tongue is a different language. Poland, having lost most of its former Ukrainian, White Russian and Lithuanian speakers to the U.S.S.R., has acquired a fairly large number of German speakers along its western border. Rumania and Czechoslovakia have lost most of their former Ukrainian speakers to the U.S.S.R. Population shifts in the very small political units mentioned in footnote 1 on p. 45 are trifling, save that the Free State of Danzig has been absorbed into Poland.

VIII

5. ASIA

Country	Approximate Population	Notes
Afghanistan	14,000,000	
Burma	21,000,000	
Cambodia	5,000,000	Formerly a part of French Indo-China.
Ceylon	9,000,000	
China (People's Republic)	640,000,000	Mainland, or Communist, China. The population total includes the populations of Manchuria (the former Manchukuo; about 45,000,000); Inner Mongolia, (about 6,000,000); and Tibet (over 1,000,000). The very approximate distribution of the major Chinese dialects is as follows: Mandarin (Kuo-yü), 465,-000,000; Cantonese, 50,000,000; Wu, 45,000,000; Min, 45,000,-000; Miao-Hakka, 25,000,000; others, 10,000,000.
China (Republic of)	10,000,000	Nationalist China, holding effective authority only over the island of Taiwan, or Formosa. Language: Chinese, mostly of the Mandarin variety.
Cyprus	600,000	Ultimate political status not as yet determined.
Malayan Federation	7,000,000	Including former British Malaya and Straits Settlements, but not Singapore; member of British Commonwealth of Nations.
Hong Kong	3,000,000	
India	400,000,000	Since the partition of the former British Dominion of India into the separate Republics of India and Pakistan, the two countries are separate nations, though both form part of the British Commonwealth of Nations.

Iran	20,000,000	
Iraq	5,000,000	
Israel	2,000,000	Coincides roughly with the former Palestine, with addition of Negev region. Language: Hebrew, with Arabic and English as widespread secondary languages.
Japan	95,000,000	
Jordan	2,000,000	Formerly part of French mandated area. Language: Arabic, with some French and English influence.
Korea	30,000,000	Republic of Korea (South Korea), 22,000,000; People's Democratic Republic of Korea (North or Communist Korea), 8,000,000.
Laos	3,000,000	Formerly a part of French Indo-China.
Lebanon	2,000,000	Formerly part of French mandated area. Language: Arabic, with some French and English influence.
Muscat and Oman	600,000	
Nepal and Bhutan	10,000,000	
Outer Mongolia	1,000,000	Officially, Mongolian People's Republic. Language: Mongol, with Chinese fairly widespread, and some Russian influence.
Pakistan	90,000,000	Formerly part of British Dominion of India. Languages: Indo-Aryan tongues, with predominance of Urdu in West Pakistan, of Bengali in East Pakistan; English fairly widespread.
Portuguese Asia	1,000,000	
Sa'udi Arabia	7,000,000	
Singapore	1,500,000	Political status not yet fully de-

X

		termined. Languages: Malay and Chinese; English superimposed.
Syria	4,000,000	Formerly part of French mandated area. Egypt and Syria have now united to form the United Arab Republic. Language: Arabic, with some French and English influence.
Thailand	22,000,000	
Turkey (including European Turkey)	25,000,000	
U.S.S.R. in Asia	45,000,000	Includes Asiatic portion of Russian S.F.S.R. (about 13,000,-000); Armenian S.S.R. (2,000,-000); Georgian S.S.R. (4,000,-000); Azerbaijan S.S.R. (4,-000,000); Uzbek S.S.R. (7,500,-000); Turkmen S.S.R. (1,500,-000); Kazakh S.S.R. (9,000,-000); Kirghiz S.S.R. (2,000,-000); Tadjik S.S.R. (2,000,-000).
Vietnam	22,000,000	Formerly part of French Indo-China. North Vietnam (Communist area, also known as Vietminh), 12,000,000; South Vietnam (Republic of Vietnam), 10,000,000. Language: Vietnamese (or Annamese), Mon-Khmer dialects; French superimposed.
Yemen	4,500,000	

British possessions and protectorates mentioned in footnote 3, page 52 (Aden, Bahrein, Kuwait, Trucial, Qatar, etc.) now have an aggregate population of well over 1,000,000. Language: Arabic; English superimposed.

Major political shifts since 1944 include the separation of India and Pakistan; the separate statehood of India, Pakistan, Burma, Ceylon, the Malayan Federation, French Indo-China (now four separate states: North Vietnam, South

Vietnam, Cambodia, Laos), North and South Korea, Israel, Lebanon, Jordan and Syria, with the subsequent fusion of Syria and Egypt into the United Arab Republic.

Linguistic changes are insignificant by comparison. In all Arabic-speaking states, Arabic is now the official as well as the national language. Hindi is making slow progress as the common language of India, and is now spoken, even as an acquired tongue, by no more than half the population. Urdu, the official language of Pakistan, has been forced to recognize the equal rights of Bengali in East Pakistan. Singhalese, the official language of Ceylon, encounters opposition from the speakers of Tamil. Hebrew is the official tongue of Israel; Cambodian (of the Mon-Khmer family) of Cambodia; Vietnamese of Vietnam. Chinese and Russian have somewhat extended their influence, but the old languages of colonization (English, French, Portuguese) are still very much alive and in use.

6. AFRICA

Country	Approximate Population	Notes
Algeria	10,000,000	
Angola	5,000,000	
Basutoland	700,000	
Bechuanaland	400,000	
Belgian Congo	14,000,000	
Cameroons	5,500,000	Political status as yet undetermined, both for British and French areas.
Central African Federation	8,000,000	Including Northern and Southern Rhodesia and Nyasaland.
Egypt	25,000,000	Now united with Syria into the United Arab Republic.
Ethiopia	20,000,000	Including the former Italian colony of Eritrea.
French Equatorial Africa	5,000,000	Now mostly absorbed into the French Union.

French West Africa	20,000,000	Now mostly absorbed into the French Union.
Gambia	400,000	
Ghana	5,000,000	Including the former Gold Coast, portions of Togoland, and other areas.
Guinea	1,000,000	Recently made into an independent republic out of former French areas.
Guinea, Portuguese; Madeira and Cape Verde Islands; Príncipe, São Tomé	1,000,000	Languages: Sudanese-Guinean in Guinea, with Portuguese superimposed; Portuguese elsewhere.
Guinea, Spanish; Ifni, Río de Oro	300,000	Languages: Bantu in Guinea; Arabic and Berber dialects in Ifni and Río de Oro; Spanish superimposed.
Kenya	7,000,000	
Liberia	3,000,000	
Libya	1,500,000	
Madagascar	5,000,000	
Morocco	9,000,000	Including both former French Morocco and former Spanish Morocco.
Mozambique	6,500,000	
Nigeria	34,000,000	Political status not yet fully determined.
Sierra Leone	2,500,000	
Somaliland	1,500,000	Former Italian colony, now independent.
Somaliland, British	700,000	
Somaliland, French	100,000	
Sudan	10,000,000	Formerly Anglo-Egyptian Sudan; now an independent nation.
Swaziland	300,000	
Tanganyika	9,000,000	
Tunisia	4,000,000	Former French possession; now fully independent.

XIII

Togoland	1,000,000	Now a fully independent nation.
Uganda	6,000,000	
Union of South Africa	15,000,000	Including former Southwest Africa.
Zanzibar	400,000	Languages: Bantu (especially Swahili); English superimposed.

Major political shifts include independent nationhood for the following nations: Ethiopia (for ten years an Italian colony; now again independent, and joined by Eritrea, another former Italian colony of longer standing); Ghana; Guinea; Libya (formerly an Italian colony); Morocco (including both former French and former Spanish areas); Somaliland (formerly an Italian colony); the Sudan; Tunisia; Togoland. There are further the union of the Rhodesias, Northern and Southern, and of Nyasaland into a Central African Federation; and the full absorption of Southwest Africa into the Union of South Africa. Areas where additional political changes appear likely as we write are: Algeria; the Belgian Congo; the Cameroons; Nigeria; Sierra Leone. With the exception of Guinea, areas included in French West Africa and French Equatorial Africa, along with Madagascar, have joined the French Union. The languages of colonization and former colonization (English, French, Portuguese, Italian, Spanish, Afrikaans) are still very much in use. Little if any attempt has been or is being made to use native languages as official or national tongues, save for Arabic in Morocco, Tunisia, Libya and the Sudan; this despite the fact that Hausa could well function in the region of the Gulf of Guinea, and Swahili along the East African coast from Somaliland south.

7. OCEANIA

Country	Approximate Population	Notes
Australia	10,000,000	
British North Borneo	500,000	
Brunei	50,000	

Caroline, Marianas, Marshall Islands	120,000	Now taken over by U.S.A.; English superimposed on native Micronesian dialects.
Dutch New Guinea	1,000,000	Papuan dialects; Dutch superimposed.
Fiji Islands	400,000	
French Oceania	50,000	
Gilbert and Ellice Islands	50,000	
Guam	70,000	
Hawaii	700,000	Now a State of the Union.
Indonesia	85,000,000	With the exception of Dutch New Guinea, which has remained under Dutch rule, the Republic of Indonesia coincides with the former Dutch East Indies. Language: Indonesian (Bahasa Indonesia, largely based on Malay); Malay, Dutch and, to a lesser degree, English are still widespread. Distribution of major local languages, all of the Indonesian branch of the Malayo-Polynesian family, is roughly as follows: Javanese, 45,000,000; Sundanese, 15,000,000; Madurese, 7,000,000; Balinese, 5,000,000; Dayak and Batak, between 1,000,000 and 2,000,000 apiece; others, 10,000,000.
New Caledonia	100,000	
New Guinea	1,500,000	Icluding Bismarck Archipelago, under Australian administration.
New Hebrides	60,000	
New Zealand	2,500,000	Including Cook Islands.
Papua	500,000	
Philippines	25,000,000	Now fully independent, with Tagalog as the official language; English and Spanish are still quite in use. Distribution of the

major Philippine languages, all of the Indonesian branch of the Malayo-Polynesian family: Tagalog, 8,000,000; Bisaya, 8,000,000; Ilocano, 3,000,000; others 6,000,000.

Samoa and West Samoa	120,000
Sarawak	700,000
Solomon Islands	150,000
Timor (Portuguese)	500,000
Tonga	100,000

The major political changes in this area are: 1. the arising of the Republic of Indonesia out of the former Dutch East Indies, with the creation of Bahasa Indonesia to serve as an official tongue; 2. the independence of the Philippines, with the adoption of Tagalog as the official language. The languages of colonization and former colonization (English, French, Dutch, Portuguese) are still very much in evidence, along with traces of older colonizing languages (German, Spanish, Japanese).

TABLE II — LANGUAGE TYPES AND LANGUAGE FAMILIES (see pp. 25-39 of text)

(All population figures are based on United Nations 1960 estimates, with a slight projection, based on existing trends, into the future)

The picture of the world's languages and language families has, of course, little or nothing to do with the political scene. But numerical shifts in the number of speakers of given languages are significant, even politically, since they may be the forerunners of shifts in political power.

Again, for purposes of comparison, we have preferred to leave unchanged our set-up of language types, language families and numbers of speakers as they appeared in 1944

XVI

(pages 25-39). Note the numerical changes, the only truly significant shifts in the entire picture.

Note also that we have not hesitated to duplicate where bilingualism enters the situation. The number of *native* speakers of English, in 1960, hovers around the 270,000,000 mark; to these, however, are added the 30 million people, more or less, who speak English as an acquired language, although these 30 million also appear under their own mother-tongues. Native speakers of French do not exceed 65 million; but who can deny the existence of at least 15 million additional people throughout the world who speak French fluently, though their native language is something else? Native speakers of Russian probably do not go much beyond 100 million; but practically every one of the 200,000,000 or more inhabitants of the U.S.S.R. has learned enough Russian to be able to handle his own affairs in that language. German, the native tongue of 90 million Germans, Austrians and Swiss, is also handled reasonably well by some 30 million other people (mostly central Europeans, Czechs, Hungarians, Yugoslavs, Poles, Danes, Hollanders, Swedes, and others; as well as people of German stock in North and South America and elsewhere). The reader is therefore warned that our figures are padded to make allowance for those who speak with reasonable fluency languages that are not native to them.

* * *

The total number of speakers of Indo-European languages appearing on p. 25 now closely approaches 1,500,-000,000, about half of the world's total population.

Their present distribution, in comparison with the figures appearing on pages 28-29, is as follows:

Armenian	4,000,000	
Albanian	2,000,000	
Greek	10,000,000	
Celtic	5,000,000	
Indo-Iranian	390,000,000	(250,000,000 in India; 90,000,-000 in Pakistan; 10,000,000 in Nepal and Bhutan; 5,000,000

XVII

		in Ceylon; 20,000,000 in Iran; 14,000,000 in Afghanistan).
Balto-Slavic	320,000,000	(200,000,000 for Russian; 40,-000,000 for Ukrainian; 10,000,-000 for Byelorussian; 30,000,-000 for Polish; 14,000,000 for Czech and Slovak; 18,000,000 for Serbo-Croatian and Slovenian; 8,000,000 for Bulgarian; 3,000,000 for Lithuanian; 2,-000,000 for Latvian. Note that the figures for Ukrainian, Byelorussian, Lithuanian and Latvian duplicate part of the Russian total).
Romance	400,000,000	(160,000,000 for Spanish; 80,-000,000 for French; 80,000,000 for Portuguese; 60,000,000 for Italian; 20,000,000 for Rumanian).
Germanic	460,000,000	(300,000,000 for English; 120,-000,000 for German; 20,000,-000 for Dutch, Flemish and Afrikaans; less than 20,000,000 for the Scandinavian languages)

*   *   *

The Semito-Hamitic group, described on pages 29-30, now comprises about 120,000,000 speakers, with Arabic coming close to the 90 million mark, Hebrew accounting for 3 million, and Ethiopian, Libyco-Berber and Kushitic languages accounting for the rest.

*   *   *

The Ural-Altaic group, described on pages 30-31, has now perhaps 75,000,000 speakers, of whom Finnish, Karelian, Estonian and Lapp account for some 6 million, Hungarian for 13 million, Turkish for 25 million, and various Uralic and Altaic tongues of the U.S.S.R., Mongolia and Manchuria for 32 million.

XVIII

The Japanese-Korean family (pages 31-33) now numbers about 125,000,000 speakers, about 95 million of whom are Japanese and 30 million Koreans.

*　　*　　*

The Sino-Tibetan family (pages 32-33) now comes close to 700,000,000 speakers, of whom about 650 million are Chinese, 20 million Burmese, 20 million Thai, and several million of other related tongues, including about one million speakers of Tibetan.

*　　*　　*

The Dravidian family (pages 33-34) at present numbers about 130 million speakers.

*　　*　　*

Malayo-Polynesian at the present time has risen to about 130,000,000 speakers, with the Indonesian branch in heavy predominance (85 million in Indonesia, 25 million in the Philippines, 5 million in Madagascar).

*　　*　　*

The African Negro languages described on page 35 now number about 140,000,000 speakers (90 million of Sudanese-Guinean languages, 50 million of Bantu, less than one million of Hottentot-Bushman).

*　　*　　*

Other statistical revisions are as follows:

p. 63	English — 270,000,000
	German — 90,000,000
p. 64	Dutch and Flemish — 17,000,000
	Afrikaans — 3,000,000
	Swedish — 8,000,000
	Danish — 4,500,000
	Norwegian — 4,000,000
	Icelandic — 200,000
	English — 270,000,000
p. 65	U. S. A. — 180,000,000

XIX

XX

Tunisia — 4,000,000; French Somaliland — 100,000.

Asia — Cambodia, 5,000,000; Laos — 3,000,-000; North Vietnam — 12,000,000; South Vietnam — 10,000,000; Syria — 4,000,000; Lebanon — 2,000,000; Jordan — 2,000,000.

Oceania — French Oceania, New Caledonia, New Hebrides, West Samoa, etc. — 250,000.

Western Hemisphere — Canada — 5,000,000; Haiti, 3,500,000; Guadeloupe, Martinique, French Guiana — 1,000,000.

Other facts and figures unchanged.

p. 227   Spanish — *Europe* — Spain — 30,000,000.

Africa — Canary Islands, Río de Oro, Spanish Guinea — 1,000,000.

North America — Mexico — 32,000,000.

Central America — Canal Zone — 70,000; Costa Rica — 1,000,000; Guatemala — 3,500,-000; Honduras — 2,000,000; Nicaragua — 1,500,000; Panama — 1,000,000; Salvador — 1,500,000.

West Indies — Cuba — 6,000,000; Dominican Republic — 3,000,000; Puerto Rico — 2,500,000.

South America — Argentina — 21,000,000; Bolivia, 3,500,000; Chile — 7,500,000; Colombia — 13,500,000; Ecuador — 4,000,000; Paraguay — 2,000,000; Peru — 10,000,000; Uruguay—3,000,000; Venezuela—6,000,000.

Other facts and figures unchanged.

p. 269   Portuguese — *Europe* — Portugal and Azores — 9,000,000; Galicia — 3,500,000.

Asia — Goa, Damau, Diu, Macao—1,000,000.

Africa — Portuguese Guinea — 500,000; Angola — 5,000,000; Mozambique — 6,500,000; Madeira, Cape Verde, São Tomé, Príncipe — 500,000.

XXI

Oceania — Portuguese Timor — 500,000.
South America — Brazil — 65,000,000.
Other facts and figures unchanged.

p. 313   Italian — *Europe* — Italy — 50,000,000;
Switzerland — 500,000
Africa — former colonial language of Libya
(1,500,000); Ethiopia and Eritrea (20,000,-
000); Somaliland (1,500,000).

p. 351-352   Languages of the Slavic Group.
Russian (Great Russian) — official and prin-
cipal language of U.S.S.R. (European popula-
tion — 160,000,000; Asiatic population —
45,000,000). Native Great Russian speakers —
over 100,000,000. Spoken as acquired language
by another 100,000,000.
Ukrainian — 40,000,000.
Byelorussian (White Russian) — 10,000,000.
Polish — 30,000,000.
Czech and Slovak — 14,000,000.
Serbo-Croatian and Slovenian — 18,000,000.
Bulgarian — 8,000,000

p. 376   U.S.S.R. population — 205,000,000
Russian speakers — 100,000,000 native; 100,-
000,000 acquired.
Ukrainian 40,000,000.
Byelorussian — 10,000,000.

pp. 419-420   Greek — 10,000,000
Albanian — 2,000,000
Finnish — 4,500,000
Estonian — 1,000,000
Hungarian — 13,000,000
Turkish — 25,000,000
Other facts and figures unchanged.

pp. 457-458   Persian — 20,000,000
Pushtu — 13,000,000
Hindustani — 200,000,000 (Hindi — 150,-

000,000, more or less evenly divided between native speakers and those who have acquired the language; Urdu (mostly in West Pakistan) — 50,000,000).
Bengali — 85,000,000 (Calcutta region of India, East Pakistan).
Bihari — 35,000,000
Marathi (Maharashtrian) — 35,000,000
Punjabi — 25,000,000
Rajasthani — 20,000,000
Gujarati — 20,000,000
Oriya — 15,000,000
Assamese — 10,000,000
Sindhi — 7,000,000
Singhalese — 7,000,000
Kashmiri — 3,000,000

DRAVIDIAN LANGUAGES OF INDIA:

Tamil — 40,000,000
Telugu — 45,000,000
Canarese (Kanarese, Kannada) — 20,000,000
Malayalam — 20,000,000

SINO-TIBETAN LANGUAGES

Chinese — 650,000,000
Tibeto-Burmese — 20,000,000
Thai — 20,000,000

JAPANESE-KOREAN LANGUAGES

Korean — 30,000,000
Japanese — 95,000,000
p. 459
p. 482 Malay (Indonesian) — 90,000,000
Hindustani — 125,000,000 native speakers (75,000,000 Hindi, 50,000,000 Urdu), plus 75,000,000 non-native speakers.

XXIII

CHAPTER I

LANGUAGE TYPES AND LANGUAGE FAMILIES

What languages are to be studied in connection with our post-war needs? Gray's *Foundations of Language* (p. 418) tentatively places the total number of present-day spoken languages, exclusive of minor dialects, at 2,796 — a staggering total, when we consider the amount of effort required to master even one foreign tongue. Obviously, a wise choice is imperative.

But fortunately for the practical linguist, there are "key" languages, which open up to us vast areas of the earth. THE MAN WHO HAS SOME PRACTICAL ACQUAINTANCE WITH ENGLISH, FRENCH, GERMAN, SPANISH, POR-TUGUESE, ITALIAN, RUSSIAN, AND JAPANESE IS, ROUGHLY SPEAKING, IN A POSITION TO MAKE HIS WAY AROUND THE WORLD. If to this knowledge he adds a smattering of Arabic, Chinese, Malay, and Dutch, and the ability to identify a few other tongues, so that he can distinguish between Polish and Czech, Swedish and Danish, Finnish and Hungarian, at least in their written form, his linguistic educa-tion, for purely utilitarian purposes, is completed.

Can this be demonstrated?

The impressive total of 2,796 tongues, mentioned above, includes over a thousand American Indian languages, whose present-day speakers number a few thousand or even a few hundred each. Over five hundred "languages" are spoken by African Negro tribes; nearly five hundred more by the natives of Australia, New Guinea, and the islands of the Pacific. Sev-eral hundred others are little-known tongues spoken by isolated groups in Asia. All these can safely be disregarded for the purpose on hand.

This does not mean that they are scientifically unimportant. Some of them, though spoken by small and semi-savage groups, are of the highest interest to the professional linguist by reason of their peculiar structure, and to the psychologist and anthropologist because of the mental processes they betoken. But our present aim is immediate use. Whether from a military, economic and political standpoint, or from a cultural one, we find that the world's truly significant languages now number less than one hundred.

We also find that not all of these significant languages are of equal importance. The number of speakers has something to do with this. For *practical* purposes, in spite of the civilization behind it and the contribution it has made to the vocabularies of all civilized modern tongues, Greek, with its seven or eight million present-day speakers, cannot be ranged alongside of Spanish, whose speakers number well over a hundred million. Political and cultural influence also comes into play. Dutch may be the language of only some nine million speakers in Holland, but it is current, side by side with native Malay languages, in the Dutch colonial empire (Java, Sumatra, Borneo, Celebes, etc.), with over 60,000,000 inhabitants. French is a mighty and widely spoken language in its own right (42,000,000 Frenchmen, plus about six million French speakers in Belgium and Switzerland, plus the speakers of French in Canada and in the French colonial possessions); but in addition, French is also a current tongue among the more cultured classes of numerous European countries, so that it may be, and frequently is used as a means of common intercourse between, say, an American who has learned it in the schools and a native Pole or Italian or Hollander. This matter of bilingualism (one individual speaking two languages) and polylingualism (several languages spoken by the one person) will have to be taken into account as our study proceeds, particularly when we come to countries which are or have been colonial possessions. While it is true, for instance, that India's 390,000,000 inhabitants are linguistically divided among three groups (Indo-Aryan, Dravidian and Munda), it is also true that the use of English is widespread by reason of the long British occupation of the Indian Peninsula. This leads necessarily to a certain amount of duplication in enumerating the speakers of various tongues. We can list the majority of Czecho-Slovakia's former 15,000,000 inhabitants among the speakers of Slavic tongues, but it is also true that more than half of them can be reached with German. In Budapest, the Hungarian capital, it was the writer's experience that four out of every five people approached responded to German. The bald figures of the number of native speakers of a given language, therefore, very often do not tell the whole story. Certain languages spread far beyond their national or colonial borders, and can be used, with greater or lesser effectiveness, in other lands as well.

What of the matter of facility in acquiring foreign tongues for practical purposes? Are some languages inherently "easy", others inherently "difficult"? While it is true that some tongues *seem* to possess a more simple structure than others, no language is intrinsically difficult to its own speakers, who have acquired and used it, and only it, from childhood. *Speaking* Chinese is not difficult to the Chinese speaker, though *writing* it may be. To him, the complicated tones[1] which we describe as "sing-song" and master only with the greatest difficulty are the most natural thing in the world; he has learned to produce them and use them in the proper place ever since he first began to use his vocal organs. "Ease" or "difficulty" in acquiring a language is not something intrinsic, but something which functions with reference to one's own previous linguistic habits. The more a tongue resembles our own, in sounds, in grammatical structure, in vocabulary, the "easier" it is to us; the more it diverges from our own, the "harder" it becomes. To the speaker of a language like English, the grammatical structure of a language like French is comparatively

1—Cf. p. 32.

easy ("I have laid the book on the table" can be translated absolutely word for word into French); German, which says "I have the book on the table laid", seems a little harder; Latin, requiring "Book on table laid-I", is harder still. On the other hand, German *ich habe — gelegt* and *das Buch* come considerably closer to English "I have laid" and "the book" than French *j'ai posé* and *le livre,* or Latin *librum* and *posui,* with the result that for the example in question, the advantage of similarity in French word-order is offset by the advantage of similarity in German vocabulary, and the beginner would be tempted to say: "French and German are about equally difficult". But the minute it is pointed out to him that French translates "of the book", "to the book" more or less literally, while German effects a change in the article and the ending of the noun, and omits "of" and "to", he will vote in favor of French as the "easier" language.

What governs similarity between two languages in sounds, grammatical structure and vocabulary? The answer to this question leads us into a discussion of linguistic classification. A few extremists among language scientists are of the opinion that all languages go back to one original common stock, which in the course of thousands of years and countless prehistoric migrations has evolved into the various language types of today. The process by which this took place would be, according to them, one of infinite differentiation and change. But the divergences and differences among the world's languages seem too radical and far-reaching to be accounted for by any such process, no matter how drastic or prolonged. On the other hand, it is undeniable that a somewhat comparable process has, so to speak, taken place under our eyes in the case of several languages whose history can be traced. This is true, for example, of French, Spanish, Portuguese and Italian, stemming from an original Latin during the course of the last two thousand years, or of English and German, originally far closer than they are today. This means that even if languages cannot be reduced to one single, common ancestry, they can at least be grouped into large family units, the members of which bear enough of a fundamental resemblance to one another to be described as proceeding from a common ancestor, or "parent-language", frequently unknown because no written[2] trace of it has come down to us, but which can be hypothetically reconstructed.

This means that language goes through a constant process of change or evolution. The English of today is no longer the English of Shakespeare, which requires a certain amount of study and even the occasional help of a glossary to be fully understood; still less is it the English of Chaucer, or of the Anglo-Saxon days before the Norman conquest of England. Nor will the English of tomorrow be the English of today. New words, new expressions, even new grammatical constructions are constantly being added to the language, while old ones drop out, become "obsolete", then "archaic", and finally require the aid of a dictionary to be understood. The slang of today may become the colloquialism of tomorrow and the correct literary form of a hundred years hence. As the present-

2. Language, be it noted, comes in two forms, the spoken and the written. The former, of course, invariably precedes the other. People learn to speak before they learn to write, and spoken languages antedate their written counterparts. The latter assume varied forms. The alphabet we use in English is current in a great many languages (French, Spanish, Italian, etc.) ; in others it diverges slightly (German) ; the divergence is still greater in others (Greek, Russian) ; while in Hebrew and Arabic the alphabetic kinship is almost completely disguised. The writing of languages like Chinese and Japanese not only bears no resemblance to, but has no kinship with our own. Note also the different values of the same alphabetic symbol in different languages, or even in the same language (Eng. *far*, *bat*, *fare*, *all*, etc.). Occasionally, the same language is written in different alphabets, according to the religious or cultural background of its speakers; such is the case with Serbo-Croatian, written in Roman characters by the Catholic Croats and in Cyrillic characters by the Greek Orthodox Serbs; or with Hindustani, written in Devanagari characters (derived from Sanskrit) by its speakers of the Hindu faith (in which case it is also called Hindi), and in Arabic script by its Muhammadan speakers (in which case it is also called Urdu).

day speaker delves back into his own language of past centuries, it becomes increasingly more difficult to him, until the
point is reached where it is a "foreign" tongue. The cultured
English speaker can struggle backwards as far as the English
of Chaucer, but when he comes to "Beowulf" he needs a course
in Anglo-Saxon. The cultured French speaker can make his
way back with ease to the fifteenth-century French of Villon,
and with considerable difficulty to the eleventh-century "Song
of Roland"; but if he goes back beyond the ninth century he
finds himself in a Latin atmosphere, and has to study the language once spoken on his own soil, and from which his own
language proceeds, just as he would a foreign, though related,
tongue.

The present-day geographical aspect of languages within
the same family bears some similarity to the historical picture
of a single language throughout its evolution. Starting with
English, we find sufficient striking resemblances in German,
Dutch and Scandinavian to permit even the layman to classify
these tongues as closely related. The resemblances are almost
equally striking when we come to French, Spanish, Italian,
Portuguese. As we wander further afield, into Greek, Russian, and some of the languages of India, we can, if properly
trained, still detect a sufficient number of similarities to enable us to class these languages as originally akin to our own.

On the other hand, we come across a certain number of
languages which differ so radically in structure and vocabulary
that we can safely decide they do not belong to our group.
Yet some of these languages show the same striking similarities among themselves that are shown by English and German,
or by French and Spanish. Such is the case, for instance, with
Finnish and Hungarian, or with Hebrew and Arabic. The result is that languages have been classified into families and
sub-families. The classification is imperfect, particularly in
the case of the less known and less important languages. It is
fairly exact for languages which have been and are the vehicles
of important civilizations.

The linguistic family to which English, French, German,

Spanish, Italian, Portuguese and Russian belong is called Indo-European, by reason of the fact that its members stretch across all of Europe and west central Asia to northern India. The term "Indo-Germanic" is preferred by the Germans, ostensibly because Icelandic, the westernmost member of the family, belongs to the Germanic subdivision. The term "Aryan" has also been used, but here we run into a major difficulty. "Aryan" is also used in referring to a somewhat hypothetical race: the race which, it is supposed, originally spoke the "Aryan" parent-language. Such a race, speaking such a language, may have existed, though the evidence is far from absolute. But if there is one thing of which we are mathematically sure in the field of language, it is that race and language do not necessarily coincide; a Negro whose ancestors came from Africa, a Jew whose forebears spoke a Semitic language, can (and do) today speak perfect Indo-European English and have no recollection of their ancestral tongues; an Aztec Indian of Mexico may speak Indo-European Spanish with no memory or trace of his ancestral American Indian language. The nations or groups that today speak Indo-European languages are not at all necessarily of "Aryan" stock. The description of the ideal "Aryan" (tall, blond, long-skulled) certainly does not fit the majority of the peoples living in central or southern Europe, who nevertheless speak pure Indo-European languages. The fact of the matter seems to be that races have an inherent tendency to become mixed, and languages to be borrowed, assimilated and appropriated by people who originally did not speak them. "Aryan", therefore, is best discarded,[3] and Indo-European is best taken as a purely linguistic term, with no racial connotation.

It is undeniable, on the other hand, that the greatest contributions to civilization, both ancient and modern, have been

3. Save in one legitimate linguistic connection: the Indo-European languages of northern India are often described, as a group, as "Indo-Aryan". But even this term is becoming obsolete.

made by peoples speaking Indo-European tongues, with Semitic speakers as closest rivals. It is also true that of all the language-families the Indo-European is the one which has received the most careful scrutiny at the hands of linguists, and concerning the classification and subdivisions of which we are most certain. Lastly, it is true that an absolute majority of the world's chief present-day languages, both from the standpoint of number of speakers and that of cultural, political and economic importance, belongs to this group.

English is, in many ways, a fair representative of Indo-European. Its numerical strength and power of expansion, its influence upon civilization and the destinies of the world, are characteristic. Its vocabulary, which represents an almost equal blending of the two greatest Indo-European subdivisions, the Germanic and the Latin-Romance (with considerable additions from Greek and other sources), tends to make it international in scope. Its rich variety of sounds is such that its speakers can adapt themselves with comparative ease to the sounds of many foreign tongues. On the other hand, its alphabetic notation is far from perfect, and very distressing to the foreigner, and even to the native (the process of learning to "spell" goes on through grammar school, high school and college, and is often not quite completed by the time the student emerges with a university degree). On the structural side, modern English displays a process of simplification[4] of orig-

4. The process is perhaps better described as one of analysis (breaking up a thought-concept into several words representing its component parts: "I" "have" "ended") versus the old Indo-European system of synthesis (gathering together the complete concept into a single word: Latin *fini-v-i*). It means, in the case of nouns, using position ("Peter sees the boy"; "The boy sees Peter") and prepositions ("to the boy", "of the boy") instead of case-endings indicating subject, object, "of", "to", etc. (as with Latin *puer, puerum, pueri, puero*); in the case of verbs, using pronouns ("I", "you", "he", etc.) and auxiliaries ("shall", "will", "have", etc.) in the place of suffixes carrying those meanings (Latin *fini-v-i*). Note that even in modern English the two systems, synthetic and analytic, occasionally appear side by side ("the boys' books", or "the books of the boys").

inal Indo-European grammatical forms which sets it rather far away from the original Indo-European type (much farther away, for instance, than modern Russian, or even German); in this, it is accompanied, though not all the way, by the major Romance tongues.

The original Indo-European type is described as "inflectional", which means that it indicates grammatical relations by means of endings, or "suffixes", which are added on to the "roots" of words. Latin, for example, takes a root *mur-*, "wall", and indicates that it is the subject of the sentence by adding *-us* (*murus*), or that it is the object by adding *-um* (*murum*); "of the wall" is indicated by the ending *-i* (*muri*); "to the wall" by *-o* (*muro*). In the case of verbs, Latin uses a root like *fini-*, "end", adding an ending *-o* (*fini-o*) which at the same time marks the present tense and the first person singular ("I end"); for the future ("I shall love"), Latin adds to the root *ama-* a suffix *-b-*, indicating futurity, and another suffix *-o*, indicating "I" (*amabo*); while for the past tense ("I ended") the root *fini-* receives the suffixes *-v-* and *-i* (*finivi*); different personal suffixes are used throughout, eliminating the need for subject pronouns ("you ended", *fini-v-isti;* "he ended", *fini-v-it;* "we ended", *fini-v-imus;* "they ended", *fini-v-erunt*). Old English (or Anglo-Saxon) had a very similar structure, but modern English has largely discarded it (*'s* in the possessive case, *-s* in the third person singular of the present tense, *-d* in the past tense of verbs, are vestiges of the older system). This process of simplification has gone on, to some extent, in all Indo-European languages, but in some to a far greater degree than in others. The Romance languages, for example, have simplified their structure even more than English for what concerns the noun, but practically not at all for what concerns the verb. The Slavic languages, on the other hand, have a comparatively simplified verb, but retain a full "inflectional" system for the noun. German effects a minor degree of simplification in both, but still retains a good deal of the original inflectional structure.

From a practical standpoint, this means that the English speaker will encounter little difficulty with the Romance noun ("dog", Spanish *perro;* "of the dog", *del perro;* "to the dog", *al perro;* "dogs", *perros;* "of the dogs", *de los perros;* "to the dogs", *a los perros*); but he will meet considerable hardship with the Romance verb ("I loved", Spanish *amé;* "you loved", *amaste;* "he loved", *amó;* "we loved", *amamos;* "they loved", *amaron*). He will experience trouble with the Slavic noun ("dog", Russian *pyos;* "of the dog", *psa;* "to the dog", *psu*); but he will breathe more easily when he sees: "I loved", *ya lyubil;* "you loved", *ty lyubil;* "he loved", *on lyubil.* German *der Hund* ("dog", subject); *den Hund* ("dog", object); *des Hundes* ("of the dog"); *dem Hunde* ("to the dog"); and *ich liebte, du liebtest, er liebte* for "I", "you", "he", "loved", will prove moderate stumbling-blocks.

When we come to other linguistic families, the difficulties encountered will be much greater. In the first place, the vocabulary resemblances to which we are accustomed in German, French, Spanish, Italian, and, to a lesser degree, in Russian or Greek, are largely, almost totally, absent. Secondly, we meet a grammatical structure which bears no resemblance to ours. Japanese, for instance, utterly fails to recognize our concept of gender (masculine, feminine, neuter), and has very vague notions about number (singular, plural). It does not care much for our "personal" verb ("I", "you", "we" do something), but prefers to use a different verb altogether, according as the subject is the speaker (in which case the verb is a "humble" verb), or the person addressed (in which case it is a "polite" or "respectful" verb). Hungarian attaches prepositions and possessive adjectives to the noun ("house", *ház;* "in the house", *ház-ban;* "arm", *kar;* "my arm", *kar-om*).

But here, our process of choice and elimination comes to our rescue. Of the world's *chief* languages, only a few that are not Indo-European combine numerical strength, cultural importance, and practical value. Very few of them are "irreplaceable", in the sense that a good many of their speakers cannot be reached through the medium of another, more accessible tongue. The chapter on geographical distribution will tell us which they are, and why they are irreplaceable.

Meanwhile, for the sake of curiosity, we present a table of the world's chief linguistic families with their main subdivisions. This table is not exact, and it is far from complete. Nevertheless, it is imposing. Read it, but do not attempt to memorize it.

I — INDO-EUROPEAN.

Location: nearly all of Europe; southwestern Asia as far as northeastern India, inclusive; the entire western hemisphere; Australia, New Zealand, Tasmania; South Africa; spoken in the form of superimposed languages of colonization (English, French, Dutch, Portuguese, Italian, Spanish) throughout Africa, India, southeastern Asia, the islands of the Pacific.

Number of speakers: nearly 1,000,000,000.

Structure: originally inflectional and synthetic; modified to varying degrees in the direction of simplification (analysis; cf. p. 20), with the loss of inflectional endings, and the use of word-order to indicate grammatical relations.

Main branches:

a) Germanic:[5] Northern (or Scandinavian): Icelandic, Dano-Norwegian, Swedish.

Western: English, High and Low German,[6] Dutch-Flemish.

5. A third branch of Germanic, the Eastern, represented by ancient Gothic, has disappeared.
6. Yiddish, which has no national territory, is fourteenth-century German adopted by the northern Jews (Ashkenazim) in the course of their migrations; it is written with a modified Hebrew alphabet and mingled with words borrowed from Hebrew, Slavic, English, etc.

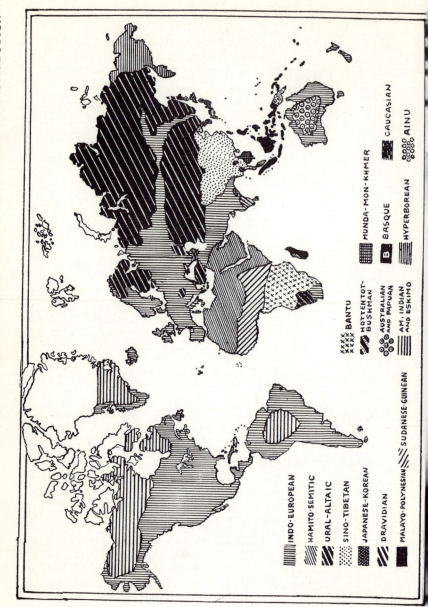

b) Romance:[7] Hispanic: Spanish,[8] Portuguese, Catalan.[8]
   French: French, Provençal.
   Italian.
   Roumanian.

c) Celtic: Goidelic: Scots Gaelic, Irish Gaelic (Erse), Manx.
   Brythonic: Welsh, Breton.

d) Balto-Slavic: Baltic: Lithuanian, Lettish.
   Slavic: Eastern: Russian, Ukrainian, White
   Russian.
   Western: Polish, Czech, Slovak.
   Southern: Serbo-Croatian, Slovene,
   Bulgarian.

e) Greek.

f) Albanian.

g) Armenian.

h) Iranian: Persian, Kurdish, Balochi, Afghan (or Pushtu).

i) Indo-Aryan languages of northern India and southern
   Ceylon; among the better known are: Hindi, Urdu, Bengali, Panjabi, Rajasthani, Marathi, Gujarati, Singhalese. The language of the Gypsies also belongs to this
   group.

★ ★ ★

7. Or Italic. Latin is the direct ancestor of all the languages of this branch; in ancient times, there was another Italic subdivision, the Oscan-Umbrian, which Latin absorbed. Additional minor Romance branches are the Rhetian (Rumansh, Ladin) of southeastern Switzerland, the Italian Tyrol and Friuli, and the Logudorese-Campidanese of Sardinia.

8. Judaeo-Spanish, also called Sephardic, Sephardí or Ladino (do not confuse with Ladin, above), is the Romance counterpart of Germanic Yiddish; it is a medieval Spanish retained by migrating southern Jews (Sephardim) after their expulsion from Spain, and carried to various localities along the Mediterranean coast, notably Salonika, Monastir and Constantinople; its borrowed elements are mainly Turkish, Greek and Hebrew; it also is written with a modified Hebrew alphabet. Some doubt exists whether Catalan should be classed with the Hispanic languages or with Provençal.

A glance at this chart shows us the varying practical importance of these branches and their languages, both from the standpoint of number of speakers and from that of political, economic and cultural worth. The total number of Armenian speakers does not exceed 4,000,000, that of Albanian speakers 2,000,000. Greek, despite its tremendous contribution to civilization in ancient times, has today perhaps 8,000,000 speakers. The Celtic languages taken together do not exceed 4,000,000 speakers, though an attempt is being made at the present time by the Irish Free State Government to reintroduce Irish Gaelic (Erse) as the spoken language of Eire. The Baltic tongues (Lithuanian and Lettish) count approximately 4,000,000 speakers, the Iranian tongues of Iran, Afghanistan and Baluchistan perhaps 30,000,000.

On the other hand, the Indo-Aryan vernaculars of India are estimated to be spoken by some 250,000,000 people, and their cultural background runs back to the Sanskrit of the sacred Vedic writings; but the colonial status of India, and the existence of an extremely large number of diverging dialects robs them of much of the importance to which their numerical strength would otherwise entitle them.

The Slavic languages number nearly 200,000,000 speakers, of whom nearly 150,000,000 are located on Soviet soil. The Romance languages with their Latin background and, approximately, 100,000,000 Spanish speakers, 70,000,000 French speakers, 50,000,000 Portuguese speakers, 50,000,000 Italian speakers, share with the Germanic branch the distinction of being, *par excellence*, the tongues of modern culture, civilization, and political and economic expansion. Among the Germanic tongues, English, with over 200,000,000 speakers and vast colonial and commercial influence, and German, with approximately 100,000,000 speakers, are the leaders, though Dutch, with its colonial empire of 60,000,000 and some 9.000,-000 native speakers in Holland, is a tongue of considerable importance.[9] The total number of Scandinavian speakers is about 15,000,000.

II — SEMITO-HAMITIC.

Location: the peninsula of Arabia; Iraq, Palestine and Syria; northern Africa (Egypt, Libya, Algeria, Tunisia, Morocco, the Sahara); Ethiopia, Eritrea and Somaliland; Zanzibar and Madagascar; Malta.

Number of speakers: approximately 75,000,000.

Structure: the main characteristic of this family is the word-root consisting of three consonants, with shifting vowels to carry accessory meanings; e. g., Arabic root *k-t-b*, "write"; *kataba*, "he has written"; *kutiba*, "it has been written"; *yaktubu*, "he will write"; *yuktabu*, "it will be written"; *'aktaba*, "he has made someone write"; *kitābun*, "writing", "book"; *kātibun*, "writer"; *katbun*, "act of writing".

Main branches:

a) Semitic:[10] Northern: Hebrew.

   Southern: Arabic, Ethiopian (Tigre, Amharic, etc.).

b) Hamitic: Libyco-Berber (Kabyle, Shilh, Tuareg, etc.).

   Kushitic (Somali, Galla, etc.).

   Coptic.[11]

9.   Flemish, a variant of Dutch, is spoken in Belgium by perhaps 5,000,000 people, most of whom, however, can also be reached through French.   Afrikaans, the language of the South African Boers, is a dialect of Dutch.   It is still used by some 3,000,000 people.

10.   An Eastern branch, represented by ancient Akkadian (Assyrian, Babylonian) has become extinct.   The northern branch, of which Hebrew is the modern representative, formerly comprised several important tongues which have disappeared in the course of history; among the better known are: Canaanite, Moabite, Phoenician (with a variant, Punic, spoken by the Carthaginians), Aramaic, Syriac (the last still spoken by about 100,000 people).   Phoenician speakers seem to have been the initiators of the alphabet which, with considerable modifications and in different forms, is in use among most Indo-European and Semitic languages today.

11.   The ancestor of medieval Coptic, still used as a liturgical language in parts of Egypt, is the ancient Egyptian of the hieroglyphic inscriptions.

Arabic, which spreads across northern Africa and the Arabian peninsula, is by far the most important of these languages, both from the standpoint of number of speakers and that of expansional power and influence. As the sacred language of Muhammadanism, it influences, linguistically and psychologically, hundreds of millions. Palestinian Hebrew is in the nature of a rejuvenated artificial language, with perhaps 1,000,000 speakers. The other tongues of this group are relatively unimportant and can, to varying degrees, be replaced by the languages of colonization (English in Egypt, Italian in Eritrea and Somaliland, etc.).

III — URAL-ALTAIC.

Location: Finland, Karelia, Estonia; northern Norway and Sweden; Hungary; eastern European Russia; Turkey; Soviet Asia, Mongolia, Chinese Turkestan, Manchukuo.

Number of speakers: about 60,000,000.

Structure: "agglutinative"; this means that the process of adding endings to a word-root, which appears in Indo-European, is carried on to a far greater degree, suffix upon suffix being attached to the root to carry a variety of meanings: Turkish *at*, "horse"; *at-ım*, "my horse"; *at-lar-ım*, "my horses"; *sev*, root carrying general meaning of "love"; *sev-mek*, "to love"; *sev-dir-mek*, "to make to love"; *sev-me-mek*, "not to love"; *sev-il-eme-mek*, "to be impossible to be loved"; *sev-il-dir-eme-mek*, "to be impossible to be made to be loved". Another interesting characteristic of this group is "vowel harmony"; this means that if the root word contains a "front vowel",[12] all added suffixes must also contain front vowels; but if the root has a "back vowel",[12] the suffixes must do likewise: Hungarian *kéz*, "hand" (with the front vowel *e*); *ház*, "house"

---

12. The "front vowels" are the ones pronounced in the front part of the mouth; in most languages of this group, *e, i, ä, ö, ü,* are considered front vowels; the "back vowels" are the ones pronounced in the back part of the mouth; they are *a, o, u,* and Turkish *ı*.

(with the back vowel *a*); "in the hand" is *kéz-ben* (with the suffix *ben* containing the front vowel *e*); but "in the house" is *ház-ban* (with suffix changed to contain the back vowel *a*). A third widespread feature of this group is the absence of the concept of gender (masculine, feminine, neuter).

Main branches:
a) Uralic (or Finno-Ugric): Finnish (with Karelian and Estonian).
Lapp (with some languages of northeastern European Russia, such as Mordvinian, Cheremiss, Votyak).
Hungarian (or Magyar), Ostyak.
Samoyed.
b) Altaic: Turkish (allied to Turkish are various languages of the Tatars, Turcomans, and Kirghiz).
Mongol (Kalmuk, Buryat, etc.).
Tungus (Manchu).

★ ★ ★

The geographical extent of this group is imposing, since it stretches from northern and central Europe, across northern Asia, to the shores of the Pacific. But its speakers are not numerous, nor do they have great cultural, political, or economic importance. Finnish, Hungarian and Turkish are the only languages of this group to have attained statehood or cultural prestige. The Asiatic members of the group, being for the most part located on Soviet soil, are replaceable by Russian, while Manchu, the tongue of Manchukuo, is replaceable by Chinese and Japanese.

IV — JAPANESE-KOREAN.

Location: Japan, Korea. Japanese is also current in Formosa, Manchukuo, the Caroline and Marshall Islands, large sections of formerly occupied China, and, to a certain extent, in those territories which Japan recently held (Dutch East Indies, French Indo-China, Thailand, Malaya, Burma, Philippines).

Number of speakers: over 100,000,000.

Structure: agglutinative (but to a lesser degree than the Ural-Altaic languages); no distinction of gender or number; "impersonal" verb, different terms being used in the same meaning to convey shades of respect, humility, etc. Despite similarities of structure, many linguists doubt the connection between Japanese and Korean.

Main branches:

a) Japanese.
b) Korean.

★ ★ ★

The former military, political and economic status of Japan, added to the imposing number of Japanese speakers and the areas where Japanese is current, makes this language one of primary importance.

V — SINO-TIBETAN.

Location: China; Tibet; Burma; Thailand (Siam); northern Indo-China; Manchukuo; Sinkiang.

Number of speakers: nearly 500,000,000.

Structure: monosyllabic (words of one syllable, which are invariable and do not add on endings; grammatical relations are generally indicated by the position of the word in the sentence (cf. English "give me the *jack*", where "jack" is understood to be a noun; "we must *jack* up this car", where "jack" is understood as a verb; "this is a *jack-knife*", where "jack" is an adjective); in addition, these languages make use of *tone* (the pitch, or the rising and falling inflection of the voice) to distinguish among different meanings of what would otherwise be the same word: Chinese *fu*, pronounced with a high, even pitch, means "man"; with a slight and quickly rising pitch, "fortune"; with a slowly falling and then rising inflection, "prefecture"; with an abruptly falling inflection, "rich".

Main branches:
a) Chinese.
b) Tibetan-Burmese.
c) Siamese (or Thai).

★ ★ ★

Chinese, with some 450,000,000 speakers and a rich background of ancient civilization, is probably destined to become one of the world's most important languages. The difficulties that strew the path of the student of Chinese are: 1. the extremely large number of dialects, many of them mutually incomprehensible; 2. the tone system, which runs contrary to our linguistic habits; we are accustomed to using high, low, rising and falling inflections of the voice to express emphasis and different feelings ("*I* have seen John"; "I *have* seen John"; "I have *seen* John"; "I have seen *John*"; "*Jo-/* where are you?" "*Jo-* How could you?"), and find it very difficult to use them otherwise; 3. the complicated system of writing, with no less than 3,000 commonly used characters, which are combined to represent not *sounds*, but individual *words*. This system, with modifications, has been borrowed by the Japanese.

VI — DRAVIDIAN.

Location: southern India, northern Ceylon.
Number of speakers: nearly 100,000,000.
Structure: moderately agglutinative (e. g., noun-root, plus sign of plural, plus case-ending, which is the same for the plural as for the singular); gender not by sex, but by caste ("superior" and "inferior" beings, with women, and even goddesses, often ranged among the latter, in the same classification with inanimate objects).

Main branches: a) Tamil.
                b) Telugu.
                c) Brahui.
                d) Canarese.
                e) Gond.
                f) Bhil.
                g) Malayalam (do not confuse with Malay).

★ ★ ★

These languages, which share with the Indo-European tongues of northern India major control over the Peninsula's 390,000,000 speakers, are relatively unimportant. English is superimposed as a language of colonization.

VII — MALAYO-POLYNESIAN.

Location: Malay Peninsula; East Indies (Java, Sumatra, Borneo, Celebes, Bali, etc.); Philippines; Madagascar; New Zealand (Maori); Samoa, Hawaii, Tahiti, and, generally, the islands of the Pacific.

Number of speakers: about 90,000,000.

Structure: two-syllable root; no endings attached to nouns; concept of gender and number generally absent.

Main branches:

a) Indonesian: Dutch East Indies; Malaya; Madagascar; Philippines (Tagalog, Bisaya, etc.).
b) Melanesian: New Hebrides; Fiji Islands; Solomon Islands; etc.
c) Micronesian: Gilbert, Marshall, Caroline Islands, etc.
d) Polynesian: Samoa, New Zealand, Tahiti, Hawaii, etc.

★ ★ ★

The extremely large number of separate languages in this family makes any kind of systematic study for practical purposes difficult. Javanese, Malayan and Hawaiian can, to some extent, be reduced to a systematic arrangement. The languages of colonization (English, Dutch, Japanese, French, etc.) are everywhere superimposed.

VIII — AFRICAN NEGRO.

Location: Africa, south of the Sahara and west of Ethiopia.

Number of speakers: about 100,000,000.

Structure: no definite classification can be given. Some of these languages are characterized by the placing of nouns into distinct classes (man, tree, water, etc.), each of which receives a special distinguishing syllable or sound which is prefixed to nouns of that class and to adjectives associated with them, with a change of prefix to indicate the plural: Swahili *m-thu m-zuri*, "handsome man"; *wa-thu wa-zuri*, "handsome men"; *n-iumba n-zuri*, "pretty house"; *ma-niumba ma-zuri*, "pretty houses". Adverbs often take the same prefix as the verbs they modify: *ku-fa ku-zuri*, "to die beautifully".

Main groups:
a) Sudanese-Guinean (Nubian, Masai, Hausa, Yoruba, Mandingo, etc. .Many linguists reject Sudanese-Guinean unity).
b) Bantu (Ruanda, Swahili, Zulu, Herero, Umbundu, etc.).
c) Hottentot-Bushman.

★ ★ ★

Because of their great variety and low cultural, political and economic status, these tongues are relatively unimportant (though two of them, Swahili and Hausa, with 8,000,000 and 13,000,000 speakers, respectively, are worthy of some attention). They are everywhere in the process of being superseded by the languages of colonization (English, French, Portuguese, etc.).

IX — AMERICAN INDIAN.

Location: Western Hemisphere.

Number of speakers: undetermined, but probably does not exceed 10,000,000 at the present time, many of whom are bilingual (English in Canada and U. S. A., Spanish or Portuguese in Latin America).

Structure: enormous variations, but in the case of a large number of these languages it is characterized by "polysynthetism" ("polvsynthetic"); this means that words seldom have individual status, but become significant only when placed in a sentence; or, to put it another way, the entire sentence forms one word-unit, with none of its component parts enjoying true separate existence: Oneida *g-nagla-sl-i-zak-s*, "I am looking for a village"; *g-* carries the meaning of "I"; *nagla* conveys the idea of "living"; *sl* is a suffix giving *nagla* the force of a noun (therefore, *nagla* plus *sl* convey the idea of "village"); *i* is a verbal prefix, indicating that *zak* is to convey a verbal idea; *zak* carries the meaning of "looking for"; *s* is the sign of continued action. None of these parts would convey any very definite meaning if used by itself.

Main groups: classification is almost impossible; among the better known linguistic tribes of North America are the Eskimo, the Algonquian (Blackfoot, Cheyenne, Arapahoe, Cree, Ojibwa, Delaware, etc.), the Iroquois (Huron, Wyandot, Cherokee, etc.), and the Uto-Aztec; Central America has, among others, the Mayan, Mixtec and Zapotec; South America, the Arawak, Araucanian, Carib, Chibcha, Quechua, Tupi-Guaraní, etc.

★ ★ ★

The practical and cultural importance of the American Indian languages is small, and they are everywhere superseded by Indo-European tongues of colonization which have become the national languages of the overwhelming majority of the inhabitants (English, Spanish, Portuguese, etc.).

X — OTHER GROUPS.

The *Ainu* of northern Japan (20,000 speakers, who belong to a mysterious white race); the *Hyperborean* tongues of northeastern Siberia (a few thousand speakers); the *Basque* of northeastern Spain and southwestern France (less than

1,000,000); the *Caucasian* group of the Caucasus region in the Soviet Union (Georgian, Lesghian, Avar, Circassian, etc.; perhaps 2,000,000); the *Mon-Khmer, Annamese* and *Munda* tongues of southeastern Asia (perhaps 20,000,000 or 30,000,-000, most of them in eastern India and French Indo-China); the native tongues of Australia and New Guinea (*Papuan*), with a few hundred thousand apiece, all form separate linguistic groups, but have little practical importance.

Ainu has a curious duplication of the French-Celtic expression for "eighty" ("four twenties"); Basque has a structure somewhat reminiscent of the polysynthetism of some American Indian languages (*ponet-ekila-ko-are-kin*, "with the one who has the cap", literally: "cap-with-the-of-with"); the Caucasian tongues enjoy an unparalleled richness of consonant sounds and grammatical genders, together with a peculiar structure ("I make my father happy" has to be translated by "through me — contented — makes — self — father"); some native Australian tongues can count only up to three, with the result that "seven" has to be rendered by "pair-pair-pair-one", and "fifteen" by "hand-side-side-and-foot-half".

But while these tongues are an object of great curiosity to the scientist, their political, economic and cultural value is so small, and they are so encroached upon by neighboring and colonizing languages (Japanese for Ainu; Russian for the Hyperborean and Caucasian tongues; Spanish and French for Basque; English and French for Mon-Khmer, Annamese and Munda; English for Australian) that they can safely be disregarded by the practical linguist.

SUMMARY

Our analysis of the world's linguistic picture for practical purposes has considerably narrowed down our search for the important languages. While it is conceivable that a situation may arise in which there is a need for Ainu, or a native Australian tongue, or an African Negro dialect, or an American Indian language, we find that the practically significant lan-

guages can be determined and isolated. "Practical significance" hinges on a number of factors; numerical strength is
important, but only if accompanied by continued cultural and
economic development and political unity, so that the language
becomes standardized and assumes a definite current and literary form; otherwise, the rise of infinite dialects renders the
language difficult of access, while political instability leads to
the superimposition of another conquering or colonizing tongue.
Such is the case with India's Indo-Aryan and Dravidian languages, and, to a far lesser degree, with Chinese. Culture,
civilization, literature are of importance, but they must be accompanied by expansive power in the political and economic
fields, or the number of speakers will remain small, and the
practical importance of the language low; Greek is a good example of this. Political unity and power, force of expansion
and commercial and economic penetration, when accompanied
by the numerical factor and a cultural background, lead to
practical importance.

The languages that combine all these factors, though to
varying degrees, in the Indo-European group, are "Germanic"
English and German; "Romance" Spanish, French, Portuguese
and Italian; "Slavic" Russian. In the Semitic group, Arabic
is the only tongue that can at the present time lay claim to a
first-class position; but the fact that it has been partly replaced
by European languages of colonization robs it of the dominant
position it has held in the past. Among the Asiatic groups,
Japanese and Chinese combine the various factors that appear
significant.

In a second division, we may place Dutch and, perhaps,
Polish; while a third group might include, for Indo-European,
the Scandinavian tongues (Dano-Norwegian, Swedish, Ice-
landic), Roumanian, the minor Slavic languages (Czech, Serbo-
Croatian, Bulgarian), Greek, and Lithuanian; for Ural-Altaic,
Finnish, Hungarian and Turkish; for the languages of the Far
East, Malay.

Tongues like Albanian, Armenian, the Celtic languages,

Persian, a few vernaculars of India, Palestinian Hebrew, Siamese, Burmese, are linguistic stragglers from the standpoint of practical importance.

The key position of certain languages is now clear. English, German, French, Spanish, Portuguese, Italian, Russian and Japanese occupy these key posts. Arabic, Chinese, Malay, and Dutch, even if acquired in the form of a smattering, help to fill the gaps. The ability to identify forty or fifty of the remaining languages, so that we can distinguish between Bulgarian and Serbian, Greek and Albanian, Turkish and Persian, at least in written form, completes all that is needed for a utilitarian linguistic education.

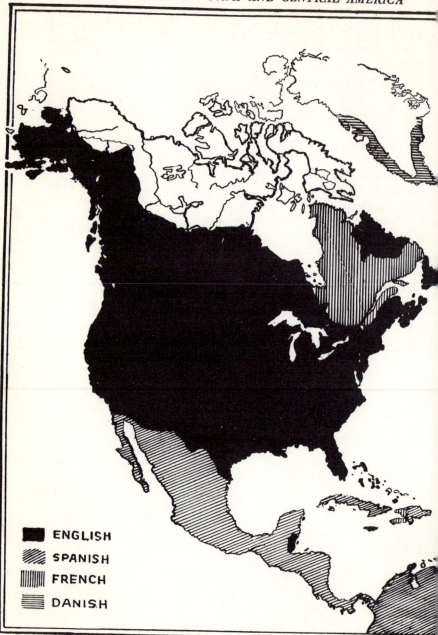

ENGLISH
SPANISH
FRENCH
DANISH

CHAPTER II

GEOGRAPHY AND LANGUAGES

So far we have grouped languages by family units. Geographical distribution now claims our attention. What languages are current in each of the political divisions of the various continents? What secondary, auxiliary or colonial languages may we expect to be able to use, if a country's primary national tongue is not available to us? In dealing with the geographical problem, we shall find it convenient to take the world's pre-war political arrangement, regardless of military occupations, even those that occurred prior to the actual outbreak of hostilities, such as Germany's seizure of Czecho-Slovakia.

1. NORTH AMERICA

Country	Approximate Population	Language(s)
Alaska	70,000	English.
Bermudas	30,000	English.
Canada (including Labrador and Newfoundland)	12,000,000	English, with perhaps 3,000,000 French speakers located primarily in the Province of Quebec, and to some extent in Ontario; many of them can be reached with English.
Greenland	20,000	Danish.
Mexico	20,000,000	Spanish.
U. S. A.	132,000,000	English.

English serves the purpose practically everywhere in North America, save in Greenland (Danish), Mexico (Spanish), and French-speaking sections of Canada. Foreign-speech groups in the U. S. A. and Canada are picturesque and interesting, but inconsequential for practical purposes. English can to some extent be used in Mexico and Greenland, and largely in French-speaking Canada. For North America, as well as for Central and South America, little mention need be made of Eskimo or American Indian languages, the importance of which is extremely limited.

2. CENTRAL AMERICA AND WEST INDIES.

Country	Approximate Population	Language(s)
Bahamas	70,000	English.
British Honduras	60,000	English and Spanish.
Canal Zone	50,000	English and Spanish.
Costa Rica	600,000	Spanish.
Cuba	4,200,000	Spanish.
Dominican Republic	1,600,000	Spanish.
Guadaloupe and Martinique	600,000	French.
Guatemala	3,000,000	Spanish.
Haiti	3,200,000	French.
Honduras	1,000,000	Spanish.
Jamaica	1,200,000	English.
Leeward Islands	100,000	English.
Nicaragua	1,100,000	Spanish.
Panama	700,000	Spanish.
Puerto Rico	2,000,000	Spanish and English.
Salvador	1,700,000	Spanish.
Virgin Islands	25,000	English and Danish.
Windward Islands	300,000	English.

★   ★   ★

Spanish, English and French, in the order mentioned, are the essential languages in this area. English can to some extent be used in all Spanish and French-speaking sections.

3. SOUTH AMERICA.

Country	Approximate Population	Language(s)
Argentina	13,000,000	Spanish
Bolivia	3,300,000	Spanish.
Brazil	44,000,000	Portuguese.
Chile	4,600,000	Spanish.
Colombia	8,700,000	Spanish.
Ecuador	3,000,000	Spanish.
Guiana, British	350,000	English.
Guiana, Dutch	200,000	Dutch.
Guiana, French	50,000	French.
Paraguay	1,000,000	Spanish.
Peru	6,800,000	Spanish.
Uruguay	2,100,000	Spanish.
Venezuela	3,500,000	Spanish.

★ ★ ★

The South American picture is one of division between Spanish (roughly 46,000,000 speakers) and Portuguese (44,-000,000), with the latter concentrated in a single country, Brazil. The American Indian languages, which are on their way to complete extinction in North America, are perhaps a little more alive here (Quechua, for example, has nearly 4,000,000 speakers); but their extreme diversity and the fact that many of their speakers can be approached through the medium of the official tongue renders them of scant practical import-ance. English and French are current among the higher ranks of society in all Latin-American countries; Italian and German are fairly current in some sections of Brazil (São Paulo, Rio Grande do Sul); Italian to some extent in Argentina.

★ ★ ★

The Western Hemisphere as a whole shows a preponder-ance of English (about 145,000,000 speakers), followed by Spanish (83,000,000) and Portuguese (44,000,000). French

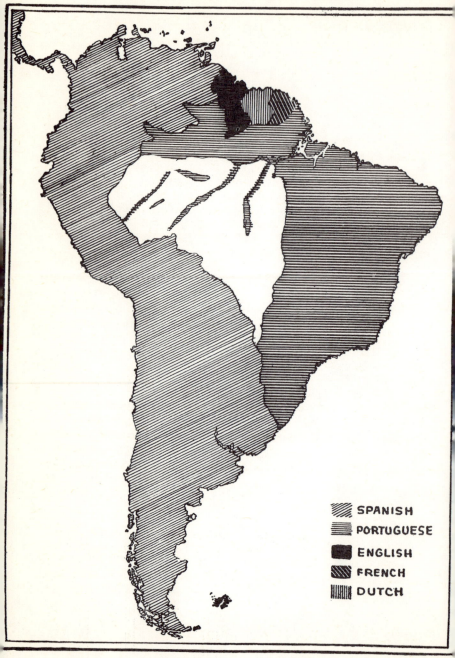

SPANISH
PORTUGUESE
ENGLISH
FRENCH
DUTCH

(8,000,000), Dutch (about 200,000) and Danish (less than 50,000) constitute hemispheric linguistic minorities.

4. EUROPE

Country[1]	Approximate Population	Language(s)
Albania	1,100,000	Albanian (with Italian, Greek, Turkish, Serbo-Croatian to some extent current).
Belgium	8,500,000	French and Flemish (over one-half of the population has Flemish for its native tongue, but French is everywhere current).
Bulgaria	6,500,000	Bulgarian (with Turkish along Black Sea coast).
Czechoslovakia	15,000,000	Czech (of which Slovak is a variant; German everywhere current, particularly in Sudeten areas; Hungarian in southern section, and Ukrainian in extreme east).
Denmark	4,000,000	Danish (German fairly current, especially in southern section, Schleswig).
Estonia	1,000,000	Estonian (with Russian and German fairly widespread).
Finland	4,000,000	Finnish (with Swedish, Russian and German fairly current).
France	42,000,000	French (linguistic minorities, Bretons, Basques, Catalans, Alsatians, Italians, etc., normally speak French as well).

1. Such small political units as Andorra (6,000: Spanish, French, Catalan); Danzig (400,000: German and Polish); Gibraltar (21,000: Spanish and English); Liechtenstein (10,000: German); Monaco (24,000: French and Italian); San Marino (14,000: Italian), need not be discussed.

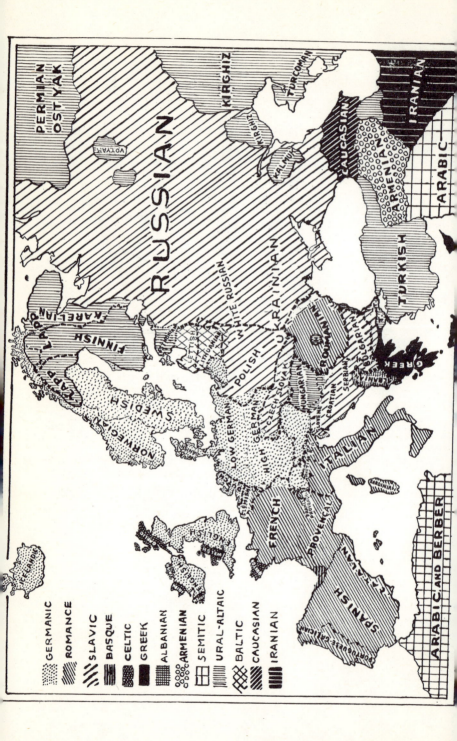

Germany (including Austria)	76,000,000	German (small linguistic minorities in East Prussia, Silesia, etc., normally speak German as well).
Great Britain and Northern Ireland	47,000,000	English (Welsh and Gaelic speakers normally speak English as well).
Greece	7,500,000	Greek (small Turkish, Albanian, Bulgarian minorities).
Hungary	9,500,000	Hungarian (Slovak, German and Roumanian minorities; German quite current).
Iceland	120,000	Icelandic, Danish.
Ireland (Eire)	3,000,000	English, Erse (or Irish Gaelic; very few inhabitants of Eire fail to speak and understand English).
Italy	45,000,000	Italian (linguistic minorities, Germans in Alto Adige, Slovenes in Istria, Croatians in Zara, etc., normally speak Italian as well).
Latvia	2,000,000	Latvian (or Lettish; Russian and German fairly current).
Lithuania	3,000,000	Lithuanian (Russian, German, Polish current).
Luxembourg	300,000	German, French (population fairly bilingual).
Netherlands	9,000,000	Dutch (a large number of Hollanders are equipped with German, French, or English).
Norway	3,000,000	Norwegian (a variant of Danish); Lapp in the far north; German and English have some currency).
Poland	35,000,000	Polish (linguistic minorities very large: German in Polish Corridor and western provinces; Lithuanian, White Russian and Ukrainian in eastern sections; German and Russian current among a good many Poles; about 3,000,000 Yiddish speakers).

Portugal (including Azores)	8,000,000	Portuguese (Spanish generally understood).
Roumania	20,000,000	Roumanian (linguistic minorities very large: Hungarian and German in Transylvania; Ukrainian in Bessarabia; Bulgarian in Dobruja and Bessarabia, etc.).
Soviet Union (in Europe)	130,000,000	Russian (linguistic minorities heavy, but scattered; Caucasian and Armenian in Caucasus; Ural-Altaic in Karelia, north and northeast, etc.; generally accessible through Russian; Russian's kindred tongues, Ukrainian and White Russian, number 28,000,000 and 5,000,000 speakers, respectively).
Spain	25,500,000	Spanish (Catalan speakers in east, Basques in northeast, normally accessible through Spanish; Galicians in northwest through Spanish or Portuguese).
Sweden	6,500,000	Swedish (Lapp in extreme north; German has a certain amount of currency).
Switzerland	4,500,000	German, French, Italian, Rumansh (all four languages are official; over 3,000,000 Swiss speak German; French speakers number over 2,000,000. Italian and Rumansh speakers nearly 1,000,000).
Yugoslavia[2]	16,000,000	Serbo-Croatian, Slovene (very large linguistic minorities, consisting of German, Bulgarian, Hungarian, Albanian, Turkish, Roumanian and Italian speakers; German is quite current in areas formerly forming part of Austro-Hungarian Empire).

2.   For Turkey, see Asia, p. 52.

A linguistic survey of Europe shows English to be officially current among some 50,000,000 speakers, and widely spoken and understood outside of its own territory. German includes over 80,000,000 native speakers, and gives access to at least 20,000,000 or 30,000,000 more, in addition to being a "cultural" language (though to a lesser degree than French). French, with some 50,000,000 speakers in France, Belgium and Switzerland, pervades the upper and middle classes of most European countries. Italian gives access to some 50,-000,000 European speakers; Russian to over 100,000,000; Spanish to about 25,000,000; while perhaps 30,000,000 can be reached with Polish.

Among the minor European tongues that do not have much European currency outside of their own national territory are Hungarian (13,000,000); Dutch-Flemish (13,000,-000); Serbo-Croatian and Slovene (16,000,000); Roumanian (16,000,000); Czech and Slovak (12,000,000); Swedish (7,-000,000); Dano-Norwegian, Portuguese, Bulgarian and Greek, with about 7,000,000 each; and Finnish (4,000,000). But some of these languages, notably Portuguese and Dutch, have vast non-European ramifications in colonial or former colonial territories.

Europe is one of the most polylingual of continents. Outside of the general knowledge of French, German, and/or English possessed by most people of culture, many border areas are bilingual, trilingual, even quadrilingual, while the everyday necessities of peoples living together in a crowded area have led to the speaking of one or two additional languages by large segments even of uneducated people in many European countries. If you do not know the national language of the country you are in, don't give up hope; try the languages you do know; they very often work successfully.

INDO-EUROPEAN
URAL-ALTAIC
HAMITO-SEMITIC
CAUCASIAN
DRAVIDIAN
SINO-TIBETAN
POLYNESIAN
HYPERBOREAN
JAPANESE-KOREAN
MUNDA
MON-KHMER
ANNAMESE
AINU
SUDANESE-GUINEAN

5. ASIA.

Country	Approximate Population	Language(s)
Afghanistan	12,000,000	Pushtu and Persian.
Burma	16,000,000	Burmese (with English superimposed).
Ceylon	6,000,000	Singhalese (Indo-Aryan) in south; Tamil (Dravidian) in north; English superimposed.
China	425,000,000	Chinese (Ural-Altaic dialects in Chinese Turkestan and Mongolia; Tibetan in Tibet; Thai dialects in southeastern sections and Hainan; Japanese to some extent current in Japanese-seized territory; European languages, especially English, in foreign concessions and coastal cities). The principal Chinese dialects (Mandarin, now the official tongue, or Kuo-yü: 280,000,000; Cantonese: 38,000,000; Wu of Shanghai: 34,000,000; Min of Fukien: 30,000,000) are not mutually intelligible.
Cyprus	400,000	Greek (Turkish, English superimposed).
Malaya (including Straits Settlements)	5,500,000	Malayan (Indonesian), Chinese, and Mon-Khmer dialects (English superimposed).
French Indo-China	24,500,000	Annamese and Mon-Khmer dialects (French superimposed).
Hong Kong	1,500,000	Chinese (English, Japanese superimposed).
India	390,000,000	Indo-Aryan tongues (Panjabi, Bengali, Hindi, Urdu, etc.) in north; Dravidian languages (Tamil, Telugu, Canarese, etc.) in south; scattered Munda groups, mostly in northeast; English superimposed.

Iran	15,000,000	Persian, Kurdish. French is current among the upper classes.
Iraq	4,500,000	Arabic, Kurdish, Turkish.
Japan (including Karafuto)	73,000,000	Japanese (Ainu in Yezo and Karafuto, the southern part of Sakhalin Island).
Korea	25,000,000	Korean (Japanese superimposed).
Manchukuo	43,000,000	Manchu (of the Ural-Altaic family; less than 500,000); Chinese (about 40,000,000); Japanese superimposed.
Nepal and Bhutan	6,000,000	Indo-Aryan and Tibetan dialects.
Oman	500,000	Arabic.
Palestine	1,500,000	Arabic (Hebrew and English superimposed).
Portuguese Asia	1,000,000	Indo-Aryan dialects in Goa, Damau and Diu; Chinese in Macau (Portuguese superimposed).
Saudi Arabia (including Hejaz)	5,500,000	Arabic.
Soviet Union in Asia	41,000,000	Ural-Altaic and Hyperborean dialects (Ostyak, Samoyed, Turcoman, Kirghiz, Mongol, Tungus, Yukagir, etc.; Russian everywhere superimposed).
Syria and Lebanon	4,000,000	Arabic (French superimposed).
Taiwan (Formosa)	5,500,000	Indonesian dialects and Chinese (Japanese superimposed).
Thailand (Siam)	16,500,000	Siamese (Thai) and Mon-Khmer dialects.
Transjordan	500,000	Arabic (English superimposed).
Turkey (including European Turkey)	18,000,000	Turkish (a Ural-Altaic language; Indo-European Armenian and Kurdish in the eastern sections).
Yemen[3]	3,500,000	Arabic.

3. British possessions in and near Arabia (Aden, Bahrein Island, Kuwait) have a total of some 300,000 Arabic speakers, with English superimposed.

The linguistic picture of Asia is at least as involved as that of Europe. Northern Asia (Siberia, Union of Soviet Republics) is almost solidly Ural-Altaic, but with a strong Russian infiltration which is particularly noticeable along the courses of the great rivers (Ob, Lena, Yenisei), and in the larger cities and towns. The Ural-Altaic tongues extend down into Chinese Turkestan, Mongolia and Manchuria.

Chinese, with its mighty mass of speakers, predominates in most of east central continental Asia. But politically Chinese territory is abundantly strewn with other linguistic groups; the Ural-Altaic dialects mentioned above, and Chinese's kindred tongues, Tibetan and Thai, in southwestern and southeastern China, respectively.

The Indo-Aryan and Dravidian languages of India and Ceylon account for most of India's 390,000,000 speakers, but colonizing English forms a strong super-layer, as it does also in Burma and Malaya.

Japanese, with over 70,000,000 native speakers, also permeates Korea, Formosa, Manchukuo and, to a lesser degree, other lands of former Japanese occupation.

Arabic is current in the entire Arabian Peninsula, Iraq, Syria, Palestine and Transjordan, with English in the last two countries, French in Syria, and Hebrew in Palestine as superimposed tongues. The influence of Arabic is also strongly felt in Indo-European Afghanistan, Iran, and northern India, and, in fact, wherever the Muhammadan faith has followers.

Ural-Altaic Turkish, with Indo-European Armenian and Kurdish spoken on its national territory; Sino-Tibetan Thai, current in Siam and parts of southeastern China; Annamese in French Indo-China; Mon-Khmer dialects in Indo-China, Thailand and Malaya; Munda dialects in India; Indonesian Malayan in Malaya; Indo-European Persian and Pushtu, may be said to constitute a secondary group of Asiatic tongues.

Among the languages of colonization, first place belongs to English, which pervades India, Ceylon, Burma, Malaya, Cyprus, Hong Kong, Palestine, Transjordan and sections of

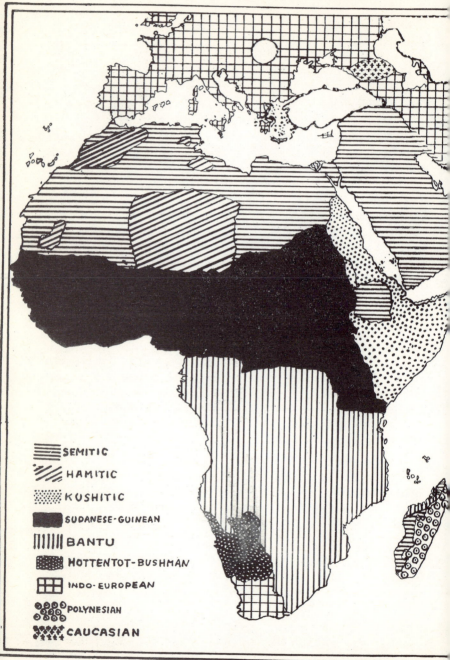

SEMITIC
HAMITIC
KUSHITIC
SUDANESE-GUINEAN
BANTU
HOTTENTOT-BUSHMAN
INDO-EUROPEAN
POLYNESIAN
CAUCASIAN

Arabia (Aden, Bahrein, Kuwait). French appears in Indo-China, Syria, and one or two cities of India (Pondichéry) and China (Kwangchowan); Portuguese in Goa, Damau and Diu, on the western coast of India, and in Chinese Macau; Russian throughout the Asiatic territory of the Soviet Union, and, to some extent, in Mongolia.

6. AFRICA

Country	Approximate Population	Language(s)
Algeria	8,000,000	Arabic and Berber (French superimposed).
Anglo-Egyptian Sudan	6,500,000	Arabic, Kushitic (Beja, etc.), and Sudanese-Guinean dialects, especially Nubian.
Angola	3,500,000	Bantu (Portuguese superimposed).
Basutoland	600,000	Bantu (English superimposed).
Bechuanaland	300,000	Bantu (English superimposed.
Belgian Congo	14,000,000	Bantu, Sudanese-Guinean (French superimposed).
Cameroons	2,600,000	Sudanese-Guinean and Bantu dialects (French superimposed).
Egypt	17,000,000	Arabic and Kushitic dialects (English, French, Greek, Italian superimposed). Nubian (Sudanese-Guinean) in Upper Egypt.
Ethiopia (including Eritrea and Italian Somaliland)	12,000,000	Ethiopian (Amharic, Tigre, etc.); Kushitic dialects (Galla, Somali, etc.); Sudanese-Guinean dialects in extreme west; Italian superimposed.
French Equatorial Africa	3,500,000	Sudanese-Guinean; Arabic in north; Bantu in extreme south (French superimposed).
French West Africa (Dahomey, Fr. Sudan, Fr. Guinea, Ivory Coast, Niger, Togo, Senegal)	16,000,000	Arabic, Berber, Sudanese-Guinean (French superimposed).
Gambia	200,000	Sudanese-Guinean (English superimposed).

Gold Coast	4,000,000	Sudanese-Guinean (English superimposed).
Guinea, Portuguese	400,000	Sudanese-Guinean (Portuguese superimposed).
Guinea, Spanish	150,000	Bantu (Spanish superimposed).
Ifni	20,000	Berber and Arabic (Spanish superimposed).
Kenya	3,500,000	Bantu (English superimposed).
Liberia	2,000,000	Sudanese-Guinean (English superimposed).
Libya	1,000,000	Arabic, Berber (Italian superimposed).
Madagascar	3,800,000	Malagasy (Indonesian); French superimposed.
Morocco	7,000,000	Arabic, Berber (French superimposed).
Mozambique	4,500,000	Bantu (Portuguese superimposed).
Nigeria	22,000,000	Sudanese-Guinean (English superimposed).
Nyasaland	1,600,000	Bantu (English, Afrikaans, superimposed).
Rhodesia	3,000,000	Bantu (English, Afrikaans, superimposed).
Rio de Oro	30,000	Arabic (Spanish superimposed).
Sierra Leone	2,000,000	Sudanese-Guinean (English superimposed).
Somaliland, British	350,000	Kushitic (English superimposed).
Somaliland, French	50,000	Kushitic (French superimposed).
Southwest Africa	300,000	Bantu, Hottentot-Bushman (English, German superimposed).
Spanish Morocco	800,000	Arabic, Berber (Spanish superimposed).
Swaziland	150,000	Bantu (English superimposed).
Tanganyika	5,300,000	Bantu (English superimposed).
Tunisia	3,000,000	Arabic, Berber (French, Italian superimposed).
Uganda	3,800,000	Sudanese-Guinean, Bantu (English superimposed).
Union of South Africa	10,700,000	Bantu, Hottentot-Bushman (English, Afrikaans superimposed).

Linguistically, northern Africa, as far as the Tropic of Cancer and beyond, is solidly Semito-Hamitic, with Semitic Arabic stretching from the Sinai Peninsula to the Atlantic coast, and Hamitic Berber intermingled with it in the interior, particularly in the Sahara, in Algeria and Morocco. Hamitic Kushitic and Semitic Ethiopian languages appear in the area east of the Nile and extend down to the southern borders of Ethiopia and Italian Somaliland and beyond. The rest of the continent is divided between two great African Negro groups, the Sudanese-Guinean and the Bantu, with the dividing line between them a little to the north of the Equator on the western coast and a little to the south of it on the eastern. Hottentot-Bushman appears only in a restricted section of Southwest Africa.

The languages of colonization are of particular importance in this continent. They are not everywhere equally widespread, however, ranging from the strong position which English holds in South Africa to the very thin veneer of French and Flemish in the Belgian Congo, and from the native-tongue status of French and Italian among a quarter of Tunisia's inhabitants to the military outpost and trading-post function of English in Uganda, Kenya and Tanganyika.

English appears in the Anglo-Egyptian Sudan, Gambia, the Gold Coast, Kenya, Liberia, Nigeria, Nyasaland, Sierra Leone, British Somaliland, Tanganyika, Uganda, and all of South Africa (the Union of South Africa, including the Transvaal, the Cape of Good Hope, the Orange Free State and Natal; Rhodesia, Swaziland, Bechuanaland, Basutoland, and Southwest Africa). In South African territory, English shares with a variant of Dutch (Afrikaans) the honor of having become a national language by virtue of white settlers who now number over one-fourth of the total population.

French is current in Algeria, the Cameroons, French Equatorial and West Africa, Madagascar, French Morocco, French Somaliland and Tunisia; in the Belgian Congo, it forms, with Flemish, the language of colonization.

Italian appears in Libya, Eritrea, Italian Somaliland, and, to some extent, in Ethiopia and Tunisia.

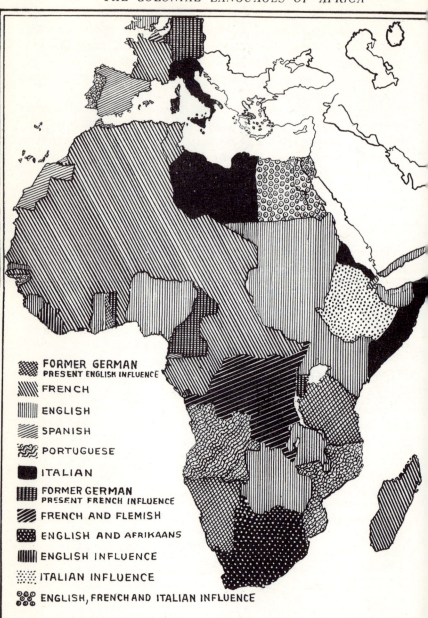

FORMER GERMAN
PRESENT ENGLISH INFLUENCE

FRENCH

ENGLISH

SPANISH

PORTUGUESE

ITALIAN

FORMER GERMAN
PRESENT FRENCH INFLUENCE

FRENCH AND FLEMISH

ENGLISH AND AFRIKAANS

ENGLISH INFLUENCE

ITALIAN INFLUENCE

ENGLISH, FRENCH AND ITALIAN INFLUENCE

Portuguese appears in Angola, Portuguese Guinea and Mozambique, and is the national language in the Cape Verde and Madeira Islands (about 250,000 inhabitants each).

Spanish is current in Spanish Morocco, the Canary Islands, Ifni, Rio de Oro and Spanish Guinea.

Lastly, German very occasionally appears in Germany's former colonial possessions of the days prior to the first world war: the Cameroons, Togoland (now divided between French West Africa and British Gold Coast), Southwest Africa, Nyasaland and Tanganyika.

Egypt (predominantly Arabic in speech) is a land where English, French, Greek and Italian are fairly current.

7. OCEANIA.

Country	Approximate Population	Language(s)
Australia	7,000,000	English (with native Australian languages approaching extinction).
Bismarck Archipelago	250,000	Melanesian (English and German superimposed).
British North Borneo	300,000	Indonesian (English superimposed).
Brunei	40,000	Indonesian (English superimposed).
Caroline Islands	40,000	Micronesian (Japanese superimposed).
Cook Islands	15,000	Polynesian (English superimposed).
Dutch East Indies (Java, Sumatra, Borneo, Celebes, Neth. New Guinea, Bali, Madura, Flores, western Timor, Amboina, etc.)	60,000,000	Indonesian languages and dialects (save for the interior of New Guinea, where Papuan is spoken); these are Javanese (over 20,000,000) and Sundanese (6,000,000) in Java; Balinese (3,000,000) in Bali; Madurese (3,000,000) in Madura; Dayak in Borneo; Atchin, Minangkabau and Batak in Sumatra; Macassar, etc., in Celebes; Dutch and Malay everywhere superimposed).

Fiji Islands	200,000	Melanesian and Hindustani (English superimposed).
French Oceania	45,000	Polynesian (French superimposed).
Gilbert and Ellice Islands	35,000	Micronesian and Polynesian (English superimposed).
Guam	25,000	Micronesian (English superimposed).
Hawaiian Islands	500,000	Polynesian (English, Japanese, Chinese, Korean superimposed).
Labuan	10,000	Indonesian (English superimposed).
Marianas Islands	70,000	Micronesian (Japanese superimposed).
Marshall Islands	10,000	Micronesian (Japanese superimposed).
New Caledonia	65,000	Melanesian (French and English superimposed).
New Guinea	750,000	Papuan (English superimposed).
New Hebrides	45,000	Melanesian (English and French superimposed).
New Zealand	1,600,000	English (Polynesian Maori on the way to extinction).
Palau	6,000	Micronesian (Japanese and German superimposed).
Papua	275,000	Papuan (English superimposed).
Philippine Islands	16,000,000	Indonesian (about 50 different dialects: Bisaya - about 7,000,000; Tagalog - about 4,000,000; Ilocano - about 2,300,000; etc. English and Spanish superimposed).
Samoa	13,000	Polynesian (English and German superimposed).
West Samoa	60,000	Polynesian (French superimposed).
Sarawak	450,000	Indonesian (English superimposed).
Solomon Islands	140,000	Melanesian (English superimposed).
Timor (Portuguese)	500,000	Indonesian (Portuguese superimposed).
Tonga	35,000	Polynesian (English superimposed).

Oceania shows a predominance of Malayo-Polynesian, indigenous to all the Oceanic Islands with the exception of Australia (native Australian languages) and New Guinea (Papuan). The division of the Malayo-Polynesian tongues into Indonesian, Melanesian, Micronesian and Polynesian is somewhat arbitrary (being to some extent geographical and racial rather than linguistic), and not very important, in view of the innumerable diverging dialects. Indonesian Javanese, accounting for some 20,000,000 people, is the most important of these languages.

Among the languages of colonization, English is by far the most widespread, having become the language of the majority of the inhabitants in Australia and New Zealand, where colonists originally from Britain and their descendants far outstrip the native populations in number. It also forms a superimposed layer in Hawaii, the Philippines, the northern sections of the island of Borneo (Sarawak, British North Borneo), eastern Papua (New Guinea and Papua Territories), and about half of the minor islands and groups.

Dutch, current in the Dutch East Indies (Java, Sumatra, Celebes, southern Borneo, western Papua, Bali, Madura, western Timor, Amboina, etc.) is second only to English in importance.

Japanese, current in all the Japanese-mandated islands (Caroline, Marianas, Marshalls, etc.) and, to some extent, in seized territory, runs third.

French appears in Tahiti, New Caledonia, parts of the New Hebrides and Samoa, etc.; Portuguese in the eastern section of Timor. Vestiges of former colonial occupations appear in the half million Spanish speakers of the Philippines and the occasional traces of German in former German colonial possessions (Bismarck, Caroline, Marianas, Marshall Islands, Samoa, New Guinea, etc.).

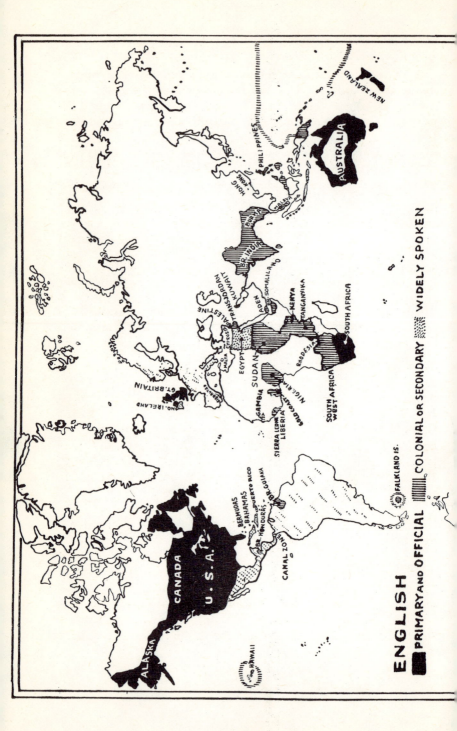

CHAPTER III

LANGUAGES OF THE GERMANIC GROUP

Of the three leading Indo-European divisions (Germanic, Romance, Slavic), the Germanic holds first place in point of numbers and political and commercial importance, vying for cultural first honors with the Romance group. Its main modern subdivisions are English, German, Dutch-Flemish, Dano-Norwegian, Swedish and Icelandic. Of these, the first three belong to the West Germanic family, while the others are of the Scandinavian, or North Germanic variety.

English, with over 200,000,000 native speakers, located principally on the North American continent, the British Isles, South Africa, Australia and New Zealand, is also by far the most important and far-reaching among the tongues of colonization in Asia, Africa and Oceania. It is, furthermore, the language of commercial intercourse *par excellence.* During its past history, it differentiated itself from its sister Germanic tongues by the inclusion of larger numbers of borrowed words, especially from the Latin-Romance languages, and this mixture gives it a distinctive international flavor that makes it ideal for general use throughout the world.

German, with over 80,000,000 native speakers in the Reich and Switzerland, serves also as a tongue of international exchange throughout Central Europe, being used as a secondary language by large sections of the populations of countries that formerly formed part of the Austro-Hungarian Empire (Hungary, Czechoslovakia, Yugoslavia), and, to a lesser degree, of Poland, the Netherlands, Denmark, Norway, Sweden, Finland, Lithuania, Latvia, Estonia, etc. As a "cultural" language, German is current among large segments of the more learned classes of other European countries and of North and South America, while German emigration to the New World and former colonization of African and Oceanic territories account for additional millions of people who can be reached with German.

Dutch, with its Belgian variant, Flemish, is the native tongue of some 13,000,000 people in Europe, while the Dutch colonial empire and the Belgian Congo comprise some 80,000,000 people in part accessible through Dutch and Flemish. Afrikaans, the South African variety of Dutch, is still in fairly general use throughout the Union of South Africa, Rhodesia and neighboring territories, side by side with English.

As compared with the West Germanic languages, the tongues of the Scandinavian group have relatively few speakers. Swedish is the native tongue of about 6,500,000, and is used by considerable segments of the population of western and southern Finland and the Aaland Islands. Danish and Norwegian have a joint speaking population of some 7,000,-000, and Danish is, in addition, used to some extent in Greenland, Iceland and the Virgin Islands. Icelandic is the tongue of only 100,000 people in Iceland. The Faroe Islands, north of Scotland, use a dialect intermediate between Danish and Icelandic.

ENGLISH — DISTRIBUTION AND VARIETIES

English, the mother-tongue of over 200,000,000 people scattered all over the six continents, displays local differences which, while not so radical as those appearing in other languages concentrated in much smaller areas, nevertheless render mutual understanding difficult at times. These differences appear, for the most part, in the fields of pronunciation and vocabulary, with grammar more generally standardized in countries settled by people of Anglo-Saxon blood. Grammatical standardization does not hold, however, for lands where English has become a secondary tongue, acquired by the native populations in "Pidgin" forms.

U. S. A.

For practical purposes, it may be said that American Indian languages have disappeared from United States soil. 'It is estimated that less than a quarter of a million American Indians now exist in the U. S., and a considerable number of them are acquainted only with English).

The English of America's 140,000,000 inhabitants, despite local features of intonation and pronunciation (Southern "drawl"; New England "twang"; Middle Western strongly marked *r;* New York *thoity-thoid* for "thirty-third"; "Bostonese"; "Brooklynite"; etc.), and occasional vocabulary and semantic divergences,[1] has become one of the world's most standardized tongues, by reason of generally high levels of communications, transportation and education. Many of its current slang expressions and colloquialisms are unintelligible or only semi-intelligible to inhabitants of other parts of the English-speaking world.[2]

1. E. g., Southern "to carry" for "to take" ("he carried me to the dance"; "carry me back to Old Virginny"); "falling weather" for "rainy weather"; "you-all" for a plural "you"; East Texas "gallery" for "porch"; Mid-Western "get shut of" for "get rid of" and "to jin" for "to do odd jobs"; New England's "tonic" for "soft drink"; New York's "stoop" for "porch". Among rapidly disappearing local forms may be cited the picturesque expressions for "small portion" current in the Cumberlands, Great Smokies and Ozarks, respectively: *smidgen, canch, tiddy-bit;* while "cow" is *cow-beast, cow-brute* and *she-cow. To lollygag* for "to make love", *bumbershoot* for "umbrella" and *schnicklefritz* for "German" are reported from the Ohio Valley.

2. A few examples of words and expressions for which the average non-American English speaker needs a glossary are: *ballyhoo, bellhop, co-ed, bughouse, flivver, flop-house, four-flusher, go-getter, goo* and *gooey, hayseed, joint, lobbying, sissy, smart Aleck, sorehead, traffic jam, wisecrack, wiseguy; to be* (two dollars) *shy, to bump off, to discombobulate, to get a line on, to get a load of, to get next to, to get stuck with, to get the drop on, to gouge, to hornswoggle, to monkey with, to pitch woo, to shoot craps, to smooch, to soak* (somebody), *to spoof, to stay put, to whoop things up; fresh* ("he's a fresh

GREAT BRITAIN

The population of Great Britain, including Scotland, Wales and Northern Ireland, is about 47,000,000. Practically all of these people, to whom may be added Eire's 3,000,000, speak English.[3] However, on its far more limited territory, the English of Britain displays far greater local divergences than does the English of America. The English dialects are powerful realities, based on strong features of individual pronunciation, grammar and vocabulary divergence. The following are only a few scattered examples:

The Shetland Islands pronounce "shall" and "should" as *sall* and *soud*. The western part of Scotland has *ba'el* for "battle" and *be'er* for "better". The Braid Scots dialect uses *lippen* for "believe", *aboon* for "above" and *till* for "to". Cornwall has *dafter* for "daughter". In Ulster, the demonstratives "that", "those" appear as *yon, thon;* in northern England, "these" and "those" are *thee, thir,* and in Wexford "this" or "that" is *thik;* the English Midlands use *chilt, ged, wod* for "child", "get", "what"; Yorkshire has *hoo* for "she" and *han, liven, shan* for "have", "live", "shall"; Gloucestershire has *her* for "she" and *thak* for "that", while the southwest of England turns "parlor" into *palder.* The pronunciation of a Yorkshireman is normally totally incomprehensible to the average American. We are somewhat more familiar with the Scottish "burr", the Irish "brogue", and the "Cockney" of London. From the standpoint of syntax, dialectal English occasionally produces a somewhat weird effect. The following signalled conversation between two Brit-

---

guy"), *hard-boiled, no-account, ornery, pesky, rambunctious, swelegant.*

3. Celtic speakers (Irish, Welsh and Scots) in the British Isles are normally bilingual. and to a majority of them, English is more familiar than their own Celtic tongues. See p. 446-450 for the Celtic languages of the British Isles.

ish naval officers, both from Somersetshire, as their ships were about to go into action, is reported from the Mediterranean: "I be relying on you". — "Doan 'ee worry; we got they in the bag."

Outside of dialectal forms and intonations, the "King's English" itself will occasionally disturb the American speaker of English. First and foremost, there is the matter of enunciation, which in British English is normally more clipped, incisive and staccato than in its American counterpart, with far more modulation of tone and rise and fall in the pitch of the voice. The pronunciation of individual words and groups of sounds diverges (*laugh, branch, bath, vase*, etc., pronounced in Britain with the *a* of "father"). Note also the British pronunciation of "clerk" (*clark*), "Derby" (*Darby*), "schedule" (*shedule*), "lieutenant" (*leftenant;* but a pronunciation similar to our own prevails for the rank in the British Navy), "figure" (*figger*), etc. Many words are differently stressed (British *nécess'ry, papá, mammá, prímarily, témporarily, fináncier*). Many spelling divergences occur (British *labour, favour, honour, connexion, inflexion, gaol, waggon, kerb, programme, jewellery, tyre, grey, cheque*). In grammar, such expressions as "His Majesty's Government *are* in favour of this measure" occasionally come up to make us realize that there is a difference.

Of far greater interest and importance, however, are the numerous semantic[4] differences between the two chief varieties of English. Most of these have fortunately been codified. Only a few of the most significant and important appear here.[5]

---

4. *Semantic* — pertaining to the meanings of words.

5. For a fairly complete discussion, cf. H. W. Horwell, *An Anglo-American Interpreter*, Oxford, 1939.

TRANSPORTATION

American	British
information bureau,	*inquiry office*
ticket agent,	*booking clerk* (pron. *clark*)
conductor,	*guard*
right of way,	*permanent way*
freight car,	*goods waggon*
ties,	*sleepers*
sleeper,	*sleeping car*
tracks,	*metals*
all aboard!,	*take your seats!*
gangway!, one side!,	*by your leave!*
on time,	*to time*
street-car,	*tram*
subway,	*underground*
underpass,	*subway*
comfort station,	*public convenience*
top (car),	*hood*
hood,	*bonnet*
fender,	*wing*
gas, gasoline,	*petrol*
rumble seat,	*dickey*
spark plug,	*sparking plug*
storage battery,	*accumulator*
windshield,	*windscreen*
muffler,	*silencer*
gear shift,	*gear lever*
sedan,	*saloon car*
parking-place,	*car-park*
truck,	*lorry*
dirt road,	*unmetalled road*
traffic jam,	*traffic block*

COMMUNICATIONS

information,	*inquiry*
hello!,	*are you there?*
line's busy,	*number's engaged*
hook-up,	*relay*
are you through?,	*have you finished?*
you're connected,	*you are through*

BUSINESS AND OCCUPATIONAL

employment bureau,	*registry office*
white-collar job,	*black-coat job*
to fire, to lay off,	*to stand off*
salary, wage,	*screw*
payroll,	*wage sheet*
saloonkeeper,	*publican, licensed victualler* (pron. *vittler*)
financial editor,	*city editor*
city editor,	*chief reporter*
legal holiday,	*bank holiday*
check,	*draft* (or *cheque*)
instalment plan,	*hire system*
billboard,	*hoarding*

ATTIRE

garters,	*sock suspenders*
suspenders,	*braces*
wash rag,	*face flannel*
vest,	*waistcoat* (pron. *weskit*)
undershirt,	*vest*
raincoat,	*mackintosh, mack*
slacks,	*bags*
run (stocking),	*ladder*
derby,	*bowler*
permanent,	*perm*
nail polish,	*nail varnish*

HOUSEHOLD

radio,	*wireless set*
tubes,	*valves*
wrench,	*spanner*
ash can, junk heap,	*dust bin*
overnight bag,	*attaché case*
baby carriage,	*pram*
hot water heater,	*geyser* (pron. *geezah*)
flashlight,	*electric torch*
thumbtack,	*drawing pin*
chicken yard,	*fowl run*
writing desk,	*bureau*
sideboard,	*dresser*
apartment,	*flat*
single room,	*apartment*
apartment house,	*block of flats*
transient,	*temporary guest*
room clerk,	*reception clerk* (pron. *clark*)

AMUSEMENTS

to stand in line,	*to queue up*
orchestra,	*stalls*
aisle,	*gangway*
to buy (ticket),	*to book*
movies,	*cinema*
intermission,	*interval*
dance-hall,	*dancing saloon*

SHOPS

candy store,	*sweet shop*
drug store,	*chemist's*
dime store,	*bazaar*
chain store,	*multiple shop*
paper stand,	*kiosk*
hardware store,	*ironmonger's*
fruit store,	*fruiterer's*
dry goods store,	*draper's*

FOODS AND AGRICULTURAL PRODUCTS

string beans,	*French beans*
beets,	*beet root*
romaine,	*cos*
lima beans,	*flat beans*
egg-plant,	*aubergine*
catnip,	*catmint*
alfalfa,	*lucerne*
roast,	*joint*
fruit,	*dessert*
dessert,	*sweet*
pie,	*tart*
muffins,	*crumpets*
biscuits,	*scones* (pron. *scawns*) —, *muffins*
crackers,	*biscuits*
syrup,	*treacle*
peanuts,	*monkey nuts*

EDUCATIONAL, LEGAL AND POLITICAL

private school,	*non-provided* (or *public*) *school*
to flunk (active),	*to plough*
to bone up on,	*to swot up*
parole,	*ticket of leave*
to mend fences,	*to nurse one's constituency*
full dinner pail,	*big loaf*
to run for,	*to stand for*
soap-box,	*tub-thumping*

NUMBERS

billion,	*milliard*
trillion,	*billion*
wad of bills,	*sheaf of notes*
146 lbs.,	10 *stone* 6

SLANG AND COLLOQUIAL

to pick on,	*to drop on*
roughhouse,	*bear garden*
hick,	*chaw-bacon*
rubberneck,	*nosy parker*
easy mark,	*mug*
dough,	*dibs*
to doll up,	*to dress up to the nines*
cute,	*dinky*
shark, crackerjack,	*dab*
beat it!,	*hop it!*
hell!,	*'struth!*
guy,	*bloke, cove*
wallop the guy!,	*biff the bloke!*
dumb-bell,	*silly coot*
to get results, to raise money,	*to work the oracle*
to pull a boner,	*to make a bloomer*
magistrate, judge,	*beak*
to bawl out,	*to tell off*
to kick about,	*to boggle about*

MISCELLANEOUS

sidewalk,	*pavement*
mail box,	*pillar box*
pack of cigarettes,	*packet of cigarettes*
in the next block,	*beyond the next turning*
to mail,	*to post*
to pry open,	*to prize open*

AUSTRALIA

Australia's 7,000,000 people are almost completely of British stock and English speech (the native population is estimated at less than 100,000, and speaks a multitude of imperfectly known Australian languages). In pronunciation, intonation and vocabulary, the English of Australia is distinctively individual, but comes closer to that of the British Isles than to that of America. An entire series of localisms, mainly of the slang variety, appears. Some of the interesting expressions from the "Land Down Under", recently codified in magazine and newspaper articles, are the following (where possible, the American slang equivalent is given):

American	*Australian*
frontier, wilderness,	*outback, back-blocks, never-never country*
bush-hut,	*humpy*
hobo,	*swagman*
hobo's bundle,	*Waltzing Matilda, bluey*
riverbed pool or offshoot,	*billabong*
food,	*tucker*
knapsack,	*tuckerbag*
canned meat,	*tinned dog*
swimming-suit,	*cossie*
lamb, sheep,	*jumbuck*
"rookie",	*drogo*
inferior,	*sprog*
"babe", "gal", 'dame", "jane",	*sheila, cliner, sninny*
delectable femininity,	*nice bit of skirt*
crazy about,	*shook on*
"to smooch",	*to smooge*
high-powered lover, "yes-man",	*smooger*
jilted "jane",	*battered bun*
party, "blowout",	*shivoo*
"spread",	*beano*
wine,	*plonk*
beer glass,	*butcher*
drunk, "plastered",	*shikkered*
in the D. T.'s,	*in the rats*
speakeasy,	*sly grog shop*
to go on a spree,	*to go on a larrikin*

to go Dutch,	*to go whacks*
"to treat",	*to shout*
"Dutch treat",	*Scotch shout*
egg,	*goog*
jug,	*flanagan*
barrel,	*kiligan*
money,	*oscar*
ready cash,	*rhino*
copper penny,	*brownie*
threepence,	*triddlybit, traybit*
sixpence,	*zack, tanner*
shilling,	*deener, bob*
pound (money),	*fiddlydid, quid*
to borrow, to beg,	*to bot*
rest period,	*spello*
pal, "side-kick",	*cobber*
"good guy",	*fair stick*
true blue.	*dinkie die*
nose, "beak",	*boko*
hoodlum,	*larrikin*
gang of hoodlums,	*push of larrikins*
racket,	*lurk*
revolver, "gat",	*squirt*
to hit, to attack,	*to stouch*
to steal,	*to shake*
"cops",	*johns*
cattle-stealing,	*duffing*
kibitzer,	*nark*
"lowdown", absolute truth,	*dinkum oil, the straight griffin*
hard work,	*yakka*
"stuffed shirt",	*wowser*
big boss,	*head serang*
horse,	*moke, brumby, gee-gee*
tea-can,	*billy*
the "blues",	*the joes*
"lip", "back-talk",	*chivvy*
high-pressure talk,	*spruik*

"scram",	*imshi*
"to shoot off one's mouth",	*to mag*
to get angry,	*to get all wet*
to tease,	*to poke borax at*
to poke fun at,	*to sling off*
teasing, badinage,	*chiacking*
to take a mean advantage of,	*to show a point on*
all mixed up,	*humpty do*
"got a nerve",	*got a hide*
to look over,	*to take a squiz*
to brood over something,	*to chew the rag*
to give up,	*to drop the bundle*
hard hit,	*stonkered*
stupid, "dumb",	*dill*
half-wit,	*shingle-short*
had his day,	*done his dash*
to go broke,	*to go bung*
Holy Jiminy!,	*God stone the crows!*
great, "swell",	*ding dong, dinkum, bonzer, bosker, boshter, slap-up*
bad, "lousy", "rotten"	*cow, (fair cow, lousy cow)*
everything O. K.,	*curling the moe, she's right*
yes, O. K.,	*ribuck*
thanks,	*ta*
"yoohoo",	*cooee*
within hearing distance of,	*within cooee of*
Chinaman's chance,	*Buckley's chance*
Jap,	*Nip*
Italian, "Wop",	*Dingbat*
Englishman,	*Pommy*
Scotchman,	*Geordie*
Chinese,	*Chow*
Anzac,	*Digger*
New Zealander,	*Enzedder*

To all of this may be added a wealth of terms which Australia shares with Britain: *bloke* for "guy", *dinkie* for "cute," *ta-ta* for "bye-bye" are typical of these.

NEW ZEALAND

Of New Zealand's 1,600,000 inhabitants, less than 100,000 are of native (Maori) stock. Their speech belongs to the Polynesian variety of Malayo-Polynesian. The remaining million and a half are of British stock and English speech. Intonation and pronunciation, while distinctive, are closer to American than to British (*dance, path,* with the *a* of *bat,* not of *father*). The vocabulary often coincides with America's rather than with Britain's (*radio, pack of cigarettes, to mail,* in preference to *wireless, packet, to post*). Localisms generally coincide with those of Australia (*bosker* and *dinkum* for "swell", *cobber* for "side-kick", *wowser* for "blue nose" or "stuffed shirt", *cow* for "lousy", etc.). The following list seems to have originated with New Zealand. Items marked with an asterisk are common to Australia as well, and subsequent research may reveal that this is also true of others of the terms listed:

American	*New Zealand*
hut,	*whare*
lost, strayed,	*bushed*
to go native,	*to go back to nature*
"atta boy!",	*kapai!*
stranger,	*paheka*
prestige, "rep",	*mana*
hello!,	*tenakoe!*
"big chief",	*rangitira*
gas, gasoline,	*benzine*
to argue,	*to argue the toss**
farmer,	*cocky**
sharecropper,	*sharemilker*
large-scale sheep farmer,	*squatter*
ill, bad,	*crook (to feel crook)**
work,	*graft (hard graft)**
man,	*joker*
candy,	*lollies*

position,	*pozzie*
to boast, to brag,	*to skite*
ruined, upset over something,	*up the pole**
sure!,	*too right!*
mid-morning tea,	*smoke-oh* (or *smoko*)*
English immigrant,	*Homey*
girl,	*tart*
penny,	*brown*
to move house,	*to up stick*
half-baked,	*half-pie*
food,	*kai*
money,	*hoot*
to be good at,	*to be pie on*
good luck!,	*kia ora!*
G. I., doughboy,	*kiwi*

SOUTH AFRICA

The South African racial and linguistic situation is not quite so favorable to English as is the case with the other British Dominions. Out of a total of nearly 11,000,000 inhabitants of the Union of South Africa, it is estimated that about 2,500,000 are whites, about equally divided between the descendants of the Dutch-speaking Boers, who still use Afrikaans, and settlers of British origin. Probably a majority of white South Africans are bilingual. Naturally enough, a great many words and expressions have crept into the English of South Africa from Afrikaans, Bantu and other sources. The following "Afrikanderisms" are of interest:

American	*South African*
there is a flood,	*the river is down*
town-lots,	*stands*
to steal,	*to jump*
I. O. U.,	*good-for*
he threw a rock at me,	*he threw me with a rock*

to run over,	*to tramp*
in the house,	*by the house*
snooper, stool-pigeon,	*trap*
thief,	*goniv*
loot,	*goniva*
G. I., doughboy,	*springbok ·*

(*of Dutch origin*)

American	*South African*
early dawn,	*schimmel day*
farmyard,	*erf*
armed camp,	*lager*
rascal,	*schelm, skelm*
to travel,	*to trek*
gulley,	*sloot, sluit*
land measure,	*morgen*
depression between hills,	*kloof*
pound (for animals)	*schut, skit*
open country,	*veld*
boss,	*baas*
precipice,	*kranz*
3-bushel measure,	*muid*
fenced-off field,	*camp, kraal*
are you coming along?,	*are you going with?*
bogus, counterfeit,	*snyde*
conservative,	*dopper*

(*of Bantu origin*)

army,	*impi*
gully, arroyo,	*donga*
council, pow-wow,	*indaba*
sour milk,	*amasi*
thanks,	*inkosi*[6]

6. This Zulu word, meaning "chief", "bestower of benefits", ultimately has become an acknowledgement of a benefit received.

(of Portuguese origin)

nursemaid,	*ayah*
girl,	*nooi*
straw hat,	*sambriero*

(of Malay origin)

pickles, chutney,	*atjar, blatjang*
stamp,	*tjap, chop*
jacket,	*baatje*
all-leather whip,	*sjambok*
hut,	*pondok, pondhock*

CANADA

Of Canada's 12,000,000 people, some 3,000,000 are of French speech, and they are located for the most part in the provinces of Quebec and Ontario. Native American Indian and Eskimo languages account for a little over 100,000 speakers. The remaining population is of English speech, and the brand of English is so close to that of the United States that in a British-compiled dictionary of Canadianisms containing approximately one thousand terms, only some three dozen are found which are not common to both countries (subsequent research may reveal that even a few of these are):

American	*Canadian*
commercial traveller, drummer,	*bagman*
gin,	*blue ruin*
pig,	*Cincinnati olive*
pig's feet,	*Cincinnati oysters*
Newfoundland,	*Codland*
third-class coach,	*colonist car*
farmer, "hick",	*corntossle*
parson, "sky pilot",	*devil-dodger*
beer and gin mixed.	*dog's nose*

church,	*doxology works, gospel factory*
strong whiskey,	*forty-rod*
spoon, fork,	*gob-stick*
millionaire,	*gold-bug*
American flag, "Old Glory",	*gridiron*
Fourth of July,	*rebel picnic*
liquor dregs	*heel taps*
English resident of long standing,	*improved Britisher*
day's work,	*jig*
half-breed,	*metis*
land, real estate,	*mud*
newcomer, "greenhorn",	*new chum* (appears in other British Dominions, notably Australia)
in fine health,	*out of sight*
egg yolk in whiskey,	*prairie oyster*
teetotaler,	*pump-sucker*
small-town mayor,	*reeve*
to stand treat,	*to stand sam*
carpenter,	*shavings*
drunk, "stewed",	*slewed*
iced liquor,	*snow-broth*
raisin pudding,	*spotted dog*
tramp,	*sundowner*
to be under the influence of liquor,	*to have the sun in one's eyes*
dollar bill,	*toadskin*
colored man,	*unbleached American*

ANGLO-INDIAN (HOBSON-JOBSON)[7]

In the course of their long occupation of British India, British soldiers, officials and residents have developed a series

7. The origin of this term used to describe the slang of India is said to be the Muhammadan rallying-cry: *Ya Hassan! Ya Hussein!*

of words and expressions, mostly drawn from the native languages and dialects, a few of which have found their way into the English of other lands; among colloquial expressions claimed to be of Indian origin are: *cheese*, in the expression "he's the big cheese" (the *cheese* represents Hindustani *chīz*, "thing"); *dam* in "I don't give a dam" (the *dām* is an Indian coin); *grass widow*, a term said to have been coined by British officers to designate those military wives who sojourned in the cool, grassy hill-country while their husbands sweltered in the dusty plains. *Betel, bungalow, mango, cheroot, pariah, curry, tiffin* (lunch), *griffin* (newcomer, "greenhorn") are among the words which have passed from native languages or officers' slang into Anglo-Indian, and thence into common English.

Among expressions which have remained local are: *to dumb-cow*, "to browbeat" (Hindustani *dam khānā*, "to eat one's breath", "to be silent", probably crossed with the English "cow"); *to foozilow*, "to flatter"; *to puckerow*, "to lay hold of"; *bahadur*, "stuffed shirt"; *bobachu*, "kitchen"; *mort-de-chien*, "cholera" (despite its French appearance, this comes from Portuguese *mordexim*, borrowed from Marathi *modwashī*); *outcry*, "auction"; *summer-heat*, "hat" (borrowed from Portuguese *sombrero*); *goddess*, "girl", (borrowed from Malay *gādīs*); *gym-khana*, "athletic meet"; *country* in the sense of "local".

Anglo-Indianisms are exceedingly numerous by reason of the fact that they vary from locality to locality, as do the native languages.

ENGLISH AS A COLONIAL, SECONDARY AND CULTURAL LANGUAGE

The total populations of American Western Hemisphere possessions outside of U. S. soil (Alaska, Canal Zone, Puerto Rico, Virgin Islands) amount to over 2,000,000. Approximately the same figure applies to British possessions in the Western Hemisphere outside of Canada and Newfoundland

(Bahamas, Bermudas, British Guiana, British Honduras, Jamaica, Leeward and Windward Islands, etc.).

In Asia, the total populations of British dominions, colonies and dependencies run to about 430,000,000 (Burma, Ceylon, Cyprus, Malaya and Straits Settlements, Hong Kong, British India, Nepal, Bhutan, Palestine, etc.).

British African possessions and Egypt account for some 70,000,000, while in Oceania, exclusive of the white populations of Australia and New Zealand, there is a total of about 3,000,000. In our own Pacific possessions (Guam, Hawaii, Philippines, Samoa, etc.) there is a total population of about 17,000,000

This makes English by far the most widespread of the world's colonial languages, since it affects, by reason of their colonial or semi-colonial status, a total of some 520,000,000 people. How many of these people can actually be reached with English is a matter which varies widely according to locality. A large majority of the 4,000,000 people listed for the Western Hemisphere use English as a primary or secondary language. In Cyprus, Hong Kong and Palestine, the use of English is widespread. In British India, Ceylon, Malaya and Burma, only a small fraction of the native populations has English even as a secondary tongue; but the point has been made that this small fraction includes practically all the people who are instrumental in determining their countries' policies, or who have any degree of international cultural, economic or political standing. The situation in Africa and Oceania is somewhat similar. A larger proportion of the native population in Egypt and the Union of South Africa can be reached with English than is the case in such colonies as Nigeria and Kenya. In our own Pacific possessions the use of English is quite widespread; this is particularly true of Hawaii.

For the use of English as a secondary or cultural language outside of British and American territory, no precise figures are available; but it is probable that English is at least on a par with French and German. Considerable segments of the more cultured classes in the countries of continental Europe, Latin America and Asia are accessible by means of it.

"PIDGIN" ENGLISH

The word "pidgin" is a Cantonese corruption of the English "business", and the term seems to have originated in the South China trade ports, where a compromise language between the natives and the English-speaking traders was deemed necessary. Broadly speaking, Pidgin is English adapted to native habits of thought, syntax, and pronunciation; but these are far from the same everywhere, and so, correspondingly, is Pidgin.[8]

Chinese-English Pidgin abounds in picturesque expressions, many of which reflect Chinese syntax as applied to English words; among them are: *all-same, blongey* (belong), *catchee* (to have), *chin-chin* (worship), *numpa one first chop* (super-

8. It may be noted that there are not only numerous varieties of Pidgin English, but also Pidgins of other tongues. The most important of these is Pidgin Malay, called by the Dutch *pasar* (or *bazaar*) *Malay*, a compromise form of various Malayo-Polynesian dialects, which extends throughout British Malaya, the Dutch East Indies, and is understood as far as the Philippines. A *petit nègre* (French pidgin) appears in the French West African colonies. Several forms of Portuguese Pidgin are in existence, in Senegambia, São Tomé, Cochim, Diu, Mangalore, etc. A Tagalog-Spanish pidgin appears in the Philippines. The Negro-English of Dutch Guiana, interspersed with Dutch and Portuguese words, also falls under the Pidgin classification, as does a variety of English Pidgin current along the entire West African coast from the Union of South Africa to the Equator. (A few typical expressions from this area are: *Who dat man?* for "Who goes there?"; *to dash* for "to tip somebody"; *chop-chop* for "meal"; and *one-time* for "hurry up"). *Papiamento* is a picturesque Spanish Pidgin used by the native population of Curaçao, Dutch West Indies. The French Creole of Haiti and Mauritius, the Dutch Creole of Georgetown and the former Danish West Indies, the Portuguese Creole of the Cape Verde Islands, may all be said to some extent to fall under the Pidgin classification.

fine), *chop-chop* (quickly), *bull-chilo* (boy), *cow-chilo* (girl), *dlinkee* (drink), *flower-flag-man* (American), *fo what?* (why), *have got wata top-side* (crazy), *larn-pidgin* (apprentice); *long-side* (with); *one piecee* (one, referring to objects); *one fella* (one, referring to persons); *what side?* (where?); *top-side piecee Heaven-pidgin man* (bishop); *ah say* (Englishman; "I say"); *ah kee* (Portuguese; "*aqui*", "here").

The Pidgin *par excellence* is the English variety current in the Melanesian Islands (Solomons, Fiji, New Hebrides, etc.). This linguistic form, which has in some localities become fully standardized and has even been reduced to rules of grammar and syntax, has forms fully as picturesque as those of China. A few of these are: *put clothes belong-a table* (set the table); *water he kai-kai him* (the water ate him up; he drowned); *man belong bullamacow him stop* (the butcher is here); *this fellow hat belong you?* (is this your hat?); *what for you kinkenau knife belong me?* (why did you swipe my knife?). A physician sent by the Rockefeller Foundation to the Melanesian Islands to eradicate the hookworm, quotes his own Pidgin description of his employer and mission as he gave it *verbatim* to the natives: "Master belong me him make im altogether kerosene, him make im altogether benzine. Now he old feller. He got im plenty too much belong money. Money belong him allesame dirt. Now he old feller, close up him he die finish. He look about. Him he tink, 'Me like make im one feller something, he good feller belong altogether boy he buy im kerosene blonga me.' Now gubment he talk along master belonga me. Master belonga me him he talk, 'You, you go killim altogether senake (snake) belong bell' (belly) belong boy belong island.' "

From New Guinea come other interesting samples: *cut 'im grass belong head belong me* (cut my hair); *capsize 'im coffee 'long cup* (pour the coffee); *new fellow moon he come up* (it's the first of the month); *skin belong you 'im stink* (you need a bath); *make 'im die machine* (stop the machine); *two clock he go finish, three clock he no come up yet* (it's half past two); *shoot 'im kaikai* (serve the dinner); *me cross too much along you* (I'm very angry with you). Among quaint and suggestive individual expressions, we find: *time belong lim-limbu* (holiday); *kiranki* (irritable); *cus-cus* (office worker); *dim-dim* (white man); *lap-lap* (calico waistcloth); *make 'im paper* (contract); *clothes-sleep* (pajamas); *long long along drink* (drunk); *machine belong talk* (typewriter); *cow oil* (butter); *turn 'im neck belong 'im* (change one's mind); *handkerchief* (or *pants*) *belong letter* (envelope); *screw belong leg* (knee); *pull pull* (flower).

The Australian blackfellows use a variety of Pidgin that largely coincides with the Melanesian and New Guinea brands, but sometimes contributes its own special expressions: *sing 'im longa dark fella* (mosquito); *paper-yabber longa big fella hawk* (air-mail); *kill 'im stink fella* (disinfectant); *think fella too much* (intellectual); *eat 'im wind cart* (automobile); *big fella fire snake* (train); *big fella talk talk watch 'im that one* (high-pressure salesman).

Beche la Mer, or "Sandalwood English", is the form taken by Pidgin in the southern islands of Polynesia (Samoa, Tahiti, etc.). The addition of *-um* to verbs is characteristic (*eatum, callum, catchum*). So are expressions such as: *water belong stink* (perfume); *apple belong stink* (onion); *'im fellow coconut 'im bad* (he has a headache); *belly belong me walk about too much* (I have a stomach-ache).

One of the favorite processes of Pidgin is that of repetition to express intensity or thoroughness: *you go go go* (keep on going); *bamboo belong look-look* (spyglass); *wash-wash* (to bathe, in contradistinction to *wash*); *talk-talk* (long palaver, as against mere *talk*). This is reminiscent of what goes on in many more cultured tongues (Italian *gli ho parlato piano piano*, "I spoke to him very softly"; *un uomo alto alto*, "a very tall man").

Other curious parallels appear: *me-fellow, you-fellow, 'em-all* ("we", "you" plural, "they"; cf. Southern *you-all*, French *nous autres*, Spanish *vosotros*, etc.); *how much clock?*

("what time is it?"; cf. German *wie viel Uhr?*); the Pidgin use of *bel'* (*belly*) to denote the seat of the emotions corresponds to the ancient Greek belief that the stomach was the place where emotions were born and bred; while the use of *bone* to indicate courage ('*im got plenty bone*), or the lack of it (*bone belong 'im allesame water*, "he's scared to death"), has a curious correspondence in our own use of *backbone* and *spineless*, as well as in slang *tough guy*.

The Islands, moreover, have received contributions to their Pidgin from non-English sources. A Frenchman is variously described as *man-a-wiwi* (man of "oui, oui"), *montour* ("bonjour"), *montwar* ("bonsoir"); in Java, he is known as *orang deedong* (*orang* is Malay for "man", and *deedong* is the French *dites donc*). Local variations of Pidgin include such different forms as *kai-kai*, *chow-chow*, *kau-kau*, *fu-fu*, used on different islands with the meaning of "to eat".

Hawaii supplies us with what may be described as our own American variety of Pidgin. The Hawaiian language does not permit two consonants to follow each other unless a vowel intervenes, and many consonants, including b, d, f, g, j, r, s, t, v, do not appear in the language. The result is that when a Hawaiian attempts to say "Merry Christmas!" his rendition is *Mele Kalikimaka*. The names of the months, all of which are borrowed from English, appear as follows: *Ianuali, Pepeluali, Malaki, Apelila, Mei, Iune, Iulae, Aukake, Kemakemapa, Okakopa, Nowemapa, Kekemapa*. Among native words and expressions that have crept into the English of American residents are the following:

how are you?,	*pehea oe?*
clever, smart,	*akamai*
beautiful,	*nani*
old-timer,	*kamaaina*
angry,	*huhu*
greenhorn,	*malihini*
trouble,	*pilikia*
woman,	*wahini*

man,	*kane*
come in and eat!,	*hele mai e ai!*
flower,	*pua*
lie,	*hoopunipuni*
hot,	*wela*
thanks,	*mahalo nui*
hello!, good-bye!,	*aloha oe!*
yes,	*no*
crazy,	*pupule*
wreath,	*lei*
verandah,	*lanai*
feast, spread,	*luau*
pig,	*puaa*
food,	*kaukau*
stomach,	*opu*
boy,	*keikikane*
hat,	*papale*
quick,	*wikiwiki*

IMMIGRANT DIALECTS

These partake of the nature of Pidgin, since they represent a compromise between two languages. The infiltration of words generally runs, however, from English to the immigrant's native tongue, which in the course of time becomes honeycombed with English words and expressions. A few infiltrations run the other way,[9] but they are comparatively insignificant. With the restriction of immigration, the immigrant dialects of the United States are in the process of extinction, since they are for the most part a first-generation phenomenon. Similar unstable immigrant dialects appear in other countries to which large numbers of immigrants have gone in the past (South America, particularly Argentina; France, etc.).

9. *Kibitzer, hamburger, frankfurter, spiel, hoosegow, pickaninny, spaghetti, broccoli* are a few examples. The infiltrations lead even to the coining of new words, as when English *talk* or *gab* is combined with German *Fest,* or English *tender* with the suffix of Italian *maccheroni,* already anglicized to *macaroni* (*tenderoni*).

THE SCANDINAVIAN TONGUES
DANISH, NORWEGIAN,[10] SWEDISH, ICELANDIC

General Characteristics.

While the close relationship among these three languages is evident, considerable divergences appear between Icelandic, which is extremely archaic and conservative of ancient speech-forms, and the other three. To cite a few examples:

1. In the matter of gender, Swedish, Danish and Norwegian combine masculine, feminine and common nouns into a single "gender" form, which is opposed to "neuter" nouns;[11] Icelandic preserves the three grammatical genders, masculine, feminine and neuter, and these fall into distinct declensional schemes, with appropriate endings.

2. In the matter of declension, Swedish, Danish and Norwegian have no true declensional scheme, save for the addition of -s for the possessive and of a plural ending (-or, -ar, -er, -n in Swedish; -r, -er, -e in Dano-Norwegian; with or without "umlaut")[12]; Icelandic has a full-fledged declensional

10. Danish was at one time the official and literary language of Norway; but popular spoken Norwegian (Landsmål) diverged considerably. The present day literary Norwegian language is largely a compromise between the former official Danish and the popular spoken tongue.

11. The distinction is based mainly on natural gender; but the "gender" class may include animals and things, such as "fish" or "book", while the "neuter" class sometimes includes persons and animals, such as "child" and "sheep". Modern Norwegian has re-established a separate feminine form, which had always been in popular use.

12. By "umlaut" is meant a change in the vowel of the root, such as appears in Eng. *mouse, mice,* or in German *Hand, Hände,* or in Swed. *son, söner* (son, sons), or in Danish *Fod, Födder* (foot, feet), or in Icelandic *hjarta, hjörtu* (heart, hearts). The umlaut change is said to be caused by the influence of a following front vowel, belonging to an inflectional ending or some other suffix (this vowel often disappears after causing the change of the root-vowel, as has occurred in Eng. *foot, feet*); it is also described as a phenomenon of "anticipation", whereby the vocal organs begin to prepare themselves for the

system, with four cases (nominative, genitive, dative, accusative) and separate endings; compare:

Swedish: *dag*, "day"; possessive *dags*; plural *dagar*; possessive pl. *dagars*; Danish: *Dag*; possessive *Dags*; plural *Dage*; possessive pl. *Dages*;

Icelandic:	Singular	Plural
Nominative	*dagur*	*dagar*
Genitive	*dags*	*daga*
Dative	*degi*	*dögum*
Accusative	*dag*	*daga*

On the other hand, all the Scandinavian languages agree in having a *suffixed* definite article, which in Swedish, Danish and Norwegian is -*en* (or -*n*) for "gender" nouns, -*et* (or -*t*) for "neuter" nouns in the singular; in the plural, -*ena* (or -*na*) in Swedish, -*ene* (or -*ne*) in Danish and Norwegian (e. g., Swed. *stol*, "chair"; *stolen*, "the chair"; *bord*, "table", *bordet*, "the table"). Icelandic has a *fully inflected* definite article, which is added on to the *fully inflected* noun; e. g.:

	Singular
Nominative	*heimur-inn*, "the world"
Genitive	*heims-ins*, "of the world"
Dative	*heimi-num*, "to the world"
Accusative	*heim-inn*, "the world" (obj.)
	Plural
Nominative	*heimar-nir*, "the worlds"
Genitive	*heima-nna*, "of the worlds"
Dative	*heimu-num*, "to the worlds"
Accusative	*heima-na*, "the worlds" (obj.)

Another general characteristic of the Scandinavian languages is a passive voice formed by changing the -*r* of the active

---

sound of the vowel of the ending while they are still engaged in pronouncing the vowel of the root.

to -*s* (-*st* in Icelandic): Swed. *jag kallar*, "I call"; *jag kallas*, "I am called"; Danish *jeg kalder*, "I call"; *jeg kaldes*, "I am called"; Icel. *elskar*, "he loves"; *elskast*, "he is loved".

Accentuation generally on the initial syllable (save in borrowed words and in verbs compounded with a prefixed preposition; but in Icelandic even the latter are stressed on the first syllable), and "strong" and "weak" verbs (as in Eng. *break, broke, broken* vs. *love, loved, loved*), being common to all the Germanic tongues, are also characteristic of the Scandinavian group.

Other points of similarity and divergence will be noted in the discussion of the individual languages. Some idea of the resemblances and differences among these tongues, and of their relationship to other Germanic languages, may be noted from the following list:

English	Dutch	German	Dano-Nor.[13]	Swedish	Icelandic
friend	vriend	Freund	Ven (venn)	vän	vinur
dog	hond	Hund	Hund	hund	hundur
girl	meisje	Mädchen	Pige (pike)	flicka	stúlka
mother	moeder	Mutter	Moder (mor)	moder (mor)	móðir
father	vader	Vater	Fader (far)	fader (far)	faðir
daughter	dochter	Tochter	Datter	dotter	dóttir
foot	voet	Fuss	Fod (fot)	fot	fótur
night	nacht	Nacht	Nat (natt)	natt	nótt
cold	koud	kalt	kold (kald)	kall	kaldur
large	groot	gross	stor	stor	stór
good	goed	gut	god	god	góður
break	breken	brechen	bryde (bryte)	bryta	brjóta
find	vinden	finden	finde (finne)	finna	finna
run	loopen	laufen	löbe (löpe)	springa, löpa	hlaupa
fall	vallen	fallen	falde (falle)	falla	falla
die	sterven	sterben	dö	dö	deyja
one	een	ein	een (en)	en	einn
two	twee	zwei	to	två	tveir
three	drie	drei	tre	tre	þrír
four	vier	vier	fire	fyra	fjórir
five	vijf	fünf	fem	fem	fimm
six	zes	sechs	sex (seks)	sex	sex
seven	zeven	sieben	syv (sju)	sju	sjö
eight	acht	acht	otte (åtte)	åtta	átta
nine	negen	neun	ni	nio	níu
ten	tien	zehn	ti	tio	tíu
eleven	elf	elf	elleve	elva	ellefu
twelve	twaalf	zwölf	tolv	tolv	tólf
thirteen	dertien	dreizehn	tretten	tretton	þrettán
twenty	twintig	zwanzig	tyve (tjue)	tjugo	tuttugu
hundred	honderd	hundert	hundrede (hundre)	hundra	hundrað
thousand	duizend	tausend	tusind (tusen)	tusen	þúsund

13. The Norwegian form appears in parentheses only where it diverges from the Danish.

SWEDISH

ALPHABETIC NOTATION — as in English, but with the following added symbols: å (= h*o*pe or *o*ho); ä (= c*a*re or b*e*t); ö (= French eu or German ö, long or short).

Notes on Sounds.

All Swedish vowels, including å, ä, ö, may be long (especially in stressed, open syllables) or short; o often = st*oo*l or w*oo*d; u often = French n*u*it.

Swedish y = French u, long or short.

g before e, i, y, ä, ö, and gj in all positions = Eng. y (*göra*, "do", pronounced "yöra"; *gjort*, "done", pron. "yurt").

h is silent before j (*hjul*, "wheel", pron. "yul").

j = Eng. y.

k before e, i, y, ä, ö, and kj in all positions = t + German i*ch* (*köpa*, "buy", pron. tchöpa"; *kjol*, "skirt", pron. "tchul"").

r is trilled.

sk before e, i, y, ä, ö, and sj, skj, stj in all positions = Eng. sh (*skön*, "beautiful", pron. "shön"; *sju*, "seven", pron. "shu"; *skjuta*, "shoot", pron. "shuta").

w appears only in proper names, where it is pronounced as v.

z = Eng. *s*o.

ACCENTUATION — The stress is normally on the first syllable of the word, but in words of more than one syllable there is also a musical "pitch", with complicated rules; e. g., *flicka*,

"girl", is pronounced *fli*   *cka.*   /   *i*

GRAMMATICAL SURVEY

Articles.

Indefinite (Eng. "a", "an") - *en* for "gender" nouns (masc., fem., common); *ett* for "neuter" nouns: *en gosse*, "a boy"; *en flicka*, "a girl"; *en stol*, "a chair"; *ett barn*, "a child"; *ett brev*, "a letter".

Definite (Eng. "the") - add *-en* (or *-n*) for singular gender nouns; *-et* (or *-t*) for singular neuter nouns; *-na* (*-a*, *-ena*, *-en*) for plural nouns:

stolen (stol-en), "the chair"; *gossen* (gosse-n), "the boy"; *flickan* (flicka-n), "the girl";

barnet (barn-et), "the child"; *arbetet* (arbete-t), "the work"; *stolarna* (stolar-na), "the chairs"; *flickorna* (flickor-na), "the girls".

If an adjective precedes the noun, use the "prepositive" form of the definite article (*den, det,* pl. *de*) before the adjective, as well as the suffixed article after the noun: *den dåliga gossen,* "the bad boy"; *det snälla barnet,* "the good child".

Nouns.

The plural is formed generally by the addition of *-or, -ar, -er,* or *-r.*[14] To this ending, *-na* is generally added to supply the article: *flicka,* "girl"; *flickan,* "the girl"; *flickor,* "girls"; *flickorna,* "the girls"; *gosse,* "boy"; *gossen,* "the boy"; *gossar,* "boys"; *gossarna,* "the boys".

The possessive case is formed by adding *-s* (*no* apostrophe) to the nouns, singular or plural: *gossens syster,* "the boy's sister"; *flickornas moder,* "the girls' mother".

Adjectives.

The adjective normally precedes the noun it modifies. When the definite article is *not* used, or when the adjective is a *predicate* adjective (i. e., follows the verb "to be"), it takes the following endings:

	Singular	Plural
"Gender"	-	*-a*
"Neuter"	*-t*	*-a*

en varm dag, "a warm day"; *ett stort* (stor-t) *bord,* "a big table"; *varma dagar,* "warm days"; *stora bord,* "big tables"; *dagen är varm,* "the day is warm"; *dagarna äro varma,* "the days are warm".

14. Neuter nouns ending in consonants and some gender nouns take no ending in the plural; *bord,* "table"; *bord,* "tables"; the suffixed article for these nouns is *-en* in the plural: *bordet,* "the table"; *borden,* "the tables". A very limited number of nouns take *-n*.

When the noun has the definite article, the prepositive form of the article is also used before the adjective, and the adjective has an invariable form ending in *-a*:
den varma dagen, "the warm day"; *de varma dagarna*, "the warm days".

The neuter form of the adjective, ending in *-t*, usually serves also as an adverb: *dålig*, "bad", *dåligt*, "badly".

The comparative and superlative are generally formed by adding *-are* and *-ast*, respectively: *rik*, "rich"; *rikare*, "richer"; *rikast*, "richest"; *mera*, "more", and *mest*, "most", are also used: *älskad*, "beloved"; *mera älskad*, "more beloved"; *mest älskad*, "most beloved".

Pronouns.
Personal:

jag, "I"	*mig*, "me"
du, "you" (sub.)[15]	*dig*, "you" (obj.)[15]
han, "he"	*honom*, "him"
hon, "she"	*henne*, "her"
den, det, "it"[16]	

vi, "we"	*oss*, "us"
ni, "you" (sub. pl.)[15]	*er*, "you" (obj. pl.)
de, "they"	*dem*, "them"

Possessive:

Gender Sg.	Neuter Sg.	Plural	Meaning
min	*mitt*	*mina*	"my"
din	*ditt*	*dina*	"your" (familiar sg.)
hans	*hans*	*hans*	"his", "of him"
hennes	*hennes*	*hennes*	"her", "hers", "of her"

15. The plural forms *Ni, Er* replace the singular *du, dig* in polite conversation. They may or may not be capitalized.

16. Use *den* for singular "gender" nouns referring to inanimate objects, *det* for singular neuter nouns; as in Eng., there is no distinction between subject and object "it".

dess	*dess*	*dess*	"its"
vår	*vårt*	*våra*	"our"
er (*Eder*)	*ert* (*Edert*)	*era*(*Edra*)	"your", plur. and polite sing.
deras	*deras*	*deras*	"their", "of them"
sin	*sitt*	*sina*	"his", "her", "their"[17]

Demonstrative:

denna (or *den här*), "this" (with gender nouns); *detta* (or *det här*), with neuter nouns.
dessa (or *de här*), "these".
den (or *den där*), "that" (with gender nouns); *det* (or *det där*), with neuters.
de (or *de där*), "those".

Relative and Interrogative.

som, "who", "which", "that"
vars, "whose", "of which"
vad, "what", "that"
vem?, "who?", "whom?"
vems?, *vilkas?*, "whose?", "of whom?"
vad?, "what?"
vilken?, (neuter *vilket?*, plural
  vilka?), "which?"

Verbs.

"to be"-Present: *jag, du* (*Ni*), *han är*, "I, you, he" "am, are, is".
            vi, ni, de äro, "we, you, they are".
      Past: *jag, du* (*Ni*), *han var*, "I, you, he" "was, were .
            vi, ni, de voro, "we, you, they were".
"to have" -Present: *jag, du* (*Ni*), *han har*, "I, you, he had".
            vi, ni, de ha, "we, you, they had".
      Past: *jag, du, han, vi, ni, de hade*, "I, you, he,
            we, you, they had".

17. These forms appear only when the possessor is the subject of the clause, but cannot be used to modify the subject: *hennes far har gått ut*, "her father has gone out"; *hon har sett sin far*, "she has seen her (own) father"; *hon träffade hennes far*, "she met her (someone else's) father".

The negative is expressed by using *inte* (or *icke*) after the simple verb (*jag har inte*, "I have not"; *jag talar icke*, "I do not speak"); or after "to have" in a compound tense (*jag har icke talat*, "I have not spoken").

For the interrogative form, invert subject and verb: *har jag?*, "have I?", "do I have?", "am I having?".

The infinitive usually ends in -*a*; "to" is expressed by *att*: *att tala*, "to speak"; *att resa*, "to travel".

The present indicative singular usually ends in -*ar* or -*er*; the plural in -*a*: *jag, du, han talar, reser*, "I, you, he speak(s), travel(s)"; *vi, ni, de tala, resa*, "we, you, they speak, travel". The use of the singular form of the verb with plural subject pronouns is frequent in the spoken tongue.

The past indicative usually ends in -*ade*, -*de*, or -*te*:[18] *jag, du, han, vi, ni, de talade, hörde, reste*, "I, you, he, we, you, they spoke, heard, travelled".

The supine (roughly corresponding to Eng. past participle) usually ends in -*at*, -*t*, -*tt*:[19] *talat, rest, sett*, "spoken", "travelled", "seen".

Compound tenses are formed, as in Eng., by combining "to have" with the supine: *jag har talat*, "I have spoken"; *jag hade talat*, "I had spoken".

The future is formed by using *komma att* or *skola* followed by the infinitive: *jag kommer att tala*, or *jag skall tala*, "I shall speak"; *vi komma att resa*, or *vi skola resa*, "we shall travel".

18. As in all Germanic languages, many verbs have a "strong" past; this means that instead of adding an ending, they change the vowel of the root; note Eng. *take, took; write, wrote; hold, held;* and compare the Swedish equivalents: *taga, tog; skriva, skrev; hålla, höll.*

19. The supine of "strong" verbs usually ends in -*it*: *tagit, skrivit, hållit,* "taken", "written", "held"; such verbs, however, also have a past participle ending in -*en* (neuter -*et*; plural -*na*): *tagen, skriven, hållen;* the supine, which is invariable, is mainly used to form compound tenses with *att ha,* "to have"; the past participle, which is declined and agrees with the subject, is mainly used with *att bliva,* "to become", to form the passive.

The imperative ends in -a, or has no ending: *tala!*, "speak!"; *hör!* "listen!"; *låt oss tala*, "let us speak".

To form the passive, add -s to active forms, dropping the -r of the present: *jag kallar*, "I call"; *jag kallas*, "I am called"; *jag kallade*, "I called"; *jag kallades*, "I was called"; *jag kommer att kalla*, "I shall call"; *jag kommer att kallas*, "I shall be called".

The passive may also be formed by using *att bliva*, "to become", with the past participle, which agrees with the subject: *gossen blir funnen*, "the boy is found"; *barnet blev funnet*, "the child was found".

Man with the active is often used in a passive sense: *man talar svenska* (or *svenska talas*), "Swedish is spoken".

"By" with the passive is expressed by *av*: *saken ordnas nu av honom*, "the matter is now being arranged by him".

DANISH AND NORWEGIAN

ALPHABETIC NOTATION — as in Swedish, but with the following divergences:[20] aa corresponds to Swedish å; æ corresponds to Swed. ä; both ö and ø correspond to Swed. ö.

SOUNDS

For the vowels, cf. Swedish (p. 92). There are, however, numerous minor variations.

Among consonant groups, gj is generally pronounced as a hard g by the Danes, but as y (as it is in Swedish), by the Norwegians.

In the groups eg, egl, egn, the eg is usually pronounced ai.

skj = sk, not sh, in Danish (but = sh in Norwegian). Danish often drops the j even in writing (Danish *skœlde,* "to scold", Nor. *skjelle,* pron. *shelle*).

kj usually = k, in Danish (but like German i*ch* in Norwegian).

sj = sh, as in Swedish.

The musical pitch of Swedish appears also in Dano-Norwegian, to a greater extent in Norwegian than in Danish, where it has practically disappeared, save dialectally.

GRAMMATICAL SURVEY

Nouns and Articles.

The gender system and the articles are generally as in Swedish. Indefinite article - *en* for "gender" nouns; *et* for "neuter" nouns: *en Pige,*[21] "a girl"; *et Bord,* "a table".

---

20. Modern Norwegian regularly uses å, æ, ø, though aa and ö may be found in earlier writings. Danish capitalizes common nouns, and is more prone than Norwegian to use Gothic instead of Roman script.

21. Forms given as examples are in Danish orthography. Norwegian does not capitalize nouns; *en Pige* would appear in Nor. as *en pike,* *Flaade* as *flåte, Tand* as *tann, Stole* as *stoler,* etc.

Definite article (suffixed) - *-en* (*-n*) for "gender"; *-et* (*-t*) for "neuter" nouns; *-ne* (*-ene*) for plural nouns: *Stolen,* "the chair"; *Stolene,* "the chairs"; *Brevet,* "the letter"; *Brevene,* "the letters".

The plural is formed by the addition of *-r, -er, -e* (with or without umlaut), or by leaving the singular form unchanged: *Flaade,*[21] "fleet"; *Flaader,* "fleets"; *Flaaden,* "the fleet"; *Flaaderne,* "the fleets"; *Stol,* "chair"; *Stole,* "chairs"; *Stolen,* "the chair"; *Stolene,* "the chairs"; *Tand,*[21] "tooth"; *Tænder,* "teeth"; *Tanden,* "the tooth"; *Tænderne,* "the teeth"; *Ord,* "word"; *Ord,* "words"; *Ordet,* "the word"; *Ordene,* "the words".

The possessive is formed, as in Swedish, by adding *-s*: *Hus,* "house", *Huset,* "the house"; *Husets,* "the house's"; *Husene,* "the houses"; *Husenes,* "of the houses" (Norwegian often dispenses with the possessive, replacing it by a preposition: *taket på huset,* "the roof of the house", rather than *husets tak,* "the house's roof").

Adjectives

Generally as in Swedish. When the article is not used, or when the adjective is a predicate adjective, the endings are:

	Singular	Plural
Gender	-	*-e*
Neuter	*-t*	*-e*

en lang Dag, "a long day"; *et langt Bord,* "a long table"; *lange Dage,* "long days"; *lange Borde,* "long tables".

When the modified noun is to be used with the definite article, the prepositive form of the article (*den, det, de*) is used before the adjective, which is then invariable and ends in *-e*. In these cases, Danish prefers to omit the suffixed article, while Norwegian prefers the Swedish custom of using a double article: Danish *den store Mand;* Norwegian *den store mannen,* "the big man".

Comparative and superlative are usually formed by the addition of *-ere* (*-re*) and *-est* (*-st*): *söd,* "sweet"; *södere.*

"sweeter"; *sødest,* "sweetest". The neuter form of the adjective in *-t* usually serves as an adverb: *smuk,* "beautiful"; *smukt,* "beautifully" (Norwegian *pen, pent*).

Pronouns.

Personal.

jeg, "I"	*mig,* (N. *meg*) "me"
du,[22] "you" (sub.)	*dig,* (N. *deg*), "you" (obj.)
han, "he"	*ham,* "him"
hun, "she"	*hende,* (N. *henne*) "her"
den, det, "it"	
vi, "we"	*os,* (N. *oss*), "us"
I, "you" (sub. pl.; N. *dere*)	*jer,* "you" (obj. p.; N. *dere*)
de, "they"	*dem,* "them"

Possessive.

Gender Sg.	Neuter Sg.	Plural	Meaning
min	*mit* (N. *mitt*)	*mine*	"my"
din	*dit* (N. *ditt*)	*dine*	"your" (fam. sg.)
hans	*hans*	*hans*	"his", "of him"
hendes (N. *hennes*)	*hendes* (N. *hennes*)	*hendes* (N. *hennes*)	"her", "hers", "of her"
dens, dets	*dens, dets*	*dens, dets*	"its" (use *dens* for "gender", *dets* for "neuter" possessor
vor (N. *vår*)	*vort* (N. *vårt*)	*vore* (N. *våre*)	"our", "ours"
jer (N. *deres*)	*jeres* (N. *deres*)	*jeres* (N. *deres*)	"your", "yours" (fam. pl.)

22. In polite conversation, *De, Dem* (lit. "they", "them"), spelled with a capital and used with a *singular* verb, replace *du, dig, I, jer: taler De det danske Sprog?,* "do you speak the Danish language?".

deres	*deres*	*deres*	"their", "theirs", "of them"
sin	*sit*	*sine*	"his", "her", "its", "their" (with varying usage)

Demonstrative.

denne	*dette*	*disse*	"this", "these"
den	*det*	*de*	"that", "those"

Relative and Interrogative.[23]

som,	"who", "which", "that"
hvis,	"whose", "of which"
hvad,	"what", "that"
hvem?,	"who?, "whom?"
hvis?,	"whose?"
hvad?,	"what?"
hvilken?, (hvilket, hvilke)	"which?"

Verbs.

"to be" — Present (all numbers and persons): *er;* Past (all numbers and persons): *var.*

" to have" — Present: *har;* Past: *havde* (all persons and numbers; Nor. uses *hadde* instead of *havde*).

Negative — *ikke* after verb: *jeg har ikke,* "I have not". The infinitive usually ends in *-e: at elske,* "to love".

The present indicative usually ends in *-er (-r); jeg, du, han elsker,* "I, you, he love(s)"; *vi, I, de elsker,* "we, you they love".

The past usually ends in *-ede* (N. *-et*):[24] *jeg, du,* etc. *elskede,* "I, you, etc. loved".

23. In all forms beginning with *hv-*, the *h-* is silent. Norwegian prefers *hva* to *hvad*, and *hva for en* to *hvilken*.

24. "Strong" verbs usually change the root vowel and take no ending: *synge, sang,* "sing, sang"; *drikke. drak,* "drink, drank"; *give, gav* (N. *gi, ga*) "give, gave".

The supine ends in -*et*: *elsket*, "loved".

Compound tenses are formed by using "to have" with the supine: *jeg har elsket*, "I have loved"; *jeg havde elsket*, "I had loved".

The future is formed by using *skal* (plural *skal* or *skulle*) or *vil* (plural *vil* or *ville*) with the infinitive: *jeg skal elske*, or *jeg vil elske*, "I shall love".

The imperative usually has no ending in the singular: *tal!*, "speak!"

The passive adds -*s* or -*es* to active forms, dropping -*r* of the present: *jeg kaldes*, "I am called"; *jeg kaldedes*, "I was called"; *der skrives meget i vor Tid*, "much is written in our time".

Or it may be formed by using *bliver* (N. *blir;* past *blev*), or *være* ("to be"), with the past participle: *jeg bliver elsket, jeg er elsket*, "I am loved". "By" is expressed by *af: Brevet blev sendt af Soldaten*, "the letter was sent by the soldier".

IDENTIFICATION OF SWEDISH, DANISH AND NORWEGIAN

Swedish is more apt to use å, ä, ö; Danish aa, æ, ø; a mixture of the two series of symbols (å, æ, ø) usually indicates a Norwegian written document.

Swedish often uses -*a* endings where Danish and Norwegian use -*e;* this is particularly the case with the plural of nouns and adjectives, and in many verb-forms; Swedish and Norwegian often use final double consonants which in Danish regularly appear as single consonants.

Musical patterns distinguishing otherwise identical words are found in Swedish and, to a lesser degree, in Norwegian, but not in Danish, which uses a glottal stop instead.

Note the different written form of these extremely common words, with Swedish and Norwegian using a final double consonant where Danish uses a single:

English	Swedish	Danish	Norwegian (where it diverges from Danish)
and	*och*	*og*	
a (neuter)	*ett*	*et*	*ett*
not	*icke*	*ikke*	
I	*jag*	*jeg*	
	av	*af*	*av*
up	*upp*	*op*	*opp*
to	*till*	*til*	
to	*att*	*at*	*å*

COMMON PHRASES

	Swedish	Norwegian
good morning	*god morgon*	*god morgen*
good evening	*god kväll, god afton*	*god aften*
good night	*god natt*	*god natt*
good-bye	*adjö*	*adjø* (D. *far vel*)
how are you?	*hur står det till?*	*hvordan står det til?*
well, thank you	*tack, bra*	*godt, takk*
please	*var så god och*	*vær så snill å*
you're welcome	*ingen orsak*	*ingen årsak* (D. *jeg beder*)
perhaps	*kanske*	*kanskje* (D. *maaske*)
here is	*här är*	*her er*
there is	*där är*	*der er*
where is?	*var är?*	*hvor er?*
how do I go to..?	*hur kommer man till?*	*hvordan kommer jeg til?*
yes	*ja*	*ja*
no	*nej*	*nei*
very	*mycket*	*meget*
how much is it?	*hur mycket kostar det?*	*hvor meget koster det?*
why?	*varför?*	*hvorfor?*
when?	*när?*	*når?*
now	*nu*	*nu*
always	*alltid*	*alltid*
where?	*var?*	*hvor?*
because	*därför att*	*fordi*
today	*i dag*	*idag*
yesterday	*i går*	*igår*
tomorrow	*i morgon*	*imorgen*

tonight	*i natt, i kväll*	*i aften, i kvell*
to the right	*till höger*	*tilhøyre*
to the left	*till vänster*	*tilvenstre*
what time is it?	*vad är klockan?*	*hva er klokken?*
it is 7 o'clock	*den* (or *klockan*) *är sju*	*klokken er sju*
I'm hungry	*jag är hungrig*	*jeg er sulten*
I'm thirsty	*jag är törstig*	*jeg er tørst*
I'm cold	*jag fryser*	*jeg fryser*
I'm warm	*jag är varm*	*jeg er varm*
I'm ill	*jag är sjuk*	*jeg er syk*
do you speak Swedish?	*talar Ni svenska?*	*snakker De svensk?*
what is your name?	*vad heter Ni?*	*hva heter De?*
certainly	*ja visst*	*sikkert, javisst*
give me	*giv mig*	*gi meg*
show me	*visa mig*	*vis meg*
tell me	*tala om för mig*	*fortell meg*
do you understand?	*förstår Ni?*	*forstår De?*
I don't understand	*jag förstår inte*	*jeg forstår ikke*
do you know?	*vet Ni?*	*vet De?*
I don't know	*jag vet inte*	*jeg vet ikke*
very little	*mycket litet*	*meget lite*
excuse me!	*förlåt!, ursäkta!*	*unnskyld!*
don't mention it	*ingen orsak*	*ingen årsak*
what do you want?	*vad önskas?*	*hva ønsker De?*
never mind	*det gör ingenting*	*det gjør ikke noe*
I'm sorry!	*så tråkigt!*	*beklager!*
too bad!	*det var synd!*	*det var synd!*
what is the matter?	*hur är det fatt?*	*hva er i veien?*
it's fine weather	*det är vackert väder*	*det er godt vær*
at home	*hemma*	*hjemme*
come in!	*stig in!, kom in!*	*komm inn!*
stop!	*stanna!*	*stopp!*
listen!	*hör på!*	*hør!*
look out!	*se upp!*	*vær forsiktig!*
		(D. *pas paa!*)
your health!	*skål!*	*skål!*

ICELANDIC

ALPHABETIC NOTATION — as in English, but c, q, w do not appear in native words. Additional symbols: á, é, í, ó, ú, ý, æ, ö, đ, þ.

SOUNDS.

Vowels bearing the accent mark are often long, or pronounced as diphthongs (e. g., á = Eng. c*ow*). Vowels not bearing the accent mark may be long or short.

Long é = *y*es (it is often spelled je: *mér* or *mjer*).

Short u = (approximately) French f*eu;* long ú = Eng. m*oo*n.

Y, ý = Eng. p*i*n, machine, not French u, as in Swedish.

æ = f*i*ve; ö as in German.

đ = Eng. ba*the;* þ = Eng. *th*in.

g after a vowel and before i or j = Eng. y (*kragi*, "collar", pronounced "krayi").

g at the beginning of a word and followed by e or i = gy (*gefa*, "to give", pronounced "gyefa").

j = Eng. y.

r is trilled.

z = Eng. *s*on.

    A noteworthy feature of Icelandic pronunciation is the "interrupted" vowel; before kk, pp, tt, kl, kn, vowels are followed by an h-sound (*rjetta*, "to hand", pronounced "ryeh-ta"; *uppi*, "up", pron. "uh-pi").

GRAMMATICAL SURVEY

Articles and Nouns.

    No indefinite article is used: *bátur*, "boat", "a boat".

    The definite article is fully declined, whether it precedes or is suffixed to the noun. The latter is also fully declined. The four cases are: nominative, genitive, dative, accusative. Masculine, feminine and neuter gender appears. For the declension of a noun with suffixed article, cf. p. 89. The full declension of the prefixed article used if an adjective precedes the noun, is as follows:

	Singular			Plural		
	Masc.	Fem.	Neut.	Masc.	Fem.	Neuter
Nom.	*hinn*	*hin*	*hið*	*hinir*	*hinar*	*hin*
Gen.	*hins*	*hinnar*	*hins*	*hinna*	*hinno*	*hinna*
Dat.	*hinum*	*hinni*	*hinu*	*hinum*	*hinum*	*hinum*
Acc.	*hinn*	*hina*	*hið*	*hina*	*hinar*	*hin*

If the article is suffixed, its initial *h-* invariably drops out; also the *i* if the noun ends in a vowel, or after the *-r* of a nominative or accusative plural. The article is prefixed when an adjective stands before the noun, suffixed otherwise: *faðir*, "father"; *faðirinn*, "the father"; *hinn ríki faðir*, "the rich father".

Nouns of the three genders fall into various declensional schemes, of which the following are typical (the endings are given in the following order: Singular: nom., gen., dat., acc.; Plural: nom., gen., dat., acc.):

Generally for nouns ending in vowels:

Masculine: *tími*, "time" - *tím-i, -a, -a, -a; tím-ar, -a, -um, -a*;

Feminine: *tunga*, "tongue" - *tung-a, -u, -u, -u; tung-ur, -na, -um, -ur*;

Neuter: *auga*, "eye" - *aug-a, -a, -a, -a; aug-u, -na, -um, -u.*

Generally for nouns ending in consonants:

Masculine: *heimur*, "world" - *heim-ur, -s, -i, -; heim-ar, -a, -um, -a* (but many such nouns have *-ar* in the genitive singular, *-ir* or *-ur* in the nominative plural);

Feminine: *tíð*, "time" - *tíð, -ar, -, -; tíð-ir, -a, -um, -ir* (many have *-ar* or *-ur* in the nominative plural);

Neuter: *skip*, "ship" - *skip, -s, -i, -; skip, -a, -um, -.*

There are numerous deviations from these schemes.

Adjectives.

These normally precede and agree with the noun they modify. They have a "strong" and a "weak" declension, according as they are used without or with the article. The "strong" declension employs different series of endings somewhat akin to those of the nouns, while the weak, which is more commonly used, generally follows this scheme:

	Singular			Plural
	Mas.	Fem.	Neut.	
Nom.	-i	-a	-a	
Gen.	-a	-u	-a	
Dat.	-a	-u	-a	-u for all genders and
Acc.	-a	-u	-a	cases.

The comparative is formed by the addition of *-ri* or *-ari* (*-ra* or *-ara* in the neuter singular); the superlative by the addition of *-stur* or *-astur*, feminine *-st* or *-ust*, neuter *-st* or *-ast*; *ríkur*, "rich"; *ríkari* (neuter singular *ríkara*), "richer"; *ríkastur* (fem. *ríkust*, neut. *ríkast*; fully declined, with a "strong" and a "weak" scheme), "richest".

The adverb usually ends in *-a*: *víður*, "wide", *víða*, "widely".

Pronouns.

Personal.

	First Person			Second Person		
	Singular	Dual[25]	Plural	Singular	Dual	Plural
Nom.	ieg	við	vjer	þú	þið	þjer
Gen.	nín	okkar	vor	þín	ykkar	yðar
Dat.	mjer	okkur	oss	þjer	ykkur	yður
Acc.	mig	okkur	oss	þig	ykkur	yður

Third Person

	Masc.	Fem.	Neuter	Masc.	Fem.	Neuter
	Singular			Plural		
Nom.	hann	hún	það	þeir	þaer	þau
Gen.	hans	hennar	þess	þeirra	þeirra	þeirra
Dat.	honum	henni	því	þeim	þeim	þeim
Acc.	hann	hana	það	þá	þaer	þau

25. The "dual" number refers to two: "we two", "you two".

Possessive.

minn,[26] "my", "mine"	*okkar,* "our", "ours"
þinn,[26] "your", "yours"	*ykkar, ydar,* "your", "yours"
hans, "his"	
hennar, "her", "hers"	*þeirra,* "their", "theirs"
þess, "its"	
sinn,[26] "his", "her", "their" (own)	

Demonstrative.

þessi, þessi, þetta, "this"; plural: *þessir, þessar, þessi,* "these"; *sá, sú, það,* "that"; plural: *þeir, þaer, þau,* "those". These demonstratives are fully declined; only the nominative forms are given here, in the masculine, feminine and neuter.

Relative.

sem (indeclinable), "who", "which", "that"

Interrogative.

hver?, or *hvor?,* "who?", "whom?"
hvað? (indeclinable), "what?"
hvaða? (indeclinable), "which?"

Verbs.

"to be": Present - *er, ert, er, erum, eruð, eru.*
        Past - *var, varst, var, vorum, voruð, voru.*
"to have": Present - *hefi, hefir, hefir, höfum, hafið, hafa.*
        Past - *hafði, hafðir, hafði, höfðum, höfðuð, höfðu.*
        The infinitive usually ends in *-a* or *-ja: elska,* "to love":
        Present: *elsk-a, -ar, -ar, -um, -ið, -a.*
        Past: *elsk-aði, -aðir, -aði, 'unpn-*   [27] *·npn- 'pnpn-*

26. Fully declined; only the nominative masculine singular form is given here. The other possessives are invariable.

27. Strong verbs change the root vowel and add no ending: *finn, fann,* "find, found"; *gef, gaf,* "give, gave". Note that there are many other patterns besides the conjugational scheme outlined above.

Compound tenses are formed by combining *hafa*, "to have", with the supine, which frequently ends in *-að*: *hefi kallað*, "I have called"; *hafði elskað*, "I had loved".

The future is formed by combining *munu* or *skulu* with the infinitive: *mun kalla* or *skal kalla*, "I shall call".

The imperative singular adds *-a* or has no ending; the imperative plural adds *-ið*.

The passive is formed by adding *-st*, dropping the *-r* of active forms; *kallast*, "I am called". It may also be formed by using *vera*, "to be", or *verða*, "to become", with the past participle.

IDENTIFICATION

Written Icelandic is easily identified by its symbols đ, þ, which do not appear in any other modern language; also by the typical *-ur* ending of many masculine nouns and adjectives.

SAMPLES OF THE
WRITTEN SCANDINAVIAN LANGUAGES — John 3.16

Swedish: Ty så älskade Gud världen, att han utgav sin enfödde Son, på det att var och en som tror på honom skall icke förgås, utan hava evigt liv.

Danish: Thi saaledes elskede Gud Verden, at han gav sin Søn den enbaarne, for at hver den, som tror paa ham, ikke skal fortabes, men have et evigt Liv.

Norwegian: For så har Gud elsket verden at han gav sin Sønn, den enbårne, forat hver den som tror på ham, ikke skal fortapes, men ha evig liv.

Icelandic: því að svo elskaði Guð heiminn, að hann gaf son sinn eingetinn, til þess að hver, sem á hann trúir, glatist ekki, heldur hafi eilíft líf.

("For God so loved the world that he gave his only-begotten Son, that whosoever believeth in him may not perish, but may have everlasting life.")

DUTCH

ALPHABETIC NOTATION — as in English; q, x, y appear only in foreign words. Vowel *quality* (*not* length) is indicated by doubled vowels (*maan*, "moon", vs. *man*, "man").

SOUNDS

All vowels are short, save occasionally before r.

aa and a[28] = f*a*ther (r*aa*d, "advice");

ee and e[28] = f*a*te (h*ee*t, "hot");

oo and o[28] = *o*ver (*o*ver);

ie and i[28] = mach*i*ne (z*ie*k, "ill");

uu and u[28] = French t*u* (*u*ren, "hours");

a[29] = c*o*t (k*a*t, "cat").

e[29] = n*e*ck (n*e*k)[30].

o[29] = c*o*ffee (k*o*ffie).

i[29] = p*i*t (p*i*t).

u[29] = b*u*ck (st*u*k, "piece").

oe = b*oo*k (b*oe*k).

eu = French *eu* or German *ö* (d*eu*r, "door").

au, ou, auw, ouw = h*ow* (p*au*s, "pope"; *ou*d, "old"; g*auw*, "quick"; vr*ouw*, "woman".

ei, ij = p*ai*n (h*ij* z*ei*, "he said").

ui = Fr. d*eui*l.

28. The double vowel always has the value described above. For the single vowel, the value described normally occurs when the vowel is followed by a consonant which is followed by another vowel (r*a*-men, gel*o*-ven). There is no difference of sound between the *aa* of *raam* and the *a* of *ramen*, or between the *oo* of *kool* and the *o* of *kolen*. See also spelling rules on p. 111.

29. The second value described for the single vowel normally occurs when the following consonant is final in the word (gek), or when the vowel is followed by a double consonant (gek-ken) or by two different consonants (straf-te).

30. e = b*a*con, in prefixes (be-, ge-, ver-); in suffixes and inflectional endings (-en, -de, -ten, etc.); and in articles (de, het, een).

ieuw = leeway (n*ieuw*, "new").

eeuw = wayward (l*eeuw*, "lion").

g and ch = German a*ch*, but more quickly and energetically
      pronounced (gebra*ch*t, "brought").

sch = s + Dutch ch; (*sch*ip, "ship"); but in final position,
      = Eng. hi*ss* (fle*sch*, "bottle").

j = *y*es (*j*ullie, "you").

sj = *s*ure (als*j*eblieft, "please").

th = t (only in foreign words and contractions: *th*ee, "tea";
      *th*uis, contraction for *te huis*, "at home").

v = sound intermediate between v and f (*v*ol, "full").

w = *v*ine (*w*ijn, "wine").

A double vowel before a final consonant is usually spelt
single when an ending beginning with a vowel is added (*raam,*
"window", plural *ramen*); this does not reflect any change of
sound.

A single final consonant following a single vowel as described in n. 29 is spelt double when an ending beginning with
a vowel is added (*gek*, "crazy", plural *gekken*); this does not
reflect any change of sound.

Final f and s usually change to v and z, respectively, when
an ending beginning with a vowel is added, and this change in
spelling does reflect a change in sound (*huis*, "house", plur.
huizen; duif, "dove", plur. *duiven*). Final -*b* and -*d* are
sounded as -*p* and -*t*, respectively.

The stress is usually on the first syllable (save for words
with the prefixes *be-, ge-, er-, her-, on-, ont-, ver-*, which are
never stressed).

GRAMMATICAL SURVEY

Articles and Nouns.

There are three genders, masculine, feminine and neuter;
but many inanimate objects are masculine or feminine. The
spoken language makes no distinction between masculine and
feminine, the definite article *de* being used for both and remaining uninflected in speech. The written language displays

traces of a case-system similar to that of German, with so-called "nominative", "genitive", "dative" and "accusative"; the spoken tongue, however, has reduced these forms to a state very similar to that of English.

The definite article is *de* for masculine and feminine singular nouns and for all plural nouns, *het* (*'t*) for neuter singulars.

The indefinite article is *een* (pronounced th*e n*ew) for all nouns.

Proper names and some other nouns denoting persons have a genitive (or possessive) form ending in *-s* or *-es;* this is often replaced by the uninflected noun preceded by *van* (the father's daughter, the daughter of the father: *de vaders dochter* or *de dochter van de vader* (colloquially, a form like *de man z'n dochter,* the man his daughter, is sometimes heard).

While the written language has traces of an old dative, the spoken tongue indicates the indirect object exactly as English does, either by placing it before the direct object (I have written Uncle John a letter, *ik heb Oom Jan een brief geschreven;* note the position of the participle); or by using the preposition *aan* (I have written a letter *to* Uncle John, *ik heb een brief aan Oom Jan geschreven*).

The plural is formed in most cases by the addition of *-en,* less frequently by that of *-s* (*-s* appears in the plural of nouns ending in *-je*[31], *-el, -em, -en, -aar, -ier, -er, -erd, -aard*).

Adjectives.

The only inflectional ending of the adjective is *-e:* good, *goed;* the good man, *de goede man.*

An adjective used with a neuter singular noun does not take the *-e* unless the definite article or a demonstrative precede: *een groot huis,* "a large house"; *het groote huis,* "the large house".

If the adjective is used as a predicate it takes no ending:

---

31.   *-je* is a diminutive suffix, conferring neuter gender upon all words to which it is added. Note also that in the word-list (pp. 119-121) neuter nouns are indicated thus: (n.).

het huis is groot, "the house is large"; *de huizen zijn groot,* "the houses are large".

Comparative and superlative are formed by adding *-r* (or *-er*) and *-st*, respectively: *warm, warmer, warmst,* "warm, warmer, warmest"; *meer* ("more") and *meest* ("most") may also be used.

The adjective without an ending is often used as an adverb: *zij is mooi,* "she is beautiful"; *zij zingt mooi,* "she sings beautifully". Note - *zoo* - *als,* "as - as"; *niet zoo* - *als,* "not so - as"; *dan,* "than". See page 91 for Numerals (note: 14 — *veertien;* 40 — *veertig;* 80 — *tachtig*), and note the following:

drie paar handschoenen, "three pairs of gloves";
vijf en dertig huizen, "35 houses"; (lit. "five and thirty");
zes voet hoog, "six feet high"; (lit. "six foot");
hoe laat is het?, "what time is it?"; (lit. "how late is it?");
het is zes uur, "it is 6 o'clock"; (lit. "it is six hour");
het is tien minuten voor (over) zeven, "it is ten to (past) seven";
het is half zes, "it is 5:30"; (lit. "it is half six").

Pronouns.

Personal.

ik, 'k, "I"	*mij, me,* "me"
jij, je, U, "you"[32]	*jou, je, U,* "you" (obj.)
hij, "he"	*hem,* "him"

32. Where alternative forms in *-ij, -e* appear (*wij, we*), the first is more, the second less emphatic. For the second person "you", *jij, je* are used as familiar forms in the singular (*je bent,* "you are"; a singular "you", familiarly addressed); *jullie* and *jelui* are plural familiar forms, and take the verb in the second or *third person plural* (*jullie hebt* or *hebben,* "you have"; more than one person addressed, familiarly); the polite form of address is *U* with the second or third person singular of the verb, and no distinction between singular and plural (*U bent* or *U is,* "you are"; one or more people, politely addressed); if a distinction between singular and plural is desired, use *de dames,* "the ladies" or *de heeren,* "the gentlemen", with the third plural verb: *de heeren hebben,* "you gentlemen have".

zij, ze, "she"	*haar,* "her"
het, '*t,* "it"	*het,* '*t,* "it"
wij, we, "we"	*ons,* "us"
jullie, jelui, U, "you"	*jullie, jelui, je, U,* "you" (obj.)
zij, ze, "they"	*hen,* "them"; *hun,* "to them"

Possessive.

mijn, "my", "mine"	*onze, ons,* "our", "ours"
jouw, "your", "yours"	*uw,* "your", "yours" (plural possessor)
zijn, "his"	*hun,* "their", "theirs"
haar, "her", "hers"	

These appear without the article if they are used as adjectives, with the article if they are used as pronouns: *mijn zusters en de uwe,* "my sisters and yours"; *dit boek is het mijne,* "this book is mine".

Demonstrative.

deze, (neut. sg. *dit*), "this", "these"
die, (neut sing. *dat*), "that", "those"

Interrogative and Relative.

welke?, "which?" (neut. sg. *welk?*)
wat voor een?, "what kind of?"
wie?, "who?"
wiens?, "whose?"
wat?, "what?"
die, (neut. sg. *dat*), "which", "that", "who", "whom"
wiens, "whose" (fem. and plural *wier*)
wie, "he who"
wat, "that which"

Note that *wat* changes to *waar* when used with a preposition, and that the latter is suffixed: *waarin,* "in which", "wherein".

Note also: *elkander,* "each other"; *zelf,* "self"; *dezelfde* (neuter *hetzelfde*), "the same"; *zulk* or *zoo een* (often contract-

ed to *zoo'n*), "such", "such a"; *zich*, "himself", "themselves";
iemand, "somebody"; *iets*, "something"; *niets*, "nothing";
men, "one", "they"; *elk*, "each"; *ieder*, "every"; *iedereen*,
"everybody"; *niemand*, "nobody".

Verbs.

zijn or *wezen*, "to be": Present: *ik ben*, "I am"; *jij bent* (fam.),
U is (polite), "you are"; *hij, zij, het is*, "he, she, it is"; *wij,
jullie, zij zijn*, "we, you, they are". Past: singular *was*, plural
waren.

hebben, "to have": Present: *ik heb, jij hebt* (*U heeft*), *hij*
(*zij, het*) *heeft; wij, jullie, zij hebben*. Past: singular *had*,
plural *hadden*.

The infinitive normally ends in *-en*: *voeren*, "to lead".

The present indicative normally has no ending in the first
person singular, *-t* in the second and third singular, *-en* in the
plural: *ik voer*, "I lead", *U voert*, "you lead", *hij voert*, "he
leads"; *wij, jullie, zij voeren*, "we, you, they lead".

The past has the endings *-de* (sg.), *-den* (plural): *ik
voerde, hij voerde, wij voerden*, "I", "he", "we" "led". The
d of the past ending becomes *t* if the root of the verb ends in
-ch, -f, -k, -p, -t, -s or *-sch*: *straffen*, "to punish"; *ik strafte*, "I
punished".[33]

The past participle normally ends in *-d* or *-t* (see above;
also note 33), with the prefix *ge-*: *voeren*, "to lead", *gevoerd*,
"led"; *straffen*, "to punish", *gestraft*, "punished".

Compound tenses are formed, as in English, by combining
the verb "to have" with the past participle: *hij heeft gebroken*,
"he has broken". But many intransitive verbs use "to be" as an
auxiliary: *hij is gestorven*, "he has died"; *ik ben geweest*, "I
have been".

33. Strong verbs change the root vowel and add no ending in the
singular of the past; they also add *-en* in the past participle instead of
-d or *-t*: *breken*, "to break", *brak*, "broke", *gebroken*, "broken";
drinken, "to drink", *dronk*, "drank", *gedronken*, "drunk"; *geven*, "to
give", *gaf*, "gave", *gegeven*, "given".

The future is formed by using *zal* (plural *zullen*) with the infinitive: *ik zal voeren*, "I shall lead". The conditional is formed by using *zou* (plural *zouden*) with the infinitive: *ik zou voeren*, "I should lead".

The imperative singular consists of the simple root of the verb: *voer!*, "lead!"; for the plural, add *-t* (*voert!*).

The passive is formed by using *worden*, "to become", with the past participle; the present of *worden* is *word* (plural *worden*); the past is *werd* (plural *werden*): *ik word gestraft*, "I am punished"; *zij werden door mij gestraft*, "they were punished by me".

The negative is formed by using *niet* after the verb. Note the position of *niet* in the following examples: *ik leer mijn les niet*, "I do not learn my lesson"; *ik heb mijn les niet geleerd*, "I haven't learnt my lesson".

IDENTIFICATION

Written Dutch is easily identified by its use of certain vowel groups: *aai, ooi, oei, eeuw, uw, auw, ouw, ieuw, ij*. Note that no accent marks or diacritic signs appear in standard modern Dutch. In the spoken language, perhaps the most characteristic trait is the guttural sound of *g* and of *ch* in the *sch* group; the latter is similar to a quick clearing of the throat immediately following an *s*-sound.

SAMPLES OF WRITTEN DUTCH AND AFRIKAANS

Dutch: Want alzoo lief heeft God de wereld gehad, dat Hij zijn eengeboren Zoon gegeven heeft, opdat een ieder, die in hem gelooft, niet verloren ga, doch eeuwig leven hebbe.

Afrikaans: Want so lief het God die wêreld gehad, dat Hy sy eniggebore Seun gegee het, sodat elkeen wat in Hom glo, nie verlore mag gaan nie, maar die ewige lewe kan hê.

WRITTEN AND SPOKEN DUTCH
EXPRESSIONS AND WORDS

Dutch shows a very pronounced difference between "written language" and "spoken language".[34] The latter is not to be confused with slang; it is perfectly legitimate Dutch, spoken by well-educated people, who would feel silly or pedantic expressing themselves in the words of the written tongue (to cite an example from English, the literary "the fire was extinguished" would normally appear in speech as "the fire was put out"). Similarly, Dutch has two expressions for each of thousands of meanings. A few striking ones follow:

English	Written Dutch	Spoken Dutch
good morning	*goeden morgen*	*goeiemorgen*
good afternoon	*goeden middag*	*goeiemiddag*
good evening	*goeden avond*	*goeienavend*
good night	*goede nacht*	*goeienacht*
good-bye	*vaarwel*	*dag*
thank you	*ik dank U*	*dank U wel*
you're welcome	*tot Uw dienst*	*niet te danken*
please	*als het U belieft*	*alsjeblieft*
very gladly	*zeer gaarne*	*heel graag*
perhaps	*wellicht*	*misschien*
here is	*alhier is*	*hier is*
there is	*aldaar is, er is*	*daar is, er is*
where is?	*waar is?*	*waar is?*
how do I go to - ?	*hoe ga ik naar - ?*	*hoe kom ik naar - ?*

34. The root of this difference lies in the fact that the written language has its roots in the Flemish of Flanders and Brabant, which, down to the sixteenth century, were economically and politically, as well as culturally, on a higher plane than the provinces that today constitute Holland; but it is the dialects of the latter that gave rise to spoken Dutch. Reference has already been made to the declensional scheme of written Dutch, which resembles German, while spoken Dutch has discarded it, and achieved a grammatical structure somewhat similar to that of English. In vocabulary, the differences are even more glaring. The formal expressions of the written tongue are jokingly referred to as *stadhuiswoorden*, "city hall words", or what Americans would describe as "three-dollar words".

yes	*ja, jawel*	*ja*
no	*neen*	*nee*
how are you?	*hoe gaut het met U?*	*hoe gaat 't ermee?*
very well	*zeer wel*	*heel goed*
how much is it?	*wat is de prijs?*	*wat kost 't?*
why?	*warom, weshalve?*	*waarom?*
when?	*wanneer?*	*wanneer?*
where?	*waar?*	*waar?*
because	*daar*	*omdat*
today	*heden*	*vandaag*
tomorrow	*morgen*	*morgen* (silent *-n*)
yesterday	*gisteren*	*gisteren* (silent *-n*)
now	*thans*	*nu, nou*
on the right	*aan de rechterzijde*	*aan de rechterkant*
to the right	*naar rechts*	*rechtsaf*
on the left	*aan de linkerzijde*	*aan de linkerkant*
to the left	*naar links*	*linksaf*
straight ahead	*rechtuit*	*rechtuit*
what time is it?	*hoe laat is het?*	*hoe laat is 't?*
it is now - o'clock	*het is thans - uur*	*'t is nu - uur*
I'm hungry	*ik heb honger*	*'k heb honger*
I'm thirsty	*ik heb dorst*	*'k heb dorst*
I'm cold	*ik ben koud*	*'k heb 't koud*
I'm warm	*ik ben warm*	*'k heb 't warm*
I'm ill	*ik ben ziek (ongesteld)*	*'k ben ziek*
what's your name?	*hoe is Uw naam?*	*hoe heet U?*
my name is -	*mijn naam is -*	*'k heet -*
do you speak - ?	*spreekt U - ?*	*spreekt U - ?*
certainly	*welzeker, zeker*	*zeker, en of!* (and how!)
give me	*geef mij*	*geef me*
let me see	*toon mij*	*laat me - zien*
tell me	*zeg mij*	*vertel me*
do you understand?	*verstaat U?*	*begrijpt U?*
I don't understand	*ik versta (het) niet*	*ik begrijp 't niet*
do you know?	*weet U?*	*weet U?*
I don't know (it)	*ik weet (het) niet*	*'k weet ('t) niet*
very little	*zeer gering*	*heel weinig*
excuse me	*verschoon mij*	*pardon, neem me niet kwalijk*
don't mention it	*het beteekent niets*	*'t beteekent niets*
what do you want?	*wat is er van Uw dienst?, wat wenscht U?*	*wat wilt U?, wat blieft U?*

it's fine weather	het is schoon weder	lekker weertje
never mind	het komt er niet op aan	't komt er niet op aan
I'm sorry	ik betreur het	't spijt me
I'm glad	het verheugt mij	'k ben blij
too bad!	ocharme!	o jee!, 't is me toch wat!, 't is zonde!
what's the matter?	wat is er aan de hand?	wat scheelt eraan?
already	reeds	al
home	woning	huis (n)
wheel	rad (n)	wiel (n)
kiss	kus	zoen
brother	broeder	broer
to turn	wenden	draaien
face	gelaat (n)	gezicht (n)
to think	meenen	denken
you	gij	jij, je
to marry	huwen	trouwen
food	spijs	eten (n)
gladly	gaarne	graag
to die	sterven, overlijden	doodgaan
beautiful	schoon[35]	mooi
but	doch	maar
to throw	werpen	gooien
entirely	geheel	heelemaal
to get	ontvangen	krijgen
quickly	snel, vlug	gauw
soon	weldra	gauw
to try	pogen	probeeren
to leave	vertrekken	weggaan
to send	zenden	sturen
profession	beroep (n)	vak (n)
to show	toonen	laten zien
often	vaak	dikwijls
to weep	weenen	huilen
bicycle	rijwiel (n)	fiets

ADDITIONAL WORDS AND PHRASES

waiter!, *aannemen!*

there's a wind blowing, *'t waait*

it's raining, *het regent*

a cup of coffee, *'n kop (kopje) koffie*

come in!, *binnen!*

35. In spoken Dutch, this word means "clean".

knife, *mes* (n.)

spoon, *lepel*

fork, *vork*

napkin, *servet* (n.)

dish, *bord* (n.)

meat, *vleesch* (n.)

bread, *brood* (n.)

wine, *wijn*

milk, *melk*

breakfast, *ontbijt* (n.)

dinner, *middagmaal,*
    middageten (n.)

supper, *avondmaal,*
    avondeten (n.)

woman, *vrouw*

child, *kind* (n.)

girl, *meisje* (n.)

boy, *jongen*

family, *gezin* (n.)

war, *oorlog*

peace, *vrede*

army, *leger* (n.)

navy, *vloot*

rifle, *geweer* (n.)

soldier, *soldaat*

enemy, *vijand*

eye, *oog* (n.)

elbow, *elleboog*

mouth, *mond*

ear, *oor* (n.)

leg, *been* (n.)

head, *hoofd* (n.)

arm, *arm*

finger, *vinger*

tooth, *tand, kies*

neck, *hals*

hat, *hoed*

coat, *jas*

handkerchief, *zakdoek*

shoe, *schoen*

brush, *borstel*

sign, *teeken* (n.)

place, *plaats*

interpreter, *tolk*

language, *taal*

trouble, *last*

bath, *bad* (n.)

match, *lucifer*

fire, *vuur* (n.)

paper, *papier* (n.)

tree, *boom*

cow, *koe*

horse, *paard* (n.)

animal, *dier, beest* (n.)

city, *stad*

village, *dorp* (n.)

street, *straat*

way, *weg*

train, *trein*

newspaper, *krant*

shop, store, *winkel*

office, *kantoor* (n.)

money, *geld* (n.)

guilder, *gulden*

1/4 guilder, *kwartje* (n.)

1/10 guilder, *dubbeltje* (n.)

1/20 guilder, *stuiver*

work, *werk* (n.)

church, *kerk*

country, *land* (n.)

people, nation, *volk* (n.)

police, *politie*

box, *doos*
bag, *zak*
pack, parcel, *pak* (n.)
to live, *leven*
to work, *werken*
to put, *zetten*
to make, *maken*
to want, *willen*
to write, *schrijven* (*ee-e*)
to take, *nemen* (*a-o*)
to look, *kijken* (*ee-e*)
to stand, *staan* (*stond, gestaan*)
to go, *gaan* (*ging, gegaan*)
to come, *komen* (*kwam, gekomen*)
to say, *zeggen* (*zei, gezegd*)
to do, *doen* (*deed, gedaan*)
to see, *zien* (*zag, gezien*)
to eat, *eten* (*at, gegeten*)
to buy, *koopen* (*kocht, gekocht*)
to keep, *houden* (*hield, gehouden*)
to ask, *vragen* (*vroeg, gevraagd*)
nice, *aardig, leuk*
awful, *erg*
strong, *sterk*
tired, *moe*
true, *waar, echt*
wet, *nat*
dry, *droog*
empty, *leeg*
alone, *alleen*
other, *ander*
dear, *lief*
high, *hoog*

low, *laag*
dark, *donker*
dirty, *vuil*
difficult, *moeilijk*
dead, *dood*
enough, *genoeg*
bad, *slecht*
young, *jong*
old, *oud*
small, *klein*
white, *wit*
green, *groen*
red, *rood*
yellow, *geel*
black, *zwart*
blue, *blauw*
brown, *bruin*
still, *nog*
always, *altijd*
again, *weer*
very, *erg*
so, *zoo*
also, *ook*
or, *of*
for, *want*
if, *als*
without, *zonder*
with, near, *met, bij*
through, *door*
to, towards, *naar*
at, *aan*
for, before, *voor*
on, *op*
against, *tegen*
of, from, *van*
after, *na*

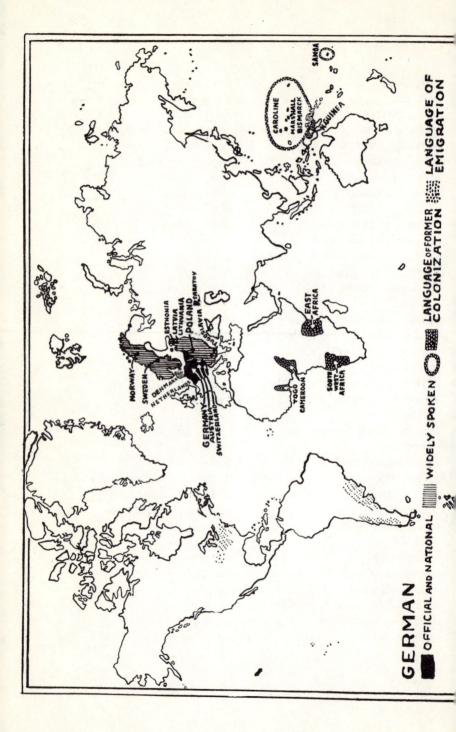

GERMAN

OFFICIAL AND NATIONAL ▓ WIDELY SPOKEN ⬭ LANGUAGE OF FORMER ▨ LANGUAGE OF COLONIZATION ░ EMIGRATION

NORWAY
SWEDEN
DENMARK
NETHERLANDS
GERMANY
AUSTRIA
SWITZERLAND

ESTHONIA
LATVIA
LITHUANIA
POLAND
SLAVIA
BESSARABIA

TOGO
CAMEROON
EAST AFRICA
SOUTH WEST AFRICA

CAROLINE
MARSHALL
BISMARCK
NEW GUINEA
SAMOA

CHAPTER IV

GERMAN

SPEAKERS AND LOCATION

(All population figures are approximate)

Europe — Germany (including Austria and Sudeten areas) — 80,000,000; Switzerland — 3,000,000; scattered groups in Luxembourg, Belgium (Eupen and Malmedy), France (Alsace-Lorraine), Italy (Alto Adige, Asiago), Polish Corridor, Danzig, Russia (Saratov region and Ukraine), Roumania (Transylvania), Hungary, Yugoslavia — perhaps a total of 5,000,000.

   Used widely as a secondary language in the Netherlands, Denmark, Norway, Sweden, Finland, Estonia, Latvia, Lithuania, Poland, Czechoslovakia, Hungary, Yugoslavia.

   As a cultural and commercial language, widely spoken and understood throughout Europe.

Africa — Language of former colonization in Togoland, Cameroon, Southwest Africa, Tanganyika.

Oceania — Language of former colonization in Bismarck, Caroline, Marianas, Marshall, Solomon Islands, Palau, New Guinea, Samoa.

Western Hemisphere — Spoken by several millions of German immigrants and their descendants in North and South America, particularly the U. S. A., Brazil (São Paulo, Rio Grande do Sul), Argentina, Chile.

   As a cultural language, spoken and understood by some millions of people in North and South America.

ALPHABET AND SCRIPT

𝔄, 𝔅, ℭ, 𝔇, 𝔈, 𝔉, 𝔊, ℌ, ℑ, 𝔍, 𝔎, 𝔏, 𝔐, 𝔑, 𝔒, 𝔓, 𝔔, ℜ, 𝔖, 𝔗, 𝔘, 𝔙, 𝔚, 𝔛, 𝔜, 𝔷, 𝔄, 𝔒, ü.

a, b, c, d, e, f, g, h, i, j, k, l, m, n, o, p, q, r, ſ (s), t, u, v, w, x, y, z, ä, ö, ü, ß, ch, ck, tz.

a, b, c, d, e, f, g, h, i, j, k, l, m, n, o, p, q, r, s, t, u, v, w, x, y, z, ä, ö, ü, ss (sz), ch, ck, tz.

a			n
b			o
c			p
d			q
e			r
f			s
g			t
h			u
i			v
j			w
k			x
l			y
m			z

[handwritten script specimens: Ä Ä ä ü. Ö Ö ö ö. Ü ü. / Tz = Tz. ſt = ſt, ſs ſs ſs = ſz. ſch. ſch. ſch.]

Notes on ſ, s, ſſ, ß, ß.

s is used at the end of a word or stem-syllable; ſ in all other cases: **es, was, auslachen, hinaus gehen**; but **bist, ſehen, Unſinn, Roſe, ſtehen**.

ß is regularly used for ss; it is however, changed to ſſ inside the word after a *short* vowel when an ending beginning with a vowel is added: **Schloß**, castle, pl. **Schlöſſer** (short ö); but **Fuß**, foot, pl. **Füße** (long ü); **ſtoßen**, to push (long o), but **laſſen**, to let (short a).

t and z are always joined together (ß): **jetzt**, now; **trotzdem**, although.

SOUNDS

Vowel sounds: usually short when followed by a double consonant: **Waſſer, Bett, Hand**; otherwise long, especially if doubled or followed by h: **Vater, Boot, wohl**.

Long	Short
a = *f*ather (**Vater**)	= *a*ha (**Waſſer**)
e = th*ey* (**zehn**)	= m*e*t (**Fenſter**)[1]
i = mach*i*ne (**ihnen**)	= p*i*n (**bin**)
o = b*o*re (**loben**)	= s*o*n (**voll**)
u = r*u*le (**gut**)	= p*u*t (**Mutter**)
ä = th*e*re (**wählen**)	= m*e*t (**Männer**)

ö = sound intermediate between German o and German e; like French eu

(**Höhle**)   (**öffnen**)

ü = sound intermediate between German u and German i; like French u

(**Hüte**)   (**Hütte**)

1. Final unstressed e = bac*o*n (**Ecke**).

äu, eu = t*oi*l (Häufer, treu)
ei = m*i*ne (ein)
ie = mach*i*ne (viel)

Consonant sounds: b, d, f, h, l, m, n, p, q, t, x, approximately as in English.

c: before a, o, u, or consonant, = k (Cafe, Creme);
before e, i, ä, ö = ts (Cicero, Cäſar).

ch: *after* a, o, u = Scots lo*ch* (Nacht, ſuchen); harsh guttural sound; *after* e, i, or consonant = sound intermediate between k and sh (nicht, manch); the nearest English equivalent is *h*uge.

g: when final, especially after e or i, pronounce like German ch as above; otherwise, like Eng. *go*.

j: = Eng. *y*et (ja).

r: guttural, as in French, or trilled, as in Italian.

ſ: at beginning of words, or between vowels = *z*eal (ſehen, Roſe); before t and p at beginning of syllable = Eng. *sh*ore, *s*ure (ſtehen, ſprechen); elsewhere, = Eng. *s*it (was).

ſch: = Eng. *sh*ore (Schiff).

ti before vowels, = Eng. *tsy* (Nation).

v: = Eng. f (Vogel).

w: = Eng. v (wir).

z: = Eng. ts in hear*ts* (Herz).

Sounds not appearing in native German words: all English vowel sounds outside of the above listed; *ch*air, *j*est, plea*s*ure, *th*in, *th*is, *w*ater, American r. German sounds not appearing in English: ö, ü, ach, ich, German r.

CAPITALIZATION, SYLLABIFICATION, ACCENTUATION, PUNCTUATION.

Use capitals for *all* nouns, proper or common (der Vater; das Bett); also for Sie (polite "you") Ihr (polite "your"). Do not use capitals for ich ("I"), or for adjectives of nationality, unless used as nouns (**ein Deutscher**, "a German"; **ein deutscher Knabe**, "a German boy").

Divide compound words according to their component parts (**hin-aus**, **Diens-tag**); otherwise, a single consonant sound between two vowels goes with the following vowel, not with the preceding (**Bü-cher, ei-nen**).

The accent regularly falls on the first syllable of the word, save in words having as a prefix **be-, emp- ent-, er-, ge-, miß-, ver-, zer-** (**anfangen, arbeiten, Buchstabe**; but **bekannt, Entwicklung, gehört, zerbrechen**).

Use commas to set off subordinate clauses: **der Mann, der diesen Brief geschrieben hat, ist angekommen**, "the man who wrote this letter has arrived".

Use exclamation mark in imperative sentences and at the beginning of letters: **Kommen Sie her!**, "Come here"; **Lieber Karl!**, "Dear Charles,".

SAMPLE OF WRITTEN GERMAN; USE FOR PRACTICE READING.

Ja, es war wirklich so. Der General wußte es denn auch bereits seit zwei Tagen: es waren drei Fälle von Influenza unter den Soldaten ausgebrochen. Man hatte erst an Hitzschlag gedacht; die Leute waren in einem Manöver gewesen, die Sonne hatte heiß gebrannt, als schösse sie mit mörderischen Pfeilen. Aber nun schüttelten die Ärzte die Köpfe: wo hatten sich die Kerls nur die Krankheit geholt? Jedenfalls außerhalb des Lagers. Die strengsten Absperrungsmaßregeln wurden auf der Stelle durchgeführt. Urlaub gab's nicht mehr; kein Soldat durfte das Lager verlassen; die Posten wurden verdoppelt; keinem Fremden wurde es erlaubt, einen Soldaten zu besuchen. Auf diese Weise suchte man, die Verbreitung der Pest zu verhindern.

GRAMMATICAL SURVEY

1. *Nouns and Articles.*

German has three genders, masculine, feminine and neuter. Nouns denoting males are usually masculine, those denoting females feminine. Nouns which in English are neuter, however, may be masculine or feminine in German (der Löffel, "the spoon", masculine; die Gabel, "the fork", feminine; das Messer, "the knife", neuter). Nouns with the diminutive suffixes -chen and -lein must be neuter even if they indicate persons (das Mädchen, "the girl"; das Fräulein, "the miss", "the young lady", both neuter). Abstract nouns are usually feminine (die Liebe, "love"; die Freiheit, "freedom", both feminine). Learn nouns with their respective articles, der for masculines, die for feminines, das for neuters.

There are four cases in German, nominative, genitive, dative and accusative. The nominative and the accusative correspond, respectively, to the English subjective and objective; the genitive indicates possession and often translates the English "of", while the dative translates "to" with verbs of saying, giving, etc.[2]

Definite Article ("the")

	Masc. Sg.	Fem. Sg.	Neut. Sg.	Pl.
Nom.	der	die	das	die
Gen.	des	der	des	der
Dat.	dem	der	dem	den
Acc.	den	die	das	die

2. "To" indicating motion towards, however, is usually translated by a preposition (nach with the dative, auf with the accusative, etc.), while "to" meaning "in order to" is translated by um....zu: ich gehe nach Hause, in die Schule, auf das Land, "I am going home, to school, to the country"; ich bin gekommen, um den Brief zu schreiben, "I came to write the letter". Note also: meines Vaters Geld, "my father's money", or das Geld meines Vaters, "the money of my father"; ich gab dem Knaben (dat.) einen Pfennig (acc.), " I gave the boy a penny".

Indefinite Article ("a", "an")

	Masc.	Fem.	Neut.
Nom.	ein	eine	ein
Gen.	eines	einer	eines
Dat.	einem	einer	einem
Acc.	einen	eine	ein

Declension of Nouns.

In the genitive singular, most masculine and neuter nouns add -ß (-eß if monosyllabic; a few masculines ending in -e add -n), while feminine nouns remain unchanged: der Bruder, "the brother", des Bruders, "of the brother", "the brother's"; der Mann, "the man", des Mannes, "of the man", "the man's"; der Knabe, "the boy", des Knaben, "of the boy", "the boy's"; die Tochter, "the daughter"; der Tochter, "of the daughter"; die Frau, "the woman", der Frau, "of the woman".

The dative and accusative singular usually have the same form as the nominative:[3] dem Bruder, "to the brother", den Bruder, "the brother" (obj.); dem Mann(e), "to the man", den Mann, "the man" (obj.); der Tochter, "to the daughter", die Tochter, "the daughter".

Plural endings are: nothing or -e (with or without umlaut); -er (with umlaut if the vowel permits); -en (without umlaut). Nouns that have the first three plural endings take on an additional -n in the dative plural: Bruder, plural nom. die Brüder, gen. der Brüder, dat. den Brüdern, acc. die Brüder; Mann, pl. nom. die Männer, gen. der Männer, dat. den Männern, acc. die Männer; Tochter, plural nom. die Töchter, gen. der Töchter, dat. den Töchtern, acc. die Töchter; Bank, plural Bänke in nom., gen.

3. In nouns of one syllable, addition of -e is customary in the dative: dem Mann or dem Manne, "to the man". Nouns that add -n in the genitive do so also in the dative and accusative: dem Knaben, "to the boy"; den Knaben, "the boy" (obj.).

and acc., 𝕭änfen in dat.; 𝕭oot, plural 𝕭oote, with 𝕭ooten in the dat.; 𝕱rau, plural 𝕱rauen; 𝕭ett, plural 𝕭etten.[4]

2. *Adjectives and Adverbs.*

The adjective usually precedes the noun, and is declined. The ending of the adjective is determined by the presence or absence of a declensional ending on a *preceding* word, such as the definite or indefinite article, the demonstrative and possessive adjectives. If such preceding word has no ending, or if there is no preceding word, the adjective takes an ending in accordance with the following scheme:[5]

	Masc. Sg.	Fem. Sg.	Neut. Sg.	Plural (all genders)
Nom.	-er	-e	-es	-e
Gen.	-en	-er	-en	-er
Dat.	-em	-er	-em	-en
Acc.	-en	-e	-es	-e

𝕸anch guter 𝕸ann, "many a good man" (manch is indeclinable in this use, and has no ending; hence the adjective gut takes on the masc. sg. -er ending); welch gutes 𝕶ind! "what a good child!" (welch has no ending, hence gut takes on the neuter sg. -es); ein junges 𝕸ädchen, "a young girl" (ein, in the neuter singular form, has no ending; hence junges); die 𝕰ibe

4. Nouns given in the vocabulary appear, with their article, in the nominative singular form; the genitive singular ending, if any, follows; then the nominative plural ending, if any, with indication of umlaut where the latter occurs; from these key forms, the entire declension of the noun can be determined; thus der 𝕭ruder, -s, ¨—; this indicates -s in the genitive singular, no plural ending, save the universal -n in the dative plural, but umlaut throughout the plural; die 𝖀hr, —, -en; this indicates a single form throughout the singular, -en and no umlaut throughout the plural.

For *practical* purposes, don't be too terrified about making a mistake in an ending or gender; the chances are you will still be understood, and probably corrected; the Germans themselves occasionally make a slip of this kind.

5. This set of endings, characteristic of adjectives and most pronouns, is worth memorizing.

guter Männer, "the oaths of good men" (there is no article or pronoun preceding guter, which therefore takes the -er genitive plural ending).

If the preceding word has a declensional ending, the ending of the adjective is -e in the nominative singular masculine, feminine and neuter, and in the accusative singular feminine and neuter, -en in all other cases: der gute Mann, "the good man" (der has characteristic masc. sg. nom. ending, hence the weak -e instead of the strong -er is used for gut); jedes deutsche Mädchen, "every German girl" (-es on jedes; therefore only -e for the adjective); jenes gute Kind, "that good child"; meines guten Bruders, "of my good brother" (-es on the possessive, therefore -en on the adjective); einer schönen Frau, "of" or "to a beautiful woman" (-er of article causes the adjective to take weak -en instead of strong -er ending); die Worte der tapferen Soldaten, "the words of the brave soldiers" (der causes "brave" to take on -en; if the expression were "the words of brave soldiers", der would disappear, and tapferen would change to tapferer). Remember again that for practical purposes an error of ending is usually inconsequential.

The predicate adjective is invariable, and takes no ending: die Männer sind gut, "the men are good"; die Mädchen sind schön, "the girls are pretty".

The invariable adjective without any ending is generally used as an adverb: er ist gut, "he is good"; er lernt gut, "he learns well".

The comparative and superlative are formed by adding -er (-r) and -est (-st), respectively, usually with umlaut: alt, "old", älter, "older", ältest, "oldest"; kurz, "short"; kürzer, "shorter"; kürzest, "shortest"; frei, "free", freier, "freer", freiest, "freest". Comparative and superlative adjectives are regularly declined: ein kürzeres Buch, "a shorter book"; des freiesten Staates, "of the freest state".[6]

6. When used after the verb "to be", without a clause or phrase following, the superlative is preceded by am instead of the definite article, and takes the ending -en: dieses Haus ist am höchsten, "this

3. *Numerals.*

a) Cardinal (indeclinable outside of ein (for which see p. 129), and Million)

1 — ein (eins when not followed by noun)		13 — dreizehn	
2 — zwei		14 — vierzehn	
3 — drei		15 — fünfzehn	
4 — vier		16 — sechzehn	
5 — fünf		17 — siebzehn	
6 — sechs		18 — achtzehn	
7 — sieben		19 — neunzehn	
8 — acht		20 — zwanzig	
9 — neun		21 — einundzwanzig	
10 — zehn		22 — zweiundzwanzig	
11 — elf		30 — dreißig	
12 — zwölf		40 — vierzig	
		50 — fünfzig	

60 — sechzig
70 — siebzig
80 — achtzig
90 — neunzig
100 — hundert
200 — zweihundert
1000 — tausend
5000 — fünftausend
1,000,000 — eine Million
3,000,000 — drei Millionen

---

house is the highest"; but dieses Haus ist das höchste in der Stadt, "this house is the highest in the city".
Note: ebenso....wie, "as....as"; als, "than"; diese Arbeit ist ebenso schwer wie die deinige, "this work is as hard as yours"; meine Arbeit ist schwerer als die deinige, "my work is harder than yours".

b) Ordinal (add -te to cardinal up to 20th, save for exceptions below; -ſte from 20th on; ordinal numerals are declined like adjectives).

1st — ber erſte	8th — ber adjte
2nd — ber zweite	10th — ber zehnte
3rd — ber britte	12th — ber zwölfte
4th — ber vierte	20th — ber zwanzigſte
5th — ber fünfte	100th — ber hunberſte

c) Others.

bie Hälfte (noun), halb (adjective), "half": bie Hälfte bes Budjes, "half of the book"; eine halbe Seite, "half a page"
einmal, "once"; zweimal, "twice"; breimal, "three times"; hunbertmal, "a hundred times"; bas erſte Mal, "the first time"; zuweilen, "sometimes"; anberthalb, "one and a half"; breieinhalb, "three and a half".

ein Glas Waſſer, "a glass *of* water"; eine Taſſe Kaffee, "a cup *of* coffee"; ſieben Pfunb Fleiſch, "seven pounds of meat"; zwei Dutzenb Eier, "two dozen eggs"; brei Fuß hoch, "three feet high"; voll Kartoffeln, "full of potatoes".

4. *Pronouns.*

a) Personal.

Singular

Nom. idj, "I"; bu, "you"[7]; er, "he"[8]; ſie, "she"[8]; es, "it"[8]

Dat.[9] mir, "to me"; bir, "to you"; ihm, "to him"; ihr, "to her"; ihm, "to it"

Acc. midj, "me"; bidj, "you"; ihn, "him"; ſie, "her"; es, "it"

7. In polite address, singular or plural, use Sie (nom. and acc.), Ihnen (dat.), with the *third person plural* of the verb: bu biſt gut, "you are good", familiar singular; ihr ſeib gut, "you are good", familiar plural; Sie ſinb gut, "you are good", polite singular or plural.
8. The German pronoun must be of the same gender as the noun it stands for: idj habe ben Fiſch gegeſſen; er iſt gut, "I have eaten the fish; it (lit. "he"; Fiſch is masculine in German) is good.
9. The genitive is omitted, as it is usually supplied by the possessive adjective-pronoun.

Plural

Nom. wir, "we"; ihr, "you"[7]; fie, "they" (all genders)
Dat. uns, "to us"; euch, "to you"; ihnen, "to them"
Acc. uns, "us"; euch, "you"; fie, "them"

An object pronoun, dative or accusative, follows the verb; in compound tenses, it is placed immediately after the auxiliary; if two object pronouns are used together, the accusative comes before the dative: er zeigt es, "he shows it"; er hat es mir nicht gezeigt, "he did not show it to me".

If the pronoun in English is the object of a preposition and refers to things (not to persons), omit it altogether in German and use instead da(r) combined with the preposition: darauf, "on it"; daraus, "out of it"; damit, "with it"; but mit ihm, "with him".

b) Possessive.

mein,	"my", "mine"	unfer,	"our", "ours"
dein,	"your", "yours"	euer,	"your", "yours"
fein,	"his", "its"	ihr,	"their", "theirs"
ihr,	"her", "hers"	Ihr,	"your", "yours" (polite, singular or plural)

When used as adjectives before the noun, these possessives are declined like ein (p. 129): ich habe meinen Hut nicht, "I haven't my hat"; ich habe es meinem Vater gegeben, "I gave it to my father".

When used as pronouns, they usually take the definite article and are declined like adjectives in a "weak" position (p. 131); that is to say, they take -en throughout, save in the nominative singular of the three genders and in the accusative feminine and neuter, where the ending is -e. They may also insert -ig- before these endings: diese Bücher und die deinen (or die deinigen) "these books and yours"; hier ist mein Hut, aber den Ihren (or den Ihrigen) kann ich nicht finden, "here's my hat, but I can't find yours".

c) Demonstrative.

biefer, "this", "these"; jener, "that", "those". They are declined like the definite article ber (p. 128), save that the neuter singular nominative and accusative has -es instead of -as (biefes, jenes).

berfelbe, "the same", berjenige, "the one", are declined as though article and adjective were separate: bemfelben Manne, "to the same man"; biejenigen auf bem Tifche, "the ones on the table". "The one" may also be expressed by ber, bie, bas, but in this meaning the genitive forms are beffen (masc. and neut. sg.), beren (fem. sg.), berer (plural), and the dative plural is benen. ber or welcher, "who", "which", "that".

d) Relative.

The relative ber is declined like the definite article, but with a genitive beffen for masc. and neut. sg., and beren for fem. sg. and all plurals, and a dat. plural benen. Welcher is declined like the definite article, but with -es in neuter nom. and acc. (welches): bas Haus, bas (or welches) ich gekauft habe, "the house I bought"; bie Frau, bie (or welche) ich fah, "the woman I saw"; ber Knabe, beffen Hut ich fand, "the boy whose hat I found"; ber Held, ben (or welchen) ich kenne, "the hero whom I know". Note that the relative pronoun must be used in German, even where it is understood in English.

was, "what", "that" (the latter meaning only after neuter adjectives and pronouns): ich fah, was bu getan haft, "I saw what you did"; bas Befte, was ich habe, "the best I have". It is also used after etwas (something), alles (everything), nichts (nothing): alles, was bu haft, "all that you have".

When the English relative pronoun follows a preposition and refers to objects (not to persons), it is customary to omit the relative and use instead wo(r), combining it with the preposition: bas Haus, worin ich wohne, "the house in which I live" (bas Haus, in bem ich wohne is permissible).

e) Interrogative.

wer (gen. weffen, dat. wem, acc. wen), "who?", "whose?", "whom?"; wer hat es getan?, "who did it?"; wem haft bu meinen

Hut gegeben?, "to whom did you give my hat?; wen haſt du geſehen?, "whom did you see?"; weſſen Hut iſt das?, "whose hat is that?"

was, "what": was haſt du geſehen? "what did you see?" (as object of preposition, referring to things, use wo(r): womit haſt du es getan?, "with what did you do it?")

welcher (declined like the relative welcher), "which?": welches Buch meinen Sie?, "which book do you mean?"

was für ein, "what kind of?": was für einen Hut trug er? "what kind of a hat was he wearing?" (omit ein in the plural: was für Waffen ſind das? "what kind of weapons are those?"

5. *Verbs.*

German verbs fall into two categories, "weak" and "strong". The weak verbs form their past tense by the addition of endings and effect no change in the root vowel, while the strong generally add no ending in the first and third persons singular, and regularly change the vowel of the root. In the past participle, weak verbs add -(e)t, strong verbs -en. Some strong verbs also effect a change in the root vowel of the present tense, in the second and third persons singular. Verbs appearing in the vocabulary are given only in the infinitive form if weak (e. g. lieben); if strong, the third person singular of the present is given, if a root-vowel change appears in the second and third singular (remember that whatever root-vowel change appears in the third singular appears also in the second singular); also the past, first person singular, and the past participle (e. g. ſprechen, ſpricht, ſprach, geſprochen); if no root-vowel change occurs in the present, only the infinitive, past and past participle are given (e. g. bringen, brachte, gebracht; finden, fand, gefunden).

The infinitive regularly ends in -en: lieben, "to love"; ſehen, "to see"; ſprechen, "to speak".

The present participle regularly ends in -end: liebend, "loving"; gehend, "going". It is most frequently used as an adjective, and agrees with the noun it modifies: ein durch die Stadt flieſſender Fluſʒ, "a river flowing through the city". It is *never* used with the verb "to be", as in Eng. "I am going", "I was going"; translate such expressions by the ordinary present or past: idⱼ geⱼe, idⱼ ging. The Eng. "do" of questions is likewise omitted: ſeⱼe idⱼ?, "do I see?"

1. Present Indicative (meaning: I love, am loving, do love)

Weak: lieben, "to love"		Strong: ſeⱼen, "to see"	
idⱼ lieb-e,	I love	idⱼ ſeⱼ-e,	I see
du lieb-ſt,[10]	you love (fam. sg.)	du ſieⱼ-ſt,	you see
er lieb-t,[10]	he loves	er ſieⱼ-t,	he sees
wir lieb-en,	we love	wir ſeⱼ-en,	we see
iⱼr lieb-t,[10]	you love (fam. pl.)	iⱼr ſeⱼ-t,	you see
ſie lieb-en,	they love	ſie ſeⱼ-en,	they see
Sie lieb-en,	you love (pol. sg. or pl.)	Sie ſeⱼ-en,	you see (pol. sg. or pl.).

Irregular:[11] ſein, "to be"		ⱼaben, "to have"	
idⱼ bin,	I am	idⱼ ⱼabe,	I have
du biſt,	you are (fam. sg.)	du ⱼaſt,	you have (fam. sg.)
er iſt,	he is	er ⱼat,	he has
wir ſind,	we are	wir ⱼaben,	we have
iⱼr ſeid,	you are (fam. pl.)	iⱼr ⱼabt,	you have (fam. pl.)
ſie ſind,	they are	ſie ⱼaben,	they have

10. A few verbs the stem of which ends in a cluster of consonants require the insertion of -e- before the -ſt of the second singular and the -t of the third singular and second plural: warten, du warteſt, er wartet, iⱼr wartet.

11. The so-called modal auxiliaries (for the use of which see p. 142) dürfen, "may", "be permitted"; können, "can", "be able"; mögen, "may", "like to"; müſſen, "must", "have to"; ſollen, "shall", "to be to"; wollen, "will", "want to" are conjugated like regular weak verbs in the plural of the present indicative and throughout the past; in the singular of the present they take the following forms: dürfen - darf, darfſt, darf; können - kann, kannſt, kann; mögen - mag, magſt, mag; müſſen - muß, mußt, muß; ſollen - ſoll, ſollſt, ſoll; wollen - will, willſt, will.

Werden, "to become", used as an auxiliary in the formation of the future and of the passive, has werde, wirſt, wird, with a past wurde.

2. Past Indicative[12] (meaning: I was seeing, used to see)

Weak: lieben

ich lieb-te,	I used to love
du lieb-teſt,	you used to love
er lieb-te,	he used to love
wir lieb-ten,	we used to love
ihr lieb-tet,	you used to love
ſie lieb-ten,	they used to love
Sie lieb-ten,	you used to love (polite)

Strong, ſehen

ich ſah,	I was seeing, used to see
du ſahſt,	you were seeing
er ſah,	he was seeing
wir ſahen,	we were seeing
ihr ſaht,	you were seeing
ſie ſahen,	they were seeing
Sie ſahen,	you were seeing (pol.)

Irregular: ſein   haben

ich war,	I was, used to be	ich hatte,	I had, used to have
du warſt,	you were (fam. sg.)	du hatteſt,	you had
er war,	he was	er hatte,	he had
wir waren,	we were	wir hatten,	we had
ihr wart,	you were (fam. pl.)	ihr hattet,	you had
ſie waren,	they were	ſie hatten,	they had

3. Future (meaning: I shall speak) and Conditional (meaning: I should speak)

The future is formed by combining the present of werden,
"to become", with the infinitive; the conditional by the past

12. The German past (ich liebte, ich ſah) generally indicates the
sort of continued or repeated past action that English normally indicates
by using "used to" or "was" with the present participle. The normal
English past ("I loved", "I saw") is best translated by the German
present perfect, which translates also the English present perfect:
ich habe geliebt, "I loved" or "I have loved"; ich habe geſehen, "I
saw" or "I have seen".

subjunctive of werden with the infinitive. The infinitive stands at the end of the clause: id) werde diefeß Bud) nid)t lefen, "I shall not read this book"; id) würde Deutfd) fpred)en, wenn eß leid)ter wäre, "I should speak German if it were easier".

Future

id) werde fpred)en,	I shall speak
bu wirft fpred)en,	you will speak
er wird fpred)en,	he will speak
wir werden fpred)en,	we shall speak
ibr werdet fpred)en,	you will speak
fie werden fpred)en,	they will speak

Conditional

id) würde fpred)en,	I should speak
bu würdeft fpred)en,	you would speak
er würde fpred)en,	he would speak
wir würden fpred)en,	we should speak
ibr würdet fpred)en,	you would speak
fie würden fpred)en,	they would speak

4. Compound Tenses (meaning: I have, had, shall have, should have spoken)

These are formed, as in English, by using the auxiliary haben ("to have") with the past participle; the latter stands at the end of the clause or sentence: id) habe deinen Bruder nid)t gefeben, "I didn't see your brother". Many intransitive verbs indicating motion (geben, "to go", fommen, "to come", etc.) and change of state (fterben, "to die", werden, "to become"), also fein, "to be" and bleiben, "to remain", use fein, ("to be") as an auxiliary instead of haben: id) bin gegangen, "I went"; er war gefommen, "he had come"; fie ift geworden, "she has become"; find Sie gewefen?, "have you been?"; such verbs are indicated in the vocabulary thus: fommen, fam, gefommen (fein).

The past participle ends in -(e)t in the case of weak verbs, -en in the case of strong verbs; with ge- prefixed in both cases unless the accent fails to fall on the initial syllable (see page 127): lieben, p. p. geliebt; haben, p. p. gehabt; feben, p. p.

gefeßen; fein, p. p. gewefen. The past participle used with an auxiliary is invariable, but if it is used as an adjective, it agrees with its noun: ein gut gefdriebenes Buch, "a well written book".
Present Perfect: idf habe geliebt, "I have loved", "I loved"; idf habe gefeßen, "I have seen", "I saw"; idf bin gegangen, "I have gone", "I went"; idf bin gewefen, "I have been", "I was".
Past Perfect: idf hatte gefprochen, "I had spoken"; idf hatte gelobt, "I had praised"; idf war gewefen, "I had been"; idf war gegangen, "I had gone".
Future Perfect: idf werde geliebt haben, "I shall have loved"; idf werde gewefen fein, "I shall have been".
Perfect Conditional: idf würde gefeßen haben, "I should have seen"; idf würde gegangen fein, "I should have gone".

5. Imperative (meaning: see!)

The second singular (familiar singular) normally is the same as the second singular of the present with the final -ft removed:[13] höre! or hör! (from hören), "listen!"; fieß!, "see!" (second singular present of feßen is fießft).

The second plural (familiar plural), and the polite form with Sie have the same form as the corresponding persons in the present: liebt!, lieben Sie!, "love!", feßt!, feßen Sie!, "see!"

"Let us" is translated by laß (fam. sg.), laßt (fam. pl.) or laffen Sie, followed by uns and the infinitive: laß uns gehen, "let us go"; laffen Sie uns fprechen, "let us speak".

6. Reflexive verbs.

The reflexive is more extensively used in German than in English.[14] The reflexive pronouns are the same as the

13. Exceptional is fei!, "be!", from fein (2nd sg. present bift).
14. E. g., fidf freuen, "to rejoice": idf freue midf, du freuft didf, er freut fidf, etc. The reflexive is also generally used in expressions referring to parts of the body, which take the definite article instead of the possessive, and a dative reflexive pronoun with the verb; idf habe mir das Bein gebrochen, "I broke my leg" (lit. "I broke *the* leg *to* myself").

accusative pronouns (mich, dich, uns, euch), save in the third
person, where sich is used for both numbers and all genders.
The dative pronoun is occasionally called for by the sense of
the expression (sich denken, "to imagine"; literally, "to think to
oneself"), and in this case the dative pronouns are used (mir,
dir, uns, euch), but sich is still used in the third person.

7. Passive.

The passive voice is formed by using werden ("to become") with the past participle;[15] ich werde geliebt, "I am
loved"; ich wurde geliebt, "I was loved"; ich werde geliebt werden,
"I shall be loved"; ich bin geliebt worden,[16] "I have been loved";
ich war geliebt worden, "I had been loved"; ich werde geliebt
worden sein, "I shall have been loved".

"By" is normally translated in the passive by von with the
dative: ich werde von meiner Mutter geliebt, "I am loved by
my mother".

Man ("one", "somebody") with the active often replaces
the passive when the doer of the action is not expressed: man
fragte dich, you were asked"; hier spricht man Deutsch, "German is
spoken here".

8. Subjunctive.

The German subjunctive has six tenses, one corresponding
to each tense of the indicative. Its forms frequently coincide
with those of the indicative; in the present tense and past tense
the endings are normally -e, -est, -e, -en, -et, -en, and in the past
tense of strong verbs there is a tendency to take umlaut wherever possible (Pres. Subj. of sehen: seh-e, -est, -e, -en, -et, -en;
Past Subj. säh-e -est, -e, -en, -et, -en). The subjunctive is often

15. Distinguish carefully between the two uses of werden as an
auxiliary: with the *infinitive* to form the future (ich werde sehen, "I
shall see"), and with the *past participle* to form the passive (ich werde
gesehen, "I am seen"). In the future passive, both uses appear (ich
werde gesehen werden, "I shall be seen").

16. The normal past participle of werden is geworden, but the form
worden is used instead in the formation of the passive.

used in subordinate clauses, especially after verbs of saying, thinking, asking, and the like: er glaubte, daß ich krank sei, "he thought I was ill"; er sagte, daß ich kein Geld hätte, "he said I had no money". Using the indicative instead of the subjunctive form is not an unforgivable crime.[17]

9. Modal Auxiliaries.

See note 11 for the conjugation of these verbs. In their compound tenses, these verbs use a form which resembles the infinitive instead of the past participle: ich werde sprechen dürfen (instead of gedurft), "I shall be allowed to speak"; ich habe schreiben können (instead of gekonnt), "I have been able to write".

In translating the English "will", wollen normally indicates willingness, werden simple futurity: er wird morgen schreiben, "he will write tomorrow"; but willst du für mich arbeiten? "will you work for me?"; wollen wir jetzt nach Hause gehen?, "shall we go home now?"

Mögen, especially with gern, has the meaning of "to be glad to, happy to": ich mag gern mit Ihnen gehen, "I'll gladly go with you".

10. Prefixes.

Verbs compounded with the prefixes be-, emp-, ent-, er-, ge-, miß-, ver-, zer-, (the same ones that do not take the accent; see p. 127) normally do not take ge- before the past participle: verstehen, "to understand", past participle verstanden, "understood"; erzählen, "to tell", p. p. erzählt, "told".

Verbs compounded with all other prefixes separate the prefix from the verb in the simple tenses, and place it at the end of the clause; anfangen, "to begin": present, ich fange an,

17. Note that the würde used to form the conditional (ich würde sehen, "I should see") is the past subjunctive of werden.
The present subjunctive of sein is irregular: sei, seiest, sei, seien seiet, seien. The past subjunctive is regular: wäre. Haben has hab and hätte, both regular.

"I begin"; past, ich fing an, "I began"; ich fange heute diese Arbeit an, "I am beginning this work today".

In the past participle, these verbs insert -ge- between the prefix and the verb (angefangen, "begun"), while if the infinitive is used in a construction requiring zu, the latter is also inserted between the prefix and the verb: er wünscht heute anzufangen, "he wishes to begin today".

11. Word Order.

If the subject does not begin the sentence, the subject and verb are usually inverted (save after aber, und, and relative pronouns): jetzt bin ich fertig, "now I am ready"; einen guten Hut suche ich, "I'm looking for a *good* hat".

In dependent clauses, the verb usually comes at the end of the clause: ich weiß nicht, wo Sie Ihren Hut gekauft haben, "I don't know where you bought your hat".

If the dependent clause precedes the main clause, both the above rules normally apply: als ich ihn sah, ging er nach Hause, "when I saw him, he was going home".

VOCABULARY

Nouns are given with their respective article (indicating gender) in their nominative singular form, followed by the genitive ending (if any), followed by the plural ending (if any), with indication of umlaut change where this occurs.

Verbs are given in the infinitive form alone, if they are "weak"; thus, to love, lieben, indicates a past liebte and a past participle geliebt. If the verb is "strong", the third person singular of the present indicative appears (indicating that the same change takes place in the second singular), provided there is a change of root vowel in those two forms; the past and past participle are then given; if the verb is conjugated with sein, the latter appears in parentheses at the close; thus, to fall, fallen, fällt, fiel, gefallen (sein).

1. *World, Elements, Nature, Weather, Time.*

world, die Welt, -, -en
earth, die Erde, -
air, die Luft, -, ˙˙-e
water, das Wasser, -s, -
fire, das Feuer, -s, -

light, das Licht, -es, -er
sea, das Meer, -es, -e
sun, die Sonne, -, -n
moon, der Mond, -es, -e
star, der Stern, -es, -e

sky, heaven, der Himmel, -s, -
wind, der Wind, -es, -e
weather, das Wetter, -s, -
snow, der Schnee, -s
to snow, schneien
rain, der Regen, -s, -
to rain, regnen
cloud, die Wolke, -, -n
cloudy, bewölkt
fog, der Nebel, -s, -
ice, das Eis, -es
mud, der Schlamm, -es
time, die Zeit, -, -en
year, das Jahr, -es, -e
month, der Monat, -s, -e
week, die Woche, -, -n
day, der Tag, -es, -e
hour, die Stunde, -, -n
minute, die Minute, -, -n
morning, der Morgen, -s, -
noon, der Mittag, -es, -e
afternoon, der Nachmittag, -es, -e
evening, der Abend, -s, -e
night, die Nacht, -, ̈-e
midnight, die Mitternacht, -, ̈-e
Sunday, der Sonntag
Monday, der Montag

Tuesday, der Dienstag
Wednesday, der Mittwoch
Thursday, der Donnerstag
Friday, der Freitag
Saturday, der Samstag,
   der Sonnabend
January, der Januar, -s
February, der Februar, -s
March, der März, -es
April, der April, -s
May, der Mai, -es
June, der Juni, -s
July, der Juli, -s
August, der August, -s
September, der September, -s
October, der Oktober, -s
November, der November, -s
December, der Dezember, -s
Spring, der Frühling, -s, -e
Summer, der Sommer, -s, -
Fall, der Herbst, -es, -e
Winter, der Winter, -s, -
North, der Norden, -s
South, der Süden, -s
East, der Osten, -s
West, der Westen, -s

"It is warm", "it is cold", etc. are literally translated: es ist warm, es ist kalt.

(On) Monday we went home, (am) Montag gingen wir nach Hause; (on) the first of January, 1943, den (or am) ersten Januar neunzehnhundertdreiundvierzig.

The genitive form of days of the week, ending in -s, indicates customary action: Montags kommt er hierher, he comes here Mondays.

2. *Family, Friendship, Love.*

family, die Familie, -, -n
husband, der Gatte, -n, -n; der
  Mann, -es, ̈-er
wife, die Gattin, -, -nen; die Frau,
  -, -en
parents, die Eltern
father, der Vater, -s, ̈-

mother, die Mutter, -, ̈-
son, der Sohn, -es, ̈-e
daughter, die Tochter, -, ̈-
brother, der Bruder, -s, ̈-
sister, die Schwester, -, -n
uncle, der Onkel, -s, -
aunt, die Tante, -, -n

nephew, der Neffe, -n, -n
niece, die Nichte, -, -n
cousin, der Vetter, -s, -n; die
    Cousine, -, -n
grandfather, der Großvater, -s, ··-
grandmother, die Großmutter, -, ··-
grandson, der Enkel, -s, -
granddaughter, die Enkelin, -, -nen
father-in-law, der Schwiegervater,
    -s, ··-
mother-in-law, die Schwieger-
    mutter, -, ··-
son-in-law, der Schwiegersohn,
    -es, ··-
daughter-in-law, die Schwiegertoch-
    ter, -, ··-
brother-in-law, der Schwager, -s, ··-
sister-in-law, die Schwägerin, -,
    -nen
man, der Mann, -es, ··-er
woman, die Frau, -, -en; das
    Weib, -es, -er
child, das Kind, -es, -er
boy, der Knabe, -n, -n; der Junge,
    -n, -n
girl, das Mädchen, -s, -
sir, Mr., der Herr, -n, -en (in

direct address, unless name
    follows, mein Herr)
lady, Madam, Mrs., die Dame, -,
    -n; die Frau, - ,-en (in direct
    address, unless name follows,
    gnädige Frau)
Miss, young lady, das Fräulein,
    -s, - (in direct address, unless
    name follows, gnädiges Fräu-
    lein)
friend, der Freund, -es, -e; die
    Freundin, -, -nen
servant, der Diener, -s, -; der Be-
    diente, -n, -n; das Dienstmädchen,
    -s, -
to introduce, vorstellen
to visit, besuchen
love, die Liebe, -
to love, lieben
to fall in love with, sich verlieben
    in (acc.)
to marry, heiraten
sweetheart, darling, der Schatz,
    -es, ··-e; das Liebchen, -s, -;
    der Liebling, -s, -e
kiss, der Kuß, -es, ··-e
to kiss, küssen

3. Speaking Activities.

word, das Wort, -es, ··-er (-e)
language, die Sprache, -, -n
to speak, sprechen, spricht, sprach,
    gesprochen
to say, sagen
to tell, relate, erzählen
to inform, berichten; sagen
to call, rufen, rief, gerufen
to be called, one's name is, heißen,
    hieß, geheißen (my name is
    William, ich heiße Wilhelm)
to greet, grüßen
to name, nennen, nannte, genannt
to listen to, zuhören (fol. by

dative)
to hear, hören
to understand, verstehen, verstand,
    verstanden
to mean, meinen, bedeuten
to ask (for something), bitten, bat,
    gebeten (um etwas)
to answer, antworten; erwidern
to thank, danken (I thank you for
    that, ich danke Ihnen dafür)
to complain (about), sich beklagen
    über
to cry, shout, schreien, schrie, ge-
    schrien

4. *Materials.*

gold, das Gold, -es
silver, das Silber, -s
iron, das Eisen, -s
steel, der Stahl, -es
copper, das Kupfer, -s
lead, das Blei, -es
tin, der Zinn, -es
oil, das Öl, -es
gasoline, das Benzin, -s
coal, die Kohle, -, -n
fuel, der Brennstoff, -es, -e
wood, das Holz, -es, ¨-er

silk, die Seide, -, -n
cotton, die Baumwolle, -
wool, die Wolle, -
cloth, das Tuch, -es, ¨-er
to cut, schneiden, schnitt, geschnitten
to dig, graben, gräbt, grub, gegraben
to sew, nähen
to mend, flicken
to darn, stopfen

5. *Animals.*

animal, das Tier, -es, -e
horse, das Pferd, -es, -e
dog, der Hund, -es, -e
cat, die Katze, -, -n
bird, der Vogel, -s, ¨-
donkey, der Esel, -s, -
mule, das Maultier, -es, -e; der Maulesel, -s, -
cow, die Kuh, -, ¨-e
ox, der Ochse, -n, -n
pig, das Schwein, -es, -e
chicken, das Huhn, -es, ¨-er
hen, die Henne, -, -n
rooster, der Hahn, -es, ¨-e

sheep, das Schaf, -es, -e
goat, die Ziege, -, -n; die Geiß, -, -e
mouse, die Maus, -, ¨-e
snake, die Schlange, -, -n
fly, die Fliege, -, -n
bee, die Biene, -, -n
mosquito, gnat, die Schnake, -, -n; die Mücke, -, en; der Moskito, -s, -s
spider, die Spinne, -, -n
louse, die Laus, -, ¨-e
flea, der Floh, -es, ¨-e
bedbug, die Wanze, -, -n

6. *Money, Buying and Selling.*

money, das Geld, -es, -er
coin, die Münze, -, -n; das Geldstück, -es, -e
dollar, der Dollar, -s, -
cent, der Cent, -s, -
mark, die Mark, -, -
pfennig, der Pfennig, -s, -e
bank, die Bank, -, -en
check, der Scheck, -es, -s; die Bankanweisung, -, -en

money order, die Postanweisung, -, -en
to earn, verdienen
to gain, to win, gewinnen, gewann, gewonnen
to lose, verlieren, verlor, verloren
to spend, ausgeben, gibt aus, gab aus, ausgegeben
to lend, leihen, lieh, geliehen
to owe, schulden; schuldig sein

to pay, zahlen; bezahlen

to borrow, borgen (he borrowed two marks from me, er hat zwei Mark von mir geborgt)

change, das Kleingeld, -es

to change, exchange, tauschen; umtauschen; wechseln

to return, give back, zurückgeben, gibt zurück, gab zurück, zurückgegeben

price, der Preis, -es, -e

expensive, dear, teuer; kostspielig

cheap, billig

store, shop, der Laden, -s, ¨-; das Geschäft, -es, -e

piece, das Stück, -es, -e (a piece of bread, ein Stück Brot)

slice, die Scheibe, -, -n; das Stück

pound, das Pfund, -es, -e

package, das Paket, -es, -e; das Bündel, -s, -; das Päckchen, -s, -

bag, der Sack, -es, ¨-e

box, die Schachtel, -, -n; die Dose, -, -en

basket, der Korb, -es, ¨-e

goods, die Ware, -, -n

to go shopping, einkaufen gehen

to sell, verkaufen

to buy, kaufen (- a ticket, eine Fahrkarte lösen)

cost, die Kosten (pl.); der Preis

to cost, kosten

to be worth, wert sein; gelten, gilt, galt, gegolten

to rent, hire, mieten, vermieten

to choose, wählen

thief, robber, der Dieb, -es, -e; der Räuber, -s, -

to steal, stehlen, stiehlt, stahl, gestohlen

police, die Polizei, -

policeman, der Polizist, -en, -en; der Schupo, -s

honest, redlich; ehrlich; zuverlässig

dishonest, unehrlich

7. *Eating and Drinking.*

to eat, essen, ißt, aß, gegessen

breakfast, das Frühstück, -s, -e

to eat breakfast, frühstücken

lunch, dinner, das Mittagessen, -s, -

to eat lunch, to dine, zu Mittag essen

supper, das Abendbrot, -es, -e

to eat supper, Abendbrot essen; zu Abend essen

meal, die Mahlzeit, -, -en

dining-room, das Eßzimmer, -s, -; der Speisesaal, -s, -säle

menu, die Speisekarte, -, -n

waiter, der Kellner, -s, -

waitress, die Kellnerin, -, -nen

restaurant, das Restaurant, -s, -e; das Gasthaus, -es, ¨-er

bill, die Rechnung, -, -en

to pass, reichen

tip, das Trinkgeld, -es, -er

to drink, trinken, trank, getrunken

water, das Wasser, -s, -

wine, der Wein, -es, -e

beer, das Bier, -es, -e

coffee, der Kaffee, -s

tea, der Tee, -s, -e

milk, die Milch, -

bottle, die Flasche, -, -n

spoon, der Löffel, -s, -

teaspoon, der Teelöffel, -s, -

knife, das Messer, -s, -

fork, die Gabel, -, -n

glass, das Glas, -es, ¨-er

cup, die Tasse, -, -n

napkin, die Serviette, -, -n

salt, das Salz, -es, -e
pepper, der Pfeffer, -s, -
plate, dish, der Teller, -s, -
bread, das Brot, -es, -e
butter, die Butter, -
roll, das Brötchen, -s, -
sugar, der Zucker, -s, -
soup, die Suppe, -, -n
rice, der Reis, -ses
potato, die Kartoffel, -, -n
vegetables, das Gemüse, -s, -
meat, das Fleisch, -es
beef, das Rindfleisch, -es
steak, das Rumpfstück, -es, -e
chicken, das Huhn, -es, ¨-er
chop, das Kotlett, -s, -e
mutton, das Hammelfleisch, -es
lamb, das Lammfleisch, -es
veal, das Kalbfleisch, -es
pork, das Schweinefleisch, -es
sausage, die Wurst, -, ¨-e
ham, der Schinken, -s, -
bacon, der Speck, -es
egg, das Ei, -es, -er

fish, der Fisch, -es, -e
fried, gebraten
cooked, gekocht
boiled, gedämpft
roast, geröstet
baked, gebacken
sauce, die Soße, -, -n (die Sauce)
salad, der Salat, -es, -e
cheese, der Käse, -s, -
fruit, das Obst, -es
apple, der Apfel, -s, ¨-
pear, die Birne, -, -n
grapes, die Weintrauben
peach, der Pfirsich, -es, -e
strawberry, die Erdbeere, -, -n
nut, die Nuß, -, ¨-e
orange, die Apfelsine, -, -n
lemon, die Zitrone, -, -n
juice, der Saft, -es, ¨-e
cherry, die Kirsche, -, -n
dessert, der Nachtisch, -es, -e; die
    Nachspeise, -, -n
pastry, das Gebäck, -es; das Back-
    werk, -es
cake, der Kuchen, -s, -

8. *Hygiene and Attire.*

bath, das Bad, -es, ¨-er
to bathe, baden
shower, das Sturzbad, -es, ¨-er;
    das Brausebad, -es, ¨-er; die
    Dusche, -, -n
to wash, (sich) waschen, wäscht,
    wusch, gewaschen (I wash my
    hands, ich wasche mir die Hände)
to shave, (sich) rasieren
barber, der Friseur, -s, -e
mirror, der Spiegel, -s, -
soap, die Seife, -, -n
razor, das Rasiermesser, -s, -
safety razor, der Rasierapparat, -s,
    -e; das Sicherheitsrasiermesser,
    -s, -

towel, das Handtuch, -es, ¨-er
comb, der Kamm, -es, ¨-e
brush, die Bürste, -, -n
toothbrush, die Zahnbürste, -, -n
scissors, die Schere, -, -n
to wear, tragen, trägt, trug,
    getragen
to take off, ausziehen, zog aus,
    ausgezogen (- one's hat, den
    Hut abnehmen)
to change, (sich) umziehen, zog
    um, umgezogen
to put on, (sich) anziehen, zog an,
    angezogen (I was putting on my
    coat, ich zog den Rock an)
clothes, die Kleider

hat, der Hut, -es, ¨-e
suit, der Anzug, -es, ¨-e
coat, der Rock, -es, ¨-e
suspenders, die Hosenträger
vest, die Weste, -, -n
pants, die Hosen
underwear, die Unterwäsche, -
glove, der Handschuh, -es, -e
socks, die Socken
stocking, der Strumpf, -es, ¨-e
shirt, das Hemd, -es, -en
collar, der Kragen, -s, -
tie, die Kravatte, -, -n; der Schlips, -es, -e
overcoat, der Mantel, -s, ¨-; der Überzieher, -s, -
raincoat, der Regenmantel, -s, ¨-
pocket, die Tasche, -, -n
handkerchief, das Taschentuch, -s, ¨-er

purse, die Handtasche, -, -n
button, der Knopf, -es, ¨-e
shoe, der Schuh, -es, -e
boot, der Stiefel, -s, -
pocket-book, die Brieftasche, -, -n
pin, needle, die Nadel, -, -n
tie-pin, die Kravattennadel, -, -n
safety-pin, die Sicherheitsnadel, -, -n
umbrella, der Regenschirm, -es, -e
watch, die Uhr, -, -en
chain, die Kette, -, -n
ring, der Ring, -es, -e
eyeglasses, die Brille, -, -n
slippers, die Hausschuhe; die Pantoffeln
bath-robe, der Bademantel, -s, ¨-
dressing-gown, der Schlafrock, -es, ¨-e

9. *Parts of the Body.*

head, der Kopf, -es, ¨-e
forehead, die Stirn, -, -en
face, das Gesicht, -es, -er
mouth, der Mund, -es, -e
hair, das Haar, -es, -e
eye, das Auge, -s, -n
ear, das Ohr, -es, -en
tooth, der Zahn, -es, ¨-e
lip, die Lippe, -, -n
nose, die Nase, -, -n
tongue, die Zunge, -, -n
chin, das Kinn, -es, -e
cheek, die Wange, -, -n
mustache, der Schnurrbart, -es, ¨-e
beard, der Bart, -es, ¨-e
neck, der Hals, -es, ¨-e
throat, die Gurgel, -, -n
stomach, der Magen, -s, -

arm, der Arm, -es, -e
hand, die Hand, -, ¨-e
elbow, der Ellbogen, -s, -
wrist, das Handgelenk, -es, -e
finger, der Finger, -s, -
nail, der Nagel, -s, ¨-
shoulder, die Schulter, -, -n
leg, das Bein, -es, -e
foot, der Fuß, -es, ¨-e
knee, das Knie, -es, -e
back, der Rücken, -s, -
chest, breast, die Brust, -, ¨-e
ankle, das Fußgelenk, -es, -e
body, der Körper. -s, -; der Leib, -es, -er
blood, das Blut, -es
skin, die Haut, -, ¨-e
heart, das Herz, -ens, -en
bone, der Knochen, -s, -

10. *Medical.*

doctor, der Doktor, -s, -en; der
   Arzt, -es, ˮ-e
drug-store, die Apotheke, -, -n
hospital, das Spital, -es, ˮ-er; das
   Krankenhaus, -es, ˮ-er
medicine, die Medizin, -, -en; die
   Arznei, -, -en
pill, die Pille, -, -n
prescription, das Rezept, -es, -e
bandage, der Verband, -es, ˮ-e
nurse, die Krankenschwester, -, -ı
ill, krank
fever, das Fieber, -s, -
illness, die Krankheit, -, -en

swollen, geschwollen
wound, die Wunde, -, -n
injury, die Verletzung, -, -en
wounded, verwundet
injured, verletzt
head-ache, das Kopfweh, -es; die
   Kopfschmerzen (pl.)
tooth-ache, das Zahnweh, -es; die
   Zahnschmerzen (pl.)
cough, der Husten, -s, -
to cough, husten
lame, lahm
burn, die Brandwunde, -, -n
pain, der Schmerz, -es, -en
poison, das Gift, -es, -e

11. *Military.*

war, der Krieg, -es, -e
peace, der Friede(n), -ns, -n
ally, der Verbündete, -n, -n
enemy, der Feind, -es, -e
army, die Armee, -, -n; das Heer,
   -es, -e
danger, die Gefahr, -, -en
dangerous, gefährlich
to win, siegen; gewinnen, gewann,
   gewonnen
to surround, einkreisen; umzingeln;
   umgeben, gibt um, gab um,
   umgegeben
to arrest, verhaften
to kill, töten
to escape, entkommen (with dative)
to run away, fliehen, floh, geflohen
   (sein); sich retten; davonrennen,
   rannte davon, davongerannt
   (sein)
to lead, führen
to follow, folgen (sein); he followed me, er ist mir gefolgt

fear, die Angst, -, ˮ-e; die Furcht, -
prison, das Gefängnis, -ses, -se
prisoner, der Gefangene, -n, -n
comrade, "buddy", der Kamerad,
   -en, -en
battle, die Schlacht, -, -en
to fight, kämpfen
to take prisoner, gefangen nehmen
   (nimmt, nahm, genommen)
to capture, einnehmen, nimmt ein,
   nahm ein, eingenommen
to surrender, sich ergeben, ergibt
   sich, ergab sich, sich ergeben;
   sich aufgeben, gibt sich auf, gab
   sich auf, sich aufgegeben
to retreat, sich zurückziehen, zog
   sich zurück, sich zurückgezogen
soldier, der Soldat, -en, -en
private, der Gemeine, -en, -en
corporal, der Gefreite, -n, -n
sergeant, der Feldwebel, -s, -
lieutenant, der Leutnant, -s, -s
   (1st, -, der Oberleutnant)
captain, der Hauptmann, -es, ˮ-er

major, der Major, -s, -e; der Kommandant, -en, -en
colonel, der Oberst, -en, -en
general, der General, -s, ̈-e (Lt. Maj., Col.-Gen., Generalleutnant, Generalmajor, Generaloberst)
officer, der Offizier, -s, -e (staff -, der Stabsoffizier; non-com. -, der Unteroffizier)
squad, die Rotte, -, -n
company, die Kompagnie, -, -n
battalion, das Bataillon, -s, -e
regiment, das Regiment, -s, -er
brigade, die Brigade, -, -n
division, die Division, -, -en
troops, die Truppen
reenforcements, die Verstärkungen
infantry, die Infanterie, -
cavalry, die Kavallerie, -
artillery, die Artillerie, -
engineers, die Pioniere
Alpine troops, die Gebirgstruppen
tank corps, die Panzerdivisionen; die Panzertruppen
motorized, motorisiert
mounted, beritten
fortress, die Festung, -, -en
sentinel, die (Schild)wache, -, -n
to stand guard, Wache halten; auf (dem) Posten stehen
guard, die Wache, -, -n
to be on duty, den Dienst haben
sign-post, der Schildposten, -s, -; das Schild, -es, -er; der Wegweiser, -s, -
headquarters, das Hauptquartier. -s, -e
staff, der Stab, -es, ̈-e
retreat, der Rückzug, -es, ̈-e
advance, der Vormarsch, -es, ̈-e
forced march, der Eilmarsch, -es, ̈-e
to quarter, einquartieren

to forage, mausern; Proviant beschaffen
casualties, die Verluste (pl.)
wounded, die Verwundeten
missing, die Vermißten
dead, die Toten
militia, die Landwehr, -
military police, die Feldgendarmerie
truce, der Waffenstillstand, -es
navy, die Marine, -; die Flotte, -, -n
sailor, der Matrose, -n, -n; der Seemann, -s, ̈-er
marine, der Marinesoldat, -en, -en
naval officer, der Seeoffizier, -s, -e; der Offizier-zur-See
engineer, der Ingenieur, -s, -e
cadet, der Kadett, -s, -en
lieutenant, der Leutnant-zur-See
captain, der Kapitän, -s, ̈-e
admiral, der Admiral, -s, -e
warship, das Kriegsschiff, -es, -e
battleship, das Schlachtschiff, -es, -e
cruiser, der Kreuzer, -s, -
aircraft carrier, das Flugzeugmutterschiff, -es, -e
destroyer, der Zerstörer, -s, -
submarine, das U-Boot, -s, -e; das Unterseeboot
transport, das Truppentransportschiff, -es, -e
mine-sweeper, der Minensucher, -s, -
auxiliary, das Hilfsschiff, -es, -e
convoy, das Geleit, -es, -e; das Schiffsgeleit; der Geleitzug, -es, ̈-e
escort, die Begleitung, -, -en
weapon, die Waffe, -, -n
rifle, das Gewehr, -s, -e
revolver, der Revolver, -s, -
bayonet, das Seitengewehr, -s, -e;

das Bajonett, -s, -e
cannon, das Geschütz, -es, -e
ammunition, die Munition, -, -en
supplies, die Vorräte
cartridge, die Patrone, -, -n
bullet, die Kugel, -, -n
belt, der Gürtel, -s, -
knapsack, der Rucksack, -s, ¨-e
tent, das Zelt, -es, -e
map, die (Land)karte, -, -n
camp, das Lager, -s, -
rope, der Strick, -es, -e; das Seil,
   -es, -e
flag, die Fahne, -, -n
helmet, der Helm, -es, -e
uniform, die Uniform, -, -en
truck, der Lastkraftwagen, -s, -
shell, das Geschoß, -es, -e
tank, der Tank, -s; der Panzer
   (wagen)
to load, laden, lädt, lud, geladen
to bomb, shell, bombardieren;
   beschießen, beschoß, beschossen
to fire, shoot, feuern; schießen,
   schoß, geschossen
fire!, Feuer!
attention!, Achtung!
forward!, Vorwärts!
halt!, Halt!
bomb, die Bombe, -, -n
to shoot (military execution).
   hinrichten

spy, der Spion, -s, -e
help, aid, die Hilfe, -, -n
airplane, das Flugzeug, -es, -e
fighter plane, das Jagdflugzeug
bombing plane, das Kampfflugzeug
dive-bomber, das Sturzkampfflug-
   zeug (das Stuka)
glider, das Gleitflugzeug
airport, der Lufthafen, -s, ¨-
landing field, der Landungsplatz,
   -es, ¨-e
emergency landing, die Notland-
   ung, -, -en
gasoline, der Brennstoff, -es; das
   Benzin, -s
pilot, der Pilot, -en, -en
machine-gun, das Maschinen-
   gewehr, -es, -e
machine gunner, der Maschinen-
   gewehrschütze, -en, -en
parachute, der Fallschirm, -es, -e
paratroopers, die Fallschirmtruppen
to take off, abfliegen, flog ab, ab-
   geflogen (sein)
to land, landen
anti-aircraft fire, die Flak
air warden, die Luftschutzwache,
   -, -n
air-raid shelter, der Luftschutzraum,
   -es, ¨-e; die Luftschutzstelle, -,
   -n

12. Travel.

customs, das Zollamt, -es, ¨-er
passport, der (Reise)paß, -es, ¨-e
ship, das Schiff, -es, -e
steamer, der Dampfer, -s, -
stateroom, die Kajüte, -, -n; die
   Kabine, -, -n
berth, die Schlafstelle, -, -n
to travel, reisen (sein)
trip, voyage, die Reise, -, -n
to leave, depart, abfahren, fährt

ab, fuhr ab, abgefahren (sein);
   wegfahren (sein)
to arrive, ankommen, kam an,
   angekommen (sein)
to ride (a conveyance), fahren,
   fährt, fuhr, gefahren
railroad, die Eisenbahn, -, -en
station, der Bahnhof, -es, ¨-e
platform, der Bahnsteig, -es, -e
track, die Schiene, -, -n; das

Geleise, -s, -
train, der Zug, -es, ⸚-e
ticket, die Fahrkarte, -, -n
to buy a ticket, eine Fahrkarte
    lösen
compartment, das Abteil, -es, -e
all aboard!, Einsteigen!
all out!, Aussteigen!
dining-car, der Speisewagen, -s, -
sleeper, der Schlafwagen, -s, -
car, coach, der Wagen, -s, -; der
    Waggon, -s, -s

trunk, der Koffer, -s, -
valise, der Handkoffer, -s, -
baggage, das Gepäck, -s
porter, der Gepäckträger, -s, -
bus, der Omnibus, -es, -e
street-car, die Straßenbahn, -, -en
    die Elektrische, -n, -n
automobile, das Automobil, -(e)s,
    -e; der Kraftwagen, -s, -
taxi, die Taxe, -, -n
driver, der Schofför, -s, -e
to drive, steuern; fahren

13. *Reading and Writing.*

to read, lesen, liest, las, gelesen
newspaper, die Zeitung, -, -en
magazine, die Zeitschrift, -, -en
book, das Buch, -es, ⸚-er
to write, schreiben, schrieb, ge-
    schrieben
to translate, übersetzen
pencil, der Bleistift, -es, -e
chalk, die Kreide, -
blackboard, die Tafel, -, -n
ink, die Tinte, -
pen, die Feder, -, -n
fountain pen, der Füllfederhalter,
    -s, -; die Füllfeder, -, -n

paper, das Papier, -(e)s, -e
writing paper, das Schreibpapier,
    -(e)s, -e
post-card, die Postkarte, -, -n
envelope, der Briefumschlag, -es,
    ⸚-e; das (Brief)kuvert, -s, -s
letter, der Brief, -es, -e
post-office, das Postamt, -es, ⸚-er;
    die Post, -
stamp, die Briefmarke, -, -n; die
    Freimarke, -, -n
letter-box, der Briefkasten, -s, -
to mail, einstecken; absenden
address, die Adresse, -, -n

14. *Amusements.*

to smoke, rauchen
cigar, die Zigarre, -, -n
cigarette, die Zigarette, -, -n
tobacco, der Tabak, -s
match, das Streichholz, -es, ⸚-er
give me a light, geben Sie mir
    bitte Feuer
theatre, das Theater, -s, -
movies, das Kino, -s, -s
dance, der Tanz, -es, ⸚-e
to dance, tanzen
to have a good time, sich amü-
    sieren, sich gut unterhalten

ticket, das Billet, -tes, -te; die Ein-
    trittskarte, -, -n
pleasure, das Vergnügen, -s, -
to play, spielen
to sing, singen, sang, gesungen
song, das Lied, -es, -er
to take a walk, spazierengehen,
    ging spazieren, spazierengegangen
    (sein)
ball, der Ball, -es, ⸚-e
beach, der (Meeres)strand, -es,
    ⸚-e
to swim, schwimmen, schwamm,

geſchwommen (ſein)
game, das Spiel, -s, -e
sand, der Sand, -es
refreshment, die Erfriſchungen (pl.)
saloon, die Kneipe, -, -n; das

Wirtshaus, -es, ˙˙-er; die Bier-
ſtube, -, -n
picnic, das Picknick, -s, -s; die
Landpartie, -, -n; der Ausflug,
-es, ˙˙-e

15. Town and Country.

place, spot, der Platz, -es, ˙˙-e; der Ort, -es, -e
city, die Stadt, -, ˙˙-e
street, die Straße, -, -n
sidewalk, der Bürgerſteig, -es, -e; das Trottoir, -s, -s
intersection, die Kreuzung, -, -en
block, der Häuſerblock, -es, -s; das (Häuſer)quadrat, -es, -e
school, die Schule, -, -n
church, die Kirche, -, -n
building, das Gebäude, -s, -
cathedral, der Dom, -es, -e
corner, die Ecke, -, -n
harbor, der Hafen, -s, ˙˙-
hotel, das Hotel, -s, -s; der Gaſthof, -es, ˙˙-er
office, das Büro, -s, -s; das Amt, -es, ˙˙-er

river, der Fluß, -es, ˙˙-e
bridge, die Brücke, -, -n
country, das Land, -es, ˙˙-er
village, das Dorf, -es, ˙˙-er
road, die Landſtraße, -, -n; die Autobahn, -, -en; der Weg, -es, -e
mountain, der Berg, -es, -e (- range, das Gebirge, -s, -)
grass, das Gras, -es, ˙˙-er
yard, der Hof, -es, ˙˙-e
hill, der Hügel, -s, -
lake, der See, -s, -n
forest, wood, der Wald, -es, ˙˙-er
field, das Feld, -es, -er
flower, die Blume, -, -n
tree, der Baum, -es, ˙˙-e
stone, der Stein, -es, -e
rock, der Felſen, -s, -

16. House.

door, die Tür, -, -en
to open, öffnen; aufmachen
to close, ſchließen, ſchloß, ge-ſchloſſen; zumachen
key, der Schlüſſel, -s, -
to go in, eintreten, tritt ein, trat ein, eingetreten (ſein)
house, das Haus, -es, ˙˙-er (at home, zu Hauſe; he is going home, er geht nach Hauſe)
to go out, hinausgehen, ging hinaus, hinausgegangen (ſein)
cottage, das Landhaus, -es, ˙˙-er
hut, die Hütte, -, -n

to live (in), wohnen
staircase, die Treppe, -, -n
to go up, hinaufſteigen, ſtieg hinauf, hinaufgeſtiegen (ſein)
to go down, hinunterſteigen, ſtieg hinunter, hinuntergeſtiegen (ſein); hinuntergehen (ſein)
room, das Zimmer, -s, -
toilet, der Abort, -es, -e; die Toilette, -, -n
kitchen, die Küche, -, -n
table, der Tiſch, -es, -e
chair, der Stuhl, -es, ˙˙-e
to sit down, ſich ſetzen; Platz

nehmen, nimmt, nahm,
genommen
to stand, ſtehen, ſtand, geſtanden
wall, die Wand, -, ``-e
lamp, die Lampe, -, -n
candle, die Kerze, -, -n; das Licht,
-s, -er
closet, der Schrank, -es, ``-e
window, das Fenſter, -s, -
to rest, ruhen; ſich ausruhen
roof, das Dach, -es, ``-er
to be sitting, ſitzen, ſaß, geſeſſen
bed, das Bett, -s, -en (to or in bed,
zu Bett)
pillow, das (Kopf)Kiſſen, -s, -
blanket, die Decke, -, -n
sheet, das Leintuch, -es, ``-er

mattress, die Matratze, -, -n
bedroom, das Schlafzimmer, -s, -
to go to bed, ſchlafen gehen, ging,
gegangen (ſein)
to go to sleep, einſchlafen, ſchläft
ein, ſchlief ein, eingeſchlafen
(ſein)
to sleep, ſchlafen, ſchläft, ſchlief,
geſchlafen
to wake up, aufwachen (ſein)
to awaken (transitive), wecken
to get up, aufſtehen, ſtand auf,
aufgeſtanden (ſein)
to dress, ſich anziehen, zog ſich an,
ſich angezogen; ſich ankleiden
clock, die Uhr, -, -en
alarm clock, der Wecker, -s, -

17. *Miscellaneous Nouns.*

people, die Leute (pl.); die Men-
ſchen (people say so, man ſagt
es)
thing, das Ding, -es, -e; die Sache,
-, -en
name, der Name, -ns, -n
number, die Nummer, -, -n; die

Zahl, -, -en
life, das Leben, -s, -
death, der Tod, -es
work, die Arbeit, -, -en
luck, das Glück, -es
bad luck, das Unglück, -es; das
Pech, -es

18. *Verbs — Coming and Going.*

to come, kommen, kam, gekommen
(ſein)
to go, gehen, ging, gegangen (ſein)
to be going to (use present or
future of following verb; I am
going to speak to him to-
morrow, morgen ſpreche ich mit
ihm, or morgen werde ich ihn
ſprechen)
to run, rennen, rannte, gerannt
(ſein); laufen, läuft, lief,
gelaufen (ſein)
to walk, (zu Fuß) gehen

to go away, fortgehen, ging fort,
fortgegangen (ſein); weggehen
(ſein)
to fall, fallen, fällt, fiel,
gefallen (ſein)
to stay, remain, bleiben, blieb,
geblieben (ſein)
to follow, folgen (dat.)
to return, zurückkehren (ſein);
(come back, zurückkommen; go
back, zurückgehen) (ſein)
to arrive, ankommen, kam an,
angekommen (ſein)

19. *Verbs — Looking and Seeing.*

to see, ſehen, ſieht, ſah, geſehen

to look (at), anſehen (he is looking at me, er ſieht mich an);
blicken; ſchauen

to look for, ſuchen (I am looking
for him, ich ſuche ihn)

to look, seem, appear, ſcheinen,
ſchien, geſchienen; ausſehen,
ſieht aus, ſah aus, ausgeſehen

to recognize, erkennen, erkannte,
erkannt

to take for, nehmen für, nimmt
für, nahm für, für — genommen

to laugh, lachen

to smile, lächeln

to laugh at, auslachen

20. *Verbs — Mental.*

to make a mistake, ſich irren

to hope, hoffen

to wait (for), warten (auf);
erwarten

to think (of), denken, dachte, gedacht (an with acc.)

to believe, glauben (I believe him,
ich glaube ihm; I believe it,
ich glaube es)

to like, gern(e) haben; gefallen,
gefällt, gefiel, gefallen (I like
him, er gefällt mir)

to wish, wünſchen

to want, wollen, will, wollte, ge-
wollt

to need, brauchen

to know (a person), kennen,
kannte, gekannt

to know (a fact), wiſſen, weiß,
wußte, gewußt

to know how to, können, kann,
konnte, gekonnt

to understand, verſtehen, verſtand,
verſtanden

to remember, ſich erinnern an

to forget, vergeſſen, vergißt, ver-
gaß, vergeſſen

to permit, allow, let, laſſen, läßt,
ließ, gelaſſen; erlauben (he
permitted me to do it, er hat es
mir erlaubt)

to promise, verſprechen, verſpricht,
verſprach, verſprochen

to forbid, verbieten, verbot, verboten

to learn, lernen

to feel like, Luſt haben (I feel
like doing it, ich habe Luſt, es
zu tun)

to fear, be afraid, ſich fürchten (I
am afraid of my brother, ich
fürchte mich vor meinem Bruder)

to be right, recht haben

to be wrong, unrecht haben

21. *Verbs — Miscellaneous.*

to live, leben

to die, ſterben, ſtirbt, ſtarb, ge-
ſtorben (ſein)

to work, arbeiten

to have just (use eben; I have
just read the book, ich habe
eben das Buch geleſen)

to give, geben, gibt, gab, gegeben

to take, nehmen, nimmt, nahm,
genommen

to begin, anfangen, fängt an,
fing an, angefangen

to finish, beendigen; aufhören (he finished reading, er hörte auf zu lesen)

to continue, keep on, fortfetzen; weitermachen; (I kept on reading, ich las immer weiter)

to help, helfen, hilft, half, geholfen (he helps me, er hilft mir)

to lose, verlieren, verlor, verloren

to find, finden, fand, gefunden

to try, verfuchen

to leave (an object), laffen, läßt, ließ, gelaffen

to show, zeigen

to meet, begegnen (dat.); treffen, trifft, traf, getroffen

to do, tun, tat, getan

to make, machen

to have done, machen laffen (he had a letter written, er hat einen Brief fchreiben laffen)

to be able, can, können, kann, konnte, gekonnt

to put, ftellen; legen; fetzen

to carry, tragen, trägt, trug, getragen

to keep, behalten, behält, behielt, behalten

to hold, halten, hält, hielt, gehalten

to bring, bringen, brachte, gebracht

to stop (self), ftehen bleiben, blieb, geblieben (fein)

to stop (another) aufhalten, hält auf, hielt auf, aufgehalten

to stop doing, to cease, aufhören

to cover, bedecken

to get, obtain, bekommen, bekam, bekommen

to get, become, werden, wird, wurde, geworden (fein)

to hide, verftecken; verbergen, verbirgt, verbarg, verborgen

to break, brechen, bricht, brach, gebrochen; zerbrechen

to hurry, eilen; fich beeilen

to deliver, liefern

to catch, fangen, fängt, fing, gefangen

to belong, gehören

to lay, legen

to send, fchicken; fenden, fandte, gefandt

22. *Adjectives.*[18]

small, klein

large, tall, groß

high, hoch (use hoh-er, -e, -es before a noun; comp. höher; sup. höchft)

short, kurz (opposite of long); klein (opposite of tall)

low, niedrig

long, lang

wide, broad, breit; weit

narrow, eng

deep, tief

heavy, fchwer

light (in weight), leicht

clean, rein; fauber

dirty, fchmutzig

fresh, frifch

cool, kühl

cold, kalt

warm, warm

18.   Note the tendency of adjectives to take umlaut in the comparative and superlative where the root vowel presents the umlaut possibility: groß, größer, größt; lang, länger, längft; kurz, kürzer, kürzeft.

hot, heiß
damp, feucht
wet, naß, feucht
dry, trocken
full, voll (full of wine, voll
  Wein)
empty, leer
dark, dunkel
light, bright, clear, hell; klar
fat, stark; dick
thick, dick
thin, dünn
round, rund
square, viereckig
flat, flach
soft, weich
hard, hart
quick, schnell
slow, langsam
ordinary, gewöhnlich
comfortable, bequem
uncomfortable, unbequem
near, nah(e) (comp. näher; sup.
  nächst)
distant, entfernt; weit
right, recht
left, link
poor, arm
rich, reich
beautiful, schön
pretty, hübsch; nett; niedlich
ugly, häßlich
sweet, süß
bitter, bitter
sour, sauer
salty, salzig
young, jung
old, alt
new, neu
good, gut
better, besser
best, best
bad, schlecht
worse, schlimmer

worst, schlimmst
fine, "regular", fein; echt
first, erst
last, letzt
strong, stark; kräftig
weak, schwach
tired, müde
alone, allein
same, derselbe (dieselbe, dasselbe,
  pl. dieselben)
true, wahr; richtig; treu
false, wrong, falsch; unwahr
sure, sicher
easy, leicht
hard, difficult, schwer; schwierig
happy, lucky, glücklich (to be
  lucky, Glück haben)
unhappy, unlucky, unglücklich (to
  be unlucky, Unglück haben)
glad, merry, fröhlich; lustig
sad, traurig
free, frei
stupid, dumm
silly, blöde; unsinnig
crazy, verrückt
drunk, betrunken
polite, höflich
good-natured, gemütlich
rude, unhöflich
kind, liebenswürdig
pleasant, angenehm; nett
unpleasant, unangenehm
lonesome, einsam
foreign, fremd; ausländisch
friendly, freundlich
hostile, unfreundlich; feindlich
charming, reizend; hold
afraid, ängstlich (to be -, Angst
  haben)
ready, bereit; fertig
hungry, hungrig (to be -, Hunger
  haben)
thirsty, durstig (to be -, Durst
  haben)

funny, komisch; lächerlich; amüsant
possible, möglich
impossible, unmöglich
brave, tapfer
cowardly, feig

quiet, ruhig
noisy, laut; geräuschvoll
living, lebendig
dead, tot

23. *Colors.*

white, weiß
black, schwarz
red, rot
green, grün
blue, blau

yellow, gelb
gray, grau
brown, braun
pink, rosa
purple, purpurrot, lila

24. *Nationalities.*[19]

American, amerikanisch; der Amerikaner, -s, -; die Amerikanerin
English, englisch; der Engländer, -s, -; die Engländerin
French, französisch; der Franzose, -n, -n; die Französin
German, deutsch; der Deutsche, -n, -n; die Deutsche, -n, -n
Spanish, spanisch; der Spanier, -s, -; die Spanierin
Russian, russisch; der Russe, -n, -n; die Russin
Italian, italienisch; der Italiener, -s, -; die Italienerin
Japanese, japanisch; der Japaner, -s, -; die Japanerin
Chinese, chinesisch; der Chinese, -n, -n; die Chinesin
Dutch, holländisch; der Holländer, -s, -; die Holländerin
Norwegian, norwegisch; der Norweger, -s, -; die Norwegerin
Swedish, schwedisch; der Schwede, -n, -n; die Schwedin
Finnish, finnisch; der Finnländer, -s, -; die Finnländerin
Belgian, belgisch; der Belgier, -s, -; die Belgierin
Polish, polnisch; der Pole, -n, -n; die Polin
Danish, dänisch; der Däne, -n, -n; die Dänin
Swiss, schweizerisch; der Schweizer, -s, -; die Schweizerin
Portuguese, portugiesisch; der Portugiese, -n, -n; die Portugiesin
Yugoslav, jugoslawisch; der Jugoslawe, -n, -n; die Jugoslawin

19. The adjective is given first, then the noun, in masculine and feminine form (all feminines in -in form their plural in -innen). Note the difference in the use of these forms: the American Navy, die amerikanische Flotte; I am an American, ich bin Amerikaner. Note also the fact that the noun is capitalized, while the adjective is not. For names of languages, use the adjective form as a noun, capitalizing it save after the preposition auf, "in": English (the English language), das Englisch(e); to speak German, Deutsch sprechen; in German, auf deutsch; into German, ins Deutsche.

Bulgarian, bulgarifdj; der Bulgare, -n, -n; die Bulgarin
Czech, tſchechiſch; der Tſcheche, -n, -n; die Tſchechin
Greek, griechiſch; der Grieche, -n, -n; die Griechin
Turkish, türkiſch; der Türke, -n, -n; die Türkin
Roumanian, rumäniſch; der Rumäne, -n, -n; die Rumänin
Hungarian, ungariſch; der Ungar, -s, -en; die Ungarin
Austrian, öſterreichiſch; der Öſterreicher, -s, -; die Öſterreicherin
Malay, malayiſch; der Malaye, -n, -n; die Malayin
Persian, perſiſch; der Perſer, -s, -; die Perſerin
Arabian, Arab, Arabic, arabiſch; der Araber, -s, -; die Araberin
Jewish, Hebrew, jüdiſch; hebräiſch; der Jude, -n, -n; die Jüdin; der
    Hebräer, -s, -; die Hebräerin
Australian, auſtraliſch; der Auſtralier, -s, -; die Auſtralierin
African, afrikaniſch; der Afrikaner, -s, -; die Afrikanerin
Canadian, kanadiſch; der Kanadier, -s, -; die Kanadierin
Mexican, mexikaniſch; der Mexikaner, -s, -; die Mexikanerin
Cuban, kubaniſch; der Kubaner, -s, -; die Kubanerin
Brazilian, braſilianiſch; der Braſilianer, -s, -; die Braſilianerin
Argentinian, argentiniſch; der Argentinier, -s, -; die Argentinierin
Chilean, chileniſch; der Chilene, -n, -n; die Chilenin
Peruvian, peruaniſch; der Peruaner, -s, -; die Peruanerin
Puerto Rican, portorikaniſch; der Portorikaner, -s, -; die Portorikanerin

25. *Adverbs and Adverbial Expressions.*

today, heute
yesterday, geſtern
tomorrow, morgen
day before yesterday, vorgeſtern
day after tomorrow, übermorgen
tonight, heute Abend; heute
    Nacht
last night, geſtern Abend (Nacht)
this morning, heute Morgen
in the morning, morgens; am
    Morgen
in the afternoon, nachmittags; am
    Nachmittag
in the evening, abends; am Abend
in the night, nachts; in der Nacht
this afternoon, heute Nachmittag
tomorrow morning, morgen früh
tomorrow night, morgen Abend
    (Nacht)

early, früh
late, ſpät
already, ſchon
no longer, nicht mehr
yet, still, noch (one more, noch ein;
    something more, noch etwas;
    many more, noch viele)
not yet, noch nicht
now, jetzt
then, dann; da
afterwards, nachher
just now, ſoeben
before, earlier, vorher
never, nie, niemals (never again,
    nimmermehr)
always, immer
forever, (auf) ewig
soon, bald
often, oft

sometimes, manchmal
seldom, selten
usually, gewöhnlich; meistens
from time to time,
   von Zeit zu Zeit; ab und zu
occasionally, gelegentlich
fast, quickly, schnell
slowly, langsam
long ago, längst
here, hier; her
there, da
over there, dort; da drüben
down there, drunten
here and there, hier und da;
   hin und wieder
to and fro, hin und her
near by, in der Nähe; nah
far away, in der Ferne; weit
   entfernt
up (stairs), oben
down (stairs), unten
ahead, in front, vorne
behind, in back, hinten
forward, vorwärts
back, backward, rückwärts
outside, draußen
inside, drinnen
everywhere, überall
also, too, auch
therefore, also; folglich
yes, ja
no, nein
not, nicht
very, much, sehr
little, not much, wenig
well, gut
badly, schlecht
better, besser

worse, schlimmer
only, nur
more, mehr
less, weniger
as - as, so - wie
as much (many) - as, so viel(e)
   - wie
how much?, wieviel?
how many? wie viele?
how?, wie?
too much (many), zu viel(e)
really, truly, wirklich
about, approximately, ungefähr
rather, ziemlich
somewhat, etwas
so much (many), so viel(e)
as, like, wie
besides, außerdem
finally, in short, endlich; kurz
almost, fast; beinah(e)
quite, altogether, ganz
gladly, gern(e)
certainly, gewiß; sicher(lich)
at once, gleich; sofort
at all, irgend (anything at all,
   irgend etwas; not at all, gar
   nicht)
hardly, kaum
aloud, laut
of course, natürlich
suddenly, plötzlich
perhaps, maybe, vielleicht
a little, ein wenig
together, zusammen
again, wieder (again and again
   repeatedly, immer wieder)
at least, wenigstens
for lack of, aus Mangel an

26. Conjunctions.[20]

and, und
but, aber
or, oder
why?, warum?
why!, na! (doch! to refute a negative statement)
because, weil; da
if, wenn[21] (as if, als wenn, als ob)
whether, ob[22]
before, ehe; bevor
when, as, than, als
as long as, so lange (wie)

where, wo (whence, woher; whither, wohin)
until, bis
although, obgleich; obwohl; obschon
unless, wenn nicht; ausgenommen; es sei denn daß
while, indem; während
when?, wann?
that, daß[22]
for, denn; weil
after, nachdem
as soon as, sobald

27. Indefinite Pronouns and Adjectives.

such, solch (such a soldier, solch ein Soldat)
all kinds of, allerlei
all, everything, all; alles (everything good, alles Gute)
all, whole, entire, ganz (all the world, die ganze Welt)
everyone, alle (all the men, all die Leute)
something, etwas (something bad, etwas Schlechtes)
someone, jemand
nothing, nichts (nothing new, nichts Neues)
no one, niemand
no (adjective), kein

either - or, entweder - oder
neither - nor, weder - noch
each, every, jeder (jede, jedes)
(an)other, (ein) anderer
much, lots of, viel (lots of good, viel Gutes)
some, einige
few, wenige
many, viele (many a soldier, manch ein Soldat)
several, a few, mehrere
little, not much, wenig (not much new, wenig Neues)
both, beide (both the men, die beiden Männer)
enough, genug

20. Note that in all dependent clauses the verb is placed at the end of the clause, and if a compound tense is used, the auxiliary follows the participle: he must come, because I'm going home, er muß kommen, weil ich nach Hause gehe; I came before he went home, ich bin angekommen, ehe er nach Hause gegangen ist.

21. Usually takes the subjunctive when English uses "should" or "would": if I had time, I should do it, wenn ich Zeit hätte, so täte ich es (so würde ich es tun).

22. Usually takes the subjunctive after verbs of saying, thinking, asking: he thought that I was sick, er glaubte, daß ich krank sei; he asked me whether I was sick, er fragte mich, ob ich krank sei.

28. *Prepositions.*[23]

of (use the genitive case); **von** is occasionally used: the streets of Paris, **die Straßen von Paris**

from, out of, **von** (d.); **aus** (d.)

to (use the dative case, unless motion is implied); **zu** (d.); **an** (d. or a.); **nach** (d.): I go to him, **ich gehe zu ihm**; I go to the window, **ich gehe an das Fenster**; I go to Berlin, **ich gehe nach Berlin**; I go home, **ich gehe nach Hause**; to school, **in die Schule.**

at, **an** (d. or a.); at the window, **am Fenster**; at school, **in der Schule**; at the post-office, **auf der Post**; at home, **zu Hause.**

with, **mit** (d.)

without, **ohne** (a.)

in, **in** (d. or a.); in the country, **auf dem Lande**; in the streets, **auf den Straßen**; in German, **auf deutsch**

on, upon, **auf** (d. or a.); on Sunday, **am Sonntag**; on foot, **zu Fuß**

over, above, across, **über** (d. or a.)

for, **für** (a.)

until, up to, as far as, **bis** (a.); **bis zu** (d.); until four o'clock, **bis vier Uhr**; as far as the school, **bis zur Schule**

since, **seit** (d.)

toward, **zu**; **an**; **bis**; **bis an**; **bis zu**; **wider** (a.)

between, **zwischen** (d. or a.)

among, **unter** (d. or a.)

near, **nahe** (d.); **bei** (d.); he stands near me, **er steht nahe bei mir**

by, **von** (d.); it was done by him, **es wurde von ihm getan**

far from, **weit von**

before, in front of, **vor** (d. or a.)

after, **nach** (d.)

opposite, **gegenüber**; opposite me, **mir gegenüber**

back of, behind, **hinter** (d. or a.)

under(neath), below, **unter** (d. or a.)

instead of, **(an)statt** (g.)

beside, next to, **neben** (d. or a.); **bei** (d.)

inside of, **innerhalb** (g.)

outside of, **außerhalb** (g.)

at the house of, **bei** (d.)

on account of, because of, **wegen** (g.)

through, by means of, **durch** (a.)

against, **gegen** (a.); **wider** (a.)

on the other side of, **jenseits** (g.)

on this side of, **diesseits** (g.)

in spite of, **trotz** (g.)

about, around, **um** (a.)

concerning, **von** (d.); **über** (a.)

in order to, **um - zu**

during, **während** (g.)

---

23. The case required by each preposition (genitive, dative or accusative) is indicated thus: (g.), (d.), (a.). Prepositions taking either the dative or the accusative are used with the former when place where, but no motion, is implied, the latter when there is motion: he stood in the room, **er stand im Zimmer**; he was going into the room, **er ging in das Zimmer.** Note **am** for **an dem**, **im** for **in dem**, **ins** for **in das**, **aufs** for **auf das**, etc.; these combinations are optional.

29. *Special Expressions and Idioms.*

good morning, guten Morgen!
good day, guten Tag!
good evening, guten Abend!
good night, gute Nacht!
good-bye, auf Wiedersehen!
I'll see you later, bis auf Weiteres!
I'll see you tomorrow, bis (auf) Morgen!
I'll see you tonight, bis zum Abend!; bis heute Abend!
just now, gerade jetzt
hello, hallo! (on the telephone - hier Herr followed by speaker's name)
how are you?, wie geht's?
I'm (very) well, es geht mir (sehr; ganz) gut
I'm (much) better, es geht mir (viel) besser
what time is it?, wieviel Uhr ist es?; wie spät ist es?
it's six o'clock, es ist sechs Uhr
at six o'clock, um sechs (Uhr)
at about six, ungefähr um sechs (Uhr); um sechs Uhr ungefähr
at half past six, um halb sieben
at a quarter to six, um dreiviertel sechs; um viertel vor sechs
at a quarter past six, um viertel sieben; um viertel nach sechs
last year, letztes Jahr
next year, nächstes Jahr
every day, jeden Tag; täglich
all (the whole) day, den ganzen Tag
please, bitte!
tell me, sagen Sie mir!
bring me, bringen Sie mir!
show me, zeigen Sie mir!
thank you, danke (schön)
don't mention it, bitte schön; bitte sehr; nichts zu danken; gern geschehn
will you give me?, wollen (würden) Sie mir - (bitte) geben?
pardon me, entschuldigen Sie (bitte)! ; verzeihen Sie!
it doesn't matter, es macht nichts aus
never mind, lassen Sie es gut sein!
I'm sorry, es tut mir leid
I can't help it, ich kann mir nicht helfen (I can't help doing it, ich kann
    nicht umhin es zu tun)
it's nothing, es ist ja wirklich gar nichts
what a pity!, wie schade!
it's too bad, das ist schade
I'm glad, es freut mich; ich freue mich
I have to, ich muß

I agree (all right; O. K.), das ift mir recht; (ich bin) einverftanden
where is (are)?, wo ift (find)?
there is (are) (pointing out), da ift (find)
there is (are) (stating), es gibt; es ift (find)
where are you going?, wohin gehen Sie?
which way? (direction), wo?; wohin?; (fashion), wie?; auf welche
    Weife?
this (that) way (direction), in diefer (jener) Richtung; hierher; da
    drüben
this (that) way (fashion), auf diefe (jene) Weife; fo
to the right, nach Rechts
to the left, nach Links
straight ahead, gerade aus
come with me, kommen Sie mit (mir)!
what can I do for you?, womit kann ich dienen?; wie kann ich Ihnen
    behilflich fein?
what is it?, what is the matter?, was ift los?; was geht denn da vor?
what is the matter with you?, was fehlt Ihnen?
what do you want?, was wünfchen (wollen) Sie?
what are you talking about?, wovon reden Sie?; was erzählen Sie
    denn da?; worum handelt es fich eigentlich?
what does that mean?, was heißt das?
what do you mean?, was wollen Sie damit fagen?; wie meinen Sie?
how much is it?, wieviel (koftet es)?
anything else?, what else?, noch etwas?, was noch?
nothing else, nichts mehr
do you speak German?, fprechen Sie Deutfch?
a little, ein wenig
do you understand, verftehen Sie?
I don't understand, ich verftehe nicht
speak more slowly, fprechen Sie langfamer!
do you know?, wiffen Sie?
I don't know, ich weiß nicht
I can't, ich kann nicht
what do you call this in German?, wie heißt das auf deutfch?
I'm an American, ich bin Amerikaner
I'm (very) hungry, ich bin (fehr) hungrig; ich habe (großen) Hunger
I'm (very) thirsty, ich bin (fehr) durftig; ich habe (großen) Durft
I'm sleepy, ich bin fchläfrig
I'm warm, mir ift warm (I'm cold, mir ift kalt)
it's warm (cold, windy, sunny, fine weather, bad weather), es ift
    warm (kalt, windig, fonnig, fchönes Wetter, fchlechtes Wetter)
it's forbidden, es ift verboten (unterfagt); no smoking, Rauchen
    verboten

luckily, fortunately, glücklicherweise

unfortunately, unglücklicherweise; leider

is it not so?, nicht wahr? (use this invariable expression wherever English repeats the question: you are going, aren't you?; he is, isn't he?)

not at all, gar nicht; nicht im geringsten

how old are you?, wie alt sind Sie?

I'm twenty years old, ich bin zwanzig Jahre alt

how long have you been here?, wie lange sind Sie (schon) hier?

how long have you been waiting?, wie lange warten Sie schon?

as soon as possible, so bald wie möglich

come here, kommen Sie (hier) her!

come in! eintreten!; herein!

look!, sehen Sie!

look out!, careful!, Vorsicht!; Achtung!

just a moment!, einen Augenblick!

darn it!, verdammt!; verflucht!

darn the luck!, zum Teufel noch mal!

for heaven's sake!, um Gottes Willen!

gangway!; one side!, aufpassen, bitte!; passen Sie auf!; Achtung!; Vorsicht!

as you please, wie es Ihnen beliebt

listen!, hören Sie mal!

look here!, say!, sagen Sie mal!

may I introduce my friend?, darf ich meinen Freund vorstellen (bekannt machen?)

glad to meet you, es freut mich Sie kennen zu lernen; sehr angenehm

no admittance, kein Eingang!; Eintritt verboten!

notice!, Bekanntmachung!

nonsense!, Unsinn!

to your health!, prosit!; prost!

I should like to, ich möchte (gern)

as quickly as possible, so schnell wie möglich

stop!, halt!

keep right (left), rechts (links) fahren!

entrance, Eingang

exit, Ausgang

hurry!, beeilen Sie sich!

warning!, Achtung!; Vorsicht!

CHAPTER V

LANGUAGES OF THE ROMANCE GROUP

This large and important language group, vying with the Germanic for first place in number of speakers and cultural importance among the Indo-European families, is characterized by descent from a common and almost fully known ancestor, Latin, in its Classical and Vulgar varieties. Of the five national languages of this group (French, Spanish, Portuguese, Italian, Roumanian) the first four are numerically and culturally of somewhat comparable importance, each within its own sphere.

French, the native tongue of nearly 60,000,000 people in France, Belgium, Switzerland, Canada and Haiti, is also an extremely widespread cultural and secondary tongue (it has been estimated that perhaps 50,000,000 additional people throughout the world can be reached with it), and a language of colonization second only to English in importance (the colonial populations under French rule amount to over 80,000,000 people).

Spanish, the national tongue of Spain (over 25,000,000) and the official tongue of the Spanish colonies (about 1,000,000), is also the primary language of Mexico, most of Central America and the Antilles, and of South America outside of Brazil and the Guianas. The total number of Spanish speakers in the Western Hemisphere is over 80,000,000.

Portuguese serves Portugal (about 8,000,000) and the Portuguese colonies (nearly 11,000,000). As the national tongue of Brazil (44,000,000), Portuguese reaches a total population of over 60,000,000.

Italian, the national tongue of Italy (45,000,000), is usable in Italy's colonial empire (Dodecanese, Libya, Italian

East Africa, etc. — about 13,000,000), and is current among large immigrant groups in North and South America, totalling perhaps 10,000,000.

The rich cultural background of all these languages gives them added importance.

Roumanian, the fifth tongue of the group, serves perhaps 16,000,000 of pre-war Roumania's 20,000,000 inhabitants, with additional small and isolated groups on Russian, Yugoslav, Hungarian, Greek and Italian territory.

Rumansh (Ladin, Rhetian), in its Engadine-Grisons variety, may be termed a sixth national tongue, its use having recently been made official in Switzerland. Swiss native speakers of Rumansh, however, number less than 50,000, and a far larger number of Rumansh speakers (about 1,000,000) is located on Italian soil, in the plain of Friuli and the valleys of the Trentino.

Among non-national Romance varieties which nevertheless possess a cultural and literary background are Provençal (once a fairly unified, literary language spoken throughout southern France; today only a series of local dialects); Catalan (spoken in Catalonia, Andorra, the southeastern Pyrenean region of France, the Balearic Islands, and extending, with slight variations, into the Spanish region of Valencia); Sardinian (spoken in central and southern Sardinia, and differing so radically from Italian that it can in no way be classed as an Italian dialect); Galician (used in the extreme northwest of Spain and forming part of the Portuguese rather than of the Spanish dialectal system). Some dialects of French (Picard, Norman, Walloon, Lorrain, etc.) and of Italian (Sicilian-Calabrian, Neapolitan-Abruzzese, Venetian, and the so-called Gallo-Italian dialects — Piedmontese, Lombard, Emilian and Ligurian) display such strong divergences from the national tongues that one may safely assert that political circumstances alone have prevented them from developing into national languages.

The following series of words will serve to illustrate the

major points of similarity and divergence among the national Romance languages, and their relationship to the original Latin and to one another. Other resemblances and differences will become evident in the course of the discussion of the individual languages.

English	Latin	French	Spanish	Portuguese	Italian	Roumanian
all	*totus*	*tout*	*todo*	*todo*	*tutto*	*tot*
arm	*brachium*	*bras*	*brazo*	*braço*	*braccio*	*braţ*
black	*niger*	*noir*	*negro*	*negro*	*nero*	*negru*
bread	*panis*	*pain*	*pan*	*pão*	*pane*	*pâine*
breast	*pectus*	*poitrine*	*pecho*	*peito*	*petto*	*piept*
cold	*frigidus*	*froid*	*frío*	*frio*	*freddo*	*frig*
come	*venire*	*venir*	*venir*	*vir*	*venire*	*veni*
daughter	*filia*	*fille*	*hija*	*filha*	*figlia*	*fiică*
do	*facere*	*faire*	*hacer*	*fazer*	*fare*	*face*
dog	*canis*	*chien*	*perro*	*cão*	*cane*	*câine*
drink	*bibere*	*boire*	*beber*	*beber*	*bere*	*bea*
ear	*auricula*	*oreille*	*oreja*	*orelha*	*orecchia*	*ureche*
earth	*terra*	*terre*	*tierra*	*terra*	*terra*	*pământ*
eye	*oculus*	*oeil*	*ojo*	*olho*	*occhio*	*ochiu*
father	*pater*	*père*	*padre*	*pai*	*padre*	*tată*
foot	*pes*	*pied*	*pie*	*pé*	*piede*	*picior*
full	*plenus*	*plein*	*lleno*	*cheio*	*pieno*	*plin*
gold	*aurum*	*or*	*oro*	*ouro*	*oro*	*aur*
good	*bonus*	*bon*	*bueno*	*bom*	*buono*	*bun*
green	*viridis*	*vert*	*verde*	*verde*	*verde*	*verde*
hand	*manus*	*main*	*mano*	*mão*	*mano*	*mână*
heat	*calor*	*chaleur*	*calor*	*calor*	*calore*	*căldură*
horse	*caballus*	*cheval*	*caballo*	*cavalo*	*cavallo*	*cal*
iron	*ferrum*	*fer*	*hierro*	*ferro*	*ferro*	*fier*
king	*rex*	*roi*	*rey*	*rei*	*re*	*rege*
laugh	*ridere*	*rire*	*reír*	*rir*	*ridere*	*râde*
life	*vita*	*vie*	*vida*	*vida*	*vita*	*viaţă*
man	*homo*	*homme*	*hombre*	*homem*	*uomo*	*om*
milk	*lac*	*lait*	*leche*	*leite*	*latte*	*lapte*
night	*nox*	*nuit*	*noche*	*noite*	*notte*	*noapte*

English	Latin	French	Spanish	Portuguese	Italian	Roumanian
ox	bos	boeuf	buey	boi	bue	bou
one	unus	un	uno	um	uno	un
two	duo	deux	dos	dois	due	doi
three	tres	trois	tres	três	tre	trei
four	quattuor	quatre	cuatro	quatro	quattro	patru
five	quinque	cinq	cinco	cinco	cinque	cinci
six	sex	six	seis	seis	sei	şase
seven	septem	sept	siete	sete	sette	şapte
eight	octo	huit	ocho	oito	otto	opt
nine	novem	neuf	nueve	nove	nove	nouă
ten	decem	dix	diez	dez	dieci	zece
hundred	centum	cent	ciento	cento	cento	sută
thousand	mille	mille	mil	mil	mille	mie

Additional points of resemblance and difference may be gathered from the following translations of John 3.16 (*For God so loved the world that He gave His only begotten Son, that whosoever believeth in Him should not perish, but have everlasting life*):

Latin: *Sic enim Deus dilexit mundum, ut Filium suum unigenitum daret, ut omnis, qui credit in eum, non pereat, sed habeat vitam aeternam.*

French: *Car Dieu a tellement aimé le monde, qu'il a donné son Fils unique, afin que quiconque croit en lui ne périsse point, mais qu'il ait la vie eternelle.*

Provençal (modern; Grasse): *Car Diéu a tant ama lou mounde que i'a douna soun Fiéu soulet, per que tout ome que crèi en éu noun perigue, mai ague la vido eternalo.*

Catalan: *Car talment ha estimat Déu el món, que donà son Fill unigènit, a fi que tot el qui creu en ell no es perdi, ans tingui vida eterna.*

Spanish: *Porque de tal manera amó Dios al mundo, que dió a su Hijo unigénito, para que todo aquel que cree en él, no perezca, mas tenga vida eterna.*

Portuguese: *Porque assim amou Deus ao mundo, que lhe*

deu seu Filho unigénito, para que todo o que crê nêle não pereça, mas tenha a vida eterna.

Italian: *Infatti Dio ha talmente amato il mondo da dare il suo Figliuolo unigenito, affinchè chiunque crede in Lui non perisca, ma abbia la vita eterna.*

Roumanian: *Fiindcă atât de mult a iubit Dumnezeu lumea, că a dat pe singurul Lui Fiu, pentru că oricine crede în El, să nu piară, ci să aibă viaţa vecinică.*

Rumansh (Lower Engadine): *Perche cha Deis ha tant amâ il muond, ch'el ha dat seis unigenit figl, acio cha scodün chi craja in el non giaja a perder, ma haja la vita eterna.*

Among grammatical characteristics common to all the Romance languages may be mentioned: a) the reduction of grammatical genders to a masculine-feminine system, with the old Latin neuter gender generally discarded, and Latin neuter nouns becoming either masculine or feminine:[1] b) the disappearance of the Latin inflectional system for nouns and adjectives, so that there are today no separate "cases" for nouns in the Romance languages, which indicate case-relations, even more exclusively than English, by means of word-order and prepositions;[2] c) retention of the inflectional system for verbs, which are generally used (save in French) without the subject pronoun, since distinctive endings for persons and numbers still appear.

1. A few traces of the Latin neuter appear today, in some Italian and Roumanian irregular plurals (It. *il braccio, le braccia*; Roum. *braţul, braţele*); in the Spanish "neuter" article *lo* and the Spanish and Portuguese "neuter" demonstrative pronouns (*esto, eso, aquello; isto, isso, aquilo*); in a few French forms like *ceci* and *cela:* etc. But for practical purposes, it may be asserted that the neuter gender has disappeared from the Romance tongues.

2. Roumanian is an exception to this, having retained a separate nominative-accusative and genitive-dative, as well as occasional vocative forms. Roumanian also distinguishes itself from its sister Romance tongues by using a definite article which is added on to the noun, instead of being used before the noun. Considerable trace of the Latin inflectional system still appears in Romance personal pronouns (e. g., French *il, le, la, lui; ils, les, leur, eux, elles*).

In syntax, word-arrangement within the sentence, use of verb-tenses and moods, the Romance languages, possessing a common point of departure and having enjoyed very close cultural relations throughout their history (with the exception of Roumanian), are fairly close to one another, so that literal word-for-word translation from one to another is usually possible; this applies more to the literary and cultivated than to the lower-class language.

Vocabulary resemblances are fairly common, as may be seen from the list of words in ordinary use given above. Striking divergences also appear, however. [3] The vocabularies of Spanish and Portuguese have borrowed extensively from Arabic, those of French and Italian from Germanic, and that of Roumanian from Slavic.

Some degree of mutual comprehensibility, especially among the more cultured classes, is fairly general for Spanish, Portuguese and Italian, but does not extend to French and Roumanian without special study.

Distinctive of the written languages are the symbols *ç* in Portuguese and French; *ñ* in Spanish; *ã, õ, lh, nh* in Portuguese; *ă, ş, ţ* in Roumanian.

Distinctive of the spoken tongues are the nasal sounds of French and Portuguese; the middle vowels (represented in writing by *u, eu, oeu*) of French; the *â, î* of Roumanian (a sound which Roumanian shares with Russian, and the closest English approximation to which is the *y* of "rhythm"); the clearly audible double consonant sounds of Italian; the guttural *j* of Spanish; the uvular *r* of Parisian French, in contrast to the trilled *r* of the other languages (the trilled *r* is quite common in provincial French).

---

3. The word for "bat", for instance, is *chauve-souris* in French, *murciélago* in Spanish, *pipistrello* in Italian; while *negro* may be used for "black" in Portuguese, the more common word is *prêto*, which would be incomprehensible elsewhere save in Spanish (*prieto*), where it is far less commonly used.

ROUMANIAN

ALPHABETIC NOTATION — as in English; k, q, w, y appear only in foreign words. Additional symbols: ă, â, î, ş, ţ.

SOUNDS

a = f*a*ther; ă = bac*o*n; both â and î = sound somewhat similar
     to Eng. rhythm; there is no difference between â and î;
     î is used initially (*în*); â generally within the word
(*cânta*).
e initially often = *ye*s; elsewhere, = m*e*t; i = mach*i*ne; o
     = *o*r; u = f*oo*d.
c before a, o, u or consonant (and also ch before e, i) = *c*old.
c before e, i = *chi*ll.
g before a, o, u or consonant (and also gh before e, i) = *g*o.
g before e, i = *g*in.
j = plea*s*ure.
s = *s*o, never ro*s*e.
ş = *s*ure.
ţ = hear*ts*.
     There is no definite rule of accentuation; the accent
generally falls on the last, second from last, or third from last
syllable; words of two syllables are generally accented on the
first; words ending in -ar, -at, -el, -esc, -et, -ent, -ez, -os, are
generally stressed on the last syllable. The only written accent
is ` , used on the final vowel of verb-forms when no other
diacritic mark appears (*cântà*, "to sing").

GRAMMATICAL SURVEY

Articles and nouns.

     There are in Roumanian two cases, a nominative-accusa-
tive and a genitive-dative (separate vocative forms also
appear).

There are only two genders, masculine and feminine. [4]
Outside of natural gender, nouns ending in consonants are
generally masculine, those in -*ă* generally feminine. The
indefinite article is *un* (gen.-dat. *unui*) for the masculine; *o*
(gen.-dat. *unei*) for the feminine: *un amic*, "a friend"; *unui
amic*, "to, of a friend"; *o mamă*, "a mother"; *unei mame*,
"to, of a mother".

The definite article is added on to the noun. Masculine
nouns ending in -*e* add *le* (*rege*, "king"; *regele*, "the king");
masculine nouns ending in consonants add -*ul* (*domn*, "gentleman"; *domnul*, "the gentleman"; *cal*, "horse"; *calul*, "the
horse"). Feminine nouns ending in -*ă* change -*ă* to -*a* (*mamă*,
"mother"; *mama*, "the mother"; *soră*, "sister"; *sora*, "the
sister"); feminine nouns ending in -*e* add -*a* (*carne*, "meat";
carnea, "the meat"; *servitoare*, "maid"; *servitoarea*, "the
maid").

The genitive-dative case is indicated in the masculine by
adding the article -*lui* if the noun ends in a vowel, -*ului* if it
ends in a consonant (*regelui*, "of, to the king"; *domnului*, "of,
to the gentleman"; *calului*, "of, to the horse"). In the feminine,
it is indicated by changing -*ă* or -*e* to -*ei* (*mamei*, "of, to the
mother"; *sorei*, "of, to the sister"; *servitoarei*, "of, to the
maid").

In the plural, masculine nouns ending in -*e* change -*e* to -*i*,
while those ending in consonants add -*i* (*domn*, pl. *domni*,
"gentlemen"; *rege*, pl. *regi*, "kings"). To this -*i*, another -*i* is
added for the article (*domnii*, "the gentlemen"; *regii*, "the
kings"); but to form the genitive-dative, the second -*i* is replaced by -*lor* (*domnilor*, "of, to the gentlemen"; *regilor*, "of,
to the kings"). Feminine nouns in -*ă* change to -*e* in the plural
(*mamă*, pl. *mame*, "mothers"; those in -*e* remain for the most
part unchanged: *servitoare*, pl. *servitoare*); the definite article
is then suffixed by adding -*le* (*mamele*, "the mothers";
servitoarele, "the maids"), or -*lor* if the genitive-dative form

4.　But see end of n. 5.

is desired (*mamelor,* "of, to the mothers"; *servitoarelor,* "of, to the maids".[5]

Adjectives.

These agree with their nouns, both in the attributive and in the predicate position (*caii sunt buni,* "the horses are good"). In the attributive position, the adjective may precede or follow the noun; if the adjective precedes, it takes the definite article instead of the noun: *fratele bun* or *bunul frate,* "the good brother"; *fratelui bun* or *bunului frate,* "of or to the good brother"; *mama bună* or *buna mamă,* "the good mother"; *mamelor bune* or *bunelor mame,* "of or to the good mothers".

The comparative is formed by prefixing *mai* to the positive (*mai bun,* "more good", "better"); the superlative by using *cel* (fem. *cea,* masc. pl. *cei,* fem. pl. *cele*) before the comparative: *cel mai bun,* "best".

aşa de....ca, "as....as": *boul este tot aşa de tare ca şi calul,* "the ox is as strong as the horse".

de cât, "than": *boul este mai tare de cât calul,* "the ox is stronger than the horse".

The adjective without an ending is generally used as an adverb: *el scrie grozav,* "he writes horribly".

Numerals.

1 — *un* (fem. *una*)	5 — *cinci*
2 — *doi* (fem. *două*)	6 — *şase*
3 — *trei*	7 — *şapte*
4 — *patru*	8 — *opt*

5.   There are many exceptions to the above rules (e. g., *soră,* "sister", pl. *surori; carne,* "meat", pl. *cărnuri; cal,* "horse", pl. *cai*). The rules are further complicated in the case of many nouns by the change of final *-t, -d, -s* to *-ţ, -z, -ş,* respectively, before the plural *-i* (*frate,* "brother", pl. *fraţi; urs,* "bear", pl. *urşi*).   Several nouns that are masculine in the singular become feminine in the plural (*braţul,* "the arm"; *braţele,* "the arms"; and since these are derived mainly from Latin neuters, some Roumanian grammarians choose to describe them as forming a third, "*ambigen*", or "neuter" gender.

9 — *nouă*	30 — *trei-zeci*
10 — *zece*	40 — *patru-zeci*
11 — *un-spre-zece*	100 — *o sută*
12 — *doi-spre-zece*	200 — *două sute*
20 — *două-zeci*	1000 — *o mie*
23 — *două-zeci şi trei*	2000 — *două mii*

1,000,000 — *un milion*

Pronouns.

Personal.

Singular

	First Person		Second Person
Nom.	*eu*, "I"		*tu*, "you"
Dat.	*mie*, "to me"		*ţie*, "to you"
	(*mi, îmi*)		(*ţi, îţi*)
Acc.	*mine, pe mine*		*tine, pe tine*
	(*mă*), "me"		(*te*), "you"

Third Person

el, "he"		*ea*, "she"
lui, "to him"		*ei*, "to her"
(*'i, îi*)		(*'i, îi*)
pe el, "him"		*pe ea*, "her"
(*îl*)		(*o*)

Plural

	First Person		Second Person
Nom.	*noi*, "we"		*voi*, "you"
Dat.	*nouă*, "to us"		*vouă*, "to you"
	(*ni*)		(*vi*)
Acc.	*pe noi*, "us"		*pe voi*, "you"
	(*ne*)		(*vă*)

Third Person

ei, "they", m.		*ele*, "they", f.
lor, "to them"		*lor*, "to them"
(*li*)		(*li*)
pe ei, "them", m.		*pe ele*, "them" f.
(*'i, îi*)		(*le*)

The subject pronouns may be omitted: *el a auzit,* or *auzit,* "he has heard". The forms given above in parentheses are used as direct or indirect objects with verb-forms, which they normally precede, save in the imperative. Often both the prepositive object pronoun and the longer form following the verb are used: *Dumnea-Voastră nu m'aţi văzut pe mine,* "you didn't see me". *Dumnea-Voastră* ("Your Lordship") with the second person plural of the verb is generally used in polite address. In writing, it is generally abbreviated to *Dv.* or *Dvs.*

Possessive.

	Mas. Sg.	Fem. Sg.	Mas. Pl.	Fem. Pl.
"my", "mine"	*meu*	*mea*	*mei*	*mele*
"your", "yours"	*tău*	*ta*	*tăi*	*tale*
"his", "her"	*său*	*sa*	*săi*	*sale*
"our", "ours"	*nostru*	*noastră*	*noştri*	*noastre*
"your", "yours"	*vostru*	*voastră*	*voştri*	*voastre*
"their", "theirs"	*lor*	*lor*	*lor*	*lor*

The article is used with the noun when the possessives are used as adjectives: *amicul tău,* "your friend". When they are used as pronouns, prefix *al, a, ai, ale: calul vecinului vostru şi al meu,* "your neighbor's horse and mine".

Demonstrative.

	Mas. Sg.	Fem. Sg.	Mas. Pl.	Fem. Pl.
"this", "these"	*acest*	*această*	*aceşti*	*aceste*
"that", "those"	*acel*	*acea*	*acei*	*acele*

Relative and Interrogative.

care or *ce,* "who", which", "that"; *cine?,* "who?"; *pe cine?,* "whom?"; *cui?,* "to whom?"; *a cui?* "whose?"; *ce?,* "what?"; *care?,* "which?".

Verbs.

a fi, "to be": Present: *sunt, eşti, este, suntem, sunteţi, sunt*
           Imperfect: *eram, erai, erà, eram, eraţi, erau*
a aveà, "to have": Present: *am, ai, a* (or *are*), *avem, aveţi, au.*
           Imperfect: *aveam, aveai, aveà, aveam, aveaţi,*
                      aveau.

There are four conjugations, ending respectively in *-à, -ì, -eà, -e*: *cântà,* "to sing"; *dormì,* "to sleep"; *tăceà,* "to be silent"; *vinde,* "to sell".

The present indicative normally has no ending in the first singular and third plural (*dorm,* "I or they sleep"); *-i* in the second singular (*dormi, taci*); *-ă* for *-à* verbs, *-e* for others in the third singular (*cântă, tace, vinde*); *-ăm* for *-à* verbs, *-im* for *-ì* verbs, *-em* for others in the first plural (*cântăm, dormim, vindem*); *-aţi, -iţi, -eţi* in the second plural (*cântaţi, dormiţi, vindeţi*).

Other tenses include an imperfect; a past; a future (which is formed with "to want": *voi, vei, va, vom, veţi, vor,* followed by the infinitive: *voi cântà,* "I shall sing"); compound tenses formed with *aveà,* "to have", followed by the past participle (*am cântat,* "I have sung"; *am dormit,* "I have slept"; *am tăcut,* "I have kept silent"); subjunctives, regularly preceded by *să* (*să aud,* "that I hear"); and conditionals (*aş, ai, ar, am, aţi, ar* followed by the infinitive: *aş cântà,* "I should sing"). The passive is formed by "to be" with the past participle (*sunt lăudat,* "I am praised"; *fui lăudat,* "I was praised"). A reflexive conjugation appears, similar to that of other Romance languages, with dative or accusative pronouns (see pages 176-7) and *se* in the third person: *se spală,* "he washes himself"; *pentru ce nu te speli?,* "why don't you wash yourself?"; *spală-te!,* "wash yourself!"

IDENTIFICATION

The symbols *ă, ş, ţ* are characteristic of Roumanian. Typical are also the *-ul, -lui, -lor* endings of nouns.

SAMPLE OF WRITTEN ROUMANIAN

Limba Românească	The Roumanian Language

Mult e dulce și frumoasă
  Limba, ce vorbim!
Altă limbă armonioasă
  Ca ea nu găsim!
Saltă inima 'n plăcere,
  Când o ascultăm,
Și pe buze aduce miere,
  ' Când o cuvântăm.
Românașul o iubeste
  Ca sufletul său,
O! vorbiți, scriți românește,
  Pentru Dumnezeu!

Very sweet and beautiful is
  the language that we speak!
Another harmonious language
  like it we do not find!
The heart leaps up in pleasure
  when we listen to it,
And to the mouths it brings honey,
  when we speak it.
The Roumanian loves it
  as his own breath (of life),
Oh! speak, write Roumanian,
  for (the love of) God!

VOCABULARY

(Mainly of Latin origin, but with strong Slavic infiltrations; note synonyms from two sources: *față* or *obraz*, "face"; *timp* or *vreme*, "time").

și, "and"
că, "that"
sau, "or"
când, "when"
pentru ce?, "why?"
pentru că, "because"
despre, "about"
bucuros, "gladly"
astăzi, "today"
ieri, "yesterday"
mâine, "tomorrow"
acolo, "there"
aproape, "near"
a da, "to give"
cât?, "how much?"
mult, "much"
foarte, "very"
da, "yes"
nu, "not", "no"
nimic, "nothing"

bine, "well"
acum, "now"
la dreapta, "to the right"
la stânga, "to the left"
jos, "down"
acasă, "at home"
apă, "water"
cuțit, "knife"
ou, "egg"
vin, "wine"
ceaiu, "tea"
furculiță, "fork"
pâine, "bread"
poame, "fruit"
bere, "beer"
lingură, "spoon"
ceașcă, "cup"
unt, "butter"
lapte, "milk"
cafea, "coffee"

a sta, "to stand"
poate, "perhaps"
cu, "with"
fără, "without"
în, "in"
în loc de, "instead of"
sub, "under"
rău, "bad", "badly"
unde?, "where?"
acì, "here"
sus, "up"
afară, "out"
a mânca, "to eat"
a se jucà, "to play"
îmi place, "I like"
mi-e frig, "I'm cold"
mi-e cald, "I'm warm"
mi-e somn, "I'm sleepy"
mi-e bine, "I'm well"
mi-e foame, "I'm hungry"
vă rog, "please"
cât e ceasul? "what time is it?"
ce seară frumoasă! "what a
    beautiful evening!"
totdeauna, "always"
niciodată, "never"
înainte de, "before"
în faţa, "in front of"
în dosul, "behind"
albastru, "blue"
roşu, "red"
alb, "white"
galben, "yellow"
bună dimineaţa, "good morning"
bună ziua, "good day"
bună seara, "good evening",
    "good night"
la revedere, "good-bye"

ce mai faceţi?, "how are you?"
mulţumesc, "thank you"
noroc!, "your health!", "good
    luck!"
scuzaţi-mă, "excuse me"
cât costă?, "how much is it?"
prea scump, "too much"
vorbiţi englezeşte?, "do you speak
    English?"
îmi pare rău, "I'm sorry"
aţi înţeles?, înţelegeţi?, "do
    you understand?"
nu înţeleg, "I don't understand"
vorbiţi mai încet, "speak more
    slowly"
cum vă numiţi?, "what is your
    name?"
mă numesc —, "my name is —"
adu-mi, "bring me"
puteţi să-mi daţi?, "can you give
    me?"
cât timp?, "how long?"
la şase şi jumătate, "at half past
    six"
la şase fără un sfert, "at a quarter
    to six"
sunt bolnav, "I am ill"
care este drumul spre —?, "which
    is the way to —?"
nu e aşa?, "isn't it so?"
unde este?, "where is?"
pe aici, "this way"
poftiţi înăuntru!, "come in!"
domnule, "sir"
domnişoară, "miss", "young
    lady"
destul!, "enough!"

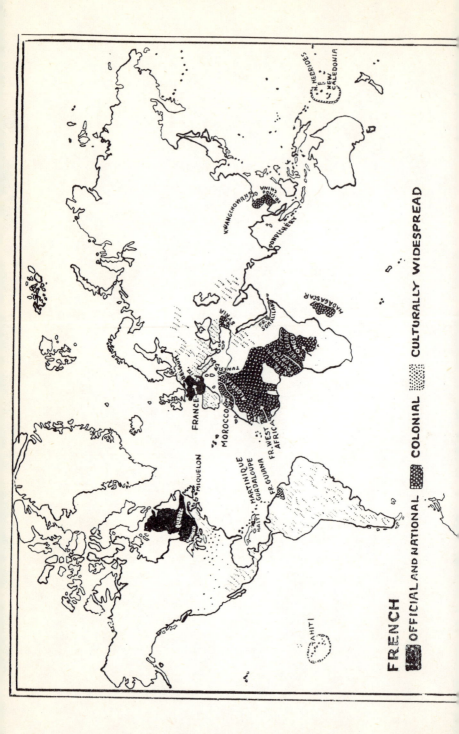

FRENCH

OFFICIAL AND NATIONAL ■ COLONIAL ▨ CULTURALLY WIDESPREAD ▦

CHAPTER VI

FRENCH

SPEAKERS AND LOCATION

(All population figures are approximate)

Europe — France — 42,000,000; Belgium — 4,500,000; Switzerland — 2,000,000; scattered groups of French speakers in extreme northwestern Italy (Val d'Aosta, Pinerolo); spoken side by side with German, but not so extensively, in Luxembourg. Widely used as a secondary, cultural, diplomatic and commercial language throughout continental Europe, particularly in Italy, the Netherlands, Portugal, Spain, Poland, Russia.

Africa — Language of colonization in the following countries: Algeria (8,000,000); Belgian Congo (14,000,000); Cameroon (2,500,000); French Equatorial Africa (3,500,000); French West Africa (16,000,000); Madagascar (4,000,000); Morocco (7,000,000); Tunisia (3,000,000); French Somaliland (50,000). Widely used as a secondary and cultural language in Egypt.

Asia — Tongue of colonization in French Indo-China (24,500,-000); Syria and Lebanon (4,000,000); French cities on the coasts of India and China (Pondichéry, Kwang-chowan, etc. — about 500,000). Used as cultural language in other Asiatic countries, notably Turkey, Iran, Japan, China.

Oceania — Tongue of colonization in French Pacific possessions (French Oceania, New Caledonia, New Hebrides, West Samoa, etc. — about 250,000).

Western Hemisphere — Canada (Quebec and Ontario) —

3,000,000 (an additional 1,000,000 in New England); Haiti — 3,000,000. Tongue of colonization in French American possessions (Guadaloupe, Martinique, French Guiana — about 750,000). Widely used as a cultural, secondary and diplomatic tongue in all countries of Latin America, especially Argentina and Mexico, and as a cultural language in the U. S. A. and English-speaking Canada.

ALPHABET AND SOUNDS

a, b, c, d, e, f, g, h, i, j, l, m, n, o, p, q, r, s, t, u, v, x, y, z (k and w appear only in a few words of foreign origin: *képi, kilo, wagon*).

Vowel sounds: usually short (never as short as English short vowels), but occasionally prolonged in stressed syllable; length is to be learned by observation.

    a = h*a*t (this is the more usual value: l*à*); or
       = f*a*ther (this is less frequent: p*a*s; but it is normal when the vowel bears the circumflex accent: *âge*).
    e = m*e*t, when the vowel bears the grave or circumflex accent (p*è*re, fen*ê*tre), also when it does not come at the end of the syllable (cf. Syllabification, p. 187: let-tre, inté*re*s-sant, al*er*-te, a-m*er*);
       = first part of *a* in Eng. g*a*te when the vowel bears the acute accent (ferm*é*); also in final *-er* and *-ez* of verb forms (aim*er*, aim*ez*);
       is completely silent in *-e* and *-es* endings of words of more than one syllable (ami*e*, ball*e*, port*es*); also in the third plural endings of verbs (port*ent*);
       = th*e* (with a slight projection of the lips) in most other positions (l*e*, r*e*mettre).
    i = mach*i*ne (v*i*e, *i*l).
    o = b*ou*ght (m*o*de); or
       = first part of *o* in Eng. g*o* (n*o*s; the latter value is rarer, but always appears when the vowel is the last *sound* in the word, or bears the circumflex accent:

nôtre, with closed sound, as opposed to notre, with
open sound).

u = sound intermediate between f*ee*d and f*oo*d (m*u*r,
t*u*). Place tongue in position for f*ee*d, lips in position for f*oo*d.

ai, at the end of a verb-form = first part of g*a*te
(j'aur*ai*).

ai, in other positions, and ei in all positions = met (f*ai*re,
av*ai*t, n*ei*ge).

au, eau = first part of g*o* (*au*ssi, b*eau*).

ou = f*oo*d (*ou*blier).

eu, oeu = sounds intermediate between g*a*te and g*o*, or
between m*e*t and m*u*d; the first sound (g*a*te, with
projected lips) occurs more frequently when it is the
final sound in a word (p*eu*, v*oeu*); the latter (m*e*t,
with projected lips) when another sound follows in
the same word (h*eu*re, s*eu*l).

oi = *wa*sp (m*oi*); *we*nt if nasalized (m*oi*ns).

Nasal Vowels: these occur, usually, when the vowel is
followed by m or n in the same syllable (b*on*, *in*-téres*sant*; cf.
Syllabification, p. 187); but not if the m or n is doubled
(bonne, homme), in which cases the vowel is pronounced by
itself, at the close of the syllable, and the double m or n is
joined to the next vowel (bo-nne, ho-mme). To produce the
nasal vowel sound, shut off partly the passage between nose
and mouth as the vowel is uttered, and refrain completely from
pronouncing the n or m:

an, am, en, em = f*a*ther, with nasal connection partly shut off
(*an*-glais, ch*am*p, *en*-core, *em*-bêter).

on, om = g*o*, with nasal connection partly shut off (*on*, *om*-
bre).

in, im, ain, aim, ein = h*a*t, with nasal connection partly shut
off (f*in*, *im*-possible, m*ain*, s*ein*).

un, um = m*e*t, with projected lips, and with nasal connection
partly shut off (*un*, l*un*-di, par-f*um*).

Consonant sounds: b, d, f, l, m, n, p, s, t, v, x, y, z, approximately as in English;[1] (d and t, however, are pronounced with tip of tongue touching back of upper teeth, not the palate).

c: before a, o, u or consonant, = cold (comment).
c: before e, i = ice (ici); ç always = ice (ça).
ch: = sure (charbon).
g: before a, o, u or consonant, = go (garçon).
g: before e or i, = pleasure (gilet).
gn: = canyon (agneau).
h: is normally silent (homme).
j: = pleasure (jeune).
ill, and final -il preceded by a vowel = machine quickly follow-
      ed by you (fille, travail).[2]

r: is rolled, with the uvula vibrating toward the palate, like a
      gentle clearing of the throat in its upper part: rare.

q: as in English, but a following u is normally silent(qui pron.
      kee; quatre pron. katr); u is also generally silent
      after g (guerre).
th: = tea (thé).

1. The final consonant of a word is generally silent (finit, pron. fini), but final c, f, l, r are usually sounded (lac, neuf, tel, par); -r, however, is silent in the infinitive ending -er (parler, pron. parlé) and in the ending -ier; the addition of -s does not change the sound of the final consonant (petit or petits, both pron. peti); but the addition of an -e does, causing an otherwise silent final consonant to be pronounc- ed (petite or petites, both pron. petit); laid (ugly) and its masc. pl. form laids are both pronounced lè; but the fem. sg. and pl., laide, laides, are both pronounced lèd.

      A final consonant, which would otherwise be silent in accordance with the above, is often carried over to the next word if the latter begins with a vowel or h and forms part of the same thought-unit; *les hommes avaient pris cette énorme table* is pronounced lé zom zavè pri sè ténorme table. In such linking, final s and x are pronounced as z when carried over, d is pronounced as t, f occasionally as v (*les* by itself is lé, but *les hommes* is lé zom; *grand* by itself is grã, but *grand homme* is grã tom; *neuf* is nöf; but *neuf hommes* is nö vom).

2. Important exceptions, in which the ill is sounded like machine followed by lamb, are: *mille* (one thousand); *tranquille* (quiet); *ville* (city); *village* (village).

CAPITALIZATION, SYLLABIFICATION, ACCENTUATION

Do not capitalize *je* (I), names of days and months (*lundi, janvier*); adjectives of nationality (*français*), even if used as names of languages (*le français; il parle français*): but capitalize if the adjective of nationality refers to people: *le Français*, the Frenchman; *les Français*, the French.

In dividing a word into syllables, make sure that a single consonant between two vowels goes with the *following*, not with the preceding vowel (*gé né ral*, as against Eng. gen er al); this rule, of great importance in all Romance languages, is doubly important in French, because upon it often depends the nasalization or non-nasalization of the preceding vowel: *main*, with nasalized ai, and silent n; but *lai-ne*, with no nasalization and n fully pronounced; *in-té-res-sant*, with nasalized i and a, and neither n pronounced, but *i-nu-ti-le*, with no nasalization of i and n fully pronounced with the following u.

French stresses all syllables of a word about equally; this means more emphasis on the final syllable than appears in English, and gives the impression that French stresses the last pronounced syllable in the word. The accent marks of French have already been described (acute: ´; grave: `; circumflex: ^). They do not indicate stress on the vowel over which they appear, but serve only to differentiate among the various possible sounds for that vowel. The circumflex may appear on any vowel, which is then often long. The acute and the grave usually appear over the vowel e; but the grave is also occasionally used on other vowels to distinguish between two words having the same pronunciation but different meanings: *où*, where; *ou*, or; *là*, there; *la*, the.

The cedilla (ç) appears only with c and indicates that the c is sounded like s before a, o or u (*reçu*).

The diaeresis (¨) is used over a vowel to prevent it from combining with the preceding vowel(*Noël*, pron. No el, not Nöl).

The apostrophe indicates that a vowel has been dropped

before another vowel or an h (*l'assiette* for *la assiette*; *l'homme* for *le homme*).

English sounds not appearing in French: all vowels save above; *ch*urch; *g*in; *th*in; *th*is; American r.

French sounds not appearing in English: eu, oeu; u; nasalized vowels; French r.

SAMPLE OF WRITTEN FRENCH; USE FOR PRACTICE READING.

Coûte que coûte, il fallait donner le signal aux avions anglais, qui ne pouvaient pas tarder à apparaître dans le ciel sombre et orageux de la nuit. Le tas de bois était là, tel que l'avait soigneusement arrangé la mère Francois avant la tombée du soleil. Mais comment s'en approcher? Comment y mettre le feu avec ces précieuses allumettes qu'on avait si long-temps conservées pour la besogne? Cette sentinelle allemande, placée à cet endroit où l'on n'avait jamais placé de sentinelle auparavant, restait là, debout, immobile. Pierrot prit une résolution soudaine. La main droite dans la poche de son pantalon, les doigts crispés autour du manche du couteau, il se dirigea lentement, en sifflant, vers le Boche, qui, sans ouvrir la bouche, sans faire un mouvement, le regardait venir. — Bonsoir, monsieur, — lui dit Pierrot, — Est-ce qu'il me serait permis de ramasser quelques morceaux de ce bois? On a froid là-bas. — L'autre fit un vague geste de consentement, lui tourna le dos, et se mit à regarder attentivement du côté de la mer. On connaissait bien Pierrot, depuis les premiers jours de l'occupa-tion; et d'ailleurs, ce n'était qu'un garçon de quinze ans.

GRAMMATICAL SURVEY

1. *Nouns and articles.*

French has only two genders, masculine and feminine. Nouns denoting males are normally masculine, those denoting females feminine. For nouns which in English are neuter, the

article, definite or indefinite, indicates the French gender. The
definite article is *le* for masculine singular nouns, *la* for feminine singulars; both masculine and feminine singular nouns
beginning with vowels and (usually) h take *l'*; the plural of
the definite article is *les*, used without exception for all plural
nouns.[3] The indefinite article is *un* for masculine nouns, *une*
for feminine nouns. Most French nouns form their plural by
the addition of a silent *-s*.[4]

le livre, the book	*les livres*, the books	*un livre*, a book
la porte, the door	*les portes*, the doors	*une porte*, a door
l'homme, the man	*les hommes*, the men	*un homme*, a man
l'eau, the water	*les eaux*, the waters	*une eau*, a water

2.   *Adjectives and Adverbs.*

French adjectives take the same gender and number as the
nouns they modify, regardless of position. Normally, the
adjective adds *-e* for the feminine singular (unless it already

3.   *Le* and *les* (but not *la* or *l'*) combine with the prepositions *de*,
"of", and *à*, "to", in the following forms: *de le* become *du; de les*
become *des; à le* become *au; à les* become *aux* (*du père*, of the father;
des hommes, of the men; *de la mère*, of the mother; *des femmes*, of the
women; *au colonel*, to the colonel; *aux officiers*, to the officers).

   Du, de la, de l', des are used with the meaning of "some", "any":
donnez-moi de l'eau, give me (some) water; *avez-vous du vin?*, have
you (any) wine?; *il a vu des hommes*, he saw some men. If the
sentence is negative, however, *de* alone, without the article, is used to
express "some", "any": *je n'ai pas de vin*, I haven't any wine, I have
no wine; *nous n'avons pas de lait*, we haven't any milk, we have no
milk.

4.   Nouns ending in *-s, -x, -z* remain unchanged in the plural (*le
nez*, the nose; *les nez*, the noses; *la voix*, the voice, *les voix*, the
voices). Most nouns ending in *-al* change *-al* to *-aux*: *le cheval*, the
horse, *les chevaux*, the horses. Most nouns ending in *-au, -eu, -ou*, add
-x instead of *-s* to form the plural: *le bateau*, the boat; *les bateaux*, the
boats; *le feu*, the fire; *les feux*, the fires; *le bijou*, the jewel; *les
bijoux*, the jewels.

ends in *-e*, like *triste;* fem. same); silent *-s* for the masculine plural;[5] *-es* for the feminine plural.

le grand homme, the great man
les grands hommes, the great men
la grande femme, the great woman
les grandes femmes, the great women
la femme est grande, the woman is great
les hommes sont grands, the men are great

Adjectives usually follow the noun, but a few commonly used ones precede (*bon,* good; *mauvais,* bad; *petit,* small, *grand,* large, great, tall).

The comparative is generally formed by placing *plus* (more) before the adjective; the superlative by using the definite article before the comparative: *un gros livre,* a big book; *un plus gros livre,* a bigger book; *le plus gros livre,* the biggest book; *un garçon intelligent,* an intelligent boy; *un garçon plus intelligent,* a more intelligent boy; *le garçon le plus intelligent de la classe,* the most intelligent boy in the class.[6]

The adverb is generally formed by adding *-ment* to the feminine singular form of the adjective: *grand,* great; fem. sg. *grande;* adverb *grandement,* greatly; *facile,* easy, fem. sg. the same; adverb *facilement,* easily.

3. *Numerals.*

a) Cardinal.[7]

1 — *un, une*	3 — *trois*
2 — *deux*	4 — *quatre*

5. But the same rules that apply to the plural of nouns generally apply to the plural of adjectives (see note 4). Remember that the addition of *-s* does not change the sound of the preceding consonant, that of *-e* does: *laid, laids,* pron. *lè; laide, laides,* pron. *lèd.*

6. Note the double use of the definite article, also the use of *de* for "in" after a superlative.

7. Use these in dates, save for "the first": *le premier juin,* June 1st; *le vingt-cinq juin,* June 25th.

5 — *cinq*[8]
6 — *six*[8]
7 — *sept*
8 — *huit*[8]
9 — *neuf*
10 — *dix*[8]
11 — *onze*
12 — *douze*
13 — *treize*
14 — *quatorze*
15 — *quinze*
16 — *seize*

17 — *dix-sept*
18 — *dix-huit*[8]
19 — *dix-neuf*
20 — *vingt*
21 — *vingt et un*[8]
22 — *vingt-deux*
30 — *trente*
40 — *quarante*
50 — *cinquante*
60 — *soixante*
70 — *soixante-dix*[8]
71 — *soixante et onze*

72 — *soixante-douze*
80 — *quatre-vingts*[8]
81 — *quatre-vingt-un*[8]
90 — *quatre-vingt-dix*[8]
91 — *quatre-vingt-onze*
92 — *quatre-vingt-douze*
100 — *cent*[8]
101 — *cent un*
200 — *deux cents*[8]
205 — *deux cent cinq*[8]
1000 — *mille* (*mil* in dates)
5000 — *cinq mille*
1,000,000 — *un million* (*de*)
1,000,000,000 — *un milliard* (*de*)

8. *Et* connects the two parts of 21, 31, 41, 51, 61, 71; **hyphens** connect the two parts of other compound numerals. Use *-s* in **80** and plural hundreds unless other numerals follow. The final *-q* of *cinq* and the final *-t* of *huit* are usually sounded. The *-x* of *six* and *dix* is silent when a following noun begins with a consonant; sounded like *-z* when the following noun begins with vowel or h; sounded like hard *-s* when there is no following noun.

b) Ordinal.

1st — *premier* (fem. *première*)	9th — *neuvième*
2nd — *second* or *deuxième*	10th — *dixième*
3rd — *troisième*	11th — *onzième*
4th — *quatrième*	19th — *dix-neuvième*
5th — *cinquième*	21st — *vingt et unième*
7th — *septième*	22nd — *vingt-deuxième*

(Drop final vowel of cardinal and add *-ième*, changing *f* of *neuf* to *v*, and *q* of *cinq* to *qu*; use *second* for the second of two, *deuxième* where more than two are involved).

c) Others.

half — *la moitié* (noun): *la moitié de ma classe,* half of my class;

half — *demi* (adjective); invariable before the noun, and attached by a hyphen: *une demi-heure,* half an hour; adds *-e* if it follows a feminine noun: *une heure et demie,* an hour and a half.

a pair of — *une paire de;* a dozen eggs — *une douzaine d'oeufs;* a score of men — *une vingtaine d'hommes;*

once — *une fois;* twice — *deux fois;* three times — *trois fois;* the first (last) time — *la première (dernière) fois.*

4 *Pronouns.*

a) Personal — Subject.

I, *je*	we, *nous*
you, *tu*[9]	you, *vous*[9]
he, it, *il*[9]	they (masc.), *ils*
she, it, *elle*[9]	they, (fem.), *elles*

These are regularly used with the verb: *il parle,* he speaks.

9. Use *tu* with the second singular of the verb only in familiar conversation; *vous* with the second plural of the verb is the general polite way of addressing either one or more people. *Il* translates "it" when the noun is masculine in French, *elle* when it is feminine: *voyez-vous le livre? Il est sur la table,* do you see the book? It is on the table; *où est la table? Elle est dans la salle,* where is the table? It is in the room.

b) Personal; Direct and Indirect Object.

me, to me, *me*	us, to us, *nous*
you, to you, *te*	you, to you, *vous*
him, it, *le*	them, *les*
her, it, *la*	to them, *leur*
to him, to her, *lui*	

These precede the verb (*je le vois*, I see him; *il me donne le livre*, he gives me the book), save in the imperative *affirmative*, where the object pronouns are attached to the verb by a hyphen, and *moi* and *toi* replace *me* and *te* (*prenez-le*, take it; *donnez-moi le livre*, give me the book). In the imperative *negative*, the general rule holds (*ne le prenez pas*, don't take it; *ne me donnez pas le livre*, don't give me the book). If the direct and indirect object pronoun are used together, put the indirect before the direct (*il me le donne*, he gives it to me; *je vous les donne*, I give them to you), unless both are third person (*je le lui donne*, I give it to him; *vous les leur donnez*, you give them to them), or the imperative *affirmative* is used (*donnez-les-nous*, give them to us; but *ne nous les donnez pas*, don't give them to us).

Y, "there", "in that place", "to that place", and *en* "of it", "of them", "some", "any" (the latter meanings when the noun does not appear), follow the same rules of position, being placed after all other pronouns: *je l'y ai vu*, I saw him there; *il m'en a donné*, he gave me some. *Y* also means "to it", "to them", referring to inanimate objects: I am going to it, *j'y vais*.

c) Personal (with prepositions or alone).

I, me, *moi*	we, us, *nous*
you, *toi*	you, *vous*
he, him, *lui*	they, them (masc.), *eux*
she, her, *elle*	they, them (fem.), *elles*

avec moi, with me; *sans toi*, without you; *pour eux*, for them; *qui avez-vous vu? Eux*, whom did you see? Them; *qui est là? Moi*, who is there? I.

d) Possessive.

1. *With the noun (adjectives)*:

Masc. Sg.	Fem. Sg.	Plural		Singular	Plural
my,	*mon*	*ma*	*mes*	our,	*notre*	*nos*
your,	*ton*	*ta*	*tes*	your,	*votre*	*vos*
his,						
her,	*son*	*sa*	*ses*	their,	*leur*	*leurs*
its,						

mon frère, my brother; *ses soeurs,* his sisters; *nos parents,* our parents; *leurs livres,* their books; *leur soeur,* their sister; *ma mère,* my mother.

2. *Without the noun (pronouns)*:

	Masc. Sg.	Fem. Sing.	Masc. Pl.	Fem. Pl.
mine,	*le mien*	*la mienne*	*les miens*	*les miennes*
yours,	*le tien*	*la tienne*	*les tiens*	*les tiennes*
his,				
hers,	*le sien*	*la sienne*	*les siens*	*les siennes*
its,				
ours,	*le nôtre*	*la nôtre*	*les nôtres*	*les nôtres*
yours,	*le vôtre*	*la vôtre*	*les vôtres*	*les vôtres*
theirs,	*le leur*	*la leur*	*les leurs*	*les leurs*

mon frère et le tien, my brother and yours; *ses livres et les vôtres,* his books and yours.

e) Demonstrative.

1. *With noun (adjectives)*:

this, that,[10] *ce, cet* (both forms are masc. sg.; use *ce* before a consonant, *cet* before a vowel or (usually) h: *ce livre,* this or that book; *cet homme,* this or that man;

10. Differentiate between "this" and "that", "these" and "those", by using -*ci* (here) or -*là* (there) after the noun, if such differentiation is really required: *ce livre-ci,* this book; *ce livre-là, that* book.

cette (fem. sg.): *cette femme,* this woman, that woman;

these, those,[10] *ces: ces hommes,* these *or* those men; *ces femmes,* these *or* those women.

2. *Without noun* (*pronouns*):

this, that, this one, that one, the one,[11] *celui* (masc.), *celle* (fem.);

these, those, the ones,[11] *ceux* (masc.), *celles* (fem.).
    mon livre et celui qui est sur la table, my book and the one which is on the table; *tes soeurs et celles de ton ami,* your sisters and those of your friend (your friend's).

this (referring not to a specific person or thing, but to a general situation or idea), *ceci: ceci ne me plaît pas,* this does not please me;

that (general situation or idea), *cela* or *ça: cela va bien,* that's all right.

f) Relative.

who, which, that (subject), *qui: l'homme qui est arrivé,* the man who came; *le livre qui est sur la table,* the book which is on the table.

whom, which, that (object), *que: l'homme que vous avez vu,* the man (whom) you saw; *le livre que vous avez pris,* the book (which) you took.[12]

whose, of which, of whom, *dont: l'homme dont vous avez parlé,* the man of whom you spoke; *l'homme dont vous avez pris le livre,* the man whose book you took (note that the word-order calls for a shift from "whose" to "of whom": the man of whom you took the book).

---

11. Append *-ci* or *-là* to these forms unless a preposition or relative pronoun follows: *tes livres et ceux-ci,* your books and these.

12. Note that the relative pronoun cannot be omitted in French.

which (generally used after prepositions, referring to things; use *qui* after prepositions referring to persons), *lequel, laquelle, lesquels, lesquelles*: *la maison dans laquelle je demeure*, the house in which I live (observe that the *le-* and *les-* of these forms combine with a preceding *de* and *à*: *duquel, desquels, auquel, auxquelles*, etc.).

g) Interrogative.

who?, *qui?* or *qui est-ce qui?*: *qui* (*est-ce qui*) *est arrivé?*, who arrived?

whom?, *qui?* or *qui est-ce que?*: *qui avez-vous vu?* or *qui est-ce que vous avez vu?*, whom did you see?

what? (subject), *qu'est-ce qui?*: *qu'est-ce qui s'est passé?*, what happened?

what? (object), *que?* or *qu'est-ce que?*: *qu'avez-vous vu?* or *qu'est-ce que vous avez vu?*, what did you see?

which?, which one?, which ones?, *lequel, laquelle, lesquels, lesquelles?*: *laquelle de ses soeurs connaissez-vous?*, which one of his sisters do you know?

5. *Verbs.*

French verbs fall into four main classes, distinguished by the infinitive endings *-er, -ir, -re, -oir*, respectively (*parler, finir, vendre, recevoir*). The infinitive is the form generally used after prepositions (*pour parler*, in order to speak; *sans finir*, without finishing). A present participle, ending in *-ant* (*-issant* for *-ir* verbs) is used after the preposition *en* with the meaning of "by", "while" (*en vendant*, by or while selling). This form cannot be used with "to be" in the English sense of "I am speaking", which is translated by the simple present (*je parle*). The subject pronoun is normally used in French.

1. Present Indicative (meaning: I speak, am speaking, do speak).

to speak, *parler*

I speak, *je parl-e*
you speak, *tu parl-es*
he speaks, *il parl-e*
we speak, *nous parl-ons*
you speak, *vous parl-ez*
they speak, *ils parl-ent*

to sell, *vend-re*

I sell, *je vend-s*
you sell, *tu vend-s*
he sells, *il vend*
we sell, *nous vend-ons*
you sell, *vous vend-ez*
they sell, *ils vend-ent*

to finish, *fin-ir*

I finish, *je fin-is*
you finish, *tu fin-is*
he finishes, *il fin-it*
we finish, *nous fin-issons*
you finish, *vous fin-issez*
they finish, *ils fin-issent*

to receive, *rec-ev-oir*

I receive, *je reç-ois*
you receive, *tu reç-ois*
he receives, *il reç-oit*
we receive, *nous rec-evons*
you receive, *vous rec-evez*
they receive, *ils reç-oivent*

to be, *être: je suis, tu es, il est, nous sommes, vous êtes, ils sont.*
to have, *avoir: j'ai, tu as, il a, nous avons, vous avez, ils ont.*
to go, *aller: je vais, tu vas, il va, nous allons, vous allez, ils vont.*
to know, *savoir: je sais, tu sais, il sait, nous savons, vous savez,
ils savent.*

to say, *dire: je dis, tu dis, il dit, nous disons, vous dites, ils
disent.*

to do (make), *faire: je fais, tu fais, il fait, nous faisons, vous
faites, ils font.*

2. Negative and Interrogative Forms.

The negative is normally formed by placing *ne* before the
verb and *pas* after it: *je ne parle pas*, I don't speak. If a compound tense is used, *pas* is placed between the auxiliary and
the past participle: *je n'ai pas parlé*, I haven't spoken. Other
negative particles (*point*, at all; *jamais*, never; *personne*, nobody; *rien*, nothing) may replace *pas*: *je ne parle point*, I'm
not speaking at all; *je ne l'ai jamais vu*, I have never seen him;

je n'ai rien vu, I have seen nothing; but *personne* follows the
past participle: *je n'ai vu personne*, I have seen no one.

The interrogative may be formed by inverting subject and
verb, if the subject is a *pronoun*: *vous parlez*, you are speaking;
parlez-vous?, are you speaking?[13] If the subject is a *noun*, this
is usually isolated by a comma at the beginning of the sentence,
and the question is then formed with the appropriate pronoun:
votre frère, parle-t-il français?, does your brother speak
French? An alternative method, which works for both noun and
pronoun subjects, is to prefix *est-ce que* (literally, "is it that?")
to the declarative form: *est-ce qu'il est ici?*, is he here (lit.
is it that he is here?) ; *est-ce que votre frère parle français?*,
does your brother speak French? (lit. is it that your brother
speaks French?).

3.   Imperfect (meaning: I was speaking, used to speak).

The endings, for all verbs, are *-ais, -ais, -ait, -ions, -iez,
-aient* (*je parl-ais, tu parl-ais*, etc.; *je vend-ais, tu vend-ais*,
etc.) ; *-ir* verbs insert *-iss-* throughout before the ending (*je
fin-iss-ais, tu fin-iss-ais*, etc.); *-oir* verbs use the full stem
(*je rec-ev-ais, tu rec-ev-ais*, etc.).   *Etre* has *j'étais*, etc.; *dire*
has *je dis-ais*; *faire* has *fais-ais*.

4.   Past (meaning: I spoke).

This tense seldom appears save in books, being replaced
in conversation by the present perfect.   Its forms are:
parl-er: *je parl-ai, tu parl-as, il parl-a, nous parl-âmes, vous
        parl-âtes, ils parl-èrent.*
fin-ir: *je fin-is, tu fin-is, il fin-it, nous fin-îmes, vous fin-îtes,
        ils fin-irent.*
vend-re: *je vend-is, tu vend-is, il vend-it, nous vend-îmes, vous
        vend-îtes, ils vend-irent.*

13.   Note the hyphen used in these cases of inversion, also the letter
-t-, inserted between the verb and the pronoun when the former ends
and the latter begins with a vowel: *a-t-il?*, has he?; *parle-t-il?*, does
he speak?

rec-ev-oir: *je reç-us, tu reç-us, il reç-ut, nous reç-ûmes, vous reç-ûtes, ils reç-urent.*

être has *je fus; avoir* has *j'eus; savoir* has *je sus; dire* has *je dis; faire* has *je fis; aller* is regular (*j'allai*).

5. Future and Conditional (meaning: I shall speak, I should speak).

The future endings are: *-ai, -as, -a, -ons, -ez, -ont.* These are added not to the stem, but to the *full infinitive* (*je parler-ai,* I shall speak; *tu finir-as,* you will finish); *-re* verbs, however, lose the final *e* (*je vendr-ai,* I shall sell), while *-oir* verbs lose the *oi* (*je recev-r-ai,* I shall receive).

The conditional endings are precisely the same as those of the imperfect: *-ais, -ais, -ait, -ions, -iez, -aient;* but they are added to the *full infinitive* instead of to the stem, with loss of *e* for *-re* verbs and loss of *oi* for *-oir* verbs; whatever irregularities appear in the future will also appear in the conditional: *je parler-ais,* I should speak; *tu finir-ais,* you would finish; *il vendr-ait,* he would sell; *nous recev-r-ions,* we should receive.

The future and conditional of *être* are *je serai* and *je serais;* of *avoir, j'aurai* and *j'aurais;* of *aller, j'irai* and *j'irais;* of *savoir, je saurai* and *je saurais;* of *faire, je ferai* and *je ferais;* of *dire, je dirai* and *je dirais.*

6. Compound Tenses.

These are formed, as in English, by using *avoir,* "to have", with the past participle. The latter ends in *-é* for *-er* verbs, (*parl-é,* spoken), in *-i* for *-ir* verbs (*fin-i,* finished), in *-u* for *-re* and *-oir* verbs (the latter, however, drop *-ev-*: *vend-u,* sold; *reç-u,* received).

A certain number of intransitive verbs denoting motion (*aller,* to go, *venir,* to come, etc.), change of state (*devenir,* to become; *mourir,* to die, etc.), also *rester,* "to remain", "to stay", and *tomber,* "to fall", (but not *être,* "to be") take *être* as an auxiliary instead of *avoir.*[14]

Present Perfect: I have spoken, I spoke, *j'ai parlé, tu as parlé, il a parlé, nous avons parlé, vous avez parlé, ils ont parlé;* I have come, *je suis venu, tu es venu, il est venu, nous sommes venus, vous êtes venus, ils sont venus* (and note *elle est venue, elles sont venues; je suis venue* if a woman is writing).

Past Perfect: I had spoken, *j'avais parlé,* etc.; I had come, *j'étais venu,* etc.

Future Perfect: I shall have spoken, *j'aurai parlé;* I shall have come, *je serai venu.*

Conditional Perfect: I should have spoken, *j'aurais parlé;* I should have come, *je serais venu.*

7.   Imperative.[15] (meaning: speak!; let us speak).

	Familiar Singular	Plural and Polite Sg.	"let us"
-er verbs:	parl-e	parl-ez	parl-ons
-ir verbs:	fin-is	fin-issez	fin-issons
-re verbs:	vend-s	vend-ez	vend-ons
-oir verbs:	reç-ois	rec-ev-ez	rec-ev-ons

14.   The past participle conjugated with *avoir* is invariable if the direct object follows, but agrees with the direct object if the latter precedes: *j'ai vu les hommes,* I saw the men; but *je les ai vus,* I saw them; *les hommes que j'ai vus,* the men I saw. When *être* is used, the past participle agrees with the subject: *elle est arrivée,* she arrived; *ils sont sortis,* they went out. Incorrect agreement of the past participle is not an unforgivable crime, particularly since the agreement appears in writing, but not in speech, the endings being normally silent.

15.   Remember: 1. that object pronouns *follow* the imperative affirmative and are attached by hyphens, with *moi* and *toi* replacing *me* and *te*: *parle-moi,* speak to me; *donnez-moi,* give me; *lave-toi,* wash yourself; 2. that the direct object always precedes the indirect object pronoun in the imperative affirmative: *vendez-le-moi,* sell it to me; *vendons-les-leur,* let us sell them to them; 3. that in the negative imperative object pronouns precede the verb in the more customary indirect-direct order (unless both are third person): *ne me le donnez pas,* don't give it to me; *ne le lui donnez pas,* don't give it to him.

être:	*sois*	*soyez*	*soyons*
avoir:	*aie*	*ayez*	*ayons*
savoir:	*sache*	*sachez*	*sachons*
aller:	*va*	*allez*	*allons*
dire:	*dis*	*dites*	*disons*
faire:	*fais*	*faites*	*faisons*

8. Reflexive.

French uses many verbs reflexively which are not so used in English (*je me suis levé ce matin*, I got up this morning: *se lever*, to get up, lit. to get oneself up). The reflexive pronouns are:

myself, to myself, *me*
yourself, to yourself, *te*
ourselves, to ourselves, *nous*
yourselves, to yourselves, *vous*
himself, herself, itself, themselves, to himself, to herself, to itself, to themselves, *se*

These pronouns may be direct or indirect: *je me lave,* I wash myself; but *je me lave les mains,* I wash *to* myself the hands (I wash my hands).

The auxiliary used with reflexive verbs is *être,* but the past participle agrees as though *avoir* were used; that is, agreement is not with the subject, but with the preceding direct object, which may or may not be the reflexive pronoun: *elle s'est lavée,* she washed herself; *elle s'est lavé les mains,* she washed her hands (no preceding direct object; *se* is indirect); *les mains qu'elle s'est lavées étaient couvertes de sang,* the hands she washed were covered with blood (agreement not with *elle,* subject; nor with *se,* indirect object, but with *que,* direct object, which refers to "hands", feminine plural).

In the plural, reflexive forms may have a reciprocal meaning (each other, to each other, one another, to one another): they saw each other, *ils se sont vus;* they shook hands, *ils se sont serré la main.*

9. Passive.

This is formed, as in English, by *être*, "to be" with the past participle. The latter agrees with the subject:*il est puni,* he is punished; *elle sera punie,* she will be punished; *elles ont été punies par leur père,* they have been punished by their father. The passive is often avoided, however, especially when "by" does not appear, by using: 1. *on* ("one", "man", "somebody") with the active: *ici on parle français,* French is spoken here (lit. one speaks French here); 2. the reflexive: *ces choses ne se font pas,* these things aren't done (lit. these things don't do themselves).

10. Subjunctive.

The French subjunctive has four tenses, and is frequently used in subordinate clauses. For the present subjunctive, the endings are: *-e, -es, -e, -ions, -iez, -ent* (-*ir* verbs insert *-iss-* throughout; *-oir* verbs have *-oiv-* in the singular and third plural, *-ev-* in first and second plural): that I speak, *que je parle, que tu parles, qu'il parle, que nous parlions, que vous parliez, qu'ils parlent;* that I finish, *que je finisse;* that I sell, *que je vende;* that I receive, *que je reçoive.*

The present perfect subjunctive is formed with the present subjunctive of *avoir* (or *être*) and the past participle: that I have spoken, *que j'aie (tu aies, il ait, nous ayons, vous ayez, ils aient) parlé;* that I have come, *que je sois (tu sois, il soit, nous soyons, vous soyez, ils soient) venu (venue, venus, venues).* The other two tenses are normally avoided in conversation and ordinary writing.

VOCABULARY [16]

16. The gender of nouns is indicated by the article (*le, la*); **nouns** beginning with vowels or *h* and taking the article *l'* are *masculine* unless otherwise indicated.

Note that nouns and *masculine* adjectives ending in *-s, -x, -z,* remain unchanged in the plural (*la voix, les voix*); that most nouns and masculine adjectives ending in *-au* and *-al* change to *-aux* in the plural (*beau, beaux; le cheval, les chevaux*); that nouns and masculine adjectives ending in *-eu* add *-x* in the plural (*le feu, les feux*).

Note that adjectives ending in *-e* remain unchanged in the feminine (*triste*); that adjectives ending in *-x* change to *-se* in the feminine (*heureux, heureuse*); *-en* to *-enne* (*italien, italienne*); *-el* to *-elle* (*naturel, naturelle*); *-ier* to *-ière* (*premier, première*); *-f* to *-ve* (*neuf, neuve*). The plurals are then independently formed (*heureux,* plu. *heureux; heureuse,* plu. *heureuses*).

Other exceptional irregularities in feminine and plural formation are separately given in the vocabulary.

Verbs ending in *-er* which have *e*-mute as the last vowel in the stem change it to *è* whenever another *e*-mute appears in the ending (*mener;* Pres. *mène, mènes, mène, menons, menez, mènent;* Fut. *mènerai*). Verbs ending in *-eler* and *-eter,* however, more generally double the *l* or *t* under the same circumstances (*appeler;* Pres. *appelle, appelles, appelle, appelons, appelez, appellent;* Fut. *appellerai*).

Verbs ending in *-er* which have *é* as the last vowel in the stem also change it to *è* when *e*-mute appears in the ending, but not in the future and conditional (*espérer;* Pres. *espère, espères, espère, espérons, espérez, espèrent;* but Fut. *espérerai*).

Verbs ending in *-cer* change *c* to *ç* when *a* or *o* follows (*avancer;* 1st pl. *nous avançons;* Impf. *j'avançais;* etc.).

Verbs ending in *-ger* insert *-e-* when *a* or *o* follows (*manger;* 1st pl. *nous mangeons;* Impf. *je mangeais;* etc.).

Most verbs ending in *-yer* change *y* to *i* before *e*-mute (*ennuyer;* Pres. *ennuie, ennuies, ennuie, ennuyons, ennuyez, ennuient;* etc.).

Other important verbal irregularities are given in the vocabulary; note that the conditional *always* follows the future, so that a future *ferai* for the verb *faire* implies a conditional *ferais.* There is never any irregularity in the *endings* of these two tenses.

If a verb is conjugated with *être*, the latter appears in parentheses; thus, to stay, *rester* (*être*). This indication is not given in the case of reflexive verbs, which are *always* conjugated with *être*.

1. World, Elements, Nature, Weather, Time, Directions.

world, *le monde*

earth, *la terre*

air, *l'air*

water, *l'eau* (fem.)

fire, *le feu*

light, *la lumière*

sea, *la mer*

sun, *le soleil*

moon, *la lune*

star, *l'étoile* (fem.)

sky, *le ciel*

wind, *le vent*

weather, time, *le temps*

snow, *la neige*

to snow, *neiger*

rain, *la pluie*

to rain, *pleuvoir* (Pres. *pleut*;

  Fut. *pleuvra*; P. p. *plu*)

cloud, *le nuage*

cloudy, *nuageux, couvert*

fog, *le brouillard*

ice, *la glace*

mud, *la boue*

morning, *le matin, la matinée*

noon, *midi*

afternoon, *l'après-midi*

evening, *le soir*

night, *la nuit*

midnight, *minuit*

North, *le nord*

South, *le sud, le midi*

East, *l'est*

West, *l'ouest*

year, *l'an*

month, *le mois*

week, *la semaine*

day, *le jour, la journée*

hour, *l'heure* (fem.)

minute, *la minute*

Sunday, *le dimanche*

Monday, *le lundi*

Tuesday, *le mardi*

Wednesday, *le mercredi*

Thursday, *le jeudi*

Friday, *le vendredi*

Saturday, *le samedi*

January, *janvier*

February, *février*

March, *mars*

April, *avril*

May, *mai*

June, *juin*

July, *juillet*

August, *août*

September, *septembre*

October, *octobre*

November, *novembre*

December, *décembre*

Spring, *le printemps*

Summer, *l'été*

Fall, *l'automne*

Winter, *l'hiver*

For "it is warm", "it is cold", etc., see p. 224.

No capitals for seasons, months, days of week.

I shall see him *on* Monday, *je le verrai lundi*; last Monday, *lundi dernier*; next Monday, *lundi prochain*; every Monday, *tous les lundis*; on May 5th, 1943, *le cinq mai dix-neuf cent quarante-trois*.

2. Family, Friendship, Love.

family, *la famille*

husband, *le mari*

wife, *la femme*

parents, *les parents*

father, *le père*

mother, *la mère*

son, *le fils*
daughter, *la fille*
brother, *le frère*
sister, *la soeur*
uncle, *l'oncle*
aunt, *la tante*
nephew, *le neveu*
niece, *la nièce*
cousin, *le cousin* (fem. *la cousine*)
grandfather, *le grand-père*
grandmother, *la grand'mère*
grandson, *le petit-fils*
granddaughter, *la petite-fille*
father-in-law, *le beau-père*
mother-in-law, *la belle-mère*
son-in-law, *le beau-fils, le gendre*
daughter-in-law, *la belle-fille, la
bru*
brother-in-law, *le beau-frère*
sister-in-law, *la belle-soeur*
man, *l'homme*
woman, *la femme*
child, *l'enfant*
boy, *le (petit) garçon*

girl, *la jeune fille, la (petite) fille*
lady, *la dame*
young lady, *la demoiselle*
sir, Mr., gentleman, *monsieur*[17]
madam, Mrs., *madame*[17]
Miss, *mademoiselle*[17]
friend, *l'ami* (fem. *l'amie*)
servant, *le* or *la domestique, la
servante, la bonne*
to introduce, *présenter*
to visit, *visiter, faire une visite*
love, *l'amour*
to love, *aimer*
to fall in love with, *tomber
amoureux de (être)*
to marry, *épouser, se marier avec*
sweetheart, *l'amoureux* (f e m.
*amoureuse), le fiancé (la
fiancée), le bien-aimé (la bien-
aimée), l'ami (l'amie)*
kiss, *le baiser*
to kiss, *embrasser*
beloved, darling, *chéri (-e)*

3. *Speaking Activities.*

word, *le mot, la parole*
language, *la langue*
to speak, *parler*
to say, *dire* (Pres. *dis, dis, dit,
disons. dites, disent;* Impf.
disais; P. p. *dit;* Impv. *dis,
dites)*
to tell, *dire, raconter, conter* (I
told him, *je lui ai dit)*
to inform, *communiquer à, rensei-
gner*
to call, *appeler*
to be called, one's name is, *s'ap-*

peler (my name is John, *je
m'appelle Jean)*
to greet, *saluer*
to name, *nommer*
to cry, shout, *s'écrier*
to listen to, *écouter* (I listen *to*
him, *je l'écoute)*
to hear, *entendre*
to understand, *comprendre* (Pres.
*comprends, comprends, com-
prend, comprenons, comprenez,
comprennent;* Impf., *compre-
nais,* P. p. *compris)*

17. These terms are abbreviated in writing to *M., Mme* and *Mlle,*
respectively. In speaking directly, the name which in English normally
follows is generally left out: Mr. Smith, have you a book? *Monsieur,
est-ce que vous avez un livre?*

to mean, *vouloir dire* (Pres., *veux dire, veux.., veut.., voulons.., voulez.., veulent ..;* P. p. *voulu*)

to ask (someone), *demander* (*à*); to ask a question, *poser une question*

to ask for, *demander* (he asked me for a pencil, *il m'a demandé un crayon*)

to answer, *répondre* (I answered my brother, *j'ai répondu à mon frère*)

to thank, *remercier* (I thanked him for the book, *je l'ai remercié du livre*)

to complain, *se plaindre* (Pres. *plains, plains, plaint, plaignons, plaignez, plaignent;* Impf. *plaignais;* P. p. *plaint*)

4. Materials.

gold, *l'or*
silver, *l'argent*
iron, *le fer*
steel, *l'acier*
copper, *le cuivre*
tin, *l'étain, le fer-blanc;*
lead, *le plomb*
oil, *l'huile* (fem.)
gasoline, *l'essence* (**fem.**)
coal, *le charbon*

wood, *le bois*
silk, *la soie*
cotton, *le coton*
wool, *la laine*
cloth, *l'étoffe* (fem.), *le drap*
to cut, *couper*
to dig, *creuser*
to sew, *coudre*
to mend, *raccommoder*

5. Animals.

animal, *l'animal*
horse, *le cheval*
dog, *le chien*
cat, *le chat*
bird, *l'oiseau*
donkey, *l'âne*
mule, *le mulet*
cow, *la vache*
ox, *le boeuf*
pig, *le cochon*
chicken, *le poulet*
rooster, *le coq*

hen, *la poule*
sheep, *le mouton, la brebis*
goat, *la chèvre*
mouse, *la souris*
snake, *le serpent*
fly, *la mouche*
bee, *l'abeille* (fem.)
mosquito, *le moustique*
spider, *l'araignée* (fem.)
louse, *le pou*
flea, *la puce*
bedbug, *la punaise*

6. Money, Buying and Selling.

money, *l'argent*
coin, *la pièce* (*de monnaie*)
dollar, *le dollar*
cent, *le sou*
bank, *la banque*

check, *le chèque*
money order, *le mandat* (*de poste*), *le mandat-poste*
to earn, to gain, to win, *gagner*
to lose, *perdre*

to spend, *dépenser*

to lend, *prêter*

to borrow, *emprunter* (I borrowed 10 francs *from* him, *je lui ai emprunté dix francs*)

to owe, *devoir* (Pres. *dois, dois, doit, devons, devez, doivent;* Impf., *devais;* P. p. *dû*)

to pay, *payer*

to give back, *rendre*

exchange, *le change* (exchange office, *bureau de change*)

to change, exchange, *changer*

change, small change, *la monnaie* (change me a dollar, *faites-moi la monnaie d'un dollar*)

honest, *honnête*

dishonest, *pas honnête, voleur*

price, cost, *le prix*

to cost, *coûter*

expensive, *cher*

cheap, *bon marché*

store, *le magasin, la boutique* (department store, *g r a n d magasin*)

7. *Eating and Drinking.*

to eat, *manger*

to eat breakfast, to eat lunch, *déjeuner*

breakfast, *le petit déjeuner*

lunch, *le déjeuner*

supper, *le souper*

to eat supper, *souper*

dinner, *le dîner*

to dine, *dîner*

meal, *le repas*

dining-room, *la salle à manger*

waiter, *le garçon*

waitress, *la servante, la serveuse*

restaurant, *le restaurant*

menu, *le menu*

bill, check, *l'addition* (fem.)

to pass (a dish), *passer*

piece, *le morceau*

slice, *la tranche*

pound, *la livre*

package, *le paquet*

basket, *le panier*

box, *la boîte*

bag, *le sac*

goods, *la marchandise*

to go shopping, *faire des achats* (*emplettes*)

to sell, *vendre*

to buy, *acheter*

to rent, *louer*

to be worth, *valoir* (Pres. *vaux, vaux, vaut, valons, valez, valent;* Impf. *valais;* Fut. *vaudrai;* (it is worth while doing it, *il vaut la peine de le faire*)

to choose, *choisir*

thief, robber, *le voleur*

to steal, *voler*

police, *la police, la sûreté*

policeman, *l'agent (de police), le sergent de ville*

state trooper, *le gendarme*

tip, *le pourboire*

to drink, *boire* (Pres. *bois, bois, boit, buvons, buvez, boivent;* Impf. *buvais;* P. p. *bu*)

water, *l'eau* (fem ·

wine, *le vin*

beer, *la bière*

coffee, *le café*

tea, *le thé*

milk, *le lait*

bottle, *la bouteille*

spoon, *la cuiller* (pronounced *cuillère*)

teaspoon, *la cuiller à thé*

knife, *le couteau*

fork, *la fourchette*

glass, *le verre*

cup, *la tasse*
napkin, *la serviette*
salt, *le sel*
pepper, *le poivre*
plate, dish, *l'assiette* (fem.), *le plat*
bread, *le pain*
roll, *le petit pain*
butter, *le beurre*
sugar, *le sucre*
soup, *le potage*
rice, *le riz*
potatoes, *les pommes de terre*
vegetable, *le légume*
meat, *la viande*
beef, *le boeuf*
steak, *le bifteck*
chicken, *le poulet*
chop, *la côtelette*
veal, *le veau*
lamb, *l'agneau*
pork, *le porc*
sausage, *le saucisson, la saucisse*
ham, *le jambon*
bacon, *le lard*

egg, *l'oeuf* (-*f* pron. in sg., silent in pl. *les oeufs*)
fish, *le poisson*
fried, *frit*
boiled, *bouilli*
roast, *rôti*
roast beef, *le rosbif*
baked, *au four* (baked apple, *une pomme cuite*)
broiled, *grillé*
sauce, *la sauce*
salad, *la salade*
cheese, *le fromage*
fruit, *le fruit*
apple, *la pomme*
pear, *la poire*
peach, *la pêche*
grapes, *le raisin*
strawberries, *les fraises*
nut, *la noix, la noisette*
orange, *l'orange* (fem.)
lemon, *le citron*
juice, *le jus*
cherries, *les cerises*
dessert, *le dessert*
pastry, *le gâteau, la pâtisserie*

8. *Hygiene and Attire.*

bathroom, *la salle de bain*
bath, *le bain*
to bathe, *se baigner*
shower, *la douche*
to wash, *se laver*
to shave, *se raser, se faire la barbe*
barber, *le coiffeur, le barbier*
mirror, *le miroir*
soap, *le savon*
razor, *le rasoir*
safety razor, *le rasoir mécanique* (*de sûreté*)
towel, *la serviette, l'essuie-mains*
comb, *le peigne*
brush, *la brosse*
scissors, *les ciseaux*

to wear, *porter*
to take off, *ôter*
to change, *changer de*
to put on, *mettre* (Pres. *mets, mets, met, mettons, mettez, mettent*; Impf. *mettais*, P. p. *mis*)
clothes, *les habits, les vêtements*
hat, *le chapeau*
suit, *le complet*
coat, *la jaquette, le veston*
vest, *le gilet*
pants, *le pantalon*
undershirt, *la sous-chemise*
drawers, *le caleçon*
glove, *le gant*
socks, *les chaussettes*

stockings, *les bas*
shirt, *la chemise*
collar, *le faux-col*
tie, *la cravate*
overcoat, *le pardessus*
raincoat, *l'imperméable*
pocket, *la poche*
handkerchief, *le mouchoir*
button, *le bouton*
shoe, *le soulier*
boot, *la botte*
pocket-book, *le porte-monnaie*

purse, *la bourse*
pin, *l'épingle* (fem.)
safety pin, *l'épingle de sûreté*
needle, *l'aiguille* (fem.)
umbrella, *le parapluie*
watch, *la montre*
chain, *la chaîne*
ring, *la bague*
eyeglasses, *les lunettes, les lorgnons*
slippers, *les pantoufles*
dressing-gown, *la robe de chambre*

9. Parts of the body.

head, *la tête*
forehead, *le front*
face, *le visage, la figure*
mouth, *la bouche*
hair, *les cheveux*
eye, *l'oeil* (pl. *les yeux*)
ear, *l'oreille* (fem.)
tooth, *la dent*
lip, *la lèvre*
nose, *le nez*
tongue, *la langue*
chin, *le menton*
cheek, *la joue*
mustache, *la moustache*
beard, *la barbe*
neck, *le cou*
throat, *la gorge*
arm, *le bras*
hand, *la main*

elbow, *le coude*
wrist, *le poignet*
finger, *le doigt*
nail, *l'ongle*
leg, *la jambe*
foot, *le pied*
knee, *le genou*
back, *le dos*
shoulder, *l'épaule* (fem.)
chest, *la poitrine*
ankle, *la cheville*
body, *le corps*
bone, *l'os* (-*s* pron. in sg., silent in pl. *les os*)
skin, *la peau*
heart, *le coeur*
stomach, *l'estomac*
blood, *le sang*

10. Medical.

doctor, *le médecin, le docteur*
drug-store, *la pharmacie*
hospital, *l'hôpital, la clinique*
first-aid station, *le poste de secours*
medicine, *le médicament*
pill, *la pilule*
prescription, *l'ordonnance* (fem.)
bandage, *la bande, le pansement*

nurse, *l'infirmier, l'infirmière, le (la) garde-malade*
ill, *malade*
illness, *la maladie*
fever, *la fièvre*
swollen, *enflé*
wound, *la blessure*
wounded, *blessé*

head-ache, *le mal de tête* (I have
  a **head-ache**, *j'ai mal à la tête*)
tooth-ache, *le mal de dents*
cough, *la toux*

to cough, *tousser*
lame, crippled, *boiteux, estropié*
burn, *la brûlure*
pain, *la douleur, le mal*
poison, *le poison*

11. Military.

war, *la guerre*
peace, *la paix*
ally, *l'allié*
enemy, *l'ennemi*
army, *l'armée* (fem.)
danger, *le danger*
dangerous, *dangereux*
to win, *triompher, gagner, rem-
  porter (la victoire)*
to surround, *entourer*
to arrest, *arrêter*
to kill, *tuer*
to escape, *échapper, s'échapper,
  s'évader*
to run away, *se sauver*
to lead, *mener, conduire*
to follow, *suivre* (Pres. *suis, suis,
  suit, suivons, suivez, suivent;*
  Impf. *suivais;* P. p. *suivi*)
to surrender, *se rendre*
to retreat, *se retirer, battre en
  retraite*
to bomb, shell, *bombarder*
fear, *la peur*
prison, *la prison*
prisoner, *le prisonnier*
to take prisoner, *faire prisonnier*
  (Pres. *fais, fais, fait, faisons,
  faites, font;* Impf. *faisais;* Fut.
  ferai; P. p. *fait*)
to capture, *s'emparer de, prendre*
help, aid, *le secours*
help!, *au secours!*
comrade, buddy, *le copain, le
  camarade, le compagnon*

battle, *la bataille*
to fight, *combattre, se battre*
soldier, *le soldat*
private, *le (simple) soldat*
corporal, *le caporal*
sergeant, *le sergent*
lieutenant, *le lieutenant*
captain, *le capitaine*
major, *le commandant*
colonel, *le colonel*
general, *le général*
officer, *l'officier*
company, *la compagnie*
battalion, *le bataillon*
regiment, *le régiment*
brigade, *la brigade*
division, *la division*
troops, *les troupes* (fem.)
reenforcements, *les renforts*
fortress, *la forteresse*
sentinel, *la sentinelle*
guard, *la garde*
to stand guard, to do sentry duty,
  être de garde, être de faction
to be on duty, *être de service*
sign-post, *le poteau indicateur*
navy, *la marine*
sailor, *le marin*
marine, *le soldat de marine, le
  fusilier marin*
warship, *le vaisseau (navire) de
  guerre, le cuirassé*
cruiser, *le croiseur*
destroyer, *le (contre-) torpilleur*
convoy, *le convoi*

escort, *l'escorte* (fem.), *le convoi*
weapon, *l'arme* (fem.)
rifle, *le fusil*
machine-gun, *la mitrailleuse*
cannon, *le canon*
ammunition, *les munitions*
supplies, *les vivres*, *le ravitaillement* (supply service, *l'intendance*, fem.)
cartridge, *la cartouche*
bullet, *la balle*
belt, *la cartouchière*, *la giberne*
knapsack, *le havresac*
tent, *la tente* (put up a tent, *dresser une tente*)
camp, *le camp*
map, *la carte*, *le plan* (*topographique*)
rope, *la corde*
flag, *le drapeau* (naval, *le pavillon*)
helmet, *le casque*
bayonet, *la baïonnette*

uniform, *l'uniforme*
airplane, *l'avion*
bombing plane, *l'avion de bombardement*, *le bombardier*
pursuit-plane, *le chasseur*, *l'avion de poursuite* (*chasse*)
shell, *l'obus*
bomb, *la bombe*
truck, *le camion*
tank, *le tank*, *le char d'assaut*
to load, *charger*
to shoot, to fire, *faire feu*, *tirer*, *décharger*
to shoot (military execution), *fusiller*
fire!, *feu!*, *faites feu!*
attention!, *attention!*, *garde à vous!*
forward, *en avant!*, *marche!*
halt!, *halte!*, *halte-là!*
air-raid shelter, *l'abri*
spy, *l'espion*

12. Travel.

customs, *la douane*
passport, *le passeport*
ship, *le vaisseau*, *le navire*, *le paquebot*
steamer, *le vapeur*
stateroom, *la cabine*
berth, *la couchette*
to travel, *voyager*
trip, voyage, *le voyage*
to leave, *partir* (Pres., *pars*, *pars*, *part*, *partons*, *partez*, *partent*); (*être*)
to arrive, *arriver*; (*être*)
to ride (a conveyance), *aller en* (Pres. *vais*, *vas*, *va*, *allons*, *allez*, *vont*; Impf. *allais*; Fut. *irai*); (*être*)
railroad, *le chemin de fer*

station, *la gare*
track, *la voie*, *le rail*
train, *le train*
platform, *le quai*
ticket, *le billet*
compartment, *le compartiment*
all aboard, *en voiture!*
dining-car, *le wagon-restaurant*
sleeper, *le wagon-lit*
car, *le wagon*, *la voiture*
trunk, *la malle*
valise, *la valise*
baggage, *les bagages*
porter, *le porteur*
bus, *l'autobus*, *l'omnibus*
street-car, *le tramway*, *le tram*
automobile, *l'auto*, *l'automobile* (fem.)

taxi, *le taxi*
driver, *le chauffeur, le conduc-
teur*

13. *Reading and Writing.*

to read, *lire* (Pres. *lis, lis, lit,
lisons, lisez, lisent;* Impf. *lisais;*
P. p. *lu*)
newspaper, *le journal*
magazine, *la revue*
book, *le livre*
to write, *écrire* (Pres. *écris, écris,
écrit, écrivons, écrivez, écrivent;*
Impf. *écrivais;* P. p. *écrit*)
to translate, *traduire* (Pres. *traduis, traduis,* etc., like *conduire*
above)
pencil, *le crayon*

to drive (car), *conduire* (Pres.
*conduis, conduis, conduit, con-
duisons, conduisez, conduisent;*
Impf. *conduisais;* P. p. *conduit*)

chalk, *la craie*.
blackboard, *le tableau* (*noir*)
ink, *l'encre* (fem.)
pen, *la plume* (fountain-, *le stylo*)
envelope, *l'enveloppe* (fem.)
paper, *le papier* (writing—, *le
papier à écrire*)
letter, *la lettre*
post-office, *la poste*
stamp, *le timbre, le timbre-poste*
letter-box, *la boîte aux lettres*
to mail, *mettre à la poste*
address, *l'adresse* (fem.)
post-card, *la carte postale*

14. *Amusements*

to smoke, *fumer*
cigar, *le cigare*
cigarette, *la cigarette*
tobacco, *le tabac*
match, *l'allumette* (fem.)
give me a light, *du feu, s'il vous
plaît*
theatre, *le théâtre*
movies, *le cinéma*
dance, *la danse, le bal*
to danse, *danser*
to have a good time, *s'amuser*
ticket, *le billet*
pleasure, *le plaisir*
to play (music), *jouer de*

to sing, *chanter*
song, *la chanson*
to play (a game), *jouer à*
game, *le jeu, la partie*
ball, *la balle*
to take a walk, *se promener, faire
une promenade*
beach, *la plage*
to swim, *nager*
sand, *le sable*
refreshment, *le rafraîchissement*
saloon, *le bar, le bistro*
picnic, *le pique-nique, l'excursion*
(fem.)

15. *Town and Country.*

place, spot, *le lieu, l'endroit*
city, *la ville*
street, *la rue*
sidewalk, *le trottoir*

road, *la route, le chemin*
intersection, *le carrefour*
harbor, *le port*
block, *l'îlot, le pâté de maisons*

school, *l'école* (fem.)
church, *l'église* (fem.)
cathedral, *la cathédrale*
building, *l'édifice, le bâtiment*
corner, *le coin, l'angle*
hotel, *l'hôtel*
office, *le bureau*
river, *le fleuve, la rivière* (small stream)
bridge, *le pont*
country, *la campagne*

mountain, *la montagne*
grass, *l'herbe* (fem.)
yard, *la cour*
hill, *la colline*
lake, *le lac*
forest, *la forêt, le bois*
field, *le champ*
tree, *l'arbre*
flower, *la fleur*
rock, *le rocher, le roc*
stone, *la pierre*

16. *House.*

house, *la maison* (at home, *à la maison;* to go home, *aller à la maison*)
roof, *le toit*
door, *la porte*
key, *la clef*
to open, *ouvrir* (Pres. *ouvre, ouvres, ouvre,* etc.; Impf. *ouvrais;* P. p. *ouvert*)
to close, *fermer* (to lock, *fermer à clef*)
to go into, *entrer dans* (he entered the room, *il est entré dans la salle*); (*être*)
to go out, *sortir* (Pres. *sors, sors, sort, sortons,* etc.; Impf. *sortais*); (*être*)
to go home, *rentrer;* (*être*)
to live in, *habiter, demeurer dans*
staircase, *l'escalier*
to go up, *monter* (to go up to,.. *à*) (*être*)
to go down, *descendre;* (*être*)
cottage, *la maisonnette*
room, *la pièce*
toilet, *les cabinets, le W. C.* (pronounce *double vé cé*)
wall, *le mur*
window, *la fenêtre*
bedroom, *la chambre à coucher*

bed, *le lit*
pillow, *l'oreiller*
cover, blanket, *la couverture*
sheet, *le drap*
mattress, *le matelas*
clock, *la pendule*
alarm-clock, *le réveille* (*-matin*)
candle, *la bougie, la chandelle*
to stand, *se tenir debout, être debout*
to rest, *se reposer*
to go to bed, to lie down, *se coucher*
to sleep, *dormir* (to fall asleep, *s'endormir*) Pres. *dors, dors, dort, dormons,* etc., Impf. *dormais,* etc.
to wake up, *se réveiller*
to get up, *se lever*
to get dressed, *s'habiller*
kitchen, *la cuisine*
table, *la table*
to sit down, *s'asseoir* (Pres. *assieds, assieds, assied, asseyons,* etc.; Impf. *asseyais;* Fut. *assiérai;* P. p. *assis*)
chair, *la chaise*
lamp, *la lampe*
closet, *l'armoire* (fem.)

17. *Miscellaneous Nouns.*

people, *les gens, le monde, on*
thing, *la chose*
name, *le nom*
luck, *la (bonne) chance* (to be
lucky, *avoir de la chance*)
bad luck, *la mauvaise fortune, la
guigne*

number, *le nombre, le numéro, le
chiffre*
life, *la vie*
death, *la mort*
work, *le travail* (pl. *travaux*)

18. *Verbs—Coming and Going.*

to come, *venir* (Pres. *viens, viens,
vient, venons, venez, viennent;*
Impf. *venais;* Fut. *viendrai;*
P. P. *venu*) ; (*être*)
to go, to be going to, *aller* (Pres.
vais, vas, va, allons, allez, vont;
Impf. *allais;* Fut. *irai*) ; (*être*)
to stay, *rester;* (*être*)
to return, *retourner, rentrer, re-
venir;* (*être* for all three)
to run, *courir* (Pres. *cours, cours,
court, courons, courez, courent;*

Impf. *courais;* Fut. *courrai;*
P. p. *couru*)
to walk, *marcher, aller* (*être*) *à
pied*
to fall, *tomber;* (*être*)
to follow, *suivre* (Pres. *suis, suis,
suit, suivons, suivez, suivent;*
P. p. *suivi*)
to arrive, *arriver;* (*être*)
to go away, to leave, to set out,
partir (Pres. *pars, pars, part.
partons,* etc.; Impf. *partais*) ;
(*être*) *s'en aller*

19. *Looking and Seeing.*

to see, *voir* (Pres. *vois, vois, voit,
voyons, voyez, voient;* Impf.
voyais; Fut. *verrai;* P. p. *vu*)
to look at, *regarder* (I am looking *at* him, *je le regarde*)
to look for, *chercher* (I am looking *for* her, *je la cherche*)
to laugh, *rire* (Pres. *ris, ris, rit,
rions, riez, rient;* Impf. *riais;*

P. p. *ri*)
to laugh at, *se moquer de,* (*se*)
rire de
to smile, *sourire* (like *rire*)
to look, seem, *sembler, avoir l'air*
(he looks ill, *il a l'air malade*)
to recognize, *reconnaître* (like
connaître)
to take for, *prendre pour*

20. *Verbs—Mental.*

to make a mistake, *se tromper*
to hope, *espérer*
to wait for, *attendre*
to think, *penser* (—of, *penser à;*
I am thinking of him, *je pense
à lui*)
to think of (have an opinion).

penser de (what do you think
of him?, *que pensez-vous de
lui?*)
to believe, *croire* (Pres. *crois,
crois, croit, croyons, croyez,
croient;* Impf. *croyais;* P. p.
cru)

to like, *aimer* (I like this hat, *j'aime ce chapeau*)

to wish, *désirer* (I should like, *je voudrais*)

to want, *vouloir* (Pres. *veux, veux, veut, voulons, voulez, veulent;* Fut. *voudrai;* P. p. *voulu;* Impv. *veuillez,* have the kindness to..)

to know (a fact), *savoir* (Pres. *sais, sais, sait, savons, savez, savent;* Fut. *saurai;* Impv. *sache, sachez;* P. p. *su*). Use *je savais* for "I knew", *j'ai su* for "I found out"

to know how, *savoir* (plus infinitive) ; I know how to dance, *je sais danser*

to know (a person), *connaître* (Pres. *connais, connais, connaît, connaissons,* etc.; Impf. *connaissais;* P. p. *connu;* use *je connaissais* for "I knew",

j'ai connu for "I met", socially)

to remember, *se souvenir de* (like *venir*), *se rappeler* (I remember it, *je m'en souviens*)

to forget, *oublier*

to permit, allow, *permettre* (like *mettre*)

to forbid, *défendre* (I forbid *him* to come, *je lui défends de venir*)

to promise, *promettre* (like *mettre*)

to learn, *apprendre* (like *prendre*)

to feel like, *avoir envie de* (I feel like going, *j'ai envie d'aller*)

to understand, *comprendre* (like *prendre*)

to be afraid, *avoir peur* (he is afraid of it, *il en a peur;* he is afraid of her, *il a peur d'elle*)

to be right, *avoir raison*

to be wrong, *avoir tort*

to need, *avoir besoin de*

21. *Verbs—Miscellaneous.*

to live, *vivre* (Pres. *vis, vis, vit, vivons, vivez, vivent;* Impf. *vivais;* P. p. *vécu*)

to survive, *survivre* (like *vivre*)

to die, *mourir* (Pres. *meurs, meurs, meurt, mourons, mourez, meurent;* Impf. *mourais;* Fut. *mourrai;* P. p. *mort*) ; (*être*)

to work, *travailler*

to give, *donner*

to take, *prendre* (Pres. *prends, prends, prend, prenons, prenez, prennent;* Impf. *prenais;* P. p. *pris*)

to show, *montrer*

to begin, to start, *commencer, se mettre à*

to finish, *finir, achever*

to continue, to keep on, *continuer* (*à*)

to help, *aider*

to hide, (*se*) *cacher*

to lose, *perdre*

to find, *trouver, retrouver*

to leave (a thing), *laisser* (a place), *quitter, partir de;* (*être*)

to try, *essayer de, chercher à*

to meet, *rencontrer*

to put, place, *mettre* (Pres. *mets, mets, met, mettons, mettez, mettent;* P. p. *mis*)

to do, to make, *faire* (Pres. *fais, fais, fait, faisons, faites, font;* Impf. *faisais;* Fut. *ferai;* P. p. *fait*). *Faire venir,* to send for

(send for the doctor, *faites venir le médecin*)

to have done, *faire faire* (have
the letter written, *faites écrire
la lettre*)

can, to be able, *pouvoir* (**Pres.**
*peux, peux, peut, pouvons,
pouvez, peuvent;* Impf. *pouvais;*
Fut. *pourrai;* P. p. *pu*)

to carry, *porter*

to bring (things), *apporter*

to bring (people), *amener*

to stop, *arrêter* (*s'arrêter* for self;
to stop writing, *cesser d'écrire*)

to cover, *couvrir* (P. p. *couvert*)

to get, obtain, *obtenir*

to hold, *tenir* (Pres. *tiens, tiens,
tient, tenons, tenez, tiennent;*
Fut. *tiendrai;* P. p. *tenu*)

to get, become, *devenir* (like
venir); (*être*)

to break, *rompre, casser, briser*

to hurry, *se dépêcher*

to send, *envoyer*

to belong, *appartenir* (like *tenir*)

to have just, *venir de* (he has
just finished it, *il vient de le
finir*); (*être*)

to accept, *accepter*

to refuse, *refuser*

22. Adjectives.

small, *petit*

big, large, tall, *grand*

short (stature), *petit, bas*

short (length), *court* (brief, *bref,*
fem. *brève*)

low, *bas* (fem. *basse*)

heavy, *lourd*

light (weight), *léger* (fem. *légère*)

long, *long* (fem. *longue*)

fat, bulky, *gros* (fem. *grosse*)

wide, *large*

narrow, *étroit*

clean, *propre*

dirty, *sale*

cool, *frais* (fem. *fraîche*)

cold, *froid*

warm, *chaud*

damp, *humide*

wet, *mouillé*

dry, *sec* (fem. *sèche*)

full, *plein, rempli*

empty, *vide*

dark, *noir, obscur, sombre*

light (color), *clair*
(to grow light, *faire jour*)

thick, *épais* (fem. *épaisse*)

thin, *mince, maigre, svelte*

round, *rond*

square, *carré*

flat, *plat*

deep, *profond*

soft, *mou* (*mol* before vowel or
h, fem. *molle*)

hard, *dur*

quick, lively, *rapide, vif*

slow, *lent*

ordinary, *ordinaire, commun,
quelconque*

comfortable, *confortable, com-
mode* (I am —, *je suis bien*)

uncomfortable, *incommode, gê-
nant*

near, *prochain*

distant, *lointain*

right, *droit*

left, *gauche*

poor, *pauvre*

rich, *riche*

beautiful, *beau* (*bel* before vowel or *h;* fem. *belle*)

pretty, *joli*

ugly, *laid*

sweet, *doux* (fem. *douce*)
bitter, *amer* (fem. *amère*)
sour, *aigre*
salt, *salé*
young, *jeune*
old, *vieux* (*vieil* before vowel or
 h; fem. *vieille*); *âgé*
new, *neuf* (fem. *neuve*), *nouveau*
 (*nouvel* bef. vowel or *h*; fem.
 nouvelle)
good, *bon* (fem. *bonne*)
better, *meilleur* (best, *le*....)
bad, *mauvais*
worse, *pire* (worst, *le*....)
fine, *excellent*
first, *premier* (fem. *première*)
last, *dernier* (fem. *dernière*)
strong, *fort*
weak, *faible*
tired, *fatigué*
alone, *seul*
same, *même*
easy, *facile*
hard, difficult, *difficile, pénible*
happy, lucky, *heureux*
sad, *triste*
merry, *gai*
free, *libre*
crazy, *fou* (fem. *folle*)
silly, *sot* (fem. *sotte*)
drunk, *ivre, gris, grisé, soûl*
 (*saoûl*)
polite, *poli*

rude, *impoli, grossier* (fem. *-ère*)
pleasant, *agréable*
unpleasant, *désagréable*
lonesome, *solitaire*
upset, *agité, ému, bouleversé*
true, *vrai*
false, *faux* (fem. *fausse*), *hypo-crite*
foreign, *étranger* (fem. *-ère*)
friendly, *amical*
kind, *aimable*
hostile, *hostile, ennemi*
unlucky, unhappy, *malheureux*
charming, *charmant*
afraid, *timide, peureux*
ready, *prêt*
hungry, *affamé* (to be hungry,
 avoir faim)
thirsty, (to be—, *avoir soif*)
right, (to be—, *avoir raison*)
wrong, (to be—, *avoir tort*)
afraid, (to be—, *avoir peur*)
funny, *drôle, comique*
possible, *possible*
impossible, *impossible*
brave, *courageux, hardi, brave*
cowardly, *lâche, poltron*
quiet, *calme, tranquille*
noisy, *bruyant*
living, *vivant*
dead, *mort*
suitable, *convenable*

23. *Colors.*

white, *blanc* (fem. *blanche*)
black, *noir*
red, *rouge*
green, *vert*
blue, *bleu* (to feel blue, *avoir le
 cafard*)

yellow, *jaune*
gray, *gris*
brown, *brun, marron*
rose (pink), *rose*
purple, *pourpre*

24. *Nationalities.*

Use no capital for the adjective or for the language. Use capital for people.

Names of languages are used *with* the article unless they *immediately* follow the verb *parler* or the preposition *en;* he speaks English, *il parle anglais;* he speaks English well, *il parle bien l'anglais;* English is difficult, *l'anglais est difficile;* he answered me in English, *il m'a répondu en anglais.*

American, *américain*
English, *anglais*
French, *français*
German, *allemand*
Spanish, *espagnol*
Russian, *russe*
Italian, *italien*
Japanese, *japonais*
Chinese, *chinois*
Dutch, *hollandais*
Norwegian, *norvégien*
Swedish, *suédois*
Finnish, *finnois, finlandais*
Belgian, *belge*
Polish, *polonais*
Danish, *danois*
Swiss, *suisse* (fem. *suissesse*)
Portuguese, *portugais*
Yugoslav, *yougoslave*
Bulgarian, *bulgare*
Czech, *tchécoslovaque*
Greek, *grec* (fem. *grecque*)

Turkish, *turc* (fem. *turque*)
Roumanian, *roumain*
Hungarian, *hongrois*
Austrian, *autrichien*
Malay, *malais*
Persian, *perse*
Arabian, Arabic, Arab, *arabe*
Jewish, Hebrew, *juif. hébreu, israélite*
Australian, *australien*
Canadian, *canadien*
Mexican, *mexicain*
Brazilian, *brésilien*
Argentinian, *argentin*
Chilean, *chilien*
Peruvian, *péruvien*
Cuban, *cubain*
Egyptian, *égyptien*
Tunisian, *tunisien*
Algerian, *algérien*
Moroccan, *marocain*

25. *Adverbs and Adverbial Expressions.*

today, *aujourd'hui*
yesterday, *hier*
tomorrow, *demain*
day before yesterday, *avant-hier*
day after tomorrow, *après-demain*
tonight, *ce soir*
last night, *hier soir*
this morning, *ce matin*
in the morning, *le matin*
all morning, *toute la matinée*

tomorrow morning, *demain matin*
in the afternoon, *l'après-midi*
tomorrow afternoon, *demain (dans l') après-midi*
in the evening, *le soir*
all evening, *toute la soirée*
tomorrow evening, *demain soir*
early (at an early hour), *de bonne heure;* (ahead of time), *en avance*

on time, *à l'heure*

late (at a late hour), *tard;* (delayed), *en retard*

already, *déjà*

yet, still, *encore*

no longer, *ne....plus* (he is no longer working, *il ne travaille plus*)

not yet, *pas encore* (he hasn't come yet, *il n'est pas encore arrivé*)

now, *maintenant, à présent*

afterwards, then, *puis, alors*

never, *jamais* (use *ne* before verb; he is never here, *il n'est jamais ici*)

always, *toujours*

forever, *à jamais, pour toujours*

soon, *bientôt*

often, *souvent*

seldom, *rarement*

usually, *d'ordinaire*

fast, *vite, rapidement*

slowly, *lentement*

here, *ici*

there, *là*

over there, *là-bas*

near by, *tout près*

far away, *loin, très loin*

up, *en haut*

down, *en bas*

ahead, *en avant*

behind, *en arrière*

forward!, *en avant!*

back, *en arrière*

outside, *dehors*

inside, *dedans*

opposite, *en face*

here and there, *ça et là, par-ci, par-là*

this way, *par ici, de ce côté*

everywhere, *partout*

where, *où*

also, *aussi* (but at beginning of sentence means "therefore")

yes, *oui*

no, *non*

very, *très*

much, very much, *beaucoup* (never use *très* with it)

well, *bien*

badly, *mal*

better, *mieux*

worse, *pis* (so much the worse, *tant pis!*)

more, *plus* (with adjectives and adverbs)

more than, *plus que* (before numbers use *plus de*)

less, *moins* (less than, *moins que;* with numbers use *moins de*)

as - as, *aussi - que* (he is as strong as I, *il est aussi fort que moi*)

as much - as, as many - as, *autant que* (he has as much money as I, *il a autant d'argent que moi*)

how much?, how many?, *combien (de)*, (how many soldiers?, *combien de soldats?*)

how?, *comment?*

too much, *trop (de)*, (he has too much money, *il a trop d'argent*)

too many, *trop (de)*; (she has too many friends, *elle a trop d'amis*)

so much, so many, *tant (de)*

as, like, *comme*

so, *ainsi*

besides, furthermore, *d'ailleurs, de plus, en outre*

finally, *enfin*

only, *seulement*

almost, *presque* (but when something almost happened, *manquer; il a manqué de tomber*, he almost fell)

gladly, *volontiers*

certainly, *certainement, sans doute*
at once, *tout de suite, immédiate-ment*
at all, *du tout*
hardly, *à peine*
aloud, *à haute voix, tout haut*
of course, *naturellement, bien en-tendu*
suddenly, *tout à coup*
about, *vers, à peu près* (with numerals: about ten, *à peu près dix*; with time: about six o'clock, *vers six heures*)
perhaps, maybe, *peut-être*

a little, *un peu*
again, *encore* (once again, *encore une fois*)
really, truly, *vraiment*
together, *ensemble*
at least, *au moins*
for lack of, *faute de*
a long time ago, *il y a longtemps*
repeatedly, *maintes fois*
therefore, *par conséquent, donc*
farther away, *plus loin*
occasionally, *de temps en temps*
entirely, altogether, *tout à fait*

26. Conjunctions.

and, *et*
but, *mais*
if, *si*
or, *ou*
why, *pourquoi*
because, *parce que*
why! par exemple!, comment!
before, *avant que*[18]
when, *quand*[19], *lorsque*[19]
than, *que* (use *de* before numbers)
where, *où*[19]
until, till, *jusqu'à ce que*[18]
although, *bien que*,[18] *quoique*[18]

unless, *à moins que*[18]
while, *pendant que*[19]
that, *que*
for, since, because, *puisque*
after, *après que*[19]
as soon as, *aussitôt que*,[19] *dès que*[19]
as long as, *pendant que*,[19] *tandis que*[19]
provided that, *pourvu que*[18]
so that, *pour que*,[18] *afin que*[18]
without, *sans que*[18]

27. Indefinite Pronouns and Adjectives.

such a, *un tel*
all kinds of, *toutes sortes de*
everything, *tout*
everyone, *tout le monde*
all, *tout, tous*
each, every, (adj. *chaque*, pron. *chacun*)

something, *(quelque chose)* (something interesting to read, *quelque chose d'intéressant à lire*)
someone, *quelqu'un*
some, *quelques* (plus noun; he has some friends, *il a quelques*

18. The subjunctive is used after these conjunctions; before he comes, *avant qu'il vienne.*
19. When these conjunctions refer to future time, the future *must* be used: I shall see him when he comes, *je le verrai quand il viendra.*

amis; in a partitive sense use *de* plus article: we bought some coffee, *nous avons acheté du café;* when referring to a noun previously mentioned, use *en:* has he any money?; yes, he has (some), *oui, il en a)*

a few, *quelques* (adj.); *quelques-uns* (pron.)

enough, *assez de*

enough! *assez!, ça suffit!*

nothing, *rien* (like *quelque chose*); nothing good, *rien de bon;* nothing to do, *rien à faire*

no one, *personne* (in sentence it is placed after verb, and the verb itself is preceded by *ne:* (*je ne vois personne,* I don't see anyone, I see no one)

neither..nor, *ne..ni..ni* (he has seen neither my baggage nor my ticket, *il n'a vu ni mes bagages ni mon billet)*

another (additional) *encore un* (different one), *un autre*

much, many, lots of, *beaucoup de*

both, *les deux, tous les deux*

several, *plusieurs*

little, few, *peu de* (he has little money, *il a peu d'argent;* he has few friends, *il a peu d'amis)*

28. *Prepositions.*

of, from, *de* (with masc. sing. article *le* contracts to *du; il parle du garçon,* he speaks of the boy; with plural article *les* contracts to *des: il parle des hommes,* he speaks of the men)

to, at, *à* (with masc. sing. article *le* contracts to *au: il va au musée,* he goes to the museum; with plural article *les* contracts to *aux: il parle aux femmes,* he speaks to the women. — Must be used with noun indirect object: he gives John the money, *il donne l'argent à Jean)*

to, at (meaning the home or place of business or store, or other occupancy) *chez; il va chez Jean,* he is going to John's house; *elle va chez mon ami,* she is going to my friend's; *on parle librement chez les Américains,* one speaks freely among Americans.

with, *avec*

in (within), *dans, en*

on, *sur*

under, *sous*

above, *au-dessus de*

below, *au-dessous de*

for, in order to, *pour* (*c'est pour moi,* it is for me; *il travaille pour réussir,* he works in order to succeed)

by, *par*

without, *sans*

until, *jusqu'à*

since, *depuis*

towards, *vers*

between, *entre*

among, *parmi*

near, *près de*

far from, *loin de*

before, *avant*

in front of, opposite, *devant*

after, *après*

back of, *derrière*

through, across, *à travers*

against, *contre*

by means of, *au moyen de*

in spite of, *en dépit de, malgré*   next to, beside, *à côté de*
about, around, *autour de*   facing (opposite), *en face de*
because of, on account of, *à cause*   instead of, *au lieu de*
     de   on the other side of, *de l'autre*
during, *pendant*   *côté de*

29. *Special Idioms and Expressions.*

good morning, good afternoon, good day, *bonjour*
good evening, good night, *bonsoir* (to one retiring, *bonne nuit*)
good-by, *au revoir* (to one whom you expect not to see for a long
     time, or again, *adieu*)
see you later, *à bientôt, à tout à l'heure*
see you to-morrow, *à demain*
see you tonight, *à ce soir*
just now, *tout à l'heure* (just a moment ago, *il y a un instant*)
hello!, *hola!* (on the telephone: *allô!*)
how are you?, *comment allez-vous?, comment vous portez-vous?*
how goes it?, *comment ça va?, ça va?*
I'm well, *je vais bien*
I'm (much) better, *je vais (beaucoup) mieux*
what time is it?, *quelle heure est-il?*
it is two o'clock, *il est deux heures*
it is twelve (noon), *il est midi*
it is twelve (midnight), *il est minuit*
it is half past two, *il est deux heures et demie*
it is a quarter past two, *il est deux heures et quart*
it is ten past two, *il est deux heures dix*
it is a quarter to two, *il est deux heures moins le quart*
it is five to two, *il est deux heures moins cinq*
at two o'clock, *à deux heures*
at about two, *vers deux heures*
last year, *l'année dernière*
next year, *l'année prochaine*
every day, *tous les jours*
the whole day, *toute la journée*
please, *s'il vous plaît* (preceding or following any request)
tell me, *dites-moi, ayez la bonté de me dire*
bring (to) me, *apportez-moi* (will you give me?, *voulez-vous me*
     donner?)
show (to) me, *montrez-moi, indiquez-moi* (will you point out to me.
     voulez-vous m'indiquer?)
thank you, *merci* (....very much, *merci bien*)

don't mention it, *il n'y a pas de quoi* (usually shortened to *pas de quoi*), *de rien*

pardon me, *pardon, pardonnez-moi, excusez-moi*

it doesn't matter, *n'importe, cela ne fait rien* (I don't care, *ça m'est égal, je m'en fiche, je m'en moque*)

I'm sorry, *je le regrette, j'en suis désolé*

I can't help, *je ne peux m'empêcher de* (infinitive)

it's nothing, *ce n'est rien*

what a pity!, too bad!, *quel dommage! c'est dommage!*

I'm glad, *cela me fait plaisir, j'en suis content*

I have to, *il me faut* (I have to leave, *il me faut partir*)

I agree (all right, O. K.), *d'accord, entendu*

where are you going?, *où allez-vous?*

where is?, *où est?*

where are?, *où sont?*

here is, here are, *voici*

there is, there are, *il y a* (use *voilà* if pointing out)

which way?, *par où?, par quel chemin?, de quel côté?*

to the right, *à (la) droite*

to the left, *à (la) gauche*

straight ahead, *tout droit*

this way, (direction), *par ici, de ce côté*

this way, (manner), *de cette façon*

that way, (direction), *par là*

come with me, *venez avec moi, accompagnez-moi* (follow me, *suivez-moi*)

what can I do for you?, *que désirez-vous?, que puis-je faire pour vous?*

what is it?, *qu'est-ce que c'est?* (what is the matter?, *qu'est-ce qu'il y a?*)

what is the matter with you?, *qu'avez-vous?*

what do you want?, *que voulez-vous?, que désirez-vous?*

how much is it?, *combien?*

anything else?, *rien d'autre?, encore quelque chose?, c'est tout?*

nothing else, *rien d'autre, c'est tout*

do you speak French?, *parlez-vous français?*

a little, *un peu*

speak (more) slowly, *parlez (plus) lentement, s'il vous plaît*

do you understand?, *comprenez-vous?*

I don't understand, *je ne comprends pas*

do you know?, *savez-vous?*

I can't, *je ne peux pas* (I don't know (how), *je ne sais pas*)

what do you call this in French?, *comment s'appelle ceci en français?*

how do you say ....in French?, *comment dit-on ..en français?*

what does that mean?, *qu'est-ce que ça veut dire?*
what do you mean?, *que voulez-vous dire?*
what are you talking about?, *de quoi parlez-vous?*
I am an American, *je suis Américain*
I'm (very) hungry (thirsty, sleepy, warm, cold), *j'ai (bien) faim (soif, sommeil, chaud, froid)*
it's warm (cold, windy, sunny, fine weather, bad weather), *il fait chaud (froid, du vent, du soleil, beau temps, mauvais temps)*
it's forbidden, *c'est (il est) défendu* (no smoking, *défense de fumer*)
luckily, *heureusement*
unfortunately, *malheureusement*
is it not so?, *n'est-ce pas?* (use this invariable phrase wherever English repeats the verb: you went, *didn't you?*; he is here, *isn't he?*)
not at all, *pas du tout*
how old are you?, *quel âge avez-vous?*
I'm twenty years old, *j'ai vingt ans*
how long have you been here?, *depuis quand (combien de temps) êtes-vous ici?*
how long have you been waiting? *depuis combien de temps (quand) attendez-vous?*
as soon (quickly) as possible, *le plus tôt possible, au plus tôt*
come here!, *venez ici!*
come in!, *entrez!* (stop!, *arrêtez!*)
look!, *regardez!*
careful!, look out!, *prenez garde!, attention!, gare!*
for heaven's sake!, *par exemple!*
in any case, *en tout cas*
let me hear from you, *donnez-moi de vos nouvelles*
glad to meet you, *enchanté (de faire votre connaissance)*
no admittance! *défense d'entrer!*
notice!, *avis (au public)!*
nonsense!, *allons donc!*
it was in fun, *c'était pour rire*
I'm in a bath of perspiration, *je suis en nage*
I have no change, *je n'ai pas la (petite) monnaie*
what else?, *quoi encore?*
you don't say so!, *pas possible!, sans blague!*
listen!, look here!, say!, *dites donc!*
just a second!, *un instant!*
gangway!, one side!, *circulez!, attention!, laissez passer!*
your health!, *à votre santé!* (reply: *à la vôtre!*)
I should like to, *je voudrais*

hurry!, *dépêchez-vous!*
keep right (left), *tenez la droite* (*gauche*)
entrance, *entrée* (exit, *sortie*)

30. *Slang Words and Expressions.*

fellow, "guy", *type* ("nice guy", *bon type, bon zig;* "awful guy",
    sale type, sale zig; "what a guy!", *quel type!*)
nerve, "crust", *culot, toupet* ("what a nerve!", *quel culot!*)
scoundrel, "louse", *canaille, salaud, saligaud*
greenhorn, "sucker", "dumb-bell", *cornichon, veau*
old fogy, *vieille momie*
soldier, doughboy, *poilu; pioupiou* (infantry only)
fatty, "greaseball", *gros patapouf, boule-de-suif*
captain, "boss", "old man", *vieux, capiston*
joint, "dump", *cambuse, boîte* ("what an awful dump!", *quelle sale*
    boîte!)
drunkard, "boozehound", *biberon, soûlot, soûlard*
to have a "swell" time, to "get plastered", *faire la bombe*
substitute, "sub", *bouche-trou*
"jalopy", *bagnole, vieux clou*
"bike", *bécane*
"gadget", *machin*
money, "dough", *pognon, du pèse*
tobacco, *perlot*
cigarette, "butt", *sèche, mégot*
pay-day, *sainte touche*
luck, *veine, filon*
noise, quarrel, *potin, tapage*
coffee, *cahoua* (bad coffee, *bain de pied, lavasse*)
smart, *calé*
funny, *rigolo*
wonderful, "swell", *épatant, formidable*
to have the blues, *avoir le cafard* (moon, *la cafarde*)
don't bother me!, "scram!", *fiche-moi la paix!*
get the devil out of here!, *fiche le camp!*
it's all the same to me, *c'est kif-kif*
to crack a smile, *faire risette*
cheese it, the cops!, *vingt-deux les flics!*
hell!, *zut!*
give me a ring, *donnez-moi un coup de téléphone*

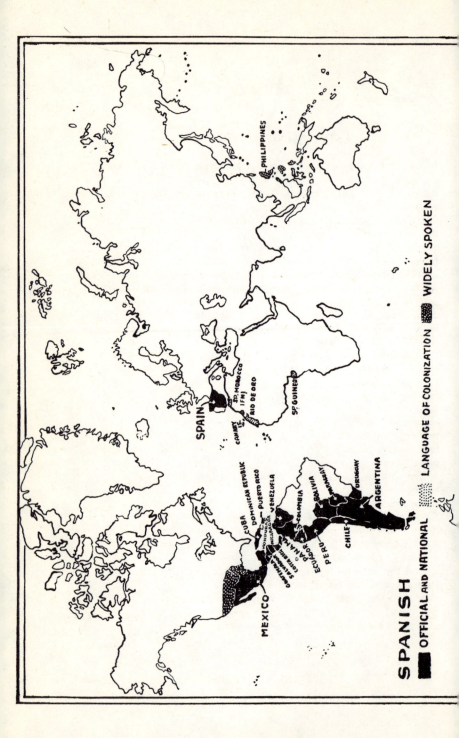

SPANISH

■ OFFICIAL AND NATIONAL ▨ LANGUAGE OF COLONIZATION ▨ WIDELY SPOKEN

SPAIN

CANARY IS.
SP. MOROCCO (IFNI)
RIO DE ORO
SP. GUINEA

PHILIPPINES

MEXICO

CUBA
DOMINICAN REPUBLIC
PUERTO RICO
HONDURAS
GUATEMALA
NICARAGUA
SALVADOR
COSTA RICA
PANAMA
VENEZUELA
COLOMBIA
ECUADOR
PERU
BOLIVIA
PARAGUAY
CHILE
URUGUAY
ARGENTINA

CHAPTER VII

SPANISH

SPEAKERS AND LOCATION

(All population figures are approximate)

Europe — Spain (25,500,000).

Africa — Canary Islands (650,000); Rio de Oro (30,000); Spanish Guinea (150,000); Spanish Morocco (800,000).

North America — Mexico (20,000,000).

Central America — Canal Zone (50,000); Costa Rica (600,000); Guatemala (3,000,000); Honduras (1,000,000); Nicaragua (1,100,000); Panama (700,000); Salvador (1,700,000).

West Indies — Cuba (4,200,000); Dominican Republic (1,600,000); Puerto Rico (2,000,000).

South America — Argentina (13,000,000); Bolivia (3,300,000); Chile (4,600,000); Colombia (8,700,000); Ecuador (3,000,000); Paraguay (1,000,000); Peru (6,800,000); Uruguay (2,100,000); Venezuela (3,500,000).

Current to some degree in other areas, including Philippine Islands and southwestern U. S. (New Mexico, Texas, Arizona, California).

ALPHABET AND SOUNDS

a, b, c, ch, d, e, f, g, h, i, j, l, ll, m, n, ñ, o, p, q, r, rr, s, t, u, v, x, y, z (k and w do not appear in native Spanish words).

Vowel sounds: a=far; e=first part of *a* in gate; i, y=machine; o=or; u=food.

Consonant sounds: ch, f, l, m, n, p, x, y, approximately as in English.

b or v: at beginning of word (*b*ien, *v*aca), or after a consonant (cor*b*ata, en*v*iar)=strongly pronounced *b*;

between vowels (ca*b*allo, bra*v*o)=*v*, pronounced not by placing lower lip in contact with upper teeth, but by placing lips almost together, as for Eng. w; lips are held back, however, not protruded. Note that in words beginning with *b* or *v*, the sound may vary accordingly as the word is preceded or not by another word ending in vowel: vaca=*b*aca, but la vaca=la*v*aca.

c: before a, o, u or consonant,=k (*c*aballo, *c*osa, *c*riado); before e or i,=*th*in (*c*ielo).

d: between vowels,=*th*is (ama*d*o); elsewhere, as in Eng., but with tip of tongue touching back of upper teeth, not palate(bon*d*ad).

g: before a, o, u or consonant,=*g*o (*g*abán, la*g*o, *g*ritar); before e or i,=strongly aspirated *h*ouse (*g*eneral, *g*iro).

h: is always silent, as in *h*onest (*h*ierro).

j: =*h*ouse, strongly aspirated (*j*inete, *j*oven).

ll: =mi*lli*on (*ll*eno, caba*ll*o).

ñ: =o*ni*on (a*ñ*o).

q: as in Eng.; used only before *ue, ui*, in which groups the *u* is silent (*qu*e, *qu*ien=ke, kyen), as it is also in the groups *gue, gui* (*gu*erra, *gu*isar).

r: trilled, as in British ve*r*y (ca*r*o).

rr: more strongly trilled, as in Irish bego*rr*a (ca*rr*o).

s: always as in thi*s*, never as in ro*s*e.

t: as in Eng., but tip of tongue touches back of upper ˈeeth, not palate (*t*engo, ma*t*ar).

z: =*th*in.

Sounds not appearing in Spanish: all Eng. vowel sounds outside of five listed above; *sh*ame, plea*s*ure, *j*est, ro*s*e, *v*at, American *r*.

Spanish sounds not appearing in English: b or v between vowels; note differences between Sp. and Eng. t, d, r, rr.

SPELLING, SYLLABIFICATION, ACCENTUATION, PUNCTUATION

No double consonants appear in Sp., save ll, rr (special sounds); nn (rare), cc (first *c*=k, second *c*=th; acción =a*kth*yon).

In dividing a word into syllables, a single consonant between two vowels goes with the following vowel, not with the preceding; pronounce Sp. *general* as *ge ne ral*, not *gen er al*, as in Eng.

The only written accent of Sp. is the acute: '. If a word ends in a vowel, in *n* or in *s*, the stress is on the next to the last syllable, and the accent is *not* written: *caballo, tienen, pesos*. If a word ends in any consonant but *n* or *s*, the stress is on the last syllable, and the accent is *not* written: *azul, primer*. If a word is stressed otherwise than in accordance with the above two rules, the accent *is* written: *pidió, carbón, francés, dólar, cárcel, último, dólares.*[1]

Punctuate as in Eng., save that Sp. uses *inverted* question and exclamation marks at beginning of interrogative or exclamatory sentences: *¿Cómo está usted?; ¡Cómo me gusta!*

SAMPLE OF WRITTEN SPANISH; USE FOR PRACTICE READING

¡Buenos días, Don José! ¿Cómo está usted?—¡Hola, Manuel! ¿Cómo estás?—Muy bien, gracias; ¿y su señora esposa?—Está en Guatemala con mis dos hijos, pero escribe que todos, gracias a Dios, están bien. ¿Qué tal en tu casa? —Bastante bien. Pero, dígame, ¿ha leído usted esto? Es un artículo en el periódico de hoy, la última edición de esta ma-

---

1. The accent mark appears on a few words to distinguish them from other words similar in appearance and pronunciation, but different in meaning: *sé* (I know), *se* (self); *este* (this, adjective), *éste* (this one, pronoun); also to separate two vowels that would otherwise combine into a diphthong (*vacío*, empty, would without the accent mark be pronounced *vacio* = *bathyo*).

ñana, anunciando que ha estallado la guerra en Europa.—Pero,
¿tú crees[2] todo lo que lees[2] en los periódicos?—Esta vez parece que dicen la verdad. Las tropas alemanas ya están inva-
diendo a Polonia. Francia e Inglaterra amenazan con decla-
rarle la guerra a Alemania. Todavía no se sabe lo que van a
hacer las demás naciones.—Pero, ¡parece mentira! ¿Cómo es
posible? ¿Para esto van a servir los adelantos de nuestra ci-
vilización?—Pues, ¡así es! Ya no hay remedio.

GRAMMATICAL SURVEY

1. *Nouns and Articles.*

Sp. has only two genders, masculine and feminine. Nouns
denoting males are masculine, those denoting females feminine. For nouns which in Eng. are neuter, the Sp. ending
often helps to determine the gender. Nouns ending in -*o* (plural -*os*) are usually masculine, those in -*a* (plur. -*as*) feminine.
The gender of nouns ending in -*e* (plur. -*es*), and of those
ending in consonants (plural formed by adding -*es* to the final
consonant) will be determined by observation.[3]

The definite article is *el* (plur. *los*) for masculine nouns,
la (plur. *las*) for feminines. The indefinite article is *un* (masc.),
una (fem.). *Unos, unas* may be used to mean "some".

la casa, the house	*los libros,* the books
el libro, the book	*las casas,* the houses
el hijo, the son	*los hijos,* the sons
la hija, the daughter	*las hijas,* the daughters
el padre, the father	*los padres,* the fathers
la madre, the mother	*las madres,* the mothers
el general, the general	*los generales,* the generals
la mujer, the woman	*las mujeres,* the women

2. Pronounce both e's separately: *cre es, le es.*

3. Nouns ending in -*ión,* -*d* or -*z* are usually feminine. Nouns ending
in -*z* change to -*c* before adding -*es* for the plural: *vez,* plural, *veces.*

un libro, a book
una casa, a house
unos hijos, some sons
unas hijas, some daughters
un padre, a father
una madre, a mother
unos generales, some generals
unas mujeres, some women

2. *Adjectives and Adverbs.*

Adjectives agree with the nouns they modify. Like nouns, they have the endings *-o* (fem. *-a;* masc. plur. *-os;* fem. plur. *-as*); or *-e* (no difference between masc. and fem.; plur. *-es*); or consonant (plur. *-es*). Agreement with the noun does not necessarily mean identical endings; the adjective may be of the *-e* (plur. *-es*) type, while the noun is of the *-o* (plur. *-os*) type. Adjectives usually follow the noun, though a few common ones precede:

el libro rojo (red); *los libros rojos*
la casa roja; las casas rojas
el libro verde (green); *los libros verdes*
la casa azul (blue); *las casas azules*

To form the comparative degree, Sp. usually places *más* (more) before the adjective; to form the superlative, the definite article is placed before the comparative; *un libro claro* (a clear book); *un libro más claro* (a clearer book); *el libro más claro* (the clearest book).

The adverb is generally formed by adding *-mente* to the feminine singular form of the adjective: *claro;* adverb: *claramente* (clearly). If two or more adverbs appear together, *-mente* is added only to the last one, while the others retain the form of the feminine singular adjective: he spoke clearly and distinctly, *habló clara y distintamente.*

3. *Numerals.*

a) Cardinal[4].

1—*uno*[5] (fem. *una*)	22—*veinte y dos*
2—*dos*	(or *veintidós*)
3—*tres*	30—*treinta*
4—*cuatro*	40—*cuarenta*
5—*cinco*	50—*cincuenta*
6—*seis*	60—*sesenta*
7—*siete*	70—*setenta*
8—*ocho*	80—*ochenta*
9—*nueve*	90—*noventa*
10—*diez*	100—*ciento*[6]
11—*once*	200—*doscientos*[7]
12—*doce*	300—*trescientos*
13—*trece*	400—*cuatrocientos*
14—*catorce*	500—*quinientos*
15—*quince*	600—*seiscientos*
16—*diez y seis*	700—*setecientos*
(or *dieciséis*)	800—*ochocientos*
17—*diez y siete*	900—*novecientos*
18—*diez y ocho*	1000—*mil*
19—*diez y nueve*	2000—*dos mil*
20—*veinte*	100,000—*cien mil*
21—*veinte y uno*	1,000,000—*un millón (de)*[8]
(or *veintiuno*)	

4. Use these in dates, save for "the first": *el primero de mayo,* May first; *el dos de mayo,* May 2nd; also generally instead of ordinals beyond 10th: *calle cincuenta y tres,* fifty-third street.

5. Use *un* before a masc. sing. noun: *tengo un libro,* I have one book; there is no distinction between "one book" and "a book".

6. *Cien* if used immediately before the noun: *cien dólares,* $100; but *ciento sesenta dólares,* $160.

7. Plural hundreds change *-os* to *-as* if used with feminine nouns: *doscientas mujeres.*

8. *Un millón de dólares,* $1,000,000; *dos millones de dólares,* $2,000,000.

b) Ordinal.

1st—*primero*[9]	5th—*quinto*	8th—*octavo*
2nd—*segundo*	6th—*sexto*	9th—*noveno*
3rd—*tercero*[9]	7th—*séptimo*	10th—*décimo*
4th—*cuarto*		

c) Others.

half—*mitad* (noun), or *medio* (adjective): *media naranja,* half an orange; *la mitad de mi clase,* half of my class.

a pair of—*un par de*   a dozen—*una docena de*
once—*una vez*   twice—*dos veces*   three times—*tres veces*
the first time—*la primera vez*   sometimes—*algunas veces*
next time—*la próxima vez*   again—*otra vez*

4. *Verbs.*

Sp. verbs fall into three main classes, with the infinitive ending respectively in *-ar, -er, -ir* (to take, *tomar;* to sell, *vender;* to live, *vivir*).

Only the most frequently used tenses are given below. In the present indicative ("I take, am taking, do take"), present subjunctive ("I may take") and singular imperative ("Take!") of a large number of verbs, there is a change in the last vowel of the root[10] whenever that vowel is stressed (this happens in the first, second and third persons singular and third person plural of the present indicative and present subjunctive, and in the singular imperative); such verbs are called *radical-changing.* They are otherwise regular, save that a few of them effect a change in a few other forms (3rd sing. and 3rd plur. of the past tense, etc.). Radical-changing verbs appearing in the vocabulary are indicated by the changed vowel in parentheses: to count, *contar (ue);* this means that whenever the *o* is stressed,

9. Use *primer, tercer,* before masculine singular noun: *el primer libro* or *el libro primero.*

10. Root - what is left of the verb when the infinitive ending is removed; the root of *sentir* is *sent-.*

it changes to *ue,* and that the first singular present indicative, consequently, is *cuento.* Other important irregularities are also noted in the vocabulary.

1. Present Indicative (meaning: I take, am taking, do take)

Regular:		Radical-Changing:	
to take, *tomar*		to count, *contar* (*ue*)	
I take,	*tom-o*[11]	I count,	*cuent-o*
you take	*tom-as*[12]	you count,	*cuent-as*
he, she takes,	*tom-a*[12]	he, she counts,	*cuent-a*
(you take)		(you count)	
we take,	*tom-amos*	we count,	*cont-amos*
you take,	*tom-áis*[12]	you count,	*cont-áis*
they (you) take,	*tom-an*[12]	they (you) count,	*cuent-an*

Regular:		Radical-Changing:	
to sell, *vender*		to lose, *perder* (*ie*)	
I sell (am selling),	*vend-o*	I lose, am losing,	*pierd-o*
you (familiar) sell,	*vend-es*	you (fam.) lose	*pierd-es*
he, she sells,	*vend-e*	he, she loses,	*pierd-e*
you (polite) sell,		you (polite) lose,	
we sell,	*vend-emos*	we lose,	*perd-emos*
you (plur. fam.) sell,	*vend-éis*	you lose,	*perd-éis*
they, you sell,	*vend-en*	they, you lose,	*pierd-en*

11. Ordinarily Sp. makes no use of subject pronouns (cf. p. 241), since the endings supply the meaning "I", "he", etc. The pronouns may be used for stress (*yo tomo, I* am taking), or for clearness (*ella toma,* "she is taking," as against "he is taking"). The Sp. present may have the meaning "I take", "I am taking", "I do take".

12. The second person singular is used in addressing intimate friends, relatives, children, inferiors, animals. The more normal way of addressing people with whom one is not on an extremely familiar basis is to use the *third* singular of the verb with *usted* (abbreviated in writing to *Ud., Vd.*). The same remark applies to the plural, where the second person is even more generally avoided: you (several persons) are taking, *ustedes toman;* in preference to *tomáis.*

Regular: Radical-changing:

to live, *vivir*	to feel, *sentir* (*ie*)	to sleep, *dormir* (*ue*)	to ask for, *pedir* (*i*)
viv-o	*sient-o*	*duerm-o*	*pid-o*
viv-es	*sient-es*	*duerm-es*	*pid-es*
viv-e	*sient-e*	*duerm-e*	*pid-e*
viv-imos	*sent-imos*	*dorm-imos*	*ped-imos*
viv-ís	*sent-ís*	*dorm-ís*	*ped-ís*
viv-en	*sient-en*	*duerm-en*	*pid-en*

to be,	*ser*[13]	*estar*[13]	to have,	*tener*[14]	*haber*[14]
I am,	*soy*	*estoy*	I have,	*tengo*	*he*
you are,	*eres*	*estás*	you have,	*tienes*	*has*
he, she is,	*es*	*está*	he, she has,	*tiene*	*ha*
we are,	*somos*	*estamos*	we have,	*tenemos*	*hemos*
you are,	*sois*	*estáis*	you have,	*tenéis*	*habéis*
they are,	*son*	*están*	they have,	*tienen*	*han*

13. *Ser* must be used to translate "to be" whenever:

a) a predicate *noun* follows: he is a general, *es general;*
b) material or origin is indicated: the watch is of gold, *el reloj es de oro;*
c) time is expressed: it is one, it is two, *es la una, son las dos.*
 Estar must be used to translate "to be" whenever:
a) health is involved: he is well, *está bien;*
b) location is expressed: he is here, *está aquí.*

If a predicate *adjective* follows, *ser* expresses a more permanent or inherent, *estar* a more temporary or occasional quality; she is pretty, *es bonita;* she is young, *es joven;* she is merry, *está alegre;* the milk is hot, *la leche está caliente.* Hence, either verb may be used with certain adjectives: ice is cold, *el hielo es frío;* the water is cold, *el agua está fría.*

14. *Haber* is " to have" used as an auxiliary: I have slept, *he dormido.* *Tener* indicates possession: I have a book, *tengo un libro;* it also has a variety of idiomatic uses (cf. p. 266): I am hungry, *tengo hambre* (literally, I have hunger); I am 20 years old, *tengo veinte años* (literally, I have 20 years).

2. Imperfect Indicative[15] (meaning: I was taking, I used to take).

	-ar verbs	-er and -ir verbs	ser[16]
I was taking, used to take,	tom-aba	vend- or viv-ía	era (I was, used to be)
you were taking, used to take,	tom-abas	vend- or viv-ías	eras
he, she was taking, used to take,	tom-aba	vend- or viv-ía	era
we were taking, used to take,	tom-ábamos	vend- or viv-íamos	éramos
you used to take,	tom-abais	vend- or viv-íais	erais
they used to take,	tom-aban	vend- or viv-ían	eran

3. Past Indicative (meaning: I took).

	-ar verbs	-er and -ir verbs	radical changing[17]
I took,	tom-é	vend- or viv-í	ped-í
you took,	tom-aste	vend- or viv-iste	ped-iste
he, she took,	tom-ó	vend- or viv-ió	pid-ió
we took,	tom-amos	vend- or viv-imos	ped-imos
you took,	tom-asteis	vend- or viv-isteis	ped-isteis
they took,	tom-aron	vend- or viv-ieron	pid-ieron

15. In the imperfect, future and conditional, radical-changing verbs never have the radical change.

16. *Estar, tener, haber* are regular: *estaba, tenía, había.* Only three verbs have irregular imperfects: *ir,* to go, *iba; ser,* to be, *era; ver,* to see, *veía.*

17. *-ir* radical-changing verbs which change *e* to *ie* when stressed also have *i* instead of *e* in the third singular and third plural of the past: *sentí,* but *sintió, sintieron; -ir* verbs which change *o* to *ue* have *u* in the same forms: *dormí,* but *durmió, durmieron; -ar* and *-er* radical-changing verbs are regular in the past tense.

	ser	estar		*tener*	haber
I was[18]	*fuí*	*estuve*[19]	I had,	*tuve*[19]	*hube*[19]
you were,	*fuiste*	*estuviste*	you had,	*tuviste*	*hubiste*
he, she was,	*fué*	*estuvo*	he, she had,	*tuvo*	*hubo*
we were,	*fuimos*	*estuvimos*	we had,	*tuvimos*	*hubimos*
you were,	*fuisteis*	*estuvisteis*	you had,	*tuvisteis*	*hubisteis*
they were,	*fueron*	*estuvieron*	they had,	*tuvieron*	*hubieron*

4. Future (meaning: I shall take), and Conditional (meaning: I should take).[20]

Future *Conditional*

I shall take,	*tomar-é*	I should (would) take,	*tomar-ía*
(sell, live),	(*vender*)-*é*	(sell, live),	(*vender*)-*ía*
	(*vivir*)-*é*		(*vivir*)-*ía*
you will take,	*tomar-ás*	you would take,	*tomar-ías*
he, she will take,	*tomar-á*	he, she would take,	*tomar-ía*
we shall take,	*tomar-emos*	we should (would) take,	*tomar-íamos*
you will take,	*tomar-éis*	you would take,	*tomar-íais*
they will take,	*tomar-án*	they would take,	*tomar-ían*

5. Compound Tenses (meaning: I have, had, shall have, should have taken).

Compound tenses are formed by using *haber* with the past participle of the verb (ending in -*ado* for -*ar* verbs, -*ido* for others: taken, *tomado*; sold, *vendido*; lived, *vivido*); thus:

Present Perfect: I have taken, *he tomado*; you have taken, *has tomado*, etc.

Past Perfect: I had taken, *había tomado*; you had taken, *habías tomado*, etc.

18. For "I was" and "I had", the imperfects *era, estaba, tenía*, which indicate *continued* action in the past, occur more frequently than the pasts *fui, estuve, tuve. Fui* is also used as the past tense of *ir*, "to go".
19. Nearly all irregular pasts ending in unaccented -*e* have this set of endings: -*e*, -*iste*, -*o*, -*imos*, -*isteis*, -*ieron*.
20. Note that future and conditional endings are added to the *entire* infinitive, not to the stem alone. Radical-changing verbs are quite regular in these tenses. *Ser* and *estar* are regular (*seré, estaré; sería, estaría*); *haber* has *habré, habría*; *tener* has *tendré, tendría*.

Future Perfect: I shall have taken, *habré tomado*, etc.
Conditional Past: I should (would) have taken, *habría tomado*, etc.

Many past participles are irregular; some will be given in the vocabulary; none of the verbs given so far has an irregular past participle.

6. Imperative (meaning: take!).

Regular

	-ar	-er	-ir
Familiar Singular	—*tom-a*	*vend-e*	*viv-e*
Familiar Plural	—*tom-ad*	*vend-ed*	*viv-id*
Polite Singular	—*tom-e*	*vend-a*	*viv-a*

(Polite imperative forms are normally followed by *usted*)

| Polite Plural | —*tom-en* *vend-an* *viv-an* |

(Polite plural forms are normally followed by *ustedes*)

Radical-Changing

	-ar	-er	-ir	
Familiar Singular	*cuent-a*	*pierd-e*	*sient-e*	*pid-e*
Familiar Plural	*cont-ad*	*perd-ed*	*sent-id*	*ped-id*
Polite Singular	*cuent-e*	*pierd-a*	*sient-a*	*pid-a*

(Polite singular forms are normally followed by *usted*)

| Polite Plural | *cuent-en* | *pierd-an* | *sient-an* | *pid-an* |

(Polite plural forms are normally followed by *ustedes*)

7. Negative.

This is regularly formed by prefixing *no* (not) to the verb: *tomo*, I take; *no tomo*, I do not take; *tome Ud.*, take (imperative); *no tome Ud.*, do not take.

8. Reflexive verbs.

Eng. uses some verbs reflexively (I see myself, I speak to myself). In Sp., the number of reflexive verbs is much larger (Eng. I bathe, but Sp. *me baño*, lit. I bathe myself).

Reflexive forms, in the plural, are often used with a reciprocal meaning (each other, one another, to each other, to one another).

The reflexive **pronouns are:**

me, myself, to myself	*nos,* ourselves, to ourselves
te, yourself, to yourself	*os*, yourselves, to yourselves

se, himself, herself, themselves, yourself, yourselves (polite);
    to himself, etc.

Reflexive pronouns, like all object pronouns (cf. p. 241), come directly before the verb (I bathe, *me baño*), except in the infinitive (to bathe, *bañarse*), gerund (bathing, *bañándose*)[21], and imperative affirmative, both familiar and polite (bathe!, *báñate*, fam.; *báñese Ud.*, pol.); but not imperative negative (do not bathe! *no te bañes, no se bañe Ud.*).

I see myself,	*me veo*
you see yourself,	*te ves*
he (she) sees himself (herself),	*se ve*
we see ourselves, or each other,	*nos vemos*
you see yourselves, or each other,	*os veis*
they see themselves, or each other,	*se ven*
I do not speak to myself,	*no me hablo*
you do not speak to yourself	*no te hablas*
he (she) does not speak to himself (herself)	*no se habla*
we do not speak to ourselves, or each other,	*no nos hablamos*
you do not speak to yourselves, or each other,	*no os habláis*
they do not speak to themselves, or each other,	*no se hablan*

21. The gerund (or present participle) is formed by adding *-ando* to the root of *-ar* verbs, *-iendo* to that of *-er* and *-ir* verbs: taking, *tomando*; selling, *vendiendo*; living, *viviendo*. It may be used alone, with the meaning of "by" or "while" (by taking, while taking, *tomando*), or

9. Passive.

The reflexive is often used in Sp. where a passive would appear in Eng. This is particularly true when the subject of the Eng. passive verb is a thing: books are sold here, *aquí se venden libros* (lit. books sell themselves here). Otherwise, the passive is generally formed with the verb "to be" (*ser*), and the past participle, being used as a predicate adjective, agrees with the subject: my parents were killed by the robbers, *mis padres fueron matados por los ladrones*.

10. Subjunctive.

The Sp. subjunctive has four tenses, and is frequently used in subordinate clauses. For the present subjunctive, the ending are normally:
for *-ar* verbs: *-e, -es, -e, -emos, -éis, -en*; I may take, *tome, etc.*[22]
for *-er* and *-ir* verbs: *-a, -as, -a, -amos, -áis, -an*; I may sell, *venda,* etc.

The imperfect subjunctive ends in *-ase* or *-ara* for *-ar* verbs, *-iese* or *-iera* for the others: I might take, *tomase* or *tomara*. The present perfect subjunctive uses the present subjunctive of *haber* (*haya*), with the past participle (*haya tomado*, I may have taken); the past perfect subjunctive has the imperfect subjunctive of *haber* (*hubiese* or *hubiera*) with the past participle (I might have taken, *hubiese tomado* or *hubiera tomado*).

---

with the verb *estar* to form a progressive conjugation (I am taking, *estoy tomando*); but the progressive meaning can also be rendered by the plain verb (*tomo*, I am taking).

22.   Note that it is really the third person singular and plural of the present subjunctive that are used as polite imperatives: *tome Ud., tomen Uds.* The second person singular and plural of the subjunctive are used as familiar imperatives in the negative: do not take, *no tomes.*

5. *Pronouns.*

a) Personal Pronouns (Subject).

I, *yo*	we, *nosotros*
you (fam.), *tú*	you (fam. plur.), *vosotros*
he, *él*	they (masc.), *ellos*
she, *ella*	they (fem.), *ellas*
you (pol.), *usted*	you (pol. plur.), *ustedes*

These are generally used only for emphasis or clarification: I take, *tomo; I* take, *yo tomo;* she takes (in opposition to "he takes"), *ella toma.*

b) Personal Pronouns (Direct Object).

me, *me*	us, *nos*
you (fam.), *te*	you, (fam. plur.), *os*
him, you (pol.), *le*	them, you (pol.), *les*
her, *la*[23]	them (fem.), *las*[23]
it, *lo*	them (plural of *lo*), *los*

Indirect object pronouns are the same as the direct (to me, *me*, etc.), save that *le* is generally used with the meanings of "to him", "to her", "to it", "to you" (pol.), and *les* with the meaning of "to them" in all connections and "to you" (pol. plur.).

Direct and indirect object pronouns precede the verb, save in the infinitive, gerund and imperative affirmative: *me ve,* he sees me; *lo tiene,* he has it; *le da el libro,* he gives him the book; but *quiero tomarlo,* I wish to take it; *¡tómalo!,* take it!; *estoy tomándolo,* I am taking it. If a direct and an indirect object pronoun are used together, the indirect normally precedes the direct (he gives it to me, *me lo da;* he wishes to give it to me, *quiere dármelo*); and if the indirect is *le* or *les,* it is changed to *se* (he gives it to him, *se lo da,* instead of *le lo da*).

23. Use *la* and *las* referring to nouns which in Sp. are feminine; I see it (the house), *la veo;* I see it (the book), *lo veo.*

c) **Personal** Pronouns with Prepositions.

These are the same as the subject pronouns, save that *mi*
replaces *yo*, and *ti* replaces *tú*; for me, *para mí*; for you, *para
ti*; for him, *para él*; for her, *para ella*; etc.

d) Possessive Adjectives and Pronouns.

Adjectives.

my, *mi*, plur. *mis*: (*mi libro, mi casa, mis libros, mis casas*)
your (fam.), *tu*, plur. *tus*: (*tu libro, tus casas*)
his, her, your, their[24]: *su*, plur. *sus*
our, *nuestro* (*nuestra, nuestros, nuestras*): (*nuestra casa*)
your, *vuestro* (*vuestra*, etc.): (*vuestras casas*)

Pronouns.

mine, *el mío, la mía, los míos, las mías*: (your books and mine,
       tus libros y los míos)
yours, *el tuyo, la tuya, los tuyos, las tuyas*.
his, hers, theirs, yours (pol.), *el suyo, la suya, los suyos, las
       suyas*[25]
ours, *el nuestro, la nuestra, los nuestros, las nuestras*
yours, *el vuestro, la vuestra, los vuestros, las vuestras*
       The article is usually omitted after the verb *ser*: *el libro
es mío.*

e) Demonstrative Adjectives and Pronouns.

Adjectives.

this, these, *este, esta, estos, estas*: (this book, *este libro*, these
       houses, *estas casas*)
that, those (near you), *ese, esa, esos, esas*: (that house of yours,
       that house near you, *esa casa*)

24. Distinguish by using *de él, de ella, de Ud., de ellos, de ellas,
de Uds.*, if necessary: her book, *su libro* or *el libro de ella*; their
books, *sus libros* or *los libros de ellos*.

25. Distinguish by using *de él*, etc.; my books and hers, *mis libros
y los suyos* or *mis libros y los de ella.*

that, those (yonder), *aquel, aquella, aquellos, aquellas*: (those
   men over there, *aquellos hombres*)

   Pronouns.

this one, these, *éste, ésta, éstos, éstas*: (your book and this one,
   tu libro y éste)

that one, those (near you), *ése, ésa, ésos, ésas*: (my book and
   that one by you, *mi libro y ése*)

that one, those (yonder), *aquél, aquélla, aquéllos, aquéllas*:
   (our books and those over there, *nuestros libros y aquéllos*)

   "Neuter" pronouns, *esto, eso, aquello* are used to refer
not to specific objects, but to a general situation or state of
affairs: this pleases me, I like this, *esto me gusta*; I don't
like that (what you have said), *eso no me gusta.*

   To translate "the one", "the ones", Sp. generally uses
the definite article (*el, la, los, las*): my book and the one
which is on the table, *mi libro y el que está en la mesa*; my
book and my brother's (the one of my brother), *mi libro y el
de mi hermano.*

   f) Relative and Interrogative Pronouns.

who, whom, that, which, *que*[26]; the man who is here, *el hombre
   que está aquí*; the letter you wrote, *la carta que Ud. escribió.*[27]

whom (after prepositions), *quien*: the man to whom I spoke,
   el hombre a quien hablé.

whose, *cuyo, cuya, cuyos, cuyas*: the man whose house I saw,
   el hombre cuya casa he visto.

who?, *¿quién?* (plur. *¿quiénes?*): who is here? *¿Quién está
   aquí?*; who are those men? *¿Quiénes son aquellos hombres?*

whom?, *¿a quién?* (pl. *¿a quiénes?*): whom did you see? *¿A
   quién vió Ud.?*

what?, *¿qué?*: what did you write?, *¿Qué escribió Ud.?*

26.   *El cual, la cual, los cuales, las cuales,* or *el que, la que, los que,
las que,* are occasionally used instead of *que* to refer to the more
distant of two possible antecedents: I spoke to the boy's mother, who
came to see me, *hablé con la madre del muchacho, la cual vino a verme.*
27.   Note that the relative pronoun cannot be omitted in Sp.

which?, which one?, which ones?, *¿cuál?* (plur. *¿cuáles?*): to
which one of my friends did you give the book? *¿A cuál
de mis amigos dió Ud. el libro?*
whose?, *¿de quién?*: whose house is that? (whose is that
house?), *¿De quién es aquella casa?*

AMERICAN VARIETIES OF SPANISH

The Spanish used in the various countries of Spanish
America has local peculiarities of pronunciation, grammar and
vocabulary. These differences, while interesting and striking,
are not so fundamental as those found in some other languages
(e.g., Italian, with its numerous dialects, many of which are
mutually incomprehensible). Several of the Spanish-American
peculiarities of pronunciation are current in Spain itself, notably
the southern part of the country (Andalusia), and seem to have
been imported by original Spanish settlers coming to America
from various sections of Spain.[28] Only a few major peculiarities
of Spanish-American speech are listed, and many of them are
common to the vulgar pronunciation of Spain as well.

PRONUNCIATION.

Spanish America generally discards the Castilian sound
of *th* in *th*in (represented by *z*, or by *c* before *e* and *i*), and
replaces it with the sound of *s* (*c*ielo; Castilian *th*yelo; Sp. Am.
*s*yelo). This leads to occasional confusion of words which in
Castilian would be differentiated by sound (*casa*, "house";
caza, "hunt"), and to the replacement of one member of the
pair by another word (*cacería*, "hunt", in Sp. Am.)

28. In Spain, local dialects (Andalusian, Asturian, Aragonese, etc.)
do not diverge from standard Castilian any more than do our southern,
middle western or New England forms of speech from standard
"American" English. Galician, Catalan and Basque are notable exceptions; but Galician (spoken in the northwestern corner of Spain)
is really a dialect of Portuguese, not of Spanish; Catalan (eastern
Spain) is rated as a separate Romance language; Basque (northeastern corner of Spain, southwestern corner of France) not only
is not a Romance language, but does not even belong to the Indo-
European family.

2. The Castilian sound of *ll* is usually *y* in Sp. **Am.** (caba*ll*o; Cast. kava*lly*o; Sp. Am. kava*y*o). In sections **of** Argentina, etc., this sound further changes to that of *s* in "pleasure", or even to that of *g* in "gin" (kava*zh*o, kava*j*o).

3. The sound of *g* before *e* or *i*, or of *j*, which is in Castilian a harsher guttural than English *h*, is in most Spanish American countries pronounced more weakly, so as to be very similar to Eng. *h* (*general*: Cast. *kh*eneral, Sp. Am. *h*eneral). The *j* of *reloj* ("watch", "clock") is often silent in Sp. Am., so that the word sounds as though spelled *reló*.

4. At the end of a word, *s*, which is strongly pronounced in Castilian, either becomes *h* or disappears in most Sp. **Am.** countries (*dos pesos* sounds like *doh pesos* or *doh pesoh*).

5. Between vowels, *d*, which in Castilian sounds like *th* of "this", often disappears altogether in Sp. Am. and **Spain** (*amado* pronounced *amao*).

6. *Pa* for *para* (*pa nada* or *pa naa* instead of *para nada*); *gweno* for *bueno; gwevo* for *huevo*, etc. are occasionally heard in Sp. Am. as well as in Spain.

7. Sections of Argentina have a habit of stressing object pronouns which are added on to verbs: *vamonós, digalé* for *vámonos* ("let's go", "let's get out"), *dígale* ("tell him").

Other sections of South America, and even of Spain, share this peculiarity.

GRAMMAR.

1. Considerable confusion appears in forms of address in various Sp. Am. countries. While *vosotros* with the second person plural of the verb is generally avoided, so that a mother who would address one of her children as *tú* (with the second singular verb) addresses more than one of them as *ustedes* (with the third plural), Argentina prefers *vos* in addressing one person, *ustedes* more than one.

2. *Mosotros, mos,* are sometimes heard in the place of *nosotros. nos* ("we", "us"). The uneducated of Spain, however, often use these same forms.

3. Argentina tends to avoid the future (*tomaré*, "I shall take"), using in its place *voy a tomar* ("I am going to take"). Colombia prefers *voy y tomo* ("I go and take"), or *voy ir tomando* ("I am going to go taking").

4. While Castilian uses the *-se* and *-ra* forms of the past subjunctive (cf. p. 240) about equally, Sp. Am. normally prefers the *-ra* form.

VOCABULARY.

Local words (frequently of Indian origin) are current in one country and not in others; many of them designate local objects. Only a few examples can be given. An illiterate farm hand is a *peón* in Mexico, but a *guaso* or *roto* in Chile, a *guajiro* in Cuba, a *jíbaro* in Puerto Rico. "Dairy" (Spain *lechería*) is *tambo* in Argentina. Chile uses *donde* ("where") in the sense of "at the house of", and goes so far as to combine, in the same meaning, *donde está, donde estaba* (literally "where was") into *ontá, ontaba*. Colombia has *desecho* for *senda* ("jungle trail"). Cuba uses *tabaco* ("tobacco") in the sense of "cigar" (Spain *cigarro*), and *cigarro* in the sense of "cigarette" (Spain *cigarrillo*). *Monte*, which in Spain has rather the meaning of "mountain", is used in Sp. Am. in the sense of "jungle", "wild country", while Chile uses *cerro* (Spain "hill") for mountain (Spain *montaña, monte*). *Papa* for *patata* ("potato"), *manteca* (which in Spain would mean "fat", "grease") for *mantequilla* ("butter") are in general use. *A la pampa*, "in the open"; *es muerto, es nacido*, instead of *ha muerto, ha nacido* ("he died", "he was born"); *achicar* ("to kill", slang for *matar*); *cada nada* ("every little trifle"); *hasta cada rato* ("in a little while", instead of Castilian *en un rato, dentro de un rato*); *pararse* (literally "to stop") used for *levantarse* ("to get up"); *truje* for *traje* ("I brought"; past tense of *traer*, "to bring"); *vido* for *vió* ("he saw"; third singular past tense of *ver*), are among forms frequently used in Spanish America. A few of them (*cigarro, monte, papa, manteca, truje, vido, es nacido, ontaba*) occasionally appear also in the speech of the illiterate in Spain.

VOCABULARY [29]

1. *World, Elements, Nature, Weather, Time, Directions.*

world, *el mundo*
earth, *la tierra*
air, *el aire*
water, *el agua* (fem.; *el* used for
    euphony before stressed *a*)
fire, *el fuego*
light, *la luz* (pl. *luces*)
sea, *el* (*la*) *mar* (masc. or fem.)
sun, *el sol*
moon, *la luna*
star, *la estrella*
sky, *el cielo*
wind, *el viento*
weather, time, *el tiempo*
snow, *la nieve*
to snow, *nevar* (*ie*)
rain, *la lluvia*
to rain, *llover* (*ue*)
cloud, *la nube*
cloudy, *nublado*
fog, *la niebla*
ice, *el hielo*
mud, *el barro, el fango, el lodo*
morning, *la mañana*
noon, *el mediodía*
afternoon, evening, *la tarde*
night, *la noche*
midnight, *la medianoche*
North, *el norte*
South, *el sur*
East, *el este*

West, *el oeste*
year, *el año*
month, *el mes*
week, *la semana*
day, *el día* (masc.)
hour, *la hora*
minute, *el minuto*
Sunday, *el domingo*
Monday, *el lunes* (pl. *los lunes*)
Tuesday, *el martes* (*los* -)
Wednesday, *el miércoles* (*los* -)
Thursday, *el jueves* (*los* -)
Friday, *el viernes* (*los* -)
Saturday, *el sábado*
January, *enero*
February, *febrero*
March, *marzo*
April, *abril*
May, *mayo*
June, *junio*
July, *julio*
August, *agosto*
September, *septiembre*
October, *octubre*
November, *noviembre*
December, *diciembre*
Spring, *la primavera*
Summer, *el verano*
Fall, *el otoño*
Winter, *el invierno*

29. Irregularities in the plural of nouns are indicated: *la luz* (pl. *luces*). Radical-changing verbs are indicated by (*ue*), (*ie*), (*i*), according to the nature of the change. Important verbal irregularities are given in parentheses.

Note that verbs ending in -*car* change *c* to *qu* before *e*-endings (*buscar*, Past 1st sg. *busqué*, Polite Imperative *busque*); verbs ending in -*gar* insert *u* after *g* before *e*-endings (*entregar*, Past *entregué*, Pol. Impv. *entregue*); verbs ending in -*zar* change *z* to *c* before *e*-endings (*empezar*, Past *empecé*, Pol. Impv. *empiece*).

For "it is warm", "it is cold", etc., see p. 266.
No capitals for seasons, months, days of week.
I shall see him *on* Monday, *le veré el lunes;* last Monday, *el lunes pasado;* next Monday, *el lunes que viene;* Monday morning, *el lunes por la mañana;* every Monday, *todos los lunes;* on May 5th, 1943, *el cinco de mayo de mil novecientos cuarenta y tres.*

2. *Family, Friendship, Love.*

family, *la familia*
husband, *el marido*
wife, *la mujer, la esposa*
parents, *los padres*
father, *el padre*
mother, *la madre*
son, *el hijo*
daughter, *la hija*
brother, *el hermano*
sister, *la hermana*
uncle, *el tío*
aunt, *la tía*
nephew, *el sobrino*
niece, *la sobrina*
cousin, *el primo, la prima*
grandfather, *el abuelo*
grandmother, *la abuela*
grandson, *el nieto*
granddaughter, *la nieta*
father-in-law, *el suegro*
mother-in-law, *la suegra*
son-in-law, *el yerno*
daughter-in-law, *la nuera*
brother-in-law, *el cuñado, el her-*
mano político
sister-in-law, *la cuñada*
man, *el hombre*
woman, *la mujer*
child, *el niño*
boy, *el muchacho*
girl, *la muchacha*
sir, Mr., *el señor*[30]
madam, Mrs., *la señora*[30]
Miss, young lady, *la señorita*[30]
friend, *el amigo, la amiga*
servant, *el criado, la criada*
to introduce, *presentar*
to visit, *visitar*
love, *el amor*
to love, *amar, querer* (*ie*) (Past, *quise;* Fut. *querré*) [31]
to fall in love with, *enamorarse de*
to marry, *casarse con* (he married her: *se casó con ella*)
sweetheart, *el novio, la novia*
kiss, *el beso*
to kiss, *besar*
dear, beloved, *querido; amado*

30. Use the definite article with *señor, señora, señorita,* save in speaking directly to the person: Mr. Lopez has a book, *el señor López tiene un libro;* Mr. Lopez, have you a book? *Señor López, ¿tiene Ud. un libro?*

31. Whenever there is an irregularity in the future, the same irregularity appears in the conditional: *querer,* Fut. *querré,* Cond. *querría.*

3. Speaking Activities.

word, *la palabra*
language, *la lengua; el idioma*
to speak, *hablar*
to say, *decir* (Pres., *digo, dices, dice, decimos, decís, dicen;* Past, *dij-e, -iste, -o, -imos, -isteis, -eron;* Fut., *diré;* Impv., *di, diga*)
to tell, *decir, contar* (*ue*)
to inform, *informar; comunicar* (see n. 29)
to call, *llamar*
to be called, one's name is, *llamarse* (my name is John, *me llamo Juan*)
to greet, *saludar*
to name, *nombrar*
to cry, shout, *gritar*
to listen to, *escuchar* (I listen *to* her, *la escucho*)

to hear, *oír* (Pres., *oigo, oyes, oye, oímos, oís, oyen;* Impv., *oye, oiga*)
to understand, *comprender, entender* (*ie*)
to mean, *querer decir* (see p. 257 for *querer;* I don't know what you mean, *no sé lo que Vd. quiere decir*), *significar* (see note 29; do not use when the subject is a person)
to ask for, *pedir* (*i*), (He asked me for a pencil, *me pidió un lápiz*)
to ask (a question), *preguntar*
to answer, *responder, contestar*
to thank, *dar las gracias* (I thanked him for the book, *le di las gracias por el libro*)
to complain, *lamentarse, quejarse*

4. Materials.

gold, *el oro*
silver, *la plata*
iron, *el hierro*
steel, *el acero*
copper, *el cobre*
tin, *el estaño*
lead, *el plomo*
oil, *el aceite, el petróleo*
gasoline, *la gasolina, la bencina, la nafta*

coal, *el carbón*
wood, *la madera, la leña*
silk, *la seda*
cotton, *el algodón*
wool, *la lana*
cloth, *el paño*
to cut, *cortar*
to dig, *cavar*
to sew, *coser*
to mend, *remendar*

5. Animals.

animal, *el animal*
horse, *el caballo*
dog, *el perro*
cat, *el gato*
bird, *el pájaro*
donkey, *el burro, el asno*
mule, *el mulo*

cow, *la vaca*
ox, *el buey*
pig, *el cerdo, el puerco, el cochino*
chicken, *el pollo*
hen, *la gallina*
rooster, *el gallo*
sheep, *la oveja*

goat, *la cabra*
mouse, *el ratón*
snake, *la culebra*
fly, *la mosca*
bee, *la abeja*

mosquito, *el mosquito*
spider, *la araña*
louse, *el piojo*
flea, *la pulga*
bedbug, *la chinche*

6. Money, Buying and Selling.

money, *el dinero*
coin, *la moneda*
dollar, *el dólar, el peso, el duro*
  (Spain, 5 *pesetas* make 1 *duro*)
cent, *el centavo, el céntimo*
bank, *el banco*
check, *el cheque*
money order, *el giro postal*
to earn, to gain, to win, *ganar*
to lose, *perder (ie)*
to spend, *gastar*
to lend, *prestar*
to borrow, *pedir (i) prestado* (he
  borrowed $2 from me, *me pi-
  dió dos dólares prestados*)
to owe, *deber*
to pay, *pagar* (see n. 29)
to give back, *devolver (ue)* ; P. p.
  devuelto
change, *la vuelta*
to change, exchange, *cambiar*
honest, *honrado, sincero*
dishonest, *poco honrado, falso*
price, *el precio*
cost, *el coste, el costo*
to cost, *costar, (ue)*

expensive, *caro, costoso*
cheap, *barato*
store, *la tienda*
piece, *el pedazo, el trozo*
slice, *la tajada, la rebanada*
pound, *la libra*
package, *el paquete, el bulto*
basket, *la canasta, la cesta*
box, *la caja*
bag, *el saco*
goods, *las mercancías*
to go shopping, *ir de compras, ir
  de tiendas*
to sell, *vender*
to buy, *comprar*
to rent, to hire, *alquilar, arrendar*
to be worth, *valer* (Pres. *valgo,
  vales*, etc.; Fut. *valdré*)
to choose, *escoger* (Pres. *escojo,
  escoges*, etc.; Pol. Impv. *esco-
  ja*)
thief, robber, *el ladrón*
to steal, *robar*
police, *la policía*
policeman, *el agente de policía,
  el policía, el guardia*

7. Eating and Drinking.

to eat, *comer*
breakfast, *el desayuno*
to eat breakfast, *desayunarse*
lunch, *el almuerzo*
to eat lunch, *almorzar* (*ue* and
  see n. 29)
supper, *la cena*
to eat supper, *cenar*

dinner, *la comida*
to dine, *comer*
meal, *la comida*
dining-room, *el comedor*
waiter, *el mozo, el camarero*
waitress, *la camarera*
restaurant, *la fonda*
menu, *la lista de platos*

bill, *la cuenta*
to pass (a dish), *alcanzar* (note 29)
tip, *la propina*
to drink, *beber*
water, *el agua* (fem.)
wine, *el vino*
beer, *la cerveza*
coffee, *el café*
tea, *el té*
milk, *la leche*
bottle, *la botella*
spoon, *la cuchara*
teaspoon, *la cucharita, la cucharilla*
knife, *el cuchillo*
fork, *el tenedor*
glass, *el vaso*
cup, *la taza*
napkin, *la servilleta*
salt, *la sal*
pepper, *la pimienta*
plate, dish, *el plato*
bread, *el pan*
roll, *el panecillo*
butter, *la mantequilla*
sugar, *el azúcar*
soup, *la sopa*
rice, *el arroz*
potatoes, *las patatas, las papas*
vegetable, *la legumbre*
meat, *la carne*
beef, *la carne de vaca*
steak, *el bistec*

chicken, *el pollo*
chop, *la chuleta*
veal, *la ternera*
lamb, *el carnero*
pork, *el cerdo, el puerco*
sausage, *el chorizo, la salchicha*
ham, *el jamón*
bacon, *el tocino, la tocineta*
egg, *el huevo*
fish, *el pescado*
fried, *frito*
to cook, *cocinar, guisar*
boiled, *cocido*
stewed, *guisado*
roast, *asado*
roast beef, *el rosbif*
baked, *al horno*
broiled, *en parrilla, a la parrilla*
sauce, *la salsa*
salad, *la ensalada*
cheese, *el queso*
fruit, *la fruta*
apple, *la manzana*
pear, *la pera*
peach, *el durazno, el melocotón*
grapes, *las uvas*
strawberries, *las fresas*
nuts, *las nueces*
orange, *la naranja*
lemon, *el limón*
juice, *el jugo, el zumo*
cherries, *las cerezas*
dessert, *el postre*
pastry, *las pastas, los pasteles*

8. *Hygiene and Attire.*

bath, *el baño*
to bathe, *bañarse*
shower, *la ducha*
to wash, *lavarse*
to shave, *afeitarse*
barber, *el barbero*
mirror, *el espejo*

soap, *el jabón*
razor, *la navaja (de afeitar)*
safety razor, *la máquina de afeitar*
towel, *la toalla*
comb, *el peine, la peineta*
brush, *el cepillo*
scissors, *las tijeras*

to wear, *llevar*
to take off, *quitarse*[32]
to change, *mudarse, cambiarse*
to put on, *ponerse*[32] (Pres. *me pongo, te pones,* etc.; Fut. *me pondré;* Past *me puse;* Impv. *ponte, póngase*).
clothes, *la ropa*
hat, *el sombrero*
suit, *el traje*
coat, *la chaqueta*
vest, *el chaleco*
pants, *los pantalones*
underwear, *la ropa interior*
undershirt, *la camiseta*
drawers, *los canzoncillos*
glove, *el guante*
socks, *los calcetines*
stockings, *las medias*
shirt, *la camisa*
collar, *el cuello*

tie, *la corbata*
overcoat, *el sobretodo, el abrigo, el gabán*
raincoat, *el impermeable*
pocket, *el bolsillo*
handkerchief, *el pañuelo*
button, *el botón*
shoe, *el zapato*
boot, *la bota*
pocketbook, *el portamonedas*
purse, *la bolsa, la cartera*
pin, tie-pin, *el alfiler*
needle, *la aguja* (*de coser*)
umbrella, *el paraguas* (pl. *los ·*)
watch, clock, *el reloj*
chain, *la cadena*
ring, *la sortija*
eyeglasses, *los anteojos*
slippers, *las zapatillas*
dressing-gown, bathrobe, *la bata* (*de baño*)

9. *Parts of the body.*

head, *la cabeza*
forehead, *la frente*
face, *la cara*
mouth, *la boca*
hair, *el pelo*
eye, *el ojo*
ear, *la oreja*
tooth, *el diente, la muela*
lip, *el labio*
nose, *la nariz* (pl. *narices*)
tongue, *la lengua*
chin, *la barba*
cheek, *la mejilla, el carrillo*
mustache, *el bigote*
beard, *las barbas*
neck, *el cuello*
throat, *la garganta*
arm, *el brazo*

hand, *la mano*
elbow, *el codo*
wrist, *la muñeca*
finger, *el dedo*
nail, *la uña*
leg, *la pierna*
foot, *el pie*
knee, *la rodilla*
back, *la espalda*
chest, *el pecho*
ankle, *el tobillo*
body, *el cuerpo*
bone, *el hueso*
skin, *la piel*
heart, *el corazón*
stomach, *el estómago*
blood, *la sangre*
shoulder, *la espalda, el hombro*

32.   Note: he put on (took off) *his* hat, *se puso* (*se quitó*) *el sombrero.*

10. *Medical.*

doctor, *el médico, el doctor*
drug-store, *la botica, la droguería,
la farmacia*
hospital, *el hospital*
medicine, *la medicina, el medica-
mento*
pill, *la píldora*
prescription, *la receta*
bandage, *la venda, el vendaje*
nurse, *la enfermera, el enfermero*
ill, *enfermo*
illness, *la enfermedad, el mal*

fever, *la fiebre*
swollen, *hinchado*
wound, *la herida*
wounded, *herido*
head-ache, *el dolor de cabeza*
tooth-ache, *el dolor de muelas*
cough, *la tos*
to cough, *toser*
lame, *cojo*
burn, *la quemadura*
pain, *el dolor*
poison, *el veneno*

11. *Military.*

war, *la guerra*
peace, *la paz*
ally, *el aliado*
enemy, *el enemigo*
army, *el ejército*
danger, *el peligro*
dangerous, *peligroso*
to win, *vencer* (Pres. *venzo, ven-
ces,* etc.; Pol. Impv. *venza*)
to surround, *rodear*
to arrest, *arrestar, detener* (see
tener, p. 258)
to kill, *matar*
to escape, *escaparse (de), evadir-
se*
to run away, *escapar, huir* (Pres.,
*huyo, huyes, huye, huimos,
huis, huyen*).
to lead, *guiar, ir a la cabeza de,
conducir* (see p. 255)
to follow, *seguir (i),* Pres. 1st sg.
sigo, Pol. Impv. *siga*
to surrender, *rendirse (i)*
to retreat, *retirarse, retroceder*
to bomb, shell, *bombardear*
fear, *el miedo*
prison, *la prisión, la cárcel*

prisoner, *el prisionero*
to take prisoner, *hacer prisionero*
to capture, *capturar, apresar*
help, *la ayuda, el socorro*
comrade, buddy, *el compañero*
battle, *la batalla, el combate, la
lucha*
to fight, *combatir, pelear, luchar
con*
soldier, *el soldado*
private, *el soldado (raso)*
corporal, *el cabo*
sergeant, *el sargento*
lieutenant, *el teniente*
captain, *el capitán*
major, *el comandante*
colonel, *el coronel*
general, *el general*
officer, *el oficial*
company, *la compañía*
battalion, *el batallón*
regiment, *el regimiento*
brigade, *la brigada*
division, *la división*
troops, *las tropas*
reenforcements, *los refuerzos*
fortress, *la fortaleza*

sentinel, *el centinela;* (to do sentry duty, *estar de centinela*)

to be on duty, *estar de guardia*

guard, *el guardia*

sign-post, *el letrero*

navy, *la marina* (**de guerra**), *la armada*

sailor, *el marinero*

marine, *el soldado* **de** *marina*

warship, *el buque* (*el barco*) *de guerra*

cruiser, *el crucero*

destroyer, *el cazatorpedero, el destructor*

convoy, *el convoy*

escort, *la escolta, el convoy*

weapon, *el arma* (fem.)

rifle, *el rifle, el fusil*

machine-gun, *la ametralladora*

cannon, *el cañón*

ammunition, *las municiones*

supplies, *las provisiones, los pertrechos*

cartridge, *el cartucho*

bullet, *la bala, el proyectil*

belt, *el cinturón* (**cartridge-belt**, *la canana*)

knapsack, *la mochila*

tent, *la tienda*

camp, *el campo, el campamento*

map, *el mapa, el plano topográfico*

rope, *la cuerda*

flag, *la bandera*

helmet, *el casco*

bayonet, *la bayoneta*

uniform, *el uniforme*

airplane, *el avión, el aeroplano*

bombing plane, *el avión de bombardeo*

pursuit plane, *el avión de caza*

shell, *la granada, la bomba*

bomb, *la bomba*

truck, *el camión, el autocamión, la camioneta*

tank, *el tanque, el camión blindado*

to load, *cargar* (note 29)

to fire, to shoot, *tirar*

to shoot (military execution), *fusilar*

spy, *el espía*

fire!, *¡fuego!*

attention!, *¡atención!, ¡firmes!*

forward!, *¡adelante!*

halt!, *¡alto!, ¡alto ahí!*

air-raid shelter, *el refugio antiaéreo*

12. *Travel.*

passport, *el pasaporte*

customs, *la aduana*

ship, *el buque, el vapor*

steamer, *el vapor*

stateroom, *el camarote*

berth, *la litera*

to travel, *viajar*

trip, voyage, *el viaje*

to leave, depart, *partir, salir* (Pres. *salgo, sales,* etc.; Fut. *saldré,* Impv. *sal, salga*)

to arrive, *llegar* (note 29)

to ride, (a conveyance), *ir montado en, ir en*

railroad, *el ferrocarril*

station, *la estación*

track, *el carril, los rieles*

train, *el tren*

platform, *el andén*

ticket, *el billete*

compartment, *el compartimiento, el departamento*

all aboard, *¡viajeros al tren!*

dining-car, *el coche comedor*

sleeper, *el vagón cama*
car, coach, *el coche*
trunk, *el baúl*
valise, *la maleta*
baggage, *el equipaje*
porter, *el mozo (de equipajes)*
bus, *el autobús, el ómnibus*
street-car, *el tranvía*

automobile, *el automóvil*
taxi, *el taxí (el taxímetro)*
driver, *el chófer, el conductor*
to drive (car), *manejar, guiar, conducir* (Pres. 1st sg. *conduz-co*, Past *conduje*, Pol. Impv. *conduzca*)

13. *Reading and Writing.*

to read, *leer*
newspaper, *el periódico*
magazine, *la revista*
book, *el libro*
to write, *escribir* (P. p. *escrito*)
to translate, *traducir* (for all verbs in -*ducir*, see *conducir*, above)
pencil, *el lápiz* (pl. *lápices*)
chalk, *la tiza*
blackboard, *la pizarra, el tablero*
ink, *la tinta*

pen, *la pluma* (fountain-pen, *plumafuente, pluma estilográfica*
envelope, *el sobre*
paper, *el papel*
letter, *la carta*
post-office, *el correo*
stamp, *el sello*
letter-box, *el buzón*
to mail, *echar al correo*
address, *la dirección*
post-card, *la tarjeta* (*postal*)

14. *Amusements.*

to smoke, *fumar*
cigar, *el cigarro*
cigarette, *el pitillo, el cigarrillo*
tobacco, *el tabaco*
match, *el fósforo, la cerilla*
give me a light, *déme Ud. lumbre*
theatre, *el teatro*
movies, *el cine*
dance, *el baile*
to dance, *bailar*
to have a good time, *divertirse* (*ie*), *pasar un buen rato*
ticket, *el billete*
pleasure, *el placer, el gusto*
to play (music), *tocar* (note 29)

to sing, *cantar*
song, *la canción*
to play (a game), *jugar* (*ue*, **and** see note 29)
game, *el juego, la partida*
ball, *la pelota*
to take a walk, *pasearse, dar un paseo*
beach, *la playa*
to swim, *nadar*
sand, *la arena*
refreshment, *el refresco*
saloon, *la cantina, el bar, la taberna*
picnic, *la escursión, la partida de campo*

15. *Town and Country.*

place, spot, *el lugar, el sitio*
city, *la ciudad*
street, *la calle*

sidewalk, *la acera*
road, *la carretera, el camino*
intersection, *la bocacalle*

harbor, *el puerto*
block, *la manzana, la cuadra*
school, *la escuela*
church, *la iglesia*
cathedral, *la catedral*
building, *el edificio*
corner, *la esquina*
hotel, *el hotel*
office, *la oficina, el despacho*
river, *el río*
bridge, *el puente*
country, *el campo*

village, *el pueblo*
mountain, *la montaña*
grass, *la hierba*
yard, *el patio, el corral*
hill, *la colina*
lake, *el lago*
forest, *el bosque*
field, *el campo*
flower, *la flor*
tree, *el árbol*
rock, stone, *la piedra*
jungle, *la selva*

16. House.

door, *la puerta*
roof, *el tejado, el techo, la azotea*
to open, *abrir* (P. p. *abierto*)
to close, *cerrar* (*ie*)
key, *la llave*
to go in, *entrar en* (he **entered the**
   room, *entró en el cuarto*)
to go out, *salir de* (**Pres.,** *salgo,*
   sales, etc.; Fut. *saldré*; Impv.
   sal, salga)
house, *la casa* (at home, *en casa,*
   to go home, *ir a casa*)
cottage, *la casita* (*de campo*)
hut, *la choza, la cabaña*
to live in, *vivir en, habitar en*
staircase, *la escalera*
to go up, *subir*
to go down, *bajar*
room, *el cuarto, la habitación*
toilet, *el retrete*
kitchen, *la cocina*
table, *la mesa*

chair, *la silla*
to sit down, *sentarse,* (*ie*)
to stand, be standing, *estar de pie*
wall, *la pared*
lamp, *la lámpara*
candle, *la bujía, la vela*
closet, *el armario, la alacena*
window, *la ventana*
bed, *la cama*
bedroom, *la alcoba*
blanket, *el cobertor*
sheet, *la sábana*
mattress, *el colchón*
alarm-clock, *el despertador*
pillow, *la almohada*
to rest, *descansar*
to go to bed, *acostarse* (*ue*)
to go to sleep, fall asleep, *dormir-*
   se (*ue*)
to sleep, *dormir* (*ue*)
to wake up, *despertarse* (*ie*)
to dress, *vestirse* (*i*)
to get up, *levantarse*

17. Miscellaneous Nouns.

people, *la gente* (with **sg.** verb)
thing, *la cosa*
name, *el nombre*
luck, *la suerte* (bad luck, *la mala*
   suerte)

number, *el número*
life, *la vida*
death, *la muerte*
work, *el trabajo*

18. *Verbs — Coming and Going.*

to come, *venir* (Pres. *vengo, vienes, viene, venimos, venís, vienen;* Past. *vine;* Fut. *vendré;* Impv. *ven, venga*)

to go, *ir* (Pres. *voy, vas, va, vamos, vais, van;* Impf. *iba;* Past *fui, fuiste, fué, fuimos, fuisteis, fueron;* Fut. *iré;* Impv. *ve, vaya*) ;

(*ir a*, to be going to: I am going to eat, *voy a comer*)

to go away, *irse, marcharse*

to stay, remain, *quedarse, permanecer* (Pres. *permanezco,* Pol. Impv. *permanezca*)

to return, *volver* (*ue*) ; P. p. *vuelto* (*volver a*, to do again; he writes again, *vuelve a escribir*)

to run, *correr*

to walk, *andar, caminar, marchar, ir a pie*

to fall, *caer* (Pres. *caigo, caes,* etc.)

to follow, *seguir* (*i*) ; Pres. 1st sg. *sigo,* Pol. Impv. *siga*

19. *Verbs — Looking and Seeing.*

to see, *ver* (Pres. *veo, ves,* etc.; Impf. *veía;* P. p. *visto*)

to look at, *mirar* (I am looking at it, *lo miro*)

to look for, *buscar* (see note 29; I am looking for it, *lo busco*)

to laugh, *reír* (Pres. *río, ríes, ríe, reímos, reís, ríen:* Past 3rd sg. *rió,* 3d pl. *rieron;* Impv. *ríe, ría*)

to laugh at, make fun of, *reírse de, burlarse de*

to smile, *sonreír*

to look, seem, *parecer* (Pres. *parezco, pareces,* etc.; it seems to me, *me parece*)

to recognize, *reconocer* (Pres. *reconozco, reconoces,* etc.)

to take for, *tomar por*

20. *Verbs — Mental.*

to make a mistake, *equivocarse,* (note 29)

to hope, *esperar*

to wait (for), *esperar, aguardar* (I am waiting for her, *la espero*)

to think, *pensar* (*ie*), -of, *pensar en* (I am thinking of him, *pienso en él*)

to believe, *creer*

to like, (lit. to please), *gustar* (I like this book, *este libro me gusta,* lit. this book pleases me)

to wish, *desear, querer* (*ie*)

to want, *querer* (*ie*) ; Fut. *querré,* Past *quise*

to know (a person), *conocer* (Pres. *conozco, conoces,* etc.; use *conocía* for "I knew", *conocí* for "I met" (socially)

to know (a fact), *saber* (Pres. *sé, sabes,* etc.; Past. *supe;* Fut. *sabré;* use *sabía* for "I knew", *supe* for "I found out"; I know how to write, *sé escribir*)

to understand, *comprender, entender* (*ie*)

to remember, *recordar* (*ue*),

acordarse de (ue)
to forget, olvidar
to permit, allow, permitir
to forbid, prohibir, impedir (i)
to promise, prometer
to learn, aprender
to feel like, tener ganas de (I feel like sleeping, tengo ganas de dormir) (Pres. of tener: tengo,

tienes, tiene, tenemos, tenéis, tienen; Past. tuve; Fut. tendré; Impv. ten, tenga)
to fear, be afraid, temer, tener miedo (he's afraid of his uncle, le tiene miedo a su tío)
to be right, tener razón
to be wrong, estar equivocado, no tener razón

21. Verbs — Miscellaneous

to live, vivir
to die, morir (ue) (P. p. muerto)
to work, trabajar
to give, dar (Pres., doy, das, etc.; Past dí)
to take, tomar
to show, mostrar (ue), indicar (note 29)
to begin, to start, empezar (ie), comenzar (ie) (note 29), ponerse a
to finish, acabar (acabar de, to have just: I have just written, acabo de escribir)
to continue, continuar, seguir (i) (he kept on reading, siguió leyendo)
to help, ayudar
to hide, esconderse, ocultarse
to lose, perder (ie)
to find, hallar, encontrar (ue); encontrar also means to meet, casually, as in the street
to leave, salir, partir (use dejar for leaving objects or people)
to try, tratar de
to meet, encontrar (ue), encontrarse con; (use conocer for the social sense: la conocí ayer, I met her yesterday)
to put, place, meter, poner (Pres. pongo, pones, etc.; Past puse;

Fut. pondré; Impv. pon, ponga; P. p. puesto)
to do, to make, hacer (Pres. hago, haces, etc.; Past hice; Fut. haré; Impv. haz, haga; P. p. hecho)
to have done, mandar hacer (I have the letter written, mando escribir la carta)
can, to be able, poder (ue); (Past pude; Fut. podré)
to carry, llevar, transportar
to stop, parar (pararse or detenerse for self; use dejar de, or cesar de for "to stop doing")
to bring, traer (Pres. 1st sg. traigo; Past traje, Pol. Impv. traiga)
to cover, cubrir (P. p. cubierto)
to get, obtain, conseguir (i), obtener (like tener, below)
to hold, tener (Pres. tengo, tienes, tiene, tenemos, tenéis, tienen; Past tuve; Fut. tendré; Impv. ten, tenga)
to get, become, ponerse (he became pale, se puso pálido)
to break, quebrar, romper (P. p. roto)
to hurry, apresurarse, darse prisa
to deliver, entregar (note 29)
to send, mandar, enviar, (Pres.

envío, envías, envía, enviamos,
enviáis, envían; Impv. envía,
envíe)

to belong, pertenecer (like cono·

cer)

to accept, aceptar

to refuse, recusar, rehusar

22. Adjectives.

small, pequeño, chiquito, chico
large, great, grande (gran before
  a sg. noun, masc. or fem.)
big (bulky), grueso
tall, high, alto
short, corto, breve
low, short (stature), bajo
heavy, pesado, grueso
light, (weight) ligero
long, largo
wide, ancho
narrow, estrecho
clean, limpio
dirty, sucio
cool, fresco
cold, frío
warm, hot, caliente
damp, húmedo
wet, mojado
empty, vacío
dry, seco
full, lleno
soft, blando, muelle
hard, duro
quick, rápido, veloz (pl. veloces)
slow, lento
ordinary, ordinario, común
comfortable, cómodo
uncomfortable, incómodo, desagradable
near, cercano
distant, lejano, distante
right, derecho
left, izquierdo
poor, pobre
rich, rico
beautiful, hermoso, bello

pretty, lindo, bonito
ugly, feo
sweet, dulce
bitter, amargo
sour, agrio, acre
salt, salado, salobre
young, joven
dark, obscuro
light, bright, clear, claro
fat, gordo
thick, espeso, grueso
thin, delgado
round, redondo
square, cuadrado
flat, plano
deep, hondo
strong, fuerte
weak, débil
tired, cansado
alone, solo
same, mismo
easy, fácil
hard, difficult, difícil
happy, contento, feliz (pl. felices)
merry, alegre
sad, triste
free, libre
crazy, loco
silly, tonto, bobo, necio, estúpido
drunk, borracho
polite, cortés
rude, descortés, mal educado
pleasant, agradable, amable
unpleasant, desagradable
lonesome, solitario, triste
true, verdadero, cierto, exacto
false, falso, postizo

foreign, *extranjero, ajeno*
old, *viejo*
new, *nuevo*
good, *bueno* (*buen* **before a masc.**
sg. noun)
better, *mejor* (best, *el -*)
bad, *malo* (*mal* before masc. sg.
noun)
worse, *peor* (worst, *el -*)
fine, *óptimo, muy bueno* (for
health use *muy bien*)
first, *primero*
last, *último*
friendly, *amigable, amistoso, amigo*
hostile, *hostil, enemigo*
lucky, *afortunado, dichoso*

unlucky, *desdichado, desgraciado*
charming, *encantador* (fem. *en-
cantadora*)
afraid, *temeroso, tímido*
ready, *listo, preparado*
hungry, *hambriento,* (to be- *tener
hambre*)
thirsty, *sediento* (to be- *tener sed*)
funny, *cómico, curioso, gracioso*
possible, *posible*
impossible, *imposible*
brave, *valiente*
cowardly, *cobarde*
quiet, *tranquilo*
noisy, *ruidoso, estrepitoso*
living, *vivo*
dead, *muerto*

23. Colors.

white, *blanco*
black, *negro*
red, *rojo*
green, *verde*
blue, *azul*

yellow, *amarillo*
gray, *gris*
brown, *pardo, castaño*
rose, *rosa, color de rosa*
purple, *morado*

24. Nationalities.

Use no capital for the adjective or for the language.
Names of languages are used *with* the article unless
they *immediately* follow the verb *hablar* or the preposition *en*:
he speaks English, *habla inglés;* he speaks English well, *habla
bien el inglés;* English is difficult, *el inglés es difícil;* he
answered me in English, *me contestó en inglés.* (Adjectives of
nationality ending in consonant add *-a* to form feminine:
inglés, fem. *inglesa,* masc. pl. *ingleses,* fem. pl. *inglesas*)

American, *americano, norteameri-
cano, sudamericano*
English, *inglés*
French, *francés*
German, *alemán*
Spanish, *español*
Russian, *ruso*

Italian, *italiano*
Japanese, *japonés*
Chinese, *chino*
Dutch, *holandés*
Norwegian, *noruego*
Swedish, *sueco*
Finnish, *finlandés*

Belgian, *belga*
Polish, *polaco*
Danish, *danés*
Swiss, *suizo*
Portuguese, *portugués*
Yugoslav, *yugoeslavo*
Bulgarian, *búlgaro*
Czech, *checo*
Greek, *griego*
Turkish, *turco*
Roumanian, *rumano*
Hungarian, *húngaro*
Austrian, *austriaco*
Malay, *malayo*
Persian, *persa*
Arabian, Arabic, Arab, *árabe*
Jewish, Hebrew, *judío, hebreo*
Australian, *australiano*
Canadian, *canadiense*
Mexican, *mejicano* (*mexicano*)

Brazilian, *brasileño*
Argentinian, *argentino*
Chilean, *chileno*
Peruvian, *peruano*
Cuban, *cubano*
Puerto Rican, *puertorriqueño*
Colombian, *colombiano*
Venezuelan, *venezolano*
Bolivian, *boliviano*
Uruguayan, *uruguayo*
Paraguayan, *paraguayo*
Ecuadorian, *ecuatoriano*
Costa Rican, *costarriqueño,
costarricense*
Honduran, *hondureño*
Salvadorean, *salvadoreño*
Guatemalan, *guatemalteco*
Dominican (of Santo Domingo).
dominicano
Panamanian, *panameño*
Nicaraguan, *nicaragüense*

25. *Adverbs and Adverbial Expressions.*

today, *hoy*
yesterday, *ayer*
tomorrow, *mañana*
day before yesterday, *antes de
ayer*
day after tomorrow, *pasado mañana*
tonight, *esta noche*
last night, *anoche*
this morning, *esta mañana*
in the morning, *por la mañana*
in the afternoon, *por la tarde*
in the evening, in the night, *por
la noche*
tomorrow morning, *mañana por
la mañana*
tomorrow afternoon, *mañana por
la tarde*
tomorrow evening, *mañana por
la noche*
early, *temprano, pronto*

on time, *a tiempo*
late, *tarde*
already, *ya*
no longer, *ya no* (he is no longer
here, *ya no está aquí*)
yet, still, *todavía*
not yet, *todavía no*
now, *ahora*
afterwards, then, *después, enton-
ces*
never, *nunca, jamás* (use *no* before verb: he never comes, *no
viene nunca*)
always, *siempre*
forever, *para siempre*
soon, *pronto*
often, *a menudo*
seldom, *rara vez, raramente*
usually, *comúnmente, general-
mente*
fast, *de prisa*

slowly, *despacio*

here, *aquí*

there, *allí, allá, ahí*

over there, *allá, por allí, allá abajo*

near by, *cerca* (near here, *aquí cerca, cerca de aquí*)

far away, *a lo lejos, lejos*

up, *arriba*

down, *abajo*

ahead, in front, *por delante*

behind, in back, *por detrás*

forward, *adelante*

back, *para atrás* (go back, *¡vuelva Ud. para atrás!*)

outside, *fuera, afuera*

inside, *dentro*

opposite, *en frente*

here and there, *aquí y allá*

everywhere, *en todas partes, por todas partes*

where?, *¿dónde?, ¿a dónde?* (use "*¿a dónde?*" if there is motion)

where, *donde, adonde,* (use *adonde* for motion)

also, *también*

yes, *sí*

no, not, *no*

very, *muy*

much, *mucho* (very much, *muchísimo*)

well, *bien*

badly, *mal*

better, *mejor*

worse, *peor*

more, *más* (more than, *más que;* but use *más de* before numerals)

less, *menos*

as - as, *tan—como*

as much - as, *tanto—como*

as many—as, *tantos—como*

how much?, *¿cuánto?*

how many?, *¿cuántos?*

how?, *¿cómo?*

too much, *demasiado*

too many, *demasiados*

so much, *tanto*

so many, *tantos*

as, like, *como*

so, *así*

besides, furthermore, *además*

finally, *finalmente, en fin, por fin*

only, *solamente, sólo*

almost, *casi*

gladly, *de buena gana*

certainly, *seguramente, sin duda*

at once, *en seguida*

at all, *no por cierto, de ninguna manera*

unfortunately, *por desgracia, desgraciadamente*

hardly, *apenas*

aloud, *en voz alta, alto*

suddenly, *de repente, de pronto*

about, *de, alrededor de*

perhaps, maybe, *tal vez, quizá, acaso* (subjunctive; perhaps he will write, *tal vez escriba*)

a little, *un poco*

again, *otra vez, de nuevo*

really, truly, *de veras, verdaderamente*

together, *juntamente, juntos* (they left together, *salieron juntos*)

at least, *por lo menos, al menos*

for lack of, *por falta de*

a long time ago, *hace mucho tiempo*

repeatedly, again and again, *repetidas veces*

therefore, *por eso, por lo tanto*

further away, *mas allá*

of course, *por supuesto, claro, natural(mente)*

occasionally, *de vez en cuando*

26. Conjunctions.

and, *y*

but, *pero*

if, *si*

or, *o*

why?, *¿por qué?*

because, *porque*

why!, *¡cómo!*, *¡qué!*, *pues*

before, *antes que*[33]

when, *cuando*[33]

than, *que* (before number use *de*)

where, *donde, adonde*

until, till, *hasta que*[33]

although, *aunque*[33]

unless, *a menos que*[33], *a no ser que*[33]

while, *mientras (que)*[33]

that, *que*

for, since, *pues*

after, *después de que*[33]

as soon as, *luego que*[33]

as long as, *mientras (que)*[33]

provided that, *con tal que*[33]

in order that, *para que*[33]

so that, *de manera que*[33]

without, *sin que*[33]

27. Indefinite Pronouns and Adjectives.

everything, *todo*

everyone, *todos*

all, *todo*

each, every, *cada uno, todos*

something, *algo, alguna cosa*

some, *algunos, unos*

little (not much), *poco*

few, *pocos*

a few, *unos cuantos*

enough, *bastante, suficiente*

enough!, *¡basta!, ¡no más!*

such a, *tal*

all kinds of, *toda clase de*

someone, *alguien*

nothing, *nada*[34]

no one, *nadie*[34]

no..(adj), *ninguno*[34] (*ningún* before masc. sg. noun)

neither - nor, *ni - ni*[34]

(an)other, *otro*

much, (lots of), *mucho, muchos*

many, *muchos*

several, *varios, diversos*

both, *ambos, los dos* (fem. *las dos*)

28. Prepositions.

of, from, *de* (with masc. sg. article *el* contracts to *del*)

to, at, *a* (with masc. sg. article contracts to *al*; *must* be used with a noun indirect object: I

give John the book, *doy el libro a Juan;* also with a noun direct object if it is a person: I see John, *veo a Juan;* but not with *tener:* I have two brothers,

33. The subjunctive is used after these conjunctions *if* they express purpose, condition, supposition, concession or indefinite future time.

34. If these expressions appear *after* the verb, *no* is required before the verb: no one came, *no vino nadie* or *nadie vino.*

tengo dos hermanos)
with, *con*, (with me, *conmigo*;
  with you, *contigo*)
in, on, at, *en*
over, above, *sobre*
for, *por*, *para* (use *para* to indicate purpose or destination.
  por for exchange: I paid $2 for
  this book; it's for you, *pagué
  dos pesos por este libro; es
  para Ud.*)
by, *por*
without, *sin*
until, up to, *hasta*
since, *desde*
toward, *hacia*
between, among, *entre*
near, *cerca de*

far from, *lejos de*
before, *antes de*
after, *después de*
in front of, opposite, *delante de,
  frente a*
in back of, behind, *detrás de*
under (neath), *bajo*
through, across, *por, a través de*
against, *contra*
by means of, *por medio de*
in spite of, *a pesar de, no obstante*
about, around, *alrededor de*
because of, on account of, *por,
  a* (or *por*) *causa de*
during, *durante*
instead of, *en lugar de, en vez de*
beside, *al lado de, junto a*
on the other side of, *del otro lado
  de*

29. Special Expressions and Idioms.

good morning, good day, *buenos días*
good afternoon, good evening, *buenas tardes*
good night, *buenas noches*
good-by, *adiós, hasta la vista*
see you later, *hasta luego*
see you tomorrow, *hasta mañana*
just now, *ahora mismo* (just a moment ago, *hace poco*)
hello!, *¡hola!* (on the telephone, *¿qué hay?, ¡diga!, ¡al aparato!*)
how are you?, *¿cómo está Ud.?*
how goes it?, *¿qué tal?*
I'm well, *estoy bien*
I'm (much) better, *estoy (mucho) mejor*
what time is it?, *¿qué hora es?*
it's six o'clock, *son las seis*
at six o'clock, *a las seis*
at about six, *a eso de las seis*
at half past six, *a las seis y media*
at a quarter past (to) six, *a las seis y (menos) cuarto*
at ten minutes past (to) six, *a las seis y (menos) diez*
last year, *el año pasado*
next year, *el año que viene, el año próximo*
every day, *todos los días*

each day, *cada día*
the whole day, *todo el día*
please, will you?, *hágame Ud. el favor (de)*, *sírvase*, *tenga la bondad (de)*
tell me, *dígame* (please tell me, *hágame Ud. el favor de decirme*)
will you give me?, *¿quiere Ud. darme?*
bring (to) me, *tráigame*
show (to) me, *muéstreme*, *indíqueme*
thank you, *gracias*
don't mention it, *no hay de que*, *de nada*
pardon me, *dispense Ud.*, *perdone Ud.*
it doesn't matter, never mind, *no importa*
I'm sorry, *lo siento*
I can't help, *no puedo menos de* (I can't help saying, *no puedo menos de decir*)
it's nothing, *no es nada*
what a pity!, it's too bad!, *¡qué lástima!*, *¡es lástima!*
I'm glad, *me alegro*, *tengo mucho gusto* (to, *en* plus infinitive)
I have to, *tengo que*
I agree (all right, O. K.), *(estoy) de acuerdo*, *estoy conforme*
where are you going?, *¿a dónde va?*
here is (are), *aquí tiene Ud.*
there is, there are, *hay* (use *ahí está*, *ahí están*, if pointing out)
which way?, *¿por dónde?*
where is?, *¿dónde está?*
this way, (direction), *por aquí* (that way, *por allá*)
this way (in this fashion), *de este modo*, *de esta manera*
to the right, *a la derecha*
to the left, *a la izquierda*
straight ahead, *adelante*
come with me, *venga conmigo*
what can I do for you?, *¿en qué puedo servirle?*
what is happening?, *¿qué pasa?*, *¿qué ocurre?*, *¿qué sucede?*
what is it?, what is the matter?, *¿qué hay?*, *¿qué pasa?*
what is the matter with you?, *¿qué tiene Ud.?*, *¿qué le pasa a Ud.?*
what do you want?, *¿qué desea Ud.?*
how much is it?, *¿cuánto?*, *¿cuánto cuesta?*
anything else?, *¿algo más?*
nothing else, *nada más*
do you speak Spanish?, *¿habla Ud. español?*
a little, *un poco*
speak (more) slowly, *hable Ud. (más) despacio*
do you understand?, *¿comprende Ud.?*

I don't understand, *no comprendo, no entiendo*
do you know?, *¿sabe Ud.?*
I don't know, *no sé*
I can't, *no puedo*
what do you call this in Spanish?, *¿cómo se llama esto en español?*
how do you say - in Spanish?, *¿cómo se dice - en español?*
what does that mean?, *¿qué quiere decir eso?*
what do you mean?, *¿qué quiere Ud. decir?*
what are you talking about?, *¿de qué habla Ud.?*
I'm an American, *soy norteamericano*
I'm hungry (thirsty, sleepy, warm, cold), *tengo hambre (sed, sueño, calor, frío)* [35]
It's warm (cold, windy, fine weather, bad weather), *hace calor (frío, viento, buen tiempo, mal tiempo)* [35]
It's forbidden, *prohibido* (no smoking, *prohibido fumar*)
luckily, *afortunadamente, por fortuna, por suerte*
is it not so?, *¿no es verdad?, ¿verdad?* (use this invariable phrase wherever English repeats the verb: you went, *didn't you?*; he is here, *isn't he?*)
not at all, *de nada*
how old are you?, *¿cuántos años tiene Ud.?*
I'm twenty years old, *tengo veinte años*
how long have you been waiting?, *¿desde cuándo espera Ud.?*
how long have you been here?, *¿desde cuándo está Ud. aquí?*
as soon as possible, *lo más pronto posible, cuanto antes*
come here!, *¡venga acá (aquí)!*
come in!, *¡pase adelante!, ¡adelante!, ¡entre Ud.!*
look!, *¡mire!, ¡vea!*
careful!, *¡con cuidado!*
look out!, *¡cuidado!, ¡tenga cuidado!*
for heaven's sake!, *¡por Dios!*
heck!, darn it!, *¡caramba!*
as you please, *como Ud. quiera, como Ud. guste*
listen!, look here!, say!, *¡oiga!*
just a second!, *¡un momento!*
what kind of?, *¿qué clase de?*
gangway!, by your leave!, *¡con permiso de Ud.!, ¡paso!, ¡allá voy!*
in any case, at any rate, *en cualquier caso*
glad to meet you, *¡muchísimo gusto!*
you don't say so!, *¡parece mentira!*
notice!, *¡aviso!*

35. With these expressions, translate "very" by *mucho* (*mucha* with *hambre* and *sed, muy* with *buen tiempo* and *mal tiempo*).

to your health!, *¡a su salud!*
I should like, *quisiera*
stop!, *¡pare!*
hurry!, *¡apresúrese (usted)!*
keep to the right, *guardar la derecha*
entrance, *entrada* (exit, *salida*)
right now, *ahora mismo*
there it (he, she) goes!, *¡ahí va!*
good luck to you!, *¡que lo pase usted bien!*, *¡buena suerte!*
he was successful, *le salió bien, tuvo éxito*
of course!, you bet!, *¡claro!, ¿cómo no?, ¡ya lo creo!*
don't worry!, *¡pierda usted cuidado!*
stop your fooling! quit your kidding!, *¡déjese de bromas!*
really?, honest?, *¿de veras?*
what nonsense!, *¡qué tontería!*
man, you don't say so!, *¡hombre! ¡no me diga!*
it's all the same to me, *lo mismo me da*
what a disappointment!, what a break! (ironical), *¡qué chasco!*
there is no doubt, *no cabe duda* (I have no doubt, *no me cabe duda*)
what do you think?, *¿qué le parece?* (how do you like this, *¿qué le
    parece a usted esto?*)
of course I did it!, you bet I did it!, *¡sí que lo hice!*
to get angry, *enfadarse*; Spanish America: *ponerse bravo* (he got
    sore, *se puso bravo*)

30. *Slang Words and Expressions.*

to die, to "kick the bucket", *espichar, estirar la pata*
to kid one along, *tomar el pelo a uno*
to have pull, *tener buenas aldabas*
to get drunk, *coger un tablón*
to sleep like a log, *dormir a pierna suelta*

pal, *compinche*
joint, dive, *garito*
fatty, *gordiflón*
colored man, *morenito*
wishful thinker, *ojalatero*
"dumb", *pelmazo*
"sissy", *marica*
face, "mug", *jeta*

policeman, "cop", *guindilla*
annoying person, "pest", *calamidad*
quack, *matasanos*
money, *parné*
wild time, *parranda*
greenhorn, *pipiolo*
nerve, "gall", *tupé*
bully, *matón*

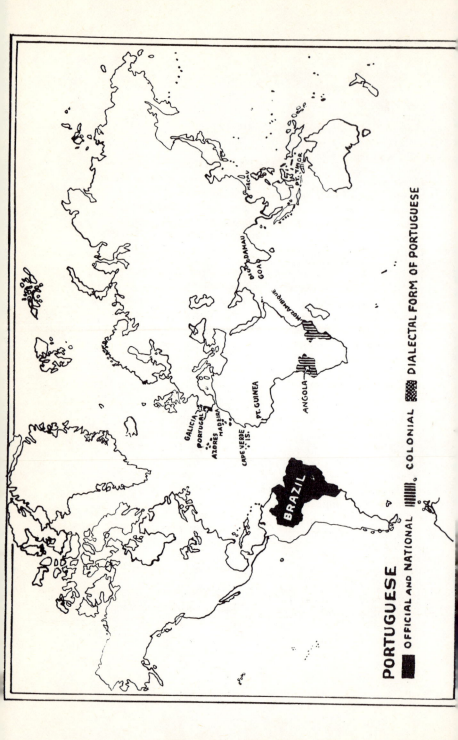

PORTUGUESE

■ OFFICIAL and NATIONAL ▥ COLONIAL ▦ DIALECTAL FORM OF PORTUGUESE

GALICIA
PORTUGAL
AZÔRES
MADEIRA
CAPE VERDE IS.
PT. GUINEA
ANGOLA
MOÇAMBIQUE
GOA
DAMAU
DIU
MACAU
PT. TIMOR
BRAZIL

Chapter VIII

PORTUGUESE

SPEAKERS AND LOCATION

(All population figures are approximate)

Europe — Portugal (including Azores) — 8,000,000; Galician, a dialect of northwestern Spain, spoken by some 3,000,000 people, is closer to Portuguese than it is to Spanish.

Asia — Goa, Damão and Diu, on the western coast of India; Macau, in southeastern China — total population, 900,000.

Africa — Angola — 4,500,000; Portuguese Guinea — 400,000; Mozambique — 4,500,000; Cape Verde and Madeira Islands, São Tomé and Príncipe, off the western coast of Africa — total population, 500,000.

Oceania — Portuguese Timor — 500,000.

South America — Brazil — 44,000,000.

North America — nearly a quarter of a million Portuguese immigrants and their descendants in the U. S. A., located mainly in California and Massachusetts.

Portuguese is also spoken in "Pidgin" or "Creole" varieties in Zanzibar, Mombasa and Melinde, on the eastern coast of Africa; in Ceylon, Mangalore, Cochin, Coromandel and other localities, in India; a Malay-Portuguese pidgin appears in Java, Malaya and Singapore.

ALPHABET AND SOUNDS

a, b, c, d, e, f, g, h, i, j, l, m, n, o, p, q, r, s, t, u, v, x, z, ã, õ, ç; (k, w and y do not appear in native Portuguese words). Vowel sounds: there is a tendency, more noticeable in Portugal than in Brazil, to prolong stressed vowels somewhat and to pronounce unstressed vowels indistinctly.

a: = f*a*ther (unstressed, it tends toward the e of th*e*) (águ*a*);

e: = m*e*t (t*e*rra), or the first part of a in g*a*te (m*e*sa);
   initial and followed by s plus consonant, it is almost silent (*e*scudo, pron. 'shkudu); final, even though followed by s, = p*i*n in Brazil, th*e* in Portugal (dent*e*, dent*e*s);

i: = mach*i*ne (f*i*lho);

o: = c*u*p (n*o*ve), or the first part of o in g*o* (n*o*vo); final, even though followed by s, = l*oo*k (amig*o*, amig*o*s);

u: = p*oo*l (m*u*ro);

ã: = f*a*ther, but followed immediately by closure of the passage between nose and mouth (irm*ã*);

õ: = c*u*p, but followed immediately by closure as above (bot*õ*es);

ou: = g*o*; but in certain words it is pronounced and even spelt oi (d*ou*s or d*oi*s);

ei: = l*a*te (l*ei*te);

Consonant sounds: b, d, f, l, m, n, p, t, v, z, approximately as in English. (Note, however, that a final -m nasalizes a preceding vowel, and is not itself pronounced: bo*m*, be*m*, fi*m*, algu*m*).

c = before a, o, u, or consonant, = *c*at (*c*asa);
   before e, i, = la*c*e (*c*idade);

ç = (used only before a, o, u) = la*c*e (ca*ç*ador);

ch and x: usually = *s*ure (*ch*amar, cai*x*a);

g: = before a, o, u, or consonant, = *g*o (*g*ula, *g*rande);
   before e, i, = mea*s*ure (*g*eral);

h: always silent (*h*ora, pronounced ora);

j: = mea*s*ure (*j*anela);

lh: = mi*ll*ion (fi*lh*o);
nh: = o*ni*on (ni*nh*o);
q: appears only before u, and = Engl. q, but the u is silent
       if e or i follow; the same applies to the gue, gui groups
       (*qua*dro, pron. *kwa*dru, but *que*rela pron. *k*erela);
r: trilled, as in British ve*r*y;
s: = *s*ure when final or followed by a consonant (e*s*cala, pron.
       '*sh*kala; dedo*s*, pron. dedu*sh*);[1]
    = pre*s*ent when between two vowels (pre*s*ente);[1]
    = *s*un elsewhere (*s*ol).

Sounds not appearing in Portuguese: all English vowel sounds
       outside of the ones mentioned above; *ch*urch; *j*est; Ameri-
       can r, *th*in, *th*is (but d between vowels (da*d*o) comes
       close to *th*is).
Portuguese sounds not appearing in English: ã, õ, Portuguese r.

SPELLING, SYLLABIFICATION, ACCENTUATION

The spelling of Portuguese is now fully standardized (at
least in theory), both in Portugal and Brazil, by mutual agreement between the two countries (1943). Alternative spellings,
however, occur in such words as *quási, quáse* (almost), *ouro,
oiro* (gold), and especially in words containing *cç* (*dire-
(c)ção*, address), where the first *c* (= k) is not pronounced,
or its pronunciation is optional, depending on local variations.
Older printed works deviate considerably from the 1943 rules,
especially in the matter of accents and double consonants (*sahir*
for *sair; secco* for the modern *sêco; janella* for *janela*). The
only double consonants permitted in the modern orthography
are: *-ss-* between vowels, indicating the sound of *s*un (no*ss*o),
whereas single *-s-* = ro*s*e (dese*j*o); *-rr-* and *-nn-* (the latter only
in a few compounds: *connosco.*

1. Note the double pronunciation of a final -s, according as a consonant or a vowel begins the next word: a*s* casas, pron. a*sh* kazash;
but a*s* amigas, pron. a*z* amigash.

A single consonant between two vowels goes with the *following*, not with the *preceding* vowel: pronounce *geral* as *ge ral; reparar* as *re pa rar; primeiro* as *pri mei ro*.

The accent regularly falls on the *next to the last* syllable in words ending in vowels (except *-ã*, which is usually stressed when final: ir*mã*), *-m* or *-s* (a*migo*, vi*a*gem, mu*lhe*res); otherwise, on the last syllable (jan*tar*). Deviations from these rules require written accents. The acute (´) is used if the vowel has an *open* sound (*o* = cup, *e* = m*e*t, etc.); the circumflex (^) if the vowel has a *closed* sound (*o* = go, *e* = g*a*te, etc.); thus, in *café*, the acute accent indicates not only that the stress falls on the last syllable, but also that the *e* has the sound of m*e*t; while in *Você*, the circumflex accent shows the place of the stress and also the fact that the *e* has the sound of the first part of g*a*te. The accent marks, acute and circumflex, are also used to distinguish between two words that would otherwise have the same spelling (*pôr*, "to put"; *por*, "for", "by"; *e*, "and"; *é*, "is"). The grave accent (`) is always used on an *unstressed* syllable, serving merely to indicate that the open sound of a vowel is kept in compound words in one of the main elements of which the acute accent appears (adverbs, augmentatives, diminutives, etc.): *má, màzinha; café, cafèzinho; pálido, pàlidamente*. It is also used to show the combination of the preposition *a* (to) with the definite article or a demonstrative pronoun (*a*, "to" plus *as*, feminine plural article, contract to *às; a* plus *aquêle*, "that", contract to *àquêle*.

The diaeresis is used to show that the *u* of the groups *qu, gu* before *e* or *i* is to be sounded, not silent (*conseqüência, tranqüilo*); it is also *optionally* used to separate two unstressed vowels that would otherwise form a diphthong (*saüdar* or *saudar; proïbido* or *proibido*). If one of the two vowels that are to be separated is *stressed*, the *acute accent* must be used (*saúde, baía*).

SAMPLE OF WRITTEN PORTUGUESE;
USE FOR PRACTICE READING.

"Senhor, pode dizer-me se esta rua conduz à praça do comércio?" — "Não, senhor. O senhor afastou-se do verdadeiro caminho; a praça acha-se no centro da cidade, numa das ruas principais, e esta estrada, em que estamos, conduz numa direcção inteiramente oposta." — "Que caminho é preciso então que eu tome?" — "Vá todo direito até à primeira ruazinha à esquerda, siga-a, ela o conduzirá a uma grande praça; quando o senhor lá tiver chegado, volte à direita e achar-se-á em face de uma grande rua ao fim da qual verá um magnífico edifício; este é o palácio da praça do comércio; o senhor não pode errar." — "Que distância pode haver daqui?" — "Pouco mais ou menos meia hora de marcha, pois eu indiquei-lhe o caminho mais curto." — "Fico-lhe muito obrigado, senhor." — "Não há de quê."

GRAMMATICAL SURVEY

1. *Nouns and Articles.*

There are only two genders in Portuguese, masculine and feminine. Nouns denoting males are masculine, those denoting females are feminine. For nouns which in English are neuter, the ending *-o* usually denotes masculine gender, *-a* feminine gender. The gender of nouns ending in *-e* or consonants must be determined by observation; learn these nouns with their definite articles. The plural of nouns is generally formed by adding *-s* to the singular if the latter ends in a vowel, *-es* if it ends in a consonant.[2]

The definite article is *o* (plural *os*) for masculine nouns, *a* (plural *as*) for feminine nouns.[3] The indefinite article is *um* for masculine nouns, *uma* for feminines.

2. Nouns ending in *-l* usually change *-l* to *-s* or *-is*: *animal*, pl. *animais*; *fuzil* ("rifle"), pl. *fuzis*; nouns ending in *-m* generally change *-m* to *-ns*: *homem*, "man", pl. *homens*; nouns ending in *-ão* usually change *-ão* to *-ães* or *-ões*: *capitão*, pl. *capitães*; *coração*, pl. *corações*; note in this connection that *-ão*, pl. *-ães* usually corresponds to a Spanish *-án*, pl. *-anes*, while *-ão*, pl. *-ões* normally corresponds to a Spanish *-ón*, pl. *-ones*; the Spanish for "nation" being *nación* (pl. *naciones*), what is the plural of Portuguese *nação?*

3. The definite article combines with certain prepositions: *de* (of, from) in combination with *o, a, os, as*, becomes *do, da, dos, das; a* (to) in the same combinations becomes *ao, à, aos, às; em* (in) becomes *no, na, nos, nas; por* (for) becomes *pelo, pela, pelos, pelas;* the woman's house, the house *of the* woman, *a casa da mulher;* the women's houses, *as casas das mulheres;* I am speaking to the man's daughter, *falo à filha do homem;* he went into the house, *entrou na casa;* by the fruit one knows the tree, *pelos frutos se conhece a árvore.*

The indefinite article combines only with *em* (*num, numa*): in a house, *numa casa.* This combination is optional (*em uma casa*).

o filho, the son	*os filhos*, the sons
a filha, the daughter	*as filhas*, the daughters
o capote, the overcoat	*os capotes*, the overcoats
o rapaz, the boy	*os rapazes*, the boys
a mulher, the woman	*as mulheres*, the women

um filho, a son
uma filha, a daughter
um capote, an overcoat
um rapaz, a boy
uma mulher, a woman

2. Adjectives and Adverbs.

The Portuguese adjective, whether attributive or predicate, agrees with the noun that it modifies; this does not necessarily mean identical endings (*o homem cruel*, the cruel man; *os homens cruéis*, the cruel men; *a mulher bonita*, the pretty woman; *as mulheres bonitas*, the pretty women). Adjectives usually follow the nouns they modify.

Adjectives ending in -*o* change -*o* to -*a* in the feminine singular, to -*os* in the masculine plural, to -*as* in the feminine plural (*novo, nova, novos, novas*); those ending in -*ão* normally change to -*ã* in the fem. sg., to -*ãos* in the masc. pl., to -*ãs* in the fem. pl. (*temporão, temporã, temporãos, temporãs*); those ending in -*e* or consonant usually remain unchanged in the feminine; in the plural, -*e* adjectives add -*s* for both genders, consonant adjectives add -*s* or -*es* (*breve, breve, breves, breves; jovem, jovem, jovens, jovens; feliz, feliz, felizes, felizes*).[4]

4. Adjectives ending in -*ês*, -*ol*, -*or*, -*um*, -*u* usually add -*a* in the feminine, especially if they denote nationality: *português, portuguesa, portugueses, portuguesas; espanhol, espanhola*. Adjectives ending in -*l* normally change -*l* to -*s*, -*is*, -*es* or -*eis* in the plural: *fácil*, pl. *fáceis; azul*, pl. *azues; civil*, pl. *civis*; while adjectives ending in -*m* form their plural in -*ns*. Note the combination of these two exceptional formations in several adjectives: *espanhol, espanhola, espanhóis, espanholas; algum, alguma, alguns, algumas*.

The comparative is usually formed by prefixing *mais* (more) to the positive: *esta rapariga é mais bonita que aquela*, this girl is prettier than that one. The superlative is formed by using the definite article before the noun or before *mais*: *é a mais bela*, she is the most beautiful; *ela é a moça mais bela que eu conheço*, she is the most beautiful girl I know.

tão - como, as - as; *tanto (tanta) - como*, as much - as; *tantos (tantas) - como*, as many - as; *menos que* - less than.

The adverb is generally formed by adding *-mente* to the feminine singular form of the adjective: *justo*, just, fem. *justa*, adverb *justamente*, justly.

3. *Numerals.*

Cardinal[5]

1 — *um, uma*	15 — *quinze*
2 — *dous (dois), duas*	16 — *dezasseis (dezesseis)*
3 — *três*	17 — *dezassete (dezessete)*
4 — *quatro*	18 — *dezóito*
5 — *cinco*	19 — *dezanove (dezenove)*
6 — *seis*	20 — *vinte*
7 — *sete*	21 — *vinte-e-um(a)*
8 — *oito*	22 — *vinte-e-dois (duas)*
9 — *nove*	23 — *vinte-e-três*
10 — *dez*	30 — *trinta*
11 — *onze*	40 — *quarenta*
12 — *doze*	50 — *cinqüenta (cincoenta)*
13 — *treze*	60 — *sessenta*
14 — *catorze (quatorze)*	70 — *setenta*

80 — *oitenta*
90 — *noventa*

5. Use these in dates, save for "the first": *o primeiro de maio*, May 1st; *o cinco de maio*, May 5th.

100 — *cem* (*cento*)[6]
200 — *duzentos*[7]
300 — *trezentos*
400 — *quatrocentos*
500 — *quinhentos*
600 — *seiscentos*
700 — *setecentos*
800 — *oitocentos*
900 — *novecentos*
1000 — *mil*
2000 — *dois mil*
1,000,000 — *um milhão* (*de*)

Ordinal.

1st - *primeiro;* 2nd - *segundo;* 3rd - *terceiro;* 4th - *quarto;*
5th - *quinto;* 6th - *sexto;* 7th - *sétimo;* 8th - *oitavo;* 9th - *nono;*
10th - *décimo;* 11th - *décimo primeiro;* 12th - *décimo segundo;*
20th - *vigésimo;* 30th - *trigésimo;* 40th - *quadragésimo;* 50th -
quinquagésimo; 60th - *sexagésimo;* 70th - *septuagésimo;* 80th -
octogésimo; 90th - *nonagésimo;* 100th - *centésimo;* 1000th -
milésimo.

Others.

half - *a metade* (noun), or *um meio* (adjective) : *a metade da
classe,* half of the class; *meia hora,* half an hour.
um par de - a pair of; *uma dúzia de* - a dozen; *uma vez* - once;
duas vezes - twice; *a primeira vez* - the first time.

6. Use *cem* immediately before the noun, or if *mil* or *milhão* follows:
cem homens, 100 men; *cem mil,* 100,000; use *cento* if a numeral
smaller than 100 follows: *cento e doze homens,* 112 men.

7. Plural hundreds change *-os* to *-as* if used with feminine nouns:
duzentas mulheres, 200 women.

4. *Pronouns.*

a) Personal (Subject)[8]

I, *eu*	we, *nós*
you (fam.), *tu*[9]	you (fam. pl.), *vós*[9]
he, *êle*	they (masc.), *êles*
she, *ela*	they (fem.), *elas*
you (polite), *Você*[9]	you (pol. pl.), *Vocês*[9]

b) Personal (Direct and Indirect Object).

me, to me, *me*	us, to us, *nos*
you, to you, *te*	you, to you, *vos*
him, it, *o*	them (masc.), *os*
her, it, *a*	them (fem.), *as*
to him, to her, to it, to you (pol.), *lhe*	to them, to you (pol. pl.), *lhes*

These normally precede the verb:[10] *êle me conhece,* he

8. These are used especially for emphasis or clarification: I speak, *falo;* I speak, *eu falo;* I should speak, *eu falaria;* he would speak, *êle falaria.*

9. *Tu* and *vós*, with the second singular and second plural of the verb, respectively, are used only in familiar conversation. One polite form of address, especially in Brazil, is *Você*, with the *third* singular of the verb, for a single person addressed, and *Vocês* with the third plural, for more than one person. The written abbreviation for the singular form is V. An even more common form of address, especially in Portugal, is *o senhor* (*a senhora, os senhores, as senhoras*) likewise with the third persons of the verb: *o senhor tem o livro?*, have you the book?; *os senhores falam português?*, do you (pl.) speak Portuguese?

10. But usage varies considerably in this respect: *digo-lhe a verdade,* I tell him the truth; *Você enganou-o,* you deceived him. In the future and conditional tenses, the pronoun is often inserted between the infinitive root and the ending: *chamarei,* I shall call; *chamá-lo-ei,* I shall call him. The negative always requires the pronoun *before* the verb: *não se deve fazer,* it must not be done. The use of the object pronoun at the very outset of the sentence is generally avoided: *vendo-lho* or *eu lho vendo,* I sell it to him (not *lho vendo*).

knows me; *eu lhe falo*, I am speaking to him. The negative *não*
("not") may appear before or after the object pronoun: *êle
não me quer pagar* or *êle me não quer pagar*, he does not want
to pay me. With the infinitive, the object pronoun regularly
follows, and is attached by a hyphen: *tenho uma graça a pedir-
lhe*, I have a favor to ask you; if the object pronoun is *o, a, os*,
or *as*, the *-r* of the infinitive is dropped, *-l* is prefixed to the
pronoun, and the final vowel of the infinitive takes a circumflex accent for *-er* verbs, an acute for *-ar* and *-ir* verbs: *quero
vender o livro*, I want to sell the book; *quero vendê-lo*, I want
to sell it; *quero comprá-lo*, I want to buy it.

c) Compound (Direct and Indirect Combined; see p. 288,
no. 3).

it to me, them to me, *mo, ma, mos, mas*: *êles mo darão*, they
will give it to me.

it to you, them to you, *to, ta, tos, tas*: *quem to prometeu?* who
promised it to you?

it to him, it to her, it to you (pol.), it to them,[11] *lho, lha*:
quero lho dar, I want to give it to him.

it to us, them to us, *no-lo, no-la, no-los, no-las*:*êles no-las
darão*, they will give them to us.

it to you, them to you, *vo-lo, vo-la, vo-los, vo-las*: *posso vo-lo
escrever*, I can write it to you.

them to him, them to her, them to you (pol.), *lhos, lhas*: *quero
lhos dar*, I want to give them to him.[11]

While a single object pronoun normally follows the infinitive (*quero vendê-lo*), a compound one more usually precedes: *quer mo dar? Não, quero vo-lo emprestar*, do you want
to give it to me? No, I want to lend it to you.

d) Personal Pronouns with Prepositions.

11. Distinguish by adding *a êle, a ela, a V., a êles, a elas*: *vendo-lho
a V.*, or *vendo-o a V.*, I sell it to you; *vendo-lho a êle* or *vendo-o a êle*,
I sell it to him. This is done only when necessary.

These are the same as the subject pronouns, save that *mim* replaces *eu*, and *ti* replaces *tu*: *fala de mim*, he is speaking about me; *lembravam-se de ti*, they remembered you. With the preposition *com* (with), the forms *migo, tigo, nosco, vosco* are used instead of *mim, ti, nos, vos*: *fala comigo*, he is speaking with me; *vai connosco*, he is going with us.

e) Possessive.

my, mine, (*o*) *meu*, (*a*) *minha*, (*os*) *meus*, (*as*) *minhas*
your, yours, (*o*) *teu*, (*a*) *tua*, (*os*) *teus*, (*as*) *tuas*
his, her, hers, its, their, theirs, your, yours (pol.),[12] (*o*) *seu*,
    (*a*) *sua*, (*os*) *seus*, (*as*) *suas*
our, ours, (*o*) *nosso*, (*a*) *nossa*, (*os*) *nossos*, (*as*) *nossas*
your, yours, (*o*) *vosso*, (*a*) *vossa*, (*os*) *vossos*, (*as*) *vossas*

These forms are used both as adjectives and as pronouns. The definite article may be used, but is more often omitted, when the possessive is an adjective: (*o*) *meu relógio*, my watch; it is regularly used when the possessive is a pronoun, save after the verb "to be": *meu relógio é melhor que o vosso*, my watch is better than yours; *esta casa é minha*, this house is mine.

f) Demonstrative.

this, these,*êste, esta, êstes, estas*: *êste livro*, this book; *que flor é esta?*, what flower is this?
that, those (near you), *êsse, essa, êsses, essas*: *essa casa*, that house of yours; *que casa é essa?* what house is that?
that, those (yonder), *aquêle, aquela, aquêles, aquelas*: *quer o senhor aquêle vinho?* do you want that wine?

"Neuter" pronouns, *isto, isso, aquilo*, refer to a general situation or state of affairs: *isto não é possível*, this is not possible; *isso não pode ser*, that can't be.

"The one", "the ones" are usually translated by the de-

12. Clarify, if necessary, by adding *de êle, de ela, de V., de êles, de elas*: *suas filhas de êle*, his daughters; *suas filhas de V.*, your daughters; or *as filhas de êle, as filhas de V.*

finite article (*o, a, os, as*), referring to persons, by *aquêle* referring to things: *o que fala é meu tio,* the one who is speaking is my uncle; *êste vinho é bom, mas aquêle que lhe dei ontem é melhor,* this wine is good, but the one I gave you yesterday is better.

g) Relative and Interrogative.

who, whom, that, which, *que*[13]: *a mulher que canta,* the woman who is singing; *a mulher que êle ama,* the woman he loves;[14] *o navio que sai,* the ship that is leaving; *o navio que V. comanda,* the ship you command.

whom (after prepositions), *quem*: *diz-me com quem andas,* tell me with whom you go.

whose, *cujo* (*cuja, cujos, cujas*): *o rapaz cujo pai é capitão,* the boy whose father is a captain.

who?, whom?, *quem?*: *quem fala português?,* who speaks Portuguese?; *a quem havemos de falar?,* to whom are we to speak?

whose?, *de quem?*: *de quem é êste livro?,* whose book is this?

what?, *que?*: *que quer o senhor?,* what do you want?; *que lições tem aprendido?,* what lessons have you learned?

which? which one? which ones?, *qual? quais?*: *qual dos irmãos morreu?* which of the brothers died?

5. *Verbs.*

Portuguese verbs fall into three main classes, with the infinitive ending respectively in *-ar, -er,* and *-ir* (to love, *amar;* to yield, *ceder;* to leave, *partir*). A considerable number of *-ir* verbs undergo changes in the vowel of the root (*u* changing to *o* when the ending has an *e: subir,* 3rd sg. *sobe; e* changing

---

13. *o qual, a qual, os quais, as quais,* or *o que, a que, os que, as que,* are occasionally used to refer to the more distant of two possible antecedents: *são os amigos de seu pai os quais saem para o Brasil,* they are his father's friends, who are leaving for Brazil.

14. Note that the relative pronoun cannot be omitted.

to *i* when the ending has *a* or *o*: *servir*, 1st sg. *sirvo*; etc.).
Numerous other irregularities appear, some of which are given
in the vocabulary.

1.   Present Indicative (meaning: I love, am loving, do love)

to love,	*am-ar*	to yield, *ced-er*		to leave,	*part-ir*

I love,	*am-o*	I yield,	*ced-o*	I leave,	*part-o*
you love,	*am-as*	you yield,	*ced-es*	you leave,	*part-es*
he loves,	*am-a*	he yields,	*ced-e*	he leaves,	*part-e*
we love,	*am-amos*	we yield,	*ced-emos*	we leave,	*part-imos*
you love,	*am-ais*	you yield,	*ced-eis*	you leave,	*part-ís*
they love,	*am-am*	they yield,	*ced-em*	they leave,	*part-em*

to be,	*ser*[15]	to be, *estar*[15]	to have,	*ter*[16]	to have, *haver*[16]
I am,	*sou*	*estou*	I have,	*tenho*	*hei*
you are,	*és*	*estás*	you have,	*tens*	*hás*
he is,	*é*	*está*	he has,	*tem*	*há*
we are,	*somos*	*estamos*	we have,	*temos*	*havemos* (*hemos*)
you are,	*sois*	*estais*	you have,	*tendes*	*haveis* (*heis*)
they are,	*são*	*estão*	they have,	*têm*	*hão*

15.   *Ser* indicates a permanent or inherent quality, and must be used
when a predicate *noun* follows; *é homem*, he is a man; *é Brasileiro*,
he is a Brazilian.   *Estar* indicates a temporary quality, location or
state of health: *está triste*, he is sad; *está cansado*, he is tired; *está no
Rio*, he is in Rio.   *Ser* is used with the past participle to form the
passive: *é louvado*, he is praised; *estar* is used with the gerund to
form the progressive: *está falando*, he is speaking.   Note that the
ordinary present indicative also expresses the progressive idea, however.   The gerund is formed by adding *-ando* to the root of *-ar* verbs
(*amar, amando*); *-endo* to the root of *-er* verbs (*ceder, cedendo*);
-indo to the root of *-ir* verbs (*partir, partindo*).

16.   *Ter* is used with the past participle to form compound tenses;
this applies to all verbs, including intransitive and reflexive forms,

2. Imperfect (meaning: I was loving, used to love)

	-ar verbs	*-er* verbs	*-ir* verbs
I used to love,	*am-ava*	*ced-ia*	*part-ia*
you used to love,	*am-avas*	*ced-ias*	*part-ias*
he used to love,	*am-ava*	*ced-ia*	*part-ia*
we used to love,	*am-ávamos*	*ced-íamos*	*part-íamos*
you used to love,	*am-áveis*	*ced-íeis*	*part-íeis*
they used to love,	*am-avam*	*ced-iam*	*part-iam*

ser: era, eras, era, éramos, éreis, eram;
estar: regular (*estava,* etc.);
ter: tinha, tinhas, tinha, tínhamos, tínheis, tinham;
haver: regular (*havia,* etc.).

3. Past (meaning: I loved)

	-ar verbs	*-er* verbs	*-ir* verbs
I loved,	*am-ei*	*ced-i*	*part-i*
you loved,	*am-aste*	*ced-este*	*part-iste*
he loved,	*am-ou*	*ced-eu*	*part-iu*

and the past participle so used is invariable: *tenho sido,* I have been; *êle os tem tido,* he has had them; *ela tem chegado,* she has arrived; *temos falado,* we have spoken; *os meninos se têm divertido,* the children have had a good time. *Ter* is also used to indicate possession (*tenho um bom amigo,* I have a good friend); with *que* and the infinitive to indicate necessity (have to): *tenho que sair,* I have to go out; and in expressions of physical feelings (*tenho fome e frio,* I am hungry and cold).

Haver is restricted in use to *haver de* followed by the infinitive (*hei de falar,* I am to speak), and impersonally in the sense of "there to be" or "ago": *havia momentos terríveis,* there were terrible moments; *haverá cem vapores no pôrto,* there will be (or must be) a hundred steamers in the harbor; *há mais de quatro meses,* more than four months ago.

we loved,	am-ámos	ced-emos	part-imos
you loved,	am-astes	ced-estes	part-istes
they loved,	am-aram	ced-eram	part-iram

ser: fui, foste, foi, fomos, fostes, foram;
estar: estive, estiveste, esteve, estivemos, estivestes, estiveram;
ter: tive, tiveste, teve, tivemos, tivestes, tiveram;
haver: houve, houveste, houve, houvemos, houvestes, houveram.

4. Future (meaning: I shall love), and Conditional (meaning:
I should love).

   The endings of these tenses are added to the entire infinitive, not to the stem:
amar- (*ceder-, partir-*) *-ei, -ás, -á, -emos, -eis, -ão* (*amarei,*
I shall love);
amar- (*ceder-, partir-*) *-ia, -ias, -ia, -íamos, -íeis, -iam* (*amaria,*
I should love).
ser, estar, ter and *haver* are regular in these tenses (*serei,
estarei,* I shall be; *seria, estaria,* I should be; *terei, haverei,*
I shall have; *teria, haveria,* I should have).

5. "Personal" infinitive.

   This is a form peculiar to Portuguese, and consists of the
infinitive to which are added the following personal endings:
nothing in the first and third singular, *-es* in the second singular, *-mos* in the first plural, *-des* in the second plural, *-em* in
the third plural: *ser, seres, ser, sermos, serdes, serem; amar,
amares, amar, amarmos, amardes, amarem.*   Its chief uses
are: 1. in exclamations: *sermos nós ricos!,* for us to be rich!
(if we only were rich!); 2. after prepositions where English
would use a gerund: *foram castigados por serem travêssos,* they
were punished for being naughty; 3. after a conjunction, to
replace a clause: *parti depois de terem falado,* I left after they
had spoken.

6. Compound Tenses.

These are formed by combining *ter* with the past participle of the verb (ending in *-ado* for *-ar* verbs, *-ido* for the others); the past participle is invariable.

Present Perfect: I have loved, *tenho amado;* I have arrived, *tenho chegado;*

Past Perfect: I had spoken, *tinha falado;* they had left, *tinham partido;*

Future Perfect: I shall have yielded, *terei cedido;*
Conditional Perfect: they would have gone, *teriam ido.*

7. Imperative.

	-ar verbs	*-er* verbs
Familiar Singular:	*am-a*	*ced-e*
First Person Plural (let us)	*am-emos*	*ced-amos*
Familiar Plural:	*am-ai*	*ced-ei*
Polite Singular:	*am-e V.*	*ced-a V.*
Polite Plural:	*am-em Vocês*	*ced-am Vocês*

	-ir verbs
Fam. Sg.:	*part-e*
1st Pl.:	*part-amos*
Fam. Pl.:	*part-í*
Pol. Sg.:	*part-a V.*
Pol. Pl.:	*part-am Vocês*

In the negative, the familiar singular and familiar plural are replaced by corresponding present subjunctive forms: *não ames, não cedas, não partas; não ameis, não cedais, não partais.*

8. Reflexive verbs.

These are conjugated with *ter;* the participle is invari-

able; the reflexive pronouns used are *me, te, se, nos, vos, se*:
êle se queixa or *queixa-se*, he complains (*queixar-se*, to complain, lit. to bemoan oneself); *os meninos se têm divertido*,
the children had a good time (amused themselves).

9. Passive.

The passive is formed with the verb *ser* combined with
the past participle, which agrees with the subject. "By" is
translated by *de* if the action is predominantly mental, by *por*
if physical: *o rapaz foi castigado de seu mestre e batido por
seu pai*, the boy was punished by his teacher and beaten by
his father.

10. Subjunctive.

The Portuguese subjunctive has six tenses, and is frequently used in subordinate clauses. For the present subjunctive, the endings normally are: for *-ar* verbs: *-e, -es, -e,
-emos, -eis, -em*: *que eu ame*, that I love; for *-er* and *-ir* verbs:
-a, -as, -a, -amos, -ais, -am: *que eu ceda*, that I yield.

The imperfect subjunctive ends in *-asse* for *-ar* verbs,
-esse for *-er* verbs, *-isse* for *-ir* verbs: *que eu amasse*, that I
should love.

The present perfect subjunctive is formed by combining
the present subjunctive of *ter* (*tenha*) with the past participle:
que eu tenha amado, that I may have loved; the past perfect
subjunctive combines the imperfect subjunctive of *ter* (*tivesse*)
with the past participle: *que eu tivesse chegado*, that I might
have arrived.

The future corresponds in form to the personal infinitive
in regular verbs, and is formed by adding *-r* to the past in
others; it is used for the most part after *se* (if) and *quando*
(when), to refer to a future possibility: *se eu partir, o diria*,
if I were to leave, I should say so.

BRAZILIAN VARIETIES OF PORTUGUESE

The Portuguese of Brazil not only differs from that of Portugal in certain points of pronunciation, grammar and vocabulary, but has local varieties of its own. Two main Brazilian varieties are recognized, the Carioca (indigenous to Rio de Janeiro) and the Paulista, current in the south of the country. In the matter of pronunciation, Brazilian appears to be more conservative of older speech-forms than Portuguese, and is characterized by a clearer, slower, and more harmonious enunciation, due in large part to the conservation of the timbre of unstressed vowels, which Portugal tends to slur and even drop (*m'nino* for *menino; pont'* for *ponte; ad'vinha* for *adivinha*). In vocabulary, on the other hand, Brazilian is distinguished not merely by archaic words, but also by numerous words borrowed from the languages of the Tupi-Guaraní Indians and the African slaves. Only a few of the major differences between Portuguese and Brazilian are listed.

PRONUNCIATION.

1. Brazilian retains the *e* in the diphthong *ei* and in the nasal diphthong *em*, while in Portugal *ei* tends toward *âi* and final *em* toward *ãi*. Brazilian, however, tends to drop the *i* of the *ei* (*beijo*, pron. *bâijo* in Portugal, *bejo* in Brazil; *também*, pron. *tambeim* in Brazil, *tambãi* in Portugal).
2. Brazilian tends to add an *i*-sound to a final stressed vowel followed by *-s* or *-z* (*voz*, pron. *voiz; gás*, pron. *gáis*).
3. The normal Portuguese diphthongs *ai, ei, ou*, tend to lose their final element in Brazilian pronunciation (*baixo*, pron. *baxo; primeiro*, pron. *primero; tirou*, pron. *tiró*).
4. In Portugal, a stressed *e* followed by *nh, lh, j, ch, x* tends to take the sound of *a*; this does not occur in Brazil (*tenho*, pron. *tanho* in Portugal; *espelho*, pron. *espalho*).

5. Brazilian tends to drop a final *-r*, while Portugal tends to add an *-i*, thus forming an extra syllable (*falar*, pron. *falari* in Portugal, *falá* in Brazil; *doutor*, pron. *doutori* in Portugal, *doutó* in Brazil).

6. In the Carioca (Rio), but not the Paulista pronunciation of Brazil, *te, ti* tend to be pronounced *che, chi*, and *de, di* tend to be pronounced *je, ji* (*antes*, pron. *anches; tio*, pron. *chio; dia*, pron. *jia*).

GRAMMAR.

1. The position of the object pronoun is more flexible in Brazil than in Portugal, with a greater tendency on the part of Brazilian speakers to place the pronoun before the verb (Portugal *o Senhor deve-me dinheiro*, Brazil *o Senhor me deve dinheiro*).

2. Brazil uses *êle, ela, êles, elas, lhe, lhes* as direct object pronouns (*vi êle*, or *eu o vi; eu lhe vi ontem na avenida; conheço ela*, or *eu a conheço*).

3. The combination pronouns *mo, to, lho*, etc. (it to me, it to you) are avoided in Brazil (*eu lhe dei isso*, or *eu lho dei*). The direct pronoun is often altogether omitted in these cases (*quer dar-me a bola? Quero dar-lhe* instead of *quero dar-lha*).

4. The preposition *em* is often colloquially used for *a* in Brazil with verbs of motion (*eu ía na cidade*, or *eu ía à cidade*).

5. In several other cases, *a* is avoided by the use of other prepositions (*consente com muita pena; pescavam de linha; tenho medo de pobreza; responda palavra por palavra*). But many of these forms are common to Portugal as well.

6. The preposition *para* tends to govern an object pronoun instead of a subject pronoun as subject of a following infinitive (*é muito para mim fazer* instead of *é muito para eu fazer*).

7. The progressive form with *estar* is more frequently used in Brazil than in Portugal, which prefers *estar* with *a* and the infinitive (*estou lendo* in Brazil, *estou a ler* in Portugal).

8. In Brazil, *ter* and *haver* are used interchangeably in the

impersonal construction "there to be" (*não tem alunos.* or *não há alunos*).

9. In Brazil, *mais* occasionally replaces *já* in negative use (*não quero mais,* or *já não quero*). Brazil also tends to double negatives (*não tem nada não*).

10. In a relative clause, Brazil often shifts the preposition to the end of the clause and adds a personal pronoun (*o livro que falei dêle,* or *o livro de que falei*).

VOCABULARY.

1. Many words in common use in Brazil are of Tupi-Guaraní origin. A few of the most common ones are: *mandioca* (a vegetable); *abacaxi* (pineapple); *sabiá, urubu* (birds); *ipé* (a tree); *jacá* (basket); *caipora* (an unlucky person); *caipira* (a "hick"); *carioca* (pertaining to Rio); *estar na pindaíba* (to "be broke").

2. Words of African Negro origin are also numerous in the tongue of Brazil: *senzala* (slave quarters); *quilombo* (communities of Negroes); *maxixe* (a dance); *samba* (a dance); *zumbi* (ghost).

3. A few archaic Portuguese forms survive in Brazil: *mas porem,* or *mas* or *porem; pro mó de,* or *por amor de; despois* for *depois.*

4. Brazilian has a particular fondness for diminutive forms, especially the ones formed with the suffix *-inho*: *doentinho* (sick); *agorinha* (right now); *pertinho* (quite close); *até loguinho* (see you later); *fique quietinho* (keep quiet); *está dormidinho* (he is asleep).

5. Among words which differ in Portugal and Brazil, the following are of interest:

English	Portugal	Brazil
girl	*rapariga*	*moça*
trolley	*carro elétrico*	*bonde*
motor-man	*guarda-freio*	*motorneiro*

police station	*esquadra*	*delegacia*
grocery store	*mercearia*	*venda*

The *moço* which means "young man" in Brazil has rather the meaning of "waiter" in Portugal; while the *fumo* which in Portugal means "smoke" has in Brazil the meaning of "tobacco", and "smoke" is *fumaça*.

It may be emphasized that a good many of the so-called "characteristics" of Brazilian appear also in Portugal, though locally and to a lesser degree.

VOCABULARY [17]

1. *World, Elements, Nature, Weather, Time, Directions.*

world, *o mundo*
earth, *a terra*
air, *o ar*
water, *a água*
fire, *o fogo*
light, *a luz*
sea, *o mar*
sun, *o sol*
moon, *a lua*
star, *a estrêla*
sky, *o céu*
wind, *o vento*
weather, time, *o tempo*
snow, *a neve*
to snow, *nevar*
rain, *a chuva*
to rain, *chover*
cloud, *a nuvem*
cloudy, *nublado*
fog, *o nevoeiro*
ice, *o gêlo*
mud, *a lama*
morning, *a manhã*
noon, *o meio dia*
afternoon, *a tarde*
evening, *a tarde, a noite*
night, *a noite*
midnight, *a meia noite*
North, *o Norte*
South, *o Sul*
East, *o Leste (Este)*

West, *o Oéste*
year, *o ano*
month, *o mês*
week, *a semana*
day, *o dia*
hour, *a hora*
minute, *o minuto*
Sunday, *o domingo*
Monday, *a segunda-feira*
Tuesday, *a terça-feira*
Wednesday, *a quarta-feira*
Thursday, *a quinta-feira*
Friday, *a sexta-feira*
Saturday, *o sábado*
January, *janeiro*
February, *fevereiro*
March, *março*
April, *abril*
May, *maio*
June, *junho*
July, *julho*
August, *agôsto*
September, *setembro*
October, *outubro*
November, *novembro*
December, *dezembro*
Spring, *a primavera*
Summer, *o verão* (pl. *-ões*)
Fall, *o outono*
Winter, *o inverno*

17. The gender of nouns is indicated by the article (*o, a,*). Note that nouns and masculine adjectives ending in *-m* regularly form their plural by changing *-m* to *-ns* (*homem,* man, pl. *homens; viajem,* trip, pl. *viajens; algum,* any, pl. masc. *alguns,* but fem. *alguma,* pl. *algumas*); nouns and adjectives ending in *-l* preceded by a *stressed* vowel normally form their plural by changing *-l* to *-is* (*animal, animais; papel, papéis; sol, sóis; cruel, cruéis*); but those

2. Family, Friendship, Love.

family, *a família*
husband, *o espôso, o marido*
wife, *a espôsa, a mulher*
parents, *os pais*
father, *o pai*
mother, *a mãe, a mãi*
son, *o filho*
daughter, *a filha*
brother, *o irmão*
sister, *a irmã*
uncle, *o tio*
aunt, *a tia*
nephew, *o sobrinho*
niece, *a sobrinha*
cousin, *o primo, a prima*

grandfather, *o avô*
grandmother, *a avó*
grandson, *o neto*
granddaughter, *a neta*
father-in-law, *o sogro*
mother-in-law, *a sogra*
son-in-law, *o genro*
daughter-in-law, *a nora*
brother-in-law, *o cunhado*
sister-in-law, *a cunhada*
man, *o homem*
woman, *a mulher*
child, *a criança*
boy, *o rapaz* (Port.), *o moço*
   (Brazil)

---

ending in *-l* preceded by an *unstressed* vowel normally change *-el* or
-il to *-eis* (*automóvel, automóveis; projéctil, projécteis; fácil, fáceis*).
Other important irregularities in the formation of the plural are
individually noted.

Important verbal irregularities are noted. Remember that the
conditional *always* follows the future, so that a future *farei* for a verb
fazer implies a conditional *faria*; there is never any irregularity in
the *endings* of these two tenses.

Verbs ending in *-car* change *c* to *qu* before *e* (*ficar*, to remain;
Past *fiquei* Pol. Impv. *fique*). Verbs ending in *-gar* change *g* to *gu*
before *e* (*pagar*, to pay; Past *paguei*, Pol. Impv. *pague*). Verbs ending in *-cer* change *c* to *ç* before *a* and *o* (*conhecer*, to know; Pres.
1st sg. *conheço*, Pol. Impv. *conheça*). Verbs ending in *-ear* usually
change *e* to *ei* when the stress falls upon it (*cear*, to dine; Pres. *ceio,
ceias, ceia, ceamos, ceais, ceiam;* Impv. *ceia* (familiar), *ceie* (polite).
Verbs ending in *-ir* which have *u* as the last vowel of the stem change
u to *o* when there is an *e* in the ending (*cubrir*, to cover; Pres. *cubro,
cobres, cobre, cubrimos, cubris, cobrem;* Impv. *cobre, cubra*).
Verbs ending in *-ir* which have *o* as the last vowel in the stem
change *o* to *u* when there is an *a* or an *o* in the ending (*dormir*, to
sleep; Pres. *durmo, dormes, dorme*, etc.; Impv. *dorme, durma*).
Verbs ending in *-ir* which have *e* as the last vowel in the stem change
e to *i* when there is an *a* or an *o* in the ending (*seguir*, to follow;
Pres. *sigo, segues, segue*, etc.; Impv. *segue, siga*).

girl, *a rapariga* (Port.), *a moça* (Brazil)
sir, Mr., *o senhor*[18]
Madam, Mrs., *a senhora*[18]
Miss, young lady, *a menina*[18], *a senhorinha*[18] (Brazil)
friend, *o amigo*
servant, *o criado, a criada*
to introduce, *apresentar*
to visit, *visitar*

love, *o amor*
to love, *amar, querer*
to fall in love with, *apaixonar-se por*
to marry, *casar, casar-se com*
sweetheart, *o namorado, a namorada*
kiss, *o beijo*
to kiss, *beijar*
dear, beloved, *querido*

3. Speaking Activities.

word, *a palavra*
language, *a língua*
to speak, *falar*
to say, *dizer* (Pres. *digo, dizes, diz, dizemos, dizeis, dizem;* Past *diss-e, -este, -e, -emos, -estes, -eram;* Fut. *direi;* Impv. *diz, diga;* P. p. *dito*)
to tell, relate, *contar*
to inform, *informar*
to call, *chamar*
to be called, one's name is, *chamar-se* (my name is John, *chamo-me João*)
to greet, *saudar* (Pres. *saúdo, saúdas, saúda, saudamos, saudais, saúdam;* Impv. *saúda, saúde*)
to name, *nomear*
to cry, shout, *chorar, gritar*

to listen to, *escutar* (*escutar a* only if one listens to a person)
to hear, *ouvir* (Pres. *ouço, ouves,* etc.; Pol. Impv. *ouça*)
to understand, *compreender, entender*
to mean, *significar, querer dizer* (use latter for persons)
to ask (a question), *preguntar, perguntar*
to ask for, *pedir* (Pres. *peço, pedes,* etc.; Pol. Impv. *peça;* he asked me *for* a pencil, *pediu-me um lápis*)
to answer, *responder*
to thank, *agradecer, ficar agradecido* (he thanked me for the book, *agradeceu-me o livro*)
to complain, *queixar-se, lamentar*

4. Materials.

gold, *o ouro* (*oiro*)
silver, *a prata*
iron, *o ferro*

steel, *o aço*
copper, *o cobre*
lead, *o chumbo*

18. Regularly used *with* the article, save when a title follows; do you speak Portuguese?, *o senhor fala português?*; good morning, doctor, *bons dias, senhor doutor.*

tin, *a folha*
oil, *o óleo*
gasoline, *a gasolina*
coal, *o corvão*
wood, *a madeira*
silk, *a sêda*
cotton, *o algodão*

wool, *a lã*
cloth, *o pano*
to cut, *cortar*
to dig, *cavar*
to sew, *coser*
to mend, *remendar*

5. Animals.

animal, *o animal*
horse, *o cavalo*
dog, *o cão* (pl. *cães*), *o cachorro*
cat, *o gato*
bird, *a ave*
donkey, *o burro*
mule, *a mula*
cow, *a vaca*
ox, *o boi*
pig, *o porco*
chicken, *a galinha, a franga*
hen, *a galinha*

rooster, *o galo*
sheep, *a ovelha*
goat, *a cabra*
mouse, *o rato*
snake, *a cobra, a serpente*
fly, *a môsca*
bee, *a abelha*
mosquito, *o mosquito*
spider, *a aranha*
louse, *o piolho*
flea, *a pulga*
bedbug, *o percevejo*

6. Money. Buying, Selling.

money, *o dinheiro*
coin, *a moeda*
dollar, *o dólar*
cent, *o centavo*
bank, *o banco*
check, *o cheque*
money order, *o vale postal*
to earn, to gain, to win, *ganhar*
to lose, *perder*
to spend, *gastar*
to lend, *emprestar*
to owe, *dever*
to pay, *pagar* (note 17)
to borrow, *pedir emprestado* (he borrowed $2 from me, *pediu-me dois dólares emprestados*)
to change, exchange, *cambiar, trocar* (note 17)

change, *o trôco*
to give back, *restituir*
price, *o preço*
expensive, dear, *caro*
cheap, *barato*
store, shop, *a loja, a tenda*
piece, *o pedaço*
slice, *a fatia, o pedaço*
pound, *a libra*
package, *o pacote*
basket, *o cêsto*
box, *a caixa*
bag, *a mala, a bolsa*
goods, *as mercadorias*
to go shopping, *fazer compras, ir às compras*
to sell, *vender*
to buy, *comprar*

to rent, hire, *alugar*
to be worth, *valer* (Pres. *valho*,
    vales, vale, valemos, etc.)
cost, *o custo*
to cost, *custar*
to choose, *escolher*
thief, robber, *o ladrão* (pl. *-ões*)

to steal, *roubar*
police, *a polícia*
policeman, *o polícia, o guarda
    civil* (pl. *civis*)
honest, *honesto*
dishonest, *deshonesto*

7. Eating and Drinking.

to eat, *comer*
breakfast, *o* (*primeiro*) *almôço*
to eat breakfast, *almoçar*
lunch, *o almôço, o lanche*
to eat lunch, *almoçar, lanchar*
supper, *a ceia*
to eat supper, *cear*
meal, *a comida*
dinner, *o jantar*
to eat dinner, *jantar*
dining-room, *a sala de jantar*
waiter, waitress, *o criado, a criada*
restaurant, *o restaurante*
menu, *a lista, a ementa*
bill, *a conta*
to pass, *passar*
tip, *a gratificação* (pl.-*ões*)
to drink, *beber*
water, *a água*
wine, *o vinho*
beer, *a cerveja*
coffee, *o café*
tea, *o chá*
milk, *o leite*
bottle, *a garrafa*
spoon, *a colher*
teaspoon, *a colher de chá*
knife, *a faca*
fork, *o garfo*
glass, *o copo*
cup, *a chávena, a chícara*
napkin, *o guardanapo*
salt, *o sal*

pepper, *a pimenta*
plate, dish, *o prato*
bread, *o pão* (pl. *pães*, "*loaves*")
butter, *a manteiga*
roll, *o pãozinho*
sugar, *o açúcar*
soup, *a sopa*
rice, *o arroz*
potatoes, *as batatas*
vegetables, *os legumes*
meat, *a carne*
beef, *a carne de vaca*
steak, *o bife*
chicken, *a galinha*
chop, *a costela*
veal, *a carne de vitela*
lamb, *a carne de cordeiro*
pork, *a carne de porco*
sausage, *a salsicha*
ham, *o presunto*
bacon, *o toucinho*
egg, *o ôvo*
fish, *o peixe*
fried, *frito*
cooked, *cozido*
boiled, *fervido*
roasted, roast, *assado*
baked, broiled, *assado no forno*
sauce, *o môlho*
salad, *a salada*
cheese, *o queijo*
fruit, *a fruta*
apple, *a maçã*

pear, *a pêra*
peach, *o pêssego*
grapes, *as uvas*
strawberries, *os morangos*
nuts, *as nozes*
orange, *a laranja*

lemon, *o limão* (pl. *-ões*)
cherries, *as cerejas*
juice, *o sumo*
dessert, *a sobremesa*
pastry, *os pastéis*

8. Hygiene and Attire.

bath, *o banho*
to bathe, *tomar banho*
shower, *o chuveiro, o banho de chuva*
to wash, *lavar*
to shave, *barbear-se, fazer a barba*
barber, *o barbeiro*
mirror, *o espelho*
soap, *o sabão*
razor, *a navalha de barba*
safety-razor, *o aparelho de barbear*
towel, *a toalha*
comb, *o pente*
brush, *a escôva*
scissors, *a tesoura (tesoira)*
to wear, *usar*
to take off, *tirar*
to change, *mudar*
to put on, *vestir* (see n. 17), *pôr* (see p. 303) ; he put on *his* hat, *êle pôs o chapéu;* he put on *his* coat, *êle vestiu o casaco;* he put on *his* gloves, *êle calçou as luvas*
clothes, *a roupa*
hat, *o chapéu*
suit, *o fato*
coat, *o casaco*

vest, *o colête*
pants, *as calças*
underwear, *a roupa de baixo*
gloves, *as luvas*
socks, *as peúgas, as meias*
stockings, *as meias*
shirt, *a camisa*
collar, *o colarinho*
overcoat, *o sobretudo*
raincoat, *a gabardina*
pocket, *a algibeira, o bôlso*
handkerchief, *o lenço*
button, *o botão* (pl. *-ões*)
shoes, *os sapatos*
boot, *a bota*
purse, *a bôlsa*
pocket-book, *a carteira*
tie, *a gravata*
pin, *o alfinete*
tie-pin, *alfinete de gravata*
safety-pin, *alfinete de dama*
needle, *a agulha*
umbrella, *o guarda-chuva*
watch, *o relógio (de algibeira)*
chain, *a cadeia*
ring, *o anel*
eyeglasses, *as lunetas, os óculos*
slippers, *as chinelas*
dressing-gown, bath-robe, *o chambre*

9. Parts of the Body.

head, *a cabeça*
forehead, *a testa*

face, *a cara*
mouth, *a bôca*

hair, *o cabelo*
eye, *o ôlho*
ear, *a orelha*
tooth, *o dente*
lip, *o lábio*
nose, *o nariz*
tongue, *a língua*
chin, *o queixo*
cheek, *as faces*
beard, *a barba*
mustache, *o bigode*
neck, *o pescoço*
throat, *a garganta*
arm, *o braço*
hand, *a mão* (pl. *as mãos*)
elbow, *o cotovêlo*

wrist, *o pulso*
finger, *o dedo*
nail, *a unha*
shoulder, *o ombro*
leg, *a perna*
foot, *o pé*
knee, *o joelho*
back, *as costas*
chest, *o peito*
ankle, *o tornozelo*
body, *o corpo*
blood. *o sangue*
skin. *a pele*
heart. *o coração* (pl. *-ões*)
stomach. *o estômago*
bone, *o osso*

10. *Medical.*

doctor, *o médico, o doutor*
drug-store, *a loja de droguista*
hospital, *o hospital*
medicine, *a medicina*
pill, *a pílula*
prescription, *a receita*
bandage, *a atadura*
nurse, *o enfermeiro, a enfermeira*
ill, *doente*
illness, *a doença*
fever, *a febre*

swollen, *inchado*
wound, *a ferida*
wounded, *ferido*
head-ache, *a dor de cabeça*
tooth-ache, *a dor de dentes*
cough, *a tosse*
to cough, *tossir*
lame, *coxo*
burn, *a queimadura*
pain, *a dor*
poison, *o veneno*

11. *Military.*

war, *a guerra*
peace, *a paz*
ally, *o aliado*
enemy, *o inimigo*
army, *o exército*
danger, *o perigo*
dangerous, *perigoso*
to win, *ganhar*
to surround, *cercar, rodear*
to arrest, *prender*

to escape, *escapar*
to run away, *fugir* (Pres. *fujo.
foges*, etc.; see note 17; Impv.
foge. fuja)
to lead, *conduzir* (3rd sg. Pres.
and Fam. Impv. *conduz*)
to follow, *seguir* (see note 17)
to surrender, *render-se*
to retreat, *retirar-se*
to bomb, to shell, *bombardear*

to kill, *matar*
fear, *o mêdo*
prison, *a prisão* (pl. *-ões*)
prisoner, *o prisioneiro*
to take prisoner, *fazer prisioneiro*
to capture, *capturar* (*caturar*)
help, aid, *o auxílio*
comrade, buddy, *o camarada*
battle, *a batalha*
to fight, *combater*
soldier, private, *o soldado*
corporal, *o cabo*
sergeant, *o sargento*
lieutenant, *o tenente*
captain, *o capitão* (pl. *-ães*)
major, *o major*
colonel, *o coronel*
general, *o general*
officer, *o oficial*
company, *a companhia*
battalion, *o batalhão* (pl. *-ões*)
regiment, *o regimento*
brigade, *a brigada*
division, *a divisão* (pl. *-ões*)
troops, *as tropas*
reenforcements, *os refôrços*
fortress, *a fortaleza, o forte*
sentinel, *a sentinela*
guard, *a guarda*
to stand guard, to do sentry duty, *guardar*
to be on duty, *estar de serviço*
sign-post, *a taboleta*
navy, *a marinha*
sailor, *o marinheiro*
marine, *o soldado de marinha*
warship, *o navio de guerra*
cruiser, *o cruzador*
destroyer, *o torpedeiro, o destró-*

ier, o contra-torpedeiro
convoy, *o combóio*
escort, *a escolta*
weapon, *a arma*
rifle, *a espingarda, o fuzil* (pl. *-is*)
machine-gun, *a metralhadora*
cannon, *o canhão* (pl. *-ões*)
ammunition, *as munições*
supplies, *os abastecimentos*
cartridge, *o cartucho*
belt, *o cinturão* (pl. *-ões*)
knapsack, *a mochila*
tent, *a tenda*
camp, *o arraial* (pl. *-ais*)
map, *o mapa*
rope, *a corda*
flag, *a bandeira*
helmet, *o capacete*
bayonet, *a baioneta*
uniform, *o uniforme*
airplane, *o avião* (pl. *-ões*)
bombing-plane, *o avião bombardeiro* (*de bombardeio*)
pursuit-plane, *o avião de caça*
shell, *a granada*
bomb, *a bomba*
truck, *o camião* (pl. *-ões*)
tank, *o tanque*
to load, *carregar* (note 17)
to shoot, to fire, *atirar, disparar*
to shoot (military execution), *fuzilar, executar*
fire!, *fogo!*
attention!, *sentido!*
forward!, *avante!, em frente!*
halt!, *alto!*
air-raid shelter, *o abrigo*
spy, *o espião* (pl. *-ões*)

12. *Travel.*

customs, *a alfândega*
passport, *o passaporte*

ship, *o navio*
stateroom, *o camarote*

berth, *o beliche*
to travel, *viajar*
trip, voyage, *a viagem*
to leave, *partir (de)*, *sair de*
to arrive, *chegar* (note 17)
to ride (conveyance), *passear de*
to ride, *andar*
railroad, *o caminho de ferro* (Pt.).
  a estrada de ferro (Br.)
station, *a estação* (pl. *-ões*)
track, *o carril*, *a calha*, *o trilho*
platform, *a plataforma*
steamer, *o vapor*
train, *o combóio* (Pt.), *o trem*
  (Br.)
ticket, *o bilhete*
compartment, *o compartimento*

all aboard!, *partida!*
dining-car, *o vagão-restaurante*
sleeper, *o vagão-leito*
car, coach, *o carro*, *o coche*
trunk, *a mala*, *o baú*
valise, *a mala de mão*
baggage, *a bagagem*
porter, *o porteiro*
bus, *o ómnibus*
street-car, *o carro elé(c)trico*
  (Pt.), *o bonde* (Br.)
automobile, *o automóvel* (note 17)
taxi, *o taxis (taxi)*
driver, *o motorista*, *o conductor*,
  o chofer
to drive (car), *guiar*, *conduzir*[19]

13. Reading and Writing.

to read, *ler* (Pres. *leio, lês, lê,*
  lêmos, ledes, lêem; Past *li,*
  lêste, leu, lêmos, lestes, leram;
  Impv. *lê, leia*)
newspaper, *o jornal* (pl. *-ais*)
magazine, *a revista*
to write, *escrever* (P. p. *escrito*)
to translate, *traduzir*[19]
pencil, *o lápis* (pl. *os lápis*)
ink, *a tinta*
pen, *a pena*
fountain-pen, *a caneta-tinteiro*
paper, *o papel*

envelope, *o sobrescrito*
letter, *a carta*
post-office, *o correio*
stamp, *o sêlo*, *a estampilha (de*
  correio)
letter-box, *a caixa do correio*
to mail, *mandar pelo correio*
address, *a direcção (direção)*, *o*
  endereço
post-card, *o bilhete postal*
book, *o livro*
chalk, *o giz*
black-board, *a pedra*

14. Amusements.

to smoke, *fumar*
cigar, *o charuto*
cigarette, *o cigarro*
tobacco, *o tabaco*, *o fumo* (Br.)

match, *o fósforo*
give me a light, *dê-me lume*
theatre, *o teatro*
movies, *o cinema*

19. Verbs ending in *-uzir* drop the *-e* in the 3rd sg. of the present and the familiar imperative: *conduz, traduz.*

dance, *a dança, o baile*
to dance, *dançar*
to have a good time, *divertir-se*
ticket, *o bilhete*
pleasure, *o prazer*
to play (music), *tocar* (n. 17)
to sing, *cantar*
song, *a canção* (pl. *-ões*)
to play (games), *jogar* (n. 17)

to take a walk, *dar um passeio*
ball, *a bola*
beach, *a praia*
to swim, *nadar*
game, *o jogo*
sand, *a areia*
refreshment, *o refrêsco*
saloon, *o bar, a taberna*
picnic, *o piquenique*

15. Town and Country.

place, spot, *o sítio, o lugar*
city, *a cidade*
intersection, *o encruzamento*
street, *a rua*
sidewalk, *o passeio*
block, *a quadra, o quarteirão*
  (pl. *-ões*)
harbor, *o pôrto*
school, *a escola*
church, *a igreja*
building, *o edifício*
cathedral, *a catedral*
corner, *a esquina*
hotel, *o hotel*
office, *o escritório*
river, *o rio*

bridge, *a ponte*
country, *o campo*
village, *a aldeia*
road, *a estrada, o caminho*
mountain, *a montanha*
grass, *a erva*
yard, *o quintal*
hill, *a colina, o monte*
lake, *o lago*
forest, wood, *o bosque*
field, *o campo*
flower, *a flor*
tree, *a árvore*
rock, stone, *a pedra*
jungle, *a selva, o sertão*

16. House.

to close, *fechar*
to open, *abrir* (P. p. *aberto*)
door, *a porta*
key, *a chave*
to go in, *entrar* (*em*)
to go out, *sair* (*de*) ; Pres. *saio,*
  sais, sai, saímos, saís, saem;
  Pol. Impv. *saia*
house, *a casa*
cottage, *a casa de campo*
hut, *a cabana*
to live (in), *morar* (*em*)

staircase, *a escadaria*
to go up, *subir*
to go down, *descer* (note 17)
room, *o quarto*
toilet, *o retrete, a latrina*
kitchen, *a cozinha*
table, *a mesa*
chair, *a cadeira*
to sit down, *sentar-se*
to stand, *estar de pé*
wall, *a parede, o muro*
bedroom, *o quarto de cama*

lamp, *o candeeiro* (*candeiro*), *a lâmpada*
candle, *a vela*
closet, *o compartimento*
window, *a janela*
to rest, *descansar*
bed, *a cama*
sheet, *o lençol* (pl. *-óis*)
pillow, *a almofada*

cover, blanket, *o cobertor, a coberta*
to go to bed, *deitar-se*
mattress, *o colchão* (pl. *-ões*)
to go to sleep, *adormecer* (n. 17)
to sleep, *dormir* (n. 17)
to wake up, *despertar*
to get up, *levantar-se*
clock, *o relógio* (*de parede*)
alarm-clock, *o despertador*

17. Miscellaneous Nouns.

people, *a gente* (always singular); how many people are coming? *quantas pessoas vêm?*
thing, *a cousa* (*coisa*)
name, *o nome*; (family name, *o apelido*)

luck, *a sorte*
bad luck, *a pouca* (*má*) *sorte*
number, *o número*
life, *a vida*
death, *a morte*
work, *o trabalho*

18. Verbs — Coming and Going.

to come, *vir* (Pres. *venho, vens, vem, vimos, vindes, vêm*; Impf. *vinha*; Past *vim, vieste, veio, viemos, viestes, vieram*; Fut. *virei*; Impv. *vem, venha*; P. p. *vindo*)
to go, *ir* (Pres. *vou, vais, vai, vamos, ides, vão*; Impf. *ia*; Past *fui, foste, foi, fomos, fostes, foram*; Impv. *vai, vá*)
to be going to, *ir* plus infinitive (I am going to dine, *vou jantar*)
to run, *correr*

to walk, *andar*
to go away, *ir-se*
to fall, *cair* (Pres. *caio, cais, cai, caímos, caís, caem*; Impf. *caía*; Past *caí*; Impv. *cai, caia*; P. p. *caído*)
to stay, remain, *ficar* (note 17)
to follow, *seguir* (note 17; *u* falls out before *a* and *o*; Pres. *sigo, segues*, etc.; Pol. Impv. *siga*)
to return, to come back, *voltar*
to arrive, *chegar* (note 17)
to go back, *regressar, voltar*

19. Verbs — Looking.

to see, *ver* (Pres. *vejo, vês, vê, vemos, vêdes, vêem*; Impf. *via*; Past *vi*; Fut. *verei*; Impv. *vê, veja*; P. p. *visto*)

to look at, *olhar*
to look for, *procurar, buscar* (n.17)
to look, seem, *parecer* (note 17)

to recognize, *reconhecer* (note 17)

to laugh, *rir* (Pres. *rio, ris, ri, rimos, rides, riem;* Impv. *ri, ria;* P. p. *rido*)

to smile, *sorrir-se* (like *rir*)

to laugh at, make fun of, *rir de, rir-se de*

to take for, *confundir por*

20. *Verbs — Mental.*

to make a mistake, *enganar-se*

to hope, *esperar*

to wait for, *esperar*

to think (of), *pensar (em)*; use *pensar de* for "to have an opinion about"; I am thinking of him, *eu penso nêle*; what do you think of him?, *que pensa o senhor dêle?*

to believe, *acreditar, crer* (Pres. *creio, crês, crê, cremos, credes, crêem;* Impf. *cria;* Past *cri, crêste, creu, cremos, crêstes, creram;* Impv. *crê, creia*)

to like, *gostar de* (I like this book, *gosto dêste livro*)

to wish, *desejar*

to need, *necessitar*

to know (a person), to meet (socially), *conhecer* (note 17)

to know (a fact), *saber* (Pres. *sei, sabes, sabe,* etc.; Past *soube, soubeste, soube,* etc.; Impv.

sabe, saiba)

to know how, *saber* plus infinitive (I know how to read, *sei ler*)

to want, *querer* (Pres. 3rd sg. *quer;* Past *quis, quiseste, quis,* etc.; Impv. *quer, queira*)

to remember, *lembrar-se de*

to forget, *esquecer de* (note 17)

to permit, allow, *permitir*

to promise, *prometer*

to understand, *entender, compreender*

to learn, *aprender*

to feel like, *ter vontade de* (I feel like eating, *eu tenho vontade de comer*)

to fear, be afraid, *temer, recear* (note 17)

to be right, *ter razão*

to be wrong, *não ter razão, estar enganado, enganar-se*

to find out, *descobrir* (no. 17)

to forbid, *proïbir*[20]

21. *Verbs — Miscellaneous.*

to live, *viver*

to die, *morrer* (P. p. *morto,* with *ser* or *estar, morrido* with *ter;* he is dead, *êle está morto;* he died, *êle tem morrido*)

to work, *trabalhar*

to give, *dar* (Pres. *dou, dás, dá, damos, dais, dão;* Past *dei, deste, deu,* etc.; Impv. *dá, dê*)

to take, *tomar*

to begin, *começar, principiar* (to begin doing, *começar a fazer*)

20. The diaeresis may be used to keep in two separate syllables two *unstressed* vowels; *proïbir = pro i bir;* if one of the two contiguous vowels is *stressed,* it takes the *acute* accent (*saúdo*).

to finish, *terminar, acabar*

to have just, *acabar de* (I have just written, *acabo de escrever*)

to continue, keep on, *continuar* (I kept on writing, *continuei a escrever* or *continuei escrevendo*)

to help, *ajudar*

to lose, *perder* (Pres. *perco, perdes*, etc.; Impv. *perde, perca*)

to find, to meet (casually), *encontrar*

to try to, *procurar*

to leave (a thing), *deixar* (use *sair de* for a place; *sair* like *cair*, p. 301)

to show, *mostrar*

to hold, *conter* (like *ter*)

to do, to make, *fazer* (Pres. *faço, fazes, faz, fazemos, fazeis, fazem*, Past *fiz, fizeste, fêz, fizemos, fizestes, fizeram*; Fut. *farei*; Impv. *faz, faça*, P. p. *feito*)

to be able, can, *poder* (Pres. *posso, podes*, etc.; Past *pude, pudeste, pôde, pudemos*, etc.; Impv. *pode, possa*)

to put, *pôr* (Pres. *ponho, pões, põe, pomos, pondes, põem*; Impf. *punha;* Past *pus, puseste, pôs, pusemos, pusestes, puseram*; Impv. *põe, ponha;* P. p. *pôsto*)

to carry, *levar*

to bring, *trazer* (Pres. *trago, trazes, traz, trazemos*, etc.; Fut. *trarei*; Past *trouxe, trouxeste, trouxe*, etc.; Impv. *traz, traga*)

to stop (self), *parar*; (another), *fazer parar*

to cover, *cobrir* (n. 17; P. p. *coberto*)

to get, obtain, *obter* (like *ter*)

to get, become, *tornar-se*

to hide, *esconder*

to break, *quebrar*

to hurry, *apressar-se* (*a* before an infinitive)

to deliver, *entregar* (note 17)

to catch, *apanhar*

to belong, *pertencer* (note 17)

to have something done, *mandar fazer* (he had a letter written, *mandou escrever uma carta*)

to lay, *pôr, colocar* (n. 17)

to send, *mandar, enviar*

to accept, *aceitar*

to refuse, *recusar*

22. *Adjectives.*

small, *pequeno*

large, big, great, *grande* (larger, *maior*, largest, *o maior*)

high, tall, *alto*

long, *comprido*

short (opp. of high), low (person) *baixo*

short (opp. of long), *curto*

heavy, *pesado*

light (weight), *leve*

wide, *largo*

narrow, *estreito*

clean, *limpo*

dirty, *sujo*

cool, *fresco*

cold, *frio*

warm, *tépido*

hot, *quente*

damp, *úmido*

wet, *molhado*

dry, *sêco*

full, *cheio*

empty, *vazio*
dark, *moreno, escuro*
light, bright, clear, *límpido*
fat, *gordo*
thick, *grosso, espêsso*
thin, *magro, delgado*
round, *redondo*
square, *quadrado*
flat, *plano*
deep, *fundo*
soft, *mole*
hard, *duro*
quick, *ligeiro*
slow, *vagaroso*
ordinary, *ordinário*
comfortable, *cómodo, confortável* (note 17)
uncomfortable, *inconfortável*
near, *próximo, cercante*
distant, *distante*
right, *direito*
left, *esquerdo*
poor, *pobre*
rich, *rico*
beautiful, *belo, formoso*
pretty, *lindo*
ugly, *feio*
sweet, *doce*
bitter, *amargo*
sour, *ácido*
salt, *salgado*
young, new, *novo*
old, *velho, antigo*
good, *bom* (fem. *boa*)
better, *melhor*
best, *o melhor*
bad, *mau* (fem. *má*)
worse, *pior*
worst, *o pior*
fine, "regular", *ótimo, bom*
first, *primeiro*
last, *último*
strong, *forte*
weak, *fraco*

tired, *cansado*
alone, *só* (fem. *só*)
same, *mesmo*
easy, *fácil* (pl. *-eis*)
hard, difficult, *difícil* (pl. *-eis*)
happy, glad, *feliz*
sad, *triste*
free, *livre*
silly, *simples, pateta, tolo, bobo*
crazy, *louco, doido*
drunk, *embriagado*
polite, *cortês* (fem. same)
rude, *rude, grosseiro*
pleasant, *agradável* (pl. *-eis*)
unpleasant, *desagradável*
lonesome, *solitário*
true, *verdadeiro*
false, *falso*
foreign, *estrangeiro*
friendly, *amigavel, amistoso, amigo*
hostile, *hostil*
lucky, *feliz*
unlucky, *infeliz*
charming, *encantador* (fem. *-a*, pl. *-es, -as*)
afraid, *medroso*
ready, *pronto*
hungry, *esfomeado* (to be—, *ter fome*)
thirsty, *sequioso, sedento* (to be—, *ter sêde*)
right (to be), *ter razão*
wrong (to be), *não ter razão, estar enganado*
funny, *cómico*
possible, *possível* (pl. *-eis*)
impossible, *impossível*
brave, *corajoso*
cowardly, *cobarde*
quiet, *quieto, sossegado*
noisy, *ruidoso*
living, *vivo*
dead, *morto*

23. *Colors*.

white, *branco*
black, *prêto*
red, *vermelho*
green, *verde*
blue, *azul* (pl. *azuis*)

yellow, *amarelo*
gray, *cinzento*
brown, *castanho*
pink, *côr de rosa*
purple, *roxo*

24. *Nationalities*.[21]

American, *americano*
English, *inglês*
French, *francês*
German, *alemão* (fem. *alemã*;
  mas. pl. *alemães*; fem. pl.
  alemãs)
Spanish, *espanhol* (*espanhola*,
  espanhóis, *espanholas*)
Russian, *russo*
Italian, *italiano*
Japanese, *japonês*
Chinese, *chinês*
Dutch, *neerlandês*, *holandês*
Norwegian, *noruego*
Swedish, *sueco*
Finnish, *finlandês*
Belgian, *belga* (fem. same; pl.
  belgas)
Polish, *polonês*, *polaco*
Danish, *dinamarquês*
Swiss, *suisso* (*suíço*)
Portuguese, *português*
Yugoslav, *iùgoslavo*

Bulgarian, *búlgaro*
Czech, *checo-eslovaco*
Greek, *grego*
Turkish, *turco*
Roumanian, *rumeno*
Hungarian, *hûngaro*
Austrian, *austríaco*
Malay, *malaio*
Persian, *persa*
Arabian, Arab, Arabic, *árabe*
Jewish, Hebrew, *hebreu* (fem.
  hebreia), *judeu* (fem. *judia*)
Australian, *australiano*
African, *africano*
Canadian, *canadiano*
Mexican, *mexicano*
Cuban, *cubano*
Brazilian, *brasileiro*
Argentinian, *argentino*
Porto Rican, *portorriquenho*
Chilean, *chileno*
Peruvian, *peruano*

21. Adjectives of nationality ending in a consonant add *-a* (*-ês* loses the accent) in the feminine: *inglês*, fem. *inglesa*, masc. plur. *ingleses*, fem. plur. *inglesas*. No capital is used, unless "Englishman" is meant. For names of languages, use no capital, and use the definite article except after *em* (in), and, usually, *falar* (to speak), *entender* (to understand), *traduzir* (to translate): *o português é uma língua fácil; eu falo português; êle responde em português*.

25. *Adverbs and Adverbial Expressions.*

today, *hoje*
yesterday, *ontem*
tomorrow, *amanhã*
day before yesterday, *ante-ontem*
day after tomorrow, *depois de amanhã*
tonight, *esta noite*
last night, *a noite passada*
this morning, *esta manhã*
in the morning, *de manhã*
in the afternoon (evening), *de tarde*
in the night, *de noite*
this afternoon, *esta tarde*
tomorrow morning, *amanhã de manhã*
tomorrow afternoon, *amanhã à tarde*
tomorrow night, *amanhã à noite*
early, *cêdo*
late, *tarde*
already, *já*
no longer, *já não* (he is no longer here, *êle já não está aqui*)
yet, still, *ainda*
not yet, *ainda não*
now, *agora*
then, *então*
afterwards, *depois*
never, *nunca, jamais* (he never comes, *nunca vem* or *não vem nunca*)
always, *sempre*
forever, *para sempre*
soon, *em breve*
only, *sòmente, só*
often, *muitas vezes, a miúdo*
usually, *usualmente*
fast, *depressa*
slowly, *vagarosamente*
here, *aqui*

there, *acolá, lá*
over (down) there, *lá-baixo*
near by, *perto*
far away, *longe*
up (stairs), *para cima, em cima*
down (stairs), *em baixo*
ahead, in front, *adiante*
behind, in back, *atrás*
forward, *para diante, em diante*
back, backward, *atrás, para trás*
outside, *fóra, para fóra*
inside, *dentro*
opposite, in front, *oposto, em frente*
here and there, *aqui e acolá*
everywhere, *em toda a parte*
where, *onde*
also, too, *também*
yes, *sim*
no, not, *não*
very, much, *muito*
little, not much, *pouco*
well, *bem*
badly, *mal*
better, *melhor*
worse, *pior*
more, *mais*
less, *menos*
so, *tão*
as - as, *tão - quanto (como)*
as much - as, *tanto - como*
as many - as, *tantos - como*
how much?, *quanto?*
how many?, *quantos?*
how?, *como?*
too much, *demasiado*
too many, *demasiados*
so much, *tanto*
so many, *tantos*
as, like, *como*
besides, *além disso*

finally, in short, *finalmente, em fim, por fim*
almost, *quási (quáse)*
gladly, *de boa vontade*
certainly, of course, *certamente*
unfortunately, *infelizmente*
at once, *de repente, já*
at all, *de todo, absolutamente*
hardly, *apenas*
aloud, *em voz alta*
suddenly, *repentinamente, de repente*
about, *àcêrca de, cêrca de*
perhaps, maybe, *talvez, acaso*

a little, *um pouco*
again, *outra vez*
really, truly, *realmente*
together, *juntos*
at least, *pelo menos*
again and again, *a miúdo, repetidas vezes*
occasionally, *casualmente*
from time to time, *de quando em quando, de vez em quando*
therefore, *portanto*
for lack of, *por falta de*
long ago, *há muito tempo*
entirely, altogether, *inteiramente*

26. Conjunctions.

and, *e*
but, *mas*
or, *ou*
why?, *porque? (porquê?* if not followed by clause)
why!, *pois!*
because, *porque*
that, *que*
where, *onde*
than, *que, de que, de* (before numerals)
since, *pois que, desde*
so that, *de maneira que*
for, *pois*
if, provided that, *se*[22]

while, as long as, *enquanto*[22]
as soon as, *logo que, assim que*[22]
when, *quando*[22]
unless, *a menos que, a não ser que*[23]
provided that, *contanto que, desde que*[23]
without, *sem que*[23]
in order that, *para que,*[23] *para*[24]
until, *até que,*[23] *até*[24]
although, *ainda que,*[23] *a pesar de*[24]
before, *antes de*[24]
after, *depois de*[24]

22. These call for the future subjunctive if future time is implied: if he doesn't come, I won't go, *se êle não vier eu não irei;* as long as he stays here, I shall stay, *enquanto êle aqui estiver, também estarei;* I shall see him when he comes, *hei-de vê-lo quando êle vier.*

23. These normally take the subjunctive: although he may do it, I shall not be angry, *ainda que o faça, não ficarei zangado;* unless he comes, I shall not go, *a não ser que êle venha eu não irei;* I did it so that he might read the letter, *fi-lo para que êle pudesse ler a carta;* he came without my seeing him, *êle veio sem que eu o tivesse visto.*

24. These are *prepositions* in Pt., and call for the personalized infinitive: I shall see him before they come, *hei-de vê-lo antes de êles*

27. *Indefinite Pronouns and Adjectives.*

such,*tal* (pl. *tais*)
all kinds of, *toda a qualidade de*
everything, *tudo*
everyone, *todo o mundo, toda a gente, todos*
something, *qualquer coisa*
someone, *alguém*
nothing, *nada*[25]
no one, *ninguém*[25]
no (adj.), *nenhum*[25]
neither - nor, *nem - nem*[25]
several, *vários*

each, every, *cada, todo*
all, *todo, todos*
(an) other, *outro*
much, lots of, *muito*
few, *poucos, uns* (fem. *umas*)
many, *muitos*
little (not much), *pouco*
both, *ambos*
enough, *bastante, suficiente*
some, *algum* (fem. *alguma*, pl. *alguns, algumas*)

28. *Prepositions.*

of, from, *de* (contracts with articles; see p. 274, n. 3)
out of, *fóra de*
to, at, *a* (contracts with articles; see p. 274; must be used with a noun indirect object: I give John the book, *dou o livro a João*)
with, *com*
in, *em* (p. 274)
without, *sem*
on, *sobre, em*
over, *em cima de*
above, *acima de*
for, *por* (for the sake of, on account of, in exchange for; p. 274); *para* (purpose, destination)

until, up to, *até*
since, *desde*
toward, *para*
between, among, *entre*
near, *perto de*
far from, *longe de*
before, *antes de*
by, *por, de* (*por* if action is physical, *de* if mental)
after, *depois de*
opposite, in front of, *em frente de*
in back of, behind, *atrás de*
under (neath), *debaixo de*
instead of, *em vez de, em lugar de*
beside, *além de*
at the house of, *em casa de*
through, *através, por*

chegarem; I saw him before they came, *ví-o antes de êles virem*; although he did it, I wasn't angry, *a pesar de êle o fazer, não fiquei zangado*; I saw him after we came, *ví-o depois de chegarmos*. Note cases where both subjunctive and infinitive may be used: I shall wait until he comes, *esperarei até que êle venha* or *esperarei até êle vir*.

25. If these are used *after* the verb, use *não* before the verb: I see nothing, *nada vejo* or *não vejo nada*.

by means of, *por meio de*

against, *contra*

across, *através*

on the other side of, *no outro lado de*

in spite of, *a pesar de*

about, *àcêrca de, cêrca de*

around, *à (em) volta de, ao redor de*

during, *durante*

because of, on account of, *por causa de*

29. Special Expressions and Idioms.

good morning, *bom dia, bons dias*

good afternoon (evening), *boa tarde*

good night, *boa noite, boas noites*

good-bye, *adeus*

I'll see you later, *até logo, até mais tarde*

I'll see you tomorrow, *até amanhã*

I'll see you tonight, *até esta noite*

just now, *agora mesmo*

hello, *alô* (on telephone, *alô, está lá;* the latter especially in Portugal)

how are you?, *como está?*

I'm well, *bem, estou bem*

I'm (much) better, *estou (muito) melhor*

how goes it?, *como vai tudo?*

what time is it?, *que horas são?*

it's six o'clock, *são seis horas*

at six o'clock, *às seis horas*

at about six, *perto das seis*

at half past six, *às seis e meia*

at a quarter to (past) six, *a um quarto para as (depois das) seis*

at ten minutes to (past) six, *a dez minutos para as (depois das) seis*

last year, *o ano passado*

next year, *o ano que vem*

every day, *todos os dias*

the whole day, *o dia inteiro*

please, *faz o obséquio, por favor, tenha a bondade*

tell me, *diga-me*

bring me, *traga-me*

show me, *mostre-me*

thank you, *obrigado, muito agradecido*

don't mention it, *não por isso*

will you give me?, *quer me dar?*

pardon me, *perdão*

it doesn't matter, *não faz diferença*

never mind, *não se incomode*

I'm sorry, *eu sinto muito, eu lamento muito*

I can't help, *não posso deixar de* (infinitive)
it's nothing, *é nada*
what a pity!, too bad!, *que lástima!, que pena!*
it's too bad, *é pena*
I'm glad, *estou contente* (*satisfeito*)
I have to, *eu tenho que, eu tenho de*
I'm agreeable, *estou de acôrdo*
where is (are)?, *onde está* (*estão*)?
where are you going?, *onde é que vai?*
here is (are), *eis aqui* (here it is, *ei-lo*)
there is (are), *há* (pointing out, *eis ali*)
which way?, *para que lado?*
this (that) way (direction), *por aqui* (*ali*)
this way (fashion), *desta maneira*
come with me, *venha comigo*
what can I do for you?, *o que posso fazer para o senhor?*
what is it?, *o que é?*
what is the matter?, *que é isso?, que há?*
what is the matter with you?, *que tem o senhor?*
what do you want?, *o que quer o senhor?*
what are you talking about?, *em que está falando?, que está dizendo?*
what does that mean?, *o que quer dizer isso?*
how much is it?, *quanto custa?*
anything else?, *mais alguma coisa?*
nothing else, *nada mais*
do you speak Portuguese?, *fala o senhor português?*
a little, *um pouco*
how do you say - in Portuguese?, *como se diz - em português?*
do you understand?, *compreende o senhor?*
I don't understand, *eu não compreendo*
do you know?, *sabe o senhor?*
I don't know, *eu não sei*
I can't, *eu não posso*
what do you call this in Portuguese?, *como se chama isto em portu-
     guês?*
I am an American, *sou norteamericano*
I'm (very) hungry, *tenho* (*muita*) *fome*
I'm (very) thirsty, *tenho* (*muita*) *sêde*
I'm (very) sleepy, *tenho* (*muito*) *sono*
I'm (very) warm, *tenho* (*muito*) *calor*
I'm (very) cold, *tenho* (*muito*) *frio*
it's (very) warm, *faz* (*muito*) *calor*
it's (very) cold, *faz* (*muito*) *frio*

it's windy, *faz vento, está ventando*
it's sunny, *faz sol, o sol brilha*
it's fine (bad) weather, *está* (or *faz*) *bom* (*mau*) *tempo*
it's forbidden, *é proïbido* (no smoking, *é proïbido fumar*)
luckily, fortunately, *afortunadamente*
unfortunately, *infortunadamente*
is it not so?, *não é verdade?, não é assim?* (use where English repeats
     the question: he is here, *is he not?*, you wrote, *didn't you?*)
not at all, *de nenhuma sorte, por nenhum modo*
how old are you?, *que idade tem?*
I'm 30 years old, *eu tenho trinta anos*
how long have you been here?, *há quanto tempo está o senhor aqui?*
how long have you been waiting?, *há quanto tempo espera o senhor?*
as soon as possible, *tão pronto quanto possível, logo que seja possível*
come here!, *venha aqui!, venha cá!*
look!, *veja!*
look out!, careful!, *cautela!, cuidado!*
come in!, *entre!, venha para dentro!*
to the right, *à direita*
to the left, *à esquerda*
straight ahead, *em frente*
just a second!, *um momento!*
what do you mean?, *que quer dizer?*
as you please, *como quizer*
speak (more) slowly, *faça favor de falar* (*mais*) *devagar*
listen!, *oiça!* (*ouça!*)
look here!, say!, *olhe!*
gangway!, by your leave!, *atenção!, com sua licença!*
for Heaven's sake!, *credo!*
darn it!, *oh, diabo!*
darn the luck!, *que má sorte!*
to your health!, *à sua saúde!*
I should like to —, *eu quisera* (*eu desejaria*)
as quickly as possible, *o mais depressa possível*
stop!, *pare!*
hurry!, *depressa!*
keep to the right (left), *siga pela direita* (*esquerda*)
entrance, *entrada*
exit, *saída*

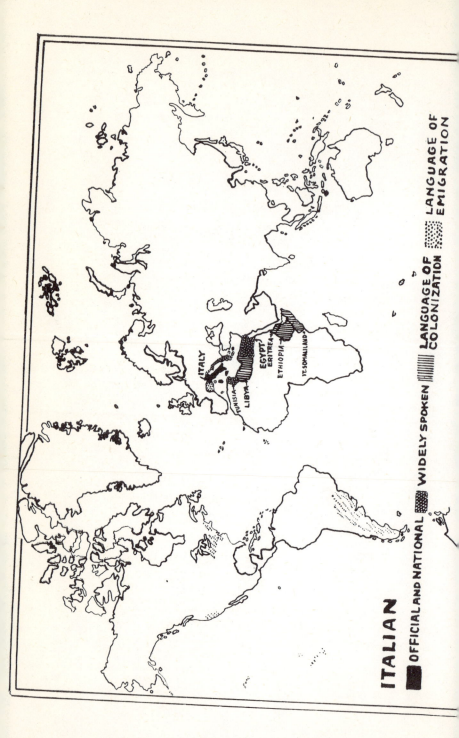

ITALIAN

OFFICIAL AND NATIONAL ■ WIDELY SPOKEN ▥ LANGUAGE OF COLONIZATION ░ LANGUAGE OF EMIGRATION ░

CHAPTER IX

ITALIAN

SPEAKERS AND LOCATION

(All population figures are approximate)

Europe — Italy (45,000,000); Switzerland (southern section: about 300,000); also spoken in Corsica and in extreme southeastern section of France, up to, but not including, Nice; widely spoken and understood, as a secondary and cultural language, along the eastern Adriatic coast (Yugoslavia, Albania, Greece), in Malta, and in the Dodecanese Islands.

Africa — colonial language of Libya (1,000,000); of Eritrea, Italian Somaliland, and, to a more limited extent, of Ethiopia (total native populations about 12,000,000); widely spoken and understood, as a secondary and cultural language, in Tunisia, Egypt, and, generally, along the European, African and Asiatic Mediterranean coast.

Western Hemisphere — spoken by large Italian immigrant groups in United States, Argentina, Brazil and Chile, amounting, with their descendants, to a total of perhaps 10,000,000.

ALPHABET AND SOUNDS

a, b, c, d, e, f, g, h, i, l, m, n, o, p, q, r, s, t, u, v, z. (The symbol j is very occasionally used with the value of y, and is generally replaced by i; the symbols k, w, x, y occur only in foreign words).

Vowel sounds: Italian vowels have, whether stressed or unstressed, equal length.

a: = f*a*ther (p*a*dre, donn*a*)

e: = m*e*t (f*e*rro, b*e*ne); or = initial part of *a* in Eng. g*a*te (fr*e*ddo, ben*e*)[1]

i: = mach*i*ne (b*i*rra)

o: = c*u*p (f*o*rte, d*o*nna); or = initial part of *o* in Eng. g*o* (m*o*ndo) [1]

u: = f*oo*d (l*u*na)

Consonant sounds: b, d, f, l, m, n, p, q, s, t, v, approximately as in English.

c: before a, o, u or consonant, and ch before e, i = *c*at (*c*aro, *c*redo, *ch*i).

c: before e, i = *ch*urch (in the groups cia, cie, cio, ciu, the i is almost silent: *ci*ascuno, pronounced *cha*skuno).

g: before a, o, u or consonant, and gh before e, i = *g*o (*g*usto, là*g*rima, lar*ghi*);

g: before e, i = *g*in (in the groups gia, gie, gio, giu, the i is almost silent: *gi*à, pronounced *ja*).

gn: = o*n*ion (a*gn*ello, pronounced a*nny*ello).

gl : = mi*lli*on (me*gli*o, pronounced me*lly*o).

h: is completely silent (*h*anno, pronounced anno); but note its uses in the ch and gh combinations above.

r: is trilled as in British ve*r*y.

sc: before e, i = *s*ure (in the groups scia, scio, sciu, the i is almost silent: *sci*acallo, pronounced *sha*kallo). Before a, o, u or consonant, sc = Eng. *sc*one.

z: = dz or ts (me*zz*o, pronounced me*dz*o; pe*zz*o, pronounced pe*ts*o). Learn by observation; the ts pronunciation generally prevails in groups of zi followed by another vowel (giusti*zi*a, pronounced justi*tsy*a).

---

1. The closed pronunciation (initial part of g*a*te and of g*o*) is always used for e and o, respectively, when unstressed. Either the open or the closed pronunciation may appear when the vowel is stressed. Learn by observation and remember that if an error is made, you will probably still be understood.

Double consonants are more strongly pronounced than single consonants: note distinction between fa*t*o (pron. fa-*t*o) and fa*tt*o (pron. fa*t*-*t*o); between a*c*e*t*o (pron. a-*che*-*t*o) and a*cc*e*tt*o (pron. a*t*-*chet*-*t*o).

English sounds not appearing in Italian: all vowel sounds save the ones described above; h; plea*s*ure; *th*in; *th*is; w; American r.

Italian sounds not appearing in English: closed sounds of e and o; Italian r; all double consonants.

CAPITALIZATION, SYLLABIFICATION, ACCENTUATION

Do not capitalize *io* ("I"); capitalize *Lei, Ella, Loro,* when they mean "you" (polite), *Suo* and *Loro* when they mean "your" (polite). Do not capitalize adjectives of nationality (*inglese*, "English") even when used as the name of a language (*parlo inglese*, "I speak English"); to indicate people, use your own choice (*gli americani* or *gli Americani*, "the Americans").

In dividing words into syllables, a single consonant between two vowels goes with the *following*, not with the preceding vowel: *generale* is to be divided and pronounced *ge ne ra le*.

The only written accent is the grave (`); this appears whenever a word of more than one syllable ending in a vowel is stressed on the final vowel: *città, perchè, tornerò*. The accent mark is also occasionally used on words of a single syllable to distinguish them from similar words having different meanings: *e*, "and"; *è*, "is"; *da*, "from"; *dà*, "gives". Otherwise, no written accent appears, and words are generally stressed on the next to the last or third from the last syllable; in these cases, the place of the accent is to be determined by observation. For the convenience of the student, the accent will be indicated when it falls elsewhere than on the second syllable from the end.

The apostrophe is used to indicate the fall of a vowel before another vowel: *l'uomo* (for *lo uomo*); *t'amo* (for *ti amo*).

SAMPLE OF WRITTEN ITALIAN;
USE FOR PRACTICE READING.

Dopo aver esaminato attentamente col canocchiale la costa della montagna, il tenente si rivolse al capitano. "Ci sono
lassù almeno due posti d'osservazione nemici; poi, tra gli
àlberi, trincee e camminamenti. Non si nascòndono troppo bene. Guardi Lei." Il capitano prese il canocchiale, guardò,
poi scosse la testa. "Ha ragione. Si vèdono persino i reticolati.
Telèfoni sùbito al comando. Dica che ci màndino due compa-
gnìe di rincalzo e una batterìa di artiglierìa da montagna. In-
tanto non possiamo muòverci. Di quante mitragliatrici dispo-
niamo?" "Sei". "Son poche. Faccia distribuire le granate
a mano, e mandi due plotoni d'esplorazione a rastrellare la
vallata." In questo istante, un sìbilo acuto fendè l'aria. La
granata nemica esplose a cinquanta passi dai due ufficiali.
"Accidenti! Ci hanno visti!" brontolò il capitano. Poi, vol-
gèndosi alla colonna, gridò: "Òrdine sparso!"

GRAMMATICAL SURVEY

1. *Nouns and Articles.*

Italian has only two genders, masculine and feminine.
Nouns denoting males are usually masculine, those denoting
females feminine. For nouns which in English are neuter, the
ending often helps to determine the gender. Nouns ending in
-o (plural changes *-o* to *-i*) are usually masculine;[2] those ending
in *-a* (plural changes *-a* to *-e*) normally feminine; the gender
of nouns ending in *-e* (plural changes *-e* to *-i*) must be determined by observation.

The indefinite article is *un* (*uno* before *s* followed by

2. A considerable number of nouns which in the singular are masculine
and end in *-o* become feminine in the plural, with change from *-o* to *-a*:
il labbro, "the lip", pl. *le labbra; il dito*, "the finger", pl. *le dita;*
such nouns are indicated in the vocabulary thus: arm, *il braccio* (pl.
le braccia).

consonant and before *z*) for the masculine; *una* (*un'* before vowels) for the feminine:

a brother, *un fratello*; a man, *un uomo*; a father, *un padre*; a mirror, *uno specchio*; an uncle, *uno zio*;

a woman, *una donna*; a mother, *una madre*; an idea, *un'idea.*

The definite article takes the following forms:[3]
Masculine singular: *l'* before vowels: the man, *l'uomo*;

lo before *s* plus consonant, or *z*: the mirror, *lo specchio*; the uncle, *lo zio.*

il in all other cases: the brother, *il fratello*; the father, *il padre.*

3. This system applies also to *quello*, 'that", "those", and to *bello*, "beautiful", "fine", when used as adjectives before the noun: that father, *quel padre*; those fathers, *quei padri*; that mirror, *quello specchio*; those mirrors, *quegli specchi*; that idea, *quell'idea*; that man, *quell'uomo*; a fine boy, *un bel ragazzo*; fine boys, *bei ragazzi*; fine men, *begli uòmini*; a fine mirror, *un bello specchio*; fine idea, *bell'idea*; fine man, *bell'uomo.*

It applies also to the article when combined with the prepositions *di*, "of"; *a*, "to"; *da*, "from", "by", "at the house of"; *in* (changed to *ne-* in combination), "in"; *su*, "on"; *con* (changed to *co-* in combination), "with"; *per* (changed to *pe-* in combination), "for", "by". This combination is compulsory with the first five prepositions mentioned, optional with the last two:

of the father, *del padre*; of the man, *dell'uomo*; of the uncle, *dello zio*; of the woman, *della donna*; of the idea, *dell'idea*; of the fathers, *dei padri*; of the men, *degli uòmini*; of the women, *delle donne*;

to the brother, *al fratello*; to the mirror, *allo specchio*; to the mirrors, *agli specchi*; to the uncle, *allo zio*;

from the son, *dal figlio*; from the daughter, *dalla figlia*; from the sons, *dai figli*; from the men, *dagli uòmini*;

in the wall, *nel muro*; in the soul, *nell'ànima*; in the trees, *negli àlberi*;

on the tree, *sull'àlbero*; on the trees, *sugli àlberi*; on the walls, *sulle mura*;

with the relatives, *coi parenti* or *con i parenti*;

for the children, *pei figli*, or *per i figli.*

Del, della, dei, etc. also translate "some" or "any", save in negative sentences: I have *some* bread, *ho del pane*; I have no bread, *non ho pane.*

Feminine singular: *l'* before vowels: the idea, *l'idea.*

                  la before consonants: the woman, *la donna;* the mother, *la madre.*

Masculine plural: *gli* before vowels, *s* plus consonant, or *z*: the men, *gli uòmini;* the mirrors, *gli specchi;* the uncles, *gli zii.*

                  i in all other cases: the brothers, *i fratelli;* the fathers, *i padri.*

Feminine plural: *le*: the mothers, *le madri;* the women, *le donne;* the ideas, *le idee.*

2. *Adjectives and Adverbs.*

Adjectives agree with the nouns they modify. Like nouns, they have the endings -*o* (feminine -*a*, masc. pl. -*i*, fem. pl. -*e*); or -*e* (no difference between masculine and feminine; plural -*i*); agreement with the noun does not necessarily mean identical endings; the noun may be of the -*a* (pl. -*e*) variety, while the adjective is of the -*e* (pl. -*i*) type: the strong woman, *la donna forte;* the strong women, *le donne forti.* Adjectives usually follow the noun, though a few common ones precede:

the red book, *il libro rosso*	the red books, *i libri rossi*
the red house, *la casa rossa*	the red houses, *le case rosse*
the green tree, *l'àlbero verde*	the green trees, *gli àlberi verdi*
the green house, *la casa verde*	the green houses, *le case verdi*

The comparative degree is formed by prefixing *più*, "more", to the positive; for the superlative, the definite article is placed before *più* or the noun: an easy book, *un libro fàcile;* an easier book, *un libro più fàcile;* the easiest book, *il libro più fàcile;* the greatest general, *il più grande generale.* "Than" is usually translated by *di*: an easier book than this, *un libro più fàcile di questo.*

The adverb is generally formed by adding -*mente* to the feminine singular of the adjective: clear, *chiaro;* clearly, *chiaramente;* strong, *forte*: strongly, *fortemente.*

3. *Numerals.*

a) Cardinal[4]

1 — *uno, una*	14 — *quattòrdici*	40 — *quaranta*
2 — *due*	15 — *quìndici*	50 — *cinquanta*
3 — *tre*	16 — *sèdici*	60 — *sessanta*
4 — *quattro*	17 — *diciassette*	70 — *settanta*
5 — *cinque*	18 — *diciotto*	80 — *ottanta*
6 — *sei*	19 — *diciannove*	90 — *novanta*
7 — *sette*	20 — *venti*	100 — *cento*
8 — *otto*	21 — *ventuno* [5]	200 — *duecento*
9 — *nove*	22 — *ventidue*	300 — *trecento*
10 — *dieci*	23 — *ventitrè*	1000 — *mille*
11 — *ùndici*	28 — *ventotto* [5]	2000 — *duemila*
12 — *dòdici*	29 — *ventinove*	1,000,000 — *un milione* (*di*)
13 — *trèdici*	30 — *trenta*	

b) Ordinal.

1st — *primo*	7th — *sèttimo*
2nd — *secondo*	8th — *ottavo*
3rd — *terzo*	9th — *nono*
4th — *quarto*	10th — *dècimo*
5th — *quinto*	11th — *undècimo* or *undicèsimo*
6th — *sesto*	20th — *ventèsimo*

Beyond 11th, ordinals are formed by dropping the final vowel of the cardinal and adding -*èsimo*: 34th, *trentaquattrèsimo*.

c) Others.

half — *la metà* (noun), or *mezzo* (adjective): *mezza mela*, half an apple; *la metà della compagnia*, half the company.

4. Use these in dates, save for "the first": May first, *il primo maggio*; May 10th, *il dieci maggio*.

5. Note the fall of the final vowel of *venti*, *trenta*, etc. in *ventuno*, *ventotto*, *trentuno*, *trentotto*.

a pair of — *un paio di*   a dozen — *una dozzina di*
once - *una volta*   twice - *due volte*   three times - *tre volte*
the first time — *la prima volta*   sometimes — *qualche volta*

4. *Pronouns.*

a) Personal (Subject).[6]

I, *io*	we, *noi, noialtri*
you (familiar), *tu*	you (fam. pl.), *voi, voialtri*
he, *egli* or *lui*	they (masc.), *essi, loro*
she, *ella* or *essa* or *lei*	they (fem.), *esse, loro*
you (polite), *Ella* or *Lei*[7]	you (pol. pl.), *Loro*[7]

b) Personal (Direct Object)

me, *mi*	us, *ci*
you (fam.), *ti*	you (fam. pl.), *vi*
him, it (standing for **an It.** masc. noun), *lo, l'*	them (It. masc.), *li* them (It. fem.), *le*
her, it (It. fem. noun), *la, l'* you (pol. sg.), *La*	you (pol. pl.), *Li, Le*

c) Personal (Indirect Object)

to me, *mi* (*me*)[8]	to us, *ci* (*ce*)
to you, *ti* (*te*)	to you, *vi* (*ve*)

6. Generally used only for emphasis or clarification: you don't know how to do it, *non sai farlo;* you don't know how to do it, *tu non sai farlo.*

7. In polite address, use *Ella* or *Lei* with the *third* person singular of the verb for a single person, *Loro* with the third plural of the verb for more than one person: *tu sei forte,* you (fam. sg.) are strong; *Lei è forte,* you (pol. sg.) are strong; *voi siete forti,* you (fam. pl.) are strong; *Loro sono forti,* you (pol. pl.) are strong.

8. If two object pronouns appear together, the indirect pronoun precedes the direct, and the form in parentheses ending in -*e* is used for the indirect instead of the form ending in -*i:* he gives me the book, *mi dà il libro;* but "he gives it to me", *me lo dà;* give him the book, *dagli il libro;* give it to him, *dàglielo.*

to him, *gli* (*glie*) [9]   to them, *loro* [10]
to her, *le* (*glie*) [9]   to you (pol. pl.) *Loro* [10]
to you (pol.), *Le* (*glie*) [9]

Direct and indirect object pronouns *precede* the verb (he sees me, *mi vede;* I give him the book, *gli do il libro*), save with the *familiar affirmative* forms of the imperative (take it!, *prèndilo!*); the infinitive (I want to see him, *voglio vederlo* or *lo voglio vedere*); and the gerund (I am speaking to him, *sto parlàndogli* or *gli sto parlando*), to all of which forms they are appended (note the double possibility when the infinitive or gerund depend on another verb). With the imperative polite or negative, the pronoun precedes: take it! (pol.), *lo prenda!;* don't take it! (fam.), *non lo prendere!;* (pol.), *non lo prenda!*

"Of it", "of them", "some" or "any" as a pronoun are expressed by *ne*, which follows other object pronouns and conforms to all the above rules: he gives me two of them, *me ne dà due;* I spoke to him of it, *gliene ho parlato.*

d) Personal (after a preposition)

me, *me*   us, *noi*
you, *te*   you, *voi*
him, *lui*   them, *loro, essi, esse*
her, *lei*   you (pol. pl.), *Loro*
it, *esso, essa*
you (pol.), *Lei*

With me, *con me;* for him, *per lui;* before them, *prima di loro.*

9. *Glie*, in writing, is always joined to a following direct object pronoun: I give it to him, *glielo do.*

10. *Loro* is an exception to all rules of position; it always follows the verb, and is never joined to anything else: I give them the book, *do loro il libro;* I give it to them, *lo do loro.*

e) Possessive.

my, mine, *il mio; la mia; i miei; le mie*
your, yours (fam. sg.), *il tuo; la tua; i tuoi; le tue*
his, her, hers, its, *il suo; la sua; i suoi; le sue*
our, ours, *il nostro; la nostra; i nostri; le nostre*
your, yours, *il vostro; la vostra; i vostri; le vostre*
their, theirs, *il loro; la loro; i loro; le loro*
your, yours (pol. sg.), *il Suo; la Sua; i Suoi; le Sue*
your, yours (pol. pl.), *il Loro; la Loro; i Loro; le Loro*

These agree with the noun they modify or replace, and regularly appear with the article, whether used as adjectives or pronouns: my book, *il mio libro;* I want mine, *voglio il mio.* The article is, however generally omitted after the verb "to be" (this book is mine, *questo libro è mio*); and before nouns of relationship in the singular, but not in the plural (my sister, *mia sorella;* my sisters, *le mie sorelle*); also in direct address (my friend!, *amico mio!*).

f) Demonstrative.

this, these, *questo* (*-a, -i, -e*): this woman, *questa donna;* here are your books; I want these, *ecco i Suoi libri; voglio questi.*

that, those, the one, the ones, *quello;* see note 3 for its forms when used as an adjective (that book, *quel libro;* those books, *quei libri;* those mirrors, *quegli specchi*); when used as a pronoun, the scheme is regular (*quello-a-i-e*): my books and the ones on the table, *i miei libri e quelli sulla tàvola.*

g) Relative and Interrogative.

who, whom, which, that, *che:* the man I saw, *l'uomo che ho visto* (note that the relative cannot be omitted); the woman who came, *la donna che è venuta. Il quale* (*la quale, i quali, le quali*), and *cui* are generally used after prepositions: the gentleman with whom I dined, *il signore con cui* (or *col quale*) *ho pranzato.*

whose, *di cui; il (la, i, le) cui; del (della) quale* (pl. *dei* or
   delle quali): the man whose sister I saw yesterday, *l'uomo
   di cui ho visto ieri la sorella; l'uomo la cui sorella ho visto
   ieri; l'uomo del quale ho visto ieri la sorella; l'uomo la
   sorella del quale ho visto ieri* (note the different word-
   orders used with each expression).
who?, whom?, *chi?*: who came?, *chi è venuto?;* whom did you
   see? *chi hai visto?*
what?, *che?* or *che cosa?*: what happened?, *che* (or *che cosa*)
   è successo?; what did you do?, *che* (or *che cosa*) *hai
   fatto?*
which?, which one?, which ones?, *quale* (pl. *quali*)?: which
   books do you want?, *quali libri vuoi?*
whose?, *di chi?*: whose house is that?, *di chi è quella casa?*

5. *Verbs.*

Italian verbs fall into three main classes, with the infinitive
ending respectively in *-are, -ere,* [11] and *-ire* [11].

1. Present Indicative.

to speak,	*parl-are*
I speak (am speaking, do speak),[12]	*parl-o*
you speak,	*parl-i*

11.   *-are* and *-ire* verbs have the stress on the *-a* and *-i*, respectively;
some *-ere* verbs have the stress on the first *e* of the ending (*godere*),
others have it on the preceding vowel of the stem (*ricèvere*), but no
difference appears outside of the infinitive. A considerable number of
-ire verbs have the following scheme of present indicative endings:
fin-isco, -isci, -isce, -iamo, -ite, -ìscono. The inserted *-isc-* reappears
in the subjunctive and imperative singular and third plural. They
are otherwise regular, and appear in the vocabulary thus: *finire (-isc-).*

12.   A progressive conjugation, formed with *stare*, "to stand", "to
be", followed by the gerund, corresponds in use to the English "I
am speaking", "I was speaking", etc. The gerund is formed by adding
-ando to the stem of *-are* verbs, *-endo* to the stem of other verbs, and is

he, she speaks,	*parl-a*
we speak,	*parl-iamo*
you speak,	*parl-ate*
they speak,	*pàrl-ano*

to receive,	*ricèv-ere*

I receive,	*ricev-o*
you receive,	*ricev-i*
he, she receives,	*ricev-e*
we receive,	*ricev-iamo*
you receive,	*ricev-ete*
they receive,	*ricèv-ono*

to sleep,	*dorm-ire*

I sleep,	*dorm-o*
you sleep,	*dorm-i*
he, she sleeps,	*dorm-e*
we sleep,	*dorm-iamo*
you sleep,	*dorm-ite*
they sleep,	*dòrm-ono*

to be, *èssere: sono, sei, è, siamo, siete, sono.*
to have: *avere: ho, hai, ha, abbiamo, avete, hanno.*
to know (a fact), to know how, *sapere: so, sai, sa, sappiamo, sapete, sanno.*

---

invariable; used by itself, it carries the meaning of "by", or "while" (by speaking, one learns, *parlando, s'impara;* while speaking, we left the house, *parlando, siamo usciti dalla casa*). The present of *stare* is: *sto, stai, sta, stiamo, state, stanno;* imperfect, future and conditional are regular (*stavo; starò; starei*). *Parlo* and *sto parlando* are interchangeable in the sense of "I am speaking"; *parlavo* and *stavo parlando* in the sense of "I was speaking".

to go, *andare*: *vado, vai, va, andiamo, andate, vanno.*
to give, *dare*: *do, dai, dà, diamo, date, dànno.*
to do, to make, *fare*: *faccio, fai, fa, facciamo, fate, fanno.*
to come, *venire*: *vengo, vieni, viene, veniamo, venite, vèngono.*
to want, *volere*: *voglio, vuoi, vuole, vogliamo, volete, vògliono*

2. Imperfect Indicative (meaning: I was speaking, used to speak):

parl-avo, -avi, -ava, -avamo, -avate, -àvano, I was speaking, used to speak
ricev-evo, -evi, -eva, -evamo, -evate, -èvano, I was receiving, used to receive
dorm-ivo, -ivi, -iva, -ivamo, -ivate, -ìvano, I was sleeping, used to sleep
"to be", *èssere*: *ero, eri, era, eravamo, eravate, èrano,* I was, etc.
"to have", *avere,* is regular: *av-evo,* etc.; so are other verbs with an irregular present: *sapevo, andavo, davo, venivo, volevo;* but *fare* has *fac-evo.*

3. Past Indicative (meaning: I spoke):

parl-ai, parl-asti, parl-ò, parl-ammo, parl-aste, parl-àrono, I spoke, etc.
ricev-ei, ricev-esti, ricev-è (or *ricev-ette*), *ricev-emmo, ricev-este, ricev-èrono* (or *ricev-èttero*), I received, etc.
dorm-ii, dorm-isti, dorm-ì, dorm-immo, dorm-iste, dorm-ìrono, I slept, etc.
èssere: *fui, fosti, fu, fummo, foste, fùrono,* I was, etc.
avere: *ebbi, avesti, ebbe, avemmo, aveste, èbbero,* I had, etc. [13]

13. Note carefully the irregular scheme of the past of *avere;* most verbs with an irregular past follow the same scheme; the irregular forms are the first singular, third singular and third plural, while the remaining three forms are quite regular; thus: to write, *scrìv-ere;* I wrote, *scrissi;* he wrote, *scrisse;* they wrote, *scrìssero;* but you wrote (sg.) *scriv-esti,* (pl.) *scriv-este;* we wrote, *scriv-emmo.* Whenever a past is irregular according to this scheme, only the first singular appears in the vocabulary (to write, *scrìvere;* Past, *scrissi*).

4. Future and Conditional (I shall write; I should write).
parl-erò, -erai, -erà, -eremo, -erete, -eranno, I shall speak, etc.
ricev-erò, -erai, -erà, -eremo, -erete, -eranno, I shall receive, etc.
dorm-irò, -irai, -irà, -iremo, -irete, -iranno, I shall sleep, etc.
èssere: sarò, sarai, sarà, saremo, sarete, saranno, I shall be, etc.
avere: avrò, avrai, avrà, avremo, avrete, avranno, I shall
     have, etc.

For the conditional of *any* verb, retain the form of the
future down to the *-r-* and add: *-ei, -esti, -ebbe, -emmo, -este,
-èbbero;* thus:

I should speak, *parler-ei;* he would speak, *parler-ebbe;* we
would sleep, *dormir-emmo;* they would be, *sar-èbbero.* It
being understood that the conditional invariably follows the
future in any irregularity the latter may have, the first person
of the future alone in the vocabulary indicates that both tenses
are irregular; thus: to come, *venire* (Fut. *verrò*) ; this indicates
that the conditional is *verrei.*

5. Compound Tenses.

These are formed as in English, by using the auxiliary
"to have" (*avere*) with the past participle. [14] Many intransitive

14.   The past participle ends in *-ato* for *-are* verbs, *-uto* for *-ere* verbs,
-ito for *-ire* verbs (spoken, *parl-ato;* received, *ricev-uto;* slept, *dorm-i-
to*).   Many past participles are irregular, and individually given in
the vocabulary.   The past participle is normally invariable (we have
spoken, *abbiamo parlato*), but changes its endings like an adjective
in the following cases:
1.   when used as an adjective: the spoken tongue, *la lingua parlata;*
2.   when used with the auxiliary "to be", in which case it must agree
with the subject; this occurs: a) with intransitive verbs of motion,
etc. as described above: the men have come, *gli uomini sono venuti;*
b) in the passive: we are loved by our parents, *noi siamo amati dai
nostri genitori;* c) in the reflexive: they got up, *si sono alzati;*
3.   when used with "to have", to agree with the *direct* object; this
agreement is compulsory if the object is a *personal direct* object
pronoun: I have seen them, *li ho visti;* optional in all other cases:
the women we saw, *le donne che abbiamo viste* (or *visto*) ; we saw
those women, *abbiamo visto* (or *viste*) *quelle donne.*

verbs of motion (to go, *andare;* to come, *venire*), change of
state (to become, *divenire;* to die, *morire*) and *èssere* itself
use *èssere* as an auxiliary instead of *avere;* in this case, the past
participle changes its ending to agree with the subject, just as
though it were an adjective: he went, *è andato;* she went, *è
andata;* we went, *siamo andati;* the ladies went, *le signore sono
andate.*

Present Perfect: *ho parlato, hai parlato, etc.,* I have spoken, I
       spoke;
       sono andato (-a), I went; *siamo andati (-e),*
       we went;

Past Perfect: *avevo ricevuto,* I had received; *avevi dormito,*
       you had slept; *ero stato,* I had been; *eravamo
       tornati,* we had come back;

Future Perfect: *avrò scritto,* I shall have written; *sarà partito,*
       he will have left;

Past Conditional: *avrei perduto,* I would have lost; *sarebbe
       andato,* he would have gone.

   6. Imperative. (meaning: speak!; let us speak)

	-are	*-ere*	*-ire*	*essere*	*avere*
Fam. Sg. [15]	*parl-a*	*ricev-i*	*dorm-i*	*sii*	*abbi*
Fam. Pl.	*parl-ate*	*ricev-ete*	*dorm-ite*	*siate*	*abbiate*
Pol. Sg.	*parl-i*	*ricev-a*	*dorm-a*	*sia*	*abbia*
Pol. P.	*pàrl-ino*	*ricèv-ano*	*dòrm-ano*	*sìano*	*àbbiano*
"let us"	*parl-iamo*	*ricev-iamo*	*dorm-iamo*	*siamo*	*abbiamo*

15. The familiar singular form is never used in the negative, being
replaced by the infinitive: don't speak!, *non parlare!;* don't sleep,
non dormire! Object pronouns are attached to the *familiar* imperatives in the *affirmative* (speak to him! *pàrlagli!; parlàtegli!;* let us
speak to him, *parliàmogli*); but precede the *polite* forms (speak to
him!, *gli parli; gli pàrlino*), and all *negative* forms, familiar or
polite (don't speak to him!; *non gli parlare; non gli parlate; non
gli parli; non gli pàrlino!;* let us not speak to him!, *non gli parlia-
mo!*)

7. Reflexive Verbs.

The reflexive is more extensively used in Italian than in English. Reflexive pronouns are: *mi, ti, si, ci, vi, si.* [16] The auxiliary used in compound tenses is *essere,* and the past participle agrees with the subject: they saw each other, *si sono visti.* [17]

I wash myself, *mi lavo*	we wash ourselves, *ci laviamo*
you wash yourself, *ti lavi*	you wash yourselves, *vi lavate*
he washes himself, *si lava*	they wash themselves, *si làvano*

I washed myself, *mi sono lavato (-a)*; we washed ourselves, *ci siamo lavati (-e)*

you washed yourself, *ti sei lavato (-a)*; you washed yourselves, *vi siete lavati (-e)*

he washed himself, *si è lavato;* she washed herself, *si è lavata;* they washed themselves, *si sono lavati (-e)*

8. Passive.

This is formed as in English, by using "to be" with the past participle; the latter agrees with the subject: we are loved by our parents, *noi siamo amati dai nostri genitori;* I was punished, *fui punito.*

A second passive form with *venire* instead of *essere* indicates more intensive and immediate action: the sentinels were killed, *le sentinelle vènnero uccise.*

The reflexive often replaces the passive, especially when the subject is a thing: Italian is spoken here, *qui si parla italiano;* these books are sold at two dollars apiece, *questi libri si vèndono a due dòllari l'uno.*

16. Note that the *-i* of all these forms changes to *-e* if another object pronoun follows: *se lo mette,* he puts it on (himself).

17. Note that in the plural, the reflexive may mean not only "ourselves", "yourselves", "themselves", but also "each other", "one another".

9. Subjunctive.

The Italian subjunctive has four tenses, and is frequently used in subordinate clauses. The endings of the present subjunctive are:

-*are* verbs: *parl-i, -i, -i, -iamo, -iate, '-ino*
-*ere* and -*ire* verbs: *ricev-* or *dorm-a, -a, -a, -iamo, -iate, '-ano*.

The imperfect subjunctive ends in -*ssi, -ssi, -sse, '-ssimo, -ste, '-ssero*, with a preceding -*a*- for -*are* verbs (*parl-assi*), -*e*- for -*ere* verbs (*ricev-essi*), -*i*- for -*ire* verbs (*dorm-issi*).

The present perfect subjunctive uses the present subjunctive of "to have" (*abbia, abbia, abbia, abbiamo, abbiate, àbbiano*) or "to be" (*sia, sia, sia, siamo, siate, sìano*), with the past participle (*abbia parlato, sia venuto*); while the past perfect subjunctive uses the imperfect subjunctive of *avere* (*avessi*) or *essere* (*fossi*), with the past participle (*avessi parlato, fossi venuto*).

I think he is speaking (will speak), *credo che parli;*
I think he spoke, *credo che abbia parlato;*
I thought he was speaking, (would speak), *credevo che parlasse;*
I thought he had spoken, *credevo che avesse parlato.*

DIALECTS

Italian has an extremely large number of widely diverging dialects, many of them mutually incomprehensible. Generally speaking, however, the standard literary speech has currency everywhere, and can be used with reasonable assurance.

The northern Italian dialects are generally identifiable by their lack of the characteristic Italian double consonant sounds and by the fall of many vowel endings (*fatto*, for example, may appear as *fato, fat, fait*). A clear, staccato pronunciation is usually indicative of northern origin. Piedmontese, Genoese, Venetian and Emilian are among the best-known dialects of this group.

The dialects south of Rome, down to the heel and toe of the boot (Neapolitan, Abruzzese, etc.) are characterized by heavy stress and prolongation of accented vowels and a general deadening of final vowels to the sound of *e* in *the* (*beelle* for Italian *bello, bella, belli, belle*). A sing-song cadence is also fairly general.

Calabria and Sicily change most *o*-sounds to *u*, and most *e*-sounds to *i* (*prufissuri* for *professore*); and change *ll* to a sound resembling Engl. *d*rink (be*d*ru for be*ll*o). A sharp, explosive pronunciation is also fairly general.

The central section of the country (Florence, Rome, etc.) generally approaches the literary standard.

VOCABULARY [18]

1. *World, Elements, Nature, Weather, Time, Directions.*

world, *il mondo*	star, *la stella*
earth, *la terra*	sky, *il cielo*
air, *l'aria*	wind, *il vento*
water, *l'acqua*	weather, time, *il tempo*
fire, *il fuoco* (pl. *fuochi*)	snow, *la neve*
light, *la luce*	to snow, *nevicare*
sea, *il mare*	rain, *la pioggia*
sun, *il sole*	to rain, *piòvere*[19] (Past *piovve*)
moon, *la luna*	cloud, *la nùvola*. [19] *la nube*

18. Irregularities in the plural of nouns are indicated thus: *il braccio* (pl. *le braccia*); this means that the plural is feminine and takes an *-a* instead of an *-i* ending. Spelling changes are also noted: *fuoco* (pl. *fuochi*).

Verbs of the *-ire* type that take *-isc-* between the root and the ending are indicated thus: to finish, *finire* (*-isc-*). Other important irregularities are also noted in parentheses. An irregular first singular in the past tense implies the same irregularity in the third singular and third plural, with the other persons regular; thus *scrivere* Past *scrissi* indicates the scheme: *scrissi, scrivesti, scrisse, scrivemmo scriveste, scrìssero* (cf. note 13). Verbs requiring *èssere* as an active auxiliary appear thus: to become, *divenire* (*èssere*). This indication is not given in the case of reflexive verbs, which are *all* conjugated with *èssere*.

19. In words of more than two syllables, if the accent falls elsewhere than on the next to the last syllable, its place is indicated thus *piòvere, nùvola*. A few other irregular accents are also indicated (*polizìa*). Note, however, that this is done only for the convenience of the student, and that Italian does not indicate the place of the accent in writing save when it falls on a final vowel (*metà, città*).

cloudy, *nuvoloso,* **coperto**
fog, *la nebbia*
ice, *il ghiaccio*
mud, *il fango*
morning, *il mattino,* **la mattina**
noon, *il mezzogiorno*
afternoon, *il dopopranzo, il pome-riggio*
evening, *la sera*
night, *la notte*
midnight, *la mezzanotte*
North, *nord, settentrione*
South, *sud, mezzogiorno*
East, *est, levante, oriente*
West, *ovest, ponente, occidente*
year, *l'anno*
month, *il mese*
week, **la settimana**
day, *il giorno*
hour, *l'ora*
minute, *il minuto*
Sunday, *la domènica*

Monday, *il lunedì*
Tuesday, *il martedì*
Wednesday, *il mercoledì*
Thursday, *il giovedì*
Friday, *il venerdì*
Saturday, *il sàbato*
January, *gennaio*
February, *febbraic*
March, *marzo*
April, *aprile*
May, *maggio*
June, *giugno*
July, *luglio*
August, *agosto*
September, *settembre*
October, *cttobre*
November, *novembre*
December, *dicembre*
Spring, *la primavera*
Summer, *l'estate* (fem.)
Fall, *l'autunno*
Winter, *l'inverno*

For "it is warm", "it is cold", etc. cf. p. 350.
No capitals for seasons, months, days of week.
I shall see him *on* Monday, *lo vedrò lunedì;* last Monday, *lunedì scorso;* next Monday, *lunedì prossimo;* every Monday, *tutti i lunedì* (nouns ending in stressed vowels usually do not change in the plural: the city, *la città;* the cities, *le città*); *on* May 5th, 1943, *il cinque maggio mille novecento quarantatrè.*

2. Family, Friendship, Love.

family, *la famiglia*
husband, *il marito*
wife, *la moglie* (pl. *mogli*)
parents, *i genitori*
father, *il padre*
mother, *la madre*
son, *il figlio* (pl. *figli*)
daughter, *la figlia*
brother, *il fratello*
sister, *la sorella*

uncle, *lo zio*
aunt, *la zia*
nephew, grandson, *il nipote*
niece, granddaughter, *la nipote*
cousin, *il cugino, la cugina*
grandfather, *il nonno*
grandmother, *la nonna*
father-in-law, *il suòcero*
mother-in-law, *la suòcera*
son-in-law, *il gènero*

daughter-in-law, *la nuora*
brother--in-law, *il cognato*
sister-in-law, *la cognata*
man, *l'uomo* (pl. *gli uòmini*)
woman, *la donna*
child, *il bambino, la bambina*
boy, *il ragazzo, il fanciullo*
girl, *la ragazza, la fanciulla*
sir, Mr., *il signore* [20]
madam, Mrs., *la signora*
Miss, young lady, *la signorina*
friend, *l'amico, l'amica* (pl. *gli amici, le amiche*)
servant, *il servo, la serva*
to introduce, *presentare*

to visit, *visitare*
love, *l'amore* (masc.)
to love, *amare, voler* [21] *bene a* (she loves him, *lo ama, gli vuol bene*)
to fall in love with, *innamorarsi di*
to marry, *sposare*
to get married, *sposarsi*
sweetheart, *il fidanzato, la fidanzata*
kiss, *il bacio* (pl. *baci*)
to kiss, *baciare*
dear, beloved, *caro*

3. Speaking Activities.

word, *la parola*
language, *la lingua*
to speak, *parlare*
to say, *dire* (Pres. *dico, dici, dice, diciamo, dite, dìcono*; Impf. *dicevo*; Fut. *dirò*; Past *dissi*; P. p. *detto*; Impv. *dì, dìte, dica*)
to tell, relate, *dire, raccontare*
to inform, *informare*
to call, *chiamare*
to be called, one's name is, *chiamarsi* (my name is John, *mi chiamo Giovanni*)
to greet, *salutare*
to name, *nominare*
to cry, shout, *gridare*
to listen to, *ascoltare* (I listen *to*

him, *lo ascolto*)
to hear, *sentire, udire* (Pres. *odo, odi, ode, udiamo, udite, òdono*)
to understand, *capire* (*-isc-*), *comprèndere* (Past *compresi,* P. p. *compreso*)
to mean, *voler dire* (cf. p. 342 for *volere*)
to ask (for), *domandare, chièdere* (Past *chiesi*, P. p. *chiesto*); the person asked is an indirect object, the thing asked for is direct: I asked him for a pencil, *gli ho domandato* (*chiesto*) *un lapis*
to answer, *rispòndere* (Past *risposi*, P. p. *risposto*); the person

20. Use the definite article with *signore, signora, signorina*, save in speaking directly to the person; *signore* usually becomes *signor* when the name follows: Mr. Bianchi has a book, *il signor Bianchi ha un libro*; Mr. Bianchi, have you a book?, *signor Bianchi, ha un libro?*; sir, have you a book?, *signore, ha un libro?*

21. Cf. p. 342 for *volere*.

answered is an indirect object:
I answered him, *gli ho risposto*
to thank, *ringraziare* (I thanked

him *for* the book, *l'ho ringra-
ziato del libro*)
to complain, *lagnarsi, lamentarsi*

4. *Materials.*

gold, *l'oro*
silver, *l'argento*
iron, *il ferro*
steel, *l'acciaio*
copper, *il rame*
tin, *lo stagno, la latta*
lead, *il piombo*
oil, *il petrolio*
gasoline, *la benzina*
coal, *il carbone*

wood, *il legno*
silk, *la seta*
cotton, *il cotone*
wool, *la lana*
cloth, *la tela, il panno*
to cut, *tagliare*
to dig, *scavare*
to sew, *cucire*
to mend, *rammendare*

5. *Animals.*

animal, *l'animale* (masc.), *la be-
stia*
horse, *il cavallo*
dog, *il cane*
cat, *il gatto*
bird, *l'uccello*
donkey, *l'àsino*
mule, *il mulo*
cow, *la vacca* (pl. *vacche*)
ox, *il bue* (pl. *buoi*)
pig, *il porco, il maiale*
chicken, *il pollo*
hen, *la gallina*

rooster, *il gallo*
sheep, *la pècora*
goat, *la capra*
mouse, *il topo*
snake, *il serpente*
fly, *la mosca* (pl. *mosche*)
bee, *l'ape* (fem.)
mosquito, *la zanzara*
spider, *il ragno*
louse, *il pidocchio* (pl. *pidocchi*)
flea, *la pulce*
bedbug, *la cimice*

6. *Money; Buying and Selling.*

money, *il danaro*
coin, *la moneta*
dollar, *il dòllaro*
cent, *il soldo*
lira (ab. 1 cent), *la lira*
centesimo (1-100th of a *lira*), *il
centèsimo*
bank, *la banca, il banco* (pl. *-che,
-chi*)
check, *l'assegno*

money order, *il vaglia* (pl. *i vaglia*)
to earn, gain, *guadagnare*
to win, *vìncere* (Past *vinsi*, P. p.
vinto)
to lose, *pèrdere* (Past *persi*, P. p.
perso; or regular, *perdei, perduto*)
to spend, *spèndere* (Past *spesi*,
P. p. *speso*)

to lend, *prestare*

to borrow, *chièdere* (*prèndere*) *in prèstito*: I borrowed $2 *from* him, *gli ho preso in prèstito due dòllari*

to owe, *dovere* (Pres. *debbo* or *devo, devi, deve, dobbiamo, dovete, dèbbono* or *dèvono*; Fut. *dovrò*)

to pay, *pagare*

to give back, *restituire* (*-isc-*) *rèndere* (Past *resi*, P. p. *reso*)

to change, exchange, *cambiare*

(small) change, *gli spìccioli*

change (of a bill), *il resto*

honest, *onesto*

dishonest, *disonesto*

price, *il prezzo*

cost, *il costo*

to cost, *costare* (*èssere*)

expensive, dear, *caro*

cheap, *ragionèvole, a buon mercato*

store, shop, *negozio, bottega* (pl. *-ghe*)

piece, *il pezzo*

7. *Eating and Drinking.*

to eat, *mangiare*

breakfast, lunch, *la colazione*

to eat breakfast, lunch, *far colazione* (cf. p. 342 for *fare*)

supper, *la cena*

to eat supper, *cenare*

dinner, *il pranzo*

to dine, *pranzare*

meal, *il pasto*

dining-room, *la sala da pranzo*

waiter, *il cameriere*

waitress, *la cameriera*

restaurant, *il ristorante, la trattorìa*

menu, *la lista delle vivande, il menù*

slice, *la fetta*

pound, *la libbra*

package, *il pacco* (pl. *pacchi*)

basket, *il canestro, il cesto*

box, *la scàtola*

bag, *il sacchetto*

goods, *la mercanzìa, la merce*

to go shopping, *andare a far còmpere* (cf. p. 341 for *andare*), *far la spesa*

to sell, *vèndere*

to buy, *comprare*

to rent, hire, *affittare, prèndere in affitto* (a conveyance, *noleggiare*)

to be worth, *valere* (Pres. 3rd pl. *vàlgono*; Fut. 3rd sg. *varrà*) (*èssere*)

to choose, *scègliere* (Pres. 1st sg. *scelgo*, 3rd pl. *scèlgono*; Past *scelsi*; P. p. *scelto*; Pol. Impv. *scelga*)

thief, robber, *il ladro*

to steal, *rubare*

police, *la polizìa*

policeman, *l'agente di polizìa, il poliziotto, il carabiniere*

bill, *il conto*

to pass (a dish), to hand, *favorire* (will you pass me the bread?, *mi vuol favorire il pane?*)

tip, *la mancia*

to drink, *bere* (Pres. *bev-o, -i, -e, -iamo, -ete '-ono*; Fut. *berrò*; Past *bevvi*; P. p. *bevuto*; Impv. *bev-i, -ete, -a*)

water, *l'acqua*

wine, *il vino*

beer, *la birra*

coffee, *il caffè*

tea, *il tè*

milk, *il latte*
bottle, *la bottiglia*
spoon, *il cucchiaio*
teaspoon, *il cucchiaìno*
knife, *il coltello*
fork, *la forchetta*
glass, *il bicchiere*
cup, *la tazza*
napkin, *la salvietta, il tovagliuolo*
salt, *il sale*
pepper, *il pepe*
plate, dish, *il piatto*
bread, *il pane*
roll, *il panino*
butter, *il burro*
sugar, *lo zùcchero*
soup, *la zuppa, la minestra*
rice, *il riso*
potatoes, *le patate*
vegetables, *i legumi, le verdure*
meat, *la carne*
beef, *il manzo, la carne di bue*
steak, *la bistecca* (pl. *-cche*)
chicken, *il pollo*
chop, *la cotoletta*
veal, *il vitello*
lamb, *l'agnello*
pork, *il maiale*

sausage, *la salsiccia*
ham, *il prosciutto* (American-style ham, *prosciutto cotto*)
bacon, *la ventresca*
egg, *l'uovo* (pl. *le uova*)
fish, *il pesce*
cooked, *cucinato, cotio*
fried, *fritto*
boiled, *bollito*
roast, roasted, *arrosto*
baked, *al forno*
broiled, *ai ferri*
sauce, *la salsa*
salad, *l'insalata*
cheese, *il cacio, il formaggio*
fruit, *la frutta*
apple, *la mela*
pear, *la pera*
peach, *la pesca* (pl. *-che*)
grapes, *l'uva*
strawberries, *le fràgole*
nuts, *le noci*
orange, *l'arancia*
lemon, *il limone*
juice, *il sugo*
cherries, *le ciliege*
dessert, *il dolce*
pastry, *le paste*

8. *Hygiene and Attire.*

bath, *il bagno*
shower, *la doccia*
to bathe, *fare un bagno*
to wash, *lavarsi*
to shave, *ràdersi* (Past *mi rasi*, P. p. *raso*)
barber, *il barbiere*
mirror, *lo specchio* (pl. *specchi*)
soap, *il sapone*
razor, *il rasoio*

safety razor, *rasoio di sicurezza*
towel, *l'asciugamano*
comb, *il pèttine*
brush, *la spàzzola*
scissors, *le fòrbici*
to wear, *portare, indossare*
to take off, *levarsi, tògliersi* (**Pres.** 1st sg. *mi tolgo*, 3rd pl. *si tòlgono*; Past *mi tolsi*; P. p. *tolto*) [22]

22. Note: he puts on *his* hat, *si mette il cappello*; I took off *my* overcoat, *mi sono tolto il* **sopràbito.**

to change, *mutarsi, cambiare di*
to put on, *indossare, mèttersi*
   (Past *mi misi;* P. p. *messo*)[22]
clothes, *i vestiti, gli àbiti*
hat, *il cappello*
suit, *il vestito, l'àbito*
coat, *la giacca* (pl. *-cche*)
vest, *il gilèt, il panciotto*
pants, *i calzoni, i pantaloni*
undershirt, *la maglia*
drawers, *le mutande*
glove, *il guanto*
socks, *i calzini*
stockings, *le calze*
shirt, *la camicia*
collar, *il colletto*
tie, *la cravatta*
overcoat, *il sopràbito*
raincoat, *l'impermeàbile*

pocket, *la tasca* (pl. *-che*)
handkerchief, *il fazzoletto*
button, *il bottone*
shoe, *la scarpa*
boot, *lo stivale*
pocket-book, *il portafogli* (pl.
   same)
purse, *la borsa*
pin, tie-pin, *la spilla*
safety pin, *spilla di sicurezza*
needle, *l'ago* (pl. *gli aghi*)
umbrella, *l'ombrello*
watch, clock, *l'orologio*
chain, *la catena*
ring, *l'anello*
eyeglasses, *gli occhiali*
slippers, *le pantòfole*
dressing-gown, *la veste da càmera*
bath-robe, *l'accappatoio*

9. Parts of the Body.

head, *il capo, la testa*
forehead, *la fronte*
face, *la faccia, il volto, il viso*
mouth, *la bocca* (pl. *le bocche*)
hair, *i capelli*
eye, *l'occhio* (pl. *gli occhi*)
ear, *l'orecchio*
tooth, *il dente*
lip, *il labbro* (pl. *le labbra*)
nose, *il naso*
tongue, *la lingua*
chin, *il mento*
cheek, *la guancia*
mustache, *i baffi*
beard, *la barba*
neck, *il collo*
throat, *la gola*
arm, *il braccio* (pl. *le braccia*)
hand, *la mano* (pl. *le mani*)

elbow, *il gòmito*
wrist, *il polso*
finger, *il dito* (pl. *le dita*)
nail, *l'unghia*
leg, *la gamba*
foot, *il piede*
knee, *il ginocchio* (pl. *le ginoc-
   chia*)
back, *il dorso, la schiena*
chest, *il petto*
ankle, *la caviglia*
body, *il corpo*
bone, *l'osso* (pl. *le ossa*)
skin, *la pelle*
heart, *il cuore*
stomach, *lo stòmaco* (pl. *gli stò-
   machi*)
blood, *il sangue*
shoulder, *la spalla*

10. *Medical.*

doctor, *il mèdico, il dottore*
drug-store, *la farmacìa*
hospital, *l'ospedale*
medicine, *la medicina*
pill, *la pìllola*
prescription, *la ricetta*
bandage, *la fasciatura*
nurse, *l'infermiere,* (-*a*)
ill, *malato*
illness, *la malattìa*
fever, *la febbre*
swollen, *gonfio, gonfiato*

wound, *la ferita*
wounded, *ferito*
head-ache, *il mal di capo, il dolor di testa*
tooth-ache, *il mal di denti*
cough, *la tosse*
to cough, *tossire* (reg. or -*isc*-)
lame, *zoppo*
burn, *la bruciatura, la scottatura*
pain, *il dolore*
poison, *il veleno*

11. *Military.*

war, *la guerra*
peace, *la pace*
ally, *l'alleato*
enemy, *il nemico* (pl. *i nemici*)
army, *l'esèrcito*
danger, *il perìcolo*
dangerous, *pericoloso*
to win, *vìncere* (Past *vinsi,* P. p. *vinto*)
to surround, *circondare*
to arrest, *arrestare*
to kill, *uccìdere* (Past *uccisi,* P. p. *ucciso*), *ammazzare*
to escape, *sfuggire* (*èssere*)
to run away, *fuggire* (*èssere*), *scappare* (*èssere*)
to lead, *condurre* (Pres. *conduc-o, -i, -e, -iamo, -ete, '-ono,* Past *con-dussi, -ducesti,* etc., Fut. *condurrò;* P. p. *condotto*)
to follow, *seguire*
to surrender, *arrèndersi* (Past *mi arresi,* P. p. *arreso*)
to retreat, *ritirarsi*
to bomb, shell, *bombardare*
fear, *la paura, il timore*
prison, *la prigione*
prisoner, *il prigioniero*

to take prisoner, *far* (or *prèndere*) *prigioniero*
to capture, *catturare*
help, *l'aiuto, il soccorso*
comrade, "buddy", *il compagno*
battle, *la battaglia*
to fight, *combàttere, bàttersi*
soldier, *il soldato, il militare*
private, *il soldato sèmplice*
corporal, *il caporale*
sergeant, *il sergente*
lieutenant, *il tenente*
captain, *il capitano*
major, *il maggiore*
colonel, *il colonnello*
general, *il generale*
officer, *l'ufficiale*
company, *la compagnìa*
battalion, *il battaglione*
regiment, *il reggimento*
brigade, *la brigata*
division, *la divisione*
troops, *le truppe*
reenforcements, *i rinforzi, le truppe di rincalzo*
fortress, *la fortezza*
sentinel, *la sentinella*

to stand guard, to do sentry duty, *far da sentinella, èssere di fazione* (*èssere*)
to be on duty, *èssere di servizio*
guard, *la guardia*
sign-post, *l'insegna* (*stradale*)
navy, *la marina*
sailor, *il marinaio*
marines, *fanterìa di marina, compagnie da sbarco*
warship, *la nave da guerra*
cruiser, *l'incrociatore* (*masc.*)
destroyer, *il cacciatorpediniere, il caccia* (pl. same)
convoy, *il convoglio*
escort, *la scorta*
weapon, *l'arma* (pl. *le armi*)
rifle, *il fucile*
machine-gun, *la mitragliatrice*
cannon, *il cannone*
ammunition, *le munizioni*
supplies, *i rifornimenti*
cartridge, *la cartuccia*
bullet, *la pallòttola, la palla*
belt, *la cintura*
knapsack, *lo zàino*
tent, *la tenda*
camp, *l'accampamento, l'attendamento*

map, *la carta*
rope, *la corda*
flag, *la bandiera*
helmet, *l'elmo, l'elmetto*
bayonet, *la baionetta*
uniform. *l'uniforme* (**fem.**)
airplane, *l'aeroplano, l'apparecchio*
bombing-plane, *l'apparecchio da bombardamento*
pursuit plane, *l'apparecchio da caccia*
shell, *la granata*
bomb, *la bomba*
truck, *l'automezzo, l'autoveicolo, il camion*
tank, *il carro armato* (*corazzato*)
to load, *caricare*
to fire, shoot, *sparare, far fuoco*
to shoot (military execution), *fucilare*
fire!, *fuoco!*
attention!, *attenti!*
forward!, *avanti!*
halt!, *alt!, alto là!*
air-raid shelter, *il ricòvero antiaèreo*
spy, *la spia*

12. *Travel.*

passport, *il passaporto*
ship, *la nave, il bastimento*
steamer, *il piròscafo, il vapore*
stateroom, *la cabina*
berth, *la cuccetta*
to travel, *viaggiare*
trip, voyage, *il viaggio*
to leave, depart, *partire* (*èssere*)
to arrive, *arrivare* (*èssere*)
to ride (a conveyance), *andare in* (cf. p. 341 for *andare*)
railroad, *la ferrovìa*

station, *la stazione*
track, *il binario*
train, *il treno*
platform, *il marciapiede*
ticket, *il biglietto*
compartment, *lo scompartimento*
all aboard!, *partenza!, in vettura!*
dining-car, *il vagone ristorante*
sleeper, *il vagone letto*
car, coach, *il vagone*
trunk, *il baùle*
valise, *la valigia*

baggage, *il bagaglio, i bagagli*
porter, *il portabagagli* (pl. same)
bus, *l'àutobus* (pl. **same**), *il torpedone*
street-car, *il tranvìa* (pl. same)

automobile, *l'automòbile* (masc. or fem.)
taxi, *la màcchina da nolo*
driver, *il conducente, l'autista* (pl. *gli autisti*)
to drive (car), *guidare, condurre*

13. *Reading and Writing.*

to read, *lèggere* (Past *lessi*, P. p. *letto*)
newspaper, *il giornale*
magazine, *la rivista*
book, *il libro*
to write, *scrìvere* (Past *scrissi*, P. p. *scritto*)
to translate, *tradurre* (cf. p. 337 for all verbs in *-durre*)
pencil, *il lapis* (pl. same), *la matita*
chalk, *il gesso*
blackboard, *la lavagna*

ink, *l'inchiostro*
pen, *la penna* (fountain -, *penna stilogràfica*)
envelope, *la busta*
paper, *la carta* (writing -, - *da scrivere, da lèttere*)
letter, *la lèttera*
post-office, *la posta, l'ufficio postale*
stamp, *il francobollo*
letter-box, *la cassetta postale*
to mail, *impostare*
address, *l'indirizzo*
post-card, *la cartolina* (*postale*)

14. *Amusements.*

to smoke, *fumare*
cigar, *il sìgaro*
cigarette, *la sigaretta*
tobacco, *il tabacco*
match, *il fiammifero*
give me a light, *mi fa accèndere?*
theatre, *il teatro*
movies, *il cìnema*
dance, *il ballo*
to dance, *ballare*
to have a good time, *divertirsi*
ticket, *il biglietto*
pleasure, *il piacere*
to play (music), *suonare*

to sing, *cantare*
song, *la canzone*
to play (a game), *giuocare a* (insert *h* before *-e* and *-i* endings)
game, *il giuoco* (pl. *i giuochi*)
ball, *la palla*
to take a walk, *fare una passeggiata, andare* (*èssere*) *a passeggio*
beach, *la spiaggia*
to swim, *nuotare*
sand, *la sabbia, l'arena*
refreshment, *il rinfresco*
saloon, *l'osterìa, il bar, la mèscita*
picnic, *la scampagnata*

15. *Town and Country.*

place, spot, *il luogo* (pl. *-ghi*) *il posto, il sito*
city, *la città* (pl. *le città*)

street, road, *la strada, la via*
sidewalk, *il marciapiede*
harbor, *il porto*

block, l'isolato
intersection, l'incrocio
school, la scuola
church, la chiesa
cathedral, la cattedrale, la basìlica,
  il duomo
building, l'edifizio
corner, l'àngolo, il cantone
hotel, l'albergo (pl. -ghi)
office, l'ufficio
river, il fiume
bridge, il ponte
country, la campagna

village, il villaggio, il paese
mountain, la montagna
grass, l'erba
yard, l'aia, il cortile
hill, la collina
lake, il lago (pl. laghi)
forest, wood, la foresta, il bosco
  (pl. -chi)
field, il campo
tree, l'àlbero
flower, il fiore
rock, stone, la pietra, il sasso

16. House.

door, la porta
to open, aprire (P. p. aperto)
to close, chiùdere (Past chiusi,
  P. p. chiuso)
key, la chiave
to go in, entrare (he entered the
  room, entrò nella stanza) (èssere)
to go out, to leave, uscire (Pres.
  esco, esci, esce, usciamo, uscite, èscono; Impv. esci, uscite,
  esca; he left the room, è uscito
  dalla stanza) (èssere)
house, la casa
roof, il tetto
cottage, la casetta
hut, la capanna
to live in, abitare in
staircase, la scala, le scale
to go up, salire (Pres. 1st sg.
  salgo, 3rd pl. sàlgono; Pol.
  Impv. salga) (èssere)
to go down, scèndere (Past scesi,
  P. p. sceso) (èssere)
room, la stanza, la càmera
bedroom, la stanza (càmera) da
  letto
toilet, il cesso, il gabinetto
kitchen, la cucina

table, la tàvola, il tàvolo
chair, la sedia, la sèggiola
to sit down, sedersi (change sed-
  to sied- whenever it is stressed),
  mèttersi a sedere (Past misi,
  P. p. messo)
to stand, be standing, stare in pie-
  di (Past stetti, stesti, stette,
  stemmo, steste, stèttero)
wall, il muro (pl. i muri or le mura)
lamp, la làmpada
candle, la candela
closet, l'armadio
window, la finestra
bed, il letto
pillow, il cuscino, il guanciale
blanket, la coperta
sheet, il lenzuolo (pl. le lenzuola)
mattress, il materazzo, la materassa
to rest, riposare, riposarsi
to go to bed, andare a letto
  (èssere)
to go to sleep, addormentarsi
to sleep, dormire
alarm-clock, la sveglia
to wake up, svegliarsi, destarsi
to get up, alzarsi, levarsi
to get dressed, vestirsi

17. *Miscellaneous Nouns.*

people, *la gente* (with sg. verb)
thing, *la cosa*
name, *il nome*
luck, *la fortuna*

number, *il nùmero*
life, *la vita*
death, *la morte*
work, *il lavoro*

18. *Verbs — Coming and Going.*

to come, *venire* (Pres. *vengo, vie-ni, viene, veniamo, venite, vèn-gono;* Past *venni;* Fut. *verrò;* P. p. *venuto;* Impv. *vieni, ven-ga*) (*èssere*)

to go, *andare* (Pres. *vado, vai, va, andiamo, andate, vanno;* Fut. *andrò* or *anderò;* Impv. *va, an-date, vada*) (*èssere*)

to be going, to use future of following verb (I am going to do it tomorrow, *lo farò domani*)

to run, *còrrere* (Past *corsi,* P. p. *corso*) (*èssere*)

to return, to go back, *ritornare* (*èssere*)

to walk, *camminare, andare a pie-di* (*èssere*)

to go away, *andàrsene* (*me ne va-do*)

to fall, *cadere* (Past *caddi,* Fut. *cadrò*) (*èssere*)

to stay, remain, *stare* (Pres. *sto, stai, sta, stiamo, state, stanno;* Past *stetti, stesti, stette, stem-mo, steste, stèttero*), *restare, rimanere* (Pres. 1st sg. *riman-go,* 3rd pl. *rimàngono;* Past *rimasi,* P. p. *rimasto,* Fut. *ri-marrò*) (*èssere* for all)

to follow, *seguire*

19. *Verbs — Looking and Seeing.*

to see, *vedere* (Past *vidi,* Fut. *ve-drò,* P. p. *veduto* or *visto*)

to look at, *guardare* (I am looking *at* him, *lo guardo*)

to look for, *cercare* (insert *h* before *e* and *i* endings; I am looking *for* it, *lo cerco*)

to laugh, *rìdere* (Past *risi,* P. p. *riso*)

to laugh at, to make fun of, *rìder-*

si di, burlarsi di

to smile, *sorrìdere* (like *rìdere*)

to look, seem, *sembrare, parere* (Pres. 1st sg. *paio,* 3rd pl. *pà-iono,* Fut. *parrò,* Past *parvi,* P. p. *parso*) (*èssere*)

to recognize, *riconòscere* (Past *riconobbi,* P. p. *riconosciuto*)

to take for, *prèndere per* (cf. p. 342 for *prèndere*)

20. *Verbs — Mental.*

to make a mistake, *sbagliarsi, fa-re uno sbaglio*

to hope, *sperare*

to wait (for), *aspettare, attèndere* (Past *attesi,* P. p. *atteso*): I

am waiting *for* him, *lo attendo*

to think, *pensare* (I am thinking *of* him, *penso a lui*)

to believe, *crèdere*

to like, *piacere* (the thing liked

is the subject, the person who likes is the indirect object: I like this book, *questo libro mi piace*; he likes me, *gli piaccio*; Pres. *piaccio, piaci, piace, piacciamo, piacete, piàcciono*; Past *piacqui*; P. p. *piaciuto*) (*èssere*)

to wish, *desiderare*

to want, *volere* (Pres. *voglio, vuoi, vuole, vogliamo, volete, vògliono*; Past *volli*; Fut *vorrò*)

to know (a person), *conòscere* (Past *conobbi*, P. p. *conosciuto*)

to know (a thing, to know how), *sapere* (Pres. *so, sai, sa, sappiamo, sapete, sanno*; Past *seppi*; Fut. *saprò*; use *sapevo* for "I knew", *seppi* for "I found out", " I learned")

to remember, *ricordare, ricordar-*

si di, rammentarsi di

to forget, *dimenticare, scordarsi di*

to permit, allow, *permèttere* (Past *permisi*, P. p. *permesso*)

to forbid, *proibire, vietare*

to promise, *promèttere* (Past *promisi*, P. p. *promesso*)

to learn, *imparare, apprèndere* (Past *appresi*, P. p. *appreso*)

to feel like, *aver voglia di, sentirsi voglia di*; I feel like sleeping, *ho voglia di dormire*

to fear, be afraid, *temere, aver paura*

to be right, *aver ragione*

to be wrong, *aver torto* (you are wrong, *Lei ha torto*)

to need, *aver bisogno di* (I need you, *ho bisogno di Lei*; I need it, *ne ho bisogno*)

21. *Verbs — Miscellaneous.*

to live, *vìvere* (Past *vissi*, Fut. *vivrò*, P. p. *vissuto*) (*èssere*)

to die, *morire* (Pres. *muoio, muori, muore, moriamo, morite, muòiono*; Fut. *morirò* or *morrò*; P. p. *morto*) (*èssere*)

to work, *lavorare*

to give, *dare* (Pres. *do, dai, dà, diamo, date, dànno*; Past *diedi, desti, diede, demmo, deste, dièdero*; Impv. Pol. *dia*)

to take, *prèndere* (Past *presi*, P. p. *preso*)

to show, *mostrare, far vedere*

to begin, to start, *cominciare, iniziare*

to finish, *finire* (*-isc-*)

to continue, keep on, *continuare, seguitare* (he kept on speaking, *continuò a parlare*)

to help, *aiutare*

to hide, *nascòndere* (Past *nascosi*, P. p. *nascosto*)

to lose, *pèrdere* (Past *persi*, P. p. *perso*, or both regular)

to find, *trovare*

to leave, *lasciare*

to try, *provare*

to meet, *incontrare* (use *conòscere* for the social sense)

to put, place, *mèttere* (Past *misi*, P. p. *messo*)

to have done, *far fare* (I have the letter written, *faccio scrìvere la lèttera*)

to do, make, *fare* (Pres. *faccio, fai, fa, facciamo, fate, fanno*; Impf. *facevo*; Past *feci, facesti*, etc.; Fut. *farò*; Impv. *fa, fate, faccia*) to be able, can, *potere* (Pres. *pos-so, puoi, può, possiamo, pote-te, pòssono*; Fut. *potrò*)

to lay, *posare*

to carry, bring, *portare*

to stop, *fermare* (*fermarsi* for self), *arrestare, arrestarsi* (use *cessare di fare* for "to stop doing")

to cover, *coprire* (P. p. *coperto*)

to get, obtain, *ottenere* (like *tene-re*, below)

to hold, *tenere* (Pres. *tengo, tieni, tiene, teniamo, tenete, tèngono*;

Past *tenni*; Fut. *terrò*; "Here! Take it!", *tieni!, tenga!*)

to get, become, *diventare, dive-nire* (like *venire*, cf. p. 341) (*èssere*)

to break, *rómpere* (Past *ruppi*, P. p. *rotto*)

to hurry, *affrettarsi, sbrigarsi*

to deliver, *consegnare*

to send, *mandare, spedire* (*-isc-*)

to belong, *appartenere* (like *te-nere*) (*èssere*)

to accept, *accettare*

to refuse, *rifiutare*

22. Adjectives.

small, *piccolo*

large, great, *grande* (*gran* before a sg. noun)

big, *grosso*

tall, high, *alto*

short, *corto*

low, short (stature), *basso*

heavy, *pesante*

light (in weight), *leggero*

long, *lungo* (pl. *-ghi, -ghe*)

wide, *largo* (pl. *-ghi, -ghe*)

narrow, *stretto*

clean, *pulito*

dirty, *sporco* (pl. *-chi, -che*)

cool, *fresco* (pl. *-chi, -che*)

cold, *freddo*

warm, hot, *caldo*

damp, *ùmido*

wet, *bagnato*

dry, *secco* (pl. *-chi, -che*), *asciut-to*

full, *pieno*

empty, *vuoto*

dark, *scuro, oscuro*

light, bright, clear, *chiaro*

fat, *grasso*

thick, *spesso, grosso*

thin, *magro, fino, sottile*

round, *rotondo*

square, *quadrato, quadro*

flat, *piatto*

deep, *profondo*

soft, *mòrbido, sòffice*

hard, *duro*

quick, *veloce*

slow, *lento*

ordinary, *ordinario*

comfortable, *còmodo*

uncomfortable, *scòmodo*

near, *vicino*

distant, *lontano*

right, *destro*

left, *sinistro*

poor, *pòvero*

rich, *ricco* (pl. *-chi, -che*)

beautiful, *bello* (cf. p. 317)

pretty, *grazioso, carino*

ugly, *brutto*

sweet, *dolce*

bitter, *amaro*

sour, *aspro, acre*

salt, *salato*

young, *giòvane*

old, *vecchio* (pl. *vecchi*)

new, *nuovo*
good, *buono* (*buon* before masc.
 sg. nouns unless they begin with
 z or s + consonant; *buon'* before fem. sg. nouns beginning
 with vowels)
better, *migliore* (best, *il* -)
bad, *cattivo*
worse, *peggiore* (worst, *il* -)
fine, "regular", *òttimo*
first, *primo*
last, *ùltimo*
strong, *forte*
weak, *dèbole*
tired, *stanco* (pl. *-chi, -che*)
alone, *solo*
same, *stesso, medèsimo*
easy, *fàcile*
hard, difficult, *difficile*
happy, glad, *contento, felice*
merry, *allegro*
sad, *triste, addolorato*
free, *libero*
crazy, *pazzo, matto*
silly, *stùpido, cretino, imbecille*
drunk, *ubriaco*
polite, *cortese, gentile*
rude, *scortese, villano, maleducato*
pleasant, *piacèvole*

unpleasant, *spiacèvole*
lonesome, *solitario, solo*
true, *vero*
false, *falso*
foreign, *straniero*
friendly, *amichèvole, amico* (pl.
 -ci, -che)
hostile, *ostile, nemico* (pl. *-ci,
 -che*)
lucky, *fortunato*
unlucky, *sfortunato, disgraziato*
charming, *incantèvole*
kind, *gentile*
afraid, *pauroso, timoroso*
ready, *pronto*
hungry, *affamato*
thirsty, *assetato*
funny, *buffo, còmico* (pl. *-ci, -che*)
possible, *possìbile*
impossible, *impossìbile*
brave, *bravo, coraggioso*
cowardly, *vigliacco* (pl. *-chi,
 -che*), *vile, codardo*
quiet, *tranquillo, quieto*
noisy, *chiassoso, rumoroso*
living, *vivo, vivente*
dead, *morto*
suitable, *adatto*

23. Colors.

white, *bianco* (pl. *-chi, -che*)
black, *nero*
red, *rosso*
green, *verde*
blue, *turchino, azzurro, celeste*

yellow, *giallo*
gray, *grigio, bigio*
brown, *marrone, bruno*
pink, *rosa*
purple, *viola, violàceo*

24. Nationalities.

Use no capital for the adjective or for the language: the
English army, *l'esèrcito inglese;* he speaks French, *parla francese.* When used as a noun to indicate people, the capital may
or may not be used: an American, *un americano, un America-*

no; the Germans, *i tedeschi, i Tedeschi.* It is perhaps more usually not used.

Names of languages are used *with* the article unless they *immediately* follow the verb *parlare* or the preposition *in:* he speaks English, *parla inglese;* he speaks English well, **parla bene** *l'inglese;* English is a difficult language, *l'inglese è una lingua difficile;* he answered me in English, *mi rispose in inglese.*

American, *americano*
English, *inglese*
French, *francese*
German, *tedesco* (pl. *-chi, -che*)
Spanish, *spagnuolo*
Russian, *russo*
Italian, *italiano*
Japanese, *giapponese*
Chinese, *cinese*
Dutch, *olandese*
Norwegian, *norvegese*
Swedish, *svedese*
Finnish, *finlandese*
Belgian, *belga* (fem. *-a,* masc. pl. *-gi,* fem. pl. *-ghe*)
Polish, *polacco* (pl. *-chi, -che*)
Danish, *danese*
Swiss, *svizzero*
Portuguese, *portoghese*
Yugoslav. *jugoslavo*

Bulgarian, *bùlgaro*
Czech, *ceco*
Greek, *greco* (pl. *-ci, -che*)
Turkish, *turco* (pl. *-chi, -che*)
Roumanian, *rumeno*
Hungarian, *ungherese*
Austrian, *austrìaco* (pl. *-ci, -che*)
Malay, *malese*
Persian, *persiano*
Arabian, Arab, Arabic, *àrabo*
Jewish, Hebrew, *ebreo, ebràico* (pl. *-ci, -che*)
Australian, *australiano*
Canadian, *canadese*
Mexican, *messicano*
Brazilian, *brasìliano, brasileno*
Argentinian, *argentino*
Chilean, *cileno*
Peruvian, *peruviano*
Cuban, *cubano*

25. *Adverbs and Adverbial Expressions.*

today, *oggi*
yesterday, *ieri*
tomorrow, *domani*
day before yesterday, *avantieri, ieri l'altro*
day after tomorrow, *dopodomani*
tonight, *stasera, stanotte*
last night, *ieri sera, ieri notte, la notte scorsa*
this morning, *stamane, stamattina*
in the morning, *di mattina*

in the afternoon, *di dopopranzo*
in the evening, *di sera*
in the night, *di notte*
this afternoon, *oggi dopopranzo*
tomorrow morning, *domani mattina*
tomorrow afternoon, *domani dopopranzo*
tomorrow night, *domani sera*
early, *presto*
on time. *a tempo*

late, *tardi*
already, *già*
no longer, *non più*
yet, still, *ancora, tuttavìa*
not yet, *non ancora*
now, *adesso, ora*
then, *allora*
afterwards, *poi, in sèguito, dopo*
never, *mai* (use *non* before verb:
   he is never here, *non è mai qui*)
always, *sempre*
forever, *per sempre*
soon, *presto*
often, *spesso*
seldom, *di rado, raramente*
usually, *di sòlito, per sòlito*
fast, *presto*
slowly, *piano, lentamente*
here, *qui, qua*
there, *lì, là*
over (down) there, *laggiù*
near by, *vicino*
far away, *lontano*
up (stairs), *su, sopra, di sopra*
down (stairs), *giù, sotto, di sotto*
ahead, in front, *davanti*
behind, in back, *di dietro*
forward, *avanti*
back, backward, *indietro*
outside, *di fuori, fuori*
inside, *dentro, di dentro*
opposite, in front, *di fronte*
here and there, *qua e là*
everywhere, *dappertutto, dovun-
   que*
where, *dove*
also, too, *anche, pure*
yes, *sì*
no, *no*
not, *non*
very, much, *molto* (very much,
   moltìssimo)
well, *bene*

badly, *male*
better, *meglio*
worse, *peggio*
only, *solo, soltanto, solamente*
more, *più*
less, *meno*
as - as, *tanto - quanto* (*come*)
as much - as, *tanto - quanto*
as many - as, *tanti - quanti*
how much?, *quanto?*
how many?, *quanti?*
how?, *come?*
too much, *troppo*
too many, *troppi*
so much, *tanto*
so many, *tanti*
as, like, *come*
so, *così*
besides, *inoltre, per di più*
finally, in short, *finalmente, infine*
almost, *quasi*
gladly, *volentieri*
certainly, *certo, certamente*
at once, *sùbito*
at all, *affatto*
hardly, *appena*
aloud, *forte*
of course, *naturalmente, ben inte-
   so*
suddenly, *d'improvviso*
about, *circa*
perhaps, maybe, *forse, chissà*
a little, *un poco, un pò*
again, *di nuovo, ancora, nuova-
   mente*
really, truly, *veramente*
together, *insieme*
at least, *almeno*
for lack of, *per mancanza di*
a long time ago, *molto tempo fa*
again and again, *ripetute volte*
therefore, *quindi, perciò*
occasionally, *di quando in quando*

26. Conjunctions.

and, *e*

but, *ma, però*

if, *se*

or, *o*

why?, *perchè?*

because, *perchè*

why!, *ma!*

before, *prima che* [23]

when, *quando*

than, *di* (use *che* before an adjective)

where, *dove*

until, *finchè*

although, *benchè, quantunque* [23]

unless, *a meno che* (use *non* before the verb) [23]

while, *mentre*

that, *che*

for, since, *poichè*

after, *dopo che*

as soon as, *appena*

as long as, *fin tanto che*

provided that, *purchè* [23]

so that, *affinchè* [23]

without, *senza che* [23]

27. Indefinite Pronouns and Adjectives.

such a, *un tale*

all kinds of, *ogni sorta di*

everything, *tutto, ogni cosa*

everyone, *tutti*

all, *tutto*

each, every, *ogni, ciascuno*

something, *qualche cosa* (something good, *qualche cosa di buono*)

someone, *qualcuno*

some, *alcuni, qualche,* (indef.)

enough, *abbastanza*

nothing, *niente, nulla* (nothing good, *nulla di buono*) [24]

no one, *nessuno* [24]

no (adj.), *nessun (-a), alcun (-a)* [24]

neither - nor, *nè - nè* [24]

(an) other, *(un) altro*

much, lots of, *molto*

many, lots of, *molti*

several, *parecchi, diversi*

little (not much), *poco*

few, *pochi*

both, *entrambi, ambedue, tutti e due*

28. Prepositions.

of, *di*

from, by, since, at the house (or place of business) of, *da*

out of, *fuori di*

to, at, *a*

with, *con*

without, *senza* [25]

in, *in*

on, over, above, *su, sopra* [25]

for, *per*

[23]. These take the subjunctive.

[24]. If these expressions appear *after* the verb, *non* is required before the verb: nothing has been done, *nulla si è fatto* or *non si è fatto nulla;* no one came, *nessuno è venuto* or *non è venuto nessuno.*

until, up to, *fino a*
toward, *verso* [25]
between, among, *tra, fra*
near, *vicino a*
far from, *lontano da*
before, *prima di*
after, *dopo di*
under (neath), *sotto* [25]
instead of, *invece di*
beside, *oltre a*
through, across, *attraverso* [25]
against, *contro* [25]

by means of, *per mezzo di*
on the other side of, *dall'altro lato di*
in spite of, *malgrado*
about, around, *attorno a*
during, *durante*
because of, on account of, *a causa di, per causa di*
opposite, in front of, *davanti a, di fronte a*
back of, behind, *dietro*[25]

29. *Special Expressions and Idioms.*

good morning, good afternoon, good day, *buon giorno*
good evening, *buona sera*
good night, *buona notte*
good-bye, *arrivederci, addìo, ciao* (the latter is also used for "hello!")
I'll see you later, *a più tardi*
I'll see you tomorrow, *a domani*
I'll see you tonight, *a stasera*
just now, *proprio adesso, proprio ora*
hello! (on the telephone), *pronto!*
how are you?, *come sta?*
how goes it?, *come va?*
I'm well, *sto bene*
I'm (much) better, *sto (molto) meglio*
what time is it?, *che or'è?, che ore sono?*
It's six o'clock, *sono le sei*
at six o'clock, *alle sei*
at about six, *verso le sei*
at half past six, *alle sei e mezzo*
at a quarter past (to) six, *alle sei e (meno) un quarto*
at ten minutes past (to) six, *alle sei e (meno) dieci*
last year, *l'anno scorso (passato)*
next year, *l'anno venturo (pròssimo, che viene)*
every day, *ogni giorno, tutti i giorni*
the whole day, *tutto il giorno, tutta la giornata*
please, *per favore, per piacere, La prego*
tell me, *mi dica*

[25]. These require *di* after them if their object is a personal pronoun: without my brother, *senza mio fratello;* without him, *senza di lui.*

bring me, *mi porti*
show me, *mi faccia vedere*
thank you, *grazie*
don't mention it, *prego, non c'è di che, niente*
will you give me?, *vuol darmi?*
pardon me, *scusi*
it doesn't matter, never mind, *non importa, non fa niente*
I'm sorry, *mi dispiace, mi rincresce*
I can't help, *non posso fare a meno di*
it's nothing, *non è niente*
what a pity!, it's too bad!, *che peccato!*
I'm glad, *mi fa piacere*
I have to, *debbo*
I agree (all right, O. K.), *(sono) d'accordo; siamo intesi*
where is (are)?, *dov'è (dove sono)?*
where are you going?, *dove va?*
there is (are), *ecco* (if pointing out), *c'è (ci sono)*
which way?, *da che parte?*
to the right, *a destra*
to the left, *a sinistra*
straight ahead, *dritto*
this (that) way (direction), *di qua (là), da questa (quella) parte*
this (that) way (fashion), *così, in questo (quel) modo*
come with me, *venga con me*
what can I do for you?, *in che posso servirla?*
what is it?, what is the matter?, *che c'è?*
what is the matter with you?, *che ha?*
what is happening?, *che succede?*
what do you want?, *che (cosa) vuole (desìdera)?*
what are you talking about?, *di che parla?*
what does that mean?, what do you mean?, *cosa vuol dire?*
how much is it?, *quanto costa?*
anything else?, *altro?*
nothing else, *nient'altro*
do you speak Italian?, *parla italiano?*
a little, *un pò*
speak (more) slowly, *parli (più) piano (lentamente)*
do you understand?, *capisce?, comprende?*
I don't understand, *non capisco (comprendo)*
do you know?, *sa?*
I don't know, *non so*
I can't, *non posso*
what do you call this in Italian?, *come si chiama questo in italiano?*

how do you say — in Italian?, *come si dice — in italiano?*
I'm an American, *sono americano*
I'm hungry (thirsty, sleepy, warm, cold), *ho fame (sete, sonno, caldo, freddo)* [26]
it's warm (cold, sunny, fine weather, bad weather), *fa caldo (freddo, sole, bel tempo, cattivo tempo)* [26]; it's windy, *tira vento*
it's forbidden, *è proibito (vietato)*; no smoking, *vietato fumare*
luckily, *per fortuna*
unfortunately, *per disgrazia*
is it not so?, *non è vero?* (use this invariable phrase wherever English repeats the verb: you went, *didn't you?*; he is here, *isn't he?*)
not at all, *niente affatto*
how old are you?, *quanti anni ha?*
I'm twenty years old, *ho venti anni*
how long have you been here?, *da quanto tempo si trova qui?*
how long have you been waiting?, *da quanto tempo aspetta?*
as soon as possible, *al più presto*
come here!, *venga qua!*
come in!, *avanti!*
look!, *guardi!*
look out! careful!, *attenzione!, attento!*
for heaven's sake!, *per carità!*
darn it!, *accidenti!* (darn the luck!, *accidenti alla fortuna!*)
gangway!, by your leave!, *permesso?*
as you wish, *come vuole*
listen!, look here!, say!, *senta! stia a sentire!, dica!*
just a minute!, *un momento!*
in any case, at any rate, *in ogni caso*
may I introduce?, *permette che Le presenti?*
glad to meet you, *fortunatissimo, piacere*
no admittance!, *vietato l'ingresso*
notice!, *avviso!*
you don't say so!, *possìbile?*
to your health!, *salute!*
I should like to, *vorrei*
as quickly as possible, *al più presto possìbile*
stop!, *ferma!*
hurry!, *(faccia) presto, si sbrighi*
keep right (left), *tenere la destra (sinistra)*
entrance, *entrata*
exit, *uscita*

---

26. With all these expressions, translate "very" by *molto*, save with *fame* and *sete (molta)*: *ho molta sete, ho molto sonno.*

CHAPTER X

LANGUAGES OF THE SLAVIC GROUP

This imposing group, extending from the shores of the Baltic and the Adriatic, across central and eastern Europe and all of northern Asia, to Kamchatka, Behring Strait and Vladivostok on the Pacific coast, comprises Russian, with its kindred East Slavic tongues, Ukrainian and White Russian; a Northwestern group that takes in Polish, Czech, Slovak, and a few minor languages (Wend or Lusatian, Kashub); and a Southern division which includes Serbo-Croatian, Slovenian and Bulgarian. The distinction among the three Slavic groups (eastern, northwestern and southern) is perhaps more geographical than linguistic.

Russian (or Great Russian) is the official and principal language of the Soviet Union, with its 130,000,000 inhabitants in Europe and 41,000,000 more in Asia. While not all of these 171,000,000 people speak Russian as a primary language, the majority of them can be reached with it. The actual number of Great Russian speakers is estimated at over 100,000,000. Ukrainian (also called Ruthenian or Carpatho-Russian in its westernmost varieties) is the tongue of some 35,000,000 more people located in southeastern Poland (formerly Galicia), the Carpathian section of Czechoslovakia, and the Russian Ukraine, as far east as the Kuban Valley and the Caucasus. About 8,000,000 more, situated in west central Russia and eastern Poland, speak White Russian. The remaining populations of the Soviet Union speak a multitude of tongues, mostly of the Ural-Altaic variety, but Russian has imposed itself as a colonizing tongue across all of Siberia, particularly along the upper courses of the great rivers and on the Pacific coast, in Transcaucasia, and in Turkestan.

Polish is the official tongue of Poland, with its 35,000,000 inhabitants, to about 25,000,000 of whom the Polish tongue is native and primary (the remainder of Poland's population speaks White Russian, Ukrainian, German, Yiddish, Lithuanian and Kashub). Some 3,000,000 Polish speakers and their descendants, incidentally, are located in the U. S. A., mostly in the mining and industrial districts of Pennsylvania, Ohio, Illinois and Michigan.

Czech, the official tongue of Czechoslovakia, is native to over 7,000,000 inhabitants of Bohemia and Moravia, while its variant, Slovak, is spoken by about 3,000,000 (the rest of Czechoslovakia's 15,000,000 inhabitants have German, Hungarian, Ruthenian and Yiddish as primary tongues). Nearly 2,000,000 Czechs and Slovaks have come to the U. S. A.

Wend (or Lusatian) is spoken by perhaps 150,000 people entirely surrounded by German speakers in the heart of the Reich, at Cottbus and Bautzen.

Approximately 12,000,000 of Yugoslavia's 16,000,000 people speak Serbo-Croatian, while 1,500,000 more use Slovene (or Slovenian), which appears also in the extreme northeast of Italy (Istria, Gorizia, Carso Plateau, Venetia northeast of Udine) and the border districts of Austria. Linguistic minorities in Yugoslavia consist of German, Hungarian, Albanian, Roumanian and Italian speakers.

Bulgarian is the language of Bulgaria's 6,500,000 inhabitants, and crosses the political borders into Yugoslav and Greek Macedonia, Roumanian Dobrudja and southern Bessarabia.

The distributional aspects of the Slavic tongues point to Russian as of primary importance, numerically, politically, economically and culturally. Polish is a somewhat distant second, while Czech and the South Slavic languages are of tertiary rank.

GENERAL CHARACTERISTICS, COMMON FEATURES, AND OUTSTANDING DIFFERENCES.

By comparison with the Germanic and Romance groups, the Slavic tongues present an archaic and conservative aspect, much closer than either of the other major groups to what must have been the original Indo-European state of affairs. Most of the Slavic languages are distinguished by a full-bodied richness of consonant sounds, with practically all consonants appearing in a double series, non-palatal and palatal (e. g., Polish *ł, l*; Serbo-Croatian *n, nj*; Czech *t, ť*). Often the palatal series is used before front vowels, the non-palatal before back vowels or where no vowel follows (e. g., Czech *druh*, comrade, but *druzi*, comrades; *voják*, soldier, but *vojáci*, soldiers). In grammar, the Slavic languages, with one exception, Bulgarian, have retained almost all of the original Indo-European system of noun declension, which means that nouns must often be learned in as many as seven cases (nominative, genitive, dative, accusative, instrumental, locative or prepositional, and vocative). The three grammatical genders, masculine, feminine and neuter, appear, but the majority of inanimate objects are masculine or feminine. The verb-system is relatively simple, only three true tenses (present, past and future) appearing in most cases, but this apparent simplicity is counterbalanced by the fact that many verbs appear in complicated double "aspects", "imperfective", to denote the action as occurring repeatedly or continually, and "perfective", to indicate that it occurs only once (e. g., Russian стучать (*stučat'*), to knock repeatedly, continually; постучать (*postučat'*), to knock once; to translate "he knocked on the door", the past of the compounded verb must be used; to translate "he was knocking when I came in", the past of the uncompounded verb appears). The Slavic languages also make abundant use of gerunds and participles, active and passive, present and past, which are often used where Germanic or Romance languages would use clauses (e. g., "he resembled a man who was losing his last hope and had left everything behind" may be translated into Russian by changing the construction to "he resembled a man losing his last hope and having left everything behind").

In sounds, in grammatical structure, and especially in vocabulary, the Slavic languages are far closer to one another than are the tongues of the Germanic or Romance groups. This similarity, in the spoken languages, is often so striking that they are to a considerable degree mutually comprehensible, and that it takes a trained ear to tell them apart. Accentuation is perhaps the best norm of general distinction. While Czech and Slovak normally accentuate on the first syllable of the word, the Polish stress regularly falls on the next to the last; the other languages, notably Russian, have a free accent, which means that words may be stressed, more or less unpredictably, on any syllable, and that the place of the accent for every given word must be individually learned. Serbo-Croatian tends to avoid final accentuation, distinguishes between long and short vowels, and has a certain amount of musical pitch; Czech and Slovak distinguish with extreme care between long and short vowels, and it is perfectly possible to have a short accented vowel and a long unaccented vowel in the same word; Polish, Bulgarian and Russian make no particular distinction between long and short vowels, but in Russian unstressed vowels tend to have a slurred and indistinct pronunciation. Polish preserves nasal vowels (ą, ę) which the other Slavic languages have changed to non-nasal sounds. Polish and Czech have a palatalized *r* (*rz, ř*) which does not appear in the other tongues.

The comparative similarity of the spoken Slavic tongues is offset by striking differences in their written appearance. Those Slavic nations which received Christianity, directly or indirectly, from Byzantium (Russians, Ukrainians, Serbs, Bulgars) have adopted a modified form of the Greek alphabet called Cyrillic, while the others (Czechs, Slovaks, Poles, Croats, Slovenes), who became Roman Catholics, use the Roman alphabet. This leads to such anomalies as a single, fairly unified spoken tongue like Serbo-Croatian appearing in written form in two alphabets (Yugoslav railway stations and postage stamps bear the identical names and inscriptions, first in

Cyrillic, then in Roman characters). The situation is further complicated by the fact that the peoples using either set of characters have devised entirely different arrangements to represent identical sounds; thus, the *ch* of *church* is represented by *cz* in Polish, by *č* in Czech and Croatian; the *ny* of *canyon* is *nj* in Croatian, *ň* in Czech, *ń* in Polish. There is a little more uniformity among the nations using the Cyrillic characters, but here too striking discrepancies appear (Russian нь, Serbian љ, to represent *ny*; Russian ть, Serbian ћ, to represent a palatalized *t*; while щ, appearing in both Russian and Bulgarian, has the value of A*shch*urch in the former, of A*sht*on in the latter).

THE CYRILLIC ALPHABETS

The letters R, S, B, in parentheses indicate that the character in question appears in Russian, Serbian, or Bulgarian; thus, Б, б (RSB) indicates that all three languages make use of the symbol; Я, я (RB) shows that the symbol is used in Russian and Bulgarian, but not in Serbian; Љ (S), that it appears only in Serbian. OR indicates that the symbol was in use in Russian prior to the Soviet orthographical reform, and that it may be encountered in pre-Soviet writings, or occasionally even today, in the writings of conservatives. Ukrainian uses Russian orthography, with Є replacing Э, and ї used to soften a preceding consonant. The values given are the more usual ones; other values will be presented under the headings of the individual languages.

Symbol		Languages using it	Customary Value
А	а		*fa*ther (R unstressed th*e*)
Б	б	(RSB)	*b*ut
В	в	(RSB)	*v*oice
Г	г	(RSB)	*g*ood
Д	д	(RSB)	*d*ear
Ђ	ђ	(RSB)	di*d* *y*ou?
Е	е	(S)	*y*et (R); m*e*t (SB)
		(RSB)	

Ё ё	(R)	yore
Ж ж	(RSB)	pleasure
З з	(RSB)	zealous
И и	(RSB)	machine
Й й	(RB)	boy
I i	(OR, Ukr)	machine
J j	(S)	young
К k	(RSB)	kiss
Л л	(RSB)	leave
Љ љ	(S)	million
М м	(RSB)	man
Н н	(RSB)	not
Њ њ	(S)	canyon
О о	(RSB)	or (R unstressed the)
П п	(RSB)	peel
Р р	(RSB)	British very
С с	(RSB)	soon
Т т	(RSB)	take
Ћ ћ	(S)	hit you
У у	(RSB)	pool
Ф ф	(RSB)	father
Х х	(RSB)	German ach
Ц ц	(RSB)	its
Ч ч	(RSB)	church
Џ џ	(S)	John
Ш ш	(RSB)	sure
Щ щ	(RB)	Ashchurch (R); Ashton (B)
Ъ ъ	(OR, B)	silent (R); but (B); silent when final
Ы ы	(R)	rhythm
Ь ь	(RB)	silent, but palatalizes preceding consonant.
Ѣ ѣ	(OR, B)	yet (R); yet, met, yard (B)
Э э	(R)	met
Ю ю	(RB)	use
Я я	(RB)	yard

Ӕ	ӕ	(B)	but
Ѳ	ѳ	(OR)	father
V	v	(OR)	machine

It will be noted that Serbian uses the single characters ђ, љ, њ, ћ, where Russian uses the combinations дь, ль, нь, ть. Croatian uses the following combinations dj, (or đ), lj, nj, ć.

★ ★ ★

Points of similarity and divergence will be noted in the discussion of the individual languages. Some of the resemblances and differences among the major national Slavic tongues may be gathered from the following list (Russian and Bulgarian are given in Cyrillic characters; Serbo-Croatian is given in the Croatian form (Roman alphabet); Polish and Czech appear in their respective Roman alphabets).

English	Russian	Polish	Czech	Serbo-Croatian	Bulgarian
bird	птица	*ptak*	*pták*	*ptica*	птица
black	чёрный	*czarny*	*černý*	*crn*	черенъ
bread	хлеб	*chleb*	*chléb*	*hljeb*	хлѣбъ
bring	носить	*nosić*	*nositi*	*nositi*	нося
brother	брат	*brat*	*bratr*	*brat*	братъ
bull	бык	*byk*	*býk*	*bik*	бикъ
clean	чистый	*czysty*	*čistý*	*čist*	чистъ
day	день	*dzień*	*den*	*dan*	день
death	смерть	*śmierć*	*smrt*	*smrt*	смърть
dog	пёс	*pies*	*pes*	*pas*	куче
drink	пить	*pić*	*piti*	*piti*	пия
eagle	орёл	*orzeł*	*orel*	*orao*	орелъ
ear	ухо	*ucho*	*ucho*	*uho (uvo)*	ухо
earth	земля	*ziemia*	*země*	*zemlja*	земя
field	поле	*pole*	*pole*	*polje*	поле
fire	огонь	*ogień*	*oheň*	*oganj*	огънь
foot	нога	*noga*	*noha*	*noga*	нога
free	свободный	*swobodny*	*svobodný*	*slobodan*	свободенъ
gold	золото	*złoto*	*zlato*	*zlato*	злато
good	добрый	*dobry*	*dobrý*	*dobar*	добъръ
grass	трава	*trawa*	*tráva*	*trava*	трѣва

green	зелёный	zielony	zelený	zelen	зеленъ
hand	рука	ręka	ruka	ruka	ржка
hard	твёрдый	twardy	tvrdý	tvrd	твърдъ
head	голова	głowa	hlava	glava	глава
heart	сердце	serce	srdce	srce	сърдце
horse	конь	koń	kůň	konj	конь
hunger	голод	głód	hlad	glad	гладъ
husband	муж	mąż	muž	muž	мжжъ
iron	железо	żelazo	železo	željezo	желѣзо
king	король	król	král	kralj	краль
knife	нож	nóz	nůž	nož	ножъ
know	знать	znać	znáti	znati	зная
leaf	лист	liść	list	list	листъ
learn	учиться	uczyć się	učiti se	učiti se	уча се
man	человек	człowiek	člověk	čovjek	човѣкъ
meat	мясо	mięso	maso	meso	месо
milk	молоко	mleko	mléko	mlijeko	млѣко
night	ночь	noc	noc	noć	нощь
nose	нос	nos	nos	nos	носъ
old	старый	stary	starý	stari	старъ
play	играть	grać	hráti	igrati	играя
read	читать	czytać	čisti	čitati	чета
rich	богатый	bogaty	bohatý	bogat	богатъ
sea	море	morze	moře	more	море
see	видеть	widzieć	viděti	vidjeti	виждамъ
sister	сестра	siostra	sestra	sestra	сестра
sky	небо	niebo	nebe	nebo	небе
small	малый	mały	malý	mali	малъкъ
son	сын	syn	syn	sin	синъ
tree	дерево	drzewo	strom	drvo	дърво
truth	правда	prawda	pravda	istina	истина
water	вода	woda	voda	voda	вода
one	один	jeden	jeden	jedan	единъ
two	два	dwa	dva	dva	два
three	три	trzy	tři	tri	три
four	четыре	cztery	čtyři	četiri	четири
five	пять	pięć	pět	pet	петь
six	шесть	sześć	šest	šest	шесть
seven	семь	siedem	sedm	sedam	седемь
eight	восемь	osiem	osm	osam	осемь
nine	девять	dziewięć	devět	devet	деветь
ten	десять	dziesięć	deset	deset	десеть
eleven	одиннадцать	jedenaście	jedenáct	jedanaest	единадесеть

twenty	двадцать	*dwadzieścia*	*dvacet*	*dvadeset*	двайсеть
hundred	сто	*sto*	*sto*	*sto*	сто
thousand	тысяч	*tysiąc*	*tisíc*	*hiljada*	хиляда

SAMPLES OF THE WRITTEN SLAVIC LANGUAGES (RUSSIAN, WHITE RUSSIAN, UKRAINIAN, BULGARIAN ARE GIVEN IN CYRILLIC CHARACTERS; SERBO-CROATIAN IS GIVEN IN THE CROATIAN VERSION, IN ROMAN CHARACTERS; POLISH, CZECH, SLOVAK, SLOVENIAN, WENDISH APPEAR IN THEIR RESPECTIVE ROMAN ORTHOGRAPHIES).

John 3.16: "For God so loved the world that He gave His only-begotten Son, that whosoever believeth in Him may not perish, but may have everlasting life"

RUSSIAN: Ибо так возлюбил Бог мир, что отдал Сына Своего единородного, дабы всякий, верующий в Него, не погиб, но имел жизнь вечную.

WHITE RUSSIAN: Бо так палюбіў Бог сьвéт, што аддаў Сына Свайго Адзінароднага, каб усякі, хто вéруе ў Яго, ня згінуў, але мéў жыцьцё вéчнае.

UKRAINIAN: Так бо полюбив Бог сьвіт, що Сина свого Єдинородного дав, щоб кожен, віруючий в Него, не погиб, а мав житте вічне.

POLISH: Albowiem tak Bóg umiłował świat, że Syna swego jednorodzonego dał, aby każdy, kto weń wierzy, nie zginął, ale miał żywot wieczny.

CZECH: Nebo tak Bůh miloval svět, že Syna svého jednorozeného dal, aby každý, kdož věří v něho, nezahynul, ale měl život věčný.

SLOVAK: Lebo tak miloval Bôh svet, že svojho jednorodeného Syna dal, aby každý, kto verí v neho, nezahynul, ale mal večný život.

WEND (or LUSATIAN): Pschetoż tak je Boh ton Sswjet lubowal, so won sswojeho jeniczkeho narodżeneho Ssyna dal je, so bychu schitzy, kiż do njeho wjerja, shubeni nebyli, ale wjeczne żiwenje mjeli.

SERBO-CROATIAN (in Croatian orthography): Jer Bog
toliko ljubi svet, da je i Sina svoga jedinorodjenoga dao, da ni
jedan koji u njega veruje ne propadne, nego da ima život
vječni.

SLOVENIAN: Kajti tako je Bog ljubil svet, da je dal Sina
svojega edinorojenega, da se ne pogubi, kdorkoli veruje vanj,
temuč da ima večno življenje.

BULGARIAN: Защото Богъ толкозъ обикна свѣта,
че отдаде Своя Единороденъ Синъ, та всѣкой,
който вѣрва въ Него, да не погине, а да има
животъ вѣченъ.

POLISH

ALPHABETIC NOTATION — a, ą, b, c, ć, d, e, ę, f, g, h, i, j, k, l, ł, m, n, ń, o, ó, p, r, s, ś, t, u, w, y, z, ź, ż, ch, cz, dz, dź, dż, sz, rz, szcz.

NOTES ON SOUNDS — Vowels are of approximately equal length; a, e, i, o, u (ó) = respectively *father*, *met*, *machine*, *or*, *moon*. ą = nasalized *or*; ę = nasalized *met* (shut passage between nose and mouth at the same time that vowel is pronounced).

c = i*ts*;

ć, ci, cz = *ch*urch (there are differences; *ch*urch is only an approximation);

g = *g*o;

j = *y*es;

l = mi*ll*i*o*n;

ł = mi*l*k; in sections of Poland, = *w*ar;

ń = ca*ny*on;

w = *v*ain;

y = p*i*n;

ź (zi), ż = mea*s*ure (two variants of approximately same sound);

ch = German a*ch*, but less guttural;

dż (dzi), dż = *j*ump (two variants of approximately same sound);

rz = s in mea*s*ure;

ś (si), sz = a*sh* (two variants of approximately same sound);

szcz = A*shch*urch.

The Polish stress normally falls on the *next to the last* syllable.

GRAMMATICAL SURVEY.

Nouns.

As in all Slavic languages there are three genders, masculine, feminine and neuter; but many inanimate objects are masculine or feminine. There is no article, definite or indefinite[1]: *król* may mean "king", "a king", "the king". Generally, nouns ending in consonants are masculine, those ending in *-a* feminine, those ending in *-o* or *-e* neuter.

Polish has seven cases (nominative, genitive, **dative**, accusative, vocative, instrumental and locative). These cases appear in nouns, adjectives and pronouns, and there is no way of avoiding them. Polish nouns fall into several distinct declensional schemes, of which only a few samples can be given.[2]

Example of the declension of a masculine noun: *wuj*, "uncle": *wuj, -a, -owi, -a, -u, -em, -u*; plural: *wuj-owie, -ów, -om, -ów, -owie, -ami, -ach.*[3]

1.   *ten* (fem. *ta*, neut. *to*) is sometimes used with the value of "the", but it is more often translated by "this".

2.   The endings of the seven cases will be given in the following order: nominative (case of subject): genitive (or possessive; translated into English by "of" or 's); dative (translated into English by "to"); accusative (case of the direct object); vocative (used in direct address: "Oh, my friend!"); instrumental (used with a variety of prepositions, especially "by", "by means of"); locative (used to denote place where, "in", "at"). These seven cases appear in all Slavic languages, with the exception of Bulgarian. The vocative for the most part has the same form as the nominative, while the accusative normally has the same form as the genitive in the case of *animate* persons or animals, as the nominative in the case of *inanimate* things. Cases are very much alive in the Slavic languages, and while an occasional slip may be forgiven, complete ignorance of case-endings is not tolerated.

3.   Note that in this noun, denoting an *animate* person, the accusative has the same form as the genitive; if the noun denoted an *inanimate* object, even though masculine in gender, the accusative would have the same form as the nominative: e. g. *piec* (masc.) "stove", acc. *piec*, not *pieca*. Note also that in Polish, when case endings are added the accent may shift from the root to the ending: thus, w*u*ja, but wuj*o*wie (italics indicate syllable to be accented). This is due to the fact that the Polish rule of accentuation is to stress the next to the last syllable, regardless whether it is part of the root or of the ending.

Example of the declension of a feminine noun: *baba,* "old
   woman".

bab-a, -y, -ie, -ę, -o, -ą, -ie; plural: *bab-y, - , -om, -y, -y,
-ami, -ach.*

Example of the declension of a neuter noun: *pole,* "field":

pol-e, -a, -u, -e, -e, -em, -u; plural: *pol-a, pól, pol-om, -a,
   -a, -ami, -ach.*

Adjectives.

These agree in gender, number, and *case* with the noun to
which they refer. They also fall into distinct declensional
schemes, of which only one type can be given here: *dobry,*
"good":

Masc. Sg.	Fem. Sg.	Neut. Sg.	Animate Masc. Pl.	Inanimate Masc. Pl.; Fem. and Neut. Pl.
dobr-y	*-a*	*-e*	*-zy*	*-e*
-ego	*-ej*	*-ego*	*-ych*	*-ych*
-emu	*-ej*	*-emu*	*-ym*	*-ym*
-ego (-y)	*-ą*	*-e*	*-ych*	*-e*
-y	*-a*	*-e*	*-zy*	*-e*
-ym	*-ą*	*-ym*	*-ymi*	*-ymi*
-ym	*-ej*	*-ym*	*-ych*	*-ych*

Comparative and superlative forms of the adjectives are
also fully declined. The comparative usually inserts *-sz-* between the root and the ending, while the superlative normally
prefixes *naj-* to the comparative: *star-y,* "old"; *star-sz-y,*
"older"; *naj-star-sz-y,* "oldest".

The adverb is generally formed by replacing the *-y* or *-i*
of the masculine singular nominative adjective ending by *-o* or
-e, respectively: *wolny,* "slow"; *wolno,* "slowly".

Pronouns.

These are all fully declined, in seven cases. Where the
declension is given, the order of the cases is the same as for
nouns

Personal.

"I", "of me", "to me", "me", etc.: *ja, mnie, mnie, mię* or
    mnie, - , mną, mnie;
"we", "of us", etc.: *my, nas, nam, nas, - , nami, nas;*
"you" (familiar singular): *ty, ciebie, tobie, ciebie* or *cię, ty,*
    tobą, tobie;
"you" (fam. pl. and polite sg.): *wy, was, wam, was, wy, wami,*
    was;
"he", "his", "to him", etc.: *on, jego, jemu, jego, - , nim, nim;*
"she", "her", "to her", etc.: *ona, jej, jej, ją, - , nią, niej;*
"it", "its", "to it", etc.: *ono, jego, jemu, je, - , nim, nim;*
"they", "of them", etc. (masc. and fem.): *oni, ich, im, ich, - ,*
    nimi, nich;
"they", etc. (neuter): *one, ich, im, je, - , nimi, nich.*

Possessive (fully declined, in seven cases).

"my": *mój,* fem. *moja,* neut. *moje;*
"your" (fam. sg.): *twój, twoja, twoje;*
"his", "her", "its", "their": *swój, swoja, swoje;*
"our": *nasz, nasza, nasze;*
"your" (plural and polite singular): *wasz, wasza, wasze.*

Demonstrative (fully declined, in seven cases).

"this", "these": *ten, ta, to;* plural: *ci, te, te;*
"that", "those": *tamten, tamta, tamto;* plural: *tamci, tamte,*
    tamte.

Relative and Interrogative (fully declined).

"who", "whose", "whom": *kto* (gen. *kogo,* dat. *komu,* acc.
    kogo, instr. and loc. *kim*);
"what", "which", "that": *co* (gen. *czego,* dat. *czemu,* acc. *co,*
    instr. and loc. *czym*).

Verbs.

These display the customary Slavic poverty of tenses,
coupled with the complication of "aspects". The infinitive
usually ends in -*ć*: *kochać,* to love.

The present indicative generally adds the endings *-m*, *-sz*, *-* , *-my*, *-cie*, *-(j)ą* to the root, which is found by dropping the *-ć* of the infinitive: *kocham, kochasz, kocha, kochamy, kochacie, kochają,* I love, you love, etc. The present of *być*, "to be", is: *jestem, jesteś, jest, jesteśmy, jesteście, są.*

The past participle is formed by adding to the stem the suffixes *-ł* (masc.), *-ła* (fem.), *-ło* (neut.), *-li* (masc. plural), *-ły* (fem. and neut. pl.): *kochał, kochała, kochało, kochali, kochały,* loved.

The past tense is formed by adding the suffixes *-m*, *-ś*, *-* , *-śmy*, *-ście*, *-* , to the past participle in the appropriate form: thus, I loved (masculine "I"), *kochałem*; (feminine "I"), *kochałam*; he loved, *kochał* (past part. without ending); she loved, *kochała*; it loved, *kochało*; we loved, *kochaliśmy* (fem. *kochałyśmy*); they loved, *kochali* or *kochały*.

The past tense of *być* is: *byłem* (fem. *byłam*); *byłeś* (f. *byłaś*); *był* (f. *była*, neut. *było*); *byliśmy* (neut. *byłyśmy*); *byliście* (*byłyście*); *byli* (*były*).

A present perfect tense is formed by combining the past of the verb with the past of *być*: *kochałem był* (fem. *kochałam była*), I have loved.

The future of *być* is: *będę, będziesz, będzie, będziemy, będziecie, będą.* Other verbs form their future by combining this future of *być* with their past participle or infinitive (both forms are current): I shall love, *będę kochał* (*kochała*), or *będę kochać.*

Other tenses include a present and a past conditional (the former is formed by inserting *-by-* between the participle and the personal ending: *kochał-by-m*, I should love; the latter by adding to the present conditional the past of *być*: *kochałbym był*, I should have loved); an imperative (*kochaj*, love thou!; *kochajcie*, love ye!, *kochajmy*, let us love); and several participles (*kochając*, loving; *kochał*, loved; *kochawszy*, having loved; *kochany*, being loved; *mając kochać*, about to love); and a gerund (*kochanie*, loving).

A complete passive voice appears, formed by means of

the verb *być* combined with the passive past participle, which
ends in *-ny* or *-ty*: *jestem kochany*, I am loved; *byłem bity*, I was
beaten; *będę chwalony*, I shall be praised.

IDENTIFICATION

In spoken form, Polish can be isolated from its kindred
Slavic languages by reason of its constant accent on the next
to the last syllable, as well as by its nasal sounds (ą, ę), which
appear in no other modern language of the group. In written
form, Polish is distinguished: 1. by the fact that it uses the
Roman alphabet; this distinguishes it at once from Russian,
Ukrainian, Serbian, Bulgarian, and restricts the possibility of
confusion to Czech, Slovak, Croatian or Slovenian; 2. by its
distinctive characters, ą, ę, ł, which appear in no other Slavic
tongue; other fairly distinctive symbols of Polish are ń, ś,
ź, ż; 3. by certain fairly distinctive consonant combinations:
dz, dź, dż, rz, szcz. Polish alone, among the national Slavic
tongues, uses *w.*

WORDS AND PHRASES

pan, pani, panna, "sir" (Mr.), "madam" (Mrs.), "Miss"
czy Pan mówi po polsku?, "do you speak Polish?"
rozumiem trochę, "I understand a little"
tak, "yes"   *nie,* "no", "not"   *proszę,* "please"
dziękuję, "thank you"
dzień dobry, "good morning"
dobranoc, "good night"
jak się Pan ma?, "how are you?"
jak się Pan nazywa?, "what is your name?"
przepraszam, "excuse me"
dobry wieczór, "good evening"
do widzenia, "good-bye"
kto tam jest? "who is there?"
która godzina teraz?, "what time is it?"
jest trzecia godzina, "it is three o'clock"

niema za co, "don't mention it"
czy pan rozumie?, "do you understand?"
nie rozumiem, "I don't understand"
ile (to kosztuje)?, "how much?"
to za drogo, "too much"
bardzo, "very much"
jak się idzie do —?, "which is the way to —?"
gdzie jest —?, "where is —?"
na zdrowie!, "to your health!"
przynieś mi, "bring me"
mów powoli, łaskawie mówić powoli, "speak more slowly"
dobrze, "all right"
jestem chory, "I am ill"

SAMPLE OF WRITTEN POLISH; USE FOR PRACTICE READING

"Kelner, proszę mi dać kartę; jestem bardzo głodny." — "Zaraz ją przyniosę, proszę Pana." — "Proszę mi przynieść kapuśniak i sztukę mięsa; chcę wołowinę smażoną." — "Mięso jest twarde dzisiaj, proszę Pana." — "Czy ma Pan pieczoną kurę?" — "Tak, Panie, mamy." — "A teraz przynieś mi Pan piwa." — "Proszę zrobić rachunek. Ile się należy?" — "Dziewięćdziesiąt centów." — "Tu jest coś dla was." — "Dziękuję Panu."

TRANSLATION

"Waiter, please give me the bill of fare; I am very hungry." — "I'll bring it at once, (please) Sir." — "Please bring me some cabbage soup and boiled beef; I want the beef well done." — "The meat is tough today, (please) Sir." — "Have you roast chicken?" — "Yes, Sir, we have." — "And now bring me some beer." — "Please make out the bill. How much is it?" — "Ninety cents." — "Here is something for you." — "Thank you, Sir."

CZECH

ALPHABETIC NOTATION — a, á, b, c, č, d, ď, e, ě, f, g, h, ch, i, í, j, k, l, m, n, ň, o, ó, p, r, ř, s, š, t, ť, u, ú, ů, v, y, ý, z, ž.

NOTES ON SOUNDS — Vowels bearing the accent mark are definitely long; the others are definitely short.   There is not much difference in *quality* between any long vowel and its corresponding short; sound a, e, i, o, u as f*a*ther, m*e*t, mach*i*ne, *o*bey, p*oo*l, prolonged or shortened, according as they bear or do not bear the accent mark.

c = i*ts*;
č = *ch*urch;
ď = di*d y*ou;
ě = *ye*s;
g = *g*o;
ch = German a*ch*;
j = *y*ear;
ň = ca*ny*on;
ř = r combined with s in mea*s*ure;
š = *s*ure;
ť = hi*t y*ou;
ú, ů = f*oo*d;
y = rh*y*thm, long or short, according as it bears or does not
        bear accent mark;
ž = mea*s*ure.

The Czech accent is normally on the *initial* syllable of the word.   The accent mark indicates length of a vowel, not the place where the stress falls.

GRAMMATICAL SURVEY.

The grammatical structure is very similar to that of Polish. The same seven cases appear, for nouns, adjectives and pronouns, and they very frequently correspond to the Polish forms. The same holds true for verb-forms.

There is no article, definite or indefinite.

Example of the declension of a masculine noun: *had,* "snake": *had, -a, -ovi* (or *-u*), *-a, -e, -em, -ovi* (or *-u*); plural: *had-i* (or *-ové*), *-ŭ, -ŭm, -y, -i* (or *-ové*), *-y, -ech.*

Example of the declension of a feminine noun: *ryba,* "fish": *ryb-a, -y, -ě, -u, -o, -ou, -ě;* plural: *ryb-y, - , -ám, -y, -y, -ami, -ách.*

Example of the declension of a neuter noun: *město,* "town": *měst-o, -a, -u, -o, -o, -em, -u;* plural: *měst-a, - , -ŭm, -a, -a, -y, -ech.*

Example of the declension of an adjective: *dobrý,* "good":

Mas. Sg.	Fem. Sg.	Neut. Sg.	Mas. Pl.	Fem. Pl.	Neut. Pl.
dobr-ý	*-á*	*-é*	*dobř-i*	*dobr-é*	*dobr-á*
-ého	*-é*	*-ého*	*dobr-ých*	*-ých*	*-ých*
-ému	*-é*	*-ému*	*-ým*	*-ým*	*-ým*
-ého	*-ou*	*-é*	*-é*	*-é*	*-á*
-ý	*-á*	*-é*	*dobř-i*	*dobr-é*	*dobr-á*
-ým	*-ou*	*-ým*	*dobr-ými*	*-ými*	*-ými*
-ém	*-é*	*-ém*	*-ých*	*-ých*	*-ých*

The verb *býti,* "to be":

Present: *jsem, jsi, jest (je), jsme, jste, jsou;*

Past Participle: *byl* (fem. *byla,* neut. *bylo;* mas. pl. *byli,* fem. pl. *byly*);

Past: *byl jsem, byl jsi, byl (byla, bylo); byli jsme; byli jste, byli (byly);*

Future: *budu, budeš, bude, budeme, budete, buďou;*

mluviti, "to speak":

Present: *mluví-m, -š, - , -me, -te, -;*

Past: *mluvil jsem;* Future: *budu mluviti.*

IDENTIFICATION

In spoken form, Czech is identified by its initial stress and by long but unaccented vowel-sounds. In written form, Czech is distinguished: 1. by the fact that it uses the Roman alphabet; 2. by its distinctive characters ě, ů, ř, which do not appear in Polish or Croatian; 3. by the large number of characters with hooks over them; Croatian shares this characteristic (č, š, ž), but note that Czech has ďˇ, ň, ťˇ, while Croatian has dj (or đ) nj, ć. It is easy to distinguish Czech from Polish by the distinctive characters of the two languages (Polish ą, ę, ł, ż; Czech ě, ů, ř); by the fact that Polish uses accents over consonants (ć, ń, ś, ź), while Czech uses hooks (č, ň, š, ž); by the fact that Polish uses consonant *combinations* (cz, dz, sz, rz, szcz) which never appear in Czech; and by the Polish use of *w* as against the Czech use of *v*.

WORDS AND PHRASES

dobrý den, "good day"; *dobré ráno,* "good morning"
dobrou noc, "good night"; *dobrý večer,* "good evening"
nazdar, "to your health, good luck"
mám hlad, "I am hungry"
kolik je hodin?, "what time is it?"
jest šest hodin, "it is six o'clock"
děkuji, "thank you"; *buďte vítán,* "you're welcome"
prosím, "please"
pán, "sir"; *paní,* "madam"; *slečna,* "miss"
jak se máte?, "how are you?; *velmi dobře,* "very well"
sbohem, (or *s Bohem*) "good-bye"
dovolte, promiňte, "excuse me"
rozumíte?, "do you understand?"
nerozumím, "I don't understand"
ano, "yes"   *ne,* "no"
kolik?, "how much?"
kudy se jde do —?, "which is the way to —?"
kde je —?, "where is —?"
mluvíte anglicky?, "do you speak English?"
mluvte pomaleji, "speak more slowly"

SERBO-CROATIAN

ALPHABETIC NOTATION[4] — a, b, v, g, d, dj (đ), e, ž, z, i, j, k, l, lj, m, n, nj, o, p, r, s, t, ć, u, f, h, c, č, dž, š.

NOTES ON SOUNDS — Vowels in Serbo-Croatian are long or short, but the fact is not usually indicated in writing. The following accent marks are occasionally used to indicate two degrees of length plus a rising or falling intonation: ˜, `, ´, ⌒.
g = *go*; dj = di*d y*ou; ž = mea*s*ure; j = *y*es; lj = mi*lli*on; nj = o*ni*on; ć = hi*t y*ou; c = i*ts*; č = *ch*urch; dž = *J*ohn; š = *s*ure.

There is no definite rule of accentuation in Serbo-Croatian, but in words of more than one syllable the stress never falls on the last, although the vowel of the last syllable may be quite long, especially in genitive plural endings and in certain verb-forms.

GRAMMATICAL SURVEY.

The general structure is similar to that indicated for Polish. The cases of nouns, adjectives and pronouns often correspond in form and use, as also do verb-forms.

Example of the declension of a masculine noun: *jelen*, "deer":
jelen, *-a*, *-u*, *-a*, *-e*, *-om*, *-u*; plural: *jelen-i*, *-a*, *-ima*, *-e*, *-i*, *-ima*, *-ima*.

Example of the declension of a feminine noun: *žena*, "woman":
žen-a, *-e*, *-i*, *-u*, *-o*, *-om*, *-i*; plural: *žen-e*, *-a*, *-ama*, *-e*, *-e*, *-ama*, *-ama*.

Example of the declension of a neuter noun: *polje*, "field":
polj-e, *-a*, *-u*, *-e*, *-e*, *-em*, *-u*; plural: *polj-a*, *-a*, *-ima*, *-a*, *-a*, *-ima*, *-ima*.

4. This is given in the Croatian version (Roman alphabet); Serbian uses Cyrillic characters, as follows: а, б, в, г, д, ђ, е, ж, з, и, j, к, л, љ, м, н, њ, о, п, р, с, т, ħ, у, ф, х, ц, ч, џ, ш.

Example of the declension of an adjective: *dobri*, "good":

Mas. Sg.   Fem. Sg.   Neut. Sg.   Mas. Pl.   Fem. Pl.   Neut. Pl.

dobr-i (*dobar*)	*-a*	*-o*	*-i*	*-e*	*-a*
-oga	*-e*	*-oga*	*-ih*	*-ih*	*-ih*
-ome	*-oj*	*-ome*	*-im*	*-im*	*-im*
-oga	*-u*	*-o*	*-e*	*-e*	*-a*
-i	*-a*	*-o*	*-i*	*-e*	*-a*
-im	*-om*	*-im*	*-im*	*-im*	*-im*
-om	*-oj*	*-om*	*-im*	*-im*	*-im*

The verb *biti*, "to be":

Present: (*je*)*sam*, (*je*)*si*, *je* (or *jest*), (*je*)*smo*, (*je*)*ste*, (*je*)*su*.
Past: *beh, beše, beše, besmo, beste, behu*; or *sam bio* (*bila*), *si bio*, etc.
Future: *biću, bićeš, biće, bićemo, bićete, biće.*
The verb *čitati*, "to read":
Present: *čita-m, -š, - , -mo, -te, -ju.*
Past: *čita-h, -še, -še, -smo, -ste, -hu.*
Present Perfect: *sam, si, je čitao* (*čitala*); *smo, ste, su čitali* (*čitale*).
Future: **ću, ćeš, će,** *ćemo, ćete, će čitati*; or *čitaću, čitaćeš, čitaće*, etc.

IDENTIFICATION

A more melodious intonation than appears in other Slavic languages is noticeable in Serbo-Croatian. An accentuation which is never final, often (but not exclusively) initial, never exclusively penultimate, also serves to identify the spoken form. In writing, Croatian uses the Roman alphabet; it may be distinguished from Polish and Czech by its use of the combinations *dj, lj, nj*. Serbian uses the Cyrillic alphabet, and can be distinguished from Russian and Bulgarian by its use of the symbols ђ, ћ, њ, љ, џ, ј.

WORDS AND PHRASES

govorite li srpski?, "do you speak Serbian?"
dobar dan, "good day"
ne govorite tako brzo, "don't speak so fast"
dobro jutro, "good morning"
kako ste, gospodjice?, "how are you, young lady?"
vrlo dobro, "quite well"
lijepo je vrijeme, "it's fine weather"
dobra večer, "good evening"
imate li dobrog vina?, "have you some good wine?"
laku noć, "good night"
ručak je gotov, "dinner is ready"
u vaše zdravlje, "to your health"
koliko je sati?, "what time is it?"
sad je osam sati, "it is 8 o'clock".
izvinite, "excuse me"
z Bogom, "good-bye"
molim vas, "please"
hvala, "thank you"
nema zašto, "don't mention it"
koliko ovo iznosi?, "how much is this?"
to je i suviše, "it's too much"
razumete li?, "do you understand?"
ne razumem, "I don't understand"
da (ne), gospodine, "yes (no), sir"
kuda se ide ka —?, "which is the way to —?"
gde je —?, "where is —?"
donesite mi, "bring me"
zar ne?, "isn't it so?"
govorite polako, "speak more slowly"
slobodno, "come in"
žao mi je, "I'm sorry"
možda, "maybe"
bolestan sam, "I'm ill"

BULGARIAN

ALPHABETIC NOTATION (in Cyrillic script; see Cyrillic chart, p. 355-357):

а, б, в, г, д, е, ж, з, и, й, к, л, м, н, о, п, р, с, т, у, ф, х, ц, ч, ш, щ, ъ, ь, ѣ, ю, я, ѫ.

NOTES ON SOUNDS — Vowels have no distinctive length or shortness.

г = *go*; ж = mea*s*ure; е = *there*; ц = i*ts*; ч = *ch*urch; ш = *s*ure; щ = *Asht*on; ъ = b*u*t; however, it is silent at the end of a word; ь is always silent; ѣ = *ye*s (occasionally *ya*rd); я = *ya*rd; ю = *you*; ѫ = b*u*t.

There is no special rule of accentuation, but, unlike Serbo-Croatian a word may have the accent on the last syllable. The syllable on which the accent falls is not indicated in writing, and must be learned for each separate word.

GRAMMATICAL SURVEY.

Bulgarian differs radically from all other Slavic tongues: 1. in having a full-fledged definite article; 2. in having reduced all case-forms to a single form (with, often, a separate vocative, and a few traces of other old cases).

The Bulgarian article is placed *after* the noun, and is attached to it. Its forms are: masc. sg., тъ; fem. sg., та; neut. sg., то; plural: masc., тѣ; fem., тѣ; neut. та.
приятель, friend, a friend; приятельтъ, the friend; приятели, friends; приятелитѣ, the friends;
глава, head, a head; главата, the head; глави, heads; главитѣ, the heads;
село, village, a village; селото, the village; села, villages; селата, the villages.

Adjectives follow these schemes, and if they precede the noun, the article is attached to them: добриятъ братъ, the good brother; братътъ е добъръ, the brother is good; добрата майка, the good mother; майката е добра, the mother is good; доброто вино, the good wine; виното е добро, the wine is good; in the plural a single form is used for all genders, even the article assuming a single form: добритѣ приятели, the good friends; добритѣ майки, the good mothers; добритѣ вина, the good wines.

The Bulgarian verb has all the complications that appear in other Slavic tongues, plus a number of tenses, both simple and compound, which no longer appear in the others (Imperfect, Pluperfect, Future Perfect, etc.). The verb "to be" has the following present tense:
съмъ, си, е, сме, сте, сѫ
The verb "to call" has the following present:
викамъ, викашь, вика, викаме, викате, викатъ

IDENTIFICATION

Bulgarian appears in Cyrillic characters. It may be distinguished from Russian by the presence of the symbols ъ, ѣ, which modern Russian has discarded, and, particularly, of the symbol ѫ. The constant appearance of the endings -тъ, -та, -то, -тѣ, -та (suffixated definite articles) also serves to inform the reader or hearer that he is dealing with Bulgarian. In speech, the fairly frequent final stress of Bulgarian will serve to distinguish it from Polish, Czech and Serbo-Croatian, though not from Russian.

WORDS AND PHRASES

азъ говоря български, "I speak Bulgarian"
все едно, "it's all the same to me"
колко е часътъ, "what is the time?"
часътъ е три, "it's 3 o'clock"
кажи де, "tell me"
внимавай!, "look out!"
сбогомъ, "good-bye"
добъръ день, "good day"
добро утро, "good morning"
добра вечерь, "good evening"
лека нощь, "good night".

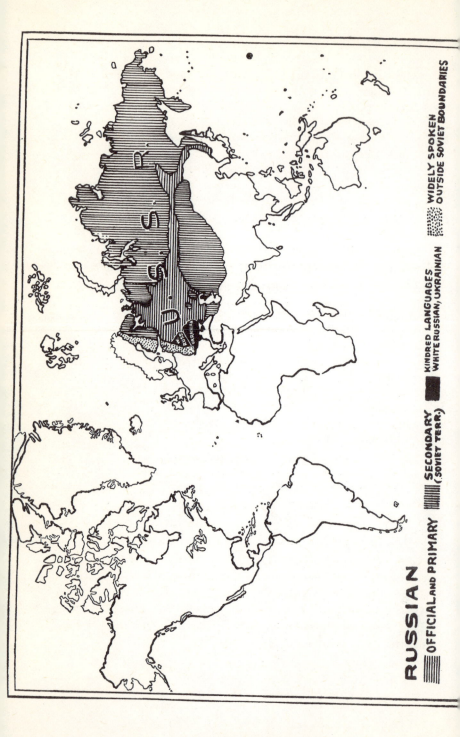

RUSSIAN

OFFICIAL and PRIMARY

SECONDARY (SOVIET TERR.)

KINDRED LANGUAGES WHITE RUSSIAN, UKRAINIAN

WIDELY SPOKEN OUTSIDE SOVIET BOUNDARIES

CHAPTER XI

RUSSIAN

SPEAKERS AND LOCATION

(All Population Figures Are Approximate)

Russian is the chief language of the Soviet Union, with a population of 171,000,000 (131,000,000 in Europe, 40,000,-000 in Asia). Russian proper (or Great Russian) is spoken as a primary language by about 100,000,000, and if its kindred tongues, Ukrainian and White Russian, are included, by over 130,000,000. It is spoken as a secondary language by over half of the remaining population of the Soviet Union, and by large numbers of people in territories once subject to Russia (Finland, Estonia, Latvia, Lithuania, Poland, Bessarabia).
The liberal linguistic and cultural policy of the Soviet Union has made many lesser tongues of the Union co-official with Russian (Ukrainian, White Russian, Georgian, Armenian, etc.). Russian settlers have, however, spread the use of Russian throughout Asiatic Russia, particularly along central Siberia, to the far eastern provinces and Vladivostok. The number of nationalities in the Soviet Union is listed at 49 basic ones (over 20,000 members), and 100 smaller ones (less than 20,000). Ukrainian speakers account for some 28,000,000; White Russian speakers are about 5,000,000. Both these languages are at least partly comprehensible to Russian speakers. The number of Russian speakers outside of Europe and Asia is not considerable, though some millions of people of Russian origin have settled in the Western Hemisphere (they come, however, largely from territories where Great Russian is not the primary tongue).

ALPHABET AND SOUNDS[1]

Аа   Бб   Вв   Гг   Дд   Ее ё

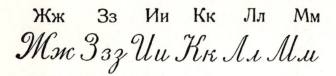

Жж   Зз   Ии   Кк   Лл   Мм

Нн   Оо   Пп   Рр   Сс   Тт

Нн Оо Пп Рр Сс Тт

Уу   Фф   Хх   Цц   Чч   Шш

Уу Фф Хх Цц Чч Шш

Щщ   Ээ   Юю   Яя   ь   ы   й   ъ

Щщ Ээ Юю Яя ь ы й ъ

1. The older Russian alphabet, used under the Tsars, contained also: the letter i, interchangeable in value, but not in use, with и; i was used regularly in connection with another vowel (Россія, today spelled Россия); the letter ъ, which was silent, but served to indicate a "hard", or non-palatal pronunciation of the preceding consonant; it appeared for the most part at the end of words, very seldom within the word; in the latter position, which is exceedingly rare, it has been retained; the letter ѣ, interchangeable in value, but not in use, with е; the letters ѵ and ѳ, interchangeable in value, respectively, with и and ф, and used in religious words borrowed from the Greek (сѵнод, synod; каѳедра, pulpit). See also Cyrillic alphabet, p. 355-357.

Vowel Sounds.

a = f*a*ther (stressed); bac*o*n, (unstressed): карандаш,[2] pencil;

e = *ye*s (more or less distinct, according as it is stressed or unstressed): есть, to eat; еда, food;

ë = *Yo*rick[3]: мёд, honey;

и = mach*i*ne: имя, name;

й = Ma*y* (this character is never used after a consonant). Май, May;

о = *o*r (stressed); bac*o*n (unstressed): хорошо, well;

у = f*oo*d: ухо, ear;

ы = rh*y*thm (this sound has no exact equivalent in English; it is best described as an attempt to pronounce f*ee*d with the front part of the mouth and f*oo*d with the back of the tongue, at the same time): был, was;

э = m*e*t: этот, this;

ь has no value of its own, but serves to palatalize the preceding consonant: говорить, to speak;

ю = *you*: люблю, I love;

я = *ya*rd: ярмарка, village fair; язык, tongue.

It is to be noted that all Russian vowels tend to have a less distinct enunciation when unstressed than when stressed; this is particularly noticeable in the case of a and о, which have practically the sound of the when unstressed (they are clearer in the syllable immediately preceding the stressed syllable).

2. The position of the accent does not appear in written Russian; the stressed vowel, in words of more than one syllable, is indicated throughout this chapter, for the convenience of the reader, by the use of heavy type.

3. ë is always stressed; the stress will therefore not be indicated on words containing ë; written Russian (save in children's books) does not generally use the double dot on ë, with the result that beginners are often left in doubt whether ë or e is indicated.

Consonant Sounds.

б, в, д, з, к, л, м, н, п, т, ф, approximately like English b, v, d, z, k, l, m, n, p, t, f, respectively.[4]

г = *go*: мно**г**о, much, many;[5]
ж = mea*s*ure: **ж**ена, wife;
р = British ve*r*y: Росси**я**, Russia;
с = *so*, in *all* positions: со**ю**з, union, alliance;
х = German a*ch*: **х**рабрый, brave; худ**о**й, bad;
ц = i*ts*: **ц**ерковь, church;
ч = *ch*ill: **ч**ёрный, black;
ш = *s*ure: **ш**есть, six;
щ = A*shch*urch; бор**щ**, beet soup; **щ**ека, cheek; **ж**енщина, woman.

There is no rule for Russian accentuation, and the place of the accent is not ordinarily indicated in writing. The stress may fall on *any* syllable, and each word must be learned with its own stress; furthermore, the stress *in the same word* often changes position according to the case-form used (му**ж**и**к**, peasant; but мужи**к**а, of the peasant), and from the singular

4. Russian consonants, however, tend to become palatalized when followed by vowels containing the *y*-sound as their first element (е, ё, и, ь, ю, я). In many cases the palatalization is instinctive for an English speaker; thus, в followed by a "hard" vowel (а, о, у, ы, э) will naturally assume the sound of in*v*oke, while if it is followed by a "soft" vowel (е, ё, и, ь, ю, я) it will naturally assume the sound of *v*iew; б will be pronounced as in *b*ooty or as in *b*eauty, respectively; п as in *p*at or in *p*ure, etc. In the case of т, д, л, н, the "soft" pronunciation, when one of the "soft" vowels follows, will go as far as hi*t y*ou, di*d y*ou, mi*lli*on, on*i*on, respectively (теперь, now; делать, to do; любовь, love; день, day).

5. Final *voiced* consonants (б, в, г, д, з, ж) tend to assume the corresponding *unvoiced* pronounciation (p, f, k, t, s, sh); thus, зуб, tooth, is pronounced *zoop*; Романов (a family name), *Románof;* друг, friend, *drook;* дед, grandfather, *dyet;* раз, time, *ras;* муж, husband, *moosh*.

to the plural (вода, water, but воды, waters). While a misplaced accent is not an unforgivable crime, some care should be taken to avoid too many wrong accentuations.

SAMPLE OF WRITTEN RUSSIAN;
USE FOR PRACTICE READING.

Мальчик рано начал учиться и с ранних лет полюбил книги, в которых описывались войны и походы. Пятнадцати лет молодой Суворов поступил на военную службу, и девять лет прослужил простым солдатом. Не было солдата исправнее его: он вставал раньше других, сам чистил себе сапоги и платье и стоял на часах во всякую погоду. Жил он вместе с простыми солдатами и ел солдатские щи и кашу; был всегда смел и весел и смешил своих товарищей весёлыми шутками и рассказами. Все любили его. Когда он стал офицером и начал командовать солдатами, всюду на войне он побеждал неприятеля. "Ребята," говорил Суворов солдатам, "всегда идите вперёд на врага. Не беспокойтесь о том, сколько перед вами неприятелей. Вы ведь пришли бить их, а не считать."

GRAMMATICAL SURVEY

1. — *Nouns.*

Russian has no article, definite or indefinite; друг means "friend", "a friend", "the friend".

There are three genders, masculine, feminine and neuter; but inanimate objects are often masculine or feminine. The ending generally helps to determine the gender of a noun. Nouns ending in consonants or -й are generally masculine, those ending in -а or -я (and most of those ending in -ь) feminine, those in -о, -е or -мя neuter.

Russian has six cases: nominative, genitive, dative, accusative, instrumental, and locative or prepositional (a separate vocative appears in a few words only, and need not be considered). These cases and their endings are alive, and have to be reckoned with; while an occasional error in case or ending is forgivable, too many such errors will make the language incomprehensible to the native.

There are numerous declensional schemes, but the following are the most common. The endings are given in the order indicated above.

Masculine Nouns.

Singular: —, -а, -у, -а or —,[6] -ом, -е;
Plural: -ы, -ов, -ам, -ов or -ы,[6] -ами, -ах.
(Decline thus: офицер, офицера, etc., officer; стол, стола, etc., table; отец, отца, etc., father).

Singular: -й, -я, -ю, -я or -й, -ем, -е;
Plural: -и, -ев, -ям, -ев or -и, -ями, -ях.
(Decline thus: герой, героя, etc., hero).

Singular: -ь, -я, -ю, -я or -ь, -ем, -е;
Plural: -и, -ей, -ям, -ей or -и, -ями, -ях.
(Decline thus: приятель, приятеля, etc., friend; рубль, рубля, etc., ruble).

Feminine Nouns.

Singular: -а, -ы, -е, -у, -ою (-ой), -е;
Plural: -ы, —, -ам, — or -ы, -ами, -ах.

(Decline thus: женщина, женщины, etc. woman; война, войны, etc.; plural войны, etc., war).

6. Masculine nouns in both singular and plural, and feminine nouns in the *plural only* make their accusative form coincide with the genitive if a living person or animal is denoted, with the nominative if an inanimate object appears; thus, the accusative of офицер and отец is офицера and отца, respectively; but the accusative of стол is стол.

Singular: -я, -и, -е, -ю, -ею (-ей), -е (if nominative has и before я, dative and prepositional have -и instead of -е);
Plural: -и, -ь, -ям, -ь or -и, -ями, -ях.

(Decline thus: пустыня, пустыни, etc., desert; Россия, Russia).

Singular: -ь, -и, -и, -ь, -ью, -и;
Plural: -и, -ей, -ям, -ей or -и, -ями, -ях.

(Decline thus: постель, постели, etc., bed; дверь, двери, etc.; plural двери, but дверей, дверям, etc., door).

Neuter Nouns.

Singular: -о, -а, -у, -о, -ом, -е;
Plural: -а, —, -ам, -а, -ами, -ах.

(Decline thus: масло, масла, etc., butter; место, места, etc., plural места, etc., place; село, села, etc., plural сёла, etc., village).

Singular: -е, -я, -ю, -е, -ем, -е (-и if nom. ends in -ие);
Plural: -я, -ей (-ий if nom. sg. ends in -ие), -ям, -я, -ями, -ях.

(Decline thus: море, моря, etc., plural моря, etc., sea; поле, поля, etc.; plural поля, etc., field; здание, здания, etc., building).

Singular: -мя, -мени, -мени, -мя, -менем, -мени;
Plural: -мена, -мен, -менам, -мена, -менами, -менах.

(Decline thus: время, времени, etc.; plural времена, времён, etc., time; имя, имени etc.; plural имена, имён, etc., name).

These schemes are perhaps less complicated than they appear at first glance. Note that in neuter nouns, and in masculine nouns denoting inanimate objects, the accusative has the same form as the nominative, while in masculine nouns denoting living things it has the same form as the genitive; note also the almost invariable -ом, -ем of the instrumental singular, the -е of the prepositional singular, the -ам or -ям of the dative plural, the -ами or -ями of the instrumental plural, and the -ах or -ях of the prepositional plural. Note also that in neuter nouns the accent of the plural is usually on a different syllable from that of the singular.

2. — *Adjectives and Adverbs.*

Adjectives agree in number, gender and *case* with the nouns they modify. The following is the most common scheme of adjective declension:

	Singular			Plural
	Masc.	Fem.	Neut.	(all genders)
Nom.	-ый	-ая	-ое	-ые
Gen.	-ого[7]	-ой	-ого	-ых
Dat.	-ому	-ой	-ому	-ым
Acc.	-ого	-ую	-ое	Genitive or Nominative,
or	-ый			according as the noun is living or inanimate
Instr.	-ым	-ой (-ою)	-ым	-ыми
Loc.	-ом	-ой	-ом	-ых

(Decline thus: ст**а**рый, old; тр**у**дный, difficult).

Two common variants of this scheme are: -ий, -яя, -ее (the "hard" vowel changes to the corresponding "soft" one throughout: а becomes я, ы becomes и, о becomes ё, у becomes ю; decline thus: р**а**нний, early); and -**о**й, -**а**я, -**о**е, genitive -**о**го, -**о**й, -**о**го, etc., like the -ый type, save that the stress is on the ending (decline thus: прост**о**й, simple).[8]

If the adjective is used after the verb "to be", it assumes the following forms: masc. sg., —; fem. sg. -а; neut. sg., -о; plural (all genders), -ы: стар, стар**а**, стар**о**, plural ст**а**ры, old; тр**у**ден, трудн**а**, тр**у**дно, plural трудн**ы**, difficult;

7. In the genitive endings -го, -его, -ого of adjectives and pronouns, the г is always pronounced as *v*.

8. If the adjective root ends in г, ж, к, х, ч, ш, щ, the following replacements must be made: и for ы, а for я, у for ю; if it ends in ц, я and ю must be replaced by а, у; if it ends in ж, ц, ч, ш, щ, о must be replaced by е; thus, вел**и**кий, вел**и**кая, вел**и**кое, great; гор**я**чий, гор**я**чая, гор**я**чее, hot. These replacements appear not only in adjectives, but in nouns, pronouns and verbs as well.

прост, проста, просто, plural просты, simple. The verb "to be" in the present tense is omitted: она—стара, she is old.

The comparative degree is generally formed by changing the ending of the adjective to -ee, which is not declined: красивый, beautiful; красивее, more beautiful; умный, intelligent; умнее, more intelligent. "Than" is expressed by чем with the nominative, or by the genitive without чем: он умнее чем я, or он умнее меня, he is more intelligent than I; железо полезнее чем серебро, or железо полезнее серебра, iron is more useful than silver. If the verb "to be" is not involved, the comparative is more usually formed by prefixing более (more) to the positive: более красивый стул, a more beautiful chair.

The superlative, both relative and absolute, is usually formed by prefixing самый to the positive: самый умный the most intelligent, extremely intelligent.

The adverb generally consists of the neuter predicate form of the adjective: хороший, good, хорошо, well; умный, intelligent; умно, intelligently; жаркий, warm; жарко, warmly.

3. — *Numerals.*

a) — Cardinal.

Outside of один, one, these are treated as nouns, are fully declined, and are followed by the *genitive* of the noun to which they refer (genitive *singular* after 2, 3, 4; genitive *plural* after all others): один дом one house; два дома, two houses; пять домов, five houses. Один, одна, одно, plural одни (meaning "alone", "some"), is otherwise declined like этот (see p. 388), but with the accent on the ending. Два, fem. две, has gen. двух, dat. двум, instr. двумя, loc. двух; три has трёх, трём, тремя, трёх; четыре has -ёх, -ём, -ьмя, -ёх. Numerals ending in -ь are declined like feminine nouns in -ь; others are declined like nouns of the corresponding classes, according to their endings.

1 = один (одна, одно)	30 = тридцать
2 = два (две, два)	40 = сорок
3 = три	50 = пятьдесят
4 = четыре	60 = шестьдесят
5 = пять	70 = семьдесят
6 = шесть	80 = восемьдесят
7 = семь	90 = девяносто
8 = восемь	100 = сто
9 = девять	200 = двести
10 = десять	300 = триста
11 = одиннадцать	400 = четыреста
12 = двенадцать	500 = пятьсот
13 = тринадцать	600 = шестьсот
14 = четырнадцать	1000 = тысяча
15 = пятнадцать	2000 = две тысячи
16 = шестнадцать	5000 = пять тысяч
17 = семнадцать	1,000,000 = миллион
18 = восемнадцать	7635 = семь тысяч
19 = девятнадцать	шестьсот тридцать
20 = двадцать	пять
21 = двадцать один	

b) — Ordinal (declined like ordinary adjectives).

1st = первый	20th = двадцатый
2nd = второй	21st = двадцать первый
3rd = третий	30th = тридцатый
4th = четвёртый	40th = сороковой
5th = пятый	50th = пятидесятый
6th = шестой	60th = шестидесятый
7th = седьмой	70th = семидесятый
8th = восьмой	80th = восьмидесятый
9th = девятый	90th = девяностый
10th = десятый	100th = сотый
11th = одиннадцатый	145th = сто сорок пятый

Use these in dates, either in the genitive, or in the neuter nominative: десятого мая or десятое мая, May 10th.

once - раз   twice - два раза   five times - пять раз
the first time - первый раз every time - всякий раз
the last time - последний раз

4. — *Pronouns*.

a) — Personal.

"I", "of me", "to me", etc. - я, меня, мне, меня, мною or
   мной, мне.
"you" (familiar), "of you", etc. - ты, тебя, тебе, тебя,
   тобою or тобой, тебе.
"he", "his", etc. - он, (н)его, (н)ему, (н)его, (н)им,
   нём.[9]
"she", "her", etc. - она, (н)ея, (н)ей, (н)её, (н)ею, ней.
"it", "its", etc. - оно, (н)его, (н)ему, (н)его, (н)им,
   нём.
"we", "of us", "to us", etc. - мы, нас, нам, нас, нами, нас.
"you" (fam. pl. and polite sg. or pl.) - вы, вас, вам, вас,
   вами, вас.
"they" - они, (н)их, (н)им, (н)их, (н)ими, (н)их.
"self", "oneself" - (no nom.), себя, себе, себя, собою
   or собой, себе.

b) — Possessive.

"my", "mine" (masc. and neut.) - мой (neut. моё), моего,
   моему, nom. or gen., моим, моём; (fem.) -
   моя, моей, моей, мою, моею or моей, моей;
   (plural, all genders) - мои, моих, моим, мои or
   моих, моими, моих.
   Твой, "your", "yours" (fam.), and свой, one's own,
are declined in the same fashion. Наш (наша, наше),
"our", "ours", and ваш (ваша, ваше), "your", "yours",
are similarly declined, but with the accent always on the root.
For "his", "her", "its", "their", use the genitive of the per-

---

9. The forms его, него; ему, нему, etc., are *not* interchangeable;
use forms with н- when the pronoun is governed by a preposition:
у него хлеб, he has bread; but у его отца хлеб, his father has bread.

sonal pronoun: **его**, of him (his); её, of her (her, hers); **его**, of it, (its); их, of them (their, theirs).

c) — Demonstrative.

this, these - **этот** (neut. **это**), **этого**, **этому**, (gen. or nom.), **этим**, **этом**; Fem. - эта, этой, этой, эту, этой, этой; Plural - эти, этих, этим, эти or этих, этими, этих.

that, those - **тот** (neut. **то**), **того**, **тому**, (nom. or gen.), тем, том; Fem. - та, той, той, ту, той, той; Plural - те, тех, тем, те or тех, теми, тех.

d) — Relative and Interrogative.

who, which, that - **который** (fully declined as a **regular** adjective; may also be used as an interrogative);

who?, whose?, to whom?, whom? - кто, кого, кому, кого, кем, ком (may also be used as a relative);

what?, which? - что, чего, чему, что, чем, чём (may also be used as a relative);

whose? - чей (fem. чья; neut. чьё; declined like мой);

what sort of? - какой (declined as a regular adjective).

NOTES ON THE USE OF THE CASES.

The nominative is the case of the subject; it is also used in the predicate nominative, after the verb "to be" (the latter is generally understood, not expressed, in the present tense): ваш сын—не маленький мальчик, your son is not a young boy; где ваш отец?, where is your father?

The genitive expresses possession: дом моего брата, the house of my brother, my brother's house. To translate the English "to have" in the sense of "to own", Russian generally uses the preposition у with the genitive case: у меня - большой дом, I have a large house (literally, to me (is) a large house); есть ли у мужика хлеб?, has the peasant the bread? (literally, is to the peasant the bread?; ли is an untranslatable interrogative particle used in questions when no other interrogative word appears). The genitive is regularly used in negative sentences, replacing the accusative: я не знал дома, I didn't know the house; у меня - нет хлеба, I have no bread (literally, to me (is) not of bread). It is used to translate "some", "any" (дайте мне хлеба, give me bread, some bread; as against дайте мне хлеб, give me *the* bread); and after adverbs of quantity (много хлеба, lots of bread, literally, much of bread). It appears with several prepositions, chief among them the у mentioned above; без, without (без книги, without a book); для, for, for the sake of (для меня, for me, for my sake); из, from, out of (из России, out of Russia); от, away from (especially a person: от моего друга, from my friend).

The dative indicates the indirect object after verbs of saying, giving, etc.: я дал мужику хлеб, I gave the peasant the bread. It is also used after certain prepositions, chief among them к (ко before troublesome consonant groups), toward: к мужику, toward the peasant; ко мне, toward me, to my house.

The accusative is the case of the direct object. Note that a separate accusative form appears only in the feminine singular; in the masculine and neuter singular, and in all plurals, the accusative takes the form of the nominative for inanimate objects, of the genitive for living persons and animals. It is also used with certain prepositions after verbs of motion, particularly в (во), in, into; на, on, onto, upon; за, behind. Note that several of these prepositions take the accusative if motion is involved, but the locative or instrumental if no idea of motion appears: он пошёл в огород, (acc.), he went into the garden; but он был в огороде (loc.), he was in the garden; он сел на стул, he sat down on the chair (acc.), but он сидел на стуле, he was sitting on the chair (loc.).

The instrumental denotes means or instrument (with, by means of): он писал карандашом, he was writing with a pencil. It is used with several prepositions, notably с (со), with, in company with: с офицером, with the officer; со мною, with me; за, behind; перед, in front of. It also appears idiomatically in certain expressions of time: завтра утром, tomorrow morning.

The locative or prepositional is *always* used with prepositions, and frequently denotes place where or in which (*not* place to which; the accusative denotes that): о (об, обо), about: о тебе, about you; об офицере, about the officer; обо мне, about me; на, on, upon: на столе, on the table; в (во), in: в городе, in the city; во мне, within me.

5. — *Verbs*.

The Russian verb has only three tenses: present, past and future. On the other hand, most verbs have a double "aspect": the "imperfective", indicating an action that is, was, or will be going on, and the "perfective", denoting an action that happened once and was completed, or that will be begun and completed; the imperfective verb is usually a simple verb, the perfective verb often (but not always) has a preposition prefixed to it (писать, to be writing; написать, to write once). The perfective verb, by its nature, cannot have a present tense, but only a past (action that was begun and finished) and a future (action that will be begun and finished); and while the past of a perfective verb is quite similar in form to the past of an imperfective verb, the perfective *future* has a set of endings similar to those of the *present* of an imperfective verb; or, to word it differently, the present *form* of the perfective verb has a future *meaning*. Thus, писать, to be writing, has a present, пишу (I am writing); a past, писал (I was writing, I used to write); and a future, буду писать (I shall be writing); but написать, the perfective counterpart of the imperfective писать, has only a past, написал (I wrote once, and finished writing); and a future with present form, напишу (I shall write once, and be finished).

The infinitive of Russian verbs usually ends in -ть (a certain number of verbs have -чь or -ти): делать, to do; говорить, to speak; жечь, to burn; нести, to carry. Its

use is similar to that of the English infinitive: **я хочу
говорить**, I wish to speak.

1. — Present Indicative.

The normal endings are: -у (or -ю), -ешь, -ет, -ем,
-ете, -ут (or -ют); or: -у (-ю), -ишь, -ит, -им, -ите,
-ат (-ят).

I do, **дела-ю**	I speak, **говор-ю**
you do, **дела-ешь**[10]	you speak, **говор-ишь**[10]
he does, **дела-ет**	he speaks, **говор-ит**
we do, **дела-ем**	we speak, **говор-им**
you do, **дела-ете**[10]	you speak, **говор-ите**[10]
they do, **дела-ют**	they speak, **говор-ят**

There are many deviations from these two fundamental
schemes; **нести** and verbs of its type have: **несу, несёшь,
несёт**, etc.; several verbs in -ть, with stress on the last vowel,
follow this scheme (**жить**, to live, has **живу, живёшь,
живёт**, etc.).

Note carefully that the *future* of perfective verbs has
precisely the same form and endings as the *present* of imperfective verbs; thus, **написать** to write (once, and be through
writing), has no present, while its future (I shall write once,
and be through) runs: **напишу, напишешь, напишет,**
etc.

The verb "to be", **быть**, has a present as follows: **есмь,
еси, есть, есмы, есте, суть**. These forms, however, are
generally understood, not expressed (**я—болен**, I am ill); the
third person singular only is regularly used in interrogative
sentences expressing possession: **есть ли у вас рубль?,**
have you a ruble? (lit. is there to you a ruble?).

10. The second person singular is used only in intimate conversation;
the second plural is regularly used in addressing a single person
politely, and in addressing more than one person, familiarly or politely.
The subject pronoun is generally used, but is sometimes omitted.

2. — Past Indicative.

This tense is formed by adding to the stem of the verb the endings -л, -ла, -ло, according to the *gender* of the subject (-ли in the plural, for all genders). This so-called past tense is really only a past participle, with predicate adjective endings, and agreement in gender and number with the subject.

I spoke, я говори-л (fem. говори-ла)
you spoke, ты говори-л (fem. говорила)
he spoke, он говорил
she spoke, она говори-ла
we spoke, мы говори-ли
you spoke, вы говори-ли
they spoke, они говори-ли

Note that this tense functions as an imperfect (I was doing, used to do) in the case of imperfective verbs; but as a past, present perfect or past perfect in the case of perfective verbs: я писал, I was writing, used to write; я написал, I wrote, have written, had written.

The past tense of быть is был (была, было, plural были). It is regularly used, not omitted as is the case with the present: я был болен, I was ill.

3. — Future.

For the future of perfective verbs, see under Present Tense. The future of imperfective verbs is formed by using the future of быть (to be), followed by the infinitive:

I shall speak, я буду говорить
you will speak, ты будешь говорить
he will speak, он будет говорить
she will speak, она будет говорить
we shall speak, мы будем говорить
you will speak, вы будете говорить
they will speak, они будут говорить

The future of perfective verbs does service for our future perfect.

4. — Conditional and Subjunctive.

The conditional idea (should, would) is normally expressed by the past tense of the verb followed by the particle бы: он делал бы, he would do, he would have done.

The subjunctive idea is generally rendered by the past tense introduced by чтобы: он написал, чтобы он купил сад, he wrote in order that he might buy the garden.

5. — Imperative.

The imperative generally ends in -й, -и, -ь (singular), and -йте, -ите, -ьте (plural): сделай, сделайте, do!; говори, говорите, speak!; неси, несите, carry!; будь, будьте, be!

6. — Participles and Gerunds.

Russian has two indeclinable gerunds, present and past: говоря, by or while speaking; поговорив, or поговоривши, having spoken.

There are four participles declined like adjectives: present active, говорящий, speaking; present passive, делаемый, being done; past active, говоривший, having spoken; past passive, читанный, having been read.

The use of gerunds and participles is quite complicated, and all the forms given above do not appear for all verbs. Generally speaking, they are very frequently used where other languages would use a subordinate clause (сказанное слово, the word that was spoken).

7. — Passive and Reflexive.

There is no true passive in Russian, save for the participial forms above indicated. The passive concept is generally rendered: 1. by a passive participle; 2. by an indefinite third person plural active (мне сказали, I was told; lit. they told me); 3. by the reflexive (это делается, this is being done, lit. this does itself).

Reflexive verbs are quite numerous. They are formed,

for all persons, by the addition of -ся (an abbreviated form of себя; -сь after vowels, except ь): умываться, to wash oneself: я умываюсь, ты умываешься, он умывается, мы умываемся, вы умываетесь, они умываются; past: я умывался (fem. я умывалась; pl. мы умывались); fut.: я буду умываться.

VOCABULARY

Nouns are generally given in their *nominative singular* form, with the root[11] separated from the ending (if any); the *genitive singular* ending follows, then the *nominative plural* ending (where a plural form is in common use); thus, язык, -а, -и, indicates a declensional scheme: - , -а, -у, - , -ом, -е; plural, язык-и, -ов, -ам, -и, -ами, -ах; мор-е, -я, -я indicates a declensional scheme мор-е, -я, -ю, -е, -ем, -е; plural, мор-я, -ей, -ям, -я, -ями, -ях. See regular declensional tables, p. 382-383.

Adjectives are given only in their *attributive nominative singular masculine* form. For declensional schemes, see p. 384. For the formation of the *predicate* forms, where these are commonly used, (1) after the adjective indicates regular formation and accentuation (thus, здоровый (1), indicates the following predicate forms: здоров, здорова, здорово, plural здоровы); (2) after the adjective indicates shift of stress from the *root* of the attributive adjective to the *ending* of the predicate adjective (thus, добрый (2) indicates the following predicate forms: добр, добра, добро, plural добры); (3) after the adjective indicates stress on the *root* in the masculine singular, neuter singular, and plural predicate

---

11. The term "root" as applied to both nouns and verbs in this vocabulary, is practically, not scientifically used; the true etymological root of ветер, for example, is ветр-, not вет-; but the latter supplies a convenient makeshift for appending genitive and plural endings -ра, -ры; the true root of the verb приходить is приход-, not прихо-; but the latter permits us to append the endings -жу, ·дишь, without entering into complicated explanations.

forms, on the *ending* in the feminine singular predicate form
(thus, НОВЫЙ (3) indicates нов, нова, ново, plural
новы; МОЛОДОЙ (3) indicates молод, молода,
молодо, plural молоды. Exceptional insertion of a vowel in
the masculine singular predicate form is indicated thus:
бедный (-ен; 3); this means that the predicate forms are
беден, бедна, бедно, plural бедны.

Verbs are given, in a few cases, in whichever aspect
(perfective or imperfective) better suits the English translation,
or is in common use. For most verbs, however, both aspects are
necessary to render the English meanings. In such cases, the
imperfective aspect appears first, the perfective follows. Where
the perfective aspect simply involves the addition of a prefix,
with no difference in the conjugational forms of the two verbs,
only the prefix is given; otherwise, all significant forms for
both verbs appear. Remember that the imperfective infinitive
normally means "to do something repeatedly, continually, or
without reference to time"; the perfective infinitive "to do
something once, at a given moment". The imperfective present
is a true present, in meaning as well as in form; the perfective
present has a future meaning, with reference to a particular
point of future time; the imperfective future, formed by means
of буду with the infinitive, refers to future action without a
definite point of time; the imperfective past is an imperfect,
usually meaning "I was doing, used to do" something; the
perfective past is an absolute past, meaning "I did, have done,
had done" (see p. 392). The forms given are the infinitive,
with the root[11] indicated; and the first and second person
singular present endings, which are to be attached to the root.
Formation and accentuation of the other forms of the present
normally follow those of the *second* singular, not those of the
first singular (note that the *third* plural normally ends in -ут
(-ют), if the second singular ends in -ешь or -ёшь; in -ат
(-ят), if the second singular ends in -ишь): thus, to come,
прихо-дить (-жу, '-дишь) indicates that endings on the
basis of '-дишь are to be attached to the working-root прихо-,

and that the full present is: прихо-жу, прихо-дишь, прихо-дит, прихо-дим, прихо-дите, прихо-дят.

The accented vowel is indicated throughout by heavy type (язык), save in cases where ё appears (ё is *always* stressed). Watch for shifting accents on different forms of the same word!

1. *World, Elements, Nature, Weather, Time, Directions.*

world, свет, -а; мир, -а
earth, земл-я, -и, '-и
air, воздух, -а
water, вод-а, -ы, '-ы
fire, ог-онь, -ня, -ни
light, свет, -а
sea, мор-е, -я, -я
sun, солнц-е, -а
moon, лун-а, -ы; месяц, -а
star, звезд-а, -ы, ··-ы
sky, неб-о, -а (pl. неб-еса, -ес)
wind, вет-ер, -ра, -ры
weather, погод-а, -ы
snow, снег, -а, -а
it is snowing, снег идёт
rain, дожд-ь, -я, -и
it is raining, дождь идёт
cloud, облак-о, -а, -а
cloudy, облачный (it's cloudy today, облачно сегодня)
fog, туман, -а, -ы
ice, лёд (льда, льд-ы)
mud, гряз-ь, -и, -и
morning, утр-о, -а, -а
noon, полд-ень, -ня, -ни
evening, вечер, -а, -а
afternoon, день (дня, дни) (in the afternoon, днём; пополудни)
night, ноч-ь, -и, -и
midnight, полноч-ь, -и
North, север, -а
South, юг, -а
East, восток, -а
West, запад, -а

time, врем-я, -ени, -ена
year, год, -а, -ы
month, месяц, -а, -ы
week, недел-я, -и, -и
day, день (дня, дни)
hour, час, -а, -ы
minute, минут-а, -ы, -ы
Sunday, воскресень-е, -я, -я
Monday, понедельник, -а, -и
Tuesday, вторник, -а, -и
Wednesday, сред-а, -ы, '-ы
Thursday, четверг, -а, -и
Friday, пятниц-а, -ы, -ы
Saturday, суббот-а, -ы, -ы
January, январ-ь, -я
February, феврал-ь, -я
March, март, -а
April, апрел-ь, -я
May, ма-й, -я
June, июн-ь, -я
July, июл-ь, -я
August, август, -а
September, сентябр-ь, -я
October, октябр-ь, -я
November, ноябр-ь, -я
December, декабр-ь, -я
Spring, весн-а, -ы, ·· -ы
Summer, лет-о, -а, -а
Fall, осень, -и, -и
Winter, зим-а, -ы, '-ы
On Monday, в понедельник
On Mondays, по понедельникам
Next Monday, в будущий понедельник

Last Monday, в прошлый
   понедельник
On Monday, May 10th, 1892, в
   понедельник, десятого мая,
   тысяча восемьсот девяносто
   второго года

2. *Family, Friendship, Love.*

family, семь-я, -и, '-и
husband, муж, -а, -ья
wife, жен-а, -ы, ̈ -ы
parents, родител-и, -ей
father, от-ец, -ца, -цы
mother, мат-ь, -ери, -ери
son, сын, -а, -овья
daughter, доч-ь, -ери, -ери
brother, брат, -а, -ья
sister, сестр-а, -ы, ̈ -ы
uncle, дяд-я, -и, -и
aunt, тёт-я, -и, -и
grandfather, дедушк-а, -и, -и
grandmother, бабушк-а, -и, -и
grandson, внук, -а, -и
granddaughter, внучк-а, -и, -и
grandchildren, внучат-а, -
nephew, племянник, -а, -и
niece, племянниц-а, -ы, -ы
cousin (masc.), двоюродный
   брат
cousin (fem.), двоюродная
   сестра
father-in-law (father of wife),
   тест-ь, -я, -и; (father of
   husband), свёк-ор, -ра, -ры
mother-in-law (mother of wife),
   тёщ-а, -и, -и; (mother of
   husband), свекров-ь, -и, -и
son-in-law, зят-ь, -я, -ья
daughter-in-law, невестк-а, -и, -и
brother-in-law, (sister's husband),

зят-ь, -я, -ья; (husband's brother), девер-ь, -я, -и
sister-in-law (husband's sister),
   золовк-а, -и, -и; (brother's
   wife), невестк-а, -и, -и
man (individual), мужчин-а, -ы,
   -ы; (human being), человек,
   -а (pl. люд-и, -ей, people).
woman, женщин-а, -ы, -ы
child, дит-я, -яти (pl. дет-и, -ей);
   ребён-ок, -ка (pl. ребят-а, -)
boy, мальчик, -а, -и
girl (small), девочк-а, -и, -и
   (young), девушк-а, -и, -и;
   девиц-а, -ы, -ы
sir, Mr.,[12] господин, -а (pl.
   господа)
Madam, Mrs.,[12] госпож-а, -и, -и
Miss, young lady,[12] барышн-я,
   -и, и; госпожа
friend (masc.), друг, -а (pl.
   друзь-я, -ей); (fem.), подруг-
   а, -и, -и
servant (masc.), слуг-а, -и, '-и;
   (fem.), служанк-а, -и, -и
to introduce, знаком-ить (-лю,
   -ишь); perfective, по-знако-
   мить
to visit, посещ-ать (-аю, -аешь);
   perf., посе-тить (-щу, -тишь)
love, люб-овь, -ви, -ви
to love, люб-ить (-лю, '-ишь)

12.   The abbreviations for господин and госпожа are Г. or Г-н, and
Г-жа, respectively (there is no abbreviation for барышня).
   Under the Soviets, it is more customary to address a man as
гражданин, -а (pl. граждан-е, — citizen); or товарищ, -а, -и
(comrade), and a woman as гражданк-а, -и, -и (citizeness).

to fall in love with, влюбл -яться
(-яюсь, -яешься) ; perf., влюб-
-иться (-люсь, '-ишься)

to marry, жен-иться (-юсь,
'-ишься) на; выхо-дить (-жу,
'-дишь) замуж за; perf. вый-ти
(-ду, -дешь) замуж за

kiss, поцелу-й, -я, -и
to kiss, цел-овать (-ую, -уешь)
perf. по-целовать
dear, beloved, дорог-ой(3) ;
любимый
sweetheart, (masc.), мил-ый, -ого,
-ые (fem.), мил-ая, -ой, -ые

3. Speaking Activities.

word, слов-о, -а, -а
language, язык, -а, -и
to speak, говор-ить (-ю, -ишь)
to say, ска-зать (-жу, '-жешь)
to tell, relate, рассказыв-ать
(-аю, -аешь) ; perf. расска-
зать (-жу, '-жешь)
to inform, сообща-ть (-ю, -ешь) ;
perf. сообщ-ить (-у, -ишь)
to call, звать (зову, зовёшь) ;
perf. по-звать
to be called, one's name is,
зваться (зовусь, зовёшься) ;
what is your name, как ваше
имя?; my name is John, моё
имя Иван
to greet, здорова-ться (-юсь,
-ешься) ; perf. по -
to name, назыв-ать (-аю, -аешь)
to cry, shout, крич-ать (-у,
-ишь) perf. по -
to listen to, слуш-ать (-аю,
-аешь) ; perf. по -
to hear, слыш-ать (-у, -ишь) ;

perf. у -
to understand, поним-ать (-аю,
-аешь) ; perf. по-нять (-йму,
-ймёшь)
to mean, означ-ать (-аю, -аешь) ;
хо-теть (-чу, '-чешь) сказать
to ask (question), спрашива-ть
(-ю, -ешь) ; perf. спро-сить
(-шу, '-сишь) ; I am asking you
where Red Square is, я Вас
спрашиваю, где Красная
Площадь
to ask for, про-сить (-шу,
'-сишь) ; perf. по-; he asked
me for 3 books, он попросил
у меня три книги
to answer, отвеча-ть (-ю, ешь) ;
perf. отве-тить (-чу, -тишь)
to thank, благодар-ить (-ю,
-ишь) (for, за with acc.) ; perf.
по -
to complain, жал-оваться
(-уюсь, -уешься) ; perf. по -

4. Materials.

gold, золот-о, -а
silver, серебр-о, -а
iron, желез-о, -а
steel, стал-ь, -и
copper, мед-ь, -и
lead, свин-ец, -ца
tin, олов-о, -а; жест-ь, -и
oil, нефт-ь, -и

gasoline, бензин, -а
coal, уг-оль, -ля
wood, дерев-о, -а
silk, шёлк, -а
cotton (raw), хлоп-ок, -ка;
(material), бумаг-а, -и
wool, шерст-ь, -и
cloth, сукн-о, -а

to cut, ре-зать (-жу, -жешь);
  perf. на -
to dig, коп-ать (-аю, -аешь);
  perf. на -
to sew, ш-ить (-ью, -ьёшь);
  perf. сшить (сошью,
сошьёшь)
to darn, штопа-ть (-ю, -ешь);
  perf. по -
to mend, чин-ить (-ю, '-ишь);
  perf. по -

5. *Animals.*

animal, животн-ое, -ого, -ые
horse, лошад-ь, -и, -и; кон-ь,
  -я, -и
dog, собак-а, -и, -и; п-ёс, -са,
  -сы
cat, кошк-а, -и, -и
bird, птиц-а, -ы, -ы
donkey, ос-ёл, -ла, -лы
mule, мул, -а, -ы
cow, коров-а, -ы, -ы
ox, вол, -а, -ы; бык, -а, -и
pig, свинь-я, -и, '-и
chicken, цыпл-ёнок, -ёнка, -ята

hen, куриц-а, -ы, куры
rooster, пет-ух, -а, -и
sheep, овц-а, -ы, '-ы
goat, коз-ёл, -ла, -лы
mouse, мыш-ь, -и, -и
snake, зме-я, -и, '-и
fly, мух-а, -и, -и
bee, пчел-а, -ы, ''-ы
mosquito, комар, -а, -ы
spider, паук, -а, -и
louse, вош-ь, -и, вши
flea, блох-а, -и, '-и
bedbug, клоп, -а, -ы

6. *Money, Buying and Selling.*

money, деньги, денег (pl.)
coin, монет-а, -ы, -ы
dollar, доллар, -а, -ы
cent, цент, -а, -ы
national currency (large), рубл-ь,
  -я, -и (small), копейк-а, -и, -и
bank, банк, -а, -и
check, чек, -а, -и
money order, почтовый перевод,
  -а, -ы
to earn, зарабатыва-ть (-ю,
  -ешь); perf. заработ-ать (-аю,
  -аешь)
to gain, выруч-ать (-аю, -аешь);
  име-ть (-ю, -ешь) прибыль;
  perf. выруч-ить (-у, -ишь)
to win, выигрыва-ть (-ю, -ешь);
  perf. выигр-ать (-аю, -аешь)
to lose, тер-ять (-яю, -яешь);
  perf. по -

to spend, тра-тить (-чу, -тишь);
  perf. по -
to lend, да-вать (-ю, -ёшь)
  взаймы; одолж-ать (-аю,
  -аешь); perf. одолж-ить (-у,
  '-ишь)
to owe, быть должным (lit., to be
  indebted)
to pay, пла-тить (-чу, '-тишь);
  perf. за -
to borrow, занима-ть (-аю,
  -аешь); perf. за-нять (-йму,
  -ймёшь); he borrowed 3 rubles
  from me, он занял у меня три
  рубля
change, мелоч-ь, -и
to change, exchange, мен-ять
  (-яю, -яешь); perf. раз -
to give back, return, отда-вать
  (-ю, -ёшь); perf. отда-ть

(-м, -шь)
price, цен-а, -ы, '-ы
expensive, dear, дорогой (3)
cheap, дешёвый (дёшев, 3)
store, shop, магазин, -а, -ы;
 лавк-а, -и, -и
piece, кус-ок, -ка, -ки
slice, лом-оть, -тя, '-ти
pound, фунт, -а, -ы
package, пакет, -а, -ы
basket, корзин-а, -ы, -ы
box, ящик, -а, -и
goods, товар-ы, -ов (pl.)
to go shopping, и-тти (-ду, -дёшь;
 past шёл, шла, шли) за
 покупками; perf. пой-ти (-ду,
 дёшь) за покупками
to sell, прода-вать (-ю, -ёшь);
 perf. прода-ть (-м, -шь)
to buy, покуп-ать (-аю, -аешь);
 perf. куп-ить (-лю, '-ишь)

to rent, hire, наним-ать (-аю,
 -аешь); perf. на-нять (-йму,
 -ймёшь)
to be worth, сто-ить (-ю, ишь);
 it is worth while writing to him,
 стоит ему написать
cost, стоимост-ь, -и, -и
to cost, сто-ить (-ю, -ишь)
to choose, выбир-ать (-аю,
 -аешь); perf. выб-рать (-еру,
 -ерешь)
thief, robber, вор, -а, -ы
to steal, вор-овать (-ую, уешь);
 perf. с -
policeman, полицейск-ий, -ого,
 -ие; милиционер, -а, -ы
police, полици-я, -и; милици-я,
 -и

honest, честный (-тен, 1)
dishonest, нечестный (-тен, 1)

7. *Eating and Drinking.*

to eat, есть (ем, ешь); past ел,
 ела, ели; perf. по -; куша-ть
 (-ю, -ешь); perf. с-
breakfast, утренний завтрак
lunch, завтрак, -а, -и
to eat breakfast, lunch, завтрака-
 ть (-ю, -ешь); perf. по -
supper, ужин, -а, -ы
to eat supper, ужина-ть (-ю,
 -ешь); perf. по -
dinner, обед, -а, -ы
to eat dinner, to dine, обеда-ть
 (-ю, -ешь); perf. по -
meal, ед-а, -ы
dining-room, столов-ая, -ой, -ые
waiter, слуг-а, -и, '-и
waitress, служанк-а, -и, -и
restaurant, ресторан, -а, -ы
menu, меню (invariable)
bill, счёт, -а, счета

to pass, перед-ать (-аю, -аешь)
tip, на-ча-й
to drink, п-ить (-ью, -ьёшь);
 perf. вып-ить (-ью, -ьешь)
water, вод-а, -ы, '-ы
wine, вин-о, -а, '-а
beer, пив-о, -а
coffee, коф-е, -я
tea, ча-й, -я, -и
milk, молок-о, -а
bottle, бутылк-а, -и, -и
spoon, лож-ка, -ки, -ки (gen. pl.
 -ек)
teaspoon, чайная ложка
knife, нож, -а, -и
fork, вил-ка, -ки, -ки (gen. pl.
 -ок)
glass, стакан, -а, -ы
cup, чаш-ка, -ки, -ки (gen. pl
 -ек)

napkin, салфетк-а, -и, -и

salt, сол-ь, -и

pepper, пер-ец, -ца

plate, dish, блюд-о, -а, -а

bread, хлеб, -а, -а

butter, масл-о, -а, -а

roll, булк-а, -и, -и

sugar, сахар, -а

soup, суп, -а, -ы

rice, рис, -а

potatoes, картофел-ь, -я

vegetables, овощ-и, -ей (pl.)

meat, мяс-о, -а

beef, говядин-а, -ы

steak, бифштекс, -а, -ы

chicken, цыпл-ёнок, -ёнка, -ята

chop, отбивная котлет-а, -ы, -ы

lamb, баранин-а, -ы

veal, телятин-а, -ы

pork, свинин-а, -ы

sausage, колбас-а, -ы, '-ы

ham, ветчин-а, -ы

bacon, сал-о, -а

egg, яйц-о, -а, '-а

fish, рыб-а, -ы, -ы

fried, жареный

cooked, приготовленный

boiled, варёный

roasted, broiled, жареный

baked, печёный

sauce, соус, -а, -а

salad, салат, -а, -ы

cheese, сыр, -а, -ы

fruit, фрукт, -а, -ы; плод, -а, -ы

apple, яблок-о, -а, -и

pear, груш-а, -и, -и

grapes, виноград, -а

peach, персик, -а, -и

strawberry, земляник-а, -и, -и

nut, орех, -а, -и

orange, апельсин, -а, -ы

lemon, лимон, -а, -ы

juice, сок, -а, -и

cherry, вишн-я, -и, -и

dessert, сладк-ое, -ого

pastry, пирожн-ое, -ого

8. *Hygiene and Attire.*

bath, ванн-а, -ы, -ы

to bathe, куп-аться (-аюсь, -аешься); perf. вы -

shower, душ, -а, -и

to wash, м-ыться (-оюсь, -оешься); perf. у -

to shave, бр-иться (-еюсь, -еешься); perf. по -

barber, hairdresser, парикмахер, -а, -ы

mirror, зеркал-о, -а, -а

razor, бритв-а, -ы, -ы
    (safety razor, безопасная бритва,

soap, мыл-о, -а, -а

towel, полотенц-е, -а, -а

comb, греб-ень, -ня, '-ни

brush, щётк-а, -и, -и

scissors, ножниц-ы, - (pl.)

to wear, но-сить (-шу, '-сишь)

to take off, сним-ать (-аю, -аешь); perf. сн-ять (-иму, -имешь); I took off *my* coat, я снял пиджак

to change, мен-ять (-яю, -яешь); perf. перемен-ить (-ю, -ишь)

to put on, надев-ать (-аю, -аешь); perf. над-еть (-ену, -енешь); I put on *my* coat я надел пиджак

clothes, одежд-а, -ы

hat, шляп-а, -ы, -ы

suit, костюм, -а, -ы

coat, пиджак, -а, -и

vest, жилет, -а, -ы

pants, брюк-и, - (pl.)

underwear, нижнее бель-ё, -я

glove, перчатк-а, -и, -и

socks, носк-и, -ов (pl.)
stockings, чул-ки, -ок (pl.)
shirt, рубашк-а, -и, -и
collar, воротник, -а, -и
tie, галстук, -а, -и
overcoat, пальто (invariable)
raincoat, дождевое пальто
pocket, карман, -а, -ы
handkerchief, носовой плат-ок,
  -ка
button, пуговиц-а, -ы, -ы
shoe, башмак, -а, -и
boot, сапог, -а, -и
purse, сумочк-а, -и, -и

pocket-book, записная книжк-а,
  -и, -и
pin, булавк-а, -и, -и
tie-pin, булавка для галстука
safety-pin, английская булавка
needle, иголк-а, -и, -и
umbrella, зонтик, -а, -и
watch, час-ы, -ов (pl.)
chain, цепочк-а, -и, -и
ring, кольц-о, **-а**, '-а (gen. pl.
  колец)
eyeglasses, очк-и, -ов (pl.)
slippers, туф-ли, -ель (pl.)
dressing-gown, bath-robe, халат,
  -а, -ы

9. *Parts of the Body.*

head, голов-а, -ы, головы
forehead, л-об, -ба, -бы
face, лиц-о, -а, '-а
mouth, р-от, -та, -ты
hair, волос, -а, -ы
eye, глаз, -а, **-а**
ear, у-хо, -ха, -ши (gen. pl. -шей)
tooth, зуб, -а, -ы
lip, губ-а, -ы, '-ы
nose, нос, -а, -ы
tongue, язык, **-а, -и**
chin, подбород-ок, -ка, -ки
cheek, щек-а, -и, ¨-и
mustache, ус-ы, -ов (pl.)
beard, бород-а, -ы, бороды
neck, ше-я, -и, -и
throat, горл-о, -а, -а
stomach, желуд-ок, -ка, -ки

arm, hand, рук-а, -и, '-и
elbow, лок-оть, -тя, '-ти
wrist, кист-ь (-и, -и) руки
finger, пал-ец, -ьца, -ьцы
nail, ног-оть, -тя, -ти
shoulder, плеч-о, **-а**, '-и
leg, foot, ног-а, -и, '-и
knee, колен-о, -а, -и
back, спин-а, -ы, '-ы
chest, груд-ь, -и, -и
ankle, щиколк-а, -и, -и
body, тел-о, -а, **-а**
blood, кров-ь, -и
skin, кож-а, -и, -и
heart, сердц-е, -а, -а (gen. pl.
  сердец)
bone, кост-ь, -и, -и

10. *Medical.*

doctor, доктор, -а, **-а**; врач, **-а,
  -и**
drug-store, аптек-а, -и, -и
hospital, госпитал-ь, -я, -я;
  больниц-а, -ы, -ы
medicine, лекарств-о, -а, -а

pill, пилюл-я, -и, -и
prescription, рецепт, -а, -ы
bandage, бинт, **-а, -ы**
nurse, сестр-а (-ы, ¨-ы) мило-
  сердия
ill, больной (2; болен)

fever, лихорадк-а, -и, -и
illness, болезн-ь, -и, -и
swollen, распухший
wound, ран-а, -ы, -ы
wounded, раненый (1)
head-ache, головная бол-ь, -и, -и
tooth-ache, зубная боль

cough, каш-ель, -ля
to cough, кашля-ть (-ю, -ешь)
lame, хромой
burn, ожог, -а, -и
pain, бол-ь, -и, -и
poison, яд, -а, -ы

11. *Military.*

war, войн-а, -ы, '-ы
peace, мир, -а
ally, союзник, -а, -и
enemy, враг, -а, -и
army, арми-я, -и, -и
danger, опасност-ь, -и, -и
dangerous, опасный (-сен, 1)
to win, побежд-ать (-аю, -аешь);
   perf. побе-дить (-жу, -дишь)
to surround, окруж-ать (-аю,
   -аешь); perf. окруж-ить (-у,
   -ишь)
to arrest, арест-овать (-ую,
   -уешь)
to kill, убив-ать (-аю, -аешь);
   perf. уб-ить (-ью, -ьёшь)
to escape, избег-ать (-аю, -аешь)
to run away, убег-ать (-аю,
   -аешь); perf. изб-ежать (-егу,
   -ежишь)
to lead, ве-сти (-ду, -дёшь);
   perf. по -; past вёл, вела,
   вели
to follow, след-овать (-ую,
   -уешь); perf. по -
fear, страх, -а, -и
prison, тюрьм-а, -ы, '-ы
captivity, плен, -а
prisoner, арестант, -а, -ы
war prisoner, пленн-ый, -ого, -ые
comrade, "buddy", товарищ,
   -а, -и
fight, битв-а, -ы, -ы
battle, сражени-е -я, -я

to fight, сраж-аться (-аюсь,
   -аешься); perf. сра-зиться
   (-жусь, -зишься)
to take prisoner, б-рать (-еру,
   -ерёшь) в плен; perf. взять
   (возьму, возьмёшь)
to surrender, сда-ваться (-юсь,
   -ёшься); perf. сд-аться
   (-амся, -ашься)
to retreat, отступ-ать (-аю,
   -аешь); perf. отступ-ить
   (-лю, '-ишь)
help, помощ-ь, -и
help!, помогите!
to help, помог-ать (-аю, -аешь);
   perf. пом-очь (-огу, -ожешь)
to capture, захватыв-ать (-аю,
   -аешь); perf. захва-тить (-чу,
   '-тишь)
soldier, private, солдат, -а, -ы
corporal, капрал, -а, -ы
sergeant, сержант, -а, -ы
lieutenant, лейтенант, -а, -ы
captain, капитан, -а, -ы
major, майор, -а, -ы
colonel, полковник, -а, -и
general, генерал, -а, -ы
officer, офицер, -а, -ы
company, рот-а, -ы, -ы
battalion, батальон, -а, -ы
regiment, полк, -а, -и
troops, войск-а, - (pl.)
brigade, бригад-а, -ы, -ы
division, дивизи-я, -и, -и

reenforcements, подкреплени-е, -я

fortress, крепост-ь, -и, -и

sentinel, часов-ой, -ого, -ые

to stand guard, to do sentry duty, сто-ять (-ю, -ишь) на часах; perf. по -

guard, страж-а, -и, -и

to be on duty, не-сти (-су, -сёшь) службу; perf. по -; past нёс, несла, несли

sign-post, указательный столб (-а, -ы)

navy, флот, -а, -ы

sailor, матрос, -а, -ы

marine, моряк, -а, -и

warship, военное суд-но, -на, -а

cruiser, крейсер, -а, -ы

destroyer, истребител-ь, -я, -и; миноноск-а, -и, -и; миdonос-ец, -ца, -цы

convoy, конво-й, -я, -и

escort, охран-а, -ы, -ы

weapon, оружи-е, -я, -я

rifle, винтовк-а, -и, -и; ружьё, -я, '-я

machine-gun, пулемёт, -а, -ы

cannon, пушк-а, -и, -и

ammunition, вооружени-е, -я, -я

supplies, снаряжени-е, -я, -я

cartridge, заряд, -а, -ы

bullet, пул-я, -и, -и

belt, пояс, -а, -а

knapsack, ран-ец, -ца, -цы

tent, палатк-а, -и, -и

map, карт-а, -ы, -ы

spy, шпион, -а, -ы

air-raid shelter, убежищ-е, -а, -а

camp, лагер-ь, -я, -я

rope, канат, -а, -ы

flag, флаг, -а, -и

helmet, каск-а, -и, -и

bayonet, штык, -а, -и

uniform, мундир, -а, -ы

airplane, аэроплан, -а, -ы; самолёт, -а, -ы

bombing plane, бомбовоз, -а, -ы

pursuit plane, истребител-ь, -я, -и

to bomb, to shell, бомбардир-овать ('-ую, '-уешь)

truck, грузовик, -а, -и

shell, снаряд, -а, -ы

tank, танк, -а, -и

to load, заряж-ать (-аю, -аешь); perf. заря-дить (-жу, -дишь)

bomb, бомб-а, -ы, -ы

to fire, to shoot, стрел-ять (-яю, -яешь); perf. выстрел-ить (-ю, -ишь)

(military execution) расстрели-ва-ть (-ю, -ешь)

fire!, огонь!

attention!, внимание!; смирно!

forward!, вперёд!

halt!, стой!

12. Travel.

passport, паспорт, -а, -а

customs, таможн-я, -и, -и

steamer, пароход, -а, -ы

ship, судн-о, -а, суда

stateroom, кают-а, -ы, -ы

berth, койк-а, -и, -и

to travel, путешеств-овать (-ую, -уешь)

trip, voyage, путешестви-е, -я, -я

to leave, depart, уезж-ать (-аю, -аешь); perf. уе-хать (-ду, -дешь)

to arrive, приезж-ать (-аю, -аешь); perf. прие-хать (-ду, -дешь)

to ride (conveyance), е-хать (-ду, -дешь)

railroad, железная дорог-а,
 -и, -и
station, станци-я, -и, -и
platform, платформ-а, -ы, -ы
track, коле-я, -и, -и; пут-ь, -и, -и
train, поезд, -а, -а
ticket, билет, -а, -ы
to buy (a ticket), в-зять (-озьму,
 -озьмёшь) билет; куп-ить
 (-лю, ´-ишь) билет
compartment, купэ (indecl.)
all aboard!, третий звонок!
car, coach, вагон, -а, -ы

dining-car, вагон-ресторан, -а
sleeper, спальный вагон
trunk, сундук, -а, -и
valise, чемодан, -а, -ы
baggage, багаж, -а
porter, носильщик, -а, -и
taxi, такси (indecl.)
bus, автобус, -а, -ы
street-car, трамва-й, -я, -и
automobile, автомобил-ь, -я, -и
driver, шофёр, -а, -ы
to drive (car), ез-дить (-жу,
 -дишь)

13. *Reading and Writing.*

to read, чит-ать (-аю, -аешь);
 perf. про-
newspaper, газет-а, -ы, -ы
magazine, журнал, -а, -ы
book, книг-а, -и, -и
to write, пи-сать (-шу, ´-шешь);
 perf. на-
to translate, перево-дить (-жу,
 ´-дишь); perf. переве-сти
 (-ду, -дёшь); past перев-ёл,
 -ела, -ели
pencil, карандаш, -а, -и
chalk, мел, -а
blackboard, чёрная доск-а, -и, -и
ink, чернил-а, - (pl.)
pen, пер-о, -а, ´-ья

fountain-pen, самопишущее
 перо
paper, бумаг-а, -и, -и
writing-paper, писчая (почтовая)
 бумага
envelope, конверт, -а, -ы
letter, письм-о, -а, ´-а
post-office, почт-а, -ы
stamp, (почтовая) марк-а, -и, -и
letter-box, почтовый ящик, -а, -и
to mail, посыл-ать (-аю, -аешь;
 perf. по-слать (-шлю, -шлёшь)
 по почте; отправ-ить (-лю,
 -ишь) по почте
address, адрес, -а, -а
post-card, открытк-а, -и, -и;
 почтовая карточк-а, -и, -и

14. *Amusements.*

to smoke, кур-ить (-ю, ´-ишь);
 perf. по -
cigar, сигар-а, -ы, -ы
cigarette, папирос-а, -ы, -ы
tobacco, табак, -а, -и
match, спичк-а, -и, -и
give me a light, дайте мне огня
theatre, театр, -а, -ы
movies, кино (indecl.)

dance, тан-ец, -ца, -цы
to dance, танц-овать (-ую.
 -уешь)
to have a good time, весел-иться
 (-юсь, -ишься); perf. по -
ticket, билет, -а, -ы
pleasure, удовольстви-е, -я, -я
ball, мяч, -а, -и
to play (music), игр-ать (-аю,

-аешь) на with prepositional
case; perf. по -
(games), игр-ать в with accusative case; perf. по -
to sing. п-еть (-ою, -оёшь)
song, песн-я, -и, -и
to take a walk. гул-ять (-яю,
-яешь); perf. по -

15. *Town and Country.*

place, spot, мест-о, -а, -а
city, город, -а, -а
street, улиц-а, -ы, -ы; переул-ок,
-ка, ки
sidewalk, тротуар, -а, -ы
harbor, гаван-ь, -и, -и
intersection, перекрёст-ок, -ка,
-ки
block, квартал, -а, -ы
school, школ-а, -ы, -ы
church, церк-овь, -ви, -ви
building, здани-е, -я, -я
cathedral, собор, -а, -ы
corner, уг-ол, -ла, -лы
(at the corner, на углу)
hotel, гостинниц-а, -ы, -ы
office, контор-а, -ы, -ы
river, рек-а, -и, '-и

16. *House.*

door, двер-ь, -и, -и
to open, открыв-ать (-аю,
-аешь); perf. откр-ыть (-ою,
-оешь)
to close. закрыв ать (-аю,
-аешь); perf. закр-ыть (-ою,
-оешь,
key, ключ. -а, -и
to go in, вхо-дить (-жу, '-дишь);
perf. вой-ти (-ду, -дёшь); past
вошёл, вошла, вошли
to go out. выхо-дить (-жу,
'-дишь'; perf. вы-йти (-йду,

beach, взморь-е, -я; берег, -а, -а
to swim, плава-ть (-ю, -ешь)
game, игр-а, -ы, '-ы
sand, пес-ок, -ка, -ки
refreshment, угощени-е, -я, -я
saloon, трактир, -а, -ы; пивн-ая,
-ой, -ые; кабак, -а, -и
picnic, пикник, -а, -и

bridge, мост, -а, -ы
(on the bridge, на мосту)
country, деревн-я, -и
village, сел-о, -а, ¨-а
road, дорог-а, -и, -и
mountain, гор-а, -ы, '-ы
grass, трав-а, -ы, '-ы
yard, двор, -а, -ы
hill, холм, -а, -ы
lake, озер-о, -а, ¨-а
forest, wood, лес, -а, -а
field, пол-е, -я, -я
flower, цвет-ок, -ка, -ы
tree, дерев-о, -а, деревья
rock, скал-а, -ы, '-ы
stone, кам-ень, -ня, -ни
jungle, джунгл-и, -ей (pl.)

-йдешь); past вышел, вышла
вышли
house, дом, -а, -а
cottage, дач-а, -и, -и
hut. изб-а, -ы, '-ы
to live (in), жи-ть (-ву, -вёшь);
perf. про -
staircase, лестниц-а, -ы, -ы
to go up, подним-аться (-аюсь,
-аешься); perf. подн-яться
(-имусь, -имешься)
to go down, спуск-аться
(-аюсь, -аешься); perf. спу-

ститься (-щусь, '-стишься)
room, комнат-а, -ы, -ы
toilet, уборн-ая, -ой, -ые
kitchen, кухн-я, -и, -и (gen. pl. кухонь)
table, стол, -а, -ы
chair, стул, -а, -ья
to sit down, с-адиться (-ажусь , -адишься); perf. с-есть (-яду, -ядешь); past сел, села, сели
to be sitting, си-деть (-жу, -дишь)
roof, крыш-а, -и, -и
to stand, be standing, сто-ять (-ю, -ишь); perf. по -
to stand up, вст-ать (-ану, -анешь)
wall, стен-а, -ы, '-ы
lamp, ламп-а, -ы, -ы
candle, свеч-а, -и '-и; свечк-а, -и, -и
closet, шкаф, -а, -ы
window, окн-о, -а, '-а
to rest, отдых-ать (-аю, -аешь); perf. отдохн-уть (-у, -ёшь)

bed, кроват-ь, -и, -и; постел-ь, -и, -и
bedroom, спальн-я, -и, -и
blanket, одеял-о, -а, -а
sheet, простын-я, -и, '-и
mattress, матрац, -а, -ы
pillow, подушк-а, -и, -и
to go to bed, лож-иться (-усь, -ишься) спать; perf. л-ечь (-ягу, -яжешь), past лёг, легла, легли
to go to sleep, и-тти (-ду, -дёшь)[13] спать; засып-ать (-аю, -аешь)
to sleep, сп-ать (-лю, -ишь); perf. по -
to wake up, просып-аться (-аюсь, -аешься); perf. просн-уться (-усь, -ёшься)
to get up, вста-вать (-ю, -ёшь); perf. вст-ать (-ану, -анешь)
to dress, одев-аться (-аюсь, -аешься)
clock, час-ы, -ов (pl.)
alarm-clock, будильник, -а, -и

17. *Nouns — Miscellaneous.*

people, люд-и, -ей (pl.)
thing, вещ-ь, -и, -и
name, им-я, -ени, -ена
luck, счасть-е, -я
bad luck, несчасть-е, -я

number, числ-о, -а, '-а; номер, -а, -а
life, жизн-ь, -и, -и
death, смерт-ь, -и, -и
work, работ-а, -ы, -ы; (labor), труд, -а, -ы

18. *Verbs — Coming and Going.*

to come, прихо-дить (-жу, '-дишь); perf. при-дти (-ду, -дёшь)
to go, хо-дить (-жу, '-дишь); и-тти (-ду, -дёшь);[13] perf.

пой-ти (-ду, -дёшь)
to be going to, (use future of perfective verb; we are going to win, мы победим)
to walk, гул-ять (-яю, -яешь);

13. The past of итти, to go, and all its compounds (which normally appear as -йти or -ити) is irregular: шёл, шла, шли.

perf. по -

to go away, ухо-дить (-жу,
'-дишь); perf. уйти

to fall, пада-ть (-ю, -ешь); perf.
упа-сть (-ду, -дёшь); past
упал

to run, бега-ть (-ю, -ешь); perf.
убе-жать (-гу, -жишь)

to stay, remain, оста-ваться
(-юсь, -ёшься); perf. оста-
ться (-нусь, -нешься)

to follow, след-овать (-ую,
-уешь); - somebody, за with
instrumental: follow me,
следуйте за мной; perf. по -

to return, come back, возвращ-
аться (-аюсь, -аешься); perf.
возвра-титься (-щусь,
-тишься)

to arrive, приезж-ать (-аю,
-аешь); perf. прие-хать (-ду,
-дешь)

to depart, уезж-ать (-аю, -аешь);
perf. уе-хать (-ду, -дешь)

19. *Verbs — Looking and Seeing.*

to see, ви-деть (-жу, -дишь);
perf. у -

to look (at), смотр-еть (-ю
'-ишь); perf. по -

to look for, и-скать (-щу,
'-щешь); perf. по -

to look. seem, выгля-деть (-жу,
-дишь)

to recognize, узна-вать (-ю,
-ёшь); perf. узна-ть (-ю,
-ешь), with added meaning of
"to find out".

to take for, приним-ать (-аю,
-аешь) за with acc.; perf. при-
нять (-му, '-мешь); past
принял

to laugh, сме-яться (-юсь,
-ёшься); perf. по - or за-

to smile, улыб-аться (-аюсь,
-аешься)

to laugh at, сме-яться, посме-
яться (-юсь, ёшься) над with
instrumental

20. *Verbs — Mental.*

to make a mistake, ошиб-аться
(-аюсь, -аешься); perf. ошиб-
иться (-усь, -ёшься)

to hope, наде-яться (-юсь,
-ешься)

to wait (for), жд-ать (-у, -ёшь);
perf. подо -

to think (of), дума-ть (-ю,
-ешь); pf. по-
(I am thinking of him, думаю
о нём; what do you think of
him?, что Вы думаете о нём?;
какого Вы о нём мнения?)

to believe, вер-ить (-ю, -ишь);
perf. по -

to like, люб-ить (-лю, '-ишь);
perf. по -

to wish, жел-ать (-аю, -аешь);
perf. по -

to want, хо-теть (-чу, '-чешь);
perf. за -

to need, нужд-аться (-аюсь,
-аешься); I need help, я
нуждаюсь в помощи; мне
нужна помощь

to know (person or fact), зн-ать
(-аю, -аешь)

to understand, поним-ать (-аю,
-аешь); perf. по-нять (-йму,
-ймёшь)

to know how to, уме-ть (-ю,
-ешь)

to remember, помн-ить (-ю,
-ишь); perf. за -

to forget, забыв-ать (-аю,
-аешь); perf. заб-ыть (-уду,
-удешь)

to permit, allow, позвол-ять
(-яю, -яешь; dative of person
allowed); perf. позвол-ить
(-ю, -ишь)

to promise, обещ-ать (-аю,
-аешь; dative of person promised)

to forbid, запрещ-ать (-аю,
-аешь; dative of person for-

bidden); perf. запре-тить
(-щу, -тишь)

to learn, уч-иться (-усь,
'-ишься); perf. на -

to feel like, хотеться
(I feel like working, мне
хочется работать; lit., it
feels to me like working)

to fear, be afraid, бо-яться
(-юсь, -ишься)

to be right, быть правым
(I am right, я прав; make
the predicate adjective agree
in gender and number with
the subject)

to be wrong, быть неправым
(she is wrong, она неправа)

21. *Verbs — Miscellaneous.*

to live, жи-ть (-ву, -вёшь)

to die, умир-ать (-аю, -аешь);
perf. умереть (умру,
умрёшь); past умер, умерла,
умерли

to work, работа-ть (-ю, -ешь)

to give, да-вать (-ю, -ёшь);
perf. да-ть (-м, -шь)

to take, б-рать (-еру, -ерёшь);
perf. взять (возьму, возьмёшь)

to begin, начин-ать (-аю, -аешь);
perf. нач-ать (-ну, -нёшь)
(I began reading, я начал
читать)

to finish, конч-ать (-аю, -аешь);
perf. конч-ить (-у, -ишь)
(he finished writing, он
кончил писать)

to continue, keep on, продолж-
ать (-аю, -аешь)
(he kept on writing, он
продолжал писать)

to help, помог-ать (-аю, -аешь)
dat. of person); perf. помо-чь

(-гу, '-жешь); past, помог,
помогла, -и

to lose, тер-ять (-яю, -яешь);
perf. по -

to find, нахо-дить (-жу, '-дишь);
perf. найти

to try, проб-овать (-ую, -уешь);
perf. по -

to leave (something), оставл-ять
(-яю, -яешь); perf. остав-ить
(-лю, -ишь)

to show, показыва-ть (-ю, -ешь);
perf. пока-зать (-жу, - '-жешь)

to meet, встреча-ть (-ю, -ешь);
perf. встре-тить (-чу, -тишь)

to do, make, дела-ть (-ю, -ешь);
perf. с -

to be able, can, мо-чь (-гу,
'-жешь); perf. с -; past мог,
могла, могли

to put, lay, кла-сть (-ду, -дёшь);
perf. полож-ить (-у, '-ишь)

to carry, нес-ти (-у, -ёшь); perf.
по -; past нёс, несла, несли

to bring, прино-сить (-шу,

'-сишь); perf. принести

to stop (another), останавлива-ть (-ю, -ешь); perf. останов-ить (-лю, '-ишь)

to stop (self), останавлива-ться (-юсь, -ешься); perf. остано-виться

to cover, покрыв-ать (-аю, -аешь); perf. покр-ыть (-ою, -оешь)

to get, obtain, получ-ать (-аю, -аешь); perf. получ-ить (-у, '-ишь)

to get, become, станов-иться (-люсь, '-ишься; generally followed by instrumental; to become obstinate, становиться упрямым); perf. ста-ть (-ну, -нешь)

to hide, пря-тать (-чу, -чешь); perf. с -

to break, лом-ать (-аю, -аешь); perf. с -

to send, посыл-ать (-аю, -аешь); perf. по-слать (-шлю, -шлёшь)

to hurry, спеш-ить (-у, -ишь); perf. по-

to deliver, доставл-ять (-яю, -яешь); perf. достав-ить (-лю, -ишь)

to catch, лов-ить (-лю, '-ишь); perf. пойм-ать (-аю, -аешь); словить

to belong, принадлеж-ать (-у, -ишь)

to have (something) done, заставл-ять (-яю, -яешь); perf. застав-ить (-лю, -ишь)

to hold, держ-ать (-у, '-ишь)

to have just (I have just written, я только что написал)

to accept, приним-ать (-аю, -аешь)

to refuse, отказыва-ться (-юсь, -ешься; followed by от with genitive)

22. *Adjectives.*

small, маленький; малый (2)
large, большой
great, великий (3)
tall, high, высокий (2)
short (opp. of tall), маленький
low, низкий (-ок, 3)
heavy, тяжёлый (2)
light (weight), лёгкий (-ок, 2)
long, длинный (-инен, 3); долгий (-ог, 3)
short (opp. of long), короткий (короток, 2)
wide, широкий (2)
narrow, узкий (-ок, 3)
clean, чистый (3)
dirty, грязный (-ен, 3)
fresh, свежий (2)
cool, прохладный ('-ен, 1)

cold, холодный (холод-ен, -на, '-о, '-ы)
warm, тёплый (-пел, 3) (warm day, жаркий день)
hot, горячий (2); жаркий (-ок, 3)
damp, сырой
wet, мокрый (3)
dry, сухой (3)
full, полный (-он, 3)
empty, пустой (3)
dark, тёмный (-ен, 2)
light, bright, clear, светлый (-ел, 2)
fat, жирный (-ен, 3) (person, толстый, 2)
thick, плотный
thin, тонкий (-ок, 2); худой (3)
round, круглый (3)

square, квадратный
flat, плоский (-ок, 3)
deep, глубокий (2)
soft, мягкий (-ок, 2)
hard, твёрдый (3)
quick, быстрый (3), скорый (1)
slow, медленный (-ен, 1)
ordinary, обыкновенный
comfortable, удобный (-бен, 1)
uncomfortable, неудобный
near, близкий (-зок, 2)
distant, далёкий (2)
right (direction), правый (3)
left, левый
poor, бедный (-ен, 3)
rich, богатый (1)
beautiful, красивый (1)
ugly, некрасивый (1)
pretty, хорошенький
sweet, сладкий (-док, 3)
bitter, горький (-рек, 3)
sour, кислый (-сел, 3)
salty, солёный (-лон, 3)
young, молодой (молод, 3)
old, старый (3)
new, новый (3)
good, хороший (2); добрый (2)
better, лучший
best, самый лучший
bad, плохой (3); худой (3)
worse, худший
worst, самый худший
fine, "regular", хороший (2)
first, первый
last, последний
strong, сильный (2)
weak, слабый (3)
tired, усталый (1)
alone, один (одна, одно)
same, самый
true, правдивый (1)

false, неверный (-ен, 3);
  ложный
easy, лёгкий (-ок, 2)
hard, difficult, трудный (-ен, 3)
happy, glad, довольный (-ен, 1)
sad, грустный (-тен, 3)
free, свободный (-ден, 1)
silly, глупый (3)
crazy, помешанный (1)
brave, храбрый (3)
cowardly, трусливый (1)
quiet, тихий (3)
noisy, шумный
kind, любезный (-ен, 1)
drunk, пьяный (2)
polite, вежливый (1)
impolite, rude, грубый (3)
pleasant, приятный (-ен, 1)
unpleasant, неприятный (-ен, 1)
lonesome, одинокий (1)
foreign, иностранный
friendly, приветливый (1);
  дружественный (-нен, 1)
hostile, враждебный (1);
  неприятельский
lucky, счастливый (1)
unlucky, несчастливый (1)
charming, очаровательный
afraid, боязливый
  (I am afraid, мне страшно)
ready, готовый (1)
hungry, голодный (-ен, 3)
thirsty (I am), мне хочется пить
funny, смешной (-он, 2)
possible, возможный (-жен, 1)
impossible, невозможный (1)
living, живой (3)
dead, мёртвый (2)
right (correct), правый (3)
  (I'm right, я прав)
wrong, неправый (3)
  (I'm wrong, я неправ)

23. *Colors.*

white, белый (3)
black, чёрный (-ен, 3)
red, красный (-ен, 2)
green, зелёный (3)
blue, синий
   (light blue, голубой)

yellow, жёлтый (2)
gray, серый (3)
brown, коричневый
pink, розовый
purple, пурпуровый; **лиловый**

24. *Nationalities.*[14]

American, американский; американ-ец, -ка, -цы
English, английский; англичан-ин, -ка, -е
French, французский; францу-з, -женка, -зы
German, немецкий; нем-ец, -ка, -цы
Spanish, испанский; испан-ец, -ка, -цы
Russian, русский; русск-ий, -ая, -ие; советский (pertaining to the
   Soviet Union; not interchangeable with русский, and never
   applied to the language)
Italian, итальянский; итальян-ец, -ка, цы
Japanese, японский; япон-ец, -ка, -цы
Chinese, китайский; кита-ец, -янка, -йцы
Dutch, голландский; голланд-ец, -ка, -цы
Norwegian, норвежский; норвеж-ец, -ка, -цы
Swedish, шведский; швед, -ка, -ы
Finnish, финский; финн, -ка, -ы
Belgian, бельгийский; бельги-ец, -йка, -йцы
Polish, польский; пол-як, '-ька, -яки
Danish, датский; датчан-ин, -ка, -е
Swiss, швейцарский; швейцар-ец, -ка, -цы
Portuguese, португальский; португал-ец, -ка, -ьцы
Yugoslav, югославянский; югославян-ин, '-ка, -е

14.   The first form given is the adjective, to be declined as such, and
to be used in connection with a noun: the American Navy,
американский флот. The second form is the noun, meaning a person
of the stated nationality: he is an American, он — американец; she is
an American, она — американка; they are Americans, они —
американцы. The name of the language is indicated by the adjective
with язык: the Russian language, русский язык; after the verb "to
speak", however, the masculine singular form of the adjective, preceded
by по and minus the -й of the ending, is used: I speak Russian, я
говорю по-русски; do you speak French? говорите ли Вы
по-французски? Nouns and adjectives of nationality are not usually
capitalized, though names of countries are.

Bulgarian, болгарский; болгар-ин, -ка, -ы
Czech, чешский; че-х, -шка, -хи
Greek, греческий; гре-к, -чанка, '-ки
Turkish, турецкий; тур-ок, -чанка, '-ки
Roumanian, румынский; румын, -ка, -ы
Hungarian, венгерский; венгер-ец, -ка, -цы
Austrian, австрийский; австри-ец, -ячка, -цы
Malay, малайский; мала-ец, -йка, -цы
Persian, персидский; перс, -иянка, -ы
Arabian, Arab, Arabic, арабский; араб, -ка, -ы
Jewish, Hebrew, еврейский; евре-й, -йка, -и
Australian, австралийский; австрали-ец, -йка, -йцы
African, африканский; африкан-ец, -ка, -цы
Canadian, канадский; канад-ец, -ка, -цы
Mexican, мексиканский; мексикан-ец, -ка, -цы
Cuban, кубанский; кубан-ец, -ка, -цы
Brazilian, бразильянский; бразильян-ец, -ка, -цы
Argentinian, аргентинский; аргентин-ец, -ка, -цы
Porto Rican, порториканский; порторикан-ец, -ка, -цы

25. *Adverbs and Adverbial Expressions.*

today, сегодня
yesterday, вчера
tomorrow, завтра
day before yesterday, третьего дня
day after tomorrow, послезавтра
tonight, сегодня вечером
last night, вчера вечером
this morning, сегодня утром
in the morning, утром
in the afternoon, днём
in the evening, вечером
in the night, ночью
this afternoon, сегодня днём
tomorrow morning, завтра утром
tomorrow afternoon, завтра днём
tomorrow night, завтра вечером
all day, весь день
all morning, всё утро
all night, всю ночь
every day, каждый день
every morning, всякое (каждое) утро

every night, каждую ночь
early, рано
late, поздно
already, уже
yet, still, ещё
no longer, больше не
not yet, нет ещё
now, теперь
then, тогда
afterwards, после
never, никогда
always, всегда
forever, навсегда
soon, скоро
often, часто
seldom, редко
usually, обыкновенно
fast, быстро
slowly, медленно
here, здесь
there, там
near by, близко
far away, далеко

up (stairs), наверху; наверх
  (motion)
down (stairs), внизу; вниз
  (motion)
ahead, in front, впереди; вперёд
  (motion)
forward, вперёд
behind, in back, сзади
back, backward, назад (motion)
outside, снаружи; наружу
  (motion)
inside, внутри; внутрь (motion)
opposite, in front, напротив
here and there, тут и там
everywhere, всюду, везде
where, где; куда (motion)
also, too, также; тоже
yes, да
no, нет
not, не
very, much, очень
little, not much, мало; не очень
well, хорошо
badly, плохо
better, лучше
worse, хуже
only, только
more (than), более (чем),
  больше
less, менее, меньше
as - as, так - как
as much - as, столько же -
  сколько (with genitive sg.)
as many - as, столько же -
  сколько (with gen. pl.)
how much?, сколько (with gen.
  sg.) ?
how many?, сколько (with gen.

pl.) ?
how?, как?
too much, слишком много
  (with gen. sg.)
too many, слишком много
  (with gen. pl.)
really, truly, действительно
so much, столько (with gen. sg.)
so many, столько (with gen. pl.)
as, like, как
besides, кроме того
finally, in short, наконец;
  в конце концов
almost, почти
gladly, с удовольствием
certainly, непременно
at once, сразу
at all, вовсе
hardly, с трудом, едва не
aloud, вслух
of course, конечно
suddenly, внезапно; вдруг
about, около
perhaps, maybe, может-быть
a little, немножко; немного
  (with gen.)
again, опять
together, вместе
at least, по крайней мере
for lack of, за недостатком
  (with gen.)
long ago, давным давно
repeatedly, часто; неодно-
  кратно; повторно
therefore, поэтому
occasionally, случайно; иногда
entirely, altogether, слишком;
  совсем

26. Conjunctions.

and, и
but, но; а
if, provided that, если
  (if with conditional usually =

  если бы with past)
or, или
why?, почему?
why!, ну что!; ну да!; что же!

because, for, потому что
before, прежде чем; до того как
when, when?, while, когда
than, чем; лучше чем; genitive case
where, where?, где; куда (motion)
whence, whence?, откуда
until, пока не; до тех пор пока не

although, хотя
unless, если только
that, что
after, после того как
as soon as, как только
as long as, пока не
without, без того чтобы (more often, не with gerund: without knowing this, не зная этого)

27. *Indefinite pronouns and Adjectives.*

such, такой
of all kinds, всякого рода
everything, всё
everyone, все
something, что-то
someone, кто-то
nothing, ничто
no one, никто
no (adj.), нет (with gen.; I have no bread, у меня нет хлеба)
some, некоторые or gen.: give me some bread, дайте мне хлеба; some men, некоторые люди

a few, several, несколько with gen.
neither - nor, ни - ни
each, every, каждый; всякий
all, весь (вся, всё, pl. все)
(an) other, другой
much, lots of, много (with gen.)
few, немного (with gen. pl.)
many, много (with gen. pl.)
little, not much, мало (with gen.)
both, оба(обе, оба) with gen. sg.
enough, довольно; достаточно (with gen.)
not enough, недостаточно (with gen.)

28. *Prepositions* (the cases taken by each preposition are indicated).

of, из (gen.); or genitive alone
from, away from, от (gen.)
outside of, вне (gen.)
to, dative; в (acc.); к (dat.); на (acc.); до (gen.)
at, у (gen.)
with, с (instr.)
as far as, until, up to, до (gen.)
without, без (gen.)
in, в (prep.)
into, в (acc.)
on, на (acc. or prep.)
over. above, над (instr.)

for, for the sake of, для (gen.)
since, с (gen.)
toward, к (dat.)
between, among, среди; посреди (gen.)
near, next to, близ (gen.); рядом с (instr.)
below, beneath, под (instr.); ниже (gen.)
by, (instrumental case)
far from, далеко от (gen.)
before, до (gen.)
after, после (gen.)

opposite, in front of, впереди (gen.)

back of, behind, позади (gen.)

under (neath), под (instr.)

instead of, вместо (gen.)

beside, кроме (gen.)

at the house of, в доме (with gen.); у (gen.)

through, сквозь (acc.)

by means of, instr.; посредством (gen.)

against, против (gen.)

across, через (acc.)

on the other side of, на другой стороне (with gen.)

in spite of, несмотря на (acc.)

about, около (gen.)

around, кругом (gen.)

during, во время (gen.)

because of, on account of, из за (gen.); на основании того что

in order to (inf.), для того чтобы (past)

29. *Special Expressions and Idioms.*

good morning, доброе утро; здравствуйте (often pronounced здрасте)

good afternoon, good day, добрый день; здравствуйте

good evening, добрый вечер

good night, спокойной ночи

good-bye, до свиданья; прощайте

I'll see you later, до скорого свидания

I'll see you tomorrow, до завтра

I'll see you tonight, до вечера

just now, только - что

hello! (on telephone), слушаю!; алло!

how are you?, как Вы поживаете?

I'm well, хорошо; мне хорошо

I'm (much) better, мне (гораздо) лучше

how goes it?, как дела?

what time is it?, который час?

it's six o'clock, шесть часов

at six o'clock, в шесть часов

at about six, около шести; часов в шесть

at half past six, в половина седьмого

at a quarter to six, без четверти шесть

at a quarter past six, в четверть седьмого

at ten minutes to six, без десяти шесть

at ten minutes past six, в десять минут седьмого

last year, в прошлом году

next year, в будущем году; на будущий год (for next year)

every day, каждый день

the whole day, весь день

please, пожалуйста (pronounce пожалста)

tell me, скажите мне

bring me, принесите мне
show me, покажите мне
thank you, спасибо; благодарю (Вас)
don't mention it, не за что; пожалуйста
will you give me?, дайте мне, пожалуйста
pardon me, извините; простите
it doesn't matter, never mind, ничего
I'm sorry, виноват
I can't help, ничего не могу (with inf.)
it's nothing, это ничего
what a pity!, как жаль!
it's too bad, ужасно!
I'm glad, я рад
I have to, мне надо; мне нужно; я должен
I agree (all right, O. K.), я согласен
here is (are), вот
there is (are), вот; там
where is (are)?, где?
where are you going?, куда Вы идёте?
which way?, по какой дороге?; в какую сторону?
this (that) way (fashion), этим путём
this (that) way (direction), в этом направлении; по этой стороне;
    в эту сторону
to the right, направо
to the left, налево
straight ahead, прямо
come with me, идите со мной
what can I do for you?, что я могу для Вас сделать?; чем я могу
    помочь?; что Вам угодно?
what is it?, что это такое?
what is the matter?, в чём дело?
what is the matter with you?, что с Вами?
what do you want?, что Вы хотите?
what are you talking about?, о чём Вы говорите?
what does that mean?, что это значит?
what do you mean?, что Вы подразумеваете?; что Вы хотите
    этим сказать?
how much (is it)?, сколько (это стоит)?
anything else?, что ещё?; что больше?
nothing else, больше ничего
do you speak Russian?, говорите ли Вы по-русски?
a little, немножко; немного
speak more slowly, говорите медленнее
do you understand?, понимаете ли Вы?

I don't understand, я не понимаю; я не понял
do you know?, знаете ли Вы?
I don't know, я не знаю
I can't, я не могу
what do you call this in Russian?, как это называется по-русски?
how do you say - in Russian?, как говорится - по-русски?
I'm an American, я — американец (американка, fem.)
I'm (very) hungry, я (очень) голоден
I'm thirsty, я хочу пить
I'm sleepy, я хочу спать
I'm warm, мне тепло
I'm cold, мне холодно
it's warm, жарко
it's cold, холодно
it's windy, ветрено
it's sunny, солнечно
it's fine weather, хорошая погода
it's bad weather, плохая погода
it's forbidden, запрещено (no smoking, курить воспрещается)
luckily, fortunately, к счастью
unfortunately, к несчастью
is it not so?, don't you?, aren't you? (etc.), не так (ли)?; не
    правда (ли)?
not at all, совсем нет; совсем не так
how old are you?, сколько Вам лет?
I'm — years old, мне — лет (replace лет with год for "one" and
    compounds of "one", with года for 2, 3, 4, and compounds)
how long have you been here?, давно ли Вы здесь?, Вы давно
    здесь?
how long have you been waiting?, сколько времени Вы ждёте?
as soon as possible, возможно скорее; поскорее
come here!, идите сюда!
come in!, войдите!
look!, посмотрите!
look out!, careful!, будьте осторожны!; осторожно!
darn it!, чорт возьми!; это — возмутительно!
for heaven's sake!, ради Бога!
glad to meet you!, очень приятно!; я очень рад!
no admittance, вход запрещён!: входить воспрещается!
notice!, объявление!
nonsense!, пустяки!; ерунда!
listen!, look here!, say!, послушайте!; скажите!
just a second!, одну минуту!
gangway!, one side!, посторонитесь!

CHAPTER XII

OTHER EUROPEAN TONGUES

The languages of Europe that do not belong to the three major branches of Indo-European (Germanic, Romance, Slavic) are fairly numerous, but relatively unimportant, from a practical standpoint. Greek and Albanian form two separate branches of Indo-European. The former is the national tongue of some 7,000,000 people in Greece and of perhaps one or two million more, located on Turkish, Bulgarian and Albanian territory, and in the politically Italian Dodecanese Islands, while the latter is spoken by over 1,000,000 people in Albania and by scattered minorities in Yugoslavia, Greece, and even in southern Italy and Sicily. Finnish, Hungarian, Turkish and Estonian belong to the great Ural-Altaic family of northern Asia, and bear some resemblance to one another in structure, though they have so diverged in vocabulary as to be mutually incomprehensible (save in the case of Finnish and Estonian). Finnish is spoken by some 4,000,000 people in Finland and by scattered minorities in Russian Karelia; Estonian by about 1,000,000 in Estonia; Hungarian, or Magyar, by over 13,000,000 people, located in Hungary and in countries bordering on Hungary (Czechoslovakia, Roumania, Yugoslavia); while Turkish is the national tongue of Turkey's 18,000,000 inhabitants, located mainly in Asia Minor, but also in European Turkey and adjacent territories (Bulgaria and Greece; Turkish linguistic minorities are to be found as far west as Albania, and as far north as Roumanian Dobrudja). The Celtic group of Indo-European appears in Ireland (Eire), where Irish (occasionally called "Erse", but not by the Irish themselves) is the official tongue, though more English than

Irish is spoken among Eire's 3,000,000 inhabitants; in the highlands of Scotland; in Wales; and in French Brittany; the number of people speaking Scots Gaelic does not exceed a hundred thousand; Welsh speakers may run up to 1,000,000, but English is current among them; Breton is spoken by over 1,000,000 people in Brittany, but most of them use French as well. Lithuanian and Lettish are the national tongues of two countries having populations of about 3,000,000 and 2,000,000, respectively; they belong to the Baltic branch of Indo-European, which is frequently joined to the Slavic in a Balto-Slavic classification. Basque, a language with no known affiliations, is spoken by perhaps half a million people in the extreme northeastern corner of Spain and the extreme southwestern corner of France, astride the Pyrenees; most Basque speakers can be approached with either Spanish or French.

From a practical standpoint, the majority of speakers of all these languages may be reached with other tongues. French and Italian are fairly current in Greece; Italian and Serbo-Croatian in Albania. Large numbers of Finns are acquainted with Russian, German and Swedish. Estonians, Latvians and Lithuanians are generally acquainted with Russian, German or Polish. Most Hungarians speak German. Celts and Basques can generally be reached with English, French and Spanish. Even in Turkey, the educated classes are generally acquainted with French, English and Italian.

GREEK

From a cultural standpoint, the most important of these minor European tongues is Greek, which has behind it a glorious past of civilization and tremendous contributions made to the world's progress. From a linguistic standpoint, Greek has made an equally vast contribution to all other civilized languages, whose scientific and literary vocabularies are replete with words borrowed from Greek. The modern Greek language differs far less from the ancient Greek of classical times than modern Italian differs from Latin, so that it is quite possible for one trained in ancient Greek to read modern Greek. Most of the innovations have been in the fields of pronunciation and vocabulary; but while the modern tongue has borrowed considerably from Turkish, Italian and other sources, the bulk of the Greek vocabulary still remains what it was in the days of Homer and Aristotle, and the student of modern Greek finds himself constantly faced with words in current popular use which have given rise to cultural terms in his own tongue (e.g. στράτευμα, pron. *strátevma,* army; compare "strategy";ἀριθμῶ, pron. *arithmó,* to count; compare "arithmetic"). There is a certain divergence between literary modern Greek, which consciously and proudly adheres to traditional forms, and the colloquial or "Demotic" variety, which introduces foreign (particularly Turkish) words, and displays a relaxation of grammatical standards and a simplification of grammatical forms (e. g. literary ποτήριον οἴνου vs. popular ποτῆρι κρασί, "glass of wine").

ALPHABET AND SOUNDS

Symbol   Value

A α = father (ἀνά, pr. **aná,** "by", "over"; cf. **analyze**).
B β = vase (6λέπω, pr. **vlépo,** "I see").
Γ γ = lo**ng**er, before γ, κ, ξ, χ; (ἔγγονος, pr. **éngonos,** "grandson").

= yes, before ε, η, ι, υ, αι, ει, οι, υι; (γῆ, pr. **yee**, "earth"; cf. **ge**ography) ;

= voiced German ich in all other positions; (γάτα, pr. **gháta**, "cat").

Δ δ = **this**, (ἐδῶ, pr. **edhó**, "here").

Ε ε = met (ἔλα, pr. **éla**, "come!").

Ζ ζ = zinc (ζώνη, pr. **zónee**, "belt"; cf. **zone**).

Η η = me (ἡμέρα, pr. **eeméra**, "day").

Θ ϑ = think (θέλω, pr. **thélo**, "I want").

Ι ι = me (δίδω, pr. **dheédho**, "I give").

Κ κ = king (κακός, pr. **kakós**, "bad"; cf. **cac**ophony).

Λ λ = low (καλός, pr. **kalós**, "good"; cf. **cal**isthenics).

Μ μ = moon (μόνος, pr. **mónos**, "alone"; cf. **mono**syllabic).

Ν ν = new (νόμος, pr. **nómos**, "law").

Ξ ξ = fix (ἔξω, pr. **ékso**, "out").

Ο ο = obey (πόλεμος, pr. **pólemos**, "war"; cf. **pol**emic).

Π π = pat (πόδι, pr. **pódhee**, "foot"; cf. tri**p**od).

Ρ ϱ = British very (παρά, pr. **pará**, "than"; cf. pa**r**allel).

Σ σ = us (σῶμα, pr. **sóma**, "body"; cf. **s**omatic). (ς final)

Τ τ = tall (ποταμός, pr. **potamós**, "river"; cf. hippo**pot**amus).

Υ υ = very, in diphthongs (αυ, ευ, ηυ), when a vowel or a voiced consonant follows (αὔριον, pr. **ávrion**, "to-morrow") ;

= father, in diphthongs (αυ, ευ, ηυ), when an unvoiced consonant follows (αὐτός, pr. **aftós**, "this") ;

= me, in all other positions (ὕλη, pr. **eélee**, "material").

Φ φ = father (φωνή, pr. **foneé**, "voice"; cf. tele**ph**one).

Χ χ = German ach, before α, ο, ω, or consonant (χάνω, pr. **kháno**, "I loose") ;

= German ich, before ε, η, ι, υ; (χέρι, pr. **chéree**, "hand"; **chir**opractor).

Ψ ψ = perhaps (ψυχή, pr. **pseecheé**, "spirit"; cf. **psycho**logy).

Ω ω = obey (ζωή, pr. **zoeé**, "life"; cf. **zoo**logy).

Special Groups:

αι = met (πηγαίνω, pr. **peeyéno**, "I go").

ει, οι, υι = me (εἶνε, pr. **eéne**, "is"; οἶνος, pr. **eénos**, "wine"; υίός, pr. **eeós**, "son").

ου = food, (βουνό, pr. **voonó**, "mountain").

μπ = **b**en**d** or em**b**er (μπαρμπέρης, pr. **barbérees**, "barber":
  μπόμπα, pron. **bómba**, "bomb").
ντ = **d**o or un**d**o (ντόμινο, pr. **dómino**, "domino"; ἔντιμος, pr.
  éndeemos, "honored").

Special characters, called breathings (' , '), appearing
over the initial vowel of a word, have no value in modern
Greek (note, however, that the second symbol had the value
of *h* in the ancient language, and that English words derived
from Greek words beginning with a vowel that has this symbol
over it appear with an *h*: ὕπνος, pr. *eépnos*, "sleep"; cf.
*hypno*tism). Three accents appear in Greek, the acute
('), the grave (`) and the circumflex (˜). All three of them
indicate the position of the stress, but there is no difference
among them in the modern tongue.[1] A semicolon (;) is the
Greek equivalent of a question mark: εἶνε κακόν;, is it bad?

GRAMMATICAL SURVEY.

Nouns and Articles.

Greek has three genders, masculine, feminine and neuter
(but inanimate objects are often masculine or feminine); and
five cases: nominative, genitive, dative, accusative and vocative. There is no indefinite article, so that ἄνθρωπος may mean
"man" or "a man". The definite article is:

	Singular			Plural		
	Masc.	Fem.	Neut.	Masc.	Fem.	Neut.
Nom.	ὁ	ἡ	τό	οἱ	αἱ	τὰ
Gen.	τοῦ	τῆς	τοῦ	τῶν	τῶν	τῶν
Dat.	τῷ	τῇ	τῷ	τοῖς	ταῖς	τοῖς
Acc.	τὸν	τὴν	τό	τοὺς	τὰς	τὰ

1. In the ancient tongue, only a long vowel could bear the circumflex
accent; the latter may therefore appear on η and ω (invariably long
vowels in ancient Greek), but not on ε and o (invariably short
vowels); in modern Greek there is no difference of length in vowels,
all vowel sounds being of medium length and clearly enunciated,
whether stressed or unstressed.

There is a large number of declensional schemes, of which the following three are samples:

Masculine: λαός, "people": λα-ός, -οῦ, -ῷ, -όν, -έ; plural: λα-οί, -ῶν, -οῖς, -ούς, -οί.

Feminine: χαρά, "joy": χαρ-ά, -ᾶς, -ᾷ, -άν, -ά; plural: χαρ-αί, -ῶν, -αῖς, -άς, -αί.

Neuter: ξύλον, "wood"; ξύλ-ον, -ου, -ῳ, -ον, -ον; plural: ξύλ-α, -ων, -οις, -α, -α.

The nominative case is primarily the case of the subject or of the predicate nominative; the accusative the case of the direct object; the genitive indicates possession. The dative is the case of the indirect object, but there is a tendency in the spoken tongue to replace it by using the preposition εἰς ("to") with the accusative; this preposition tends to lose its initial vowel sound and to combine its final s-sound with a following definite article: δίδω στὸν (for εἰς τὸν) ἄνθρωπον, I give to the man, in substitution for a more literary δίδω τῷ ἀνθρώπῳ.

Adjectives and Adverbs.

Adjectives agree in gender, number and case with the nouns they modify, and follow complex declensional schemes similar to those of the nouns: ὁ σοφὸς ἄνθρωπος, the wise man; τοῦ σοφοῦ ἀνθρώπου, of the wise man; τῷ σοφῷ ἀνθρώπῳ (colloquial: στὸν σοφὸν ἄνθρωπον), to the wise man; etc.; ἡ σοφὴ φιλενάδα, the wise girl friend: τῆς σοφῆς φιλενάδας, etc.

The comparative is generally formed by replacing the ending of the positive with -τέρος or -ώτερος; the superlative by replacing the ending of the positive with -τατος (-ώτατος); or by prefixing the article to the comparative: σοφός, wise; σοφώτερος, wiser; σοφώτατος or ὁ σοφώτερος, wisest. In colloquial Greek, πειὸ and πειὸ preceded by the definite article are also used for the comparative and superlative, respectively; πειὸ μεγάλος, larger; ὁ πειὸ καλός, the best.

The adverb is usually derived from the adjective by changing the ending of the latter to -ως: σοφός, wise; σοφῶς, wisely. A few adjectives change -ος to -α: καλός, good; καλά, well.

Numerals.

"One", "three" and "four", their compounds and plural hundreds are declined. The others are invariable.

1—ἕνας (fem. μία, neut. ἕνα)
2—δυὸ
3—τρεῖς (neut. τρία)
4—τέσσαρες (neut. -α)
5—πέντε
6—ἕξι (ἐξ)
7—ἐφτὰ (ἐπτά)
8—ὀκτὼ
9—ἐννηὰ (ἐννέα)
10—δέκα
11—ἕνδεκα
12—δώδεκα

13—δεκατρεῖς (-ία)
20—εἴκοσι
21—εἰκοσιένας
30—τριάντα
40—σαράντα
50—πενήντα
60—ἐξήντα
70—ἑβδομήντα
100—ἑκατὸ
200—διακόσιοι (-αι, -α)
1000—χίλια
2000—δυὸ χιλιάδες

1,000,000 — ἕν ἑκατομμύριον

Pronouns.

Personal.

I, ἐγώ; me, to me, ἐμένα (μοῦ); we, ἐμεῖς; us, to us, ἐμᾶς (μᾶς).
you, σύ; you, to you, ἐσένα (σοῦ); plural nom. σεῖς, acc. ἐσᾶς (σᾶς).
he, she, it, αὐτὸς (τοῦ), αὐτὴ (τῆς), αὐτὸ (regularly declined).

(Forms in parentheses are used before a verb as direct or indirect objects; but τόν, τήν, τὸ are more commonly used as direct objects).

Possessive (follow a noun or adjective, and are unaccented).

my, mine, μου; our, ours, μας.
your, yours (sg.), σου; (pl.) σας.
his, her, hers, its, their, theirs, του, της, των.
(my brother, ὁ ἀδελφός μου; his father, ὁ πατήρ του).

Interrogative and Relative.

who?, τίς; ποιός;
what?, τί; ποιό;
whom?, τίνα; ποιόν;
whose?, of whom?, τίνος;

As a relative pronoun, ποὺ is generally used in all connections: ὁ ἄνθρωπος ποὺ εἶδα, the man whom I saw.

Verbs.

The Greek verb appears in a complicated scheme of tenses and moods, with a present, an imperfect, several possible future formations, an aorist (or past), a perfect (or present perfect), and a pluperfect; the conditional is treated as a mood rather than a tense, and appears in four possible forms; there are two forms of the subjunctive, and various forms of the imperative, infinitive and participle. A full-fledged passive appears, formed in most of its tenses by the addition of endings (τιμῶ, I honor; τιμῶμαι, I am honored). In a verb such as λύω, loose, the present indicative assumes the following forms: λύ-ω, -εις, -ει, -ομεν, -ετε, -ουν. The imperfect is ἔλυον; the future (I shall be writing) is θὰ λύω, or (I shall write, at some specified time), θὰ λύσω; the aorist is ἔλυσα; the perfect ἔχω λύσει; the pluperfect εἶχον λύσει.

IDENTIFICATION

In written form, Greek is very easily identified by means of its distinctive alphabet. In spoken form, the distinctive sound of the Greek s, which is almost a sharp hiss, is of help. Distinctive words, similar to English words known to be of Greek origin, frequently appear in speech.

SAMPLE OF WRITTEN GREEK

Διότι τόσον ἠγάπησεν ὁ Θεὸς τὸν κόσμον, ὥστε ἔδωκε τὸν Υἱὸν αὐτοῦ τὸν μονογενῆ, διὰ νὰ μὴ ἀπολεσθῇ πᾶς ὁ πιστεύων εἰς αὐτόν, ἀλλὰ νὰ ἔχῃ ζωὴν αἰώνιον.

WORDS AND PHRASES

good morning, καλὴ ἡμέρα (καλημέρα)
good evening, καλὴ ἑσπέρα (καλησπέρα)
how are you? πῶς εἶσθε; τί κάνετε;   very well, πολὺ καλὰ
much better, πολὺ καλήτερα   good night, καλὴ νύκτα
please, παρακαλῶ   and, καὶ   yes, ναὶ   no, not, ὄχι
thank you very much, εὐχαριστῶ παρὰ πολὺ
I am very glad, χαίρω παρὰ πολὺ
I am hungry, πεινῶ   I am thirsty, διψῶ
I am sorry, λυποῦμαι   to your health!, εἰς ὑγείαν σας!
where are you going?, ποῦ πᾶτε;
do you speak Greek?, ὁμιλεῖτε Ἑλληνικά;
very little, πολὺ ὀλίγον
I understand, ἐννοῶ   I have not, δὲν ἔχω
what time is it?, τί ὥρα εἶνε;   it is 3 o'clock, εἶνε τρεῖς ἡ ὥρα
it is bad weather, εἶνε κακὸς καιρός
it is warm, κάμνει ζέστη   it is cold, κάμνει κρύο
it is a fine night, εἶνε ὡραία νύκτα
give me, δόσετέ μου   come here, ἐλᾶτε ἐδῶ
so long (lit. health to you!), γειά σου.

ALBANIAN

ALPHABET AND SOUNDS — There is little uniformity in the orthography of the various Albanian dialects, of which the principal two are Gheg, spoken in northern Albania, and Tosk, spoken in the south. In a form of standardized orthography adopted by the Albanian Committee in 1908, Roman characters are used, with an alphabet lacking the letter w. The seven vowels are: a, e, ë, i, o, u, y; these have approximately the sound of *father*, m*e*t, French f*eu*, ma*chi*ne, *o*bey, f*oo*d, and French s*ur*, respectively. Consonants and consonant groups are approximately as in English, with the following modifications: dh = *th*is; gj = hog-*y*ard; j = *y*es; nj = on*i*on; q = sto*ck*-*y*ard. The accent of Albanian usually falls on the next to the last syllable, but there are numerous words in which it falls on the last or third from the last.

GRAMMATICAL STRUCTURE — Albanian has two genders, masculine and feminine, with traces of a former neuter appearing only in the plural. The indefinite article is *një*, "a" or "an": *një shtëpi*, a house. The definite article is suffixed to the noun: *mik*, friend, *miku*, the friend. The case-system of Albanian includes a nominative, a genitive-dative, and an accusative: *mik*, friend; *miku*, the friend; *mikut*, of or to the friend; *mikun* or *miknë*, the friend (object).

The adjective is normally not declined, but requires a prefixed form of the article: *një njeri i mirë*, a good man (lit. a man the good). The adjective often serves as an adverb: *unë jam mirë*, I am well.

The numerals are as follows: *një, dy, tre, katër, pesë, gjashtë, shtatë, tetë, nëntë, dhjetë; një-mbë-dhjetë* (11); *njëzét* (20); *një-qint* (100); *një-mijë* (1000).

The verb shows considerable complexity of tenses and moods. The present indicative of a regular verb such as *hap*, to open, is as follows: *hap, hap, hap, hapim, hapni, hapin*. The verb "to be" has: *jam, je, është, jemi, jini, janë*. The verb "to have" has: *kam, ke, ka, kemi, kini, kanë*.

The interrogative form of the verb is formed by prefixing
a: *a jam?*, am I?; *a íshin*, are they? The negative is formed by
prefixing *s'* or *nuk*: *s'jam*, I am not; *nuk do të jem*, I shall
not be.

The vocabulary of Albanian indicates considerable borrowing from neighboring tongues (Latin, Italian, Greek, Serbo-
Croatian, Turkish). "Gold", for example, is *ar*, and "silver"
ergjënt; "dog" is *qen*, and "meat" *mish* (Slavic *myaso*);
"bad" is *i keq* (Greek *kakós*), along with a more indigenous
i lig; "body" is *trup* (Slavic); "cup" is *fildxhán* (Turkish
filján), or *kupë* (Latin *cuppa*).

SAMPLE OF WRITTEN ALBANIAN (John 3.16)

*Sepse Perëndia kaq e deshi botën, sa dha Birin' e tij
të-vetëmlíndurin, që të mos humbasë kushdó që t'i besojë
atíj, po të ketë jetë të-përjétëshme.*

WORDS AND PHRASES

greetings, hello, *t'u ngjat jeta*
good day, *mirë dita*
good evening, *mirë mbrëma*
good night, *natën e mirë*
good-bye, *lamtumirë, ditën e mirë*
thank you, *ju falem nderit*
excuse me, *më falni*
please, *ju lutem*
do you understand?, *a më kuptoni?, a mer vesh?*
I don't understand, *unë s'kuptój, unë nuk kuptój*
do you speak English?, *a flisni inglísht?*
yes, *po*
no, *jo*
how much?, *sá bën?, sá kushtón?*

EUROPEAN LANGUAGES OF THE
URAL-ALTAIC GROUP

Finnish, Hungarian and Turkish form the three western-most European spearheads of the great Ural-Altaic family of northern and central Asia. Other languages of this group are spoken in northern and eastern Europe (Lapp, Estonian, Livonian, Permian, Mordvinian, Cheremiss, etc.), but they have few speakers and scant cultural or commercial importance.

While a fairly close bond exists between Finnish, Estonian and Livonian, the unity among the other members of the family is more a matter of certain pecularities in sound and grammatical structure than of vocabulary. Indeed, some linguists reject the fundamental unity of the Ural-Altaic family, and prefer to classify the Finno-Ugric languages separately from the Altaic. Illustrative of the vocabulary differences among the three main European tongues of the group are the following:

English	Finnish	Hungarian	Turkish
apple	*omena*	*alma*	*elma*
arm	*käsivarsi*	*kar*	*kol*
fire	*tuli*	*tűz*	*ateş*
one	*yksi*	*egy*	*bir*
two	*kaksi*	*kettő*	*iki*
three	*kolme*	*három*	*üç*
four	*neljä*	*négy*	*dört*
five	*viisi*	*öt*	*beş*
six	*kuusi*	*hat*	*altı*
seven	*seitsemän*	*hét*	*yedi*
eight	*kahdeksan*	*nyolc*	*sekiz*
nine	*yhdeksän*	*kilenc*	*dokuz*
ten	*kymmenen*	*tiz*	*on*
eleven	*yksitoista*	*tizenegy*	*on-bir*
twelve	*kaksitoista*	*tizenkettő*	*on-iki*
twenty	*kaksikymmentä*	*húsz*	*yirmi*
one hundred	*sata*	*száz*	*yüz*
one thousand	*tuhat*	*ezer*	*bin*

(Languages of this group generally agree in using the *singular* after any numeral: Finnish *kolme poikaa*, three boys; Hungarian *öt fa*, five trees).

In the matter of sounds, the languages of this group generally agree in having some measure of "vowel harmony". This means that the vowel sounds are divided into two or three classes (front, pronounced in the front part of the mouth, such as *ö* or *ü;* back, pronounced in the back part of the mouth, such as *a, o, u;* and neutral, pronounced in the middle part of the mouth, such as *e*); if the root of the word has a "back" vowel, added suffixes must also contain back vowels; if a front vowel appears in the root, the vowel of the suffix must be changed so as to conform; the "middle" or "neutral" vowels, where they exist, may work with either front or back vowels. This in turn means that practically all suffixes appear in double form, with a front or neutral vowel to conform with a front vowel of the root, and with a back or neutral vowel to conform with a back vowel of the root.

In grammatical structure, these languages generally agree in rejecting the concept of gender, and in indicating noun and verb relations by the piling on of suffix upon suffix (the so-called "agglutinative" process), to a far greater degree than is the case in the Indo- European tongues.

The following is a sample of the same Biblical passage (John 3.16) in the three main Ural-Altaic tongues, with a few minor European languages of the group added for purposes of comparison:

Finnish: *Sillä niin Jumala on rakastanut maailmaa, että hän antoi ainokaisen Poikansa, jotta kuka ikinä häneen uskoo, se ei hukkuisi, vaan saisi iankaikkisen elämän.*

Estonian: *Sest nõnda on Jumal maailma armastanud, et tema oma ainusündinud Poja on annud, et ükski, kes tema sisse usub, ei pea hukka saama, waid et igawene elu temal peab olema.*

Livonian: *Sīepierast ku Jumal um nei māilmõ ārmastõn, ku um andõn āinagisyndõn Pŭoga, algõ amšti, kis uskõbõd täm pāl, milykš ukkõ lāgõ, aga amadõn volgõ igani jelami.*

Lapp: *Tastko nū rakisti Ibmil mailmi, atti son addi aidnu riegadam Parnis, amas oktage, kutte sudnji osku, kaďutussi šaddat, muttu vai son ožuši agalaš aellim.*

Hungarian: *Mert úgy szereté Isten e világot, hogy az ő egyetlenegy szülött Fiját adná, hogy minden, valaki hiszen ő benne, el ne veszszen, hanem örök életet vegyen.*

Turkish: *Zira Allah dünyayı öyle sevdi ki biricik Oğlunu verdi; ta ki ona her iman eden helâk olmayıp ancak ebedî hayata malik olsun.*

FINNISH

ALPHABET AND SOUNDS: a, d, e, g, h, i, j, k, l, m, n, o, p, r, s, t, u, v(w), y, ä, ö.

Vowels are short unless doubled.
a = h*u*t; aa = f*a*ther; e = m*e*t; ee = first part of l*a*te; i = b*i*t; ii = mach*i*ne; o = *o*bey; oo = first part of h*o*pe; u = b*u*ll; uu = b*oo*t; y = Fr. t*u*; yy = Fr. s*û*r; ä = h*a*t; ää = h*a*d (prolonged); ö = Fr. f*eu*; öö = Fr. p*eu*r. Consonants are approximately as in English; j = *y*es; h = Germ. a*ch*. All double consonants must be *sounded* double, as in Italian.

The Finnish stress is always on the first syllable of the word.

By the process of vowel harmony, the vowels are divided into: back (a, o, u); neutral (e, i); front (ä, ö, y). If the first syllable of the word has a back vowel, all other syllables must have back or neutral vowels; if a front vowel appears in the first syllable, the others must have front or neutral vowels. This means two forms to practically all endings; the ablative termination, for example is -*lta* or -*ltä*, the first reserved for words having *a, o, u* in their roots, the latter for words having ö, ä, *y*: *maa*, land; ablative *maalta;* but *työ*, work; ablative *työltä.*

GRAMMATICAL STRUCTURE.

Finnish has two numbers, but no gender distinction. Fifteen cases appear; nominative (subject); partitive (denoting "some"); genitive-accusative (denoting possession or the direct object); inessive (denoting "in"); elative (denoting "from"); illative (denoting place to which); adessive (denoting place on which, or means by which); ablative (denoting motion from); allative (denoting motion towards); abessive (denoting absence of, "without"); prolative (denoting motion along); translative (denoting a change of state); essive (denoting a continued state of being); comitative (denoting accompaniment, "with"); instructive (denoting means by which). Each case has its own ending, which is the same in the singular and in the plural. The latter is formed in the nominative by adding *-t* to the root, but in all other cases by adding *-i* to the root, then adding the same ending as in the corresponding cases in the singular; thus *puu*, "tree", has a nominative plural *puut*, but in all other plural cases *pui-*, followed by the ending of the particular case; while the ablative singular is *puu-lta*, the ablative plural is *pui-lta*. The complete declension of *puu*, is as follows, with the cases appearing in the order outlined above:

puu, -ta, -n, -ssa, -sta, -hun, -lla, -lta, -lle, -tta, (pui)-tse, -ksi, -na, (pui)-ne, -n; plural: nominative, *puut*; other cases: *pui-ta, -tten, -ssa, -sta, -hin, -lla, -lta, -lle, -tta, -tse, -ksi, -na, -ne, -n.*

The Finnish adjective is completely declined, by a process similar to that of the noun. The comparative stem is formed by adding *-mpa* (*-mpä*) to the positive; the superlative stem by adding *-impa* (*-impä*); *huono*, bad; *huonompa-*, worse; *huonoimpa-*, worst. These comparatives and superlatives are fully declined, as are also the numerals (see p. 429).

The personal pronouns, also fully declined, are: *minä*, I; *me*, we; *sinä*, you (singular); *te*, you (plural); *hän*, he, she, it; *he*, they.

The possessive is usually expressed by suffixes added to the inflected noun; these suffixes are: *-ni*, my, mine; *-mme*, our, ours; *-si*, your, yours; *-nne*, your, yours (pl.); *-nsa* (*-nsä*), his, her, its, their; e. g. *puu*, tree; partitive plural *puita*, of the trees; *puitamme*, of our trees.

Demonstratives are *tämä* (pl. *nämät, näitä*, etc.; fully inflected), this, these; *tuo* (pl. *nuot, noita*, etc.), that, those; *se* (partitive *sitä*; plural *ne, niitä*, etc.), that, those.

Interrogatives are *kuka* and *ken*, "who?", *mikä*, "what?", and *kumpi*, "which?". The chief relative is *joka*, who, which, that; all are fully inflected.

The Finnish verb has several moods and tenses, with a passive which is used only impersonally, and a negative conjugation which differs completely from the affirmative (*saavat*, they receive; but *eivät saa*, they-do-not receive). The personal endings are usually as follows: *-n, -t, -, -mme, -tte, -vat* (*-vät*). *Saa*, to receive, has, in the present indicative: *saan, saat, saa, saamme, saatte, saavat*; with a negative: *en saa, et saa, ei saa. emme saa, ette saa, eivät saa.*

IDENTIFICATION

Finnish is identified in written form by its double vowels and double consonants, by its umlauted vowels *ä* and *ö*, by its frequent *-en* endings, and by the *absence* of certain letters (b, c, f, q, x, z).

SPECIAL EXPRESSIONS

good morning, *hyvää huomenta*
how are you?, *kuinka voitte?*
very well, thank you, *vallan hyvin, kiitoksia kysymästä*
good bye, *hyvästi*
do you understand me?, *ymmärrättekö minua?*
what did you say?, *mitä te sanoitte?*
what do you want?, *mitä te tahdotte?*
I beg your pardon, *minä pyydän anteeksi*
excuse me, *suokaa anteeksi*
don't mention it, *ei ansaitse*
never mind, *se ei tee mitään*
I am glad, *se ilahduttaa minua*
I am sorry, *se pahoittaa minua*
can you tell me?, *voitteko sanoa minulle?*
no, *ei*
yes, *kyllä*
now, *nyt*
at once, *heti* (soon, *pian*)
always, *aina*
enough, *riittää*

yet, *vielä*
the weather is fine, *ilma on kaunis*
it is very cold, *on kovin kylmä*
what time is it?, *mitä kello on?*
it is five o'clock, *kello on viisi*
thank you, *kiitoksia*
which is the shortest way, *mikä on lyhin tie?*
go straight, *suoraan eteenpäin*
to the right, *oikeaan*
to the left, *vasempaan*
please, *olkaa hyvä*
good day, *hyvää päivää*
good evening, *hyvää iltaa*
good night, *hyvää yötä*
I don't understand, *en ymmärrä*
how much?, *kuinka paljon?*
it's too much, *se on liikaa*
which is the way to — ?, *mitä tietä pääsen* — ?
where is — ?, *missä on* — ?
bring me, *tuokaa*
your health!, *terveydeksenne!*
I should like, *tahtoisin* (I want, *tahdon*)
this way, *tätä tietä*
speak more slowly, *puhukaa vähän hitaammin*
do you speak English?, *puhutteko englantia?*
all right, *hyvä on*
I am ill, *olen sairas*
stop!, *seis!*
hurry!, *kiirehtikää!*
careful!, *varokaa!*
listen!, *kuulkaa!*
keep to the right, *oikealle*
entrance, *sisäänkäytävä*
exit, *uloskäytävä*
perhaps, *ehkä*
never, *ei koskaan*

HUNGARIAN

ALPHABET AND SOUNDS — a, á, b, c, d, e, é, f, g, h, i, í, j, k, l, m, n, o, ó, ö, ő, p, r, s, t, u, ú, ü, ű, v, x, y, z, cs, cz (tz), ds (dzs), gy, ly, ny, sz, ty, zs.

Vowels bearing the accent mark are long; other vowels are short.

a = not; á = father; e = met; é = fate; i = pin; í = machine; o = obey; ó = go; ö = Fr. feu; ő = Fr. peur; u = bull; ú = food; ü = Fr. tu; ű = Fr. sûr.

c, cz, tz = its; g = good; s = sure; cs = church; ds, dzs = gin; gy = did you; ly = million, or, more commonly, yard; ny = onion; sz = so; ty = hit you; zs = measure.

Double consonants must be pronounced double, as in Italian. Long vowels must be pronounced long, even though unstressed. The Hungarian stress is always on the *first* syllable of the word. Accent marks do not indicate stress, but vowel-length.

For purposes of vowel-harmony, a, á, o, ó, u, ú, are considered back vowels; é, i, í neutral; and e, ö, ő, ü, ű front. The vowel of the root determines the nature of the vowel of the suffix: *ház*, house; *ház-ban*, in the house; but *kert*, garden; *kert-ben*, in the garden.

GRAMMATICAL STRUCTURE.

Hungarian has two numbers and no concept of gender. Unlike Finnish and Turkish, however, Hungarian has both a definite and an indefinite article; the former is *a* (before consonants), *az* (before vowels), for all nouns, singular or plural: *a ház*, the house; *a házak*, the houses. The indefinite article is *egy*, which also means "one".

The plural is generally formed by the suffix -*k*, preceded by various vowels (-*ak*, -*ok*, -*ek*, -*ök*). Officially, Hungarian has four "cases", nominative, genitive, dative, and accusative; in reality, since all ideas of place where, to which, from which, etc. are indicated not by prepositions, but by suffixes, or postpositions, the actual number of possible case-forms in Hungarian equals or surpasses that of Finnish; as in Finnish, these case-endings or postpositions are added on to the plural suffix: *a ház,* the house; *a ház-ak,* the houses; *a ház-ak-nak,* to the houses; *a ház-ak-ban,* in the houses; *a ház-ak-ból,* from the houses; etc.

The adjective is invariable, unless used predicatively, in which case it takes the plural suffix, but no case-suffix: *a nagy asztal-ok,* the large tables; *az asztalok nagyok,* the tables are large. The comparative is formed by the suffix *-bb* (*-abb, -ebb*), added to the positive; the superlative by prefixing *leg-* to the comparative: *jó,* good; *jobb,* better; *legjobb,* best.

Personal pronouns are as follows: *én,* I; *nekem,* to me; *engem,* me; *mi,* we; *nekünk,* to us; *minket,* us; *te,* you (sg.); *neked,* to you; *téged,* you (acc.); *ti,* you (pl.); *nektek,* to you; *titeket,* you (acc.); *ő,* he or she; *neki,* to him or her; *őt,* him, her; *ők,* they; *nekik,* to them; *őket,* them.

The possessive pronoun consists of a series of suffixated endings: *könyv,* book; *könyv-em,* my book; *könyv-ünk,* our book; *könyv-eim,* my books; *könyv-eink,* our books.

The chief demonstratives (used *with* the article when they are adjectives) are *ez* (pronoun: *emez*), this, and *az* (pronoun: *amaz*) that: *ez az ember,* this man; *az az ember,* that man; *ezek az emberek,* these men.

Interrogative pronouns are: *ki,* who?; *mely,* which?, what?; *melyik,* which?; *mi,* what? These are turned into relatives by prefixing *a*: *aki,* who; *amely,* which, that, etc.

The Hungarian verb appears in numerous tenses and moods, with the object pronoun normally incorporated in the verb: thus, *verni,* to beat, has the following present indicative if no definite object pronoun is implied: *verek, versz, ver, verünk, vertek, vernek,* I beat, you beat, etc.; but if the meaning is "I beat it", "you beat it", etc., the forms become: *verem, vered, veri, verjük, veritek, verik.* Furthermore, the Hungarian verb may assume a variety of aspects: *ir,* he writes; *irat,* he causes to write; *irogat,* he writes (repeatedly); *irkál,* he scribbles, plays at writing; *irhat*, he may write, etc. The negative is formed by prefixing *nem*, not, to the verb: *nem ir*, he does not write.

IDENTIFICATION

Hungarian is readily identified in written form by its long and short umlauted vowels (ö, ő, ü, ű), and, to a lesser degree, by certain consonant groups (cs, gy, zs, dzs). In spoken form, stress on the first syllable, together with long vowels further on in the word, and the abundance of middle vowel sounds (ö, ü), as well as the frequent endings in *-ak, -ok, -unk, -ek, -ik*, and the relative length of Hungarian words, caused by the piling on of suffixes, give clues to the nature of the language.

SPECIAL EXPRESSIONS

please, *legyen szives, kérem;* thank you, *köszönöm*
you're welcome, *szivesen; kérem szépen*
don't mention it, *szivesen; nincs mit; nem jelent semmit; nem baj*
yes, *igen;* no, *nem*
excuse me, *bocsánat, bocsánatot kérek, bocsásson meg*
give me, *adjon kérem*
tell me, *mondja kérem*
do you speak Hungarian?, *beszél ön magyarúl?*
a little, *egy keveset*
what is the matter?, *mi a baj?, mi történt?;* nothing, *semmi*
pleased to meet you, *örvendek*
I am sorry, *sajnálom;* I am glad, *örülök*
how are you?, *hogyan érzi magát?, hogy van?*
very well, thanks, and you?, *köszönöm, nagyon jól, és ön?*
I am ill, *beteg vagyok*
good morning, *jó reggelt*
good afternoon, *jó napot*
good evening, *jó estét*
good night, *jó éjszakát*

good-bye, *viszontlátásra, Isten vele*
how much is it?, *mennyibe kerül?*
that is too much, *az drága, tul drága*
it is late, *késő van*
what time is it?, *hány óra van?*

it is ten o'clock, *tiz óra van*
what a beautiful day!, *milyen gyönyörű nap!*
perhaps, *talán*
here is, (here are), *itt van (itt vannák)*
there is, (there are), *ott van (ott vannak)*
how do I go to...?, *hogy juthatok....re(ra)?*
straight ahead, *egyenesen előre*
to the right, *jobbra*; to the left, *balra*
why?, *miért?*
when?, *mikor?*
where?, *hol?* (where is?, *hol van?*)
because, *mert*
today, *ma*
yesterday, *tegnap*
tomorrow, *holnap*
I'm hungry, *éhes vagyok*
I'm thirsty, *szomjas vagyok*
I'm cold, *fázom*; it's cold, *hideg van*
it's warm, *meleg van*; I'm warm, *melegem van*
what is your name?, *mi az ön neve?*
certainly, *persze*
show me, *mutassa nekem*
do you understand?, *érti ön?*
I don't understand, *nem értem*
do you know?, *tudja ön?*
I don't know, *nem tudom*
very little, *nagyon kevés, nagyon keveset*
what do you want?, *mit kiván ön?*; *mit parancsol?*; *mi tetszik?*
too bad!, *kár*; *igazán sajnos*; *igazán sajnálom*
it's fine weather, *szép idő*
your health!, *egészségérc!*

TURKISH

ALPHABET AND SOUNDS — a, b, c, ç, d, e, f, g, ğ, h, i, ı,
j, k, l, m, n, o, ö, p, r, s, ş, t, u, ü, v, y, z.[1]

a = *f*a*ther*; e = met or h*a*nd; i = machine; ı = Russian ы;
o = *o*bey; ö = Fr. f*eu*; u = f*oo*d; ü = Fr. m*u*r; c = *J*ohn;
ç = *ch*urch; g = *g*ood; ğ is the voiced counterpart of the
unvoiced German a*ch*; h = *h*ot or German a*ch*; j = mea*s*ure;
s = *s*on; ş = *s*ure; y = *y*es.

A circumflex accent is occasionally used on a vowel, usually to indicate palatalization of a preceding *k* or *g* (in Arabic
and Persian loan-words): *kâmil,* pron. *kjamil,* "complete".
The stress of Turkish is usually on the *last* syllable of the
word.

GRAMMATICAL STRUCTURE

Turkish has no article, definite or indefinite, and no
concept of gender. For purposes of vowel-harmony, a, o, ı, u
are considered back vowels; e, i, ö, ü front vowels.

The plural suffix is *-lar* if the preceding syllable contains
a back vowel, *-ler* if it contains a front vowel; *baba,* father;
babalar, fathers; *gün,* day; *günler,* days. Officially, Turkish has
six "cases" (nominative, genitive, dative, accusative, ablative,
locative); but since postpositions, instead of prepositions, are
used to indicate all sorts of relations (up to, with, on, without,
instead of, about, etc.), and since many of these are added on to
the noun in the plural as well as in the singular, it may almost
be said that Turkish has as many separate cases as it has postpositions. Like Finnish and Hungarian, Turkish has identical
suffixes in the singular and in the plural for its six official
cases: *-n* preceded by whatever vowel may be required by vowel
harmony is fairly universal in the genitive of both numbers;

---

1.   This is the modern romanized Turkish alphabet, devised by Mustafa
Kemal in 1928; before his time, Turkish was written in a modified
version of the Arabic alphabet.

the dative has -*a* or -*e*, according to the nature of the root-vowel; the accusative usually ends in ı, i, u, ü; while -*dan* or -*den* is universal in the ablative, and -*da* or -*de* in the locative. A typical Turkish noun, *dil*, language, has the following scheme:

Singular: *dil, -in, -e, -i, -den, -de.*

Plural: *dil-ler, -ler-in, -ler-e, -ler-i, -ler-den, -ler-de.*

The adjective is completely indeclinable: *güzel at*, a fine horse, *güzel atlar*, fine horses; *güzel atlara*, to the fine horses. The comparative is formed by placing *daha*, the superlative by placing *en*, before the positive: *güzel*, fine; *daha güzel*, finer; *en güzel*, finest.

Personal pronouns, which are declined by the same system of endings as nouns, are: *ben*, I; *biz*, we; *sen*, you (fam. sg.); *siz*, you (pl.); *o*, he, she, it; *onlar*, they.

The possessive is indicated, as customary in Ural-Altaic languages, by a suffix: *baba*, father; *babam*, my father; *baban*, thy father; *babası*, his (her) father; *babamız*, our father; *babanız*, your father; *babaları*, their father. These forms are then completely declined (*babam*, my father; *babamın*, of my father; *babama*, to my father; *babalarım*, my fathers; *babalarımın*, of my fathers; *babalarıma*, to my fathers, etc.).

The chief demonstrative pronoun is *bu* (*bunun, buna, bunu*, etc.), this, that, these, those. The chief relative is *ki*, who, which, that; the chief interrogatives are *kim*, who?; *ne*, what?; *hangi*, which?

The Turkish verb has an infinitive ending in -*mek* or -*mak*. The passive is formed by means of the suffix -*l*-, the negative by means of -*ma*- or -*me*- (*sevmek*, to love; *sevilmek*, to be loved; *sevmemek*, not to love; *sevilmemek*, not to be loved). Reciprocal, causative, reflexive, and many other forms of conjugations appear, including the "impossible" one (*sevememek*, to be unable to love). Numerous tenses and other forms appear, corresponding roughly to the various tenses, and to the indicatives, optatives and subjunctives of the Indo-European languages. A typical "present", that of *sevmek*, runs as follows: *sev-erim, -ersin, -er, -eriz, -ersiniz, -erler.*

IDENTIFICATION

Turkish, in its modern written form, may be identified by its two distinctive characters, ı and ğ. The characteristic plural in *-lar* and *-ler*, and ablatives in *-dan*, *-den* are also useful.

SPECIAL EXPRESSIONS

good morning, good afternoon, *gün aydın*
good evening, *tün aydın*
good night, *geceniz hayır olsun, allah rahatlık versin*
how are you?, *nasılsınız?*; certainly, *elbet, tabii, şüpesiz*
well, thank you, *iyiyim, teşekkür ederim*
please, *lûtfen*; you're welcome, *bir şey değil*
here is, here are, *işte burada* (here is the book — *işte kitap burada*); there is, there are, *vardır*
where is?, *nerededir?*; what is the matter?, *ne var?*
how do I go to Istanbul?, *istanbul'a nasıl gidilir?*
yes, *evet*; no, *hayır, yok*
how much is it?, *kaça? fiyatı kaça?*
why?, *niçin? neden?*; when?, *ne zaman?*; where, *nerede?*
today, *bugün*; yesterday, *dün*; tomorrow, *yarın*
to the right, *sağa*; to the left, *sola*
straight ahead, *dos doğru, doğru*
what time is it?, *saat kaçtır?*; it is 6 o'clock, *saat altıdır*
I'm hungry, *açım, acıktım, karnım aç*
I'm thirsty, *susadım*; I'm ill, *hastayım*
do you speak Turkish?, *Türkçe konuşurmusunuz?*
a little, *biraz*; very little, *çok az, pek az*
tell me, *bana söyleyiniz*; show me, *bana gösteriniz*
do you understand?, *anlıyormusunuz?*
I don't understand, *anlamıyorum*
do you know?, *biliyormusunuz?*; I don't know, *bilmiyorum*
excuse me, *afedersiniz*; don't mention it, *birşey değil*
what do you want?, *ne istiyorsunuz?*; never mind, *zarar yok*
too bad!, *çok fena, çok yazık*; I'm sorry, *müteesirim*
give me, *bana veriniz*; I want, *istiyorum*
good bye, *allaha ısmarladık*; (reply) *güle güle*

THE BALTIC LANGUAGES — LITHUANIAN, LETTISH

From a practical standpoint, these tongues are of little importance, being spoken by about 3,000,000 and 2,000,000 people, respectively. They are often linked to the Slavic tongues, from which, however, they diverge to a considerable degree. Their relationship to each other and to the languages of the Slavic group may be inferred from the following examples:

English	Lithuanian	Lettish	(Russian)
brother	brólis	brālis	(brat)
house	nãmas	nams	(dom)
mother	mótina	māte	(mat')
father	tévas	tēvs	(otéts)
fish	žuvìs	zivs	(rýba)
heart	širdìs	sirds	(sérdtse)
land	žẽmė	zeme	(zemlyá)
fire	ugnìs	uguns	(ogón')
man	výras	vīrs	(mužčína)
one	víenas	viens	(odín)
two	dù	divi	(dva)
three	trỹs	trīs	(tri)
four	keturì	četri	(četýre)
five	penkì	pieci	(pyat')
six	šešì	seši	(šest')
seven	septynì	septiņi	(sem')
eight	aštuonì	astoņi	(vósem')
nine	devynì	deviņi	(dévyat')
ten	dẽšimt	desmit	(désyat')
eleven	vienúolika	vienpadsmit	(odínnadtsat')
twelve	dvýlika	divpadsmit	(dvenádtsat')
twenty	dvìdešimt	divdesmit	(dvádtsat')
hundred	šim̃tas	simts	(sto)

Both languages are heavily inflected, with a declensional system for nouns which in Lettish includes nominative, genitive, dative, accusative and locative, and which in Lithuanian includes the same five cases with the addition of vocative and instrumental. A sample of the declensional system of the two languages is as follows:

Lithuanian: *širdìs*, heart: Singular: Nom. *širdìs*; Gen. *širdiẽs*; Dat. *šìrdžiai*; Acc. *šìrdį*; Voc. *širdiẽ*; Instr. *širdimì*; Loc. *širdyjè*; Plural: Nom. & Voc. *šìrdys*; Gen. *širdžiū̃*; Dat. *širdìms*; Acc. *šìrdis*; Instr. *širdimìs*; Loc. *širdysè*.
Lettish: *sirds*, heart: Singular: Nom. *sirds*; Gen. *sirds*; Dat. *sirdij*; Acc. *sirdi*; Loc. *sirdī*; Plural: Nom. *sirdis*; Gen. *siržu*: Dat. *sirdīm*; Acc. *sirdis*; Loc. *sirdīs*.

The verb system is fully developed in both languages, with a wealth of tenses and moods, and copious participles, gerunds, and other verbal forms.

IDENTIFICATION

Distinctive of Lithuanian are the following characters: ą, č, ę, ė, į, š, ų, ū, ž, in addition to the letters of the English alphabet outside of q, w. Lithuanian uses three accent marks to indicate an accentuation which is not merely stress, but also intonation: the grave accent (ˋ) is used only over short vowels; the acute (ˊ) indicates a long vowel with a *falling* tone of the voice; the circumflex (˜) indicates a long vowel with a *rising* tone of the voice. If a short vowel is followed in the same syllable by n, m, l or r, it is customary for the *consonant* to bear the circumflex accent: *dviẽm pir̃štam*, with two fingers. While these accent marks do not usually appear in the written language, they are fully characteristic; so are the four vowels with the hook beneath, indicating a former nasalization which today no longer exists (ą, ę, į, ų; Polish has only two such symbols: ą, ę).

Distinctive of Lettish is the fact that four vowels, if long, bear the mark of length (ā, ē, ī, ū). The following symbols appear: č, dz dž, ġ, ķ, ļ, ņ, ŗ, š, ž. The spoken accent of Lettish is invariably on the first syllable of the word, unlike that of Lithuanian, which may fall anywhere.

SAMPLES OF THE WRITTEN LANGUAGES

Lithuanian (without accent marks) : Taip Dievas mylėjo pasaulį, kad savo viengimusįjį sūnų davė, kad visi į jį tikintieji nepražūtų, bet turėtų amžinąjį gyvenimą.

Lettish: Juo tik ļuoti Dievs pasauli mīlējis, ka viņš savu vienpiedzimušuo dēlu devis, lai neviens, kas vinam tic, nepazustu, bet dabūtu mūžīguo dzīvību.

	Lithuanian	Lettish
good day, miss	*labá d* *diená, panēle*	*labdien, jaunkundz*
good morning	*lábas rýtas*	*labrīt*
good evening	*lábas vákaras*	*labvakar*
good night	*labánaktis*	*ar labunakti*
good-bye	*sú Dievú*	*ar Dievu*
please	*prašaú*	*lūdzu*
thank you	*áčiu labaí*	*pateicos*
don't mention it	*nẽr už ką*	*nav par ko*
excuse me	*dovanókite,* *átsiprašaú*	*lūdzu atvainot, ļoti* *atvainojos*
yes, sir	*taip, Támsta*	*ja, kungs*
no, madam	*ne, pónia*	*nē, kundze*
how much?	*kiek?*	*cik?*
it's too much	*taí per daúg*	*tas ir par daudz*
give me	*dúokit man*	*dodat man*
bring me	*atnéškit*	*atnesat*
do you understand?	*ar Támsta supranti?*	*vai Jūs saprotiet?*
I don't understand	*nesuprantú*	*es nesaprotu*
do you speak English?	*ar Támsta kalbí ángliškai?*	*vai runājiet angļu?*
all right	*geraí*	*labi*
which is the way to	*kurís kẽlias į —?*	*kā es varu nokļūt uz*
where is — ?	*kur —?*	*kur ir —?*
speak more slowly	*kalbékit léčiaú*	*runājiet lēnāk*
careful!	*atsargiaí!*	*uzmanaties!*

THE CELTIC LANGUAGES

These consist of Irish, the official language of Eire, with its approximately 3,000,000 inhabitants, most of whom, however, speak English as well; Scottish Gaelic, spoken by perhaps a hundred thousand people in the Highland region of Scotland; Manx, the dialect of the Isle of Man; Welsh, spoken by perhaps 1,000,000 people in Wales, who also normally speak English; and Breton, spoken in French Brittany by probably not more than 1,000,000 people most of whom also speak French. Cornish, the former Celtic tongue of Cornwall, is extinct.

While these tongues all belong to the Celtic division of Indo-European, Irish, Gaelic and Manx form part of the Goidelic group of Celtic, while Welsh, Breton, and Cornish belong to the Brythonic group. The divergences between Irish and Scottish Gaelic are less pronounced; those between Welsh and Breton more striking. In all the Celtic languages, without exception, the student is faced with exceedingly intricate rules of pronunciation, which in the Goidelic group are complicated by an orthography which is archaic and no longer corresponds to the actual pronunciation. Goidelic consonants frequently assume a double sound (described as "broad" and "slender"), according to the nature of the following vowel; all this means is that before the front vowels, e, i, there is a tendency for the consonant to assume a palatalized sound (Irish *cailín*, girl, pronounced *kolyin*). But in addition to this, the Celtic tongues often undergo aspiration or mutation ("eclipsis" or "lenition") of initial consonants in accordance with the final sound of the preceding word (Scots Gaelic *tarbh geal*, white bull, but *bó gheal*, white cow; *teine*, fire, but *ar dteine*, pronounced *ar deine*, our fire; Irish *fuil*, blood, but *ar bhfuil*, pronounced *ar wil*, our blood; Welsh *pen*, head, but *fy mhen*, my head; Breton *kalon*, heart, but *me halon*, my heart, *é galon*, his heart; these are only a few easy examples of an extremely complicated system).

The Celtic languages share with the Romance group the feature of having only two genders, masculine and feminine, and of having the adjective more frequently after than before the noun. But while Irish and Scots Gaelic have four distinct cases (nominative, genitive, dative, vocative), Welsh and Breton have practically reduced the noun to a single case. The verb system is elaborate, with abundant tenses and moods. The Brythonic tongues favor accentuation on the next to the last syllable, save for one dialect of Breton, which prefers final accentuation. The Irish accent is initial.

The relationship of the three major Celtic tongues to one another and to the other languages of the Indo-European family may be inferred from the following list of common words, and from the translations of John 3.16 which follow:

English	Irish	Welsh	Breton
arm	*brac*	*braich*	*bréac'h*
big	*mór*	*mawr*	*meûr*
black	*dubh*	*du*	*dû*
brother	*bráthair*	*brawd*	*breûr*
family	*teaghlach*	*teulu*	*tiégez*
fire	*teine*	*tân*	*tân*
friend	*cara*	*câr*	*kâr*
full	*lán*	*llawn*	*leûn*
one	*aon*	*un*	*un, an, eunn*
two	*dó* (or *dá-*)	*dau*	*daou*
three	*trí*	*trī*	*trî*
four	*ceathair*	*pedwar*	*péder*
five	*cúig*	*pump*	*pemp*
six	*sé*	*chwĕch*	*c'houéac'h*
seven	*seacht*	*saith*	*seic'h* (*seiz*)
eight	*ocht*	*w̄yth*	*eiz*
nine	*naoi*	*nāw*	*naô*
ten	*deich*	*dĕg*	*dég* (*dēk*)
eleven	*aondéag*	*un-ar-ddeg*	*unnék*
twelve	*dódhéag*	*deuddeg*	*deuzek*
twenty	*fiche*	*ugain*	*ugeṅt*
eighty	*ceithre fichid*	*pedwar ugain*	*péder ugeṅt*
hundred	*céad*	*cant*	*kaṅt*

Irish (in transcription): *óir do ghrádhuigh Dia an saoghal chómh mór sin, go dtug sé a Aon-Mhac féin, ionnas, gach duine creidfeadh ann, nach gcaillfidhe é, acht go mbéadh an bheatha shíorraidhe aige.*

Scots Gaelic: *Oir is ann mar sin a ghràdhaich Dia an saoghal, gu'n d'thug e 'aon-ghin Mhic féin, chum as ge b'e neach a chreideas ann, nach sgriosar e, ach gu'm bi a'bheatha shìorruidh aige.*

Manx: *Son lheid y ghraih shen hug Jee da'n theihll, dy dug eh e ynrycan Vac v'er ny gheddyn, nagh jinnagh quoi-erbee chredjagh aynsyn cherraghtyn, agh yn vea ta dy bragh farraghtyn y chosney.*

Welsh: *Canys felly y carodd Duw y byd fel y rhoddodd efe ei unig-anedig Fab, fel na choller pwy bynnag a gredo ynddo ef, ond caffael ohono fywyd tragwyddol.*

Breton: *Rag Doue hen deuz karet kement ar bed, ma hen deuz roet he Vab-unik, abalamour da biou benag a gredo ennhan na vezo ket kollet, mes ma hen devezo ar vuez eternel.*

SAMPLE OF PRINTED IRISH

Óir do ghrádhuig Dia an raoghal cóṁ mór rin, go dtug ré a Aon-Ṁac féin, ionnar, gach duine creideaḋ ann, nac gcaillfide é, act go mbéaḋ an beata ríorraide aige. Óir ni cum breiteaṁnar do tabairt ar an raoghal do cuir Dia a Ṁac uaiḋ; act cum go raorraide an raoghal crìḋ. An cé creidear ann ni tugtar breit air: an cé nac gcreideann atá breit tabarta air ceana féin, toirc nár creiḋ ré i n-ainm Aon-Ṁic Dé. Agur ir i reo an breit, go dtáinig an rolar ar an raoghal, agur gurḃ annra leir na daoiniḃ an dorcact 'ná an rolar; toirc a ngníoṁarta beit go h-olc. Óir gach duine cleactar an t-olc bionn fuat aige do'n trolar, agur ni tig ré cum an trolair, ar eagla go noctraide a gníoṁarta.

(Courtesy of American Bible Society)

IRISH

ALPHABET — a, b, c, d, e, f, g, h, i, l, m, n, o, p, r, s, t, u.

An accent mark over a vowel indicates length: *mór,* big. A dot over a consonant indicates aspiration; this aspiration never corresponds to the sound of the original consonant followed by *h;* an aspirated *t,* for example, has the sound of ordinary *h: teine,* fire; but *mo theine* (pronounced *mo heine*), my fire; an aspirated *m,* due to the loss of the nasal, has the sound of *v: mo mháthair* (pronounced *mo vaher,* my mother). The difficulties of Irish pronunciation, with its aspirated and eclipsed consonants and broad and slender vowels, are illustrated by the Lord's Prayer, with a guide to pronunciation:

Ar n-Athair, atá ar neamh, (go) naomhthar t'ainm;
(Ar nahir, etah er nav, gu naev-har th-an-am;)
(go)tigidh do ríoghacht;
(gu dig-ee dhu riachth;)
*(go) n déantar do thoil ar an talamh mar do-ghníthear ar
     neamh.*
(gu naenthar dhu hel er an tholav mor nihar er nav.)
Tabhair dhúinn a niugh ar n-arán laetheamhail,
(Thouar ghoon inyoo ar naraun laehooil)
agus maith dhúinn ar bh-fiacha
(ogus mah ghoon or viacha)
mar mhaithmid-ne dar bh-féicheamhnaibh féin;
(mor wahamid dhar vaehooniv faen;)
agus na léig sinn a gathughadh,
(ogus nau laeg shin a gohoo)
achd saor sinn ó olc. Amen.
(ochth saer shinn o ulk. Omaen.)

GRAMMATICAL NOTES — The definite article in Irish is *an* in the singular, *na* in the plural. The plural of nouns is often formed by the addition of *-a, -ta, -e.* Four cases (nominative, genitive, dative, vocative) are still in use.

WELSH

ALPHABET — a, b, c, ch, d, dd, e, f, ff, g, ng, h, i, l, ll, m, n, o, p, ph, r, rh, s, t, th, u, w, y.

Vowels may be long or short. Welsh u = b*u*sy or m*e*; w = g*oo*d or b*oo*n; y = f*u*r or c*u*rl; both u and y often = Fr. u. Among the consonants, c = *c*at; ch = German a*ch*; dd = *th*is; f = e*v*e; ff = *f*ire; = *g*o; ll = emphatic l; rh = aspirated r; s = *s*o.

The accent of Welsh is generally on the next to the last syllable.

GRAMMATICAL NOTES — There is no indefinite article. The definite article is *yr* before vowels, *y* before consonants, for both genders and both numbers. The most common plural endings are *-au, -on, -aid, -ydd*. There are no cases in Welsh.

SPECIAL EXPRESSIONS

please, *os gwelwch yn dda* (lit., if it seems good to you)
thank you, *diolch i chwi*(*chi*); *diolch*
you're welcome, *croeso i chi*
yes, *ie ,do, oes*
no, *na, nage, nac oes*
excuse me, *esgusodwch fi*
do you understand?, *a ddeallwch chwi?, a ydych yn deall?*
I don't understand, *ni ddeallaf, nid wyf yn deall*
do you speak Welsh?, *a siaredwch Gymraeg?, a ydych yn siarad Cymraeg?*
a little, *ychydig*
tell me, *dywedwch imi*
give me, *rhoddwch imi, rhowch imi*
too bad!, *rhy ddrwg!, gresyn!*
how much?, *faint?*
how are you?, *sut hwyl?, shwd y'ch chi?, sut 'dach chi?*
very well, *da iawn, o'r goreu*

I am ill, *yr wyf yn sal, nid wyf yn dda*
good morning, *bore da*
good day, *dydd da*
good afternoon, *prynhawn da, p'nawn da*
good evening, *dywetydd da*
good night, *nos da; nos dawch*
what time is it?, *beth yw'r amser?; faint o'r gloch yw hi?*
it is five o'clock, *y mae hi'n bump o'r gloch, pump o'r gloch
yw hi*

BRETON

ALPHABET — a, b, d, e, f, g, h, i, j, k, l, m, n, ñ, o, p, r,
s, t, u, ù, v, z, ch. The sounds are generally as in French (e. g.
j = mea*s*ure). But g = *g*o; ñ = nasal sound of n; s = *s*o;
ù = sound intermediate between u and v.
   The Breton accent is usually on the last syllable.

GRAMMATICAL NOTES — The definite article is *en*, (in
Vannes; *ar* in other dialects), for both numbers and genders.
The most common plural endings are -*éz*, -*en*, -*el*. There are no
cases in Breton.

IDENTIFICATION OF THE CELTIC LANGUAGES.

   Irish is very easily identified by its distinctive alphabet.
Welsh is identified by its use of w and y as vowels and by some
of its consonant groups (ch, ll, dd). Breton may be distinguished from its sister Celtic tongues by its frequent -*ek* ending, and
by the fact that its aspirated consonants are not marked in
writing by such combinations as mh, bh, th, etc.

BASQUE

This mysterious language of northeastern Spain and south-western France, totally unrelated to any other European tongue, appears in several dialects, spoken by perhaps 1,000,000 people on both sides of the Pyrenees.

ALPHABET AND SOUNDS — There is a standardized alphabet for Spanish Basque, now used also by the French Basques. Roman characters are used, with the five vowels pronounced approximately as in Spanish (the Soule French Basques have a tendency to give u its French value); g = *go*; z = *so*; tx = *ch*urch; j = harsh guttural h in Spain, *y*es in France; k = *c*at; *h* is generally silent in Spain, pronounced like *h*ot in France. The Basque accent is extremely indefinite, and best described as evenly distributed on all syllables of the word.

GRAMMATICAL NOTES.

The definite article of Basque is *a*, suffixated to the noun: *etxe*, house; *etxea*, the house. Suffixes indicating case-relations are added on to the noun with its article: *gizon*, man; *gizona*, the man; *gizonagandik*, for the man.

The concept of gender is wanting in Basque. The plural number is generally indicated by the suffix -*k*: *gizonak*, the men.

Case relations are indicated by a large variety of suffixes, which are added on to the noun, forming a single word with it: *zaldia*, the horse; *zaldiaren*, of the horse; *zaldika*, on horseback; *gizonakaz*, with the men; *etxeetan*, in the houses.

The adjective is invariable, and follows the noun: *gizon eder bat*, a fine man (lit. man fine a). The comparative is formed by the suffix -*go* plus the preposition *baño*, the superlative by the genitive plural ending -*en* followed by the article -*a*; *handia*, great; *zu handiago baño* (*zu baño handiago*), greater than you; *handiena*, greatest.

The Basque numerals from one to thirteen are as follows: *bat, bi, hirur, laur, bortz, sei, zazpi, zortzi, bederatzi, hamar, hamaika, hamabi, hamahirur.* "Twenty" is *hogei,* "thirty" *hogei ta hamar,* "forty" *berrogei,* "hundred" *ehun.*

The Basque verb, despite the fact that it has only two true tenses, present and past, is somewhat complicated by reason of the fact that it incorporates both subject and object pronoun: thus, *ekarri,* to bear, present *d-akar-t,* I bear it (lit. it bear I), *d-akar-k,* you bear it; *n-akar-zu,* you bear me.

A sample of Basque syntax will appear from the following literal translation of Luke 1.62 ("Then they made signs to his father how he would have him called"):

Orduan keinu egin ziezoten haren aitari,
Then sign making they were of him to the father,
nola nahi luen hura dei ledin.
how wish he would have he named he should be.

Two additional samples of Basque, one from the Spanish side of the Pyrenees (Guipuzcoa), the other from the French side (Labourdin) illustrate the nature of the language: (John 3.16):

Guipuzcoan: *Zergatik aiñ maite izan du Jaungoikoak mundua, non eman duen bere Seme Bakarra beragan fedea duan guzia galdu ez dedin, baizik izan dezan betiko bizia.*

Labourdin: *Ezen hala Iainkoak onhetsi ukan du mundua, non bere Semé bakoitza eman ukan baitu, hura baithan sinhesten duenik gal eztadin, baina bizitze eternala duenzát.*

IDENTIFICATION

The frequent recurrence of z and tz is characteristic of Basque.

CHAPTER XIII

LANGUAGES OF THE MIDDLE AND FAR EAST[1]

Asia is a vast linguistic world in its own right. The tongues of this great continent are as varied and picturesque as are their speakers, and run into the number of several hundreds, distributed among most of the world's great language families: Indo-European, Semitic, Ural-Altaic, Sino-Tibetan, Japanese-Korean, Dravidian, Malayo-Polynesian, Caucasian, Mon-Khmer, Hyperborean, Ainu.

Fortunately for the practical linguist, not all of these numerous tongues are of equal importance. The linguistic explorer in the Asiatic continent finds himself indeed faced with tongues of primary rank, numerically, commercially, politically and culturally. He also finds himself face to face with a myriad minor languages whose speakers are comparatively few in number, and which have never attained a very lofty cultural status.

Such is the case, for example, with the Ural-Altaic tongues

1. Limitations of time and space make it impossible at the present time to give the languages of Asia the treatment which the growing practical importance of many of them warrants. It is planned in the near future to offer, in separate booklets of the "World Languages Series", a presentation of Chinese, Hindustani, Arabic and Malay which will be in all respects as thorough as is that of Japanese in the present volume. A second volume of "Languages for War and Peace" is in preparation, in which will appear a more comprehensive outline of several of the Asiatic tongues cursorily treated in this chapter (notably Palestinian Hebrew, Persian, Hindustani, Bengali, Tamil, Telugu, Siamese, Burmese and Korean), as well as of certain native African tongues of strategic and commercial importance (Amharic, Swahili, Hausa, Fanti).

of Asiatic Russia, Mongolia and Manchukuo (Bashkir, Uzbeg, Turkoman, Mongol, Buryat, Yakut, Kalmuk, Manchu, Tungus, etc.). These tongues, which are members of the Altaic branch of the family, cover a tremendous extent of territory; but their speakers are relatively few, and they are divided into such a vast number of diverging and mutually incomprehensible dialects that the study of any one of them can repay only the specialist interested in their linguistic structure or in the particular area where they are spoken. Their speakers, furthermore, are partly accessible through other tongues which may be termed languages of colonization (Russian in the Soviet Union in Asia, Chinese in Mongolia and Manchukuo, Japanese in Manchukuo). Turkish, the only Asiatic tongue of this group to present a solid body of speakers and a certain amount of cultural, political and commercial importance, has already been discussed under a European heading (see p. 440).

Even less important are the mysterious Hyperborean tongues of Kamchatka and northeastern Siberia, with a few thousand speakers, and the Ainu of Japan's northern islands (Yezo and Karafuto). Here again, Russian and Japanese, respectively, supply most practical needs.

The Caucasian tongues of the Caucasus, between the Black Sea and the Caspian, are extremely picturesque and interesting from a linguistic point of view, including such languages as Georgian, Avar, Lesghian, Circassian, Mingrelian, Laz, etc. Little practical advantage is to be derived from their study, however, in view of the limited number of their speakers, their numerous dialects, and the fact that Russian may be used with comparative ease in their area.

The Mon-Khmer, Annamese and Munda groups of southeastern Asia are imperfectly known; their speakers are relatively few, while their dialectal divisions are numerous. It is even doubtful that they are related, and various linguistic affiliations are claimed for them.

Two of Asia's tongues belong to the Semitic branch of the Semito-Hamitic group, which also stretches across northern

Africa almost to the Equator on the west, slightly below it on the east. They are Hebrew, which has a rejuvenated Palestinian variety, and Arabic. Palestinian Hebrew is the ancient tongue of the Scriptures and the Mishnāh, to which the status of a living and official language has been restored by the various Jewish groups participating in the Zionist experiment, with a modernization of vocabulary, and the inclusion of such non-Biblical terms as "telephone" and "telegraph". Palestinian Hebrew is the official tongue of less than a million Jewish settlers in Palestine, and as such its practical importance is limited, particularly as many of these Jews are accessible through European tongues. It is also, however, the key to the vast treasure-house of Hebrew tradition and learning, and it may be used as a secondary cultural tongue in all Jewish communities throughout the world, particularly among the more cultured elements.

Of far greater practical importance in the Semitic group is Arabic, the sacred tongue of Islam, and the popular tongue of Morocco, Algeria, Tunisia, Libya, Egypt, Syria, Iraq and Arabia. As a religious and written language, Arabic is unified and traditional, and extends far beyond the confines of the spoken tongue, being used wherever the Muhammadan faith has followers, in the Balkans, Turkey, Iran, India, China, central and eastern Africa, Malaya and the Dutch East Indies, and even in the Philippines. As a popular spoken tongue, in the countries where it is so used, Arabic shows a series of fairly strong dialectal divergences. The spoken Arabic of Morocco, Algeria, Tunisia and Libya may be described as a western variety; Egypt and the Egyptian Sudan may be said to form a central group of spoken Arabic dialects; while Syria and Palestine, Iraq, and Arabia constitute three diverging eastern groups.

The Indo-European tongues of Asia (outside of tongues of colonization, such as Russian in Asiatic Russia, English in India, Burma and Malaya, French in Indo-China and Syria, etc.) include: 1. Armenian, the ancient and highly cultivated language of a relatively small group of speakers located astride the Russo-Turkish frontier; 2. modern Persian, the language of some 15,000,000 speakers in Iran and Afghanistan; 3. the so-called Indo-Aryan[2] languages of Afghanistan (Pushtu; about 10,000,000), southern Ceylon (Singhalese, about 4,000,000), and northern and central India (Hindustani, Bengali, Punjabi, Rajasthani, Marathi, etc.). Indo-Aryan speakers are very numerous, comprising over two-thirds of India's 390,000,000 inhabitants. It is estimated, however, that India's approximately 290,000,000 Indo-Aryan speakers are divided among seventeen major languages, not to mention numerous minor dialects.

The chief of these languages, with their approximate number of speakers, are:

Hindustani (including both Hindi and Urdu; north
    central India) — 130,000,000
Bengali (northeastern India: Bengal and the
    Calcutta region) — 60,000,000
Bihari (northeastern India, west of Bengal) — 30,000,000
Marathi (western India: the Bombay region) — 20,000,000
Punjabi (northern India: Punjab region) — 20,000,000
Rajasthani (northwestern India, south of Punjab;
    Rajputana) — 15,000,000
Gujarati (western India, north of Bombay) — 13,000,000
Oriya (eastern India, southwest of Calcutta;
    Orissa) — 10,000,000

The Dravidian speakers of southern India and northern Ceylon are estimated at nearly 100,000,000, apportioned among sixteen major languages.

Chief among these are:

Tamil (southeastern India, northern Ceylon) — 22,000,000
Telugu (southeastern India, north of Tamil; region
    of Madras) — 27,000,000

2. Because of the disagreeable connotations with which "Aryan" has been invested by certain racial theories which have nothing to do with language, "Indo-Iranian" is perhaps a better term; "Indo-Iranian", however, also includes the Iranian, or Persian branch of Indo-European.

Canarese (southwestern India, south of the Bombay
    region)   — 13,000,000
Malayalam (southwestern India, south of
    Canarese)   — 10,000,000

The vast Sino-Tibetan linguistic world includes Chinese,
Siamese (or Thai), Burmese, Tibetan and, according to some
scholars, Annamese and Cambodian. Of these languages,
Chinese, with its vast mass of perhaps 450,000,000 speakers
(subdivided, however, into several often mutually incomprehensible dialects), its ancient culture, and its growing
commercial and political worth, is by far the most important.
The Tibeto-Burmese and Thai members of the family may
be estimated to have some 20,000,000 to 30,000,000 speakers
each.   Political, economic and cultural factors all point to
Chinese, in its expanding standardized national form (Kuo-yü),
as a tongue of coming primary importance.

The Japanese-Korean group (assuming that there is a
connection between Japanese and Korean, which many scholars
deny) is represented by Korean, the tongue of some 25,000,000
people in Korea, who are for the most part accessible by means
of Japanese; and the latter language, which has some 75,000,-
000 native speakers and has recently been to some degree
current in territories having a total population of over
400,000,000.   The future of Japanese as a world language
is at present in considerable doubt; however restricted its use
may be outside of Japan proper, it will still remain the tongue
of a large population which has displayed great ingenuity and
adaptability in assimilating the mechanical aspects of western
civilization.

The Malayo-Polynesian group, subdivided into an impressive number of languages and an almost infinite variety
of dialects, is represented by the Malay-speaking portion of
the population of British Malaya, and by the entire vast island
world that stretches from Madagascar across the Indian and
Pacific Oceans to Easter Island, and from Formosa on the
north to New Zealand on the south (exclusive, however, of

Australia, Tasmania, and the interior of New Guinea). The trade language known as Pidgin (or Bazaar) Malay is generally current throughout Malaya, the Dutch East Indies and, to some extent, the Philippines, and this fairly standardized *lingua franca*, which gives access to a total population of perhaps 80,000,000 (many of whom are also accessible through tongues of colonization, such as Dutch, English and Spanish) is of great practical importance in the reconquest of this section of the world from the Japanese and in the eventual reconstruction of the entire Pacific area.

In the complex linguistic picture of the Middle and Far East, four tongues stand out as of primary practical importance at the present moment: Japanese, Chinese, Arabic and Malay.

The following comparative table of a few fundamental words in some of the major Asiatic languages will be of interest in its indications of similarities and differences among and within the various groups.

	one	three	ten	hundred	foot
(Indo-European)					
Sanskrit	ēkaḥ	trayaḥ	daša	šatam	pādaḥ
Hindustani	ēk	tīn	das	sau	pānw
Bengali	ek	tin	daṣ	šo	pā
Persian	yak	sih	dah	sad	pāi
(Semitic)					
Arabic	aḥad	thalāth	'ašr	mi''ah	qadam
(Dravidian)					
Tamil	ondrŭ	mūndrŭ	pattŭ	nūrŭ	pādam
Telugu	okaṭi	mūdŭ	padĭ	nūrŭ	kālŭ
(Sino-Tibetan)					
Chinese	⁻i	⁻san	∕shĭ	√pai	⁻chiao
Siamese	⁻nung	∕sām	⁻sip	＼rǎi	＼t'āo
Burmese	tā	＼thoun	tà s'ä	tà yā	⁻chi
Tibetan	chik	sum	chu	gya	kang-pa
(Mon-Khmer)					
Khmer	muy	bei	dàp	roy	chŏn
(Japanese-Korean)					
Japanese	hitotsu	mitsu	tō	hyaku	ashi
Korean	hăn	seit	yel	păik	pàl
(Malayo-Polynesian)					
Malay	satu	tiga	sa-puloh	sa-ratus	kaki

	tooth	father	mother	brother[3]	sister[3]
(Indo-European)					
Sanskrit	*dantaḥ*	*pitā*	*mātā*	*bhrātā*	*svasā*
Hindustani	*dāṅt*	*bāp*	*mā*	*bhāʿī*	*bahin*
Bengali	*dāṅt*	*bāp*	*mā*	*bhāi*	*bain*
Persian	*dandān*	*pidar*	*mādar*	*birādar*	*khāhar*
(Semitic)					
Arabic	*sinn*	*ab*	**umm**	*akh*	*ukht*
(Dravidian)					
Tamil	*pallŭ*	*tagappanār*	*tāyār*	*aṇṇan*	*akkāl*
Telugu	*pallŭ*	*taṇḍrĭ*	*tallĭ*	*annă*	*akkă*
(Sino-Tibetan)					
Chinese	╱*ch'ĭ*	╲*fu*	╱*mu*	⁻*hsiun*	╱*chie*
Siamese	⁻*fan*	╲*bå*	╲*mä*	╲*p'i-ch'ai*	╲*bĭ* ╱*sāo*
Burmese	╲*thwā*	*a p'e*	*a me*	*a ko*	*a* ╲*mao*
Tibetan	*so*	*a-pa*	*a-ma*	*a-jo*	*sriṅ-mo*
(Mon-Khmer)					
Khmer	*t'meñ*	*àpuk*	*mdai*	*bàṅ*	*bàṅ srey*
(Japanese-Korean)					
Japanese	*ha*	*chichi*	*haha*	*kyōdai*	*shimai*
Korean	*ī*	*àpi*	*emi*	*hyen*	*nuöi*
(Malayo-Polynesian)					
Malay	*gigi*	*bapa*	*amak*	*saudara*	*saudara*

3. It is of interest to note that in all these languages, outside of the Indo-European and Semitic ones (Sanskrit, Hindustani, Bengali, Persian, Arabic) an entirely different word is used for "brother" and "sister" according as it is an older or a younger brother or sister that is being referred to. The forms given above under Dravidian, Sino-Tibetan, Khmer, Japanese, Korean and Malay headings all indicate an older brother or sister.

THE NATIVE SCRIPTS

Asia is a land of many tongues and many writings. The two Semitic languages, Hebrew and Arabic, employ types of script which, although derived from the same original source as ours, the Phoenician alphabet, now differ widely both from ours and from each other. They both have, however, certain characteristics in common, being written from right to left and consisting of consonants only, with the vowel sounds mostly indicated by separate markings above or below the line.

The Hebrew characters, with which a good many American Jews are familiar because they are also used in printed Yiddish, are of a square type. A few letters (k, m, n, etc.) assume a different form if they occur in the final position in the word, but for the most part each letter remains uniform, while "vowel points" are optionally placed below, above, or to the left of the consonants. In Yiddish (used by Central and East European Jews, and derived for the most from medieval German), and in Ladino (used by southern or Sephardic Jews and derived from medieval Spanish) certain of the original consonants (though not the same ones in both languages) have changed their function to act as vowels, and the number of vowel-points in use has accordingly been reduced.

The Arabic script may have four separate forms for each consonant, according as it comes at the beginning, the middle or the end of a word, or is used by itself. Vowel-sounds are indicated by short oblique bars and hooks above or below the consonants, but are very frequently left out altogether, and the vowel-values are left to be supplied by the reader (this practice is also current in Hebrew texts, and is an indication of the secondary function of vowels in the Semitic languages). The Arabic script, with certain modifications, is used by a number of other tongues, and generally appears where the speakers are members of the Muhammadan faith. Among the languages often appearing in Arabic characters are the Fula, Hausa and Swahili of Central Africa; the Malay, Javanese and Sundanese of the Dutch East Indies; the Moro of the Philippines; the Urdu variety of Hindustani; other languages of India, such as Malayalam, Brahui, Tamil and Punjabi; the Persian of Iran; the Balochi of Balochistan; and several of the Turkic (Altaic) tongues of Asiatic Russia. Turkish formerly used a modified Arabic script, but discarded it in favor of Roman characters under Mustapha Kemal Ataturk.

The languages of India make use for the most part of alphabets derived from the ancient Devanagari (or Nagari) in which Sanskrit was written. Many of these languages, in fact, still use the unmodified Devanagari characters today (Hindi, to cite one example, is the Hindu version of Hindustani, while Urdu is the Moslem version; Hindi uses Devanagari in writing, rejects Arabic and Persian loan-words and retains the more ancient Sanskrit terms, but the language is fundamentally one and the same). Bengali is not only the closest numerical rival of Hindustani, but also the language whose script, while differing, diverges least from the Devanagari. In the alphabets of southern India (Tamil, Telugu, Canarese, etc.), and even of tongues outside of India, like Siamese and Burmese, descent from the Nagari characters is largely disguised. Devanagari is read from left to right. Each consonant carries inherently with it the following sound of a short *a*, while other vowel-values are indicated by separate symbols above or below the line, or by separate characters within the line.

The Chinese characters are of the ideographic variety, and are separately described under the heading of Chinese (see p. 489-492). They have been adopted, with modifications, by the Japanese, who have in part adapted the borrowed characters to a syllabic instead of an ideographic system (see p. 526-530).

Samples of some of the languages of Asia in their own characters are presented (see pp. 463, 478, 479, 480, 481, 485, 486, 490, 504, 505, 506, 529).

THE SEMITIC LANGUAGES — ARABIC, HEBREW

The two modern Semitic languages display the typical Semitic arrangement of three-consonant roots, with the vowels relegated to an internal flexional role (see p. 29); two genders, masculine and feminine, with inanimate objects distributed between them; a dual number, indicating two objects, especially ones that naturally go in pairs (hands, feet, etc.). The verb is fully inflected, with numerous separate masculine and feminine forms, especially in the third person.

SAMPLE

OF

PRINTED

ARABIC

وزي مارفع موسى التعبان فى الجبل اهوكـد الازم
يترفع ابن الانسان ۞ عشان ما يهلكش كل اللى يا آمن به
لكن تبقى له الحياه الابديه ۞ لان الله حب العالم الدرجة انه
وهب ابنه الوحدانى عشان ما يهلكش كل اللى يا آمن
به لكن تبقى له الحياه الابديه

SAMPLE OF PRINTED HEBREW

כו כי אסידחה חי עולמים : כירככה אהב האלהים
את־העולם עד־אשר נתן את־בנו את־יחידו המען לא־
יאבד כל־המאמן בו כי אסידחה חי עולמים : כי
האלהים לא־שלח את־בנו אל־העולם לדין את־העולם
בי אסל־המען ישע בו העולם : המאמן בו לא ידון
ואשר לא־אמן בו כבר נדון כי לא־האמן בשם בן
האלהים היחיד : זה הוא הדין כי האור בא אל־
העולם ויבו האדם אהבו החשך מהאור כי רעים
מעשיהם : כי כל־פעל עולה ישנא את־האור ולא יבא
לאור פן־יכחו מעשיו : אבל עשה האמת יבא לאור
למען יגלו מעשיו כי נעשו באלהים :   ודי

(Courtesy of American Bible Society)

The following comparative table will serve to give an indication of the resemblances and differences between spoken Egyptian Arabic and spoken Palestinian Hebrew.

English	Arabic	Hebrew
air	*hawā'*	*avīr*
all	*kull*	*kōl*
apple	*tuffaḥah*	*tappūakh*
ask	*sa'al*	*šā'al*
bone	*'oẓm*	*'etsem*
brother	*'akh*	*'ākh*
cut	*qaṭa'* (coll. *'aṭa'*)	*gāda'*
death	*mawt*	*māvet*
deep	*'amīq* (coll. *'amī'*)	*'āmōq*
do	*fa'al*	*pā'al*
dog	*kalb*	*kelev*
dream	*ḥulm*	*khălōm*
ear	*'uẓn*	*'ōzen*
eat	*'akal*	*'ākhal*
eye	*'ayn*	*'ayin*
father	*'ab*	*'āv*
full	*mal'ān*	*mālē'*
great	*kibīr*	*kabbīr*
one	*wāḥid*	*'ekhād*
two	*'itnēn*	*šnayim*
three	*talāta*	*šlōšāh*
four	*'arba'a*	*'arbā'āh*
five	*khamsa*	*khămīšāh*
six	*sitta*	*šiššāh*
seven	*saba'a*	*šiv'āh*
eight	*tamanya*	*šmōnāh*
nine	*tis'a*	*tiš'āh*
ten	*'ašara*	*'ăsārāh*
hundred	*miyya*	*mē'āh*
thousand	*'alf*	*'elef*

ARABIC[4]

SOUNDS AND TRANSCRIPTIONS

Vowel Sounds.

ā = f*a*ther (this sound is of comparatively rare occurrence: khā*li*ṣ, "pure"); or, much more commonly, = m*a*d (m*ā*t, "he died").

a = c*a*t (m*a*lḥ, "salt").

ē = first part of a in l*a*te (f*ē*n, "where").

e = th*e* man (m*e*naggim, "astrologer"); or = m*e*t (b*e*tna, "our house").

ī = mach*i*ne (m*ī*n, "who?").

i = t*i*n (b*i*nt, "daughter").

ō = *a*ll (*kō*ra, "ball"); or = *o*bey (*ō*da, "room").

o = g*o*ing (*o*dtna, "our room"); or = g*o*t (b*o*ṭṭāl, "evil").

ū = f*oo*d (š*ū*f, "look").

u = g*oo*d ('*u*lt, "I said").

Consonant Sounds.

Approximately as in English: b, t, g (*g*o in Egypt; *g*eneral in other localities), h, z, r, s, d, f, k, l, m, n, y, w.

ṭ = t vigorously uttered, with blade of tongue pressed against palate (*ṭ*īn, "mud").

ḍ = d, as above (*ḍ*ēf, "guest").

ṣ = s, as above (*ṣ*ūf, "wool").

ẓ = z, as above (*ẓ*ahr, "dice").

4. The form of Arabic here given is not the literary language (standardized throughout the entire Arabic world and strongly conservative), but the Egyptian spoken tongue, comprehensible, but with difficulty, in the countries to the east (Palestine, Transjordan, Iraq, Arabia) and to the west (Libya, Tunisia, Algeria, Morocco). This form has been selected because of its central position, which gives it the nature of a compromise between the eastern and the western dialects, and also because it gives direct access to more Arabic speakers than any other spoken dialect. The Arabic script, in which the literary tongue is written, is discussed elsewhere (see p. 461-462).

š = *s*ure (*š*ēkh, "sheik").
ḥ = h, stronger and more emphatic than h, but not rasped (*ḥ*usan, "horse").
' = like ḥ, but with vibration of vocal cords ('id, "feast").
kh = guttural German a*ch*-sound, or Spanish *j* (*kh*ēr, "good").
gh = like kh, but with vibration of vocal cords; somewhat similar to French uvular *r* (*gh*arb, "west").
' = catch in voice, as between the two o's of English cooperate, or between the article and the noun in German *die Eier* (*su'āl*, question).

Many Arabic consonants are emphatic, or guttural, or both. No precise English equivalent appears for ṭ, ḍ, ṣ, ẓ, all of which call for an unfamiliar position of the tongue coupled with energy of articulation. Note the three guttural gradations in h (English h); ḥ (the same, but with greater force, and yet no rasping of the throat); and kh (vigorous and rasping); as well as in the voiced g (English g*o*); ' (the voiced counterpart of ḥ); and gh (a gargling sound, with vibration of the vocal cords).

Long vowels must be pronounced long. Double consonants must be pronounced double (*'izzayyak?*, how are you?, pronounced *'iz-zay-yak*).

The accent of Arabic tends to be on the next to the last syllable; but a long vowel elsewhere in the word tends to draw accentuation to itself.

GRAMMATICAL SURVEY.

Nouns and Articles.

There are only two genders in Arabic. masculine and feminine. Nouns denoting males are usually masculine, those denoting females feminine (man, *rāgil,* masc.; girl, *bint,* fem.). Nouns denoting inanimate objects are in part masculine, in part feminine; the ending -*a* usually denotes a noun of feminine gender (table, *ṭōrōbēza;* watch, *sā'a*).

There are *three* numbers, singular, plural and *dual* (the latter denotes two objects, and is especially used for things that normally occur in pairs, such as hands, feet, etc. The dual ending is *-ēn*: hand, *īd*; two hands, *īdēn*. Feminine nouns ending in *-a* change *-a* to *-tēn* to form the dual: table, *ṭōrōbēza*; two tables, *ṭōrōbēztēn*.

Feminine nouns in *-a* form their plural by changing *-a* to *-āt*: table, *ṭōrōbēza*; tables, *ṭōrōbēzāt*; watch, *sā'a*; watches, *sā'āt*.

Masculine nouns have so-called "broken plurals", which means that the plural form is irregular, and follows no set rules that can be easily codified; they are therefore best learned in their double form, singular and plural; there is, however, very frequent change of the internal vowels: book, *kitāb*; books, *kutub*; boy, *walad*; boys, *'awlād*; dog, *kalb*; dogs, *kilāb*.

The definite article for all nouns, masculine and feminine, singular, dual and plural, is *il*: the book, *il kitāb*; the girl, *il bint*; the books, *il kutub*; the girls, *il banāt*.

The *l* of *il* is assimilated to a following s, ṣ, š, z, ẓ, t, ṭ, d, ḍ, n, r; so that *il sā'a*, "the watch", becomes *is sā'a*; *il dulāb*, "the cup-board", becomes *id dulāb*.

A noun used with the definite article and placed immediately after another noun often indicates the possessor: the man's house, *bēt ir rāgil*.

There is no indefinite article, although *wāḥid*, "one", may be used with the sense of "a certain".

Adjectives and Adverbs.

The adjective *follows* the noun, and agrees with it in gender and number: a nice book, *kitāb gamīl*; a nice watch, *sā'a gamīla*. If the noun has the definite article, this is repeated before the adjective: the nice book, *il kitāb ig gamīl*; the nice watch, *is sā'a ig gamīla*.

The feminine singular of the adjective is formed by adding *-a*: large, great, *kibīr*; fem. singular *kibīra*. The dual does not appear in adjectives, being replaced by the plural: two good men, *rāgilēn kuwayyisīn*. The plural is formed by adding *-īn*, for both genders: good boys, *'awlād kuwayyisīn*; good girls, *banāt kuwayyisīn*. But if the noun denotes an inanimate object, the feminine singular form of the adjective, ending in -a, is used with it: big books, *kutub kibīra* (or *kutub kubār;* a few adjectives, *kibīr* among them, also have broken plurals).

A predicate adjective follows the noun just like an attributive adjective, and the verb "to be" is generally understood; but in this case, only the noun has the definite article: the great man, *ir rāgil il kibīr;* the man (is) great, *ir rāgil kibīr.*

The comparative of the adjective resembles a noun plural of the "broken" type; for most adjectives, the following scheme will work: *kibīr,* big; *akbar,* bigger; *ṣaghīr,* small; *aṣghar,* smaller; *ṭawīl,* long, tall; *aṭwal,* longer, taller; the superlative is formed by placing the article before the comparative: great, *kibīr;* greater, *akbar;* greatest, *il akbar;* nice, *gamīl;* nicer, *agmal;* nicest, *il agmal.* The superlative form is seldom used colloquially, being replaced by the comparative, or by the positive with *khāliṣ,* "pure", or *'awi,* "very".

"Than" is expressed by using either the positive with *'an* (a preposition meaning "about", "over"); or the comparative with *min* (a preposition meaning "of"): greater than, *kibīr 'an* or *akbar min.*

There is no true adverb in Arabic. Adverbial expressions are usually formed by a preposition with a noun: easily, *bir-rāha;* hardly, *biz-zūr;* quickly, *bil 'agal.*

Numerals.

Cardinal[5]

1 = *wāḥid*	5 = *khamsa*
2 = *'itnēn*	6 = *sitta*
3 = *talāta*	7 = *saba'a*
4 = *'arba'a*	8 = *tamanya*

5. The singular form of the noun is used with "one": one book, *kitāb wāḥid* (or, more commonly, simply *kitāb*). The dual is used with "two": two books, *kitābēn 'itnēn* (or, more commonly, simply *kitābēn*). The plural appears with numbers from 3 to 10: three books,

9 = *tis'a*
10 = *'ašara*
11 = *ḥidāšer*
12 = *itnāšer*
13 = *talatāšer*
14 = *'arba'tāšer* (etc.)
20 = *'išrīn*
21 = *wāḥid we 'išrīn*
22 = *'itnēn we 'išrīn*
30 = *talatīn*

40 = *'arbi'īn*
50 = *khamsīn*
60 = *sittīn*
70 = *sab'īn*
100 = *miyya*
200 = *mitēn*
300 = *tultu miyya*
400 = *rub'u miyya*
1000 = *'alf*
2000 = *'alfēn*

3000 = *talāt 'ālāf*

Ordinal.

1st = *il 'awwal*
2nd = *it tāni*
3rd = *it tālit*
4th = *ir rābi'*
5th = *il khāmis*

6th = *is sātit*
7th = *is sābi'*
8th = *it tāmin*
9th = *it tāsi'*
10th = *il 'āšir*

Others.

half = *nuṣṣ*
one-fourth = *rub'a*
once = *marra wāḥda*
twice = *marratēn*
three times = *talāt marrāt*
the first time = *il marra il 'ūla*, or *'awwil marra*
the last time = *il marra il 'ākhīra*, or *'ākhir marra*

Pronouns.
Personal, Subject.

I, *ana*
you (masc. sg.), *inta, enta*

---

talāt(*a*) *kutub;* but the *singular* form of the noun is used with numbers above 10: twenty books, *'išrīn kitāb*. The final -*a* of numerals from 3 to 10 is often dropped, especially before feminine nouns and nouns beginning with vowels.

you (fem. sg.), *inti, enti*
he, it, *huwwa*
she, it, *hiyya*
we, *iḥna, eḥna*
you (plural), *intum, entum*
they, *humma, hum*

These are used alone, or as subjects of verbs. The verb is generally used without the subject pronoun, however, unless emphasis is desired.

Direct Object.

me, *-ni*
you, (masc. sg.), *-ak* (*-k* after vowels)
you, (fem. sg.), *-ik* (*-ki* after vowels)
him, it, *-u* (*-h* after vowels)
her, it, *-ha*
us, *-na*
you, (pl.), *-kum*
them, *-hum*

These forms are attached to verbs: he beat, *ḍarab;* he beat me, *ḍarab-ni.*

Possessive.

These are the same as the direct object pronoun forms given above, save that (1) they are attached to nouns; (2) *-i,* "my", replaces *-ni,* "me"; (3) attached to the preposition *li,* "to", they serve as indirect objects: *lik,* "to you"; *lihum,* "to them".

	After consonants	After vowels
my,	*-i*	*-ya*
your (masc. sg. possessor),	*-ak*	*-k*
your (fem. sg. possessor),	*-ik*	*-ki*
his,	*-u*	*-h*
her,	*-ha*	*-ha*
our,	*-na*	*-na*
your (plural possessor),	*-kum*	*-kum*
their,	*-hum*	*-hum*

Book, *kitāb;* my book, *kitāb-i;* your book, *kitāb-ak;* his book, *kitāb-u.*

Father, *āb* (in combination, *abū*) ; my father, *abū-ya;* your father, *abū-k;* her father, *abū-ha.*

These possessive forms are also used as object pronouns after prepositions: with, *ma'a;* with me, *ma'āya;* with you, *ma'-ak.* When combined with the prepositions *li, ma'a* or *'and,* the possessive forms acquire the meaning of "I have", "you have", etc.: I have a book, *'andi kitāb* (lit. a book(is) at me) ; I have a house, *lī bēt;* have you a match?, *ma'ak kabrīt?;* she has an umbrella, *'andaha šamsīyya* (*li* is generally used for big, precious or important objects, *ma'a* for small objects).

Some common prepositions are:

of, from, *min*	for, *'alašān*
to, for, *li*	in, *fi*
with, *ma'a, 'and, wayya*	over, on, *'ala*
without, *min ghēr*	

Demonstrative.

this, these, *da* (masc. sg.) ; *di* (fem. sg.) ; *dōl* (pl.)
that, those, *dukha* (masc. sg.) ; *dikha* (fem. sg.) ; *dukham* (pl.)

These normally follow the noun if used as adjectives: this house, *il bēt da.* If they precede, they are pronouns, and the verb "to be" is understood: this (is) a house, *da bēt.*

Relative.

The general relative pronoun is *illi;* the house which I saw, *il bēt illi šuftu* (lit. the house which I saw it: *šuftu* = *šuft,* I saw + *-u,* it).

If the antecedent has no definite article, *illi* is omitted: a house which I saw, *bēt šuftu* (lit. house I saw it). *Illi* may also mean "the one who": the man I saw yesterday was ill, *illi šuftu embāriḥ kān 'ayyān.*

Interrogative.

who?, whom?, whose?, *mīn*: whom did you see?, *šuft mīn?*
　　(lit. you saw whom?); whose book?, *kitāb mīn?* (lit.
　　book whose?)

what?, *ēh?*: what (is) this?, *ēh da?*; what did you say?, *'ult ēh?*

which?, *anho* (masc. sg.); *anhe* (fem. sg.); *anhum* (pl.)

Verbs.

　　The Arabic verb is a root consisting of three consonants
(*K-T-B*, write). Internal vowels, and prefixed and suffixed
vowels and consonants provide the conjugational scheme. This
three-consonant root is sometimes disguised by the fact that one
of the three consonants is a "weak" consonant, such as *w* or *y*,
which is absorbed by neighboring vowels. The verb is then
called "weak", in contrast with the "strong" verb, in which
the original three consonants stand out clearly.

　　The basic form of the verb, selected by Arabic grammarians to designate the verb itself (as we designate the infinitive, "to write") is not the infinitive, but the third singular of the
past tense; thus, the verb "to write" would be designated by
katab, "he wrote".

　　The three basic forms are the "imperfect" (usually translated by a present or future); the "perfect" (usually translated
by a past), and the imperative. A more specific future may be
formed by using the imperfect with a prefixed *ha-*.

Strong Conjugation:　　　"to write", *katab* (lit. "he wrote").

	Perfect (Past)	Imperfect (Pres.)	Imperative	Future
I	*katab-t*	*'a-ktib*		*ha-'aktib*
you (masc. sg.)	*katab-t*	*ti-ktib*	*'i-ktib*	*ha-tiktib*
you (fem. sg.)	*katab-ti*	*ti-ktib-i*	*'i-ktib-i*	*ha-tiktibi*
he	*katab*	*yi-ktib*		etc.
she	*katab-it*	*ti-ktib*		
we	*katab-na*	*ni-ktib*		
you (plural)	*katab-tu*	*ti-ktib-u*	*'i-ktib-u*	
they	*katab-u*	*yi-ktib-u*		

An active participle, "writing"; a passive participle, "written"; and a verbal noun, "act of writing", also appear. The participles are declined like adjectives.

Active participle, "writing": masc. sg. *kātib;* fem. sg. *katb-a;* pl. *katb-īn.*

Passive participle, "written": masc. sg. *ma-ktūb;* fem. sg. *ma-ktūb-a;* pl. *ma-ktub-īn.*

Verbal noun, "act of writing": *kitāb-a.*

Weak Conjugation: "to see", *šāf* (lit. "he saw")

	Perfect (Past)	Imperfect (Pres.)	Imperative	Future
I	*šuf-t*	*'a-šūf*		*ḥa-'ašūf*
you (masc. sg.)	*šuf-t*	*ti-šūf*	*šūf*	*ḥa-tišūf*
you (fem. sg.)	*šuf-ti*	*ti-šūf-i*	*šūf-i*	etc.
he	*šāf*	*yi-šūf*		
she	*šāf-it*	*ti-šūf*		
we	*šuf-na*	*ni-šūf*		
you (plural)	*šuf-tu*	*ti-šūf-u*	*šūf-u*	
they	*šāf-u*	*yi-šūf-u*		

Active participle, "seeing": masc. sg. *šāyif;* fem. sg. *šayfa;* pl. *šayfīn.*

Passive participle, "seen": none appears in this verb.

Verbal noun, "act of seeing": *šōf.*

The role played by shifting internal vowels in the conjugation of the Arabic verb is obvious. Note the difference between the strong and the weak verb appearing in the third singular and third plural of the past, where the weak verb changes the internal vowel, while the strong verb does not.

Subject pronouns are normally omitted, but may be used for emphasis or clarity: I saw, *ana šuft;* you (masc. sg.) saw, *inta šuft;* he saw, *šāf; he* saw, *huwwa šāf·*

Object pronouns are added on to the verb (see p. 470): he saw me, *šāf-ni;* I saw him, *šuft-u;* I saw you, *šuft-ak* (*šuft-ik,* if "you" is feminine) ; he saw us, *šāf-na;* we saw them, *šufna-hum.*

Negative and Interrogative.

To form the negative, use *ma* before the verb and *-š* as a suffix: he did not write, *ma katab-š;* I do not see, *ma 'ašuf-š.* With the active and passive participles, a single word, *muš,* is placed before the participle: not writing, *muš kātib;* not written, *muš maktūb.*

Interrogation is usually conveyed by the tone of the voice, or by an interrogative word: where is the city?, *il balad fēn?* (lit., the city where?).

"To Be"

In simple sentences, "to be" is generally understood: this (is) a book, *da kitāb;* the man (is) great, *ir rāgil kibīr.* This is particularly the case with the participles: it (is) written, *maktūb;* I (am) not writing, *ana muš kātib.*

"To be" is also expressed, however, particularly in tenses other than the present, by the verb *kān* (lit. "was"; note the contraction of *ḥa-* with the present in the future of this verb):

	Past	Present	Imperative	Future
I	*kun-t*	*'a-kūn*		*ḥa-kūn*
you (masc. sg.)	*kun-t*	*ti-kūn*	*kūn*	*ḥa-tkūn*
you (fem. sg.)	*kun-ti*	*ti-kūn-i*	*kūn-i*	*ḥa-tkūni*
he	*kān*	*yi-kūn*		*ḥa-ykūn*
she	*kān-it*	*ti-kūn*		*ḥa-tkūn*
we	*kun-na*	*ni-kūn*		*ḥa-nkūn*
you (plural)	*kun-tu*	*ti-kūn-u*	*kūn-u*	*ḥa-tkūnu*
they	*kān-u*	*yi-kūn-u*		*ḥa-ykūnu*

"To Have".

This is generally expressed by "to be" (*kān*) with the prepositions *'and, li* or *ma'a* (see p. 471), followed by a pronoun indicating the possessor (cf. French *un livre est à moi*): he had a book, *kān 'andu kitāb* (lit. "there was with him a book"); I had a house, *kān lī bēt;* I had a match, *kān ma'āya kabrīt.*

Progressive.

The imperfect (present) with the prefix *b-* conveys a progressive meaning: I am writing, *b-aktib.*

WORDS AND PHRASES

good morning, *ṣabāḥ il khēr*
good afternoon, *nahārak saʿīd* (to a woman, *nahārik saʿīd*)
good evening, good night, *lēltak saʿīda* (to a woman, *lēltik sa-ʿīda*)
good-bye, *maʿa is salāma*
thank you, *kattar khērak*
you're welcome, *'ahlan wa sahlan; marḥaba*
please, *min faḍlak*
very gladly, *bi kull surūr*
perhaps, *yimkin*
here, here is, *hina, 'aho* (here is the book, *il kitāb aho*)
there, there is, *hināk*
where?, where is?, *fēn?*
how do I go to..., *'izzāy 'arūḥ li...*
yes, *naʿam; aiwa*
no, *la*
how are you?, *'izzayyak?* (to fem. *'izzayyik?*; to pl. *'izzaykum?*)
very well, *kuwayyis*
how much is it?, *bi kām da?*
why?, *lēh?*
when?, *emta*
because, *'alašān*
today, *ın naharda*
tomorrow, *bukra*
yesterday, *'imbāriḥ*
to the right, *'al yimīn*
to the left, *'aš šimāl*
straight ahead, *'ala ṭūl; dughri*
what time is it?, *is sāʿa kām?*
it is now six o'clock, *dilwö'ti is sāʿa sitta*

I'm hungry, *ana ga'ān*
I'm thirsty, *ana 'ōṭšān*
I'm cold, *ana bardān*
I'm warm, *ana ḥarrān*
I'm ill, *ana 'ayyān*
what is your name?, *'ismak ēh?* (to fem. *'ismik ēh?*)
my name is..., *'ismi...*
how old are you?, *kām sana 'umrak?* (to fem. *kām sana 'umrik?*)
do you speak Arabic?, *'inta bititkallim (il) 'arabi?*
certainly, *ṭab'an; ma'lūm*
very little, *šuwayya*
give me, *'iddīni*
show me, *warrīni*
tell me, *'ulli*
do you understand?, *('inta) fāhim?*
I don't understand, *ana muš fāhim*
do you know?, *('inta) 'ārif?*
I don't know, *ana muš 'ārif*
excuse me, *wala mu'akhza; matakhiznīš*
don't mention it, *il 'afw*
what do you want?, *'inta 'āwiz ēh?*
it's fine weather, *il gaw gamīl*
never mind, *ma'lēš*
I'm sorry, *ana muṭa'assif; ana 'āsif*
I'm glad, *ana mabsūṭ*
too bad!, *zayy iz zift!; ya salām!; ya khṣāra!*
what is the matter?, *gāra eh?; ḥaṣal ēh?*
come in!, *khūš!; 'itfoḍḍal!*
get out!, *imši!; iṭlā' barra!* (fem. *iṭla'i barra!*; pl. *iṭla'u barra!*); *'ukhrug barra!*
gangway!, *riglak!; 'iw'a!*

PERSIAN

Persian normally makes no distinction of gender. The plural is formed by adding -*hā* to the singular (man, *mard;* men, *mardhā*). A special suffix -*ra* is used to indicate a definite direct object (the man, object, *mardra*). Possession is indicated by placing the possessor (noun or pronoun) after the thing possessed, with -*e-* or -*ye-* between (my money, *pūl-e-man,* lit. money-of-I). The same arrangement is generally used for attributive adjectives (the left hand, *dast-e-chap,* lit. hand-left). The comparative and superlative are usually formed by adding to the adjective the suffixes -*tar* and -*tarin* (cold, *sard;* colder, *sardtar;* coldest, *sardtarin*).

The Persian verb is relatively simple, the common endings being: -*am,* -*i,* -*ad,* -*im,* -*id,* -*and*. These are added to the two roots of the verb, present and past: to take, *gereft-an;* present root, *gir* (with a prefix *mi-*); past root, *gereft;* present, *mi-gir-am, mi-gir-i, mi-gir-ad, mi-gir-im, mi-gir-id, mi-gir-and;* past, *gereft-am, gereft-i, gereft* (-*ad* normally omitted), *gereft-im, gereft-id, gereft-and*. The prefix *mi-* used with the past turns it into an imperfect: I was taking, used to take, *mi-gereft-am*. The negative is formed by prefixing *na* (I did not take, *na gereftam*); the past participle, which is used in compound tenses, is formed by adding -*é* to the past root (taken, *gereft-é*). The verb usually comes at the end of the sentence.

WORDS AND PHRASES

good night, *shab be-khair*
what is the matter?, *ché khabar ast?*
where is?, *kujāst?;* there is, *ānjāst;* here is, *injāst*
how much?, *chagadr?,* how many?, *chand?*
I want, *mikhāham;* gangway!, *bi-zahmat rāh bedehid!*
give, *bedeh;* water, *āb;* bread, *nān;* bring, *biavar;* and, *va*
hot, *garm;* one, *yak;* two, *dō;* three, *sih;* four, *chahar;* five, *panj*
six, *shesh;* seven, *haft;* eight, *hasht;* nine, *noh;* ten, *dah*

SAMPLE OF PRINTED PERSIAN

۱٤۷   انجیل یوحنّا ۳

عیسی در جواب کنت آمین آمین بتو میکویم آکرکسی از آب وروح مولود نکردد
ممکن نیست که داخل ملکوت خدا شود * آنچه از جسم مولود شد جسم است
وآنچه از روح مولود کشت روح است * تعجب مدارکه بتو کفتم باید شا از سر نو
مولود کردید * باد هرجا که میخواهد میوزد وصدای آنرا میشنوی لیکن نمیدانی
از کجا میآید وبکجا میرود همچنین است هرک از روح مولود کردد * نیقودیموس
در جواب وی کنت چکونه ممکن است که چنین شود * عیسی در جواب وی
کفت آیا تو معلّم اسرائیل هستی واینرا نمیدانی * آمین آمین بتو میکویم آنچه میدانم
میکوئیم وبآنچه دیده ایم شهادت می دهم وشهادت مارا قبول نمیکنید * چون
شارا از امور زمینی بگن کفتم بور نکردید پس هرگاه به امور آسمانی با شا بگن رانم
چکونه تصدیق خواهید نمود * وکسی باسمان بالا نرفت مکر آنکس که از آسمان
پائین آند یعنی پسر انسان که در آسمانست * وهمچنانکه موسی مارا در بیابان بلند
نمود همچنین پسر انسان نیز باید بلند کرده شود * تا هرکه باو ایمان آرد هلاک
نکردد بلکه حیات جاودانی یابد * زیرا خدا جهانرا اینقدر محبّت نمود که پسر
یکانهٔ خودرا داد تا هرکه بر او ایمان آورد هلاک نکردد بلکه حیات جاودانی یابد *
زیرا خدا پسر خودرا در جهان نفرستاد تا بر جهان داوری کند بلکه تا بوسیلهٔ او
جهان نجات یابد * آنکه باو ایمان آرد بر او حکم نشود امّا هرکه ایمان نیاورد الآن
بر او حکم شده است بجهة آنکه باسم پسر یکانهٔ خدا ایمان نیاورده * وحکم این
است که نور در جهان آمد ومردم ظلمت را بیشتر از نور دوست داشتند از آنجا
که اعمال ایشان بد است * زیرا هرکه عمل بد میکند روشنی را دشمن دارد وپیش
روشنی نمیآید مبادا اعمال او توبیخ شود * ولیکن کسیکه براستی عمل میکند پیش
روشنی میآید تا آنکه اعمال او هویدا کردد که در خدا کرده شده است *

(*Courtesy of American Bible Society*)

THE INDO-EUROPEAN LANGUAGES OF INDIA

Numerically, the most important of these are Hindustani and Bengali, spoken in northern and northeastern India, respectively. Hindustani is subdivided into Urdu and Hindi, but the differences are more a matter of script and certain sections of the vocabulary than of geographical location.

SAMPLE OF PRINTED HINDI
(Nagari characters)

कि उस ने अपना एकलौता पुत्र दे दिया कि जो कोई
उस पर विश्वास करे वह नाश न हो पर अनन्त जीवन
पाए । परमेश्वर ने अपने पुत्र को जगत में इसलिये १७
नहीं भेजा कि जगत को दोषी ठहराए पर इसलिये कि
जगत उस के द्वारा उद्धार पाए । जो उस पर विश्वास १८
करता है वह दोषी नहीं ठहरता पर जो विश्वास नहीं
करता वह दोषी ठहर चुका इसलिये कि उस ने परमे-
श्वर के एकलौते पुत्र के नाम पर विश्वास नहीं किया ।
और दोषी ठहरने का कारण यह है कि ज्योति जगत में १९
आई है और मनुष्यों ने अंधकार को ज्योति से अधिक
प्रेम किया इसलिये कि उन के काम बुरे थे । क्योंकि जो २०
कोई बुराई करता है वह ज्योति से वैर रखता है और
ज्योति के निकट नहीं आता न हो कि उस के कामों पर
दोष लगाया जाए । पर जो सच्चाई पर चलता है वह २१
ज्योति के निकट आता है इसलिये कि उस के काम
प्रगट हों कि परमेश्वर की ओर से किए गए हैं ॥
इस के पीछे यीशु और उस के चेले यहदिया देश २२

(Courtesy of American Bible Society)

Generally speaking, the Indo-Aryan tongues of India display a tendency to reduce the ancient Indo-European cases to a single, or at most a double form (nominative and oblique), to use prepositions to replace the older case-endings, and to merge the old grammatical genders. Similar tendencies, to an even greater degree, are displayed by Persian.

The following table is of interest as indicating a few vocabulary divergences between the Hindi and the Urdu forms of Hindustani, along with the Sanskrit forms to which Hindi is partial and the Persian and Arabic forms from which Urdu

SAMPLE OF PRINTED BENGALI

১৬ কারণ ঈশ্বর জগৎকে এমন প্রেম
করিলেন যে, আপনার একজাত পুত্রকে
দান করিলেন, যেন, যে কেহ তাঁহাতে
বিশ্বাস করে, সে বিনষ্ট না হয়, কিন্তু

১৭ অনন্ত জীবন পায়। কেননা ঈশ্বর
জগতের বিচার করিতে পুত্রকে জগতে
প্রেরণ করেন নাই, কিন্তু জগৎ যেন

১৮ তাঁহার দ্বারা পরিত্রাণ পায়। যে তাঁহাতে
বিশ্বাস করে, তাহার বিচার করা যায় না;
যে বিশ্বাস না করে, তাহার বিচার হইয়া
গিয়াছে, যেহেতুক সে ঈশ্বরের একজাত

১৯ পুত্রের নামে বিশ্বাস করে নাই। আর
সেই বিচার এই যে, জগতে জ্যোতি
আসিয়াছে, এবং মনুষ্যেরা জ্যোতি হইতে

(Courtesy of American Bible Society)

has borrowed. It must be understood, however, that both Urdu and Hindi forms are generally comprehensible to all Hindustani speakers and are often interchangeably used. Sanskrit is the ancient sacred tongue of northern India, from which all Indo-Aryan tongues are at least partially derived. The Persian and Arabic elements in Urdu are due to the religious factor of Muhammadanism. Persian itself, though strictly an Indo-European tongue, is a very heavy borrower from Arabic.

English	Sanskrit	Hindi	Urdu	Persian	Arabic
arm	*bāhu*	*bāṅh*	*bāṅh*	*bāzū, saʻid*	*sāʻid*
brother	*bhrātā*	*bhāʻī*	*birādar*	*birādar*	*ʼakh*
death	*mṛtyuḥ*	*mrityu*	*maut*	*marg*	*mawt*
deep	*gambhīraḥ*	*gambhīr*	*ʻamīq*	*ʻamīq*	*ʻamīq*
ear	*karṇaḥ*	*kān*	*gosh*	*gūsh*	*ʼuzn*
eye	*nayanam*	*nayan*	*āṅkh*	*chashm*	*ʻayn*
fire	*agniḥ*	*agni*	*ātash*	*ātash*	*nār*
foot	*pādaḥ*	*paṅw*	*qadam*	*pāi*	*qadam*
friend	*mitram*	*mitra*	*dost*	*dūst*	*ḥabīb*
fruit	*phalam*	*phal*	*bar*	*bar*	*fākiha*

SAMPLE OF PRINTED URDU

(Persian-Arabic characters)

(Courtesy of American Bible Society)

HINDUSTANI

Hindustani (including both Urdu and Hindi) is the native language of some 65,000,000, but is used as a sort of *lingua franca* throughout India, particularly in the north; it has been estimated that nearly 140,000,000 can be more or less satisfactorily reached with it.

Hindustani has only two genders. Nouns denoting males are masculine, those denoting females feminine; names of inanimate objects are usually feminine if they end in *-ī, -sh,* or *-t,* otherwise masculine. The plural is regularly indicated by the suffix *-oṅ,*[1] in all cases save the nominative plural; the latter is the same as the nominative singular for masculine nouns ending in consonants (*mard,* man; *mard,* men); changes *-ā* or *-a* to *-e* in the case of masculines ending in *-ā* or *-a* (*beṭā,* son; *beṭe,* sons); adds *-āṅ* for feminine nouns ending in *-ī* or *-ū* (*beṭī,* loaf; *beṭīāṅ,* loaves); adds *-eṅ* for other feminine nouns (*bāt,* word; *bāteṅ,* words).

Suffixes, or postpositions, to indicate case-relations are added on to both the singular and the plural form of the noun, as follows: agent case ("by") or instrumental ("with"): *-ne;* genitive ("of"): *-kā, -ke, -kī;* dative ("to"): *-ko;* accusative (direct object): *-ko* or same as nom.; ablative ("from"): *-se;* locative: *-men* ("in") or *-par* ("on").[2] The declension of *mard,* "man", is as follows: Singular - Nom., *mard;* Agent or Instr., *mard-ne;* Gen., *mard-kā* (*mard-ke, mard-kī*)[3]; Dat.,

---

1.　Masculines in *-ā* or *-a* drop this vowel before adding the *-oṅ* plural oblique suffix (*beṭā,* son; *beṭ-oṅ-ne,* by the sons).

2.　Masculine nouns in *-ā* or *-a* change this ending to *-e* before adding the case-suffixes in the singular (*beṭā,* son; but *beṭe-ko,* to the son).

3.　The noun in the genitive is treated like an adjective and must, like the adjective, precede and agree in gender and number with the noun it modifies; *-kā* is therefore used before masculine nouns in the nom. sg. (*mard-kā beṭā,* the man's son); *-ke* before all other masculine noun-forms, singular or plural (*mard-ke beṭe,* the man's sons; *mard-ke*

mard-ko; Acc., *mard-ko* or *mard;* Abl., *mard-se;* Loc., *mard-men, mard-par;* Plural - Nom., *mard;* Agent or Instr., *mard-oṅ-ne;* Gen., *mard-oṅ-kā (-ke, -kī)*[3]; Dat., *mard-oṅ-ko;* Acc., *mard-oṅ-ko* or *mard;* Abl., *mard-oṅ-se;* Loc., *mard-oṅ-men, mard-oṅ-par.*

Adjectives immediately precede the noun modified, and are uninflected, unless they end in *-ā,* which then changes to *-e* and *-ī* under the same circumstances as the genitive ending *-kā* (see note 3): *khūb kitāb* (fem. nom. sg.), a fine book; *khūb kitābeṅ* (fem. nom. pl.), fine books; *khūb laṛkā* (masc. nom. sg.), a fine boy; *khūb laṛke* (masc. nom. pl.), fine boys; *baṛā mard* (masc. nom. sg.), a great man; *baṛe mard-kā* (masc. gen. sg.), of a great man; *baṛe mard* (masc. nom. pl.), great men; *baṛī kitābeṅ* (fem. nom. pl.), great books. There is no change in form to express degrees of comparison, but the comparative is expressed by putting the word with which the comparison is made in the ablative (by adding the postposition *-se*): *wuh baṛā hai,* he is great (lit., he great is); *wuh sultān-se baṛā hai,* he is greater than a king (lit., he king-than great is). The superlative is formed by prefixing to the adjective expressions like *sab-se,* "than all": *wuh sab-se baṛā hai,* he is the greatest of all (lit., he all-than great is).

Verbs have only one conjugation. The infinitive always ends in *-nā* (*girnā,* to fall; root: *gir-*); the present participle in *-tā* (*girtā,* falling); the past participle in *-ā* (*girā,* fallen). An "indefinite" present (I fall, I may fall) is formed by using the present participle with the subject pronouns[4]: I may fall, *maiṅ girtā* (*girtī*)[5]; you may fall, *tū girtā* (*girtī*);

---

beṭe-se, from the man's son); *-kī* before all feminine nouns, singular or plural (*mard-kī beṭī,* the man's daughter; *mard-kī beṭīāṅ,* the man's daughters).

4. These are: I, *maiṅ;* you (sg.) *tū;* he, she, it, *wuh;* we, *ham;* you (pl.), *tum;* they, *wuh.*

5. Participles agree with the subject in gender and number: masc. sg., *-ā;* fem. sg., *-ī;* masc. pl., *-e;* fem. pl., *-īṅ;* they (masc.) may fall, *wuh girte;* they (fem.) may fall, *wuh girtīṅ.*

etc. A more definite present (I am falling) is formed by adding
to the participle the present of the verb *honā*, "to be":[6] *maiṅ
girtā hūṅ*, I am falling. The imperfect is formed by adding
thā (fem. sg. *thī*; masc. pl. *the*; fem. pl. *thīṅ*) to the present
participle: *maiṅ girtā thā*, I was falling. The past is formed
by using the subject pronoun with the past participle (*maiṅ
girā* or *maiṅ girī*, I fell); the pluperfect by adding *thā* to the
past participle (*maiṅ girā thā*, I had fallen). The future has
the following forms: *gir-ūṅgā, gir-egā, gir-egā, gir-eṅge, gir-
oge, gir-eṅge* (change *-ā* to *-ī*, *-e* to *-īṅ* for the feminine). The
imperative has the endings: *-ūṅ, -, -e, -eṅ, -o, -eṅ*. The verb
usually comes last in the sentence, with the subject or agent
first, followed by the object, each immediately preceded by
its modifiers.

The numerals from one to ten are: *ek, do, tīn, chār, pāṅch,
chha, sāt, āṭh, nau, das*. 100 is *sau* or *sai*, 1000 is *hazār*.

COMMON WORDS AND EXPRESSIONS

what is your name?, *tumhārā kyā nām hai?*
what is the matter?, *kyā hai?*   what else?, *aur kyā?*
do you speak Hindustani?, *tum Hindūstānī bolte ho?*
a little, *wājibī*   do you understand?, *tum samajhte ho?*
to the right, *dā'eṅ*   to the left, *bā'eṅ*
darn it!, *balā se!*   I'm hungry, *mujhe bhūk lagī hai*
please tell me, *mihrbānī kar-ke bolo*   thank you, *taslīm*
what do you call this in Hindustani?, *is-ko Hindūstānī-men
    kyā kahte ho?*
it's raining, *pānī paṛtā hai*   here, *yahāṅ*
who?, *kaun?*   what?, *kyā?*   where?, *kahāṅ?, kidhar?*
    when?, *kab?*
today, *āj*   yesterday, *kal*   always, *hamesha*
quickly, *turant, jald*   no, *nahīṅ*   not, *na*   enough, *bas*
more, *ziyāda*   how much?, *kitnā?*

6. I am, *hūṅ*; you are, *hai*; he, she, it is, *hai*; we are, *haiṅ*; you
are, *ho*; they are, *haiṅ*.

THE DRAVIDIAN LANGUAGES OF INDIA

These languages, which predominate in southern India, with a total speaking population of approximately 100,000,000, are numerous. Chief among them are Tamil, Telugu, Canarese and Malayalam. It is believed that they are the descendants of the original languages of India, spoken throughout the Peninsula before the coming of Indo-Aryan-speaking invaders.

They are written in native alphabets which, while related to the Devanagari of the Indo-Aryan tongues, are so modified as to appear at first glance totally different.

SAMPLE OF PRINTED TELUGU

ఆలాగు మనుష్య కుమారుడు, ఆయనయందు విశ్వాస
ముంచు ప్రతివాడును నశించక నిత్యజీవము పొందు

16 నట్లు, ఎత్తబడ వలెను; । దేవుడు లోకమును ప్రేమించ
చెను. ఏలాగనిన, ఆయన తన జనితైక కుమారుని
యందు విశ్వాసముంచు ప్రతివాడును నశించక నిత్య

17 జీవము పొందుటకై, ఆయనను ఇచ్చెను. । లోకము
తన కుమారుని ద్వారా రక్షణ పొందుటకే కాని, లోక
మునకు తీర్పు చేయుటకు, దేవుడు ఆయనను లోకము

18 లోనికి పంపలేదు. ౹ ఆయనయందు విశ్వాసముంచు
వానికి తీర్పు చేయబడదు గాని, విశ్వసించనివాడు
దేవుని జనితైక కుమారుని నామమందు విశ్వాసముంచ
లేదు, గనుక వానికి ఇంతకు మునుపే తీర్పుచేయబడి

19 యున్నది. ౹ ఆ తీర్పు ఇదే; వెలుగు లోకములోకి
వచ్చి యున్నది గాని, మనుష్యులు, తమ క్రియలు
చెడ్డవైనందున, వెలుగుకంటే చీకటిని ప్రేమించిరి. ౹

20 దుష్కార్యములు చేయు ప్రతివాడు వెలుగును ద్వేషిం
చును. వాడు, తన క్రియలు గద్దించబడకుందునట్లు,

21 వెలుగునొద్దకు రాడు. ౹ సత్యవర్తనుడైతే, తన క్రియలు
దేవునియందు చేయబడి యున్నవని కనుపడునట్లు,
వెలుగునొద్దకు వచ్చునసెను.

(Courtesy of American Bible Society)

SAMPLE OF PRINTED TAMIL

கடவுன் தமது ஒரே பேரான குமா 16
ரனில் விசுவாசமாயிருக்கிறவன் எவ
னும் கெட்டுப்போகாமல் நித்திய ஜீவ
னைப் பெறும்படி அவரைத் தந்தருளி,
இவ்வளவாய் உலகத்தில் அன்புகூர்ந்
தார். உலகத்திற்குத் தீர்ப்பிடுவதற் 17
கென்று கடவுள் தமது குமாரன உல
கத்தில் அனுப்பாமல், உலகம் அவ
ராலே இரட்சிக்கப்படுவதற்கென்றே
அவரையனுப்பினர். அவரில் விசு 18
வாசமாயிருக்கிறவன் தீர்ப்பிடப்படா
ன்; விசுவாசமில்லாதவனே கடவுளின்
ஒரேபேரான குமாரனுடையநாமத்தில்
விசுவாசமாயிராதபடியினால் தீர்ப்பி
டப்பட்டாயிற்று. வெளிச்சம் உலகத் 19
தில் வந்திருக்கிறது, மனுஷருடைய
செய்கைகளோ பொல்லாதவைகள்.
ஆதலால் அவர்கள் வெளிச்சத்தைப்
பார்க்கிலும் இருள் அதிகமாய் விரும்
பினர்கள் ; இதுவே அந்தத் தீர்ப்பு.
தீமைமுயல்வோன் எவனும் வெளிச் 20
சத்தைப் பகைக்கிறான், தன் செய்
கைள் கண்டிக்கப்படாதபடி வெளிச்
சத்தினிடம் வராதிருக்கிறான். உண் 21
மையைச் செய்கிறவனே, தன் செய்
கைகள் கடவுளுக்குள் செய்யப்பட்ட
வைகளொன்று வெளியாகும்படி, வெ
ளிச்சத்தினிடம் வருகிறான்.

(Courtesy of American Bible Society)

A few of their distinctive features are: reluctance to permit consonants to appear in groups within the word (a group such as *skr* or *str*, for example, will not occur); double consonants, on the other hand, are frequent, but consonant sounds at the end of words are rare. The accent is not very well defined, but mostly initial. The root of a word normally remains unchanged, and suffixes (postpositions and detached particles) are added at the end. Distinction among the various parts of speech (nouns, adjectives, verbs) is not very well defined. Something corresponding to gender appears, but it is based on caste rather than sex, with rational beings in a "high-caste" classification and irrational beings and inanimate objects in a "casteless" one (women are sometimes regarded as irrational beings and placed in the casteless classification). Distinction between masculine and feminine appears only in third person pronouns. The plural is usually undetermined in the case of "casteless" objects. The adjective is undeclined. The pronoun displays a difference between "we" including the person addressed (Tamil *nām*) and "we" which excludes the person addressed (*nāngal*). The verb has an affirmative and a negative voice (Canarese, I did, *madid-enu*; I did not, *mad-enu*). Great use is made of participles, which normally take care of all subordinate clause functions.

LANGUAGES OF THE SINO-TIBETAN GROUP

CHINESE, THAI (SIAMESE), BURMESE, TIBETAN, ANNAMESE.

The languages of the Sino-Tibetan group are said to be monosyllabic (consisting of one-syllable words). Recent research, particularly in the Tibetan and Burmese fields, casts some doubt upon monosyllabism as the original state of these languages (there seem to be remnants of former inflectional prefixes and suffixes in both Tibetan and Burmese).

In a monosyllabic tongue, the number of possible sound-combinations is limited. If the language is rich in varied sounds, and consonant as well as vowel-sounds are allowed to appear at the end of the word, the combinations may run into the thousands.

If the language is relatively poor in consonant sounds, and the majority of these are excluded from the final position in the word, the number of possible combinations gets to be quite limited: such is the case with North Mandarin, the dialect on which the official Chinese language is based. Only about 420 combinations of sounds are possible in monosyllabic Mandarin, with the result that the same combination must do service for many different ideas, expressed in *writing* by totally different characters.

Tones, however, add diversification to these combinations. The fact that North Mandarin has four possible tones for each of its 420 sound-combinations immediately raises the number of possible spoken "words" to 420 x 4.

The additional fact that the monosyllabic tendency of these languages does not preclude them from putting together two or more monosyllabic words to form a "compound" which carries a different meaning from those of its constituent parts[1] adds greatly to the vocabulary.

Lastly, since the same word, in the same tone, may acquire several different meanings according to its position and use in the sentence, this process of multiplication of meanings is carried on to a point where the language has an adequate supply of words to express all necessary concepts.

Chinese being by far the most important of the Sino-Tibetan languages, and its tone system and grammatical arrangement being to some extent typical of the entire group, further clarification of these tongues will appear from the outline of Chinese.

---

1. E. g., Chinese *hsia* (under) + √*wu* (noon) = "afternoon"; note the identical process in the structure of the English word (*after* + *noon*).

CHINESE[2]

THE WRITTEN LANGUAGE

Chinese writing is largely pictographic and ideographic, with symbols representing complete *objects, words* and *ideas*, rather than *sounds*. In their origin, the Chinese characters appear to have been pure picture-writing.[3] The symbols for "sun" and "moon", for instance, were pictured representations of the objects in question ("sun" was originally a circle with a straight line in its center; "moon" was the picture of a crescent with or without a line running through it). In rapid brush-

2. Requirements of space and time preclude our giving, in this volume, the treatment that this extremely important language calls for. In the forthcoming "World Languages Series" it is planned to extend to Chinese the identical treatment that is here given to German, French, Spanish, Italian, Portuguese, Russian and Japanese.

3. The same picture-writing, though with different forms, gave rise to the ancient Egyptian hieroglyphs, the Babylonian cuneiform inscriptions, and even the Phoenician system of writing from which our own alphabet is derived, as well as to the picture-writing of the Mayas and Aztecs, which never got beyond the picture stage. People at first convey their ideas in pictorial representations of objects, and the association of a picture-symbol with the spoken sounds representing the identical object is unconscious and not at all deliberate. It is only as a certain picture-symbol gets to be constantly associated with a certain sound or set of sounds that it gets to acquire a phonetic value. In the ancient Egyptian system, for instance, the symbol for "sun" (the *spoken* word for "sun" was *ra*) got to be associated with the value of the initial *r* of *ra*, until ultimately it came to be employed whenever the sound *r* was to be represented. In Phoenician, the symbol for a house (the word for "house" was *beth*) ultimately came to have the value of the initial *b* of *beth,* and the symbol for camel (the spoken word was *gimel*) got to have the value of the initial *g* of *gimel.* The process frequently runs from a pictorial symbol representing a word to the value of a syllable (usually the initial) in that word, then to the value of the consonant in that syllable. Chinese has not advanced very far along this road, though many characters are used with a phonetic value to clarify the pronunciation of another character which might itself be ambiguous.

上帝愛世人　　作惡的恨光

新約全書　約翰福音　第三章　一百九十六

沒有上帝同在、無人能行耶穌回答說我實實在在的告訴你人若不重生、就

不能見上帝的國尼哥底母說人已經老了、如何能重生呢豈能再進母腹生

出來麼耶穌說我實實在在的告訴你人若不是從水和聖靈生的、就不能進

上帝的國從肉身生的、就是肉身從靈生的、就是靈我說你們必須重生、你不

要以爲希奇風隨着意思吹、你聽見風的響聲、卻不曉得從那裏來、往那裏去.

凡從聖靈生的、也是如此尼哥底母問他說怎能有這事呢。耶穌回答說你是

以色列人的先生、還不明白這事麼我實實在在的告訴你、我們所說的、是我

們知道的、我們所見證的、是我們見過的你們卻不領受我們的見證我對你

們說地上的事、你們尚且不信、若說天上的事、如何能信呢除了從天降下仍

舊在天的人子沒有人升過天摩西在曠野怎樣舉蛇、人子也必照樣被舉起

來叫一切信他的都得永生。○上帝愛世人、甚至將他的

獨生子賜給他們叫一切信他的不至滅亡、反得永生因爲上帝差他的兒子

降世不是要定世人的罪、乃是要叫世人因他得救信他的人不被

定罪不信的人罪已經定了、因爲他不信上帝獨生子的名光來到世間、世人

(Courtesy of American Bible Society)

writing, these symbols became conventionalized in shape, "sun" assuming the form of an upended oblong with a horizontal line through it, "moon" that of the same oblong, but open at the bottom with two horizontal lines inside. The combination of these two symbols ("sun" followed by "moon") conventionally stands for the adjective "bright", which has a pronunciation totally unrelated to that of either "sun" or "moon", while "sun" shining through "tree" gives, conventionally, the character for "east", which in the spoken language has no pronunciation connection with either "sun" or "tree".

The drawbacks of such a system of writing, largely unconnected with pronunciation, are enormous. It is estimated that to read an ordinary Chinese newspaper one must be acquainted with at least 3000 separate characters, while for works of literature and philosophy the characters run into several additional thousand.

There are corresponding advantages. The *written* language (especially literary) is standardized throughout China, regardless of *spoken* dialectal variations. A document written in literary Wen-li can be read anywhere, though if it is read aloud, local pronunciations may differ to the point of being mutually incomprehensible. The symbol for "man" is the same throughout China, though it is variously pronounced *jên, nyin, nên, lên, yên* in different provinces. It is as though the western nations were to generalize their own limited system of numerical and other symbols: "1000" is "one thousand" to the English-speaker, "tysyach" to the Russian, "mille" to the Frenchman; "$10" is "ten dollars" to the American, "diez dólares" to the Spanish speaker; "lb." is "pound" to the American, "livre" to the Frenchman; "NaCl" is "sodium chloride" to the American chemist, "cloruro di sodio" to the Italian; all who know the symbols in question understand their meaning, even though the spoken renditions of them diverge radically.

Wen-li, China's standardized, petrified literary language (which may be said to be an unspoken tongue, since its symbols carry no definite phonetic value, but only ideographic connota-

tions, differently rendered in sound in different parts of the
country) is in process of replacement by Kuo-yü, the "National
Tongue", which uses the written symbols of Wen-li, but assigns
to each of them a definite spoken value.

KUO-YÜ AND THE DIALECTS — SPEAKERS AND LOCATION

Kuo-yü is to some extent an artificial national tongue,
based primarily upon the spoken North Mandarin dialect in
its Peiping variety (North Mandarin, with comparatively slight
local variations, was the language of the majority of China's
population even before the advent of Kuo-yü).   It is now
estimated to be the language of common use of some 280,000,-
000 of China's 425,000,000 inhabitants, and tends to encroach
more and more upon the local dialects as the tendency toward
national unity grows stronger.

The main Chinese dialects which diverge to such an extent
from Kuo-yü as to be practically unintelligible are: Wu, around
the Yang-tze delta (Shanghai, Soochow), about 34,000,000;
Yüeh of Kwang-tung (Cantonese)[4], about 38,000,000; Min of
Fu-kien province, about 30,000,000. The Miao and Hakka of
southern China, with several million speakers apiece, are rated
as separate dialects of the Sino-Tibetan group. Sub-dialects
(Swatow, Amoy, Ning-po, etc.) are extremely numerous, but
they are declining in use and importance. For practical
purposes, at least two-thirds of China's population can be
reached with Kuo-yü[5].

Chinese speakers abroad are estimated at about 8,000,-
000, of whom about 6,500,000 (largely Min speakers) are in

4.   Cantonese is of special interest to Americans because the majority
of Chinese residents in the U. S. A. are from the Cantonese-speaking
region. It distinguishes itself from Mandarin especially by its use of
a larger number of tones, and by permitting such consonant sounds
as -*t* and -*p* to stand at the end of a word.

5.   The term "Chinese" as used henceforth is to be understood as referring to Kuo-yü.

other countries of Asia and in the islands of Oceania (notably Thailand, Malaya, Indo-China and the Dutch East Indies), and some 250,000 in the Western Hemisphere.

SOUNDS.[6]

Vowel sounds.

a = father
e = met
ê = us
i = machine
ĭ = pin
o = more
u = rude
ü = French u
ŭ = the; is often completely silent

Diphthongs.

ai = aisle
ao = how
ei = eight
ia = yard
iĕ = yes
iu = you
ou = toe
ua = quantity
ui = we
uo = war
iao = yowl
uei = way

Consonants.

ch = Italian cielo
ch' = church
f = four
h = house
hs = house quickly followed by house
j = pleasure, with a strong mixture of r
k = sky
k' = cat
l = low
m = moon
n = new[7]
ng = king[7]

6. In Chinese to an even greater extent than in other tongues, the English equivalents given are only approximations to the native sounds, which can accurately be acquired only from a speaker.

p = spin
p′ = pin
s = soul
sh = shore
sz = loss quickly followed by zeal
t = stem
t′ = tale
ts = that's all
ts′ = its
tz = store quickly followed by zeal
tz′ = tale quickly followed by zeal

English consonant sounds not appearing in Chinese: b, d, g, r, v, z, thing, this (a sound approximating r appears in ＼erh, and in words containing j). Note: where consonants and combinations appear with and without the accent (ch, ch′; k, k′; p, p′; t, t′, etc.), the consonant with the accent is aspirated; that is, it is given the slight puff after it which is characteristic in English when the consonant begins the word (pin = p + hin; tale = t + hale). Where the accent does not appear, the puff is missing, as is the case in English when the consonant follows an s (spin, state). Or, to put it another way, the consonants without the accent have the sounds they normally would have in Romance languages, like French or Italian (It. cielo vs. En. church; Sp. perro vs. En. pet); this softened pronunciation of the unaspirated unvoiced consonants (ch, k, p, t, ts) occasionally makes them sound to the English ear somewhat like the corresponding voiced consonants (j, g, b, d, dz).

The fact that Chinese writing has only partial phonetic value deprives spoken Chinese of a good deal of the visual support and stabilizing influence which western tongues normally derive from their written counterparts, with the result that Chinese pronunciation with respect to many consonant-sounds is somewhat vague and fluctuating. There is confusion.

7. -n and -ng are the only consonant-sounds permitted at the end of a word, save in the word ＼erh (two).

for example, among the ch, k and ts sounds, with k tending toward the sound of ch, and ch' toward the sound of ts (*Chung King* may be heard pronounced *Tsung Ching*).

TONES.

Chinese has four distinct tones. They are indicated by symbols used in front of each word:

ˉindicates that the vocable is to be pronounced on a fairly high, level note: ˉ*shĭ*, "to lose";

╱ indicates a rising inflection: ╱*shĭ*, "ten";

╲╱ indicates a slight fall followed by an immediate rise: ╲╱*shĭ*, "history";

╲ indicates an abrupt fall: ╲*shĭ*, "city", "market".

(The vocable *shĭ* has been selected because it has all four tones; but note that in addition to the meanings given, there are several other totally unrelated meanings for this same word in each one of the four tones, depending upon special use, position in the sentence, etc.).

Of interest is the fact that a few words in very common use change their tone if they precede another word having the same tone: the word for "I", for example, is ╲╱*wo;* but "I write" is ╱*wo* ╲╱*hsiĕ*, with ╲╱*wo* shifting its tone because the following word has the same tone.

Tones are, of course, best learned by contact with native speakers. Limited comprehensibility may be achieved by a foreigner even without a mastery of tones, provided there is mastery of word-order and the use of certain syntactical make-shifts, such as noun-classifiers (see p. 499).

GRAMMATICAL SURVEY.

In outlining Chinese grammar, it is necessary to eject from one's mind, to some extent, the Indo-European grammatical classifications (nouns, adjectives, adverbs, verbs, prepositions, etc.). The same Chinese word, according to its position and use, may translate an English noun, adjective, verb, or preposition; *hsia,* for instance, may mean "under" (preposition), "to descend" (verb), "bottom" (noun); the "down" concept, it will be noted, is common to all the translations. There is a striking similarity to the English process whereby "mail" can, according to its position and use, be a verb ("to mail a letter"), a noun ("by mail"), or an adjective ("mail-clerk"). In Chinese, as in English, words acquire their full significance only by reference to their position and function in the sentence.

An interesting theory advanced by some linguists is that at one time Chinese was a fully inflected, polysyllabic tongue, but that prehistorically it went through the same process that English has undergone during the last fifteen centuries and is still undergoing at present, the falling off of inflectional endings, the tendency to use one-syllable words (as evidenced by some of our popular newspaper headlines), and the consequent reliance upon word-order to clarify meanings. Whether this theory be true or not, the fact remains that there are remarkable points of contact between modern Chinese and modern American newspaper-headline English.

Word-order is of paramount importance in Chinese, and must be strictly observed. The modifier regularly precedes the modified word (adjective before noun; adverb before verb). The subject-verb-object order is rigidly adhered to.

Chinese compounds are numerous and varied; as many as four monosyllabic words sometimes go into the rendering of one idea. Two-word compounds are extremely frequent: *k'an* *chien,* literally "look-see", for "to see"; ⁻*chin* ⁻*t'ien,* "now-day" for "today" (note the similarity of formation in English; "yester-day" is "past-day" in Chinese, and "tomorrow" is "next-day").

Nouns and Articles.

Chinese has no definite article; the demonstrative √*tzŭ* however, often approaches the value of "the" rather than "this".

The numeral ⁻*i* ("one") may be used with the value of "a", "an".

The Chinese noun has no distinction of gender, number

or case; ╱*jên* may mean "man" or "men", according to the context.

The fact that a noun is in plural use may, if necessary, be indicated by (a) the use of a numeral: (b) the use of a plural demonstrative; (c) the use of an indefinite adjective, such as "many", "some"; (d) the plural suffix ⁻*mên,* ╱*mên:* eight men, ⁻*pa* ╱*jên;* these men, ╲*chê* ⁻*hsiĕ* ╱*jên;* many men, ⁻*to* ╱*jên;* men, ╱*jên* ⁻*mên.* The last form, however, is normally avoided (except in general statements), ⁻*mên* being preferably reserved for personal pronouns.

⁻*ti,* placed after the noun, indicates a genitive or possessive function, and may be said to correspond to English 's, -s': the man's house(s), the men's house(s), ╱*jên* ⁻*ti* ╱*fang* √*tzŭ.*

The fact that the noun is the subject of the sentence is indicated by its position before the verb; the fact that it is the object of the verb is indicated by its position after the verb: this man sees the child, ╲*chê* ╱*jên* ╲*k'an* ╲*chien* ╱*hai* √*tzŭ* (this man look see boy the); this boy sees the man, ╲*chê* ╱*hai* √*tzŭ* ╲*k'an* ╲*chien* ╱*jên.*

Other case-relations are indicated by separate words serving as prepositions or postpositions, placed before or after the noun they govern: to the man, √*kei* ╱*jên;* under the bridge, ╱*ch'iao* ╲*hsia* (lit. bridge under).

Adjectives and Adverbs.

The position of a word used as an attributive adjective is before the noun it modifies: the good man, √*hao* ╱*jên.*

If the adjective appears after the noun, it has the value of a predicate adjective: the man (is) good, ╱*jên* √*hao.* The verb "to be" is normally omitted in this construction.

The position of a word used as an adverb is usually before the verb: to write well, √*hao* √*hsiĕ* (lit., well, or good, to write). The same form is normally used for both adjective and adverb: slow, slowly, ╲*man.*

To form the comparative of adjectives and adverbs, the prefix ╲*kêng* is used: slower, more slowly, ╲*kêng* ╲*man.*

To form the superlative the prefix ＼*tsui* is used: slowest, most slowly, ＼*tsui* ＼*man.*

Pronouns.

Personal.

I, √*wo* (before verb)	me, √*wo* (after verb)
you (sg., subj.), √*ni* (bef. verb)	you (sg., object), √*ni* (after verb)
he, she, ‾*t'a* (bef. verb)	him, her, ‾*t'a* (after verb)
we, √*wo* ‾*mên* (bef. verb)	us, √*wo* ‾*mên* (after verb)
you (pl. subj.), √*ni* ‾*mên* (bef. verb)	you (pl. obj.), √*ni* ‾*mên* (after verb)
they, ‾*t'a* ‾*mên* (bef. verb)	them, ‾*t'a* ‾*mên* (after verb)

Possessive.

Add ‾*ti* to personal pronoun: our, ours, √*wo* ‾*mên* ‾*ti.*

Demonstrative.

this, ＼*chê*	these, ＼*chê* ‾*hsiě*
that, ＼*na*	those, ＼*na* ‾*hsiě*

Interrogative.

who?, whom?, ／*shui*
whose?, ／*shui* ‾*ti*
which?, √*na*
which one?, √*na* ‾*i* ‾*ko*

Relative.

There is no true relative pronoun in Chinese; an expression such as "the mountain which is at the center of the country" is rendered by "at country's center mountain", ＼*tsai* ／*kuo* ‾*chung* ‾*hsin* ‾*ti* ‾*shan.*

Numerals.

1	‾*i*		5	√*wu*
2	＼*erh*		6	＼*liu*
3	‾*san*		7	‾*ch'i*
4	＼*szŭ*		8	‾*pa*

9	√*chiu*	20	*erh* /*shĭ*
10	/*shĭ*	100	√*pai*
11	/*shĭ* ‾*i*	1000	‾*ch'ien*
12	/*shĭ* *erh*	10,000	*wan*

A digit before "ten" multiplies it, after "ten" is added to it: "14" is "ten four"; "40" is "four ten"; "45" is "four ten five"; "565" is "five hundred six ten five".

An ordinal numeral is usually formed by prefixing *ti* to the cardinal: fourth, *ti* *szŭ*.

Classifiers.

Classifying words are often prefixed to certain classes of nouns in Chinese, particularly after numerals. The classifier indicates that the noun specifically belongs to a certain class of objects, and removes whatever doubt might be caused by phonetic similarities; the entire expression is thereby made more definite (compare the English "five *head* of cattle"). In Pidgin English, the native tendency to use classifiers transpires in the constant use of such words as "fellow", "piecee" ("two fella man"; "five piecee shirt"). A few examples of classifiers are:

kê or *ko* (for human beings): three men, ‾*san* *ko* *jên*. ‾*chĭ* (for animals, hands, feet, etc.): five hands, √*wu* ‾*chĭ* √*shou*. *chien* (for things, clothes, etc.): four coats, *szŭ* *chien* ‾*i*.

If an adjective is used with the noun, it goes between the classifier and the noun: five large hands, √*wu* ‾*chĭ* *ta* √*shou*.

Somewhat similar in nature, but not in position, to the classifier is √*tzŭ*, which *follows* the noun and is an indication of a concrete object: house, /*fang*, or /*fang* √*tzŭ*. This "concretizer" has been compared to a definite article.

Verbs.

The Chinese verb has no tense, mood, person or number, and simply indicates the action: to write, √*hsiĕ*.

Present.

"I write", "you write", "he writes", etc. are formed by prefixing the personal pronoun to the verb: ╱wo √hsiĕ; ╱ni √hsiĕ; etc.

Past.

The force of a past is often given to a verb by adding √liao (lit. "finish"; compare Pidgin "he die finish" for "he died", "he is dead"): I wrote, ╱wo √hsiĕ ╲liao.

A secondary past, corresponding in value to the present perfect, is sometimes formed by adding ╲kuo (experience): I have written, ╱wo √hsiĕ ╲kuo. (I have had the experience of writing).

Note, however, that even without √liao or ╲kuo, a verb may receive past force from the appearance in the sentence of a word indicating past time, such as "yesterday" or "last year". The adverbial expression of time in such cases must, in accordance with the rule for the position of adverbs, immediately precede the verb: "I wrote yesterday" becomes "I past day write", √wo ╱tso ⁻t'ien √hsiĕ.

Future.

There is no specific future form, future force being given to the verb by the use in the sentence of some expression indicating future time: "I shall write tomorrow" becomes "I next day write", √wo ╱ming ⁻t'ien √hsiĕ.

Conditional.

╱ju or ╲jo, "if", or ╱ju √kuo, "if really" are the nearest approximation to a conditional; if no subject appears, ╱ju or ╲jo comes first in the sentence; otherwise, the subject precedes: if he does not come, ⁻t'a ╲jo ╲pu ╱lai.

Negative.

The negative form of the verb is produced by prefixing ╱mei or ╱pu to the verb: I do not eat, √wo ╱pu ⁻ch'ĭ.

/*mei* is especially used with the verb √*yu*, "to have", "there to be": /*mei* √*yu*, there is not, there are not. /*Pu* is never used in the past.

Interrogative.

No change in word-order occurs in an interrogative sentence, but the interrogative particle ‾*ma* (less frequently ‾*ni*) appears at the end: do you see?, √*ni* *k'an* *chien* ‾*ma*.

A question may also be formed, however, by stating the verb first in the affirmative, then in the negative: √*ni* *k'an* *chien* *k'an* /*pu* *chien*, lit. "you see not see" (do you see or don't you see?).

Reflexive.

A reflexive pronoun is formed by adding *tzŭ* √*chi* to the personal pronoun: I see myself, √*wo* *k'an* *chien* √*wo* *tzŭ* √*chi*.

WORDS AND PHRASES

good morning, /*ni* √*hao*; √*tsao* ‾*an*
good afternoon, /*ni* √*hao*; *hsia* √*wu* /*p'ing* ‾*an*
good evening, good night, /*ni* √*hao*; √*wan* ‾*an*
good-bye, *tsai* *chien*; *tsai* *hui*; (au revoir) *hui* ‾*t'ou* *chien*
thank you, *hsiĕ* *hsiĕ*
you're welcome, *pu* *yao* *k'ê* *ch'i*
please, √*ch'ing*
very gladly, /*hên* √*hsi* ‾*huan*; √*hên* ‾*kao* *hsing* ‾*ti*
perhaps, /*yĕ* √*hsü*
here is, *chê* *li* √*yu*
there is, *na* √*li* √*yu* (pointing out); √*yu* (stating)
where?, where is?, (subject) *tsai* /*na* √*li*
how do I go to...?, √*wo* √*tsen* ‾*mo* *tao*...?
yes, *shĭ* (in reply to "is" questions); √*yu* (in reply to "have" questions)

no, /*pu* *shǐ* (in reply to "is" questions) ; /*mei* √*yu* (in
     reply to "have" questions)

how are you?, /*ni* √*hao* *pu* √*hao*

very well, /*hên* √*hao*

how much is it?, *chê* *kê* ¯*to* √*shao* /*ch'ien*

why?, *wei* /*shên* ¯*mo*

when?, /*shên* ¯*mo* /*shǐ* *hou*

because, ¯*yin* *wei*

today, ¯*chin* ¯*t'ien*

tomorrow, /*ming* ¯*t'ien*

yesterday, /*tso* ¯*t'ien*

to the right, *yu* *pien*

to the left, √*tso* *pien*

straight ahead, ¯*i* /*chǐ* ¯*ti*

what time is it?, /*chi* √*tien* *chung*; /*shên* ¯*mo* /*shǐ* *hou*

it is now six o'clock, *hsien* *tsai* *liu* √*tien*

I'm hungry, √*wo* *ê* ¯*la*

I'm thirsty, /*wo* √*k'ê* ¯*la*

I'm cold, /*wo* √*lêng*

I'm warm, /*wo* √*nuan* ¯*ho*

I'm ill, √*wo* *ping* ¯*la*; /*wo* √*yu* *ping*

what is your name?, √*ni* *kuei* *hsing* (very polite); √*ni*
     hsing /*shên* ¯*mo*; √*ni* *chiao* *shên* ¯*mo* /*ming*
     ¯*tzǔ*

my name is..., √*wo* *hsing*...; √*wo* *pi* *hsing*; √*wo*
     /*ming* ¯*tzǔ* *shǐ*

do you speak...?, √*ni* *hui* ¯*shuo*... ¯*mo*

certainly, ɩ*zǔ* /*jan*

very little, /*hên* √*hsiao*

give me, /*kei* √*wo*

show me, /*kei* √*wo* *k'an*

tell me, *kao* *su* √*wo*

do you understand?, /*ni* √*tung* ¯*pu* √*tung*

I don't understand, √*wo* *pu* √*tung*

do you know?, √*ni* ¯*chǐ* ¯*tao* ¯*mo*

I don't know, √*wo* ¯*pu* ¯*chǐ* ¯*tao*

excuse me, *tui* ⁻*pu* √*ch'i*
don't mention it, ⁻*pu* *yao* /*t'i*
what do you want?, √*ni* *yao* /*shên* ⁻*mo*
it's fine weather, ⁻*t'ien* ⁻*ch'i* √*hao*
never mind, ⁻*pu* *yao* √*chin*
I'm glad, √*wo* √*hsi* ⁻*huan* /*chi* ⁻*lo*
too bad!, *t'ai* √*k'ê* ⁻*hsi*
what is the matter?, √*tsen* ⁻*mo* ⁻*la*

OTHER LANGUAGES OF THE SINO-TIBETAN GROUP
SIAMESE, TIBETAN, BURMESE

Siamese is a monosyllabic tongue and has five tones. Its system of writing is derived from the Devanagari of India and is quite complicated, with 44 consonants, 32 vowels, and the five tones mentioned above (the tones and some of the vowel-values are indicated above or below the written line.)

SAMPLE OF PRINTED SIAMESE

เพราะ ว่า พระเจ้า ทรง รัก โลก,   จน ได้ ประทาน พระบุตร์
องค์ เดียว ของ พระองค์,   เพื่อ ทุก คน ที่ วาง ใจ ใน พระบุตร์
นั้น จะ มิ ได้ พินาศ,   แต่ มี ชีวิต ชั่ว นิรันตร์.   เพราะ ว่า พระ-
เจ้า มิ ได้ ทรง ใช้ พระบุตร์ ของ พระองค์ เข้า มา ใน โลก เพื่อ จะ
พิพากษา โลก,   แต่ เพื่อ จะ ให้ โลก รอด ได้ เพราะ พระบุตร์
นั้น. ผู้ ใด ได้ วาง ใจ ใน พระบุตร์ ไม่ ต้อง ถูก พิพากษา,   แต่
ผู้ ใด มิ ได้ วาง ใจ ก็ ต้อง ถูก พิพากษา อยู่ แล้ว,   เพราะ เขา มิ
ได้ วาง ใจ ใน นาม พระบุตร์ องค์ เดียว ของ พระเจ้า.

(Courtesy of American Bible Society)

There is no gender or inflection. Possession is generally indicated by the simple expedient of placing the possessor immediately after the thing possessed (my ring, *wen k'ha*, lit. ring-me; this device appears also in Malay; see p. 511). Determinatives or classifiers are abundantly used, especially after numerals ("tiger two head" for "two tigers"; "knife three blade" for "three knives"). The adjective, which is invariable, as are all parts of speech, usually follows the noun. The numerals from one to ten are: *nung, sang, sam, si, ha, hoh, chet, pēt, kaû, sip.* Verbs have no tense or mood, such accessory

SAMPLE OF PRINTED BURMESE

၁၆ ဘုရားသခင်သည်၊ သားတော်ကို ယုံကြည် သူ တိုင်းမပျက်စီးဘဲ၊ ထာ၀ရအသက်ရစေခြင်းငှါ။ဧ၁ ပုဿသားတော်ကို အပ်ပေးသည့် တိုင်အောင်၊ ၍ လောကသားတို့အား မေတ္တာသက်တော်မူ၏။ ။

၁၇ သားတော်ကို ၍လောကကသို့ ဘုရားသခင်စေလွှတ် တော်မူသည်မှာ၊ ၍ လော ကသားတို့ကို စီရင်ဆုံး ဖြတ်စေ ရန်၊ မ ဟုတ်။ ကယ် တင် တော်မူ စေ ရန်

၁၈ တည်း။ ။ကိုယ်တော်ကို ယုံကြည်သောသူသည်၊ စီရင်ဆုံးဖြတ်ခြင်းကို့မခံရ၊ ယုံကြည်သူမှုကား၊ ဘု ရားသခင်၊ ကေပုဿသားတော်၏ နာမကိုမယုံကြည် သောကြောင့်၊ စီရင်ဆုံးဖြတ်ခြင်းကိုခံရပြီးဖြစ်၏။ ။

၁၉ တရား၊ စီရင်ဆုံးဖြတ်ခြင်းမှာ။ ၍လောကသို့အလင်း ရောက်လာရား၊လူတို့သည်၊ အပြုအမူဆိုးသွမ်းသည့် အလျောက်။ ။အလင်းထက် မှောင်မိုက်ကိုနှစ်သက်

၂၀ ကြ၏။ ။ယုတ်မာစွာပြုကုင်သူတိုင်း။ အလင်းကို ရွှုရှာလျက်၊ ကိုယ်ပြုအပြုအမူပေါ်မည့်စိုးရှို။ အလင်း

၂၁ သို့မရဉ်းဝံ့ချေ။ ။ သစ္စာသမာအတိုင်းပြုကျင့်သူမူ ကား။ ကိုယ်အးပြုအမူကို့ ဘုရားသခင်အားဖြင့် ပြုမူ ကြောင်းထင်ရှားစေရန်။ အ လင်း သို့ ချင်း လာ သ

၂၂ တည်း။ ။

အောင်တမန်လည်း။ ။ကြားရသော ဂင်လာဒအ၁င် သတ္တိသား၏ စကားသံကြ၁င့်၊ အားရ၀မ်းမြေ၁က် ၏။ ။သူ့ဖြစ်ရွှို၊ ငါ၏ ၀မ်းမြေ၁က်ခြင်းသည်။ ။ထိုအ တိုင်းစုံလင်ပြီ။ ။ကိုယ်တော်သည်၊ တိုးတက်ရမည်။ ၃၀ ငါ့မူကား။ ။ ဆုတ်ယုတ်ရမည်ဟု ဆိုပြန်၏။

အထက်မှ ကြွလာသောအရှင်သည်၊ အလုံးစုံတို့ ၃၁ ၏ အထွဋ်ဖြစ်၏။ ။ ၍ မြေကြီး မှ ဖြစ်ပွ၍ သော သူမူ ကား။ မြေကြီးနှင့်ဆိုင်သည့်အလျောက်။ ။မြေ ကြီးဆိုင် ရာများကို့သ၁ပြော၁ဆိုတတ်၏။ ။ကောင်းကင်ဘုံ့မှုကြွ လာသောအရှင်သည်။ ။ အလုံးစုံတို့ အထွဋ်ဖြစ် ၃၂ လျက်။မြင်ခဲ့၊ ကြ၁းခဲ့ရ၁ကို သက်သေခံ၁ဘ၁်မှုသ၁် လည်။ ။ မည်သူမူ မနာမယူချေ၊ ။ ။သက်သေခံတော်၃၃ မူချက်ကို နာယူလှူမူကား၊ ။ ဘုရားသခင်သည့် မှန် ကန် တော် မူ ကြေ၁င်း။ တံဆိပ်ခတ်သူဖြစ်၏။ ။ ၀ိညာဉ်တော်ကို အခြင်အတွယ်မဲ့ ပေးတော်နှု၁သည့် ၃၄ အလျောက်။ ။ ဘုရားသခင် စေလွှတ် လိုက်တော်၀နု သောအရှင်သည်။ ။ ဘုရားသခင့် ဗျ၁ဒိတ် တော်ကို ဆင့်ဆိုတတ်၏။ ။ခမည်းတော်သည် သားနော်ကို ၃၅ အားမေတ္တ၁သက်၍။ ။ အရ၁ခပ်သိမ်းကို လက်ဝတော် တွင်းသို့ အပ်နှင်းတော်မူပြီ။ ။သားတော်ကို ယုံ ၃၆

(Courtesy of American Bible Society)

ideas being conveyed by adverbial expressions. Samples of Siamese sentence-structure are:

Rao	dek-chai	sam	kon	cha	pai	chap	pla
we	boy	three	person	future	go	catch	fish

sam-rap hai paw kin.
for-to give father eat (We three boys will go and catch fish in order to feed our father).

Me tan yu ti nai.
Mother you live place where (Where does your mother live?).

Me pai ta-lat leao.
Mother go bazaar finish (Mother went to the bazaar).

A very similar structure appears in Burmese and Tibetan, which are monosyllabic and make use of word-order and tones to distinguish meanings. Traces of ancient prefixes, dropped by the modern tongues, are said to be in evidence. There is in these tongues no gender (save for an added "male" or "female" where necessary); no number (save for the use of words like "many", "heap", with the single form of the noun); and no distinction among the various parts of speech ("I go" is translated by "my going").

SAMPLE OF PRINTED KOREAN

하유위사를독하을이하   다림에심자를배모
섯죄하람주생샤사쎄나   치을못자거으암세
스케야을어자그땅상님   심가박가가로을가

신약 요한복음 매三장

二二九

죄명·혹² 자인는잇에날하곳·에본샤먼엇¹

MALAY

by

Rev. William E. Lowther, Litt. D.[1]

The Malay language is understood over a wider geographical extent in the Eastern Archipelago than any other language. It is used in the whole of the Malay Peninsula; Siam, in some of the southern parts; Indo-China, along some coasts and in some river valleys; the Straits Settlements; Sumatra; Java, in considerable part; Borneo; Celebes; Flores; Timor; and in islands too numerous to mention.

Whatever variations there may be in these regions, the Malay speaker masters in a short time. Some of the languages that bear other names are so nearly akin to Malay that the task of learning them is like the task of a Spaniard who undertakes to study Portuguese.

When the Malays became Muhammadans, in the thirteenth century, they adopted the Arabic alphabet with some modifications, and use it to this day, though there is an increasing amount of teaching and writing done with the Roman alphabet. The Arabic writing is such a poor guide to pronunciation that the student should not undertake it till he is using the language with some comfort.

The loan words of Malay are chiefly from Sanskrit and Arabic. The Malay language is dissyllabic. Monosyllables are few. Words of more than two syllables are also rare. A glance at a page of Malay will show many words that look as though they were polysyllables, but in the overwhelming majority of cases they are dissyllables with affixes. Malay is among the "easier" languages. The verb has few irregularities; there are no conjugations or declensions.

---

1. Forms in parentheses, preceded by the letters D. M., are Malay variants current in the Dutch East Indies which diverge from the Malay of British Malaya. They have been supplied by Mrs. Claire Holt, of Columbia University.

ACCENT.

The accent ordinarily falls on the syllable next to the last, but if that syllable is open and contains the vowel ĕ the accent generally falls on the last syllable. Accent is lighter in Malay than in English:

makan, eat: pronounce *má-kan;*
bĕsar, great: (ĕ in open syllable); pronounce *bĕ-sár;*
dĕndam, longings: (ĕ in closed syllable); pronounce *dĕń-dam.*

As a rule the addition of affixes to a word does not change the place of the accent:

> *makan,* **eat;**   *mákanan,* food;
> *bĕsár,* **great;**   *kĕbĕsáran;* greatness.

PRONUNCIATION.

Vowel Sounds.

> a = f*a*ther
> e = th*ey*
> i = pol*i*ce
> o = h*o*pe
> u = cr*u*de
> ua = *wa*d

ĕ represents a sound such as the one between the k and the n in German *Knabe, Knecht* (*bĕsár*, pronounced *bsár*; *dĕndam*, pron. *dń-dam; bĕtúl*, pron. *btúl*).

Consonant Sounds.

Generally as in English. Final *k* is a glottal stop. *G* is always hard. *R* is trilled more than in English. *S* in always hissed, never like *Z. Ng* as in si*ng*er; *ngg* as in fi*ng*er.

We shall now proceed to a study of the Malay language by using the Lord's Prayer as our textbook. From the fifty-nine words in it, we shall develop by far the greater part of the Malay grammar.

PERMINTAAN TUHAN
PRAYER   LORD'S

                1   2
1. *Ya Bapa   kami yang di-shurga,*
   O Father our   who   in heaven,
   3   4   5   6   7   8
2. *tĕrhormat-lah kira-nya nama-mu.*
   be hallowed we pray name your.
   9   9   10 11   12   13
3. *Datang-lah kĕrajaan-mu.*
   Come   kingdom your.
    14   15
4. *Jadi-lah kĕhĕndak-mu, di-atas bumi sĕpĕrti di-shurga*
   Become will your, at on earth as in heaven.
    16   17   18 19   20   21   22 23   24
5. *Bĕri-lah akan kami pada hari ini makanan yang*
   Give   to us at day this food which
    25   26   27   28   29 30   31   32
   sa-hari-harian.
   one day(after) day.
    33 34   35
6. *Maka ampunkan-lah hutang-hutang kami*
   ( ) forgive   debt-debt   our
    36   37   38   39
7. *sĕpĕrti kami sudah mĕngampuni orang yang bĕrhutang*
   as   we   have forgiven men who owing
   40   41   42   43   44   45   46
   pada kami.
   to us.
   47 48
8. *Jangan-lah mĕmbawa kami masok pĕnchobaan,*
   Don't   bring   us enter temptation,
    49   50   51   52   53
9. *mĕlainkan lĕpaskan-lah kami dari-pada yang jahat.*
   but   deliver   us from   who evil.
    54   55   56   57   58   59

NOUNS.

Malay words do not always fit into our English grammatical classifications. The noun does not change form to denote number, gender or case. (44) *Orang* means man, men, people. Like our word "sheep," it depends upon the context to reveal its number. When it is necessary to indicate plurality with more exactness, the words *sĕgala* and *sĕmua*, all, and *banyak*, many, may be added to the word: *sĕmua orang, sĕgala orang* (compare French *tout le monde*).

Some nouns have the faculty of indicating plurality, and also variety, by reduplication:

(44) *Orang*, man; *orang-orang*, men, mankind.

(38) *Hutang*, debt; *hutang-hutang*, debts.

(34) *Hari*, day; *sa-hari-hari*, every day, daily.

 Kuda, horse; *kuda-kuda*, horses.

 Budak, child; *budak-budak*, children.

Only observation of Malay usage will guide the student in learning the nouns that can be reduplicated. There is no rule that is fixed, other than to say that the names of living creatures may be reduplicated, and that undefined nouns standing alone may be treated as plural.

DERIVATIVE NOUNS.

The Malay system of prefixes and suffixes can change verbs and other parts of speech into nouns.

Prefix P, often with a "bridge letter," usually indicates an agent. When used with the suffix *an*, an abstract noun is formed:

 Bunoh, kill; *Pĕmbunoh*, murderer; *Pĕmbunohan*, murder.

 Ajar, teach; *Pĕngajar*, teacher; *Pĕngajaran*, teaching, doctrine.

(53) *Choba*, attempt; *Pĕnchoba*, tempter; *Pĕnchobaan*, temptation.

The suffix *an* generally denotes the thing that is affected by the action expressed by the verb:

(31) *Makan*, eat; *Makanan*, thing eaten, food.

 Minum, drink; *Minuman*, thing drunk, beverage.

The Prefix K forms nouns from verbs:

(17) *Hĕndak,* wish; *Kĕhĕndak,* will, desire.

The prefix *k* with the suffix *an* forms nouns, generally abstract, from other nouns and from other parts of speech:

(15) *Raja,* king; *kĕrajaan,* kingdom.

(59) *Jahat,* wicked; *kĕjahatan,* wickedness.

The suffix *an* with reduplication may express multiplicity:

(34, 35) *Hari,* day; (*sa-*) *hari-harian,* daily.

When two nouns stand together, the second is in the possessive case:

(31, 44) *Makanan orang,* man's food (also *orang punya makanan*).

(5, 31) *Makanan kami,* our food (also *kami punya makanan*).

The word *punya* makes any noun a possessive. The *punya* possessive must stand before its object.

PERSONAL PRONOUNS.

There is no variation in the form of the pronouns to indicate case:

sahaya, saya, aku,	I, me, my (5, 27, 41, 51, 56)
ĕngkau,	thou, thee, thine
dia,	he, she, it,
	him, her, his, its.
kita, kami,	we, us, our
kamu,	you, your
dia, dia-orang,	they, them, their

The personal pronouns are often shortened or changed in the possessive case.

(12, 13) *Nama kamu,* or *nama-mu,* your name.

(15) *Kĕrajaan kamu,* or *kĕrajaan-mu,* your kingdom.

(17, 18) *Kĕhĕndak kamu,* or *kĕhĕndak-mu,* your will.

Nama aku, or *nama-ku,* my name;

(11) *Dia* becomes *nya;*

Nama dia, or *nama-nya,* his, her, its or their name.

Kira-nya (pray, prithee), changes an imperative to a request or prayer.

RELATIVE PRONOUN.

There is only one, *yang*. It means who, which, that, what.
(6, 32, 45, 58)

DEMONSTRATIVE PRONOUNS.

(30) *Ini*, this, these; *itu*, that, those.

There are no articles, a, an, or the. The demonstratives substitute for them.

INTERROGATIVE PRONOUNS.

Siapa, who? (44, 30): *Siapa orang ini?*, who is this man?

Apa macham, what kind of? (31, 30): *Apa macham makanan ini?*, what kind of food is this?

Mana, where? (interrogative adverb): (15) *Di-mana raja itu?*, where is the king?

By adding the suffix *-kah*, we make any word interrogative: *Datang-kah orang itu?*, is that man coming?

ADJECTIVES.

The adjective normally follows the noun it qualifies: (44, 59) *Orang jahat*, the wicked man.

Orang yang jahat, the man who (is) wicked.

For reasons of emphasis it may stand elsewhere.

Comparison of adjectives:

lěbeh, lagi, more; *kurang*, less; *dari-pada*, than, from; *sama....děngan, sěpěrti*, equally....with, as....as; *sa-kali* (one time, i. e. uniquely), most, superlative **degree**, frequently used with the relative *yang*.

(59, 44, 15.)

Lěbeh   jahat   orang   ini   dari-pada   raja.
More   evil   man   this   than (the) king.

Kurang   jahat   orang   ini   dari-pada   raja.
Less   evil   man   this   than (the)   king.

(30, 44, 58, 59)

Ini-lah   orang   yang   jahat   sa-kali.
This (is the) man   who(is) evil   most.

Orang	*ini*	*sama*	*jahat*	*děngan*	*raja.*
Man	this	equally	evil		with (the) king.

Orang	*ini*	*sama*	*jahat*	*sěpěrti*	*raja.*
Man	this	as	evil		as (the) king.

ADVERBS.

Pula, again; *pun,* also; *juga,* likewise, nevertheless.

Time: *sěkarang,* now; *tadi,* just now; *kělmarin,* yesterday; *ini hari,* today; *besok,* tomorrow.

Place: *sini,* here; *sana, situ,* there; *luar,* outside; *dalam,* inside; (20) *atas,* on, above; *bawah,* below, under.

PREPOSITIONS.

(7) *di-,* at, in; (20) *atas,* on, on top of; *di-atas,* upon; (26) *akan,* to; (47) *pada,* to; (28) *pada,* to (time); (57) *dari-pada,* from (persons); *dari,* from (places), *ka-,* to (motion).

CONJUNCTIONS.

(54) *mělainkan,* but (German *sondern*); *tětapi,* but (German *aber*); *dan,* and; *atau,* or; *kalau,* if; *sěbab,* because; *supaya,* in order that.

PUNCTUATION WORDS.

In Malay, when written in the Arabic characters, there are no punctuation marks. Certain words help with the work of punctuation, introducing new sentences and paragraphs, and breaking into sentences themselves. They need not be translated. Yet they are carried over bodily into Romanized editions of Malay works and do double duty alongside the modern punctuation system.

(36) *maka,* may be translated, if at all, by the word "and".

bahwa introduces narration.

ada pun, introduces a parenthetical clause, or calls the reader back to the main story after a digression.

běrmula, takes up a new subject, paragraph, chapter.

dan lagi, continues the same subject.

These and others will become familiar in reading.

INTERJECTIONS.

There are many as in all languages.

(3)   *Ya, O!*, from the Arabic, used in prayer and in addressing holy persons.

NUMERALS.

(33) *Sa-* is a shortened form of the numeral *satu* meaning one.

1 — *satu*, or *sa-*	6 — *ĕnam*
2 — *dua*	7 — *tujoh*
3 — *tiga*	8 — *dĕlapan*
4 — *ĕmpat*	9 — *sĕmbilan*
5 — *lima*	10 — *sa-puloh* (*satu puloh*, one ten)

Bĕlas is another word for *puloh*

11 — *sa-bĕlas* (*satu* added to *bĕlas*)

12 — *dua-bĕlas*, and so on up to 19, when *puloh* returns.

With *puloh* the first number is a multiplier.

20 — *dua-puloh*	100 — *sa-ratus* (*satu ratus*)
21 — *dua-puloh-satu*	101 — *sa-ratus satu*
32 — *tiga-puloh-dua*	200 — *dua-ratus*
43 — *ĕmpat-puloh-tiga*	1000 — *sa-ribu*
54 — *lima-puloh-ĕmpat*	2000 — *dua-ribu*

And so on to 99.

ORDINAL NUMBERS.

Ordinal numbers are formed by adding the prefix *kĕ* to the cardinal numbers, and putting the relative pronoun before the new word.

3   — *tiga*   3rd — *yang kĕtiga*

1st — *yang pĕrtama* (irregular)

2nd — *yang kĕdua*

4th — *yang kĕĕmpat*

5th — *yang kĕlima*

Without the *yang*, groups are meant. Collectives: *kĕdua*, both; *kĕtiga*, all three; *kĕlima*, all five, etc.

FRACTIONS.

The prefix *pĕr* added to the cardinal numbers gives the corresponding fractions. Note following the two exceptions, *tĕngah* and *suku*.

1/2 — *sa-tĕngah* (*tĕngah* means "a half")

2/3 — *dua pĕrtiga*

3/4 — *tiga pĕrĕmpat*, or commonly *tiga-suku* (*suku* means a "quarter" in Malaya, ½ guilder or 35 cents in Java; D. M. ¼ — *sa pĕrapat*; ¾ — *tiga pĕrapat*).

4/5 — *ĕmpat pĕrlima*

6/10—*ĕnam pĕrpuloh*

VERBS.

The verb is not inflected. It cannot show number, person, or tense.

Verbs are either primitive or derivative. The primitives are verbs in their original signification (14, 16, 25, 52). The derivative verbs are made from primitive verbs, nouns and adjectives and adverbs by the application of particles (37, 43, 50, 55). Transitive verbs are formed from all other parts of speech by the addition of *-kan* and *-i*.

(37) *Ampun*, pardon (noun); *ampunkan*, pardon (verb)

(55) *Lĕpas*, after (preposition), free, loose; *lĕpaskan*, deliver (verb)

(43) *Ampun*, pardon (noun); *mĕng-ampun-i*, pardon (verb) *Jalan*, walk; *jalankan*, cause to walk.

THE PREFIX *M*

The Malays use the prefix *M* (with a bridge letter where needed) with transitive verbs in the active voice. Exception is made when the verb is in the imperative mood, in which case the particle of intensity *lah* is added. In communication between Malays and foreigners the prefix M is largely left unemployed.

(50) *Mĕmbawa*, bring; *bawa-lah*, bring (imperative; 14, 16, 25, 37, 49, 55)

BRIDGE LETTERS WITH THE PREFIX *M*

None before l, m, n, r, w, y:
> *Lihat,* see; *mĕlihat,* see
> *Makan,* eat; *mĕmakan,* eat, etc.

M before b and p; but the p drops out:
> *Bunoh,* kill; *mĕmbunoh,* kill
> *Padam,* extinguish; *mĕmadam,* extinguish

N before t, d, j, ch; but t drops out:
> *Dapat, mĕndapat,* find.
> *Churi, mĕnchuri,* steal
> *Taroh, mĕnaroh,* put.
> *Tidor, mĕnidor,* sleep.

Ng before k, g, h, or any vowel; but k drops out:
> (43) *Mĕngampuni,* from *ampun,* pardon
> *kĕpit, mĕngĕpit,* to carry under the arm
> *gigit, mĕnggigit,* to bite.

Ny before s; but s drops out:
> *Suroh, mĕnyuroh,* order

Note: it is the *unvoiced* consonant that is dropped.
Exceptions are extremely rare.

THE PASSIVE VOICE.

The passive is formed by the prefix *di-*:
(25) *Bĕri,* give; *di-bĕri,* is given.
The preposition *oleh* governs the agent:
(31, 25, 44, 26, 15) *Makanan di-bĕri oleh orang akan*
> Food was given by the man to the
> *raja.*
> king.

A passive may also be formed by using the verb *kĕna* before another verb. It also translates the English word *get*.
Dia kĕna bunoh, he was (got) killed.
Dia kĕna hukum, he was (got) punished.
Dia kĕna sakit, he got sick.
Kĕna standing alone means "hit the mark".

THE PREFIX *TĔR*

This prefix provides a past participle, but its various uses cannot be gathered up in a single term.

(9) *Hormat-lah*, honor (imperative)

Tĕrhormat-lah, may be called a past participle, yet in this case it is used in the imperative mood. Hence, honored be, or hallowed be.

Buka, open; *tĕrbuka*, opened.

THE PREFIX *BĔR*

We call the forms with *bĕr* present participles, but they do not direct the thought so much to the action itself as to the state of the persons who perform the actions.

A verb with this prefix can be expressed by our present participle:

(44) *Orang bĕrlari*, the man is running.

Lari, run; *bĕrlari*, running.

A noun with this prefix has in it the idea of possession:

(44, 45, 46) *Orang yang bĕrhutang pada kami*, the man who is having a debt toward us.

Hutang, debt; *bĕrhutang*, having a debt.

(44, 15) *Orang bĕrraja*, a man who has a king.

Verbs with this prefix may be reflexive or reciprocal.

AUXILIARIES.

(42) *Sudah*. This word indicates past time. To translate it into English, the context must tell whether to use was, did, has, or had.

The verb *habis*: *Sudah* expresses completed action in the past. *Habis* expresses more emphatically that the action is finished, utterly, entirely, once for all.

Orang sudah makan, the man has eaten.

Orang sudah habis makan, the man has completely finished eating.

Following is a list of auxiliaries with a list of English

words that will translate them. The context must guide in the choice.

Ada, is, are, was, were, possess.
Tiada, is not, will not
Akan, will, shall, would, should
(17) *Hĕndak*, will, shall, would, should
Mau, will, shall, would, should
Boleh, can, could, may, might
Dapat, can, could, may, might
Patut, ought
Mĕsti, must
Nanti, will, shall
Raja ini boleh bĕri makanan pada kami, this king can
   15   30   25   31   47   48

                                              give food to us.
Orang ini mau datang pada bapa, this man will come to
   44   30   14   47   4

                                              father.
Kami patut mĕngampuni hutang-hutang, we ought to for-
   5   43   38

                                            give debts.

The Verb *ADA*, "to be"

Ada, to be, existence in time or place.
It asserts presence or existence:
    Ada orang di-atas bumi, there are people on the earth.
       44   19 20
    Ada may be used as the equivalent of "to be" when adverbs of place follow or are understood. It is never the equivalent of "to be" followed by adjectives. The Malays join their adjectives to nouns without a copula.
It expresses progressive action when joined to another verb:
    Orang ada makan, people are eating.
      44   31
It asserts possession in the form that we call the Dative of Possession:

Pada orang ada makanan, the man has food
   47   44   31.   (to the man is food).

Colloquially this *pada* is usually suppressed, and the sentence becomes: *Orang ada makanan,* the man has food.

Ada in conversation expresses our verb *to have,* (to possess). Thus the object of a preposition becomes the subject of the sentence, and the real subject becomes the object. In good writing the verb *ada* is seldom the equivalent of the English *to have;* the *pada* is not omitted.

Ada may serve as a "Punctuation Word", introducing sentences without being necessary to their meaning. It may then be ignored in translation, or translated by some English introductory word such as "now", "there", etc.

Ada-lah nama raja itu, Raja Da'ud, now the name of that king (was) Raja Da'ud.

Ada pun pada masa itu datang-lah raja itu dari Hindi, now at that time came the king from India.

Ada may be used to round off and close a sentence with emphasis, expressing some sentiment like, "And this is the truth", or, "And this is a fact". In this case the syllable *nya* is added, *ada-nya.*

Sĕgala pĕrbuatan-nya baik   ada-nya.
   All   works   his   good   (and that is a fact).

NEGATIVE AUXILIARIES.

Tidak: Kami tidak boleh makan, we cannot eat.
Bukan: Orang ini bukan raja kami, this man is *not* our king.

Bĕlum: Not yet. Very frequently used. In a multitude of cases where we give a direct negative answer, the Malays say "not yet". Is he married? English answer: No. Malay answer, *Bĕlum,* not yet.

WORDS AND PHRASES.

Good morning, good evening, good-by, farewell, (a general greeting), *tabek.*

How do you do, how are you, how goes it, etc., *apa khabar?* (literally, what's the news?)

I am well, *khabar baik* (literally, the news is good).

What time is it?, *pukul bĕrapa?* (literally, how many strikes?).

It is two o'clock, *pukul dua* (literally, it has struck twice).

half past two o'clock, *pukul dua sa-tengah* (lit., strikes two and a half; D. M., *sa-tĕngah tiga*).

Noon (midday), *tĕngah hari.*

Midnight, *tĕngah malam.*

It is five minutes to six, *kurang lima minit pukul anam.*

It is a quarter to five, *kurang suku pukul lima* (D. M., *pukul lima kurang sa-pĕrapat*).

Next year, *tahun datang.*

Last year, *tahun lalu.*

Next month, *bulan datang.*

Last month, *bulan lalu.*

Every day, daily, *sa-hari-hari.*

The whole day, all day long, *sa-panjang hari.*

Please (try), *choba; minta* (more polite).

Tell me, *bilang pada sahaya* (D. M., *kasih* (or *bĕri*) *tahu pada saya*).

Bring, *bawa.*

Show, *tunjok.*

Thank you, *tĕrima kaseh.*

Pardon me, *sahaya minta ampun* (D. M., *maap; maaf*).

I am glad, *sahaya bĕrsuka.*

I have to, I must, *sahaya mĕsti.*

Where are you going?, *pĕrgi mana?* (D. M., *ka-mana?; pĕrgi ka-mana?*).

Which way?, *jalan mana?*

To the right, *ka-sĕbĕlah kanan.*

On the right, *di-sĕbĕlah kanan.*

To the left, *ka-sĕbĕlah kiri.*

Straight ahead, *maju; těrus.*
Here, *di-sini.*
There, *di-situ.*
In that way (manner), *bagitu.*
In this way (manner), *bagini.*
Come with me, *datang-lah sama sahaya* (D. M., *ikut saya; turut sama saya*).
What do you wish?, *apa tuan mau?*
What is that?, *apa itu?*
What is the matter with you?, *apa salah?*
What is the price?, *běrapa harga?*
Do you speak Malay?, *tuan tahu chakap Mělayu?*
A little, *sědikit.*
Speak slowly, *chakap pělan-pělan* (D. M., *minta bichara pělahan-pělahan*).
Do you understand?, *měngěrti-kah?* (D. M., *apa měngěrti?*).
I do not understand, *sahaya tidak měngěrti.*
Do you know?, *tahu-kah?* (D. M., *apa tahu?*).
I cannot, *sahaya tidak boleh* (D. M., *saya tida bisa*).
I can, *sahaya boleh* (D. M., *saya bisa*).
What is the name of that in Malay?, *apa nama itu děngan bahasa Mělayu?*
I am an American, *sahaya orang Merican.*
I am thirsty, *sahaya dahaga, sahaya haus.*
I am hungry, *sahaya lapar.*
How old are you?, *běrapa 'umur?*
I am twenty years old, *'umur sahaya dua-puloh tahun.*
How long have you lived here?, *běrapa lama-kah tuan dudok di-sini?*
Come here, *mari sini.*
Come in, *masok.*
Look!, *tengok!*
Look out!, Be careful!, *jaga baik-baik!* (D. M., *awas!; ati-ati!*).
Don't, *jangan.*
Don't forget, *jangan lupa.*
Don't run, *jangan lari.*

Go, *pĕrgi.*

Go away, *pĕrgi sana* (D. M., *pĕrgi-lah*).

Go quickly, *pĕrgi lĕkas.*

That is correct, *itu bĕtul.*

There is no more, *tiada lagi.*

Where is there a restaurant?, *di-mana rumah makan?*

I do not know, *sahaya kurang pĕreksa* (D. M., *tidak tahu;*
    bĕlum tahu; kurang tĕrang).

Call on me when you pass, *singgah sambil lalu.*

They are all alike, *sa-rupa sahaja sĕmua-nya.*

What does it contain?, *apa isi-nya?*

Have you a room vacant?, *ada bilek kosong?* (D. M., *apa ada*
    kamar kosong?).

Where does this road lead?, *jalan ini sampai ka-mana?*

I feel ill, *sahaya sakit* (D. M., *saya rasa sakit*).

What are you looking for?, *apa tuan chari?*

I think it is going to rain, *sahaya fikir mau hujan.*

Close the windows and the door, *tutup jĕndela dan pintu.*

I do not want to get wet, *sahaya ta'mau kĕna hujan.*

You ought to, *patut ĕngkau* (D. M., *patut kamu*).

What is your occupation?, *pĕkĕrjaan tuan?* (D. M., *pĕkĕrjaan*
    tuan apa?; tuan pĕkĕrjaannya apa?).

He has never seen a tiger, *dia bĕlum pĕrnah mĕlihat harimau.*

I shall remove to Singapore next month, *sahaya mau bĕrpindah*
    ka-Singapura lain bulan.

He is writing (continuous), *dia ada tulis, dia tĕngah tulis.*

to day, *ini hari*

tomorrow, *besok*

last night, *malam tadi,*
    sĕmalam

early, *siang*

now, *sĕkarang*

fast, *lĕkas*

yes, *ya*

very much, *banyak*

yesterday, *kĕlmarin*

tonight, *ini malam*

tomorrow morning, *besok*
    pagi

late, *lambat*

afterwards, *lĕpas*

slowly, *pĕlan-pĕlan*

no, *tidak*

how much, how many?,
    bĕrapa?

too much, too many, *tĕrlam-*

pau	at once, *sĕkarang ini*
small, *kĕchil*	large, *bĕsar*
poor, *miskin*	rich, *kaya*
beautiful, *elok*	ugly, *odoh*
young, *muda*	old, *tua*
good, *baik*	bad, *jahat*
strong, *kuat*	weak, *lĕmah*
white, *puteh*	black, *hitam*
red, *merah*	green, *hijau*
blue, *biru*	yellow, *kuning*
house, *rumah*	door, *pintu*
cigarette, *rokok*	cigar, *chĕrutu*
army, *tĕntĕra*	enemy, *musoh*
head, *kĕpala*	face, *muka*
mouth, *mulut*	eye, *mata*
ear, *tĕlinga*	tooth, *gigi*
arm, *lĕngan*	hand, *tangan*
foot, leg, *kaki*	bone, *tulang*
blood, *darah*	to eat, *makan*
to drink, *minum*	meat, *daging*
money, *wang*	to pay, *bayar*
expensive, *mahal*	cheap, *murah*
to sell, *jual*	to buy, *bĕli*
horse, *kuda*	dog, *anjing*
ox, *lĕmbu*	chicken, *ayam*
to speak, *chakap*	to say, *kata*
to ask, *tanya*	to answer, *jawab*
man, *orang*	woman, *pĕrĕmpuan*
child, *anak*	water, *ayer*
to come, *datang*	to go, *pĕrgi*
to see, *lihat*	to like, *suka*
to want, *mau*	to know, *tahu*
to live, *hidup*	to die, *mati*
to give, *bĕri*	to take, *ambil*
to lose, *hilang*	to find, *dapat*
to do, to make, *buat*	to carry, *bawa*

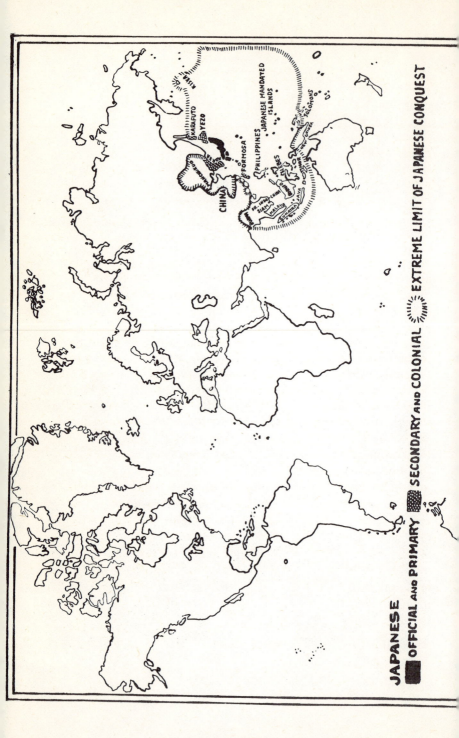

JAPANESE

■ OFFICIAL AND PRIMARY   ▨ SECONDARY AND COLONIAL   ☼ EXTREME LIMIT OF JAPANESE CONQUEST

CHINA

SIAM

KARAFUTO

YEZO

FORMOSA

PHILIPPINES

JAPANESE MANDATED ISLANDS

FR. INDO-CHINA

SIAM

MALAYA

SUMATRA

JAVA

CELEBES

BORNEO

NEW GUINEA

SOLOMONS

CHAPTER XIV

JAPANESE

BY RALPH WALKER SCOTT, PH. D.

*Professor of Romance Languages at Trinity College, Hartford, Conn.
Former Professor of Occidental Languages at Rikkyo University,
Tokyo, Japan.*

SPEAKERS AND LOCATION.

(All population figures are approximate)

Asia and Oceania — The population of the Japanese
Empire prior to the seizure of Manchukuo was estimated at
about 100,000,000, distributed as follows: Japan proper,
72,000,000; Korea, 25,000,000; Taiwan (Formosa), 5,500,-
000; Karafuto (the southern part of the island of Sakhalin),
500,000. It is fairly safe to assume that practically all of
these populations may be reached with Japanese. To these
may be added the mandated Bismarck, Caroline, Marianas,
Gilbert and Marshall Islands, with a total population of slightly
over 500,000.

The Manchukuo conquest brought about 43,000,000
people, mostly of Chinese stock and speech, under Japanese
domination. The areas of China overrun and dominated by
Japan (including the important cities of Peiping, Tientsin,
Nanking, Hankow, Shanghai, Hangchow, Wenchow, Foochow,
Amoy, Swatow, and Canton) may be estimated to have well
over 100,000,000 inhabitants. Japanese was to some extent
current in all this territory.

With Japan's entry into the war, Nippon's temporary
territorial acquisitions included Thailand (16,000,000); French
Indo-China (24,500,000); British Malaya (5,500,000);

Burma (16,000,000); Hong Kong (1,500,000); the Netherlands East Indies (60,000,000); the Philippines (16,000,000);
British possessions on the islands of Borneo and New Guinea
(about 2,000,000); Portuguese Timor (500,000); and
various South Pacific islands (Guam, New Hebrides, northern
Solomons, etc. — about 250,000). To what extent the Japanese
language has penetrated these now liberated populations totalling nearly 140,000,000 is a matter of conjecture.

Japanese speakers are fairly numerous in Hawaii, while
small Japanese communities exist in various parts of North
and South America. Exact figures are not available, but it is
unlikely that the total number of Japanese speakers outside
of Japanese-held territory exceeds 2,000,000.

THE WRITTEN LANGUAGE

The Japanese language proper has no relation whatever
to Chinese. They are as far apart as English and Japanese.
However, many Chinese words have entered into the Japanese,
just as Norman French words came into English.

Chinese literature was introduced into Japan about
300 A.D. and the Japanese adopted the Chinese system of writing. In Chinese, the written characters are symbols of ideas,
or of things. In other words, the Chinese and Japanese use
ideograms, or picture-words, to express ideas or concepts.
There are many thousands of these ideograms, and in
order to read a newspaper or non-technical book, the
student must learn three or four thousand ideograms, at least.
To read literature, he will need six or seven thousand ideograms.
Now Japanese is an inflected language and phonetic symbols
are necessary to indicate the inflections. Hence at a very early
date the Japanese began to use some ideograms phonetically.
These few phonetic characters are simplified forms of the
ideograms from which they evolved and are known as *kana*.
These *kana* characters, although phonetic, are not alphabetic,
but syllabic. That is, each *kana* character represents a syllable,
such as *ru, ju, mu, fu,* etc. There are two sets of these *kana*

characters, one known as the *kata-kana* and the other as the *hira-gana*. Each set has 48 syllabic characters in common use. The *kata-kana* is written in a square style and is now used chiefly in formal documents, in transliterating foreign names and in writing telegrams. The *hira-gana* syllabary is written cursively and is more complicated than the *kata-kana*, but is nevertheless the syllabary most commonly used by the Japanese.

The *hira-gana* syllabary is used in two ways. First, it serves to express the inflections, that is, the changing portions of Japanese parts of speech, such as verb endings. Again, in popular publications, such as newspapers and magazines, it is printed alongside of and to the right of the Chinese ideograms, in order to aid the less educated reader in making out the pronunciation of the Chinese ideogram. An example may make this clearer.

As we have just said, the Chinese ideogram is the symbol of an idea, a word picture. For example, the character 川 means river. It was originally the picture of a river, the currents of water being pictured thus 〜 . Now the ideogram is read as "river" in English and as *kawa* in Japanese. There is no way of indicating the genitive case, "of the river" (*kawa no* in Jap.) or the accusative case (*kawa wo* in Jap.). Hence we use the *hira-gana* syllabic character の to denote "of" (*no* in Jap.) and " を " to denote *wo* the Japanese sign of the accusative case or direct object. Thus *kawa no* 川 の ; *kawa wo* 川 を . In modern, written Japanese, these *hira-gana* characters are found interspersed among the Chinese ideograms in order to indicate particles, modifiers and syntactical terminations.

As we have indicated above, the *hira-gana* may also be printed to the immediate right of a more difficult Chinese ideogram in order to indicate its correct pronunciation. Thus, we may take this same ideogram 川 , although it is not a difficult one, and write the *hira-gana* to the right of it, 川 か : か , *ka* and わ *wa*, both spelling out the word *kawa*. river.

In writing Japanese, the ideograms and accompanying *kana* symbols begin at the upper right-hand corner and run down the page. The next vertical line of writing begins to the left of the first line and runs down, and so on. Japanese is thus read from top to bottom, and from right to left.

Japanese can of course be written in the Latin alphabet. The Japanese themselves have been interested in giving up the difficult and cumbersome Chinese characters and in adopting the Latin alphabet of the west. A society known as the *Rōmajikwai* (Roman Letter Society) was organized in 1885 to encourage the use of our alphabet in the place of the Chinese characters. However, the influence of custom and history have so far proved too strong, and Japan is still far from accepting our alphabet. The military defeat of Japan may well hasten the movement, however.

SAMPLE OF PRINTED JAPANESE
(in Kana-Majiri characters: mixed Chinese characters and Hiragana)

ヨハネ傳 三・二

言ふ『いかで斯る事どものあり得べき』。イエス答へて言ひ給ふ『なんぢはイスラエルの師にして猶かかる事どもを知らぬか。一一誠にまことに汝に告ぐ、我ら知ることを語り、また見しことを證す、然るに汝らその證を受けず。一二われ地のことを言ふに汝ら信ぜずば、天のことを言はんには爭で信ぜんや。一三天より降りし者、即ち人の子の他には、天に昇りしものなし。一四モーセ荒野にて蛇を擧げしごとく、人の子もまた必ず擧げらるべし。一五すべて信ずる者の彼によりて永遠の生命を得んな

『り』

一六それ神はその獨子を賜ふほどに世を愛し給へり、すべて彼を信ずる者の亡びずして永遠の生命を得んためなり。一七神その子を世に遣したまへるは、世を審かん爲にあらず、彼によりて世の救はれん爲なり。一八彼を信ずる者は審かれず、信ぜぬ者は既に審かれたり。神の獨子の名を信ぜざりしが故なり。一九その審判は是なり。光、世にきたりしに、人その行爲の惡しきによりて、光よりも暗黒を愛したり。二〇すべて惡を行ふ者は光をにくみて光に來らず、その行爲の責められざらん爲なり。二一眞をおこなふ者は光にきたる、その行爲の神によりて行ひたることの顯れん爲なり。

(Courtesy of American Bible Society)

THE JAPANESE SYLLABARIES

Hiragana	Katakana		Hiragana	Katakana
I, Yi	い	イ	Wi	ゐ	ヰ
Ro	ろ	ロ	No	の	ノ
Ha	は	ハ	O	れ	オ
Ni	に	ニ	Ku	く	ク
Ho	ほ	ホ	Ya	や	ヤ
He	へ	ヘ	Ma	ま	マ
To	と	ト	Ke	け	ケ
Chi	ち	チ	Fu	ふ	フ
Ri	り	リ	Ko	こ	コ
Nu	ぬ	ヌ	E, Ye	ゑて	エ
Ru	る	ル	Te	て	テ
Wo	を	ヲ	A	あ	ア
Wa	わ	ワ	Sa	さ	サ
Ka	か	カ	Ki	き	キ
Yo	よ	ヨ	Yu	ゆ	ユ
Ta	た	タ	Me	め	メ
Re	れ	レ	Mi	み	ミ
So	そ	ソ	Shi	し	シ
Tsu	つ	ツ	We	ゑ	ヱ
Ne	ね	ネ	Hi	ひ	ヒ
Na	な	ナ	Mo	も	モ
Ra	ら	ラ	Se	せ	セ
Mu	む	ム	Su	す	ス
U, wu	う	ウ	N	ん	ン

This arrangement of the Japanese syllabaries is the work of a ninth-century Buddhist priest, and spells out a complete poem on the frailty of human affairs.

In the Hiragana syllabary, no distinction in common usage is made between syllables beginning with *k* and those beginning with *g*, so that the symbols given above for *ka, ke, ki, ko, ku* may represent also the sounds *ga, ge, gi, go, gu;* the same lack of distinction appears between the *s* and the *z*-sounds, the *t* and the *d*-sounds, the *h, b* and *p*-sounds, and between the syllables *chi* and *ji, shi* and *zhi, tsu* and *dzu, fu, bu* and *pu.*

The Katakana syllabary distinguishes between unvoiced and voiced consonants by placing a double stroke, somewhat like our ", above and to the right of the character if this is meant to designate a voiced consonant, so that the symbols for *ka, ke, ki, ko, ku,* when accompanied by this double stroke, represent *ga, ge, gi, go, gu,* etc. Furthermore, in the Katakana, the symbols for *ha, he, hi, ho, fu,* if accompanied by a small circle above and to the right, stand for *pa, pe, pi, po, pu,* respectively. With a double stroke instead of a circle, the *h* and *f*-symbols represent *b*-sounds.

PRONUNCIATION.

Vowel Sounds.

a = c*o*t;

ā = f*a*r;

e = m*e*t;

ē (ei) = *ei*ght;

i = b*i*g (short i has a feeble sound, and tends to disappear, most frequently *within* the word, seldom at the *end* of the word; *Yamashita* is pronounced *Yamash'ta*);

ī (ii) = mach*i*ne;

o = *o*bey;

ō = h*o*ly;

u = p*u*sh (short u has a feeble sound, and tends to disappear, both within and at the end of a word (*kusa,* "grass", pron. *k'sa; desu,* pron. *des'*; it does not disappear, however, in *-ru* verb-endings);

ū = r*u*de.

Distinguish carefully between short and long vowels; many words are alike, save for long or short vowels (compare: *tori,* "bird"; *tōri,* "street"; *toki,* "time"; *tōki.*" registration"; *yuki,* "snow"; *yūki,* "courage"). The most frequently recurring long vowels are ō and ū. Pronounce the former like h*o*ly in an exclamation (Holy Jiminy!) ; the latter like food, likewise in an exclamation (We want food!).

If two vowels appear together, pronounce them separately (*ataeru*, "to give", pron. *a-ta-e-ru*).

Consonant Sounds.

b = *b*ed;
d = *d*ebt;
f = *f*ood, produced, however, by bringing the lower lip against the upper lip, not against the upper teeth, as in English;
g = *g*ave; often si*ng*
h = *h*e; this sound in the Tōkyō dialect approaches *she* (*hito*, "human being", pron. *shito* or *sh'to*) ;
j = *j*oy;
k = *k*eep;
m = *m*an;
n = *n*ame; before g, = fi*n*ger; before k, = ba*n*ker;
p = *p*en;
r = British ve*r*y; the trill is so slight that the listener is often in doubt whether the sound is r or l;
s = *s*ee;
t = *t*ale;
w = *w*ave;
y = *y*ard;
z = *z*eal;
ch = *ch*urch;
sh = *sh*ore;
ts = i*ts*;
dz = a*dz*e.

Double consonants (kk, nn, pp, mm, ss, ssh, tch, tt, tts) are fully pronounced.

In compound words, the *first* consonant of the *second* half of the compound often undergoes a change, as follows:

h, f become b (*sakura*, "cherry", plus "*hana*, "blossom", to *sakurabana*, "cherry blossom"; *te*, "hand", plus *fukuro*, "bag", to *tebukuro*, "glove") ;

k becomes g (*ko*, "small", plus *katana*, "sword", to *kogatana*, "pen-knife");

s, ts become z (*kan*, "can", plus *tsume* "packed", to *kanzume*, "canned goods");

sh, ch become j (*chika-chika*, "soon-soon", to *chikajika*);

t becomes d (*Benten* plus *tōri*, "street", to *Bentendōri*, Benten Street").

Accent.

The strong tonic accent of English is not found in Japanese, all the syllables of a word being stressed about equally, thus not "Yokoháma", as in English, but *Yókóhámá*, every syllable having equal stress.

Long vowels and vowels before double consonants tend to be stressed, thus; (*jochū* "maidservant" (the ū being long is emphasized); *jōdan* "joke" (the ō being long is slightly stressed); *máppira* "earnestly" (the syllable má is stressed as it precedes a double consonant).

When the vowels i or u, which are by nature weak, drop out entirely from a word, in pronunciation, which very frequently happens, the preceding or following vowel is stressed, in compensation for the lost vowel; thus, General Yamashita's name is pronounced *Yamáshta*, (not *Yamashíta*) the preceding *a* being stressed in compensation for the lost *i*. *Taksán* "much" for *takusan*, the *san* being stressed in compensation for lost *u*.

Within the sentence, case particles (postpositions) are especially stressed: *Watakushi wá hon wó motte imasu,* I have a book.

GRAMMATICAL SURVEY

1. — *Nouns.*

a) — Number.

The Japanese mind is not so much interested in number or quantity as ours; consequently the Japanese seldom make a distinction between singular and plural. *Hana* means "flower" or "flowers". If a distinction must be made, it is done, especially in the case of human beings, by adding *domo, tachi* or *gata* to the word, by repeating the noun, or by adding an auxiliary numeral to the noun, thus: *ko*, child; *kodomo*, children; *watakushi*, I; *watakushidomo*, we; *danna*, master; *dannagata*, masters; *hito*, man, *hitobito*, people, *hito sannin*, three persons.

b) — Gender.

There is no grammatical gender in Japanese, such as is found in French and German. The gender of Japanese words is determined by sex, as in English. Sex can be distinguished in three ways: by a sex prefix; by prefixing another word indicating gender; by using a quite different word, as in English.

The masculine prefix is *o-* (sometimes *on-*) thus:

ushi, "cow"	*o-ushi*, "bull"
inu, "dog"	*o-inu*, "male dog"
tori, "bird"	*ondori*, "cock"

The female prefix is *me-* (sometimes *men-*) thus:

tori, "bird"	*mendori*, "hen"
inu, "dog"	*me-inu*, "bitch"

One may prefix the word *otoko no*, "male" (lit., man-of), or *onna no*, "female" (lit. woman-of): *ko*, "child"; *otoko no ko*, "boy"; *onna no ko*, "girl".

Generally a different word is used as in English; thus:

otoko, "man"	*onna*, "woman"
musuko, "son"	*musume*, "daughter"
chichi, "father"	*haha*, "mother"
oji, "uncle"	*oba*, "aunt"
shinshi, "gentleman"	*shukujo*, "lady"
otto, "husband"	*tsuma*, "wife"

c) — Articles.

The Japanese language has neither a definite nor an indefinite article. *Hon* means "the book", "a book", "book", "the books", "books".

d) — Case.

Japanese may be said to have five "cases".[1] These are not indicated by real declensional endings, but by particles placed after the noun. They are as follows:

absolute: *niwa wa*, "the garden", "gardens"
nominative: *niwa ga*, "garden", "gardens" (as subject of verb)
genitive: *niwa no*, "of garden", "of gardens"
dative: *niwa ni*, "to", "for garden", "gardens"
accusative: *niwa o*, (often written *wo*, but always pronounced *o*), "garden", "gardens" (object of a verb)

The case particles call for some comment. *Wa* and *ga* both may be used after the subject of a verb. *Wa* is frequently used when the verb is negative, *ga* when it is affirmative: *hon ga arimasu*, there are books, (literally, books there-are); *hon wa arimasen*, there are no books (literally, books there-are-not).

Wa emphasizes the predicate and *ga* emphasizes the subject. *Doko e ikimasu ka?*, where are you going? (*doko* = "where"; *e* = "to"; *ikimasu* = "go"; *ka* is an interrogative particle, the sign of a question; note that "you" is left to the hearer's understanding). *Watakushi wa Yokohama e iku*, I am going *to Yokohama*, not to some other city. That is, the particle *wa* after *watakushi* emphasizes the predicate "to Yokohama". *Dare ga ikimasu ka?*, *who* is going? (*dare* = "who"). *Watakushi ga iku*, *I* am going. That is, I, not some one else, am going.

Wa may also be used when the Japanese wish to isolate the subject and then ask a question about it. *Ano hito wa, dare desu ka?* As for that man, who is he? (cf. French, *cet homme-là, qui est-il?*).

No is the usual particle used to express possession, and

---

1. The word "case" is not scientifically used, since Japanese could be said to have as many "cases" as there are separate postpositions, and these are numerous; it is employed merely as a practical make-shift, designed to clarify unfamiliar Japanese syntax through familiar Indo-European terminology.

as such is often attached to a proper noun or a pronoun: *Brown San no,* Mr. Brown's (*San,* "Mr."); *dannasan no,* "of the master", "master's"; *watakushi no,* "my", "mine" (literally, "of me")

Ni is the case particle used to indicate the indirect object: *Hon wo Suzuki san ni yarimasu,* I give the book to Mr. Suzuki. (*hon* = "book"; *yarimasu* = "give")

The dative case may denote possession. *Watakushi ni oji ga arimasu,* I have an uncle (literally, to me uncle there-is; cf. French, *ce livre est à moi*).

With verbs of existence it denotes the locative. *Tôkyô ni takusan arimasu,* there are many at Tokyo. *Tsukue no ue ni hon ga takusan arimasu,* there are many books on the top of the table (*ue* = "top"; *tsukue* = "table"; *hon* = "books"; *takusan* = "many")

Some Japanese verbs govern the indirect object, while these same verbs in English would call for some other construction, thus — *Itsu Tanaka San ni aimashita ka?,* when did you meet Mr. Tanaka? (*itsu* = "when"; *aimashita* = past of verb *au*). *Ii* or *ī* (long *i*) *o tenki ni narimasu,* the weather is turning fine (*ii* = "fine"; *o* = "honorable"; *tenki* = "weather"; *narimasu* = "is becoming").

2. — *Personal Pronouns.*

There are no real personal pronouns in Japanese, but certain expressions may be used as pronouns. Even these pronominal expressions are but little used, since Japanese is an impersonal language. The meaning is made clear by the use of humble or honorific words, or by the context. Expressions which are used as personal pronouns are as follows:

Watakushi or *watashi* = I

Anata = you (singular)

Ano o kata (that honorable person); *ano hito* (that person); *ano onna* (that woman); *ano otoko* (that man) may all be used for "he" or "she".

Are = it, of a thing far off.

Watakushi-domo or *watashi-domo* = we
Anata-gata = you (plural)
Ano hito-tachi (of persons); *are* (of things) = they.

3. — *Postpositions.*

Japanese has no prepositions, but instead employs post-positions, that is, it uses particles placed AFTER the noun or pronoun. In speaking, these postpositions are commonly stressed or accentuated. Some common postpositions are —

De — denotes means, instrument, measure, value, time.

yūbin de, by post (literally, mail by).
takushi de, by taxi
pen de kaku, to write with a pen.
dāsu de kau, to buy by the dozen (dāsu - dozen)
go sen de katta, I bought it for five cents: (go = "five"; sen = "cents"; katta = past tense of kau, to buy)
ni fun de hachi ji, two minutes to eight (ni = "two"; fun = "minute"; hachi = "eight", ji = "hour" or "o'clock"; hence, literally, two minute by eight o'clock).

Kara — denotes "from", "after", and, with the gerund of the verb, "since".

kuni kara, from home
sore kara, after that
kore kara, after this, henceforth
Yokohama kara, from Yokohama
Tōkyō e kite kara, since coming to Tokyo (kite = "coming", gerund of verb kuru, to come)

E — denotes "to", "towards", "into".

hoteru e ikimasu, I am going to the hotel.
doko e ikimasu ka, where are you going? (literally "where to", "whither")

Made — denotes "up to", "as far as".

Yokohama kara Tōkyō made, from Yokohama to Tokyo.
doyōbi made, till Saturday
suteishon made, as far as the station

To — denotes, among other things, "with", "in company with",

ano hito to sampo ni ikimasu, I am going for a walk with

that person (*sampo* = "walk"; *ano* = "that"; *to* = "with", "in the company of"; *ni* = "for" or "on")

Ni — denotes "in", "into", "for" of purpose or end.

    uchi ni, in the house, at home

    sampo ni, for a walk

    Chicago ni, in or at Chicago. Cf. *Chicago e,* to or into Chicago.

    Eigo ni yakusuru, to translate into English.

    Kono mono wa nani ni tsukaimasu ka?, what do you use this thing for? (Literally, as for this thing, what for do you use it? *Mono* = thing; *nani* = what; *ni* = for; *tsukaimasu* = use)

4. — *Verbs.*[2]

The Japanese verb is completely "impersonal". It does not indicate person or number, but only tense and mood; it does, however, include the notion of familiarity, politeness, or extreme (honorific) politeness. A so-called present indicative, such as *kakimasu,* may be translated by "I, you, he, she, we, they write or writes" (the real meaning is "there is an action of writing going on"). It is possible to "personalize" it by using a subject pronoun (*watakushi wa kakimasu,* lit. "so far as I am concerned, there is a writing"); but subject pronouns are seldom employed, it being left to the hearer or reader to figure out who does the writing from the trend of the conversation or the context. On the other hand, the use of the form *kakimasu* implies a certain amount of politeness toward the hearer; the form *kaku* has precisely the same meaning as *kakimasu,* but implies familiarity. The honorific form is seldom used (at least by foreigners), and often consists of an entirely different verb (*taberu,* "to eat", familiar; *tabemasu,* "to eat", polite; *meshiagaru,* "to eat", honorific). The familiar form would

2. The Japanese verb system is exceedingly intricate, and an extensive treatment is outside the scope of this chapter. Only those verbal forms are presented which are essential to an elementary and practical knowledge of the language.

seldom be used by a foreigner, save for the fact that it normally appears in dependent clauses, even though the verb of the main clause is polite. There is no verb form in Japanese that really corresponds to our infinitive, although for convenience's sake we shall occasionally translate the familiar present as an English infinitive.

1. — Present Tense (familiar form).

The familiar present form ends in *-u* or *-ru*. Verbs ending in *-u* have stems ending in consonants: *yob-u*, calls (stem *yob*); *ka(f)-u*[3], buys; *kak-u*, writes; *nar-u*, becomes; *hanas-u*, speaks; *mats-u*[4], waits. Most, but not all, present tense forms ending in *-eru* and *-iru* have vowel stems, the *e* or the *i* of the endings *-eru*, *-iru*, forming the vowel-stem: *mi-ru*, sees; *de-ru*, goes out; *shirase-ru*, informs. Since these forms indicate tense only, not person, they may refer to any person: *hanasu*, I, you, he, she, we, they, speaks or speak.

This familiar form is used only between members of a family or between close friends. It is given here because this familiar form of the present is the one that will always be used in a subordinate clause, even in polite conversation.

2. — Present Indicative (polite, but not honorific).

This is formed by adding *-imasu* to the stem: *kak-imasu*, I, you, we, they, write; he, she writes (in polite, but not honorific speech). If subject pronouns are really needed, they may be used, with *wa* or *ga*: *watakushi wa kakimasu*, I write; *anata wa kakimasu*, you (sg.) write; *ano hito wa kakimasu*, he writes; *watakushi-domo wa kakimasu*, we write; *anata-gata wa kakimasu*, you (pl.) write; *ano hito-tachi wa kakimasu*, they write. It must again be stressed, however, that this is not the customary practice in Japanese. If the verb-stem ends in a vowel, only *-masu* is added: *mi-masu*, I, you, etc. see. If the

3. The final *-f* of verb stems is no longer pronounced, and is generally omitted in writing.

4. The real stem is *mat-*; *t* before *u* is regularly changed to *ts*.

stem of the verb ends in *t-*, this is changed to *ch-* before the *i* of
-imasu: *matsu*, to wait (stem *mat-*), present *mach-imasu*. If
the stem of the verb ends in *s-*, this is changed to *sh-* before the
i of *-imasu*: *hanasu*, to speak (stem *hanas-*), present *hanash-imasu*.[5]

3. — Past Indicative (polite, but not honorific).

This is formed by adding *-imashita* (*-mashita* if the stem
ends in a vowel): *kaku*, to write; past *kak-imashita*; *ka(f)u*,
to buy; past *ka-imashita*; *yob-imashita*, called; *nar-imashita*,
became; *hanash-imashita*, spoke; *mach-imashita*, waited;
mi-mashita, saw; *de-mashita*, went out.

4. — Future.

There is no true future tense in Japanese, the present
being used with a future meaning as well: *kakimasu*, I, you,
etc. write or will write.

A "future of probability" is formed by adding *deshō* to
the familiar present: *kaku deshō*, I, you, etc. will probably write;
ashita hon wo kau deshō, tomorrow he will probably buy the
book (books).

Another future of probability may be formed by adding
-ō (*-yō* if the stem ends in a vowel) to the stem: *kak-ō*, will
probably write; *ka-ō*, will probably buy; *mi-yō*, will probably
see.

5. — Conditional.

A "present conditional" is formed by adding *-imasureba*
(*-masureba* if the stem ends in a vowel), or *-eba* (*-reba* if the
stem ends in a vowel). It is used with the meaning of "if" or
"when" in the dependent clause, but never in the main clause:
watakushi ga kakimasureba (*kakeba*), if (when) I write (shall
write); *ano hito-tachi ga hanashimasureba* (*hanaseba*), if

5. These changes of *t* to *ch* and *s* to *sh* before *i* are general, and
apply to all tenses and, indeed, to all words. The same is true of the
change of *t* to *ts* before *u*. See *Katakana*, p. 530-531.

(when) they speak (will speak). The main clause in these cases takes whatever tense is called for by the meaning: *Tōkyō e ikimasureba, hoteru ni tomaru*, if (when) I go to Tokyo, I shall put up at a hotel (*tomaru* is the familiar present-future, the conversation here being between intimate friends; note the complete lack of subject pronouns; the sentence could mean not only "I", but also "you", "he", "she", "we", "they'); *Tōkyō e ikimasureba* (*ikeba*), *o miyage wo motte kitte kudasai*, when you go to Tokyo, please bring me a present (*motte kitte kudasai* being the polite imperative of *motte kuru*, "to bring", the subject here is obviously "you").

A "past conditional" is formed by adding *-imashitara* (*-mashitara* if the verb-stem ends in a vowel), and conveys the meaning of "if" or "when" with reference to the past: *anata ga kaimashitara*, when you bought; *anata ga machimashitara*, when (if) you waited. The past indicative usually appears in the main clause.

A more specific "if" may be formed by using the present or past with *moshi* before the verb and *nara* after it: *moshi watakushi ga kakimasu nara*, if I write, were I to write; *moshi anata ga ikimashita nara*, if you went, if you had gone.

6. — Participle.

A familiar present participle is formed by adding *-ite* (*-te* if the verb-stem ends in a vowel): *hanasu*, to speak; *hanash-ite*, speaking; *miru*, to see; *mi-te*, seeing. This *familiar* participle is of importance in *polite* conversation because it has two important *polite* uses: 1. with the present and past of various verbs meaning "to be", to form progressive present and past tenses: *hanashite orimasu* (*oru*, to be), am, is, are speaking; *mite orimashita*, was, were seeing; 2. with *kudasai*, "please", to form a *polite* imperative: *hanashite kudasai*, please speak (lit. speaking, please).[6]

6. The following contractions take place in the formation of the participle:

If the verb-stem ends in (*f*)-, *r*- or *t*-, *-tte* replaces *-ite*, *-rite*, *-chite*:

7. — Imperative.

The ordinary way to express a polite command is by using the *familiar* participle with *kudasai*, "please", as described above: *yonde kudasai*, please call (lit. calling, please); *katte kudasai*, please buy (buying, please).

"Let us" is expressed by adding *-imashō* (*-mashō* if the verb-stem ends in a vowel): *yob-imashō*, let us call; *ka-imashō*, let us buy; *kak-imashō*, let us write. With the addition of the interrogative particle *ka*, this form serves also as a first person future interrogative, singular or plural: *yobimashō ka?*, shall I (we) call?; *ikimashō ka?*, shall I (we) go?

8. — Conjugation with *suru*, "to do".

Chinese words, which have entered the Japanese language from the fifth century on, are generally conjugated with the irregular verb *suru*, to do (make), which has the following forms:

Present, *shimasu*; Past, *shimashita*; Pres. Cond., *shimasureba*; Past Cond., *shimashitara*; Participle, *shite*.

Kenkyū suru, to study (lit. study to do); *jōdan suru*, to jest (lit. joke to make); *shūzen suru*, to repair (lit. repair to make); *sōji suru*, to clean: Pres. *sōji shimasu*, I, you, etc. clean; Past *sōji shimashita*, I, you, etc. cleaned; Pres. Cond. *sōji shimasureba*, if (when) I, you, etc. clean; Participle, *sōji shite*, cleaning; Imperative, *sōji shite kudasai*, please clean.

9. — Familiar Forms.

The polite forms so far described are the ones most commonly used. When used with reference to the first person, they

---

ka(ƒ)u, to buy; *katte* (for *kaite*), buying; *naru*, to become, *natte* (for *narite*), becoming; *matsu*, to wait; *matte* (for *machite*), waiting. If the verb-stem ends in *b-*, *-nde* replaces *-bite*: *yobu*, to call; *yonde* (for *yobite*), calling.

If the verb-stem ends in *k-*, *-ite* replaces *-kite*: *kaku*, to write; *kaite* (for *kakite*), writing.

do not cast honor upon the speaker, but upon the person spoken to.

The familiar form of the verb is used within the family circle or among intimate friends and children, or to inferiors. Its present and past tenses, however, are also used in *polite* conversation in dependent clauses.

The familiar present has been described (verb-stem plus *-u* or *-ru*), while the familiar past is obtained by changing the *-e* of the participle to *-a*:

	Familiar Present	Familiar Past
yobu, to call	*yobu,* call, calls	*yonda,* called
ka(f)u, to buy	*kau,* buy, buys	*katta,* bought
kaku, to write	*kaku,* write, writes	*kaita,* wrote
naru, to become	*naru,* become, becomes	*natta,* became
hanasu, to speak	*hanasu,* speak, speaks	*hanashita,* spoke
matsu, to wait	*matsu,* wait, waits	*matta,* waited
miru, to see	*miru,* see, sees	*mita,* saw
deru, to go out	*deru,* go out, goes out	*deta,* went out

Outside of their use in familiar conversation, these two familiar tenses are used in polite speech to replace relative clauses. Japanese has no relative pronoun, and no true relative clause. The present or past of the familiar is used instead like an adjective before the antecedent: *kinō mita hito,* the man I saw yesterday (lit. yesterday saw man; compare Eng. "the shipwrecked man" for "the man who was shipwrecked"); *kaita tegami,* the letter I (you, he, etc.) wrote (lit. wrote letter).[7]

Familiar forms are used whenever the verb is subordinate to the principal verb, especially in temporal or causal clauses: *ii o tenki ni natta kara, ikimashō,* since the weather has turned fine, let us go (*ii,* fine; *o,* honorable; *tenki,* weather; *ni natta,* familiar past of *ni naru,* to become; *kara,* since (conjunction); *ikimashō,* let us go, from *iku,* to go. See Imperative, p. 542);

7. This use of the past familiar could perhaps be compared to that of a past participle used as an adjective, and the expressions above be translated as "the yesterday seen man", "the written letter".

hon wo katta kara, since I (you, etc.) bought the book; *chichi ga matte imasu kara*, since my father is waiting; *sore ga okotta toki*, when that happened (*sore ga*, that, demonstrative pronoun in the nominative case; *okotta*, familiar past of *okoru*, to happen; *toki*, when, conjunction of time).

10. — The verb "to be".

There are three verbs meaning "to be": *aru, oru, iru*. The latter two are generally used when there is an animate subject (person or animal), *aru* when the subject is inanimate. The stem of *iru* is *i-*, that of *oru* is *or-*; both verbs are used with the familiar participle to form a progressive present and past: *yonde imasu*, I (you, etc.) am calling (*yonde*, fam. part. of *yobu*; *imasu*, present of *iru*); *matte imashita*, I (you, etc.) was waiting (*matte*, fam. part. of *matsu*; *imashita*, past of *iru*); *kaite orimasu*, I (you, etc.) am writing (*kaite*, fam. part. of *kaku*; *orimasu*, present of *oru*); *hanashite orimashita*, I (you, etc.) was speaking (*hanashite*, fam. part. of *hanasu*; *orimashita*, past of *oru*).

The verb *aru*, used for inanimate subjects, means "to be" when a predicate noun appears; all predicate nouns used with *aru* must be followed by the postposition *de*: *kore wa hon de aru*, this is a book. The meaning "to have" is implied when only the subject appears, without a predicate noun: *pen ga aru*, I (you, etc.) have a pen (pens); the literal meaning, however, is "there is (are) a pen (pens)"; *tsukue no ue ni pen ga aru*, there is (are) a pen (pens) on top of the table (lit. table-of top-on pen is; compare the use of French *avoir* in *il y a une plume sur la table*). In the sense of "to have", *aru* may be used even with animate subjects: I have many friends, *tomodachi ga takusan arimasu*; I have children, *kodomo ga arimasu*.

The postposition *de* which must accompany predicate nouns contracts with some of the forms of *aru*. The conjugation of *aru*, with and without a preceding *de*, is:

Polite Pres.	*arimasu*	*desu*	is, are
Familiar Pres.	*aru*	*da*	is, are (which is, are)
Polite Past	*arimashita*	*deshita*	was, were
Familiar Past	*atta*	*datta*	was, were (which was, were)
Probable Future	*arimashō*	*deshō*	will probably be
Probable Past	*arimashita deshō*	*deshita deshō*	probably was, were
Present Cond.	*arimasureba*	*desureba*	if (when) is, are, will be
Past Cond.	*arimashitara*	*deshitara*	if (when) was, were
Participle	*atte*	*de (datte)*	being

11. — Interrogative.

A question is indicated by the use of *ka* following the verb: *hon ga arimasu ka?*, are there books?; *doko desu ka?*, where is it?; *ikimasu ka?*, are you going?

Ne instead of *ka* is used if an affirmative answer is expected (cf. English "isn't it?", "aren't you?", or French *n'est-ce pas?*): *ii o tenki, desu ne?*, lovely weather, isn't it?

12. — Negative.

All Japanese verbs have special negative forms. The negative forms of *aru*, "to be", and *de aru*, "to be" with a predicate noun, are:

Polite Pres.	*arimasen*	*de wa arimasen*	is, are not
Familiar Pres.	*nai*	*de wa nai*	(which) is, are not
Polite Past	*arimasen deshita*	*de wa arimasen deshita*	was, were not
Fam. Past	*nakatta*	*de wa nakatta*	(which) was, were not

Probable Fut.	*nai deshō*	*de wa nai deshō*	probably won't be
(Polite)	*arimasen deshō*	*de wa arimasumai*	
Probable Past	*nakatta deshō*	*de wa nakatta deshō*	probably was, were not
Present Cond.	*nakereba*	*de (wa) nake-reba*	if (when) is (are) not
Past Cond.	*nakattara*	*de (wa) nakat-tara*	if (when) was (were) not
Participle	*nakute*	*de (wa) nakute*	not being

The negative of the polite forms of other verbs is formed by adding the following suffixes to the stem (with *i* if the stem ends in a consonant, without *i* if the stem ends in a vowel):

Present	*-(i)masen*
Past	*-(i)masen deshita*
Probable Future	*-(i)masen deshō*
Probable Past	*-(i)masen deshitarō*

Yobimasen, does not call; *machimasen deshita*, did not wait; *kakimasen deshō*, probably will not write; *mimasen*, does not see.

The negative of the familiar forms of these verbs is made by adding the familiar negative forms of *aru*, "to be", given above, with a prefixed *a*, if the stem ends in a consonant, to the stem of the verb: *yob-a-nai*, is (are) not calling; *kak-a-nai*, does (do) not write; *mi-nai*, does (do) not see; *yob-a-nakatta*, did not call; *kak-a-nakatta*, did not write; *mi-nakatta*, did not see.

The familiar negative participle is the familiar present negative plus *de* (the participle of *de aru*): *yob-a-nai de*, not calling. Another familiar negative participle is formed by adding *-(a)nakute* to the stem: *yob-a-nakute*.

13. — Passive.

The suffix *-areru* (*-rareru* if the stem ends in a vowel) forms the passive: *korosu*, to kill; *korosareru*, to be killed;

miru, to see; *mirareru,* to be seen. These passive forms are then conjugated throughout: *taberu,* to eat; *taberareru,* to be eaten, it is eaten; *miraremashita,* was (were) seen. The passive is not so frequently used in Japanese as in English.

14. — Desiderative.

The suffix *-itai* (*-tai* for verbs whose stem ends in a vowel) denotes a wish, particularly of the first person: *kakitai,* I want to write; *tegami wo kakitai,* I want to write a letter; *kaitai,* I want to buy; *mitai,* I want to see. For the negative forms, change *-(i)tai* to *-(i)taku nai.*

15. — Honorifics.

Some nouns and verbs are humble or plain in themselves, while others are honorific. In speaking of your own (and therefore humble) mother, you would use the word *haha,* but in speaking of your friend's (and therefore honorable) mother, you would use *okāsama.*

	Humble	Honorific[8]
father	*chichi*	*otōsama*
mother	*haha*	*okāsama*
husband	*shujin*	*dannasan*
wife	*kanai*	*okusan*
son	*segare, musuko*	*musukosan*
daughter	*musume*	*ojōsan*

In like manner, some verbs are honorific, such as *meshiagaru* for the usual *taberu,* to eat; *itadaku,* to receive (from honorable you), for the usual *morau. Gozaru* is the honorific verb meaning "to be" and takes the place of the usual *aru.* It is a combination of *go,* honorable, and *aru,* to be. This verb is often preceded by the particle *de,* as is the case with its more usual form *aru,* (*de aru, desu,* etc.): *ikaga de gozaimasu*

8. Observe the suffix *-san* or *sama* (sir, Mr., Madam, Mrs., Miss) in these words, and compare with Spanish *su señor padre,* or French *madame votre mère.*

ka?, how are you?; *bōshi wa doko de gozaimasu ka?*, where is your hat? (note that in both these sentences, "you" and "your" are to be inferred from the honorific nature of the verb).

5. — *Adjectives.*

In Japanese the adjective partakes of the nature of a verb; consequently all true adjectives can be conjugated. This is because the signification of "to be" or "being" is inherent in every adjective form.

Real adjectives end in *-ai, -ii, -oi* and *-ui*: *takai*, expensive; *yoroshii (ii, yoi)*, good; *kuroi*, black; *samui*, cold.

These adjectives are used as attributives, just as in English: *takai uchi*, an expensive house; *yoi hito*, a good person; *kuroi hon*, a black book.

When used in the predicate with the honorific verb *gozaru*, "to be", such adjectives take the following forms: *takō*; *yoroshiū*; *kurō*; *samū*: *samū gozaimasu*, it is cold or it is a cold day; *takō gozaimasen*, it is not expensive.

True adjectives when used as simple predicates partake of the nature of a verb and can be conjugated. The attributive form of the adjective is the present tense. Thus, *kuroi* = is black; *hana wa shiroi* = the flowers are white. Other tenses are formed by adding the following suffixes to the stem of the adjective (when one removes the final *-i* of a real adjective, one has the stem: *shiroi*, white; stem *shiro; samui*, cold; stem *samu*):

Tense	Suffix	Example
Past	-katta	*takakatta*, was expensive
Probable Future	-karō	*takakarō*, will probably be expensive
Probable Past	-kattarō	*kurokattarō*, was probably black
Present Cond.	-kereba	*kurokereba*, if it is black
Past Cond.	-kattara	*yoroshikattara*, if it was good

Adverbs are formed from adjectives by adding the adverbial suffix *-ku* to the stem of the adjective:

Adjective	Adverb
takai	*takaku*
yoroshii	*yoroshiku*
kuroi	*kuroku*
samui	*samuku*

The negative forms of the adjectival conjugation are made by combining the adverb formed from the adjective with the familiar negative forms of the verb *aru*, "to be", producing such forms as *takaku nai*, it is not expensive; *shiroku nai*, it is not white; *yoroshiku nakatta*, was not good; *samuku nai deshō*, it will probably not be cold; *kinō samuku nakatta*, it was not cold yesterday, yesterday was not a cold day.

Many nouns take the suffix *na* or *no* to form an adjectival phrase: *gin no*, of silver; *kin no*, of gold, golden; *ki no*, wooden; *kirei na*, of beauty, beautiful.

These phrases may be used as attributive adjectives: *gin no tokei*, a silver watch; *kirei na uchi*, a beautiful house; *ki no hako*, a wooden box.

6. — *Numerals.*

a) — Cardinal.

For the first ten numbers there are two sets of cardinal numerals (the short forms, *ichi*, *ni*, etc., are originally Chinese, the longer ones, *hitotsu*, *futatsu*, etc., are Japanese):

1 *ichi*	*hitotsu*	12 *jū-ni*	
2 *ni*	*futatsu*	20 *ni-jū*	
3 *san*	*mitsu*	21 *ni-jū-ichi*	
4 *shi*	*yotsu*	22 *ni-jū-ni*	
5 *go*	*itsutsu*	30 *san-jū*	
6 *roku*	*mutsu*	40 *shi-jū* (*yon-jū*)	
7 *shichi*	*nanatsu*	50 *go-jū*	
8 *hachi*	*yatsu*	60 *roku-jū*	
9 *ku*	*kokonotsu*	70 *shichi-jū*	
10 *jū*	*tō*	100 *hyaku*	
11 *jū-ichi*		200 *nihyaku*	

300	*sambyaku*	2000	*ni-sen*
600	*roppyaku*	3000	*san-zen*
800	*happyaku*	10,000	*ichi-man*
1000	*sen*	1,000,000	*hyaku-man*

Japanese has an elaborate set of auxiliary numerals in addition to the cardinal numerals. Most nouns need the first set of cardinals plus the auxiliary numeral. The order is, noun, cardinal numeral, auxiliary numeral. There are many auxiliary numerals, of which a few of the most common are given here:

Hon, for round things, such as trees, cigars, pens:
1-*ippon*; 2-*nihon*; 3-*sambon*; 4-*shihon*; 5-*gohon*; 6-*roppon*; 7-*shichihon*; 8-*hachihon*; 9-*kyuhon*; 10-*jippon*, etc. *Hamaki sambon* = three cigars; *pen ippon* = one pen.

Mai, for flat things such as letters, tickets, rugs, etc.:
1-*ichimai*; 2-*nimai*; 3-*sammai*, etc. *Kippu nimai* = two tickets.

Nin, for persons: 1-*hitori*; 2-*futari*; 3-*sannin*; 4-*yottari*; 5-*gonin*; 6-*rokunin*; 7-*shichinin*, etc. *Hito gonin* = five men or persons.

Hiki, for animals, except birds: 1-*ippiki*; 2-*nihiki*; 3-*sambiki*; 4-*shihiki*; 5-*gohiki*; 6-*roppiki*; 7-*shichihiki*, etc. *Inu sambiki* = three dogs.

Wa, for birds: 1-*ichiwa*; 2-*niwa*; 3-*samba*; 4-*shiwa*; 5-*gowa*, etc. *Tori niwa* = two birds.

Soku, for pairs of shoes, boots, socks, etc.: 1-*issoku*; 2-*nisoku*; 3-*sanzoku*; 4-*shisoku*; 5-*gosoku*, etc. *Kutsu sanzoku* = three pairs of shoes.

Fuku, for sips of tea, coffee, whiffs of tobacco, doses of medicine, etc.: 1-*ippuku*; 2-*nifuku*; 3-*sambuku*; 4-*shifuku*; 5-*gofuku*, etc. *Tabako sambuku* = three whiffs of tobacco.

Dai, for carriages, rikishas, taxis, automobiles, etc.: 1-*ichidai*; 2-*nidai*; 3-*sandai*, etc. *Takushi nidai* = two taxis; *jinrikisha ichidai* = one jinrikisha.

Hai, for cupfuls, glassfuls, etc.: 1-*ippai*; 2-*nihai*; 3-*sambai*; 4-*shihai*, etc. *Chawan nihai* = **two tea-cupfuls.**
Satsu, for books: 1-*issatsu*; 2-*nisatsu*; 3-*sansatsu*, etc. *Hon sansatsu* = three books.

b) — Ordinal.

Use *dai* before the Chinese cardinal numeral, or *me* after the Japanese cardinal numeral: first, *dai ichi* or *hitotsu me*; second, *dai ni* or *futatsu me;* etc. The cardinals are often used instead of the ordinals.

c) — Fractional.

hambun, a half
sambun no ichi, a third (literally, one of three parts: *sam* = 3; *bun* = part; *no* = of; *ichi* = one.)
shibun no ichi, a quarter
shibun no san, three quarters.

7. — *Demonstrative Pronouns*

this, *kore;*   that (by you), *sore;* that (far away), *are*

Demonstrative Adjectives
this, *kono;*   that (by you), *sono;* that (far away), *ano*

Interrogative Pronouns
who, *donata?*   which, *dore?*

Interrogative Adjectives
what kind of?, *donna?*   which?, *dono?*

8. — *Adverbs of Place*

here, *koko;* there (near you), *soko;* there (far), *asoko*
where?, *doko?, dochira?*

VOCABULARY[9]

1. *World, Elements, Nature, Weather, Time, Directions*

world, *sekai*
earth, land, *tsuchi, riku*
air, *kūki*
water, *mizu*
fire, *hi*
light, *hikari*
sea, *umi*
sun, *taiyō*
moon, *tsuki*
star, *hoshi*
sky, *sora*
wind, *kaze*
weather, *tenki*
snow, *yuki*
to snow, *yuki ga furu*
rain, *ame*
to rain, *ame ga furu*
cloud, *kumo*
cloudy, *kumotta*
fog, *kiri*
ice, *kōri*
mud, *doro*
morning, *asa*
noon, *hiru*
afternoon, *gogo*
evening, *yūgata*
night, *yoru, ban*
midnight, *yonaka*
North, *kita*
South, *minami*
East, *higashi*
West, *nishi*

time, *jikan* (o'clock, *ji*)
year, *toshi, nen* (in combination)
month, *tsuki, gatsu* (in combination)
week, *shūkan*
day, *hi, nichi* (in combination)
hour, *jikan*
minute, *fun*
Sunday, *nichiyōbi*
Monday, *getsuyōbi*
Tuesday, *kayōbi*
Wednesday, *suiyōbi*
Thursday, *mokuyōbi*
Friday, *kinyōbi*
Saturday, *doyōbi*
January, *shōgatsu, ichigatsu*
February, *nigatsu*
March, *sangatsu*
April, *shigatsu*
May, *gogatsu*
June, *rokugatsu*
July, *shichigatsu*
August, *hachigatsu*
September, *kugatsu*
October, *jūgatsu*
November, *jūichigatsu*
December, *jūnigatsu*
Spring, *haru*
Summer, *natsu*
Fall, *aki*
Winter, *fuyu*

9. Most, but not all, verbs ending in *-eru*, *-iru* are vowel-stems, and call for the shorter endings described on p. 539. In the vocabulary, these vowel-stem verbs are indicated thus: to inform, *shiraseru* (v. s.); verbs not thus marked (e. g. to relate, *kataru*) are consonant-stems, and take the longer endings.

2. Family, Friendship, Love

family, *kazoku*

husband, *shujin* (humble); *go-shujin* (polite)

wife, *tsuma, kanai* (humble); *okusama* (polite)

brother, *niisan* (elder, polite)

sister, *nēsan* (elder, polite); your brother, your sister (polite), *go kyōdai*

father, *chichi* (fam.); *otōsama* (pol.)

mother, *haha* (fam.); *okāsama* (pol.)

son, *musuko* (humble); *musuko san* (polite)

daughter, *musume* (humble); *ojōsan* (polite)

parents, *oyatachi*

uncle, *ojisan*

aunt, *obasan*

grandfather, *ojīsan*

grandmother, *obāsan*

nephew, *oi*

niece, *mei*

cousin, *itoko*

grandson, *mago*

granddaughter, *mago-musume*

father-in-law, *yōfu*

mother-in-law, *yōbo*

son-in-law, *muko*

daughter-in-law, *yome*

brother-in-law, *gi-kyōdai; gi-kei* (older); *gi-tei* (younger)

sister-in-law, *gi-kyōdai; gi-shi* (older), *gi-mai* (younger)

man, *otoko*

woman, *onna*

child, *kodomo*

boy, *otoko no ko*

girl, *onna no ko*

sir, Mr., *sama, san;* Mr. Tanaka, *Tanaka san*

Madam, Mrs., *sama, san;* Mrs. Tanaka, *Tanaka san no okusama.*

Miss, young lady, *sama, san;* Miss Hanako, *Hanako san*

friend, *tomodachi*

maid-servant, *jochū*

to introduce, *shōkai suru*

to visit, *hōmon suru*

love, *ai*

to love, *ai suru*

to fall in love with, *ai suru*

to marry, *kekkon suru*

sweetheart, *koibito*

kiss, *seppun*

to kiss, *seppun suru*

dear, beloved, *sai ai no* followed by name of speaker; *ai suru* followed by name; *chan* (after name)

3. Speaking Activities

language, *kotoba, gen-go, -go* (in compounds); English language, *ei-go;* Japanese language, *nihon-go*

to speak, *hanasu*

to say, *yū*

to tell, relate, *hanasu, kataru*

to inform, *shiraseru* (v. s.)

to call, *yobu*

to be called, one's name is, *mōshimasu* (my name is Suzuki, *watakushi wa Suzuki to mōshimasu; watakushi no na wa Suzuki desu*)

to greet, *aisatsu suru*

to give a name to, *nazukeru* (v. s.)

to name, to indicate, *nazukeru,
   shimesu*
to cry, shout, *sakebu, donaru*
to listen to, *kiku*
to hear, *kiku*
to understand, *wakaru, ryōkai
   suru*
to mean, *imi suru*

to ask (question), *kiite miru*
   (v.s.), *kiku*
to ask for, *motomeru* (v. s.)
   tazuneru (v. s.)
to answer, *kotaeru* (v. s.), *henji
   wo suru*
to thank, *orei wo yū, kansha suru*
to complain, *fuhei wo yū, kujō wo
   yū*

4. Materials

gold, *kin*
silver, *gin*
iron, *tetsu*
steel, *hagane*
copper, *akagane, dō*
lead, *namari*
tin, *suzu*
oil, *sekiyū*
gasoline, *gasorin, kihatsuyū*
coal, *sekitan*

wood, *ki*
silk, *kinu*
cotton, *wata*
wool, *yōmō, ke*
cloth, *kire, nuno*
to cut, *kiru*
to dig, *horu*
to sew, *nuu*
to mend, *naosu*

5. Animals

animal, *dōbutsu*
horse, *uma*
dog, *inu*
mule, *raba*
cat, *neko*
bird, *tori*
donkey, *roba*
monkey, *saru*
chicken, *niwatori, hiyoko*
hen, *niwatori, men-dori*
rooster, *niwatori, on-dori*
sheep, *hitsuji*
mouse, *nezumi*

snake, *hebi*
goat, *yagi*
bee, *hachi*
cow, *me-ushi*
ox, *o-ushi*
pig, *buta*
insect, *mushi*
fly, *hai*
mosquito, *ka*
spider, *kumo*
louse, *shirami*
flea, *nomi*
bedbug, *nankin mushi*

6. Money, Buying, Selling

money, *kane*
coin, *kahei*
dollar, *doru, dara*
~nt, *sento*

(national currency; large), *yen*
(national currency; small), *sen*
bank, *ginko*
check. *kogitte*

money order, *kawase*
to earn, *kasegu, mōkeru* (v. s.)
to gain, to win, *mōkeru* (v. s.)
   eru (v. s.), *uru*
to lose, *nakusu, makeru* (v. s.)
to spend money, *kane wo tsuiyasu*
   (*tsukau*)
to lend, *kasu*
to owe, *kari ga aru*
to pay money, *kane wo harau*
to borrow, *kariru* (v. s.)
to change, exchange, *torikaeru*
   (v. s.)
to give back, *kaesu*
price, *nedan*
expensive, dear, *takai*
cheap, *yasui*
change, *tsurisen*
store, shop, *mise*
piece, *kire, kake*
slice, *kire*
pound, *ei-kin, pondo*

package, *tsutsumi*
basket, *kago*
box, *hako*
goods, *shinamono*
to go shopping, *kaimono ni iku*
to sell, *uru*
to buy, *kau*
to buy (a ticket), *kippu wo kau*
to rent, hire, *yatou, kariru* (v. s.)
to be worth, *neuchi ga aru*
cost, *nedan, genka*
to cost, *kakaru; suru* (it cost $30,
   sanju doru kakarimashita, sanju
   doru shimashita)
to choose, *erabu*
thief, robber, *dorobō*
to steal, *nusumu*
policeman, *junsa*
police, *keisatsu*
honest, *shōjiki*
dishonest, *fushōjiki*

7. *Eating and Drinking*

to eat, *taberu* (v. s.)
breakfast, *asa no shokuji, asa no*
   meshi, asa no han
to eat breakfast, *asa no shokuji*
   wo suru, asa-han wo taberu
lunch, *hiru no shokuji, hiru-han*
to eat lunch, *hiru no shokuji wo*
   suru
supper, *ban-meshi, yū-han*
to eat supper, *ban-meshi wo*
   taberu, yū-han wo suru
dinner (in the evening), *yū-meshi,*
   enkai
to eat dinner, *yū-meshi wo suru*
   (*taberu*)
meal, *shokuji, meshi, han* (in
   combination)
dining-room, *shokudō*
menu, *kondate*

waiter, *kyūjinin,* waitress, *jokyū*
restaurant, *ryōri-ya*
bill, *kanjō*
to pass something, *mawasu* (please
   pass the bread, *pan wo mawa-*
   shite kudasai
tip, *kokorozuke, chippu*
to drink, *nomu*
water, *mizu*
wine, *budōshu, sake*
beer, *biru*
coffee, *kōhī*
tea, *cha*
milk, *gyūnyū*
bottle, *bin*
spoon, *saji*
teaspoon, *cha-saji*
knife, *naifu*
fork, *fōku*

glass, *koppu*
chop-sticks, *hashi*
cup (teacup), *chawan*
napkin, *nafukin*
salt, *shio*
pepper, *koshō*
plate, dish, *sara*
bread, *pcn*
butter, *bata*
roll, *chiisai pan*
sugar, *satō*
soup, *soppu, suimono, shiru*
rice, *kome* (raw), *gohan, meshi*
potatoes, *imo, jagaimo*
vegetables, *yasai*
meat, *niku*
beef, *gyūniku*
steak, *bifuteki*
chicken, *tori*
chop, *choppu*
lamb, *ko-hitsuji no niku*
veal, *koushi no niku*
pork, *tonniku, buta-niku*
sausage, *chōzume, soseiji*
ham, *hamu*
bacon, *beikon*

egg, *tamago*
fish, *sakana*
to fry, *furai ni suru, ageru*
fried, *abura de ageta, furai shita*
cooked, *ryōri shita*
boiled, *yudeta*
broiled, *yaita*
roasted, roast, *yaita, rōsu*
baked, *yaita*
sauce, *sōsu*
salad, *sarada*
cheese, *chīzu, kanraku*
fruit, *kudamono*
apple, *ringo*
pear, *nashi*
grapes, *budō*
peach, *momo*
strawberries, *ichigo*
walnuts, *kurumi*
orange, *mikan*
lemon, *remon*
juice, *shiru, tsuyu*
cherries, *sakurambō*
dessert, *dezāto*
pastry, *seiyō-gashi*
cake, *kashi*

8. Hygiene and Attire

bath, *furo*
shower, *shawa*
to bathe, *yu ni hairu, furo ni hairu*
to wash, *arau*
to shave, *soru, hige wo soru*
barber, *toko-ya*
mirror, *kagami*
soap, *shabon, sekken*
razor, *kamisori*
safety razor, *anzen-kamisori*
towel, *tenugui*
comb, *kushi*
brush, *burashi*
scissors, *hasami*

to wear (a hat), *kaburu*
to wear (a coat), *kiru*
to wear (trousers, shoes), *haku*
to take off, *nugu*
to change (clothes), *kikaeru* (v. s.)
to put on (a hat), *kaburu*
to put on (a coat), *kiru*
clothes, *yōfuku* (western), *ifuku* (Japanese)
hat, *bōshi*
suit, *mitsu zoroi no yōfuku*
coat, *uwagi*
vest, *chokki*
trousers, *zubon*

underwear, *shitagi*
glove, *tebukuro*
socks, *kutsu-shita*
stockings, *naga-kutsu-shita*
shirt, *shatsu*
collar, *kara*
tie, *nekutai, erikazari*
overcoat, *gaitō*
raincoat, *amagappa, ame no gaitō*
pocket, *poketto, kakushi*
purse, *saifu, kane-ire, kin-chaku*
handkerchief, *hankechi*
button, *botan*
shoe, *kutsu*
boot, *naga-gutsu*

pocket-book, *satsu-ire*
tie-pin, *nekkutai pin*
pin, *pin, tome-bari*
safety pin, *anzen-pin*
needle, *hari*
parasol, *higasa*
umbrella, *kōmori-gasa*
watch, *kaichū-dokei*
wrist watch, *ude-dokei*
chain, *kusari*
ring, *yubiwa*
eyeglasses, *megane*
slippers, *uwa-gutsu, surippa*
dressing-gown, *dotera*
bath-robe, *yukata*
kimono, *kimono*

9. Parts of the Body

head, *atama*
forehead, *hitai*
face, *kao*
mouth, *kuchi*
hair, *ke, kami*
eye, *me*
ear, *mimi*
tooth, *ha*
lip, *kuchibiru*
nose, *hana*
tongue, *shita*
chin, *ago*
cheek, *hō*
mustache, *kuchi-hige*
beard, *hige, ago-hige*
neck, *kubi*
throat, *nodo*
stomach, *i, hara* (colloquial)

arm, *ude*
hand, *te*
elbow, *hiji*
wrist, *te-kubi*
finger, *yubi*
nail, *yubi no tsume*
shoulder, *kata*
leg, *ashi*
foot, *ashi*
knee, *hiza*
back, *senaka*
chest, *mune*
ankle, *ashi-kubi*
body, *karada*
blood, *chi*
skin, *hifu*
heart, *shinzō*
bone, *hone*

10. Medical

doctor, *isha*
drug-store, *kusuri-ya*
hospital, *byōin*
medicine, *kusuri*
pill, *ganyaku*

prescription, *shohōsen*
bandage, *hōtai*
nurse, *kangofu, kanbyōfu*
ill, *byōki*
fever, *netsu*

illness, *byōki*
swollen, *hareta*
wound, *kizu, kega*
wounded, *kizu shita, kega shita*
head-ache, *zutsu*
tooth-ache, *ha no itami*
cough, *seki*

to cough, *seki wo suru, seki ga deru* (v. s.)
lame, *bikko*
burn, *yakedō*
pain, *kutsū, itami*
poison, *doku*

11. Military

war, *sensō*
peace, *heiwa*
ally, *dōmei-koku* (nation), *dōmei-gun* (army)
enemy, *teki, teki-gun*
army, *guntai*
danger, *kiken*
dangerous, *abunai, ayaui, kiken-na*
to win, *katsu, shōri wo eru* (v. s.)
to surround, *kakomu, torimaku*
to arrest, *kōin suru, tsukamaeru* (v. s.)
to kill, *korosu*
to escape, to run away, *nigeru* (v. s.)
to lead, *michibiku, annai suru*
to follow, *tsuite kuru, shitagau*
fear, *osore*
prison, *kangoku, keimusho*
prisoner, *horyo*
comrade, buddy, *gun-yū, tomoda-chi, doryo, nakama*
battle, *ikusa, sentō*
to fight, *tatakau, sento suru*
to take prisoner, *toriko ni suru, horyo ni suru*
to surrender, *kōsan suru, kōfuku suru*
to retreat, *taikyaku suru*
to capture, *bundori suru* (booty), *tsukamaeru*, (v. s.), *hokaku suru* (gun, tank, etc.), *senryo suru* (city, fort)
to bomb, shell, *bakudan wo tōka*

suru, *bakugeki suru, hōgeki suru*
sailor, *suifu, suihei*
marines, *kaihei*
warship, *gunkan*
battleship, *sentō-kan*
cruiser, *jun-yō-kan*
destroyer, *kuchiku-kan*
convoy, *gosō*
escort, *keibo*
weapon, *buki*
rifle, *raifurujū*
machine-gun, *kikanjū*
cannon, *taihō*
ammunition, *danyaku*
provisions, *hyōrō*
cartridge, *jitsudan*
bullet, *dangan*
belt, *obi*
knapsack, *hainō*
soldier, private, *heitai, heisotsu*
corporal, *gochō*
sergeant, *gunsō*
lieutenant, *shō-i*
captain, *taichō, tai-i, senchō*
major, *shōsa*
colonel, *taisa*
general, *taishō*
officer, *shikan*
company, *chutai*
battalion, *daitai*
regiment, *rentai*
troops, *heitai*
brigade, *ryodan*

division, *shidan*
reinforcements, *enpei, zōentai*
fortress, *shiro, yōgai*
sentinel, *bampei, hoshō*
to stand guard, *hoshō ni tatsu,
    shōhei ni tatsu*
guard, *mamoru, shugo suru*
to be on duty, *tōban de aru*
sign post, *michishirube*
navy, *kaigun*
spy, *kanchō, spai*
help (noun), *kyūyen*
tent, *tento*
military supplies, *gunjuhin*
map, *chizu*
camp, *yaei*
rope, *tsuna*
flag, *hata*
helmet, *kabuto*

bayonet, *jūken*
uniform, *gunpuku*
airplane, *hikoki*
bombing plane, *bakugeki-ki*
pursuit plane, *tsuigeki-ki*
bomb, *bakudan*
truck, *kamotsu-jidosha*
shell, *ryūdan*
tank, *tanku, sensha*
to load, (*tama wo*) *sōten suru*
to fire, shoot, *hassha suru*
to shoot (military execution),
    jūsatsu suru
fire!, *utte!*
attention!, *kiotsuke!*
forward!, *mae e!, susume!*
halt!, *tomare!*
air raid shelter, *bōkūgo*

12. Travel

passport, *ryoken*
ship, *fune*
steamer, *kisen*
stateroom, *senshitsu*
berth, *shindai*
to travel, *ryokō suru*
trip, voyage, *ryokō, kokai*
to leave, *dekakeru* (v. s.), *deru*
    (v. s.), *shuppatsu suru*
to arrive, *tsuku*
to ride (conveyance), *noru*
railroad, *tetsudō*
station, *teishajō, suteishon*
platform, *purattohōmu*
track, *senro*
train, *kisha*
ticket, *kippu*
to buy (a ticket), *kippu wo kau*

compartment, *kyakusha no shiki-
    tta-seki tokubetsu-seki*
all abord!, *ohayaku negaimasu*
dining-car, *shokudō-sha*
sleeper, *shindai-sha*
custom-house, *zeikan*
car, coach, *kyakusha*
trunk, *toranku*
valise, *kaban*
baggage, *nimotsu*
taxi, *takushi*
porter, *akabō*
bus, *basu*
street-car, *densha*
automobile, *jidōsha*
driver, *untenshu*
to drive, *unten suru*

13. Reading and Writing

to read, *yomu*
newspaper, *shimbun*

magazine, *zasshi*
book, *hon, shomotsu*

to write, *kaku*
to translate, *honyaku suru*
pencil, *empitsu*
chalk, *hakuboku*
blackboard, *kokuban*
ink, *inki*
pen, *pen*
fountain pen, *mannenhitsu*
paper, *kami*

writing paper, *hakushi, tegami no kami*
envelope, *fūtō*
letter, *tegami*
post-office, *yūbin kyoku*
stamp, *kitte*
letter-box, *yūbin-bako*
to mail, *yūbin wo dasu*
address, *banchi, jūsho, atena*
post-card, *hagaki*

14. *Amusements*

to smoke, *kitsuen suru, tabako wo nomu*
cigar, *hamaki*
cigarette, *maki-tabako*
tobacco, *tabako*
match, *matchi*
give me a light, *hi wo kudasai*
theatre, *gekijō*
movies, *katsudō shashin, eiga*
dance, *odori, dansu*
to dance, *odoru*
to have a good time, *tanoshimu*
ticket, *kippu*

pleasure, *tanoshimi*
to play (music), *hiku*
to play (games), *asobu*
to sing, *utau*
song, *uta*
to take a walk, *sampō suru*
ball, *tama*
beach, *kaigan*
to swim, *oyogu*
game, *yūgi, asobi*
sand, *suna*
refreshment, *inshoku-motsu, chaka*
saloon, *sakaba, sakaya*
picnic, *pikunikku, noasobi*

15. *Town and Country*

place, spot, *tokoro, basho*
city, *shi*
street, *machi, chō* (in combination)
harbor, *minato*
block, *chō*
sidewalk, *jindō*
intersection, *yotsukado*
school, *gakkō*
church, *kyōkai*
building, *tatemono, birujingu*
cathedral, *dai-kaidō*
corner, *kado*
hotel, *hoteru, ryokan*
office, *jimusho*
river, *kawa*

bridge, *hashi*
country, *inaka*
village, *mura*
road, *dōro, michi*
mountain, *yama*
grass, *kusa*
yard, *naka-niwa*
hill, *oka, ko-yama*
lake, *mizuumi, ko* (in comb.)
forest, wood, *hayashi, mori*
field, *hatake, nohara, hara*
flower, *hana*
tree, *ki*
rock, stone, *iwa, ishi*
jungle, *mitsurin, yabubayashi*

16. *House*

door, *to*
to open, *akeru* (v. s.)
to close, *shimeru* (v. s.)
key, *kagi*
to go in, *hairu*
to go out, *deru* (v. s.), *dekakeru* (v. s.)
house, *ie, uchi*
cottage, *inaka-ya*
hut, *koya*
to live (in), *sumu*
staircase, *kaidan, hashigodan*
to go up, *noboru, agaru*
to go down, *kudaru, oriru* (v. s.)
room, *heya*
bed-room, *nema, shinshitsu*
toilet, *benjo*
kitchen, *daidokoro*
table, *teiburu, tsukuye*
clock, *hashira-dokei*
alarm-clock, *mezamashi-dokei*
to get dressed, *kimono wo kiru*

chair, *isu*
to be sitting, *suwatte iru* (v. s.)
to sit down, *kakeru* (v. s.), *suwaru*
to stand, *tatsu*
wall, *kabe*
lamp, *rampu*
light, *akari*
candle, *rōsoku*
closet, *oshiire, todana*
window, *mado*
to rest, *yasumu*
bed, *toko*
pillow, *makura*
to go to bed, *neru* (v. s.)
to be asleep, *neiru* (v. s.)
to sleep, *nemuru*
to wake up, *me ga sameru* (v. s.)
to get up, *okiru* (v. s.)
blanket, *mōfu*
sheet, *shikifu, shītsu*
mattress, *matoresu*

17. *Miscellaneous Nouns*

people, *hito, hitobito*
thing, *mono*
name, *na, namae*
luck, *un*
bad luck, *aku-un, fu-un, fu-kō*

number, *ban, kazu*
life, *inochi, seimei*
death, *shi*
work, *shigoto, hataraki*
good luck, *ko-un, saiwai*

18. *Verbs — Coming and Going*

to come, *kuru*
to go, *iku, yuku*
to be going to, *shite iru* (I am going to write, *kaku, kakō to shite iru*)
to run, *hashiru, kakeru* (v. s.)
to walk, *aruku*
to go away, *tachisaru, itte shimau*

to fall, *korobu*
to stay, remain, *tomaru, todomaru*
to follow, *shitagau*
to return, *kaeru, modoru*
to go back, *kaette yuku*
to come back, *kaette kuru*
to arrive, *tsuku, tōchaku suru*

19. *Verbs — Looking*

to see, *miru* (v. s.)
to look (at), *miru, goran nasaru*
to look for, *sagasu*
to look, seem, *kao wo suru, mieru* (v. s.)
to recognize, *mitomeru* (v. s.).

mioboeru (v. s.)
to take for, *kangaeru* (v. s.), *omou*
to laugh, *warau*
to smile, *hohoemu, nikkori warau*
to laugh at, make fun of, *azawarau, baka ni suru*

20. *Verbs — Mental*

to make a mistake, *machigai wo suru, machigaeru* (v. s.)
to hope, *nozomu, kibō suru*
to wait (for), *matsu*
to think (of), *omou, kangaeru* (v. s.)
to believe, *shinjiru* (v. s.), *shinkō suru*
to like, *suku, suki de aru*
to wish, *-(i)tai* added to stem of verb - see p. 547.
to want, *hossuru, hoshigaru*
to want (lack), *kaku, kaite iru* (v. s.); *tarinai* (negative verb; money is lacking, he lacks money, *kane ga tarinai*)
to need, *iru* (with thing needed

as subject)
to know (person), *shitte iru*
to know (fact), *shiru*
to know how to, *dekiru* (v. s.)
to remember, *oboeru* (v. s.)
to forget, *wasureru* (v. s.)
to permit, allow, *yurusu, saseru*
to promise, *yakusoku suru*
to forbid, *kinzuru*
to learn, *narau*
to feel like, *kanzuru*
to fear, be afraid, *osoreru* (v. s.), *kowagaru*
to be right, *tadashii desu, tadashiku aru*
to be wrong, *machigatte iru, machigai desu*

21. *Verbs — Miscellaneous*

to live, *ikiru* (to have life; v. s.); *ikite iru*
to die, *shinu, nakunaru*
to work, *hataraku, shigoto wo suru*
to give, *ataeru* (v. s.), *ageru* (v. s.)
to take, *toru*
to begin, *hajimeru* (v. s.; trans.; began to write, *kaki hajimeta*)
to begin, *hajimaru* (intr.)
to finish, to end, *shimau, owaru* (finished writing, *kaki owatta*)
to continue, keep on, *tsuzukeru*

(v. s.; trans.; kept on writing, *kaki tsuzuketa*)
to continue, *tsuzuku* (intr.)
to help, *tetsudau*
to lose, *nakusu*
to lose, to be beaten, *makeru* (v. s.)
to find, *mitsukeru* (v. s.)
to try, *yatte miru* (v. s.); *kokoromiru* (v. s.)
to leave (something), *oku*
to show, *miseru* (v. s.)
to meet, *au*
to do, *suru*

to make, *koshiraeru* (v. s.)
to be able, can, *dekiru* (v. s.)
to put, *oku*
to carry, *hakobu, motte iku*
to forbid, *kinzuru*
to understand, *rikai suru, wakaru*
to bring, *motte kuru*
to stop, *tomeru* (trans.; v. s.)
to stop, *tomaru* (intrans.)
to cover, *kabuseru* (v. s.), *ōu*
to get, obtain, *morau, eru* (v. s.)
to get, become, *naru*
to hide, *kakureru* (intrans.; v. s.)
to hide, *kakusu* (trans.)
to hold, *motsu, tamotsu*

to break, *kowasu* (trans.); *kowareru* (intr., v. s.)
to hurry, *isogu* (intrans.)
to deliver (hand over), *todokeru* (v. s.)
to belong (use possessive form with verb "to be"; *kore wa watakushi no desu*, it belongs to me)
to have (something) done, *suru yō ni natte iru*
to lay, deposit, *oku*
to end, *owaru* (intrans.)
to end, *shimau* (trans.)

22. *Adjectives*

small, *chiisai, chiisana*
big, large, *ōkii, ōkina,*
great, *idai na, ōkina*
tall, high, *takai*
short (opp. of tall), low, *hikui*
heavy, *omoi*
light (weight), *karui*
long, *nagai*
short (opp. of long), *mijikai*
wide, *hiroi*
narrow, *semai*
clean, *kirei na*
dirty, *kitanai*
cool, *suzushii*
cold, *samui, tsumetai*
warm, *atatakai*
hot, *atsui*
damp, *shimeppoi*
wet, *nureta*
dry, *kawaita*
full, *ippai*
empty, *kara*
dark, *kurai*
light, bright, clear, *akarui, hareta*
fat, *futotta*
thick, *atsui*

thin, *yaseta* (of persons); *usui* (of flat things)
round, *marui*
square, *shikakui*
flat, *hiratai, taira na*
deep, *fukai*
soft, *yawarakai*
hard, *katai*
quick, *hayai*
slow, *osoi*
ordinary, *futsū no, atarimae no*
comfortable, *rāku na, kimochi yoi*
uncomfortable, *kokochi yoku nai, kimochi warui*
kind, *shinsetsu na*
right, *tadashii*
wrong, *machigatta*
near, *chikai*
distant, *tōi*
right, *migi*
left, *hidari*
poor, *bimbō na, mazushii*
rich, *kane-mochi na, yutakana, tonda*
beautiful, *utsukushii*
pretty, *kirei na*

ugly, *minikui, iyana*
sweet, *amai*
bitter, *nigai*
sour, *suppai*
salty, *shio-karai*
young, *wakai*
old, *toshiyori na, toshitotta* (persons) ; *furui* (things)
new, *atarashii*
good, *yoi, ii*
better, *motto ii, issō yoi, motto yoi*
best, *ichi-ban ii, ichi-ban yoi, mottomo yoi*
bad, *warui*
worse, *issō warui, motto warui*
worst, *mottomo warui, ichi-ban warui*
fine, "regular", *yoi, ii*
first, *hajime no, daiichi no*
last, *owari no, saigo no*
strong, *tsuyoi*
weak, *yowai*
tired, *tsukareta*
alone, *hitori*
same, *onaji*
true, *makoto no*
false, *itsuwari no, uso no*
easy, *yasashii*
hard, difficult, *muzukashii*
happy, glad, *saiwai na, yorokobashii, ureshii*

sad, *kanashii*
free, *jiyū na*
silly, *baka na*
crazy, *kichigai no*
drunk, *yopparatta*
polite, *teinei na*
rude, *burei na*
pleasant, *yukai na, tanoshii*
unpleasant, *fu yukai na*
lonesome, *samushii, sabishii*
foreign, *gaikoku no*
friendly, *shitashii, yūjō aru*
hostile, *tekii aru*
lucky, *kōun na*
unlucky, *fuun na*
charming, *kawaii*
afraid, *kowai*
ready, *yōi no dekita*
hungry, *himojii, kūfuku na* (to be hungry, *hara ga hetta*)
thirsty, *nodo ga kawaita*
funny, *okashii, kokkei na*
possible, *deki uru, dekiru, kanō na,*
impossible, *deki nai, fukanō na*
brave, *yūkan na*
cowardly, *okubyō na, hikyō na*
noisy, *yakamashii, sōzōshii*
quiet, *shizuka na*
living, *ikita*
dead, *shinda*

23. *Colors*

white, *shiroi*
black, *kuroi*
red, *akai*
green, *midori no*
blue, *aoi*

yellow, *ki iro no*
gray, *nezumi iro no, hai iro no*
brown, *cha iro no*
pink, *momo iro no*
purple, *murasaki iro no*

24. Nationalities[10]

American, *Beikoku no*
English, *Eikoku no*
French, *Furansu no*
German, *Doitsu no*
Spanish, *Supein no*
Russian, *Roshia no*
Italian, *Itarī no*
Japanese, *Nippon no*
Chinese, *Shina no*
Dutch, *Oranda no*
Norwegian, *Nōruwei no*
Swedish, *Sueiden no*
Finnish, *Finrando no*
Belgian, *Berugī no*
Polish, *Pōrando no*
Danish, *Demmāku no*
Swiss, *Suisu no*
Portuguese, *Porutogaru no*
Chilean, *Chirī no*
Peruvian, *Perū no*
Yugoslav, *Yūgōsurabia no*

Bulgarian, *Burugaria no*
Czech, *Chekku no*
Greek, *Girisha no*
Turkish, *Toruko no*
Roumanian, *Rūmania no*
Hungarian, *Hangarii no*
Austrian, *Ōsutoriya no*
Malay, *Marei no*
Persian, *Perusha no*
Arabian, Arab, Arabic, *Arabiya no*
Jewish, Hebrew, *Yudaya no*
Australian, *Gōshū no*
African, *Afurika no*
Canadian, *Kanada no*
Mexican, *Mekishiko no*
Cuban, *Kyuba no*
Brazilian, *Buraziru no*
Argentinian, *Arujentina no*
Puerto Rican, *Poruto Riko no*
Indian (Hindu), *Indo no*

25. Adverbs and Adverbial Expressions

today, *kyō, konnichi*
yesterday, *kinō, sakujitsu*
tomorrow, *asu, myōnichi*
day before yesterday, *ototoi*
day after tomorrow, *asatte*
tonight, *konban*
last night, *sakuban*
this morning, *kesa*
in the morning, *asa no uchi ni*
in the afternoon, *gogo ni*
in the evening, *yūgata ni*

in the night, *ban ni, yachū ni*
this afternoon, *kyō no gogo*
tomorrow morning, *asu no asa*
tomorrow afternoon, *asu no gogo*
tomorrow night, *asu no ban*
early, *hayaku*
late, *osoku*
already, *mō*
no longer, *mō* (followed by neg. verb, p. 545)
yet, still, *ima-motte, nao*

10. The forms given, with *no*, literally mean "of America" "of England", etc. (*Furansu no budōshu*, wine of France, French wine). The suffix *-koku* denotes "country"; for languages, drop *-koku*, if it appears, and add *-go* (*shina-go*, the Chinese language); for people, add *-jin*, "man": *Beikoku-jin*, an American; *Itarī-jin*, an Italian; if *hito* is used, retain *no*: *Beikoku no hito*.

not yet, *mada*
now, *ima*
then, *sono-toki*
afterwards, *atokara*
never, *kesshite*
always, *itsu de mo, tsune ni*
forever, *eikyū ni, itsu made mo*
soon, *sugu ni*
often, *shiba shiba, tabi tabi*
seldom, *metta ni, mare ni*
not, *nai* (see negative form of
   verb, p. 545)
very much, *taihen ni, takusan*
little, not much, *sukoshi, chotto*
well, *yoku*
badly, *waruku*
better, *issō yoku*
worse, *issō waruku*
only, *wazuka ni, tada, dake*
more, *motto*
less, *issō sukunaku*
as - as, he is *as* tall *as* I, *ano hito
   wa watakushi to onaji gurai
   sei ga takai*:
   literally, that man (*ano hito*),
   and (*to*), I (*watakushi*), same
   (*onaji*), about (*gurai*), height
   (*sei ga*), high are (*takai*)
as much - as (as many - as)
   possible, *dekiru-dake takusan*
how much?, *ikura*
how many?, *ikutsu*
how?, *donna fū ni shite, dō shite*
too much, *ammari, ōsugiru*
too many, *ammari takusan*
really, truly, *hontō ni*
usually, *futsū ni, taitei*
fast, *hayai, hayaku*
slowly, *osoku, noroku*
here, *koko ni*
there, *asoko ni*
over (down) there, *mukō ni*
near by, *chikaku ni*
far away, *tōi, tōku ni*

up (stairs), *nikai ni*
down (stairs), *kaika ni, shita ni*
ahead, in front, *mae ni, saki ni*
behind, in back, *ushiro ni, ato ni*
forward, *zenpō e, mae ni*
back, backward, *ushiro e, kōhō e*
outside, *soto ni*
inside, *naka ni*
opposite, in front, *mae ni, han
   tai ni*
here and there, *koko kashi-ko*
everywhere, *dokoni mo*
where, *doko ni*
also, too, *mata, yahari*
yes, *sayō, hai*
no, *iie*
for lack of, (something) **ga nai**
   node
occasionally, *toki doki*
all day, *ichinichi-jū*
all morning, *gozen chū*
all afternoon, *gogo jū, maru han
   nichi*
all night, *yo jū*
why?, *dōshite*
very much, *taihen*
like, *no gotoki, no yōna*
besides, *sono hoka ni*
finally, *saigo ni*
in short, *yōsuru ni*
almost, *taitei, hotondo*
gladly, *yorokonde*
certainly (it is so), *tashika ni*
at once, *sugu ni, tadachi ni*
at all, *sukoshi mo*
hardly, *hotondo . . . . de nai*
aloud, *takagoe ni*
of course, *mochiron*
suddenly, *kyū ni, totsu-zen ni*
perhaps, maybe, *tabun, osoraku*
a little, *sukoshi*
again, *mata, futatabi*
together, *issho ni*

at least, *sukunaku tomo*
long ago, *zutto mae, mukashi*
again and again, *ikudo mo,*

shiba shiba
from time to time, *tokidoki*
therefore, *yue ni, dakara*

26. Conjunctions

and, (between nouns) *to*
but, *ga*
if, *moshi* (also see conditional of verb, p. 540)
or, *ka*
why, *naze*
because, *kara, yue ni*
before, *izen ni, mae ni*
when, *toki, sono toko ni*
than, *yori*
where, *doko ni, doko*

whither, *doko e*
until, *made*
although, *tatoe—to iedomo, keredomo*
unless, *de nakereba*
while, *aida ni, uchi ni*
when, *itsu*
that, *to yū koto, to*
after, *ato ni*
as soon as, *ya ina ya, suru to sugu ni*
as long as, *no aida, kagiri*

27. Indefinite Pronouns and Adjectives

such (adj.), *sō yū yō na, sono yō na*
such (pron.), *konna mono, sonna hito*
all kinds of, *iroiro na*
everything, *nan de mo*
everyone, *dare de mo*
something, *nani ka, aru mono*
someone, *dare ka, aru hito*
nothing, *nani mo* (with neg.)
no one, *dare mo* (with neg.)
no (adj.), *sukoshi mo—nai, nani mo—nai*
some (pron.), *sukoshi, ikuraka*
neither—nor, *—mo—mo dochiramo nai* (I have neither fish nor

rice, *sakana mo kome mo dochiramo nai*)
some (adj.), *aru, nani ka*
all, *mina(n), mina no* (adj.)
other, another, *hoka no*
much, *takusan no* (adj.)
much, *takusan* (pron.)
few (adj.), *sukunai, shō-sū no*
many, *takusan*
several, *iro-iro no*
little (not much), *sukoshi*
both, *dochi mo, ryōhō tomo*
neither, *dochi mo* (with neg.)
enough, *jūbun*
each, every, *onoono no, subete no*

28. Postpositive particles and Expressions

of, *no*
from, *kara*
out of, *kara*
to, toward, *e*

on, *—no ue ni*
over, *—no ue ni*
above, *—no ue ni*
for (the sake of) *—no tame ni*

for (of price), *de*
until, up to, *made*
since, *kara*
toward, —*no hō e*
between, —*no aida ni*
among, —*no naka ni*
near, —*no chikaku ni*
before, —*no mae ni* (of place)
after, —*no ato ni*
opposite, in front of, —*no mukai ni*
back of, behind, —*no ushiro ni*
under (neath), below, —*no shita ni*
at, *de*, —*no tokoro ni*
with, *de* (means); *issho ni* (in company with)
without, —*no soto ni*, —*nashi ni*
in, *ni*
instead of, *no kawari ni*
beside, —*no soba ni*

at the house of, —*no uchi ni*
through, —*wo tōshite; -jū*
next to, —*no tsugi ni*, —*no tonari ni*
by means of, —*ni yotte, de*
against, —*ni taishite*
across, —*no mukō ni*
in spite of, —*ni mo kakawarazu*
in order to, —*no tame ni*, —*suru tame ni*
about, concerning, —*ni tsuite*
about, round about, —*no mawari ni*
around, —*no shūi ni*
during, —*no aida, -jū*
because of, on account of, —*no tame ni*
by (agent), —*ni yotte*
by (place), —*no soba ni*
by (means), *de*

29. Special Expressions and Idioms

good morning, *ohayō*
good day, good afternoon, *konnichi wa*
good evening, *komban wa*
good night, *oyasumi nasai*
good-bye, *sayōnara*
I'll see you later, *ato de o me ni kakarimashō*
I'll see you tomorrow, *myōnichi o me ni kakarimashō*
I'll see you tonight, *komban o me ni kakarimashō*
just now, *tadaima*
how are you?, *ikaga desu ka?*
I'm well, *watakushiwa jōbu desu, genki desu.*
I'm (much) better, *taihen yoku narimashita*
how goes it?, *dō desu ka?*
what time is it?, *ima nanji desu ka?*
it's six o'clock, *roku-ji desu*
at six o'clock, *roku-ji ni*
at about six, *roku-ji goro ni*
at half past six, *roku-ji han ni*
at a quarter to six, *roku-ji jū-go-fun mae ni*
at a quarter past six, *roku-ji jū-go-fun sugi ni*

at ten minutes to six, *roku-ji jippun mae ni*
at ten minutes past six, *roku-ji jippun sugi ni*
last year, *sakunen, kyonen*
next year, *rainen, myōnen*
every day, *mai-nichi*
the whole day, *ichi-nichi-jū*
please, *dōzo, kudasai* (following participle of verb)
bring me, *motte kite kudasai*
show me, *misete kudasai*
thank you, *arigatō*
don't mention it, *dō itashimashite*
will you give me?, *kudasaimasu ka?*
pardon me, *gomen nasai*
it doesn't matter, *kamaimasen*
never mind, *kamaimasen*
I'm sorry for you, *okinodoku desu*
I can't help it, *watakushi wa dō suru koto mo deki masen, shikataga-nai*
it's nothing, *nan de mo nai*
what a pity!, *oshii koto desu*
it's too bad, *oshii koto desu*
I'm glad to hear it, *sore wa nani yori de gozaimasu*
I have to, (neg. present conditional of verb followed by *nara-nai*)
I must (have to) go, *ika nakereba nara-nai*
I'm agreeable, *shōchi shimashita, yoroshii*
where is (are)?, *doko desu ka, doko ni arimasu ka?*
where are you going?, *doko e yukimasu* (or *mairimasu*) *ka?*
there is (are), *arimasu* (of inanimate things), *orimasu* (of living
    things)
there is (are), with noun or pronoun as predicate, *ga aru*
which way (to a place)?, (place) *e iku michi wa dochira desu ka?*
this (that) way (fashion), *kō yū yarikata de, kō*
this direction, *kochira e*
that direction, *achira e*
what can I do for you?, *nani ka hoshii* (*onozomi*) *desu ka? nani ka
    itashimashō ka?*
what is it?, *dō shita no desu ka?*, *nan desu ka?*
what is the matter?, *nani ga okotta no desu ka?*, *nanigoto desu ka?*,
    dō shita no desu ka?
what do you want?, *nan no goyō desu ka?*
what are you talking about?, *nani wo hanashite iru* (*irassharu*) *no
    desu ka?*
what do you mean?, what does that mean?, *sore wa dō iu wake
    desu ka?*

how much is it?, *ikura desu ka?*

anything else?, *hoka ni nanika iriyō desu ka?*

nothing else, *mō nai, mō hoka ni nani mo arimasen*

do you speak English?, *eigo ga dekimasu ka?, eigo wo hanashimasu ka?*

a little, *sukoshi dake*

do you understand?, *wakarimasu ka?*

I don't understand, *wakarimasen*

do you know, *shitte imasu ka?*

I don't know, *shirimasen*

I can't, *dekimasen*

what is your name?, *anata wa nan to osshaimasu ka?; anata no o namae wa?*

what do you call this in Japanese?, *kore wa nihon-go de nan to iimasu ka?*

I'm an American, *watakushi wa Beikoku-jin desu*

I'm hungry, *hara ga hette iru*

I'm thirsty, *nodo ga kawakimashita*

I'm sleepy, *nemutai, nemuku nari mashita* (I want to sleep, *nemuritai*)

I'm warm, *watakushi wa atatakai*

I'm cold, *watakushi wa samui*

it's warm, *atsui, atatakai*

it's cold, *samui*

it's windy, *kaze ga fuiteiru*

it's sunny, *hi ga tetteiru*

it's fine weather, *ii o tenki desu*

it's bad weather, *warui (iyana) o tenki desu*

it's forbidden, *dekimasen*

no smoking, please, *tabako goenryo kudasai*

luckily, fortunately, *un yoku, saiwai ni*

unfortunately, *ainiku, un waruku*

is it not so?, don't you?, aren't you?, *desu ne?, deshō?*

not at all, by no means, *sukoshi mo* (with negative), *chitto mo* (with negative)

how old are you?, *o toshi wa ikutsu desu ka?*

I'm eight years old, *toshi wa yattsu desu* (use second set of numerals: *hitotsu, futatsu, mittsu,* etc.)

how long have you been here?, *dono-gurai nagaku koko ni orimashita (oide deshita) ka?*

how long have you been waiting?, *dono-gurai nagaku matte imashita ka?*

as soon as possible, *dekiru-dake hayaku*

come here!, *koko e oide nasai*

come in!, *o hairi nasai*

look!, *goran nasai*
look out!, *abunai!*
for heaven's sake!, *sore wa taihen da!*
what is the matter with you?, *dō shita no desu ka?*
how do you say - in Japanese?, ...*nihon-go de nan to iimasu ka?*
gangway!, by your leave!, *o doki nasai!, gomen nasai! doite kudasai*
as you please, *anata no ii yō ni, gojiyū ni*
listen!, look here!, say!, *ano ne!, chotto!*
hello! (at telephone), *moshi-moshi*
just a second!, *chotto matte kure (kudasai)*
to the right, *migi e*
to the left, *hidari e*
straight ahead, *massugu ni*
what do you mean by this?, *kore wa dō iu wake desu ka?*
speak (more) slowly, *dōzo yukkuri hanashite kudasai*
just right, *chōdo yoi*
here is (are), *koko ni — aru*
there is (are), *asoko ni — aru*
no admittance!, *iru bekarazu!*
notice!, *chūi*
nonsense!, *baka na, detarame*
what else?, *sore kara, sono hoka*
glad to meet you, *o meni kakarete saiwai (ureshii) desu*
stop!, *tomare!, mate!*

SAMPLE JAPANESE SENTENCES AND PHRASES
ILLUSTRATING THE STRUCTURE OF THE JAPANESE
LANGUAGE.

1.   *Anata wa ikaga de gozaimasu ka?*
1.   How are you? or How do you do? *Anata wa* - you; *ikaga*
- how; *de* - a particle used in conjunction with the verb *gozaimasu* (see page 547); *gozaimasu* = present tense of polite verb
gozaru, to be; *ka* = interrogative particle.
2.   *Okusan wa ikaga de gozaimasu ka?*
2.   How is your wife? *Okusan* (polite) = your wife, (*kanai*
humble = my wife); *wa* = a postposition meaning "as for".
As for your wife, how is she?
3.   *Taihen yoku narimashita.*
3.   I feel very much better. *Taihen* = very; *yoku* = well
(adv.); *narimashita*, past tense of *naru*, to become; literally:
I have become very well.
4.   *Eigo ga dekimasu ka? Sukoshi dake.*
4.   Do you speak English? A little only. *Ei* = English; *go* =
language; *ga* postposition, sign of subject; *dekimasu* = present
of *dekiru*, to know how, to be able. Literally: Is there a know-
ing-how (to speak) English? *Sukoshi* = little; *dake* = only.
5.   *Wakarimasu ka? Wakarimasen.*
5.   Do you understand? I don't understand. *Wakarimasu* =
present of *wakaru*, to understand. *Wakarimasen* = present
negative of same verb.
6.   *Eigo ga wakaru hito.*
6.   A man who understand English, (lit. English understanding man). On this use of the plain present see pg. 544. The
postposition *ga*, sign of subject, is used, since *wakaru* is not
transitive in Japanese.
7.   *Eigo ka Fransugo ga wakaru hito wa imasen ka?*
7.   Is there anyone here who understands English or French?
Ei = English; *go* = language; *ka* = either; *Fransu* = French;
ga = sign of subject; *wakaru hito* = understanding
person (a person who understands). See pg. 543 for the

use of the plain or familiar form of a verb as the equivalent of a relative clause in English. *Imasen* = present negative of verb *iru*, to be; *ka* = sign of interrogation; *imasen ka* = is there not present? The sentence, word for word goes thus = English language or, French language, subject sign, understanding person, as for, is there not?

8. *Eigo wa sukoshi dekimasu ga Fransugo wa dekimasen.*

8. I speak a little English, but I don't speak French. Literally = English language as for, little I speak, but (*ga*) French language as for, I speak not

9. *Nihongo benkyō shite imasu.*

9. I am studying Japanese. *Nihon* = Japanese; *go* = language; *benkyō* = a studying; *shite* = doing; *imasu* = I am. *Shite* is the present participle of *suru*, to do. *Imasu* is present of *iru*, to be. The two words together form a progressive present, I am doing. *Benkyō suru* forms a so called Chinese conjugation, (see pg. 542).

10. *Ano hito wa san-nen Nihongo benkyō shimashita.*

10. He studied Japanese three years. *Ano* = that; *hito* = person; *san* = three; *nen* = years.

11. *Ano hito wa Nihon-jin desu ka?*

11. Is he a Japanese? *Jin* = man; *desu* = is. *Desu* is one of the combinations of *de aru* (see pg. 544).

12. *Hawaii ni ni-nen sunde imashita, sorekara kochira e kimashita.*

12. I lived in Hawaii for two years and then I came here. *Ni* = in; *ni-nen* = two years; *sunde* = present participle of *sumu*, to live; *imashita* = past of *iru*, to be; *sorekara* = afterwards (*sore* = that; *kara* = after); *kochira* = here, this place; *e* = to, toward; *kimashita* = past of *kuru*, to come.

13. *Anata wa dare desu ka?*

13. Who are you? *Anata* = you; *wa* = as for; *dare* = who; *desu* = are; *ka* = question. A more polite word for "who" is *donata*.

14. *Anata no namae wa?*

14. What is your name? Literally = You of name as for? *o namae* would be a more polite word.

15. *O toshi wa ikutsu desu ka?*

15.   What is your age? *O* = honorable; *toshi* = age; *ikutsu* = how many (years).

16. *Koko ni o kake kudasai.*

16.   Please sit down here. *Koko* = here; *ni* = at; *o* = honorable; *kake* = sitting (stem of *kakeru*); *kudasai* = please (polite). On the use of *kudasai*, see pg. 541.

17. *Kore wo setsumei shite kudasai.*

17.   Please explain this. *Kore* = this; *wo* = sign of object; *setsumei* = explanation; *shite* = making (pres. participle of *suru*, to make); *kudasai* = please (polite). The verb *setsumei-suru* means "to explain".

18. *Mado wo akete kudasai.*

18.   Please open the window. *Mado* = window; *wo* = sign of object of verb; *akete* = pres. part. of *akeru*, to open.

19. *Mado wo akenaide kudasai.*

19.   Please don't open the window. *Akenai de* = pres. particiciple negative. *Akenai de kudasai* = please do not open.

20. *Nodo ga kawakimashita.*

20.   I am thirsty. *Nodo* = throat; *ga* = sign of subject of verb; *kawakimashita* = past of verb *kawaku*, to become dry.

21. *Kōhi ga aru ka?*

21.   Have you any coffee? *Kōhi* = coffee; *ga* = sign of subject; *aru* = plain verb "to be" (polite verb is *gozaru*). Literally: Is there any coffee? (Addressed to a servant).

22. *Ocha ga aru ka?*

22.   Have you any tea? *ocha* = tea.

23. *Motte kite kudasai.*

23.   Please bring. *Motte* = pres. part. of *motsu*, to have in the hand; *kite* = pres. part. of *kuru* = to come. Literally: Please come bringing.

24. *Mizu wo motte kite kudasai.*

24.   Please bring some water. *Mizu* = water.

25. *Ano hito wa nani wo motte imasu ka?*

25.   What has that person (or he, or she) got? *Nani* = what. Literally: That person as for, what (sign of object of verb)

having, is he? *Motte imasu* is the present progressive form of the verb *motsu,* to have in the hand. See "Participles" pg. 541.

26. *Sandwich wo motte kimashita ka?*

26.   Did you or he or she bring a sandwich? *Kimashita* = past of *kuru,* to come. Literally: Sandwich having (or bringing) came he?

27. *Kore wa Nihongo de nan to iimasu ka?*

27.   What do you call this in Japanese? *Kore* = this; *wa* = as for; *Nihongo* = Japanese language; *de* = in, by; *nan* = what; *to* = as; *iimasu ka* = pres. tense of *iu,* to call.

28. *Kore wa nan de koshiraete arimasu ka?*

28.   Of what is this made? *Nan* = what; *de* = of, from; *koshiraete* = pres. part. of *koshiraeru,* to make, prepare; *arimasu ka* = pres. of *aru,* to be. Literally: This as for, what of, making, is it?

29. *Motto ōkii no ga arimashitara, motte kite kudasai.*

29.   If there should be a larger one, please bring it. *Motto* = more; *ōkii* = big; *no* = one; *ga* = sign of subject; *arimashitara* = past conditional of verb *aru,* to be (should there be); *motte* = bringing; *kite kudasai* = come please.

30. *Kono tegami wo yakushite kudasaimasen ka?*

30.   Won't you please translate this letter for me? *Kono* = this; *tegami* = letter; *yakushite* = pres. part. of *yakusuru,* to translate; *kudasaimasen ka* = couldn't you favor me, (present tense negative, of verb *kudasaru*). *Kudasaru,* to favor me by doing, is an honorific verb used politely of the 2nd person.

31. *Dono gurai nagaku koko ni orimashita ka?*

31.   About how long have you been here? *Dono* = how; *gurai* = about; *nagaku* = long (adverb formed from adjective *nagai,* long); *koko* = here; *ni* = at; *orimashita ka* = have you been? (past tense of *oru,* to be).

32. *Tenisu wo nasaimasu ka?*

32.   Do you play tennis? *Nasaimasu* = do you do, that is, do you play? (present of honorific verb *nasaru*).

33. *Hanako san wa piano wo nasaimasu ka?*

33.   Does Hanako play the piano? *Hana* = flower; *ko* =

sign of feminine gender; *san* = Miss; *Hanako san* = Miss
Flower (girl's name).

34. *Koto wo shite irasshaimasu ka?*

34.   Do you play the *koto* (a Japanese stringed instrument)?
Shite = pres. part. of *suru*, to do; *irasshaimasu*, present of
irassharu, polite verb, to be. The two verb forms together mean
"are you doing or playing?"

35. *Mae ni shite imashita ga ima wa shite imasen.*

35.   Formerly I played it, but now I do not play it. *Mae ni* =
formerly; *ga* = but; *ima wa* = as for now; *shite imasen* =
present negative of *shite iru*, to be doing. Literally = Formerly
I was doing it, but now I am not doing (it).

36. *Kono hen wa tori ga orimasu ka?*

36.   Are there not birds around here? *Kono* = this; *hen* =
region; *wa* = as for; *tori* = birds; *ga* = sign of subject;
orimasen ka = are there not (present negative of *oru*, to be.

37. *Kono hon wo agemashō.*

37.   I shall give you this book. *Hon* = book; *agemashō* =
future of *ageru*, a polite verb meaning humbly to present on
my part, to you, an honorable person.

38. *Ikitai desu.*

38.   I want to go. *Ikitai* = a wanting to go, the desiderative
form of *iku*, to go (see page 547); *desu* = there is. Literally:
There is a wanting to go.

39. *Mitai desu.*

39.   I want to see. *Mitai* = I want to see, desiderative of verb
miru, to see.

40. *Dare ka yonde kudasai.*

40.   Please call somebody. *Dare ka* = somebody; *yonde
kudasai* = please call, imperative of *yobu*, to call.

41. *Yūbin-kyoku wa doko ni arimasu ka?*

41.   Where is the post-office? *Yūbin-kyoku* = post-office;
doko ni = where; *arimasu* = is there, present tense of *aru*,
to be.

42. *Takushi wo yonde kite kure.*

42.   Go and call a taxi. *Takushi* = taxi; *wo* = sign of object
of verb; *yonde* = calling, pres. part. of *yobu*; *kite* = coming,

pres. part. of *kuru*, to come; *kure* = please, imperative of verb *kureru*. (*Kure* is used only to one's inferiors; cf. *kudasai*, please, the polite verb.) The combination *yonde kite kure* = to go and call (spoken to a servant).

43. *Mukō no jidōsha wa dare no desu ka?*

43. Whose automobile is that over there? *Mukō* = over there; *no* = of; *desu ka* = is it. Literally: Yonder of, auto as for, whom of, is it?

44. *Koko kara suteishon made densha ga arimasen ka?*

44. Is there not a tram-car from here to the station? *Koko* = here; *kara* = from; *suteishon* = station; *made* = toward; *densha* = tram-car (*den* = electricity, *sha* = carriage).

45. *Ano hito wa mada Kanada ni imasu ka?*

45. Is he still in Canada? *Ano* = that; *hito* = man; *mada* = still; *Kanada* = Canada; *ni* = in; *imasu* = is he; *ka* = sign of question.

46. *Ii o tenki desu ka? Warui o tenki desu.*

46. Is the weather fine? The weather is bad. *Ii* = fine; *o* = honorable; *tenki* = weather; *desu ka* = is it; *warui* = bad.

47. *Ame ga futte imashita kara, ikimasen deshita.*

47. Since it was raining, he did not go. *Ame* = rain; *ga* = sign of subject; *futte* = coming down, pres. part. of *furu*, to come down; *imashita* = was, past tense of *iru*, to be; *kara* = since; *ikimasen deshita* = he did not go, past tense negative of *iku*, to go.

48. *Myōnichi o uchi ni irasshaimasu ka?*

48. Will you be at home tomorrow? *Myōnichi* = tomorrow; *o* = honorable; *uchi* = house; *ni* = in; *irasshaimasu ka* = will you be. The verb is the present (used as the future) of the honorific verb *irassharu*, to be.

49. *Niwa ni hana ga arimasu ka? Arimasen.*

49. Have you flowers in your garden? I have none. *Niwa* = garden; *ni* = in; *hana* = flowers; *ga* = sign of subject; *arimasu ka* = are there, polite present of *aru*, to be.

50. *Motto arimashita ka?*

50. Was there any more? *Motto* = more; *arimashita* = was there, past of *aru*.

51. *Mō arimasen deshita.*
51.   There was no more. *Mō* = more; *arimasen deshita* = past negative of *aru.*
52. *Misete kudasai.*
52.   Show it to me. *Misete kudasai* = polite imperative of *miseru*, to show.
53. *Kore ikura desu ka?*
53.   How much is this? *Kore* = this; *ikura* = how much.
54. *Pen wa teburu no ue ni arimasu.*
54.   There is a pen on the table. Literally, Pen as for, table of, top on, there is. *Ue* = top.
55. *Pen ga sambon arimasu.*
55.   There are three pens. *Sambon* = three (san is three, *bon* is for *hon*, the auxiliary numeral for long, cylindrical things; (see page 550).
56. *Kippu ga ikumai arimasu?*
56.   How many tickets are there? *Kippu* = tickets; *ikumai* = how many (*iku* means "how many" and *mai* is the auxiliary numeral for flat things; see page 550).
57. *Hyakushō wa warui kodomo wo shikarimashita.*
57.   The farmer scolded the bad boy. *Hyakushō* = farmer; *warui* = bad; *kodomo* = boy; *wo* = object sign; *shikarimashita* = scolded, past of *shikaru*, to scold.
58. *Warui kodomo wa hyakushō ni shikararemashita.*
58.   The bad boy was scolded by the farmer. *Ni* = by, to denote agent; *shikararemashita* = was scolded, past tense passive of *shikaru.*
59. *Tōkyō ni Smith san no ie ga arimasu.*
59.   Mr. Smith's house is in Tokyo. *No* = of, possessive; *ie* = house.
60. *Kesa Suzuki san ga irasshaimashita ka?*
60.   Did Mr. Suzuki come this morning? *Kesa* = this morning; *irasshaimashita* = past of *irassharu*, polite verb, to come.
61. *Hon wo mi-ni ikimashita.*
61.   He went to see the books. *Hon* = books; *mi-ni* = to see. *Mi* is the stem of the verb *miru*, to see. *Ni* is a postposition that denotes purpose when used as a suffix to a verb stem.

62. *Shitte imasu ka?*

62. Do you know? *Shitte* = pres. part. of *shiru*, to know. Literally: Knowing are you?

63. *Okinodoku desu.*

63. I am sorry. *O* = honorable; *ki* = spirit; *no* = of; *doku* = poison. Literally: It is honorable poison of spirit.

64. *Kamaimasen.*

64. It doesn't matter. *Kamaimasen* = pres. negative of *kamau*, to matter.

APPENDIX A - ESPERANTO[1]

by G. Alan Connor, Director of the Esperanto Inter-
language Institute in New York, and Doris Tappan
Connor, Teacher of the International Cseh Institute
of Esperanto, the Hague, Netherlands.

★ ★ ★

[1] AUTHOR'S NOTE — In addition to the national languages, it was
thought appropriate to offer the readers of the second edition of
"Languages for War and Peace" a description of one *fully constructed*
international language (not a national tongue adapted for international
use, like Basic English). Esperanto was selected because of all the
languages answering that description, it is the only one having today
a world-wide body of living speakers and a world-wide press, and the
only one to have been widely used in international congresses. Attention
may be called to other constructed languages, such as Schleyer's
Volapük, Peano's *Interlingua* (or *Latino sine Flexione*), Jespersen's
Novial, and the latest comer in this field, Hogben's *Interglossa;* but
with the exception of Volapük, which for practical purposes came to
its end before the close of the last century, none of them has advanced
very far beyond the blue-print stage.

Inclusion of Esperanto in this work is not to be interpreted as
signifying advocacy or endorsement by the author of its principles or
method of construction, but simply as an effort on his part to introduce
his readers to the entrancing field of interlanguage construction and
planning for the adoption of a universal means of communication for
international use, as well as to supply them with the elements of a
tongue which occasionally proves of very direct, practical use under
the most unexpected circumstances.

                                                        Mario A. Pei.

SPEAKERS AND LOCATION

Esperanto is spoken and understood by some few millions who are scattered widely throughout the entire civilized world. Accurate estimates are extremely difficult to obtain because no census is possible in the usual sense of the term. The Esperanto movement is divided into many international, national and local groups. The two largest international organizations are the International Esperanto League, with headquarters in London, and the Universal Esperanto Association, with headquarters in Geneva, Switzerland. Besides these two general bodies, there are many sectional groups organized for special applications of the language, such as science, medicine, art, literature, religion, labor, teaching, etc. Then there are the national organizations with their metropolitan and local groups.

An estimate of speakers and users of Esperanto, based upon the best available authorities from all these organizations, places the number of Esperantists more or less accurately at anywhere from 6,000,000 to 8,000,000, although some estimates would place it at considerably higher figures.

The outstanding fact about the use of Esperanto throughout the world today, in comparison with the many international language projects which have claimed consideration in the past, is that Esperanto has steadily progressed since its construction in 1887, to where it is practically the only international language used and spoken in the world today. It is active and growing, with some millions of speakers, and has a considerable literature and press, whereas other projects remain in the realm of academic discussion, without a comparable literature or body of speakers.

Esperanto is described as an international auxiliary language, or more briefly as an *interlanguage*. It does not aim to replace the national tongues, but only to serve as a bridge-language between language-groups, for international inter-change such as commerce, tourism, short-wave radio, export films, international conferences, world government, and the like. It presents a new concept of easy, neutral inter-communication, on a basis of equal participation.

Europe — Esperanto was constructed in Poland in 1887, by Dr. L. L. Zamenhof, "from the fittest elements of occi-dental tongues, and with an agglutinative grammatical structure". It is chiefly a Latin-Germanic language. From Poland and Russia it spread abroad by way of Upsala University, Sweden, first throughout Europe, then to the rest of the world.

By far the largest number of Esperanto speakers are found in Europe today. And it is the small nations, more conscious of the language barriers, which have the greatest number. The Netherlands, Czechoslovakia, Denmark, Sweden, Austria, Switzerland, Hungary, Yugoslavia, and Italy show largest percentages. Then France, Germany and Great Britain.

Greatest growth during the present war is shown in Great Britain, Sweden, Switzerland and Portugal. It is interesting to note that with the recent proposal that "Basic English" be adopted as the "international language", Esperanto has made considerable progress in Great Britain itself, as a result of the discussion of the problem.

Africa — Esperanto comparatively little used, except in parts of South Africa and in the northern tier of Mediterranean countries.

Asia — Most remarkable development in Japan and China, where universities spread the movement, and a consider-able literature and press existed before the war. Chinese Esperantists continue to use Esperanto in new ways in the war against Japan, and a Chinese Esperanto journal is regularly published in Chungking.

Australia, Oceania, etc. — Australia and the Dutch East Indies
   developed Esperanto movements of some importance before the war. Various south sea islands have isolated
   groups, and several British officials have issued small
   journals from these island outposts.
Western Hemisphere — By far the largest group of Esperantists
   are found in Brazil, and one nation-wide governmental
   department uses Esperanto officially. Other countries
   with good showings are Uruguay, Argentina, Chile and
   Cuba. Development to a lesser extent in the United States,
   Canada and Mexico.

ALPHABET AND SOUNDS

a, b, c, ĉ, d, e, f, g, ĝ, h, i, j, ĵ, k, l, m, n, o, p, r, s, ŝ, t,
u, ŭ, v, z. (The symbol ĥ is also used infrequently, with the
value of Scottish *ch* in lo*ch*. It is being generally replaced by
the symbol and sound of *k*. For example: *arĥitekturo* becomes
arkitekturo, etc.) There is no q, w, x, or y in Esperanto.

Vowel sounds: a, e, i, o, u, have the vowel sounds heard
in b*a*r, b*e*ar, b*i*er, b*o*re, b*oo*r. They are like the sounds of
English ah, eh, ee, oh, oo, (the *eh* like the first part of *a* in
gate).

Consonant sounds: Pronounced as in English, except the
following:

c: is not sounded like s or k, but like *ts* in bi*ts*.
j: has the international phonetic sound of *y* in *y*es.
r: is slightly rolled, being stronger and clearer than in **English**.
ĉ, ĝ, ĵ, ŝ, and ŭ: are heard immediately following the *ee* sounds
in lee*ch*, lie*g*e, lei*s*ure, lea*sh*, and lee*w*ay. They are like the
sounds of English *ch*, *j*, *zh*, *sh*, and *w*.

SPELLING, SYLLABICATION, ACCENTUATION

Esperanto is scientifically phonetic — one letter, one sound
(approximating the basic symbols of the International **Phonetic**

Alphabet). Every word is pronounced as it is spelled. To name the letters, simply add *o* to the consonants.

There are no double consonants and no double vowels (save in compound words, where they are separately pronounced).

Each vowel constitutes a syllable, even if two or three of them are placed together. In dividing a word into syllables, a single consonant between two vowels goes with the *following*, not the *preceding* vowel. A consonant followed by *l* or *r* goes with the *l* or *r*. Otherwise, the syllable division is made before the last consonant of the group. Examples: a-e-ro, his-to-ri-o, a-ta-ki, an-gla, fin-gro, sank-ta.

The *accent* or *stress* is always on the *next to the last* syllable. Here, as in all other rules for Esperanto, there are no irregularities and no exceptions.

SAMPLE OF WRITTEN ESPERANTO; USE FOR PRACTICE READING

Facila Paragrafo

La inteligenta persono lernas la interlingvon Esperanto rapide kaj facile. Esperanto estas la moderna, kultura, neŭtrala lingvo por ĝenerala interkomunikado. La interlingvo estas simpla, fleksebla, praktika solvo de la problemo de globa interkompreno.

Anekdoto pri Profesoro kaj Studento

La telefono de la lernejo sonoris. La profesoro iris al la telefono. (Profesoro) "Jen, Profesoro Martelo." (Telefonanto) "Mi deziras informi vin, ke Karlo ne povas viziti la lernejon hodiaŭ, ĉar li estas malsana." (Profesoro) "Tion mi tre bedaŭras, mi deziras bonan resaniĝon! — Kiu estas ĉe la telefono?" (Telefonanto) "Mia patro."

GRAMMATICAL SURVEY

The grammar of Esperanto has only sixteen fundamental rules, which have no irregularities and no exceptions.

(1) There is no indefinite article; there is only a *Definite article*, *la*, alike for all sexes, cases, and numbers.

libro = book or a book   *la libro* = the book
pomo = apple or an apple   *la libroj* = the books
frato = brother, a brother   *la fratinoj* = the sisters
la fratoj amas la fratinon = the brothers love the sister.

(2) The *Noun* ends in *o*. To form the plural *j* is added. There are only two cases: nominative and accusative; the latter is obtained from the nominative by simply adding *n*.

tablo = table   *tabloj* = tables   *la tabloj* = the tables
ideo = idea   *ideoj* = ideas   *la ideoj* = the ideas

La lernanto havas krajonon kaj plumon en la poŝo.
The pupil has a pencil and a pen in his (*the*) pocket.

(3) The *Adjective* ends in *a*. It agrees in case and number with the noun. The *comparative* is made by the word *pli*; the *superlative* by *la plej*; with the comparative the conjunction *ol* is used.

bona = good   *bela* = beautiful   *dolĉa* = sweet

La inteligenta studento legas bonajn librojn.
The intelligent student reads good books.
La etaj infanoj havas belan patrinon.
The little children have a beautiful mother.
La pordo estas alta, la fenestro estas pli alta ol la pordo, kaj la muro estas la plej alta.
The door is high, the window is higher than the door, and the wall is the highest.

(4) The fundamental *Numerals* (not declined) are: *unu, du, tri, kvar, kvin, ses, sep, ok, naŭ, dek, cent, mil*. Tens and

hundreds are formed by simple junction of the numerals. To mark the ordinal *a* is added; for the multiple, *obl;* for the fractional, *on;* for the collective, *op.*

1 = *unu*	1st = *unua*
2 = *du*	2nd = *dua*
3 = *tri*	3rd = *tria*
10 = *dek*	15th = *dek-kvina*
14 = *dek-kvar*	36th = *tridek-sesa*
15 = *dek-kvin*	127th = *cent-dudek-sepa*
20 = *dudek*	1000th = *mila*
26 = *dudek ses*	2x2 = 4—*duoble du estas kvar*
37 = *tridek sep*	3 times = *trioble*
100 = *cent*	many times = *multoble*
108 = *cent ok*	1/2 = *duono*
149 = *cent kvardek naŭ*	1/12 = *dekduono*
1000 = *mil*	1/1000 = *milono*
5000 = *kvinmil*	by two's = *duope*
100,000 = *centmil*	by 6's = *sesope*
1,000,000 = *miliono*	in pairs = *duope*

(5) *Personal Pronouns*: *mi,* I; *vi,* you; *li,* he; *ŝi,* she; *ĝi,* it (thing or animal); *si,* (reflexive pronoun of third person); *ni,* we; *vi,* you (plural); *ili,* they; *oni,* one, people, they, we (indefinite pronoun of the third person); possessives are formed by adding *a.* Declensions as for nouns.

Li amas ŝin. He loves her.   *Ŝi amas lin.* She loves him.
mia libro, my book   *nia patro,* our father
Lia patro portis liajn paperojn en sia poŝo.
His father carried his (son's) papers in his (father's) pocket.

(6) The *Verb* undergoes no change with regard to person or number. Forms of the verb: time *being* (Present) takes the termination *-as;* time *been* (Past) *-is;* time *about-to-be* (Future) *-os;* Conditional *-us;* Imperative *-u;* Infinitive *-i.* Active Participles, *-ant, -int, -ont.* Passive Participles, *-at, -it, -ot.*

estas = is, are, am
estis = was, were
estos = will be
estus = should or would be
estu = be
esti = to be
amas = loves, is loving
amis = loved
amos = will love
amus = should or would love
amu = love
ami = to love
amanta = loving
aminta = having loved
amonta = about to love

estas amanta = is (am, are) loving
estas aminta = was (were) loving
estas amonta = is (am, are) about to love
amata = (being) loved
amita = having been loved
amota = about to be loved
estas amata = is (am, are) (being) loved
estas amita = has, (have) been, was (were) loved
estas amota = is (am, are) about to be loved

The negative is formed by placing *ne* before the verb: *mi ne komprenas*, I don't understand.

The interrogative is formed by prefixing the interrogative particle *ĉu* to the affirmative statement (do not invert the subject and the verb), unless another interrogative word (such as "who?", "when?", "why?") appears: *ĉu vi komprenas?*, do you understand?; but *kion ĝi signifas?*, what does this mean?

(7) The *Adverb* ends in *e;* comparison as for adjectives.

rapide = rapidly; *bele* = beautifully; *bone* = well; *persone* = personally, in person; *plezure* = with pleasure. *Mi kantas bone. Li kantas pli bone ol mi. Ŝi kantas la plej bone.* I sing well. He sings better than I. She sings the best.

(8) All *Prepositions* govern the nominative.

sur la arbo   *en la ĝardeno*   *apud la domo*
on the tree   in the garden   beside the house

(9) Every word is *pronounced* as it is *spelled.*

unu litero, unu sono = oo-noo lee-teh-ro, oo-noo so-no

(10) The *Accent* or *Stress* is always on the next to the last syllable.

universo = oo-nee-VEHR-so   *historio* = hees-toh-REE-o

(11) The *Compound Words* are formed by simple junction of the words; the chief word stands at the end. Grammatical terminations are also regarded as independent words.

> *bonintenca* = *bon-intenc-a* = well-meaning
> *remalsano* = *re-mal-san-o* = a return of illness, a relapse
> *katidineto* = *kat-id-in-et-o* = a tiny female kitten
> *kato*, cat; *ido*, offspring; *ino*, female; *eta*, tiny; *o*, substantive ending.

(12) When another *Negative Word* is present the word *ne* is left out.

> *Li ne havas ian sperton.* = He has not any experience.
> *Li havas nenian sperton.* = He has no experience.

(13) In order to show *Direction* towards, words take the termination of the accusative.

> *Li marŝis en la ĉambro.* He walked (about) in the room.
> *Li marŝis en la ĉambron.* He walked *into* the room.
> *Mi iras Parizon,* or *al Parizo.* I am going to Paris.

(14) Each *Preposition* has a definite meaning; but if the direct sense does not indicate which it should be, we use the preposition *je*, which has no meaning of its own. Instead of *je* we may use the accusative without a preposition.

al la domo = to the house   *en la taso* = in the cup
apud la pordo = by the door   *dum la tago* = during the day
de la urbo = from the city   *kun amiko* = with a friend

je la dua de Majo = May 2nd   *la duan de Majo* = May 2nd
longa je tri futoj = 3 ft. long   *longa tri futojn* = 3 ft. long
dum unu horo = during 1 hour   *unu horon* = during 1 hour

(15) The so-called *Foreign Words*, those which the majority of languages have taken from one source, undergo no change in Esperanto, beyond conforming to its orthography.

teatro = theatre   *ĉambro* = chamber
geografio = geography   *kemio* = chemistry
ekonomio = economy   *kvanto* = quantity

(16) The *Final Vowel* of the noun and of the article may sometimes be dropped and be replaced by an apostrophe.

> *Kiel ofte al stel', en la nokta ĉiel',*
> *Sub la bril' de l' brilanta trezor'.*
> How oft at a star, in the night sky,
> 'Neath the brillance of the glittering treasure.

PREFIXES AND SUFFIXES

The prefixes and suffixes provide great richness and flexibility in Esperanto. They are regarded as independent words, and they are combined with roots and other word-elements by simple junction. Try combining them with roots in the various lists of this section. They will augment your vocabulary and facility in Esperanto.

dis-   separation, dispersal: *doni*, to give; *disdoni*, to distribute.
ek-   beginning, brief action: *krii*, to cry, shout; *ekkrii*, to exclaim.
eks-   ex-, former: *prezidanto*, president; *eksprezidanto*, ex-president.
ge-   both sexes together: *patro*, father; *gepatroj*, parents.
mal-   opposite ideas: *alta*, high; *malalta*, low.

re-   back, again: *sendi,* to send; *resendi,* to send back.

-aĉ   contempt, disgust: *hundo,* a dog; *hundaĉo,* a cur.

-ad   continuation of action: *kanto,* a song; *kantado,* singing.

-aĵ   concrete ideas: *heredi,* to inherit; *heredaĵo,* heritage.

-an   inhabitant, member, adherent: *Parizo,* Paris; *Parizano,* Parisian.

-ar   a collection of things: *libro,* a book; *libraro,* a library.

-ebl   possibility, -able, -ible: *vidi,* to see; *videbla,* visible.

-ec   abstract ideas: *libera,* free; *libereco,* liberty.

-eg   enlargement, intensity: *domo,* a house; *domego,* a mansion.

-ej   place specially used for: *lerni,* to learn; *lernejo,* a school.

-em   inclination, disposition: *kredi,* to believe; *kredema,* credulous.

-er   unit, one of a collection: *sablo,* sand; *sablero,* grain of sand.

-estr   chief, leader, ruler: *ŝipo,* ship; *ŝipestro,* captain (of ship).

-et   diminution of degree: *monto,* mountain; *monteto,* a hill.

-id   descendant, young of: *kato,* cat; *katido,* a kitten.

-ig   causing something to be: *blanka,* white; *blankigi,* to whiten.

-iĝ   action of becoming: *pala,* pale; *paliĝi,* to turn pale.

-il   tool, instrument: *razi,* to shave; *razilo,* a razor.

-in   feminine gender: *koko,* a rooster; *kokino,* a hen.

-ind   worthy of: *admiri,* to admire; *admirinda,* worthy of admiration.

-ing   holder of one object: *glavo,* sword; *glavingo,* a scabbard.

-ism   "ism", theory, system: *idealo,* an ideal; *idealismo,* idealism.

-ist   trade, profession, occupation: *dento,* tooth; *dentisto,* dentist.

-uj   that which contains: *mono,* money; *monujo,* a purse.

-ul   person characterized by: *saĝa,* wise; *saĝulo,* a sage.

-um   general suffix: *kruco,* a cross; *krucumi,* to crucify

VOCABULARY

1. *World, Elements, Nature, Weather, Time, Directions.*

world, *mondo*
earth, *tero*
air, *aero*
water, *akvo*
fire, *fajro*
light, *lumo*
sea, *maro*
sun, *suno*
moon, *luno*
star, *stelo*
sky, *ĉielo*
wind, *vento*
weather, *vetero*
time, *tempo*
snow, *neĝo*
to snow, *neĝi*
rain, *pluvo*
to rain, *pluvi*
cloud, *nubo*
cloudy, *nuba*
fog, *nebulo*
ice, *glacio*
mud, *koto*
morning, *mateno*
noon, *tagmezo*
afternoon, *posttagmezo*
night, *nokto*
midnight, *noktmezo*
North, *nordo*
South, *sudo*
East, *oriento*
West, *okcidento*

year, *jaro*
month, *monato*
week, *semajno*
day, *tago*
hour, *horo*
minute, *minuto*
Sunday, *dimanĉo*
Monday, *lundo*
Tuesday, *mardo*
Wednesday, *merkredo*
Thursday, *ĵaŭdo*
Friday, *vendredo*
Saturday, *sabato*
January, *januaro*
February, *februaro*
March, *marto*
April, *aprilo*
May, *majo*
June, *junio*
July, *julio*
August, *aŭgusto*
September, *septembro*
October, *oktobro*
November, *novembro*
December, *decembro*
Spring, *printempo*
Summer, *somero*
Fall, *aŭtuno*
Winter, *vintro*
it is warm, *estas varme*
it is cold, *estas malvarme*

I shall see him *on* Monday, *Mi vidos lin lunde;* last Monday, *pasintan lundon;* next Monday, *sekvontan lundon;* Monday morning, *lunde matene;* every Monday, *ĉiulunde;* on May 5th, 1943, *la kvinan de majo, mil naŭcent kvardek tri.*

2. Family, Friendship, Love.

family, *familio*
husband, *edzo*
wife, *edzino*
parents, *gepatroj*
father, *patro*
mother, *patrino*
son, *filo*
daughter, *filino*
brother, *frato*
sister, *fratino*
uncle, *onklo*
aunt, *onklino*
nephew, *nevo*
niece, *nevino*
cousin, *kuzo, kuzino*
grandfather, *avo*
grandmother, *avino*
grandson, *nepo*
granddaughter, *nepino*
father-in-law, *bopatro*
mother-in-law, *bopatrino*
son-in-law, *bofilo*
daughter-in-law, *bofilino*

brother-in-law, *bofrato*
sister-in-law, *bofratino*
man, *viro*; (generic) *homo*
woman, *virino*
child, *infano*
boy, *knabo*
girl, *knabino*
sir, Mr., gentleman, *sinjoro*
madam, Mrs., lady, *sinjorino*
Miss, young lady, *fraŭlino*
friend, *amiko, amikino*
servant, *servisto, servistino*
to introduce, *prezenti*
to visit, *viziti*
love, *amo*
to love, *ami*
to fall in love with, *enamiĝi*
to marry, *edziĝi*
sweetheart, *amato, amatino*
kiss, *kiso*
to kiss, *kisi*
dear, beloved, *kara*

3. Speaking Activities.

word, *vorto*
language, *lingvo*
to speak, *paroli*
to say, *diri*
to tell, *diri, rakonti*
to inform, *informi*
to call, *voki*
to greet, *saluti*
to name, *nomi*
to cry, shout, *krii*
to listen to, *aŭskulti*

to hear, *aŭdi*
to understand, *kompreni*
to mean, *voli diri*
to ask for, *peti*
to ask (a question), *demandi*
to answer, *respondi*
to thank, *danki* (I thanked him
   for the book, *mi dankis lin pro
   la libro*)
to complain, *plendi*

4. Materials.

gold, *oro*
silver, *arĝento*
iron, *fero*

steel, *ŝtalo*
copper, *kupro*
tin, *stano*

lead, *plumbo*
oil, *oleo*
gasoline, *petrolo*
coal, *karbo*
wood, *ligno*
silk, *silko*
cotton, *kotono*

wool, *lano*
cloth, *ŝtofo*
to cut, *tranĉi*
to dig, *fosi*
to sew, *kudri*
to mend, *ripari*

5. Animals.

animal, *besto*
horse, *ĉevalo*
dog, *hundo*
cat, *kato*
bird, *birdo*
donkey, *azeno*
mule, *mulo*
cow, *bovino*
ox, *bovo*
pig, *porko*
chicken, *kokido*
hen, *kokino*

rooster, *koko*
sheep, *ŝafo*
goat, *kapro*
mouse, *muso*
snake, *serpento*
fly, *muŝo*
bee, *abelo*
mosquito, *moskito*
spider, *araneo*
louse, *pediko*
flea, *pulo*
bedbug, *litcimo*

6. Money, Buying and Selling.

money, *mono*
coin, *monero*
dollar, *dolaro*
cent, *cendo*
bank, *banko*
check, *ĉeko*
money order, *mandato, poŝt-mandato*
to earn, to gain, to win, *gajni*
to lose, *perdi*
to spend, *elspezi*
to lend, *alprunti*
to borrow, *deprunti*
to owe, *ŝuldi*
to pay, *pagi*
to give back, *redoni*
change, *moneto, restaĵo*
to change, *monerigi*
price, *prezo*

cost, *kosto*
to cost, *kosti*
expensive, *multekosta*
cheap, *malmultekosta*
store, *butiko*
piece, *peco*
slice, *tranĉaĵo*
pound, *funto*
package, *pakaĵo*
basket, *korbo*
box, *skatolo*
bag, *sako*
goods, *komercaĵoj*, (wares) *varoj*
to go shopping, *iri por aĉetadi*
to sell, *vendi*
to buy, *aĉeti*
to rent, to hire, *lui*
to be worth, *valori*
to choose, *elekti*

thief, robber, *ŝtelisto*
to steal, *ŝteli*
honest, *honesta*

dishonest, *malhonesta*
police, *polico*
policeman, *policano*

7. Eating and Drinking.

to eat, *manĝi*
breakfast, *matenmanĝo*
to eat breakfast, *matenmanĝi*
lunch, *tagmanĝo*, (small) *manĝeto*
to eat lunch, *tagmanĝi*, *manĝeti*
supper, *vespermanĝo*
to eat supper, *vespermanĝi*
dinner, *manĝo*, *ĉefmanĝo*
to dine, *manĝi*
meal, *manĝo*
dining-room, *manĝoĉambro*,
    manĝejo
waiter, *kelnero*
waitress, *kelnerino*
restaurant, *restoracio*
menu, *manĝokarto*, *menuo*
bill, *kalkulo*
to pass (a dish), *doni*, *transdoni*
tip, *dankmono*, *trinkmono*
to drink, *trinki*
water, *akvo*
wine, *vino*
beer, *biero*
coffee, *kajo*
tea, *teo*
milk, *lakto*
bottle, *botelo*
spoon, *kulero*
teaspoon, *kulero*, *tekulero*
knife, *tranĉilo*
fork, *forko*
glass, *glaso*
cup, *taso*
napkin, *buŝtuko*
salt, *salo*
pepper, *pipro*
plate, dish, *plado*
bread, *pano*

roll, *bulko*
butter, *butero*
sugar, *sukero*
soup, *supo*
rice, *rizo*
potatoes, *terpomo*
vegetable, *legomo*
meat, *viando*
beef, *bovaĵo*
steak, *viandtranĉaĵo*, *bifsteko*
chicken, *kokido*
chop, *kotleto*
veal, *bovidaĵo*
lamb, *ŝafidaĵo*
pork, *porkaĵo*
sausage, *kolbaso*
ham, *ŝinko*
bacon, *lardo*
egg, *ovo*
fish, *fiŝo*
fried, *fritita*
to cook, *kuiri*
boiled, *boligita*
stewed, *stufita*
roast, *rostaĵo*
roast beef, *rostbovaĵo*
baked, *bakita*
broiled, *kradrostita*
sauce, *saŭco*
salad, *salato*
cheese, *fromaĝo*
fruit, *frukto*
apple, *pomo*
pear, *piro*
peach, *persiko*
grapes, *vinberoj*
strawberries, *fragoj*
nuts, *nuksoj*

orange, *orangô*
lemon, *citrono*
juice, *suko*

cherries, *ĉerizoj*
dessert, *deserto*
pastry, *pastajo*

8. Hygiene and Attire

bath, *bano*
to bathe, *bani*
shower, *ŝprucbano, duŝo*
to wash, *lavi*
to shave, *razi*
barber, *razisto*
mirror, *spegulo*
soap, *sapo*
razor, *razilo*
safety razor, *sendanĝera razilo*
towel, *tuko*
comb, *kombilo*
brush, *broso*
scissors, *tondilo*
to wear, *porti*
to take off, *demeti*
to change, *ŝanĝi*
to put on, *surmeti*
clothes, *vestajoj*
hat, *ĉapelo*
suit, *kompleto, vesto*
coat, *jako*
vest, *veŝto*
pants, *pantalono*
underwear, *subvesto*
undershirt, *subĉemizo*
drawers, *kalsono*

glove, *ganto*
socks, *ŝtrumpetoj*
stockings, *ŝtrumpoj*
shirt, *ĉemizo*
collar, *kolumo*
tie, *kravato*
overcoat, *palto*
raincoat, *pluvpalto, pluvmantelo*
pocket, *poŝo*
handkerchief, *naztuko, poŝtuko*
button, *butono*
shoe, *ŝuo*
boot, *boto*
pocketbook, *manpoŝo, monujo*
purse, *monujo*
pin, tie pin, *pinglo, kravatopinglo*
needle, *kudrilo*
umbrella, *ombrelo*
watch, *poŝhorloĝo*
wristwatch, *manumhorloĝo*
chain, *ĉeno*
ring, *ringo*
eyeglasses, *okulvitroj*
slippers, *pantofloj*
dressing-gown, *ĉambrorobo,*
   tualet-robo
bathrobe, *banrobo*

9. Parts of the Body.

head, *kapo*
forehead, *frunto*
face, *vizaĝo*
mouth, *buŝo*
hair, *haroj*
eye, *okulo*
ear, *orelo*
tooth, *dento*
lip, *lipo*

nose, *nazo*
tongue, *lango*
chin, *mentono*
cheek, *vango*
mustache, *lipharoj*
beard, *barbo*
neck, *kolo*
throat, *gorĝo*
arm, *brako*

hand, *mano*
elbow, *kubuto*
wrist, *man-radiko*
finger, *fingro*
nail, *ungo*
leg, *kruro*
foot, *piedo*
knee, *genuo*
back, *dorso*

chest, *brusto*
ankle, *maleolo*
body, *korpo*
bone, *osto*
skin, *haŭto*
heart, *koro*
stomach, *stomako*
blood, *sango*
shoulder, *ŝultro*

10. Medical.

doctor, *kuracisto*
drug-store, *apoteko, drogejo*
hospital, *malsanulejo, hospitalo*
medicine, *medikamento, kuracilo*
pill, *pilolo*
prescription, *recepto*
bandage, *bandaĝo*
nurse, *flegistino, flegisto*
ill, *malsana*
illness, *malsano*
swollen, *ŝvelinta*

wound, *vundo*
wounded, *vundita*
head-ache, *kapdoloro*
tooth-ache, *dentdoloro*
cough, *tuso*
to cough, *tusi*
lame, *lama*
burn, *brulvundo*
pain, *doloro*
poison, *veneno*

11. Military.

war, *milito*
peace, *paco*
ally, *kunligano*
enemy, *malamiko*
army, *armeo*
danger, *danĝero*
dangerous, *danĝera*
to win, *venki*
to surround, *ĉirkaŭi*
to arrest, *aresti, kapti*
to kill, *mortigi*
to escape, *liberiĝi, eviti*
to run away, *forkuri*
to lead, *konduki, antaŭiri*
to follow, *sekvi*
to surrender, *cedi*
to retreat, *retiriĝi, returnemarŝi*
to bomb, shell, *bombardi*
fear, *timo*

prison, *malliberejo*
prisoner, *militkaptito*
to take prisoner, *kapti, ekkapti*
to capture, *kapti*
help, *helpo*
comrade, buddy, *kamarado, kunulo*
battle, *batalo, barakto*
to fight, *batali, barakti*
soldier, *soldato*
private, *soldato, simpla soldato*
corporal, *kaporalo*
sergeant, *serĝento*
lieutenant, *leŭtenanto*
captain, *kapitano*
major, *majoro*
colonel, *kolonelo*
general, *generalo*
officer, *oficiro*

company, *roto*
battalion, *bataliono*
regiment, *regimento*
brigade, *brigado*
division, *divizio*
troops, *soldataro, trupoj*
reenforcements, *refortigantoj, helptrupoj*
fortress, *fortikaĵo*
sentinel, *gardstaranto, gardsoldato*
to do sentry duty, *garde stari*
to be on duty, *dejori*
guard, *gvardio*
sign-post, *signa stango, vojmontrilo*
navy, *militŝiparo, militmaristaro*
sailor, *militmaristo*
marine, *marsoldato*
warship, *militŝipo*
cruiser, *krozŝipo*
destroyer, *detruoŝipo*
convoy, *ŝirmita kunŝiparo, konvojo*
escort, *kondukoŝipoj*
weapon, *armilo, batalilo*
rifle, *fusilo*
machine-gun, *maŝinpafilo*
cannon, *kanono*
ammunition, *municio*
supplies, *provizo, provizado*
cartridge, *kartoĉo*
bullet, *kuglo*
belt, *zono*

cartridge belt, *kartoĉozono*
knapsack, *tornistro*
tent, *tendo*
camp, *tendaro*
map, *karto, geografia karto, topografia karto*
rope, *ŝnuro*
flag, *standardo*
helmet, *kasko*
bayonet, *bajoneto*
uniform, *uniformo*
airplane, *aeroplano*
bombing plane, *bombardoplano, bombard-aeroplano*
pursuit plane, *ĉasoplano, ĉas-aeroplano*
shell, *obuso*
bomb, *bombo*
truck, *ŝarĝaŭto, ŝarĝaŭtomobilo*
tank, *kirasveturilo*
to load, *ŝargi*
to fire, to shoot, *pafi*
to shoot (military execution) *ekzekuti per pafado, fusilekzekuti*
spy, *spiono*
fire! *pafu!*
attention! *atentu!*
forward! *antaŭen!*
halt! *haltu!*
air-raid shelter, *rifuĝejo kontraŭ aeratako*

12. *Travel.*

passport, *pasporto*
customs, *dogano*
ship, *ŝipo*
steamer, *vaporŝipo*
stateroom, *kajuto*
berth, *ŝiplito*
to travel, *vojaĝi*
trip, voyage, *vojaĝo*
to leave, depart, *foriri*

to arrive, *alveni*
to ride, (a conveyance), *rajdi, veturi*
railroad, *fervojo*
station, *stacio*
track, *relvojo*
train, *vagonaro*
platform, *perono*
ticket, *bileto*

compartment, *kupeo*
all aboard!, *envagoniĝu!*
dining-car, *manĝvagono*
sleeper, *litvagono*
car, coach, *vagono*
trunk, *kofro*
valise, *valizo*
baggage, *pakaĵoj*

porter, *portisto*
bus, *aŭtobuso*
street-car, *tramo*
automobile, *aŭtomobilo*
taxi, *fiakro, taksfiakro*
driver, *ŝofero, veturigisto*
to drive (car), *veturigi, aŭtomobili*

13. Reading and Writing.

to read, *legi*
newspaper, *ĵurnalo*
magazine, *gazeto, revuo*
book, *libro*
to write, *skribi*
to translate, *traduki*
pencil, *krajono*
chalk, *kreto*
blackboard, *nigra tabulo*
ink, *inko*

pen, *plumo* (fountain pen, *fontplumo*)
envelope, *koverto*
paper, *papero*
letter, *letero*
post-office, *poŝtoficejo*
stamp, *poŝtmarko*
letter-box, *poŝtkesto*
to mail, *enpoŝtigi*
address, *adreso*
post-card, *poŝtkarto*

14. Amusements.

to smoke, *fumi*
cigar, *cigaro*
cigarette, *cigaredo*
tobacco, *tobako*
match, *alumeto*
give me a light, *donu al mi ekbruligon*
theatre, *teatro*
movies, *moviganta filmo, kino*
dance, *danco, balo*
to dance, *danci*
to have a good time, *amuziĝi*
ticket, *bileto*

pleasure, *plezuro*
to play, *ludi* (music or game)
to sing, *kanti*
song, *kanto*
game, *ludo*
ball, *pilko*
to take a walk, *promenadi*
beach, *marbordo*
to swim, *naĝi*
sand, *sablo*
refreshment, *refreŝigaĵo*
saloon, *trinkejo*
picnic, *pikniko, ekskurso*

15. Town and Country.

place, spot, *loko*
city, *urbo*
street, *strato*
sidewalk, *trotuaro*

road, *vojo*
intersection, *interkruciĝo*
harbor, *haveno*
block, *kvadrato*

school, *lernejo*
church, *preĝejo*
cathedral, *katedralo*
building, *konstruo*
corner, *angulo*
hotel, *hotelo*
office, *oficejo*
river, *rivero*
bridge, *ponto*
country, *kamparo*
village, *vilaĝo*

mountain, *monto*
grass, *herbo*
yard, *korto*
hill, *monteto*
lake, *lago*
forest, *arbaro*
field, *kampo*
flower, *floro*
tree, *arbo*
rock, *roko*
jungle, *ĵunglo*

16. House.

door, *pordo*
roof, *tegmento*
to open, *malfermi;* to close, *fermi*
key, *ŝlosilo*
to go in, *eniri;* to go out, *eliri*
house, *domo* (at home, *hejme,* to
   go home, *iri hejmen*)
cottage, *dometo, kabano*
hut, *kabano*
to live in, *loĝi en*
staircase, *ŝtuparo*
to go up, *supren iri*
to go down, *malsupren iri*
room, *ĉambro*
toilet, *necesejo*
kitchen, *kuirejo*
table, *tablo*
chair, *seĝo*
to sit down, *sidiĝi*
to stand, be standing, *stariĝi, stari*

wall, *muro*
lamp, *lampo*
candle, *kandelo*
closet, *vestejo*
window, *fenestro*
bed, *lito*
bedroom, *litoĉambro*
blanket, *kovrilo, lankovrilo*
sheet, *litotuko*
mattress, *matraco*
alarm-clock, *vekhorloĝo*
pillow, *kapkuseno*
to rest, *ripozi*
to go to bed, *enlitiĝi*
to go to sleep, fall asleep, *endor-*
   miĝi
to sleep, *dormi*
to wake up, *vekiĝi*
to dress, *vesti sin*
to get up, *levi sin*

17. Miscellaneous Nouns.

people, *popolo*
thing, *aĵo, afero*
name, *nomo*
luck, *bonŝanco* (bad luck, *mal-*
   bonŝanco)

number, *numero*
life, *vivo*
death, *morto*
work, *laboro*

18.   Verbs — Coming and Going.

to come, *veni*

to go, *iri*

to go away, *foriri*

to stay, remain, *resti*

to return, *reveni*

to run, *kuri*

to walk, *marŝi*

to fall, *fali*

to follow, *sekvi*

19.   Verbs — Looking and Seeing.

to see, *vidi*

to look at, *rigardi* (I am looking at it, *mi rigardas ĝin*)

to look for, *serĉi*

to laugh, *ridi*

to smile, *rideti*

to look, seem, *ŝajni* (it seems to me, *ŝajnas al mi*)

to recognize, *rekoni*

to take for, *supozi esti*

20.   Verbs — Mental.

to make a mistake, *erari*

to hope, *esperi*

to wait (for), *atendi*

to think, *pensi*

to believe, *kredi*

to like, *ŝati*

to wish, to want, *deziri*

to know (a person), *koni*

to know (a fact), *scii*

to understand, *kompreni*

to remember, *memori*

to forget, *forgesi*

to permit, allow, *permesi*

to forbid, *malpermesi*

to promise, *promesi*

to learn, *lerni*

to feel like, *emi* (I feel like sleeping, *mi emas dormi, mi estas dormema*)

to fear, be afraid, *timi*

to be right, *pravi*

to be wrong, *malpravi*

21.   Verbs — Miscellaneous.

to live, *vivi*

to die, *morti*

to work, *labori*

to give, *doni*

to take, *preni*

to show, *montri*

to begin, to start, *komenci* (transitive) ; *komenciĝi* (intransitive)

to finish, *fini* (tr.) ; *finiĝi* (intr.)

to continue, *daŭri* (intr.) ; *daŭrigi* (tr.)

to help, *helpi*

to hide, *kaŝi* (tr.) ; *kaŝiĝi, sinkaŝi* (intr.)

to lose, *perdi*

to find, *trovi*

to leave, *foriri* (use *forlasi* for leaving objects or people)

to try, *peni*

to meet, *renkonti*

to put, place, *meti*

to do, to make, *fari*

to have something done, *igi* (or use suffix -*ig*-; I had a letter written, *mi igis leteron skribinta* or *mi skribigis leteron;* I had them sing, *mi igis ilin kanti,* or *mi kantigis ilin*).

can, to be able, *povi*
to carry, *porti*
to stop, *halti* (use *ĉesi* for "to stop doing")
to bring, *alporti, venigi*
to cover, *kovri*
to get, obtain, *akiri*
to hold, *teni*
to get, become, *iĝi* (he became pale, *li iĝis pala, li paliĝis*)
to break, *rompi*
to hurry, *rapidi*
to deliver, *liveri*
to send, *sendi*
to belong, *aparteni*
to accept, *akcepti*
to refuse, *refuzi*
to do again, *fari denove*

22. Adjectives.

small, *malgranda, eta*
large, great, *granda*
big (bulky), *ampleksa*
tall, high, *alta*
short, *malalta*
heavy, *peza*
light (weight), *malpeza*
long, *longa*
wide, *larĝa*
narrow, *mallarĝa*
clean, *pura*
dirty, *malpura*
cool, *malvarmeta*
cold, *malvarma*
warm, hot, *varma*
damp, *malseketa*
wet, *malseka*
empty, *malplena*
dry, *seka*
full, *plena*
soft, *mola*
hard, *malmola*
quick, *rapida*
slow, *malrapida*
ordinary, *ordinara*
comfortable, *komforta*
uncomfortable, *malkomforta*
near, *proksima*
distant, *malproksima*
right, *dekstra*
left, *maldekstra*
poor, *malriĉa*

rich, *riĉa*
beautiful, *bela*
pretty, *beleta*
ugly, *malbela*
sweet, *dolĉa*
bitter, *amara*
sour, *acida*
salt, *sala*
young, *juna*
dark, *malhela*
light, bright, *hela*
clear, *klara*
fat, *grasa*
thick, *dika*
thin, *maldika*
round, *ronda*
square, *kvadrata*
flat, *plata*
deep, *profunda*
strong, *forta*
weak, *malforta*
tired, *laca*
alone, *sola*
same, *sama*
easy, *facila*
hard, *malfacila*
happy, *feliĉa*
merry, *gaja*
sad, *malgaja, malĝoja*
free, *libera*
crazy, *freneza*
silly, *malsprita, malprudenta*

drunk, *ebria*
polite, *ĝentila*
rude, *malĝentila*
pleasant, *agrabla*
unpleasant, *malagrabla*
lonesome, *soleca*
true, *vera*
false, *malvera* (spurious, *falsa*)
foreign, *fremda*
old, *maljuna*
new, *nova*
good, *bona*
better, *pli bona* (best, *la plej bona*)
bad, *malbona*
worse, *pli malbona* (worst, *la plej malbona*)
fine, *bela, bona*
first, *unua*

last, *lasta*
friendly, *amika*
hostile, *malamika*
lucky, *bonŝanca*
unlucky, *malbonŝanca*
charming, *ĉarma*
afraid, *timema*
ready, *preta*
hungry, *malsata*
thirsty, *soifa*
funny, *komika, ŝerca*
possible, *ebla*
impossible, *neebla*
brave, *kuraĝa, brava*
cowardly, *malkuraĝa*
quiet, *kvieta, trankvila*
noisy, *brua*
living, *viva*
dead, *morta*

23. Colors.

white, *blanka*
black, *nigra*
red, *ruĝa*
green, *verda*
blue, *blua*

yellow, *flava*
gray, *griza*
brown, *bruna*
rose, *rozkolora, roza*
purple, *purpura*

24. Nationalities.

Use no capital for the adjective or for the language, except in the case of *Esperanto*, which is capitalized because it originated as a pseudonym from the word *esperanto*, meaning "one who hopes".

Names of languages are used adverbially, or with the preposition: *angle* or *en la angla lingvo* — both mean "in the English language".

The forms given are nouns, indicating a person of the nationality mentioned. To form the adjective, change the ending *-o* to *-a* (French wine, *franca vino*).

U. S. A. citizen, *usonano*
American, *amerikano, nord-amerikano, sud-amerikano*
English, *anglo*
French, *franco*
German, *germano*

Spanish, *hispano*
Russian, *ruso*
Italian, *italo*
Japanese, *japano*
Chinese, *ĉino*
Dutch, *nederlandano*

Norwegian, *norvego*
Swedish, *svedo*
Finnish, *finlandano*
Belgian, *belgo*
Polish, *polo*
Danish, *dano*
Swiss, *sviso*
Portuguese, *portugalo*
Yugoslav, *jugoslavo*
Bulgarian, *bulgaro*
Czech, *ĉeho*
Greek, *greko*
Turkish, *turko*
Roumanian, *rumano*
Hungarian, *hungaro*
Austrian, *aŭstro*
Malay, *malajano*
Persian, *perso*
Arabian, Arab, *arabo*
Jewish, Hebrew, *judo, hebreo*
Australian, *aŭstraliano*
Canadian, *kanadano*

Mexican, *meksikano*
Brazilian, *brazilano*
Argentinian, *argentinano*
Chilean, *ĉilano*
Peruvian, *peruano*
Cuban, *kubano*
Puerto Rican, *portorikano*
Colombian, *kolombiano*
Venezuelan, *venezuelano*
Bolivian, *boliviano*
Uruguayan, *urugvajano*
Paraguayan, *paragvajano*
Ecuadorian, *ekvadorano*
Costa Rican, *kostarikano*
Honduran, *hondurano*
Salvadorean, *salvadorano*
Guatemalan, *gvatemalano*
Dominican (of Santo Domingo) *dominikano*
Panamanian, *panamano*
Nicaraguan, *nikaragvano*

25. Adverbs and Adverbial Expressions.

today, *hodiaŭ*
yesterday, *hieraŭ*
tomorrow, *morgaŭ*
day before yesterday, *antaŭ hieraŭ*
day after tomorrow, *post morgaŭ*
tonight, *hodiaŭ nokte*
last night, *hieraŭ nokte*
this morning, *hodiaŭ matene*
in the morning, *matene*
in the afternoon, *posttagmeze*
in the evening, *vespere*
in the night, *nokte*
tomorrow morning, *morgaŭ matene*
tomorrow afternoon, *morgaŭ posttagmeze*
tomorrow evening, *morgaŭ vespere*
tomorrow night, *morgaŭ nokte*
early, *frue*

on time, *akurate*
late, *malfrue*
already, *jam*
no longer, *ne plu*
yet, still, *ankoraŭ*
not yet, *ne ankoraŭ*
now, *nun*
afterwards, then, *poste*
never, *neniam*
always, *ĉiam*
forever, *por ĉiam*
soon, *baldaŭ*
often, *ofte*
seldom, *malofte*
usually, *kutime*
fast, *rapide*
slowly, *malrapide*
here, *ĉi tie*
there, *tie*

over there, *tie*
near by, *apude*
near here, *proksime*
far away, *malproksime*
up, *supre*
down, *malsupre*
ahead, in front, *antaŭe*
behind, in back, *malantaŭe*
forward, *antaŭen*
back, *malantaŭen*
outside, *ekstere*
inside, *interne*
opposite, *kontraŭe*
here and there, *tie kaj aliloke*
everywhere, *ĉie*
where?, *kie?* (motion, *kien?*)
where, *kie*, (motion, *kien*)
also, *ankaŭ*
yes, *jes*
no, not, *ne*
very, *tre*
much, *multe* (very much, *tre multe*)
well, *bone*
badly, *malbone*
better, *pli bone*
worse, *pli malbone*
more, *pli* (more than, *pli ol;* but use *pli da* before quantity connotations)
less, *malpli*
as - as, *tiel — kiel*
as much - as, *tiom—kiom*
as many - as, *tiom multe—kiom*
how much?, *kiom?*

how many?, *kiom?*, *kiom multe?*
how?, *kiel?*
too much, *tro multe*
too many, *tro multe, tro multaj*
so much, *tiom multe*
so many, *tiom multe, tiom multaj*
as, like, *kiel*
so, *tiel*
besides, furthermore, *plie, plue*
finally, *fine*
only, *sole*
almost, *preskaŭ*
gladly, *ĝoje, volonte*
certainly, *certe*
at once, *tuj*
not at all, *tute ne*
unfortunately, *bedaŭrinde*
hardly, *apenaŭ*
aloud, *laŭte*
suddenly, *subite*
about, *ĉirkaŭ*
perhaps, maybe, *eble*
a little, *iomete*
again, *denove*
really, truly, *vere*
together, *kune*
at least, *almenaŭ*
for lack of, *pro manko de*
a long time ago, *longe antaŭe*
repeatedly, again and again, *multfoje*
therefore, *do, tial*
further away, *pli malproksime*
of course, *kompreneble*
occasionally, *kelkfoje*

26. Conjunctions.

and, *kaj*
but, *sed*
if, *se*
or, *aŭ*
why?, *kial?*
because, *ĉar*

why, *tial, pro tio ke*
before, *antaŭ*
when, *kiam*
than, *ol*
where, *kie*
until, till, *ĝis*

although, *kvankam*

unless, *krom se, se - ne*

while, *dum*

that, *ke*

for, since, *de kiam, ĉar*

after, *post, post kiam*

as soon as, *tuj* (*post*) *kiam*

as long as, *dum*

provided that, *kondiĉe ke*

in order that, *por ke*

so that, *tiel ke*

without, *sen, sen ke*

27. Indefinite Pronouns and Adjectives.

everything, *ĉio*

everyone, *ĉiu*

all, *ĉio, ĉiuj*

each, every, *ĉiu*

something, *io*

some, *iuj, kelkaj*

little (not much), *malmulta*

few, *unuj, kelkaj*

enough, *sufiĉa*

enough!, *sufiĉe, ne pli!*

such a, *kia*

all kinds of, *ĉiaj*

someone, *iu*

nothing, *nenio*

no one, *neniu*

no.. (adj.), *neniu.., nenia..*

neither - nor, *nek - nek*

(an) other, *alia*

much (lots of), *multa*

many, *multaj*

several, *kelkaj, diversaj*

both, *ambaŭ*

28. Prepositions.

of, from, by, *de*

out from, out of, *el*

to, at, *al*

with, *kun*

in, *en*

on, *sur*

at, *ĉe*

over, above, *super*

for, *por*

without, *sen*

until, up to, *ĝis*

since, *de post, depost*

toward, *al* (or final -*n* as accusative of direction)

between, among, *inter*

near, *proksima al*

far from, *malproksima de*

before, *antaŭ*

after, *post*

in front of, opposite, *kontraŭ*

in back of, behind, *malantaŭ*

under (neath), *sub*

through, *tra*

across, *trans*

against, *kontraŭ, apud*

by means of, *per*

in spite of, *spite de*

about, around, *ĉirkaŭ*

because of, on account of, *pro*

during, *dum*

instead of, *anstataŭ*

beside, *apud*

on the other side of, *aliflanke de*

29. Special Expressions and Idioms.

good morning, *bonan matenon*

good day, good afternoon, *bonan tagon*

good evening, *bonan vesperon*

good night, *bonan nokton*
good-by, *adiaŭ*
see you later, *ĝis revido*
see you then, *ĝis la revido*
see you tomorrow, *ĝis morgaŭ*
just now, *ĵus nun*
just a moment ago, *ĵus antaŭ momento*
hello! *saluton!* (on the telephone, *saluton!*)
how are you? *kiel vi fartas?*
how goes it? *kiel ĝi iras*
I'm well, *tre bone, mi fartas bone*
I'm (much) better, (*multe*) *pli bone*
what time is it? *kioma horo?*
it's six o'clock, *estas la sesa*
at six o'clock, *je la sesa*
at about six, *proksimume je la sesa*
at half past six, *je la sesa kaj duono*
at a quarter past (to) six, *je la sesa kaj kvarono, kvarono post* (*antaŭ*)
    la sesa
at ten minutes past (to) six, *je la sesa kaj dek minutoj, dek post*
    (*antaŭ*) *la sesa*
last year, *pasintan jaron*
next year, *venontan jaron*
every day, *ĉiutage*
each day, *ĉiun tagon*
the whole day, *la tutan tagon*
please, will you? *mi petas, bonvolu*
tell me, *diru al mi* (please tell me, *bonvole diru al mi*)
will you give me? *ĉu vi bonvole donos al mi?*
bring (to) me, *portu al mi*
show (to) me, *montru al mi*
thank you, *dankon, mi dankas*
don't mention it, *tute ne, estas nenio*
pardon me, *pardonu, pardonu min*
it doesn't matter, never mind, *ne gravas, tute ne gravas*
I'm sorry, *mi bedaŭras*
I can't help, *mi ne povas ne* (I can't help saying, *mi ne povas ne diri*)
it's nothing, *estas nenio*
what a pity!, it's too bad!, *kia domaĝo!, estas domaĝe!, domaĝe!*
I'm glad, *mi ĝojas* (to, the same plus infinitive)
I have to, *mi devas*
I'm agreeable, *mi konsentas*
where are you going?, *kien vi iras?*
here is (are), *jen estas, jen!*

there is, there are, *estas*, (use *tie estas*, if pointing out)
which way?, *kien?*, *kiun direkton?*
where is?, *kie estas?*
this way (direction), *ĉi tien* (that way, *tien*)
this way (in this fashion), *tiel, tiamaniere*
to the right, *dekstren*
to the left, *maldekstren*
straight ahead, *rekten, rekte antaŭen*
come with me, *venu kun mi*
what can I do for you?, *kiel mi povas vin servi?*
what is happening?, *kio okazas?*
what is it?, what is the matter?, *kio estas?, kio okazas?*
what is the matter with you?, *kio malestas al vi?, kio okazas al vi?*
what do you want?, *kion vi deziras?*
how much is it?, *kiom?, kiom kostas?*
anything else?, *ion pli?, ĉu ion pli?*
nothing else, *nenion pli*
do you speak Esperanto?, *ĉu vi parolas esperante?*
a little, *iomete*
speak (more) slowly, *parolu (pli) malrapide*
do you understand?, *ĉu vi komprenas?*
I don't understand, *mi ne komprenas*
do you know?, *ĉu vi scias?*
I don't know, *mi ne scias*
I can't, *mi ne povas*
what do you call this in Esperanto?, *kiel oni nomas ĝin esperante?*
how do you say — in Esperanto?, *kiel vi diras — esperante?*
what does that mean?, *kion ĝi signifas?*
what do you mean?, *kion vi volas diri?*
what are you talking about?, *pri kio vi parolas?*
I'm an American (citizen of U. S. A., Esperantist), *mi estas amerikano
      (usonano, esperantisto)*
I'm hungry (thirsty, sleepy, warm, cold), *mi estas malsata (soifa,
      dormema, varma, malvarma)*
It's warm, (cold, windy, fine weather, bad weather), *estas varme
      (malvarme, vente, bona vetero, malbona vetero)*
It's forbidden, *estas malpermesite* (no smoking, *ne fumu, malpermesite
      fumi*)
luckily, *bonŝance, feliĉe*
is it not so?, *ĉu ne?* (use this invariable phrase wherever English
      repeats the verb: you went, didn't you?; he is here, isn't he?)
not at all, *tute ne*
how old are you?, *kian aĝon vi havas?, kiom da jaroj vi havas?*
I'm twenty years old, *mi havas dudek jarojn*

how long have you been waiting? *kiom longe vi atendis?*
how long have you been here?, *kiom longe vi estis ĉi tie?*
as soon as possible, *kiel eble plej baldaŭ*
come here!, *venu!, venu ĉi tien!*
come in!, *envenu!*
look!, *rigardu!*
careful!, *atentu!, zorgu!*
look out!, *zorgu vin!, gardu vin!*
for heaven's sake!, *pro Dio!, Dio mia!*
heck!, darn it!, *damnu!, kondamnu je infero!, diable!*
as you please, *kiel plaĉas al vi*
listen!, look here!, say!, *atentu!*
just a second!, *momenton!*
what kind of?, *kia?, kia speco de?*
gangway!, by your leave!, *pasejon!, kun via permeso!*
in any case, at any rate, *ĉiaokaze*
glad to meet you, *kun plezuro, mi ĝojas konatiĝi kun vi*
you don't say so!, *ĉu vere!, nekredeble!*
notice!, *avizo!*

APPENDIX B

ENGLISH

SPEAKERS AND LOCATION[1]

(All population figures are approximate)

Western Hemisphere — U. S. A. — 132,000,000; Canada, Newfoundland and Labrador — 12,000,000;[2] Alaska 70,000; Bermudas — 30,000; Bahamas — 30,000; Jamaica — 1,200,000; Leeward and Windward Islands — 400,000; British Guiana — 350,000. Official and secondary tongue in British Honduras (60,000); Canal Zone (50,000); Puerto Rico (2,000,000); Virgin Islands (25,000). Widely spoken in Mexico, Greenland, Cuba, Haiti, Dominican Republic, and Spanish and Portuguese-speaking countries of Central and South America.

Europe — Great Britain and Northern Ireland — 47,000,000; Eire — 3,000,000. Official and secondary tongue of Gibraltar (21,000); Malta (270,000). Widely spoken in Iceland and on the European continent, particularly in Belgium, Denmark, France, the Netherlands, Norway, Sweden and Switzerland. Between four and five million continental Europeans speak English.

Asia — Language of colonization in Burma (16,000,000); Ceylon (6,000,000); Cyprus (400,000); Malaya and Straits Settlements (5,500,000); Hong Kong (1,500,000); British India (390,000,000); Palestine (1,500,000);

1. See English map, p. 62.
2. Including some 3,000,000 French Canadian speakers in Quebec and Ontario, most of whom speak English as well.

Transjordan (500,000), etc. It is estimated that English is spoken by over 22,000,000 people in India and Ceylon, 1,200,000 in Burma and Malaya, 1,000,000 in Japan, 3,000,000 in China, 500,000 in the Near East.

Africa — Official, but not primary language of Liberia (2,000,000, of whom 200,000 speak English) and the Union of South Africa (10,700,000, of whom 2,150,000 speak English). Language of colonization in Anglo-Egyptian Sudan (6,500,000); Basutoland (600,000); Bechuanaland (300,000); Gambia (200,000); Gold Coast (4,000,000); Kenya (3,500,000); Nigeria (22,000,000). Nyasaland (1,600,000); Rhodesia (3,000,000); Sierra Leone (2,000,000); British Somaliland (350,000); Southwest Africa (300,000); Swaziland (150,000); Tanganyika (5,300,000); Uganda (3,800,000). Widely spoken in Egypt. The total number of English speakers throughout the African continent is estimated at over 4,170,000.

Oceania — Official and primary language of Australia (7,000,000) and New Zealand (1,600,000). Language of colonization in insular possessions of U. S. and Great Britain having total populations of 2,600,000,[3] exclusive of Hawaii (500,000) and the Philippines (16,000,000); in the former, most of the population speaks English, while in the latter over one-fourth (4,260,000) of the population speaks English.

3. Including the Bismarck Archipelago, British North Borneo, Brunei, the Cook, Fiji, Gilbert and Ellice Islands, Guam, Labuan, New Guinea, some of the New Caledonia and New Hebrides Islands, Papua, Samoa, Sarawak, the Solomon Islands, Tonga, etc.

APPENDIX C

MILITARY SLANG

Words and expressions coined by men in the armed services are picturesque, but extremely unstable, being frequently recast, dropped or added to. Some of these terms, however, may easily survive in the post-war period and become part and parcel of the spoken English of one or another section of the English-speaking world. A few such terms that have recently appeared in the press are:

U. S. FORCES (*MOSTLY AIR FORCE AND MARINES*)

to stew in one's own juice,	*to sweat out*
to wait for food,	*to sweat out a chow line*
stupid,	*knucklehead*
object, thing,	*gizmo*
a complete miss,	*Maggie's drawers*
to score a hit,	*to lay it in the black*
field shoes,	*boon dockers*
prisoner,	*brig rat*
cigarette makings,	*blanket and freckles*
O. K.,	*ding hau*
yes-man,	*ear banger*
girl friend,	*Fifi*
necktie,	*field scarf*
hand,	*glom*
candy,	*pogie bait*
stop it!,	*knock it off!*
Messerschmidt,	*tailpecker*
double fighter-plane attack on bomber,	*sister act*

BRITISH (*MOSTLY R. A. F.*)

plane,	*kite*
bomb,	*egg*
torpedo bomb,	*fish*
depth-bomb,	*ash-can*
machine-gun bullets,	*confetti*
enemy planes at 10,000 feet,	*bandits at ten grand*
non-flying airman,	*penguin*
canteen-loving flier,	*canteen cowboy*
girl friend,	*target for tonight*
two-turret tank,	*Mae West*
commando knife,	*smatchet*
target,	*rhubarb*
fed up with,	*browned off, brassed off cheesed off*
to crash,	*to prang*
here's to you!,	*cheers!*
to be skeptical,	*to take a dim view*
real truth,	*pukka gen*
wrong steer,	*duff gen*
not to have something,	*to have had it*

AUSTRALIAN

wife,	*trouble*
children,	*godfers*
walk,	*whisper*
street,	*field*
tea,	*rosie*
to play piano,	*to fancy fanny*

NEOLOGISMS

Definitely linked with the war, but of more widespread application by reason of civilian as well as military use, are terms like *G. I.* (originally "General Issue", applied to articles of military equipment, now used indifferently as a noun to apply to the soldier himself or as an adjective to describe any of his belongings or multifarious activities); *jeep* (said to be from *G. P.*, "general purpose"; this word has recently given rise to such derivatives as *jeepable, unjeepable, jeepability*, applied to roads and jungle trails); *gremlin; blitz* (noun, adjective and verb); *paratroops* and *paratrooper; fifth column; Quisling* (with a verb, *to quisle*); *selectee; war of nerves; black market* (with a derivative, *blacketeer*, in which the influence of *racketeer* is clearly perceptible); *flak* (an abbreviation for the German *Flugzeugabwehrkannonen*, anti-aircraft guns) and *ak-ak*. *To liaise* (from *liaison*; "to liaise between Washington and New York"), *to do a Dunkirk* (to retreat hurriedly), and *to coventrize* (from Coventry; to demolish completely) have also been reported. *Pill-box, fox-hole, bazooka, bulldozer* are well known.

The language of the underworld on the one hand, that of swing-crazy youthful generations on the other, are rich in neologisms the continued existence of most of which is extremely doubtful. Such innovations consist in part in the coining of new words, but to a much greater degree in changes in the meaning of existing words and combinations.

Three terms from the shady side of life which have recently come to the writer's attention are *mooch*, used not in its older slang acceptance of "to beg", but as a noun to replace *sucker*, the prospective victim of a swindle; *pitch*, the salestalk of an aggressive salesman or confidence man; and *to run someone* (in the sense of "to chase someone") *with a knife*.

From the youthful and swing-loving angle there is a choicer assortment: *what gives?* ("what's up?"; "how are you?"; the influence of German *was gibt's?* seems perceptible here); *apple-polishing* (currying favor); *corny*, or *off the cob* (silly or sentimental; *to spout corn*, or *to slide one's jib*, is to sentimentalize or to talk too much); *to collapse* (to sit down); *to be cooking with gas* (or *on the front burner*: to be doing well); *to blitz the cold-storage plant* (to raid the frigidaire); *AWOL* (no longer "absent without leave", but "a wolf on the loose"; *wolf* and *wolverine* are themselves new acceptances of age-old terms to denote the more sexily inclined of the two sexes); *burnt to a crisp* (up-to-date); *gruesome twosome* (a pair keeping steady company); *to ice up* (to give the cold shoulder to); *to woof* (to kid or to tease); *to nix* (to get rid of); *do you dig me?* ("do you get me?"). Expressions of approval are legion: *on the beam, in the groove, groovy, hard, murder, mellow, on fire, has his boots on*, etc. etc. etc.

From the more professionally musical end of the swing movement come expressions such as *jameroo* or *barrelhouse* (swing session); *'gators* and *hepcats* (fanciers of the new vogue in music); *fave* (favorite); *jive* or *jam anthems* (pieces of swing music); *killer-diller* (musical hit); *black-stick* or *agony-pipe* (clarinet); *voodoo boilers* (drums); *woodpile* (xylophone); and *to lather the moth-box* (to play the piano).

Terms like *boondoggle* and *gobbledigook* represent the recent contribution of politics to the language.

All that can be said of the above items is that they are illustrative of the growth and decay of language. The overwhelming majority of them are destined to an ephemeral life, being replaced almost as soon as they are born by new expressions that quickly gain and lose popularity. A few will find literary favor in the eyes of newspapers and magazines, become generalized throughout the English-speaking world by reason of the press, movietone and radio, and ultimately pass into the vocabulary of the standard English of the future.

A GLOSSARY OF GRAMMATICAL AND LINGUISTIC TERMS

(with partial index)

ablative — *see* **case**

absolute — *see* **case**

abstract — *see* **noun**

accent — voice-stress or voice-energy bearing upon a given part of the word; in a word like "*absolute*", the accent falls on the first syllable; in "European", on the next to the last; in "de*lay*", on the last. Frequently a sentence-stress appears as well as a word-stress; in the sentence "*I* have done it, not *you*", the words "I" and "you" bear a special stress. Some languages have more stress than others; English, for instance, has a stronger stress than French. For the accentuation of various languages, *see* pp. 67, 89, 127, 173, 187, 229, 272, 315, 323, 330, 354, 361-2, 366, 368, 371-2, 374-5, 379-81, 384, 396, 423, 427, 432, 436, 438, 440, 444, 447, 451, 465, 487, 508, 533. **Pitch,** or **pitch-accent,** is simply a musical rise in the tone of the voice, as when an Englishman says: "*Did* you really?" Pitch and stress are usually both present in any given tongue, but in different proportions. For the significant value of pitch in some languages, *see* pp. 92, 98, 102, 354, 372, 444. *See also* **tone.**

accent-mark — the written symbol used, in some languages, to indicate where the stress falls (as in Spanish *acción*, Italian *città*), or to show that the vowel over which it appears is to be given a special sound (as in French *parlé, fête, fidèle*). The more usual accent marks are the acute (´), the grave (`) and the circumflex (^). For the different values of accent marks in various tongues, *see* pp. 105, 173, 184, 187, 229, 272, 302, 315, 330, 361, 366, 368, 370-1, 423, 432, 436, 440, 444-5, 449, 494. *See also* **diacritic.**

accusative — *see* **case**

active — *see* **voice**

address, forms of — in English, it is customary to use the same form of address in the singular and in the plural, familiarly or politely (*you* have seen it); in many languages, however, a distinction is made between a singular and a plural "you" (French *tu l'as vu; vous l'avez vu*, or archaic English *thou hast seen it; ye have seen it*); a distinction is also made in many languages between a person or persons whom one wants to address familiarly, and a person or persons whom one wants to address politely; often the polite singular form coincides with the familiar plural (French *vous l'avez vu* can serve as a familiar plural, as when a mother addresses two of her children; as a polite singular, as when a tourist addresses a stranger; or as a polite plural, as when a tourist addresses two or more strangers); in other languages, special polite forms appear, generally with a form of the verb other than the second person (Spanish *usted lo ha visto*, for which the closest English literal equivalent would be "Your Honor, your Grace, has seen it"; or German *Sie haben es gesehen*, literally, "they have seen it"; or Italian *Lei*, or *Ella l'ha visto*, literally, "she has seen it"; the capitalization of *Sie* and *Lei* is merely a written-tongue convention). For the forms of polite address in various languages, *see* pp. 94, 100, 113, 133, 177, 192, 205, 234, 245, 248, 278, 391, 397, 538, 542–3. Certain languages, like Japanese, have, in addition to a familiar and a polite form of address, also an **honorific** one, reserved for cases where one wishes to be superlatively polite (*see* pp. 536, 538, 547). Compare with the various gradations of politeness implied in French *ton père, votre père, monsieur votre père*; in Italian *tuo padre, vostro padre, Suo padre, il Suo signor padre*; etc. The Japanese use of completely different verbs to express familiarity, politeness or special honor might be remotely compared with such English expressions as: "Buddy, did you get a look at the enemy?"; "Lieutenant, did you see the enemy?"; "Did your Excellency discern the enemy?"

adjective — a word used with a noun to describe it (in which case it is called a **descriptive** adjective: "the *large* book") or to limit it (in which case it may be **demonstrative:** "*this* book"; **possessive:** "*my* book"; **indefinite:** "*any* book"; **interrogative:** "*which* book?"). In some languages, the possessive adjective is accompanied by the definite article (Italian *il mio libro*, literally, "the my book"; *see* pp. 280, 322). **Numerals** ("*two* books") and **articles** ("*a* book", "*the* book") may also be said to fall under the heading of adjective insofar as they limit nouns. **Participles** are frequently used as adjectives ("the *speaking* man", "the *spoken* word"). For the peculiarities of adjectives in certain language-groups, *see* pp. 24, 35, 42.

The descriptive variety of adjective may modify its noun directly (in which case it is called **attributive:** "the *strong* man"); or indirectly, through the verb "to be" (in which case it is called **predicate:** "the man is *strong*"; *see* pp. 112, 131, 188, 231, 235, 384, 394, 437, 468, 497, 548). Furthermore, it may appear in three **degrees: positive** (strong, beautiful); **comparative** (stronger, more beautiful); **superlative** (strongest, most beautiful); for the formation of the comparative and superlative ın various tongues, *see* pp. 175, 276, 318, 363, 385, 424, 433, 441, 452, 468, 477, 497–8, 512.

In English, the adjective, save for the degrees of comparison described above, is **invariable;** that is, it does not change its form to conform with the gender and number of the noun (compare English *strong man, strong woman, strong men, strong women* with French *homme fort, femme forte, hommes forts, femmes fortes*). In many languages, notably of the Indo-European and Semitic groups, **agreement** prevails (*see* **agreement**); in some languages, the adjective agrees in the attributive, but not in the predicate position (German *guter Mann* vs. *der Mann ist gut*); most Germanic languages have two different forms for the attributive adjective, a "strong" and a "weak" form, according to what precedes the adjective (German *ein guter Mann* vs. *der gute Mann*; *see* pp. 93–4, 99, 106–7, 112, 131, 134).

For adjectives of **nationality** ("an English book"), *see* pp. 187, 218, 260, 305, 344, 412-3, 565.

In many languages, there is no clear-cut difference in form or use between certain adjectives and related nouns (English "put this letter in the *mail*"; "put this letter in the *mail*-box"); or even between adjectives and related verbs (pp. 496, 548).

See also: **agreement, case, classifier, declension, ending, gender, inflection, number.**

adverb — a word that modifies a verb ("he walked *slowly*"), an adjective ("a *very* good book"), or another adverb ("he walked *very* slowly"); the adverb usually shows time (tomorrow), place (here) or manner (badly). In English, many adverbs are formed from adjectives by the addition of the adverbial suffix –*ly* (slow, slowly); in other languages, similar suffixes are added (French *lent, lentement*); while others make no distinction of form between the adjective and the adverb (German *er ist langsam*, "he is slow"; *er geht langsam*, "he goes slowly"; *see* pp. 131, 175, 385, 427, 497); this occurs occasionally ın English ("shoot straight"; "go slow"). For the formation of adverbs in various languages, *see* pp. 35, 190, 231, 276, 318, 363, 424, 497.

adverbial expression — a group of words fulfilling the same function as a single adverb ("from time to time" = "occasionally": "over there" = "there"; "in a poor way" = "poorly").

    affiliation — *see,* **classification**

    affirmative — *see* **conjugation**

    affix — *see* **prefix, suffix,** and pp. 507–8

    agglutination — the process of adding suffixes to roots to indicate various relations of gender, number, case, etc. In English, this process is carried on to a moderate degree (*empr–ess–es*, where –*ess–* indicates feminine gender and –*es* plural number; or *sky–wards*, where –*wards* indicates direction). In the languages properly described as agglutinative, the process goes much further, with the added feature that the suffixes have greater independence, individuality and mobility (Hungarian *Magyar–ország–ban,* literally "Magyar-land-in", "in Hungary"), *See* pp. 24, 30, 32-3, 430, 437-8, 440-1.

agreement — the process whereby one part of speech, used in conjunction with another, changes its form to conform with the other; this applies especially to adjectives which, in many languages, "agree" in number and gender with the noun they modify (French *le haut mur, la haute maison, les hauts murs, les hautes maisons*); and to verbs, which agree with the subject in number and person, occasionally in gender (Spanish *yo hablo, ellos hablan;* English *I am, you are, he is*). In English, the adjective does not agree, while the only form of the verb that normally shows a change of ending to indicate agreement is the third person singular of the present (*he comes* vs. *I, you, we, they, come*). In languages, like Chinese, which do not use endings, there is no agreement of any kind. For various forms of agreement, *see* pp. 132, 136, 190, 203, 326, 384, 424, 467-8; for non-agreement, *see* p. 441.

alphabet — a set of letters or symbols purporting to represent in writing the sounds of a language; an alphabet differs from a syllabary in that the symbols of the alphabet are supposed to represent single vowel and consonant sounds, while the symbols of a syllabary represent complete syllables. The ideal, or phonetic alphabet is one in which each symbol has only one possible sound, and each separate sound is represented by a symbol; some alphabets, like the Spanish and Finnish, come close to this ideal state; others, like the English or French, are far removed from it, with individual symbols having several different sound-values (English *a* in bat, ball, fare, father), and single sounds represented by combination of symbols (English *shoot, this*). The alphabetic notation used by most western nations is called Roman. For various alphabetic notations, *see* pp. 19, 25, 27, 92, 98, 105, 110, 124-5, 172-3, 184-5, 227-8, 270-1, 313-4, 354-61, 368, 371, 378, 422, 426, 432, 436, 450-2, 461-2, 479, 528, 583. For individual alphabetic system, *see:*
Arabic, 440, 461-2, 507, 513
Canarese, 461
Cyrillic, 354-60, 371-2, 374-5, 378
Devanagari, 19, 461-2, 485, 504
Gothic, 98, 124-5
Greek, 354, 422, 426
Hebrew, 25, 27, 461-2
Irish, 448-9
Phoenician, 461, 489
Roman, 98, 354-5, 357, 366, 369, 371-2

Romanized, 461-2, 507, 513, 528
Tamil, 461, 485-6
Telugu, 461, 485
See also **picture-writing, syllabary.**

  analysis — *see* simplification
  animate — *see* noun
  antecedent — *see* pronoun (relative), and pp. 243, 471, 543
  aorist — *see* tense
  apostrophe — a mark indicating, usually, the omission of a letter
(English *mother o' mine*; French *l'homme*); see pp. 187, 315.

  apposition — *see* noun
  archaic (obsolete) — ancient or antiquated; no longer in use; as
applied to a word or form, it means that the latter was once in current
use, but has now dropped from the language (English *loveth* for *loves*;
forms like *'sblood!, 'sdeath!*). An **obsolescent** form is one which is not
yet obsolete, but is falling into disuse (English *graveyard*, generally
replaced by *cemetery*). *See* pp. 19, 287, 289, 353, 446.

  article — a form used with a noun, to give it a **definite** or an **indefinite** value (*the* man, *a* man); in English, *the* is the definite, *a* or *an*
the indefinite article.   Most western languages have the equivalents
of both, though the rules for their use are far from uniform (English,
"liberty is precious"; French, "la liberté est précieuse"; English, "Spanish is an easy language"; Spanish, "el español es una lengua fácil";
English, "he is a doctor"; Italian, "è medico"). Some languages, like
Russian, dispense with both; others, like Greek, have a definite, but no
indefinite article (*see* pp. 361, 368, 381, 423, 440, 450, 496, 534). In
several languages (Swedish, Roumanian, Bulgarian, etc.), the definite
article, instead of coming before the noun, follows it and is attached
or "suffixed" to it in writing (Roumanian *cal–ul*, literally "horse–the";
see pp. 89, 170, 174, 374-5, 427, 452, 467).   In many languages, the
article combines with certain preceding prepositions (French *du livre*,
"of the book", with *du* representing a contraction of *de le*, "of the":
see pp. 163, 188, 221, 272, 274, 317).   In some languages, the article is
used before the possessive adjective or pronoun (Italian *il mio libro*, lit.
"the my book"; *voglio il mio*, lit. "I want the mine"; *see* pp. 134, 280,
322).

  aspect — in several languages, notably the Slavic, verbs are divided
into two classes: **perfective** (indicating an action as completed) and
imperfective (indicating an action as uncompleted).   This may be
somewhat remotely compared to English "I *spoke* to him yesterday"
(where it is implied that the action of speaking was finished at the
time mentioned) vs. "I *was speaking* to him when you came in" (where
the action of speaking was left suspended). *See* pp. 353, 364, 390,
395, 437.

aspiration — the pronouncing of a consonant with a puff of breath immediately following it, as in English *pin* (*p* + *hin*) as against *spin*; *see* pp. 446, 449–51, 494.

assimilation — the change whereby one sound becomes identical with another; especially in the case of a consonant preceding another, and changing so as to conform with the other, as happened when Latin *septem*, *octo* became Italian *sette*, *otto*; *see* p. 467.

attributive — *see* **adjective**

auxiliary — a "helping" word, usually a verb, which helps another verb to show time, mood, etc. (English *have* in "I have spoken", *will* in "he will go", *be* in "to be heard"; *see* pp. 22, 139, 235, 517-8). **Modal auxiliary** is a term used especially in the grammar of the Germanic tongues to indicate all the verbs used to show the manner of the action shown by the main verb (English *can*, *may*, *ought*, *must*; German *dürfen*, *sollen*, *wollen*, *werden*, etc.; *see* pp. 137, 142). For **auxiliary numeral**, *see* **classifier.**

back vowel — *see* **vowel**

bilingual — speaking two languages, as a French Canadian who speaks English in addition to his native French, or a Belgian speaking both French and Flemish, or a South African speaking both English and Afrikaans; *see* pp. 16, 47, 49, 77.

borrowed words — *see* **loan-words**

breathings — special marks used in ancient Greek to indicate the aspiration or non-aspiration of certain vowels and consonants; *see* p. 422.

capital — while capitals exist in all languages using the Roman or similar alphabets (Cyrillic, Greek, Gothic, etc.), and are generally used at the beginning of the sentence, they are not always used identically in other connections; German, for instance, capitalizes all nouns, common as well as proper (*der Hund,* "the dog"); French does not capitalize adjectives of nationality (*un livre français,* "a French book"). For the different use of capitals in various languages, *see* pp. 98, 124, 159, 187, 218, 248, 260, 305, 331, 344, 412-3.

cardinal — *see* **numeral**

case — broadly, the grammatical function of a noun or pronoun in the sentence, as when we say that in the sentence "the boy is here", "boy" is in the nominative or subjective case, while in "I see the boy", "boy" is in the accusative or objective case. But often the distinction is one of form as well as of function or use; a **case-form** is a specific variant of the noun, adjective or pronoun, specifically indicating by its appearance (usually by its ending) the function which it is supposed to have in a sentence (subject, direct object, indirect object, etc.). English has no separate case-forms for adjectives; only two forms for nouns that differ from the general form (the possessive, or genitive, singular and plural: "the *boy's* book", "the *boys'* books", as against the general forms *boy, boys*); and as many as three for some pronouns (nominative or subjective, *I, who*; genitive or possessive, *my, whose*; accusative or objective, *me, whom*). Certain languages, particularly of the Indo-European group, have numerous case-forms for nouns and adjectives; where these exist, the following are the most common:

nominative (or **subjective**) — usually indicates that the noun or pronoun is the subject or a predicate nominative; Latin *"puer* est bonus"*, "Romulus est *puer"*; see pp. 23, 128, 388, 479-80.

genitive (or **possessive**) — indicates, among other things, ownership; English "the *boy's* house"; Latin "domus *pueri"*

dative — generally indicates that the noun or pronoun is an indirect object; English "I give *the boy* the book" (but note that in this sentence it is the position of "the boy", not its form, that tells us it is an indirect object); English often marks the dative by the preposition *to* ("I give the book *to the boy"*); Latin *"puero* librum do".

accusative (or **objective**) — indicates, usually, the direct object; in English "I see the boy", it is only the position of "the boy" that tells us it is a direct object, but in "I see him" we have the specific accusative form *him*, as well as the position; Latin *"puerum* video".

vocative — the form used in direct address; Latin "quid agis, *Petre?"* ("what are you doing Peter?"); see pp. 362, 374.

ablative, instrumental and **locative** indicate a variety of functions which English generally expresses by the use of prepositions; the ablative, originally, indicated *removal from,* or *direction away from* ("I took the book *from the boy"*); the instrumental, means by which ("I write *with a pencil"*); the locative, place where ("he is *in the city"*). These functions are merged in many languages (Latin, where the ablative takes over both instrumental and locative functions). The use of case-endings originally permitted Indo-European speakers to dispense with prepositions, but in many languages today both case-endings and prepositions are used.

The **prepositional** case of the Slavic languages is another term for the locative, used because, while prepositions appear in connection with other cases, the locative is the only one which cannot be used without a preposition.

The **absolute** case of Japanese (*see* p. 535) isolates the noun grammatically from the rest of the sentence (English "your brother, did he come today?").

The **oblique** case, in certain languages, represents a merger or falling together of the former cases outside of the nominative, which remains distinct in form (*see* pp. 479-80).

When the terms case and case-forms are applied to languages

outside of the Indo-European group, they are generally loosely used to indicate something analogous or similar, but not quite identical (*see* pp. 432-3, 436, 535).

See also pp. 89, 128, 170, 173-4, 353, 362, 369, 374, 382, 388-90, 423-4, 427, 432, 436, 440, 443-4, 447, 449-51, 479-80, 497, 510, 527, 535; and **declension, ending, inflection.**

caste — a hereditary social class; for the influence of the caste-system on language, *see* pp. 33. 487.

causative — *see* **conjugation**

cedilla — a mark placed under the letter *c* (ç) to indicate that it is to be given a special sound, usually that of *s* (pp. 187, 270), but occasionally another (p. 440). For the use of the cedilla under letters other than *c*, *see* pp. 173, 440. It is a curious fact that the cedilla was first used in Spanish, which later dropped it.

classification (or **affiliation**) of languages — the process of establishing the family relationship of a language, the larger group to which it belongs; *see* pp. 18-39, 455.

classifier (or **determinative**) — in certain languages, notably Chinese, a word which accompanies other words for the purpose of clarifying their meaning and identifying them as belonging to certain groups, like English "head" in "fifty head of cattle"; *see* pp. 495, 499, 504, 550-1.

clause — a simple sentence which serves as part of another, longer sentence; in a sentence such as "I spoke to the man whom I met yesterday", "I spoke to the man" is the **main** or **principal clause,** "whom I met yesterday" the **subordinate clause,** while the sentence as a whole is described as **complex.** Occasionally the two clauses are not one subordinate to the other, but equally independent; they can be detached from each other and each used separately as a complete **simple** sentence, as in "I met the man yesterday and I spoke to him". In this case, the sentence is called **compound** and the two clauses are described as **co-ordinate;** *see* pp. 127, 203, 220, 240, 263, 286, 329, 347, 353, 540-1, 543.

collective — *see* **numeral**

colloquialism — *see* **slang**

colonizing language (or **language of colonization**) — the tongue of a colonizing nation, which implants itself in another country, and is spoken by a minority composed of officials, soldiers, traders, missionaries, etc. Where the native population is sparse, and the colonizing tide heavy, the colonizing language may become the tongue of the majority of the inhabitants, as is the case with English in the United States, Australia, New Zealand and Canada. Elsewhere, it may remain a minority language, as is the case with English in

British India. *See* pp. 25, 35-9, 40, 43, 49, 51, 53, 55-64, 81-7, 122-3, 167, 182-3, 226-7, 244-6, 268-9, 312-3, 351, 376-7, 455-6, 459, 524-6, 609, 610.

common — *see* **gender, noun**

comparative — *see* **adjective**

complex — *see* **clause, sentence**

compound forms — words like *steam-boat, railroad, upgrade,* etc., where two separate elements enter into the composition of the one word; *see* pp. 353, 487-8, 496, 532.

compound object pronoun — *see* **pronoun**

compound sentence — *see* **clause, sentence**

compound tense — *see* **tense**

concrete — *see* **noun**

conditional — *see* **tense**

conjugation — either an arrangement of the forms of a verb, or a set of verbs having the same inflections. English has only two conjugational types, the **strong** and the **weak** (*see* **verb**); in other languages, notably the Romance, verbs are divided up among several distinct conjugational types (Spanish *-ar, -er, -ir; see* pp. 178, 196, 233, 281, 323, 425, 472, 507). In addition to conjugational types, we may speak of a verb as being conjugated, or presented, in many ways:

affirmative (states) — *I see, you see, he sees,* etc.; *see* p. 487.

negative (denies) — *I do not see, you do not see,* etc.; *see* pp. 434, 441, 545-6, 549.

interrogative (questions) — *do I see?, do you see?,* etc.; *see* pp. 428, 474, 501, 512, 535, 545.

progressive (indicates an action going on) — *I am speaking, I was speaking, I shall be speaking,* etc.; *see* pp. 137, 239, 282, 288, 323, 475, 518, 541.

reflexive (indicates that the subject acts on himself) — *I see myself,* etc.; *see* pp. 178, 201, 239, 285-6, 328, 335, 393, 441, 501.

reciprocal (two or more subjects acting on each other, therefore can be used only in the plural) — *we see each other,* etc.; *see* p. 441.

causative (indicates that the subject causes something to be done, or somebody to do something) — *see* p. 441.

conjunction — a word which connects other words or clauses, like English *and, but, if, since, though; see* p. 513.

consonant — a sound characterized by friction, squeezing, or stoppage of breath in some part of the mouth, or a letter representing such a sound; 21 of the 26 letters of the English alphabet (omitting *a, e, i, o, u*) are loosely described as consonants; *see* pp. 29, 37, 86, 126, 186, 228, 353, 361, 380, 461-2, 487-8. For **aspirated** consonants, *see* **aspiration**, and p. 494; for **broad** and **slender** consonants, in Irish, *see* pp. 446, 449; for **emphatic** consonants, in Arabic, *see* pp. 465–6; for **palatal** consonants, *see* pp. 353–4, 380, 446. For **double** consonants, *see* pp. 172, 270, 315, 329, 432, 434, 436, 466, 487, 532 (note that in some languages the written double consonant is pronounced single, as in English *butter*; in others, it is definitely given a double, or "long" pronunciation, as in Italian *otto*). For **voiced** and **unvoiced** consonants, *see* pp. 380, 494, 531 (the voiced consonant is pronounced with, the unvoiced without vibration of the vocal cords; there is no difference between *t* and *d*, *p* and *b*, *k* and *g*, save that the first member of each pair has no vibration of the vocal cords, while the second has).

coordinate — *see* **clause, sentence**

copulative — *see* **verb**

cultural language — *see* **secondary language**

cuneiform — wedge-shaped; the type of writing used by the Babylonians, Assyrians and ancient Persians, who pressed wedge-shaped writing instruments into wet clay; *see* p. 489.

dative — *see* **case**

declension — the various forms taken by a noun, adjective or pronoun to indicate case, number, gender, etc.; *see* pp. 88, 353, 362, 369, 382, 394, 423-4, 443-4, 507; *see also* **case, ending, gender, inflection, number.**

definite article — *see* **article**

demonstrative — a form that indicates or points out, like *this*, *that*; *see* **adjective, pronoun.**

derivative — a word that comes from another, as *undo* from *do*, *machinist* from *machine*, etc.; *see* p. 515.

descriptive — *see* **adjective**

desiderative — *see* **voice**

determinative — *see* **classifier**

diacritic mark — a mark accompanying a letter of the alphabet to indicate that it is to be given a special pronunciation. The **accent marks** (*q. v.*) are diacritics; so is the **tilde** of Spanish appearing over the *n* (*ñ*), the hook appearing under *a* and *e* in Polish to indicate nasalization (*ą, ę*), etc.; *see* pp. 366, 370, 440, 444, 531, 583.

diaeresis — two dots over a vowel to indicate that it is to be separated from the preceding or following vowel, and not to form a diphthong with it, as in French *naïf, Noël*, Spanish *averigüe*, English *zoölogy*, etc.; *see* p. 187.

dialect — a local form of speech, differing to a greater or lesser degree from the standard national or literary language; *see* pp. 33, 38, 51, 61, 64-7, 85-6, 168, 170, 172, 244-6, 268-70, 329-30, 427, 451-2, 455-8, 465, 488, 491-3, 507, 532. *See also* **standardization.**

diminutive — a derivative form indicating, usually by means of a special suffix, a small or dear variant of the object in question, as English *lambkin* (from *lamb*), *eaglet* (from *eagle*), *kitten* (from *cat*), or Spanish *cigarrillo* (from *cigarro*). Some languages, like Dutch,

Spanish and Italian, are more prone to use diminutives than others; within the same language, some sections are occasionally more prone to use diminutives (Mexico, for example, uses more than Spain). *See* pp. 128, 289.

diphthong — "two vowels pronounced as one", either for what concerns sound (as in French *ai*, which is equivalent in sound sometimes to *è*, sometimes to *é*; but this is more exactly described as a **digraph**); or for what concerns the combination of the two vowel-sounds in the same impulse of the voice (as in Spanish h*i*erro, where there are two separate sounds, but pronounced in one syllable). *See* pp. 184, 287, 493. *See also* **syllable.**

direct object — *see* **object**

dissyllabic — consisting of two syllables, like English *pretty*; *see* p. 507.

dual — *see* **number**

eclipsis — a phenomenon appearing especially in the Celtic tongues, whereby an initial consonant changes by reason of the original final sound of the preceding word, which is generally lost; *see* pp. 446, 449. *See also* **lenition.**

emigrant language (or **language of emigration**) — the tongue carried by emigrants from one country to another, and continuing to be spoken in communities made up of emigrants, like Italian in New York's Little Italy. *See* pp. 122–3, 312–3, 352, 377, 492, 526.

ending — that part of the word which does not belong to the root, but indicates gender, number, case, person, tense, mood, etc., like the –*s* in "he takes", the –*d* in "I loved", the –*en* in "oxen", French –*es* in *grandes*; *see* pp. 18, 30, 32, 88, 131, 170, 381, 394, 426, 434, 451, 496. **Case-endings** appear in languages where a case-system is used, like Latin mur*us*, muri, muro, mur*um*, mure, muro; *see* pp. 22, 33, 89, 362, 382, 479–80, 535; *see also* **case, conjugation, declension, gender, inflection, number, possession, suffix, tense, voice.**

familiar form of address — *see* **address**

feminine — *see* **gender**

fraction, fractional — *see* **numeral**

front vowel — *see* **vowel**

future, future anterior, future perfect — *see* **tense**

gender — the classification of nouns according to sex, real or fancied, or according to their denoting animate or inanimate objects, or according to other concepts, such as that of caste. English has a "natural" system of gender (male beings are **masculine,** female beings **feminine,** inanimate objects **neuter,** while the **common** gender is a rather vague entity including animate beings whose sex is unknown to the speaker). Some languages (Latin, German, Russian) have "grammatical" gender, whereby, even though a masculine-feminine-neuter classification exists, inanimate objects may be masculine or feminine as well as neuter (note a survival of this in English when a ship is referred to as "she"); other languages (Romance, Celtic, Semitic) have reduced their gender system to a masculine-feminine classification, with inanimate objects divided up between those two genders; others (Dutch, Scandinavian) make, in practice, only a division of animate (common) and inanimate (neuter), but with numerous animate objects in the "neuter" gender and inanimate objects in the common gender; others (Hungarian, Japanese) make no distinction of gender whatsoever; while others (Dravidian) have a gender system based on social caste (pp. 33, 487). *See* pp. 24, 31-3, 37, 88, 128, 170–1, 173, 175, 188, 230, 274, 316, 353, 361–2, 381, 423–4, 427, 430, 432, 436, 440, 446, 452, 463, 466, 477, 480, 487, 496, 504-5, 510, 534.

genitive — *see* **case**

gerund — a form of the verb used as a noun. In English the gerund ends in *–ing*, and there is no distinction in form between the gerund (*walking is good exercise, I like walking*) and the present participle (*he is walking, the walking man*), though the functions are quite distinct (the gerund is used as a noun, the present participle as an adjective). Other languages use distinct forms (Italian *parlando, siamo usciti*, "while speaking, we went out"; but *l'uomo è un animale parlante*, "man is a speaking animal"). The English gerund may be used alone, as subject or object (*walking is good; I like walking*) or after prepositions (*without walking*); in many languages, notably of the Romance group, these functions are taken over by the infinitive (Spanish *el hablar me gusta; sin hablar*); and the only function left for the gerund is to translate "by" or "while" doing something, as in the Italian example above. *See* pp. 239, 282, 321, 323, 353, 393, 444.

glottal stop — a "catch in the voice", or a complete shutting off of the breath-stream, usually before a vowel (German *die Eier, der Arme*). The glottal stop appears as a regular sound (**phoneme**) in Arabic and Malay (pp. 466, 508). It appears occasionally and accidentally in English (*coöperate*).

grammatical structure — the sum total of the features of a language (other than its sounds and its vocabulary), such as the way in which it forms and arranges its parts of speech, etc. *See* pp. 64, 67, 245, 353–4, 419, 429–30, 495.

hieroglyphic — the system of picture-writing of the ancient Egyptians. *See* pp. 29, 489, and **picture-writing.**

hiragana — one of the two Japanese syllabaries; *see* pp. 527–31, 539.

honorific — *see* **address**

identification of languages — the process of determining with what language, spoken or written, we are faced; *see* pp. 13, 15, 67, 72-3, 76,

102, 109, 116, 172, 178, 366, 369-70, 372, 375, 426, 434, 438, 442, 444, 451, 453.

ideograph — *see* **picture-writing**

idiom (or **idiomatic expression**) — a construction peculiar to one language, which cannot be directly or literally translated into another, and the meaning of which cannot be gathered from its component parts; *e. g.*, English "look out" in the sense of "be careful"; literally translated into most other languages, it will convey only its primary meaning of "look outside".

imperative — *see* **mood**
imperfect — *see* **tense**
imperfective — *see* **aspect**
impersonal — *see* **verb**
inanimate — *see* **noun**
indeclinable — *see* **invariable**
indefinite — *see* **article, adjective, pronoun**
indicative — *see* **mood**
indirect object — *see* **object**

infinitive — the form of the verb which indicates the action without reference to a subject. In English, the infinitive consists of the verb-root preceded by *to* ("to go"; *to* is omitted after certain verbs, like *can, may*). Other languages use a specific ending (French aim*er*, fin*ir*, vend*re*); others do not have a specific infinitive, but make use of other forms of the verb when they want to indicate the action in general (pp. 472, 539). For certain constructions with the infinitive, *see* pp. 233, 279, 321. Portuguese has a "personal" infinitive, with personal endings, corresponding roughly to such expressions as "for me to do", "for you to do", etc.; *see* pp. 284, 307. For the use of the infinitive in many languages as the equivalent of the English gerund, *see* **gerund.**

inflection — the process of change of endings in those forms (nouns, adjectives, pronouns, verbs, adverbs) which are composed of a root and an ending. English, for instance, inflects a noun like *boy* by adding *'s* for the possessive, *-s* for the plural, *-s'* for the possessive plural; it inflects a pronoun like *I* by changing it to *my* or *mine* in the possessive, *me* in the objective, *we* in the subjective plural, *our* or *ours* in the possessive plural, *us* in the objective plural; it inflects an adjective like *strong* by adding *-er* for the comparative, *-est* for the superlative; it inflects a verb like *love* by adding *-s* in the third person singular present, *-d* in the past, *-ing* in the present participle. Some languages, like Latin or Russian, inflect the noun, adjective and pronoun to a far greater degree than does English; others, like Chinese, have no inflection at all, but indicate all relations by separate words; such languages are called *isolating*, since no two meanings are combined in any single word, but each meaning is "isolated" in a separate word; compare the English isolating "I" "shall" "love" with the Spanish inflected *amaré.* *See* pp. 23, 25, 89, 170, 353, 463, 487-8, 496, 504, 507, 526-7. For various types and forms of inflection, *see also* **adjective, case, conjugation, declension, ending, gender, mood, noun, number, possession, pronoun, tense, verb.** For the change from **inflection** to **isolation,** *see* **simplification.**

instrumental — *see* **case**

interjection — a word isolated from the rest of the sentence, and used as an exclamation, like English "ah!", "oh!", "golly!", etc. *See* p. 514.

international language — either a language deliberately built for international use (like Esperanto, Volapük, Interglossa, etc.) or a national language adapted for international use (like Basic English or Interlingua); *see* p. 580.

interrogative — *see* **adjective, conjugation, pronoun.** Interrogation or inquiry is indicated in English by an interrogative word ("*who* did it?"); by an inversion of verb and subject ("is it?"); by the use of *do* as an interrogative auxiliary ("do you see it?"); or simply by a note of the voice ("you went there yesterday?"). Many languages use the first two and the last of these devices (the use of *do* as an auxiliary is typically English). For the written languages, note the Spanish use of an inverted question mark at the beginning of an interrogation (*¿lo vió Ud.?*), and its use of a written accent on many interrogative words (*¿cuándo lo vió?*). Some languages, like Chinese and Japanese, use special interrogative words and constructions (*see* pp. 501, 545).

intonation — *see* **pronunciation**

intransitive — *see* **verb**

invariable (or **indeclinable**) — unchanging in form. The adjective in English is invariable for what concerns gender and number (but not for what concerns degree), whereas in French it is variable, or inflected (*haut, haute, hauts, hautes*). In isolating languages, like Chinese, all words are invariable. *See* pp. 437, 441, 452, 504.

isolating — a type of language, like the Chinese, consisting exclusively of roots to which no suffixes or endings are added, so that each word is "isolated" and depends for its meaning on its position in the sentence.

kana — the Japanese system of writing, particularly the syllabaries (**hiragana, katakana**). **Kana majiri** is the full system of writing, combining Chinese ideographs and the syllabaries. *See* pp. 526–31.

katakana — one of the two Japanese syllabaries; *see* pp. 527–31, 540.

lenition (or **mutation**) — changes undergone by consonants, particularly in Celtic, by reason of position between vowels. *See* p. 446. *See also* **eclipsis.** For another meaning of **mutation,** *see* **umlaut.**

liaison — *see* **linking**

lingua franca — in the Middle Ages, a term describing a language spoken in the Mediterranean basin, consisting of Italian, with additions from other sources (Arabic, French, Greek, etc.), and serving as a tongue of general intercourse for the peoples in that area, especially traders and soldiers. Today the term is applied to any language of general intercourse serving a wide multilingual area (Pidgin English, Malay, etc.). *See* p. 459 and **trade language.**

linguistic minorities — groups of speakers of one tongue, living in a political subdivision in which another tongue has more speakers. The tongue of the linguistic minority may, however, be co-official with the majority language, as is the case with Rumansh in Switzerland, French in Canada, and Spanish in New Mexico; or it may be spoken in a section of the country, without official recognition, like Slovenian in northeastern Italy; *see* pp. 47–8, 122–3, 352, 376–7, 419.

linking (or **liaison**) — the carrying over of the final consonant of one word to the initial vowel-sound of the next, as in French *les amours*, or Italian *con essi*; the two words are thereby pronounced as a single word, with syllabic division accordingly (*lé za mour; co nes si*). Linking occurs most frequently in the Romance languages, with the added feature in French that it causes a final consonant to be pronounced that would otherwise be silent (*see* p. 186). In German, linking is normally prevented by the **glottal stop** (*q. v.*); in English, incorrect linking is occasionally heard (*Long Island,* pronounced *Long Gisland*).

literal translation — a word-for-word rendering of one language into another; often possible, in simple constructions and in related languages; generally more difficult as the construction becomes longer and more involved, and as the languages diverge; *see* pp. 18, 172.

literary language — *see* **written language**

liturgical — pertaining to religious service. Latin is used as a liturgical language in the Roman Catholic Church, regardless of the country's spoken tongue; classical Arabic is similarly used among Moslems; Sanskrit among Buddhists, even in Japan. *See* p. 29.

loan-word (or **borrowed word**) — a word which one language has taken from another. Some languages are relatively free of loan-words; others, like English, Persian, Albanian, Armenian, have borrowed over 50% of their total vocabulary. Depending on the time and circumstances of the borrowing, the loan-word assumes a more or less native appearance in the borrowing tongue; English, borrowing Italian *balcone* in the Renaissance, turned it into *balcony*, and the memory of the borrowing is popularly lost; *spaghetti* and *broccoli,* on the other hand, are recent arrivals, and their foreign, unmodified form easily identifies them as loan-words; the same word is sometimes borrowed twice, at different periods, like *macaroon* and *macaroni* (Italian *maccheroni*), or *saloon* and *salon* (French *salon*). *See* pp. 63, 77-9, 80-87, 90, 172, 378, 421, 426, 428, 440, 456, 462, 480-1, 507, 526, 542, 549-50.

locative — *see* **case**

main clause — *see* **clause**

masculine — *see* **gender**

middle vowel — *see* **vowel**

military influence — the coming into the language of words having their origin in warfare and soldiers' slang, like English *G. I.*, *jeep*, *bazooka*, or French *poilu*; *see* pp. 225, 528, 611.

modal auxiliary — *see* **auxiliary**

monogenesis — the theory that all the world's languages go back to a single common ancestor; originally embodied in the Biblical account of the Tower of Babel, it was popularly held for a long time, with Hebrew as the supposed original language, and led to very strange etymologies and derivations of words and grammatical forms on the part of medieval and Renaissance linguistic scholars; discarded in the 19th century, it has recently reappeared in the writings of a few linguists, notably A. Trombetti, but has not met with much favor in linguistic circles. *See* p. 18.

monosyllabic — consisting of a single syllable, like English *do*, *go*, *for*, *what*. Some languages, like Chinese, in their present state, consist exclusively of monosyllabic roots (which may, however, be combined into two, three and even four-word compounds having a single meaning). *See* pp. 32, 129, 487-8, 504-5, 507.

mood (or **mode**) — distinction of form or meaning in a verb to express the manner in which the action denoted is thought of (*see* pp. 172, 425-6, 434, 437, 499, 538). In English, we speak of an **indicative** mood (representing the action as a definite fact: "I am", "he loves"); a **subjunctive** mood (representing the action as hypothetical or subordinated to another action: "whether he be", "if I were"); and an **imperative** mood (expressing a command or an exhortation: "write to him", "let us go"). The subjunctive mood in English is to a large degree a grammatical name rather than an actuality, because outside of the verb *to be*, the overwhelming majority of subjunctive forms coincide with their indicative counterparts; this is not true of many other languages (*see* pp. 141, 203, 220, 240, 263, 286, 329, 347, 393). For the imperative, *see* pp. 127, 472, 542. Some languages boast of an **optative** mood, used primarily to express a wish ("would that he were here!" *see* p. 441). It may be added that in the case of languages having **desiderative**, **causative** and other similar forms, the assigning of such forms to mood, voice or conjugation is not always easy (*see* **conjugation, voice**).

mutation — *see* **lenition, umlaut**

nasal sounds — sounds appearing in practically all languages, in the production of which the connection between mouth and nose is wholly or partly shut off, with the soft palate lowered and the voice resounding in the nose; for some special nasal sounds of French, Portuguese, Polish, etc., *see* pp. 172, 184, 187, 270, 354, 361, 366, 444.

negation — denial; in simplest form, "no"; in connection with other words, represented in English by "not" and other devices (note the characteristic English use of *do* as a negative auxiliary for verbs: "I do not write"). Other languages use a variety of negative devices which do not always correspond to ours (*e. g.*, the French double negative particle in *je ne vois pas*); *see* pp. 278, 289, 321, 327, 428, 474, 477, 487, 500-1, 518, 535). Some languages, like Finnish and Japanese, instead of using negative particles with affirmative verbs, use a negative conjugation, which differs in form from the affirmative (*see* **conjugation**).

neuter — *see* **gender**

neuter article and **pronoun** — forms peculiar to some Romance languages, which have in other respects given up the neuter gender (Spanish *lo hermoso*, "that which is beautiful"; French *je n'aime pas cela*, "I don't like that"); *see* pp. 170, 280.

neutral vowel — *see* **vowel**

nominative — *see* **case**

noun — the name of a person, place, thing or quality (*John, France, bread, beauty*). In English, nouns are divided into **proper** (the name of a specific person or locality; these are capitalized: *Roosevelt, Rome*), and **common** (names of things and qualities: *iron, intelligence*). Common nouns may further be subdivided into **concrete** (denoting tangible, material things: *bread, iron*), and **abstract** (denoting intangible concepts and qualities: *freedom, beauty*; *see* p. 128).

From the standpoint of use in the sentence, a noun may be used as **subject** ("*John* is here"); **direct object** ("I see *John*"); **indirect object** ("I give *John* the book"); **object of a preposition** ("I went with *John*"); **in apposition** (describing another noun directly: "John *the apostle*"); or as a **predicate noun** (describing the subject through the verb *to be*: "John is *an apostle*").

From the standpoint of structure, a noun has **gender, number** and **case**, which means that in languages with full **declensional** systems, like Sanskrit, Greek, Latin and Russian, we may get as many as 24 different forms for the same noun, each marked by a different **ending** (*see* pp. 32, 170). Note the distinction made in some languages (Slavic, pp. 362, 382–3) between **animate** nouns (denoting a living person or animal) and **inanimate** nouns (denoting lifeless things or abstract qualities). *See also* **case, declension, ending, gender, inflection, number, object, possession, predicate, subject.**

number — the distinction in form or meaning of a noun, adjective, pronoun or verb to denote "one" or "more than one" of the objects named (*see* pp. 24, 32, 88, 188–9, 230–1, 247, 274, 463, 466–7, 496, 499, 506, 510, 533, 538). English has two numbers, **singular** (denoting one) and **plural** (denoting more than one). The more ancient Indo-European languages and the Semitic tongues also have a **dual** number (indicating two; Latin *duo, ambo* are survivals of the ancient Indo-European dual form; *see* pp. 463, 466–7). Certain Melanesian languages are said to have separate forms, especially for the pronouns, to indicate three and four of the objects in question ("we-three", "you-four"). Some tongues, like Chinese and Japanese, indicate the difference between singular and plural only when strictly necessary (*see* pp. 497, 510, 533–4). For the formation of the plural, regular and irregular, in various languages, *see* pp. 23–4, 33, 35, 88, 170, 189, 230–1, 247, 274, 449-50, 452, 477, 487, 497, 510, 533-4 (in English a "regular" plural would be one formed by the addition of *-s*, such as *boys, girls*; an "irregular" plural, one formed by other devices, such as *oxen, children, men, women, sheep, deer, mice*). For the "broken" plural forms of Arabic, *see* pp. 467–8.

numeral — a word indicating a number, like *three, third,* etc. The **cardinal** numeral is the primary number itself (*one, two, three*; it may be used as an adjective or as a noun). The **ordinal** numeral shows the order or numerical position of the noun it defines (*first, second, third*), and is used primarily as an adjective. A **collective** numeral indicates a round number, like *dozen, score* (*see* p. 514). A **fractional** numeral indicates a part of one, like *half, third, quarter. See* pp. 37, 132, 169–70, 175, 190, 232-3, 276-7, 319-20, 358-9, 385-6, 424-5, 427, 429-30, 433, 447, 452, 464, 468-9, 498-9, 504, 514, 549. For **auxiliary numerals,** *see* p. 550 and **classifier.**

object — the recipient of the action shown by the verb. In "I struck the man", "the man" directly receives the action of my striking, and is the **direct object.** In "I gave the man the book", there are two recipients involved, "the book" being primary or **direct** (what is given), "the man" being secondary or **indirect** (to whom is given). An easy way of distinguishing the indirect object from the direct is to determine before which of the two objects the preposition *to* may be correctly used ("I give the book *to* the man", "I give the book *to* him"). Different languages use different devices to mark the direct and the indirect object (position in the sentence, case-endings, prepositions, postpositions, etc.; *see* pp. 22, 23, 536).

object pronoun — *see* **pronoun**
objective — *see* **case**
oblique — *see* **case**
obsolete — *see* **archaic**
optative — *see* **mood**
ordinal — *see* **numeral**
orthography — *see* **spelling**

orthographical reform — a change in the system of spelling or writing of a language, usually aimed at obtaining a closer correspondence between symbol and sound. Turkish (*see* p. 440) and Russian (*see* pp. 355, 378, 462) have recently undergone official orthographic reforms which have made both languages far more accessible to foreign learners and far easier to their own school-children. Similar reforms have been advocated for English (notably, in recent times, by G. B. Shaw in England and former Senator R. L. Owen in the U. S.), but without success thus far. For a similar attempt in Japanese, *see* p. 528.

parent language — the language from which other tongues are descended; Latin is, for example, the parent language of the Romance tongues. In the case of many groups, a parent language, though unknown because no direct record of it has come down to us, can be more or less hypothetically reconstructed from a comparison of the known members of the group; *see* pp. 19, 27.

participle — a form of the verb used as an adjective. English has a **present active** participle (ending in –*ing*) which coincides in form with the gerund (*see* **gerund**) and a **passive** (incorrectly called **past**) participle which in weak verbs has the ending –*d* (*loved*), in strong verbs a variety of forms (the ending –*en* often appears: *written, spoken, broken,* but *bound, found, swum, sung,* etc.). Many languages have similar forms; others have additional ones (Latin, **future active** participle, *amaturus,* "about to love"). *See* pp. 353, 393, 444, 473, 487, 516-7, 541.

particle — a subordinate word, not inflected (such as a **preposition, conjunction** or **interjection**). Interrogative, negative, emphatic and other particles appear in many languages: *see* pp. 487, 501, 527, 533, 535.

passive — *see* **voice**

past, past absolute, past definite, past indefinite, past perfect — *see* **tense**

perfect — *see* **tense**

perfective — *see* **aspect**

person — the distinction between speaker (**first person:** "I", "we"); person addressed (**second person:** "you"); and person or thing spoken of (**third person:** "he", "she", "it", "they"). In many languages, the distinction of person appears in the form of the verb (then called a **personal** verb), being conveyed by a special suffix (Spanish amo, am*as,* am*a*); in others, it is primarily conveyed by a subject pronoun, as happens for the most part in English, where only the third singular present (loves) carries a personal suffix ("I love", "you love", "they love"). Some languages, like Japanese, generally leave the person to be inferred from the context (the Japanese verb is described as **impersonal**; *see* p. 538). Other languages, like the Dravidian, distinguish between **inclusive** and **exclusive** first person plural ("we" meaning "you and I", and "we" meaning "I and he, but not you"; *see* p. 487). *See also* pp. 23, 499, 515.

    personal verb — *see* **person, verb**

    personal infinitive — *see* **infinitive**

    personal pronoun — *see* **pronoun**

    phonetic writing — *see* **orthographic reform, spelling**

    pictograph — *see* **picture-writing**

    picture-writing — a writing system whereby objects have a pictorial representation, like a round disk for "sun", a crescent for "moon", etc. This seems to be the original form of all writing-systems (*see* p. 489). A **pictograph** is a symbol denoting a definite object, as described above; an **ideograph** is a conventional symbol representing something not so obvious, as when Chinese combines pictographs representing "sun" and "tree" into an ideograph representing "east" ("the sun shining through trees"), or when we use the symbol $ to represent "dollars". *See* pp. 19, 33, 461-2, 488-92, 526-7.

    pitch — *see* **accent**

    pluperfect — *see* **tense**

    plural — *see* **number**

    polite address — *see* **address**

    polylingual — speaking many tongues, like a Swiss speaking all four of the official languages of Switzerland (German, French, Italian, Rumansh); *see* pp. 16, 49.

    polysyllabic — consisting of more than one syllable, such as the word *in-tel-li-gent*; *see* pp. 496, 507.

    polysynthetic — a type of language characterized by the fusion of many semi-independent elements into a single word; *see* pp. 36–7.

    positive — *see* **adjective**

    possessive — *see* **case, adjective, pronoun**

    possession — ownership, or the denoting of ownership, as in "John's hat". For the denotation of possession in various languages, *see* pp. 23, 88, 467, 470-1, 477, 497-8, 504, 511, 518, 535-6.

    postposition — a particle placed *after* a noun to indicate a **case** relation, like the Japanese *wo* denoting that the preceding noun is a direct object. *See* pp. 436, 440, 487, 497, 533, 535, 537. A postposition differs from a **case-ending** in that it is a completely separate and independent word.

predicate — what is said about the subject, including the verb and any complements (such as objects). A noun, pronoun or adjective describing the subject through the verb *to be* (or another copulative verb: *to seem, to become*, etc.) is said to be a **predicate noun, predicate pronoun,** or **predicate adjective** ("he is *a general*"; "it is *I*"; "he is *good*"; *see* **noun, adjective**). The case of a noun in the predicate after a copulative verb is said to be the **predicate nominative** (*see* p. 424).

prefix — an element placed before the root of a word to modify its meaning, like in "*in–*", in "invoice", or the "*re–*" in "regain"; *see* pp. 35-6, 127, 142, 395, 477, 487, 505, 510-1, 515-7, 534, 589-90.

preposition — a particle showing the relation of a noun or pronoun to another element in the sentence, and indicating a relation of position, direction, time, means, etc., like *in, of, to, from, by*; *see* pp. 22, 24, 170, 288, 424, 471, 479, 497, 513; *see also* **case.**

prepositional — *see* **case**

present — *see* **tense**

present perfect — *see* **tense**

principal clause — *see* **clause**

progressive — *see* **conjugation**

pronoun — a word used instead of a noun. The various classes of pronouns are:

personal (standing for the name of a person or thing, as *I, you, it*);

possessive (indicating ownership, as *mine, yours*);

demonstrative (pointing out, as *these, those*);

relative (referring to some person or thing previously mentioned, as *who, which, that*; the person or thing referred to is called the **antecedent**; in "I saw the man who came yesterday", "man" is the antecedent of "who";

interrogative (asking a question, as "who" in "who did it?");

indefinite (like *someone, anyone*);

reflexive (like *myself, themselves* in "I see myself", "they speak to themselves").

From the standpoint of use in the sentence, the pronoun has the same functions as the noun (*q. v.*); a personal pronoun especially may be used as **subject** ("*I* am here"); **direct** or **indirect object** ("he sees *me*"; "he gives *me* the book"); **object of a preposition** ("he comes with *me*"); **predicate nominative** ("it is *I*"), etc. While practically all languages have subject personal pronouns, many often dispense with them, because the form of the verb makes it clear who the subject is (Spanish "quiero" vs. English "I love"; *see* pp. 22, 170, 177, 192, 234, 241, 278, 320, 391, 473, 538). With object personal pronouns, usage is still more varied; many languages customarily place the object pronoun *before* the verb (French "il *me* voit" vs. English "he sees *me*"; *see* pp.

177, 193, 200, 241, 278). At times the object pronoun is attached to the verb-form (Spanish "quiere ver*me*", "he wants to see *me*"; *see* pp. 470, 473, 477).   In some languages, notably Portuguese, two object pronouns (direct and indirect) are compounded, thereby appearing as a single form (*see* pp. 279, 288, 320–1).   Other languages "incorporate" the object pronoun in the verb (*see* pp. 437, 453). For the "inclusive" and "exclusive" pronouns of Dravidian, *see* p. 487.

Note that many pronouns, particularly demonstrative and interrogative, may also be used as adjectives ("I want *these*", "I want *these* books"; "*what* do you want?", "*what* books do you want?"); in some languages this double use of a single form extends also to the possessives (Italian "voglio *il mio*", "I want *mine*"; "voglio *il mio* libro", "I want *my* book").

See also **case, declension, ending, gender, inflection, number, object, possession, predicate, subject.**

pronunciation (or **enunciation**) — articulate utterance, with the proper sound and accent. **Intonation** is pronunciation with reference to the pitch or modulation of the voice. *See* pp. 65-7, 72-3, 76, 83, 287, 329–30, 379, 421, 423, 446.

proper — *see* **noun**

punctuation — the use of periods, commas, etc.   The rules of punctuation are not identical in all languages using our own or a similar alphabet; for some outstanding differences, *see* pp. 229, 423.

punctuating words — particles used in some languages to express a break in the meaning; *see* pp. 513, 518.

race — the anthropological affiliation of human beings, as distinct from their linguistic affiliations.   Despite certain politically inspired beliefs to the contrary, it is a universally recognized scientific fact that there is no connection between the two; *see* pp. 21, 36, 457.

reciprocal — *see* **conjugation**

reduplication — in certain Indo-European languages, a device for forming tenses by doubling the first consonant or syllable of the root of the verb; this occurs most frequently in the formation of the perfect tense (Latin *cu-curri*, perfect of *curro*; *de-di*, perfect of *do*). The term is also applied, however, to the doubling of any word (usually a noun) to indicate plural number or frequent occurrence; *see* pp. 85, 510-1, 534.

reflexive — *see* **conjugation, pronoun**

relative — *see* **pronoun**

religion — the influence which religious beliefs exert on language, particularly in its written form, is sometimes far-reaching; *see* pp. 19, 30, 53, 80, 354, 456, 461-2, 480, 507, 530.

root (or **stem**) — a primitive word-form, without prefix, suffix, or inflectional element, as *go, wall, good*. In inflected languages, the root is frequently accompanied by an inflectional **ending** (as aim–*s*, aim-*ing*, aim-*ed*); **isolating** languages, like the Chinese, permit no inflectional endings, and every word consists of a pure root (roots may, however, be combined into groups). The roots of Indo-European languages normally consist of both consonants and vowels, and the vowels are especially subject to modification (*see* pp. 88, 136, 143, 233, 430, 432, 436). Semitic languages have, generally, roots consisting of three consonants, with the vowels consigned to a secondary role (*see* pp. 29, 463, 472). *See also* pp. 23, 30, 33, 394, 477, 487, 539-40, 552.

secondary (or **cultural**) language — an acquired tongue, gained either through a cultural medium, such as a school, or through intercourse with the speakers; German, for example, is a widespread secondary and cultural tongue in countries like Czechoslovakia (where it is spoken by nearly 40% of the population), the Netherlands (20%), Hungary (15%), Sweden and Denmark (over 10%), etc. *See* pp. 41, 43, 45, 47-9, 52, 62-3, 81-7, 122-3, 167, 182-3, 312-3, 352, 376-7, 420, 456, 507.

semantic — pertaining to meaning; a **semantic change** in a word is a change in its meaning, as when Latin *mittere*, "to send", became French *mettre*, "to put". Words like English *knave* and German *Knabe* ("boy"), English *knight* and German *Knecht* ("serf"), English *rent* and French *rente* ("income") are illustrative of **semantic differentiation** of what was originally one and the same word in different languages; English *dame* (feminine of *sir*) and American slang *dame* illustrate semantic differentiation within the same language. *See* pp. 65, 67, 290.

sentence — a combination of words expressing a complete thought, as "I am here". For the various types of sentence, *see* **clause.**

simple sentence — *see* **clause**

simplification (or **analysis**) — the process whereby a language replaces inflectional endings with separate words conveying the meanings previously conveyed by the inflectional suffixes, as when Vulgar Latin replaces Classical genitive *muri* ("of the wall") with *de illo muro*, which later becomes Italian *de lo muro, del muro*. The opposite of analysis is **synthesis** (*q. v.*), whereby several concepts are gathered into a single word by the use of endings. The utmost in simplification is achieved by "isolating" languages, like Chinese, where every word is an unchanging, uninflected root. *See* pp. 22-3, 25, 421, 479-80.

singular — *see* **number**

slang — the jargon of a particular class, comprehensible only to members of that class; the use of new words and phrases, or of old words and phrases in a new and arbitrary, or figurative sense. **Colloquialisms** differ from slang only in degree, being more widely current and more acceptable to the more cultured speakers of a language, at least in spoken form. The dividing line between slang, colloquialism, and literary language is invariably vague and shadowy, since the slang and colloquialisms of today often supply the material for the literary language of tomorrow. Slang appears in practically all languages that boast of a literary or even a written form, though to varying degrees. *See* pp. 19, 65-6, 72-87, 225, 246, 267, 611, 613.

spelling (or **orthography**) — the *written* form of a *spoken* word (*see* **alphabet**). The spelling of some languages, like English and French, is quite complicated, in the sense that there is only a partial correspondence of written symbol and spoken sound (note the different sounds that the symbol *a* has in *father, all, bat, fare*, or the symbol *s* in *silly, rose, measure*; the fact that often a single symbol represents a double sound, like the *u* in *unite* (*yu*-nite); and the fact that often a single sound is represented by a double symbol, as is the case with the *th* of *this* or the *sh* of *shore*). Other languages, like Spanish, have a more "simple" spelling; that is, there is a closer approach to symbol-for-sound correspondence. Several languages have deliberately gone about securing a closer correspondence of this type, though no language has completely achieved it (*see* **orthographic reform**). Most languages are said to have **phonetic writing,** that is, writing which to a greater or lesser degree represents sounds (for non-phonetic writing *see* pp. 491, 493, 526, and **picture-writing**), but true phonetic writing, with absolute symbol-for-sound correspondence, has so far been achieved only through the International Phonetic Alphabet, and even there with qualifications and room for discussion. *See* pp. 22, 67, 103, 229, 271, 314, 446, 583.

standardization of language — the process whereby local and dialectal varieties of a language are done away with, usually through conscious governmental effort, and a uniform language, at least in written form, is imposed upon the population of a given area; *see* pp. 65, 465, 491.

stem — *see* **root**

strong — *see* **adjective, verb**

subject — the word, or group of words, about which something is said; in the sentence "I am here", "I" is the subject; in "to run fast is good exercise", "to run fast" is the subject. In languages having declensional forms, the noun or pronoun which is the subject goes into the nominative case (*see* **case, declension**); where declensional forms are wanting, position before the verb usually indicates the subject; in "the boy sees the man", the only thing that indicates that "the boy" is the subject and "the man" the object of the action of seeing is their relative position before and after "sees"; but in Latin the words may be arranged in any order (*virum videt puer*), since *puer* definitely informs us by its form that it is the subject, and *virum* that it is the object. *See* pp. 22-3.

subject pronoun — *see* **pronoun**

subjective — *see* **case**

subjunctive — *see* **mood**

subordinate — *see* **clause**

suffix — a letter or syllable added to the end of a word to modify its meaning; in "boys", *s* is a plural suffix; in "boy's", *'s* is a possessive suffix; in "warmly", *ly* is an adverbial suffix. *See* pp. 22–3, 30–1, 36, 85, 88, 128, 430, 432-3, 436-7, 440, 452, 470, 477, 487, 497, 510-1, 539, 549, 589-90. *See also* **ending.**

superlative — *see* **adjective**

supine — a verbal noun, or uninflected adjective, which does not exist in English. In the modern languages, like the Scandinavian, where the supine appears, it acts as a secondary past participle to form compound tenses in the active ("I have spoken"), while the past participle is used with a verb corresponding to *to be* to form the passive ("I am seen"); *see* pp. 96, 102.

syilable — a combination of sounds uttered with a single impulse of the voice, like each of the four voice-groups in *in–tel–li–gent*. In some languages, all words are **monosyllabic** (*q. v.*). In **polysyllabic** languages, **syllabification,** or **syllabic division,** is the dividing of words into syllables. This process, though unconscious in the spoken tongue, gives the language an individual flavor, marking it predominantly as a "vocalic" or "vowel" language, in which most syllables end in vowels **(open syllables),** or "consonantal", where most of the syllables end in consonants **(closed syllables).** English definitely belongs to the latter type, while Spanish and Italian just as definitely belong to the former. A good deal of the pronunciation difficulty which the English-speaking student encounters in connection with foreign languages is due to his instinctive incorrect syllabic division, which he carries over unconsciously from his native tongue; dividing the Spanish *ge–ne–ral* as we divide the English *gen-er-al*, we are *bound* to get incorrect vowel-sounds. A useful exercise in this connection is to take long foreign words, divide them correctly into syllables according to the rules of syllabification of the language in question, pronounce the syllables separately, at first very slowly, with a distinct break between each syllable, then faster and faster till the breaks are eliminated, but the correct tonality of the vowels remains. *See* pp. 35, 127, 187, 229, 272, 315, 462, 489, 508, 526–32.

syllabary — a table of indivisible syllabic characters, such as appears in Japanese; *see* pp. 462, 489, 527–32; *see also* **kana.** In many western languages of a predominantly "open-syllable" nature (*see* above), children are taught to *syllabify* rather than to *spell* (*a, e, i, o, u; ba, be, bi, bo, bu; da, de, di, do, du;* etc.).

synonym — a word having the same meaning as another word;

shun, for example, is a synonym of *avoid* ("I avoid his company", "I shun his company"). Languages whose vocabulary is made up from various sources (like English, which is composed of Anglo-Saxon, Norman-French, Latin, Greek, etc.), are particularly rich in synonyms (Spanish *escorpión*, from the Latin; *alacrán*, from the Arabic; both meaning "scorpion"). *See* p. 179.

syntax — the structure of the sentence, or the arranging of words in their proper relation; the placing of the subject before, and of the object after the verb, is a matter of syntax. *See* pp. 83-4, 172, 495-7, 527.

synthesis — combining, or putting together, numerous subsidiary meanings in one word; opposed to **analysis** or **simplification** (q. *v.*); *see* pp. 22, 25.

tense — the modification of verb-forms to express time. The fundamental divisions of time are **present** ("I do", "I am doing"); **past** ("I did"); and **future** ("I shall do"); and many languages, like Russian, go no farther; some even combine the future with the present ("I *am going* there tomorrow"); while others dispense with tenses altogether, save where a special word (*yesterday, now, next year*) conveys the time of the action. In the modern western languages, tense-forms are generally covered by the following scheme, with some tenses lacking in some tongues:

present (indicates what happens habitually, or what is happening now: "I *go* there every day"; "I *am going* there now");

imperfect (indicates what was happening, or used to happen: French "j'y *allais* quand vous êtes entré"). There is no specific form for the imperfect in English, but the meaning is conveyed by the *past progressive* ("I *was going*"), or by a circumlocution like "I *used to go*";

past (indicates what happened: "I *went* there yesterday"). This tense goes by many different names in the grammars of various languages. The German past corresponds in form to the English, but is often used as an imperfect; the French past is called **"past definite"**, and is used for the most part in book narration, being replaced in conversation by the **present perfect** or **"past indefinite"** ("I have done"); the Spanish past, called **"past absolute"**, and the Italian past (**"passato remoto"**) are similar to the English in use. Latin called this tense **"perfect"**, and Greek **"aorist"** (*see* p. 425);

future (indicates what will take place: "I *shall go* there tomorrow"). In English and German, the future is formed by means of an auxiliary verb (*shall, will, werden* + infinitive); this makes it, in a broad sense, an analytical, or "compound" tense, since it consists of two combined, but independent elements; in the Romance languages, the future is a simple, or synthetic tense (*je ferai, haré, farò*); *see* pp. 23, 178, 245, 390-1, 472, 500, 540;

Compound Tenses (*see* pp. 178, 282) are generally formed by means of an **auxiliary** (*to have, to be*; *see* **auxiliary**) + the **past participle** (**supine** in some languages; *see* **supine**); in English they are:

present perfect (indicating what has happened: "I *have done* it"). French calls this tense the **"past indefinite"**, and both French and German use it colloquially to translate both the English present perfect and the English past; in Spanish and Italian its use is very similar to English;

past perfect (indicating what had happened prior to something else that took place: "I *had seen* him before he went out"). It is often called **"pluperfect"**. The Romance languages have two past perfect tenses, one formed with the imperfect, the other with the past of the auxiliary (French pluperfect *j'avais parlé*; past anterior *j'eus parlé*; both mean "I had spoken", but the second is used primarily in a subordinate clause when there is a past in the main clause).

future perfect (indicating what will have taken place: "I *shall have finished* the work by tomorrow"). Sometimes called **"future anterior"**.

There is some dispute as to whether the **conditional present** ("he *would go* if I asked him") and the **conditional past** ("he *would have gone* if I had asked him") are to be considered as tenses of the indicative or as a separate mood. They appear in most western languages, being analytical forms in the Germanic, synthetic forms in the Romance tongues (*see* pp. 393, 425, 500, 540–1).

The tenses of the indicative, outlined above, are largely duplicated in the subjunctive, where the latter exists. German and Portuguese have six subjunctive tenses; French, Spanish and Italian have four (the future and future perfect subjunctive having disappeared from modern Spanish).

A tense distinction may also appear in the **infinitive** ("to do"; "to have done"; "to be about to do"); and in the participles ("doing"; "having done", "being about to do"; "done", "having been done", "being about to be done").

See pp. 23, 172, 353, 364, 375, 425-6, 499, 515, 538; *see also* **conjugation, mood, voice, verb**.

tilde — the sign used in Spanish over *n* (*ñ*) to indicate its palatal pronunciation; the same symbol is used by other languages over various letters to indicate various modifications of sound; *see* pp. 228, 270.

tone — the intonation or pitch of the voice; in certain languages, notably Chinese, tone serves to distinguish meaning; *see* pp. 17, 32-3, 459-60, 487-8, 492, 495-505. *See also* **accent**.

trade language — a tongue used as a medium of common intercourse among speakers of various languages in multilingual areas, like German in Central Europe, Malay in the Dutch East Indies, Pidgin in the Melanesian Islands, Hausa and Swahili in sections of Africa, etc. *See* pp. 65, 83-7, 268-9, 454, 459; *see also* **lingua franca.**

transitive — *see* **verb**

umlaut — the change of a root vowel under the influence of the vowel in the final syllable, which later often disappears; the term **mutation** is also used for this phenomenon, but lends itself to another meaning (*see* **lenition**). The phenomenon is particularly apparent in the languages of the Germanic group (English *mouse, mice; foot, feet*). The double dot over the umlauted vowel is often called the umlaut, particularly by students of German; it is, however, properly speaking, only an orthographical indication of the phenomenon itself. *See* pp. 88, 99, 130, 280-1, 292, 434, 438.

unvoiced — *see* **consonant**

verb — a word expressing an action (like *see, hear, go*), or a mode of being (like *be, seem, become*). In some languages, like Chinese, the verb is not particularly segregated from other parts of speech (this often happens in English, where the verb *to mail*, for example, is distinguished from the noun *mail* only by its use in the sentence). In other languages, the verb assumes an unequivocal form, with specialized endings (Latin ama*re*, French fini*r*, German sprech*en*). Verbs may be classified as **transitive** (where the action can be carried over to a recipient, or **object**: "I see *him*"); **intransitive** (where the action cannot be carried over to an object: "we have succeeded"); and **copulative** (where the verb simply links the subject to a modifier: "he is (seems, becomes) a soldier"). Note that in English many verbs may be used transitively or intransitively ("he has just passed", intransitive; "he has just passed me", transitive; "the swallow flies". intransitive: "he flies a plane", transitive). In some languages (French, German, Italian) many intransitive and copulative verbs form their compound tenses with "to be" instead of "to have" (*il est allé, er ist gegangen, è andato; see* **auxiliary**; *see also* pp. 139, 199, 326).

Verbs, in English and most Indo-European languages, have **person, number, tense, voice** and **mood** (*see* each item); a form like "he goes", for instance, would be described as third person, singular number, present tense, indicative mood, active voice. But in many non-Indo-European tongues, all or some of these distinctions are missing; the Japanese verb, for instance, has tense, voice and mood, but no person or number (*see* pp. 24, 32, 536, 538); the Chinese "verb" is an uninflected root having none of these distinctions, and can generally be used also as a noun, adjective, or other part of speech (*see* pp. 495–6, 499–501).

Many languages divide their verbs into classes according to forms and endings (*see* **conjugation**). The English (and, in general, the Germanic) division is into two classes, **weak** and **strong**; the weak verbs are characterized by the addition of a suffix (*-d, -ed*) in the past and passive participle (*love, loved, loved*); the strong by a change in the root vowel in these two forms (*write, wrote, written; speak, spoke, spoken*); *see* pp. 90, 101, 108, 115, 136). The Semitic languages have a similar classification, though different in form (*see* pp. 472-3). It is interesting to note that in English all the separate verb-forms that need be learned are four in the case of weak verbs (*love, loves, loving, loved*), five in the case of strong verbs (*speak, speaks, speaking, spoke, spoken*), all other forms being obtained by combining these with a few unchanging auxiliaries (*have, had, will*, etc.). *See* pp. 22-3, 32, 353, 463, 538. For the **polite, familiar,** and **honorific** verbs of Japanese, *see* pp. 24, 536, 538, 542-4, 547-8; *see also* **address.** *See also* **aspect, conjugation, ending, inflection, mood, tense, voice.**

verbal noun — a form of the verb syntactically used as a noun; that is, as subject ("*to walk* is good"; "*walking* is good"); direct object ("I like *to walk*"; "I like *walking*"); etc. *See* **gerund, infinitive, supine;** *see also* p. 473.

verbal adjective — a form of the verb syntactically used as an adjective, like "the *singing* man", "the *written* word"; *see* **participle.**

vernacular — the current spoken language of a given area, as opposed to its **written** or **literary** tongue. The vernacular is frequently characterized by **colloquialisms** and **slang** (*q. v.*).

vocabulary — the total stock of words in a language, or within the range of a given speaker. There is extreme variation in the vocabulary range of speakers of the same tongue. *See* pp. 24, 65-87, 172, 179-80, 246, 289-90, 354, 419, 421, 428-9, 456, 479, 487-8; *see also* **loan-word.**

vocative — *see* **case**

voice — a modification in the form of the verb to indicate whether the subject *does* the action (**active voice:** "I strike"), or *receives* it (**passive voice:** "I am struck"). In some languages, this is indicated by an inflectional ending (Latin *timeo*, active, "I fear"; *timeor*, passive, "I am feared"); in other languages, like English or German, by the use of an **auxiliary** (*to be, werden*) combined with the past participle. Some languages, particularly the Romance, tend to avoid the use of the passive by replacing it with an active equivalent (French *on le fera*, "it will be done") or by using the **reflexive** (Spanish *aquí se habla español*, "Spanish is spoken here"). In some languages the passive is completely wanting. The **middle voice,** which appeared in some of the older Indo-European languages, notably Greek, represents the subject as acting on or for himself, a function which has generally been taken over by the reflexive. Certain forms of the verb appearing in some languages (like the **desiderative;** *see* p. 546) may be described as voices, or as conjugations. For the **impersonal passive** of Finnish, *see* p. 434. *See* pp. 89, 141, 178, 202, 240, 286, 328, 353, 366, 393, 425-6, 434, 441, 516, 546-7. *See also* **verb.**

voiced consonant — *see* **consonant**

vowel — a sound produced without friction or stoppage; or a letter purporting to represent such a sound. The written vowels of English are *a, e, i, o, u*; but the number of spoken vowels is much greater (*a* of *father, bat, all, fare,* etc.; *e* of *let, her, even,* etc.; *i* of *it, machine,* etc.; *o* of *not, orb,* etc.; *u* of *cut, rude,* etc.). Note also that many so-called vowel-sounds are **diphthongs** (*q. v.*: *a* of *fate*; *i* of *tide*; *o* of *note*; *u* of *unity*). Many vowel-sounds that appear in English do not appear in other tongues, and *vice-versa* (*see* pp. 29, 86, 184-5, 227, 314, 361, 461-3). For the **middle** (or **front rounded**) vowels of French, German, etc., *see* pp. 172, 185, 437. Vowels may be **stressed or unstressed** (*see* pp. 268-9, 287, 314, 329-30, 354, 379), and modify their sound accordingly. They may be **long** or **short** (though some languages minimize this difference); *see* pp. 125, 354, 368, 371, 423, 436, 444, 450, 466, 531, 533. For the **vowel-harmony** of the Ural-Altaic tongues, whereby the vowel of the ending changes to harmonize with that of the root, *see* pp. 30-1, 430, 432, 436, 440; for the division of vowels in such languages into **front, back** and "**neutral**" (the last-named appearing only occasionally and functionally), *see* pp. 30-1, 430, 432, 436, 440. For the influx of front and back vowels in other language-groups, *see* pp. 88, 353. For the Indo-European (particularly Germanic) **umlaut** change, whereby the vowel of the root is modified by the influence of the vowel of the ending, *see* **umlaut.** For the **vowel-points** of the Semitic languages, *see* p. 461.

weak — *see* **adjective, verb.**

word-order — the arrangement of words in the sentence (*see* **syntax**). In some languages with scanty or non-existent flectional endings (English, Chinese) word-order is of paramount importance for intelligibility. Where flectional endings are more abundant, the importance of word-order is usually secondary. *See* pp. 18, 22, 25, 32, 141-3, 162, 170, 172, 193, 200, 278-9, 288, 320-1, 447, 467, 488; 495-501, 505.

written (or **literary**) **language** — the inscribed, legible form assumed by a tongue which has achieved a certain cultural level. Many languages of primitive groups are unwritten, and consequently highly fluctuating both in time and space, with numerous dialectal variations, a rapid rate of change, and an undetermined standard form. Where a written form, particularly of the semi-phonetic type, is achieved, the result is generally a greater stability in the spoken language, although the process of change never comes to a full stop. When the language becomes a vehicle for literature, the process of standardization, unification and stabilization goes even farther. The written tongue is, in due course of time, modified by spoken-language changes; on the other hand, the spoken tongue is often influenced by the written form. *See* **picture-writing, spelling,** and pp. 19, 29, 117, 127, 172, 180, 421, 424, 427, 444, 446, 456, 461-2, 465, 487-93; 504-7, 526-31.

ACKNOWLEDGMENTS

The list of those to whom the author is deeply indebted is long. The Japanese chapter is the personal offering of Professor Ralph Walker Scott, of Trinity College. The Malay section is the work of Dr. William Lowther. To both these sections the author's contribution was limited to details of revision and arrangement. In addition, it was deemed advisable to have most languages carefully checked by at least one cultivated native speaker, with general topics checked by scholars in the individual fields. (Many of these experts sat in as informants on the author's courses, and to them he is doubly grateful). Furthermore, the basic vocabularies of six out of the seven major languages treated were constructed, on a model prepared by the author, with the assistance of willing collaborators, who gave unstintingly of their time and labor to the success of this enterprise.

It is the author's desire, nevertheless, to assume personal responsibility for any errors or inaccuracies that may appear in the work; this owing to the fact that space limitations and the method that necessarily had to be followed made it impossible to accept many of the excellent suggestions offered by the experts, which would have contributed enormously to the completeness of the work, but would also have lengthened it beyond the bounds deemed practical.

Major Joseph B. Costanzo, M. I., U. S. A.; Professor Horatio Smith, of Columbia University; and Professor Harry Morgan Ayres, of Columbia, were of invaluable assistance to the author in the conception and planning of the entire work.

The first two chapters, dealing with linguistic families and the geography of language, were painstakingly examined and revised by Professor Louis H. Gray, of Columbia's Department of Comparative Linguistics, and Mr. Duncan MacDougald, Jr., author of "The Languages and Press of Africa".

In Chapter III, the general Germanic material was examined by Professor Carl Bayerschmidt, of Columbia, and Professor Margaret Schlauch, of New York University. The English section was accurately gone over by Professor Harry Morgan Ayres, Professor William Cabell Greet, and Professor Elliott V. K. Dobbie, all of the English Department of Columbia, while much of the material on the English of New Zealand was supplied by Miss Henrietta R. Mason, of the Columbia University Extension. Australian and Pidgin English sections were examined and revised by Mr. Edgar Sheappard Sayer, author of "Pidgin English", and the South African section by Professor C. W. de Kiewiet, of Cornell University. The Swedish material was checked by Mrs. Birgit Olson Wagner, formerly of the Swedish Consulate General, and Mr. Gunnar Hök; the Norwegian by Mr. Joseph Mendelsohn and Mr. Kurt Valner; the Danish by Dr. Viggo C. Mengers; the Icelandic by Professor Margaret Schlauch, of New York University. The Dutch section was carefully examined and revised by Professor Adriaan Barnouw, of Columbia, and Mr. Martin Zwart. Mrs. Wagner, Mr. Mendelsohn and Mr. Zwart supplied most of the material appearing in the Swedish, Norwegian and Dutch word-lists, respectively. The Scandinavian material has been revised in accordance with suggestions offered in a review by Professor Einar Haugen, of the University of Wisconsin.

The German chapter and vocabulary were examined by Professor Carl Bayerschmidt of Columbia, Dr. Frederick Rex of the Lincoln School, and Miss Rosa Hettwer of the Milwaukee High School system, with Professor Frederick Heuser, of Columbia, contributing the solution of several controversial points. The German vocabulary was constructed, on the author's model, by Private Robert L. Politzer, U. S. A., and Mr. Herbert S. Ruhé, of St. Louis, Mo.

The general Romance material in Chapter V was examined by Professor Henri F. Muller, of Columbia's Department of Romance Philology. The Roumanian section was checked and revised by Professor Leon Feraru, of Long Island University and Columbia, and Mr. A. Manoil, of the Language Units of the War Department.

The French chapter and vocabulary were examined by Professor Henri F. Muller and Professor Jeanne Vidon-Varney, of Columbia, and Miss Dorothy Rothschild of Hunter College, while the French vocabulary was constructed, on the author's model, by Dr. Nicholas J. Milella, of Cornell University's Foreign Area and Language Study Curriculum.

The Spanish chapter and vocabulary were examined by Professor Angel del Río, of Columbia, and Professor José Martel, of the College of the City of New York, while the Spanish vocabulary was constructed by Dr. Milella.

The Portuguese chapter and vocabulary were examined and extensively revised by Mr. Alexander da Rocha Prista, of Columbia, and Dr. Afranio Coutinho, editor of the Portuguese version (*Seleções*) of the "Reader's Digest"; most of the material on the Brazilian varieties of Portuguese was supplied by Mr. Antonio Cuffari, of the Foreign Area and Language Study Curriculum of Clark University, while the Portuguese vocabulary was constructed by Private Vincent Livelli, U. S. A.

The Italian chapter and vocabulary were examined by Mr. Gino Bigongiari, of Columbia, and Dr. Nicholas J. Milella, of Cornell.

The entire Slavic chapter was examined by Professor Clarence A. Manning and Dr. Arthur Coleman, both of Columbia, and Professor Roman Jakobson, of the University of Oslo and Columbia; the Polish section by Miss Christina Tolczynska, of the Bridgeport High Schools; the Czech section by Dr. Jaroslav Brož, of the Czechoslovak Consulate General; the Serbo-Croatian section by Mr. Alexander Trbović and Mr. Vlaho Vlahović, editor of "Slavonic Monthly"; and the Bulgarian section by Dr. Victor Sharenkoff, of the Research Department of the New York Public Library.

The Russian chapter and vocabulary were examined by Professor Clarence A. Manning of Columbia and Professor Paul Haensel of Northwestern University and Mary Washington College, as well as by Mrs. Elena Mogilat, of Columbia's Russian Department, and Mrs. Catherine Pastuhova, of the Foreign Area and Language Study Curriculum of Syracuse University. The Russian vocabulary was constructed, on the author's model, by Mrs. Pastuhova.

In Chapter XII, the Greek material was examined by Mr. Emanuel Athanas, of Columbia, and Mr. George Vanson; the Albanian by Mr. Nelo Drizari of Columbia; all of the Ural-Altaic material in Chapter I, II and XII, as well as the Turkish, Finnish and Hungarian sections, were examined and revised by Dr. Karl Heinrich Menges of Columbia; the Finnish section by Dr. John B. Olli of the College of the City of New York and Columbia; the Hungarian section by Mr. Elmer Sixay Dorsay, formerly of C. C. N. Y. and Columbia, and Dr. Lewis L. Sell; the Turkish section by Mr. Assim Yegenoglu, of the Language Units of the War Department. The Lithuanian and Lettish sections were examined by Professor Alfred Senn, of the University of Pennsylvania; the Celtic and Basque sections by Professor John L. Gerig of Columbia; the Welsh material by the Rev. Cynolwyn Pugh; the Basque by Mr. Juan Manuel Bilbao.

In Chapter XIII, the Arabic section was constructed with the very able assistance of Dr. Ibrahim Mansoury, of Columbia, and checked and revised by Professor Arthur Jeffery, of Columbia's Department of Semitic Languages, who also examined all the Semito-Hamitic material in Chapter I and II. Hebrew forms were checked by Professor Jeffery and Dr. Abraham Halkin, of Columbia, as well as by Rabbi Abraham Jacobson, of Temple Emanu-El, Haverhill, Mass., and Cantor Harold Greenblatt. The Persian and Indo-Aryan sections were examined by Mr. Anthony Paura, of Columbia's Department of Indo-Iranian. The Chinese section was examined and revised by Professor Luther Carrington Goodrich, of Columbia, who also supplied most of the Chinese phrase-list and examined the Sino-Tibetan material in Chapters I and II; and by Mr. Charles Wan, of the Chinese Ministry of Information in Chung King. Tibetan forms were checked by Dr. Theos Bernard. The

Malay section, as previously stated, is the work of Dr. William Lowther, of the Methodist Episcopal Church of Norwich, Conn., who spent ten years as a missionary in British Malaya; it was edited by the author, and examined by Mrs. Claire Holt, of Columbia University's Foreign Area and Language Study Curriculum, who supplied Dutch East Indies variants for British Malayan forms wherever such variants appear.

The Japanese chapter is the work of Professor Ralph Walker Scott, of Trinity College, who spent ten years as Professor of Occidental Languages in Rikkyō University in Tōkyō. It was edited by the author and examined and revised by Dr. Hachiro Yuasa, of the New York Japanese Methodist Church.

Appendix A (Esperanto) is the work of Mr. and Mrs. G. Alan Connor, respectively Director of the Esperanto Inter-language Institute in New York and Teacher of the International Cseh Institute of Esperanto of the Hague.

The Glossary was carefully examined by Professor Elliott V. K. Dobbie, of Columbia's English Department.

Lastly, the passages chosen for illustrative and comparative purposes throughout are official translations of John 3.16, appearing in the American Bible Society's splendid publication "The Book of a Thousand Tongues". To this choice, the objection may be offered that by reason of the subject-matter, the language is stereotyped and, in some cases, archaic. While this may be true in a few instances, it may be replied that nowhere else was it possible to obtain, for an entire series of languages, so homogeneous and accurate a set of individual translations. But of far greater importance is the fact that the Word of God, with its message of deathless hope to suffering humanity, seemed peculiarly fitted for a work of this kind, since it transcends national boundaries and finds an echo in the hearts of all men, irrespective of race, color, creed, speech or political belief. May this Word point to a solution of mankind's material, as well as spiritual, problems!

July 1, 1946.

                                                        Mario A. Pei

INDEX OF COUNTRIES, REGIONS, LOCALITIES, LANGUAGES, DIALECTS AND OTHER PROPER NAMES